AF605811

The Correspondence of Theodoret of Cyrus

The Collectio Sirmondiana

THE LIBRARY OF EARLY CHRISTIANITY

From *Les vrais pourtraits et vies des hommes illustres grecz, latins et payens* by André Thevet (1516–1590), vol. 1 (Kevert et Guillaume Chaudière: Paris 1584). Courtesy of The Rare Books & Manuscripts Department, Boston Public Library.

THE LIBRARY OF EARLY CHRISTIANITY

VOLUME 5

Theodoret of Cyrus

The Correspondence of Theodoret of Cyrus

Greek Text edited and translated by
JOHN F. PETRUCCIONE

Introduction by
ISTVÁN PÁSZTORI-KUPÁN

Commentary by
JOHN F. PETRUCCIONE AND
ISTVÁN PÁSZTORI-KUPÁN

The Catholic University of America Press
Washington, D.C.

The paper used in this publication meets the minimum requirements of American National Standards for Information Science—Permanence of Paper for Printed Library Materials, ANSI Z39.48-1992.
∞

ISBN (hardcover): 978-0-8132-3929-3
ISBN (eBook): 978-0-8132-3887-6
ISBN (paperback): 978-0-8132-3886-9

CONTENTS OF VOLUME 5

LIST OF ABBREVIATIONS

BIBLICAL BOOKS

OT	Old Testament
Gn	Genesis
Ex	Exodus
Lv	Leviticus
Nm	Numbers
Dt	Deuteronomy
Jos	Joshua
Jgs	Judges
Ru	Ruth
1–2Sm	The first and second books of Samuel
1–2Kgs	The first and second books of Kings
1–2Chr	The first and second books of Chronicles
Ezr	Ezra
Neh	Nehemiah
Tb	Tobit
Est	Esther
Jdt	Judith
1–2Mc	The first and second books of Maccabees
Jb	Job
Ps(s)	Psalms
Prv	Proverbs
Eccl	Ecclesiastes
Song	Canticle of Canticles, Song of Songs
Wis	Wisdom of Solomon
Sir	Wisdom of Jesus ben Sirach, Ecclesiasticus

Is	Isaiah
Jer	Jeremiah
Lam	Lamentations
Bar	Baruch
Ep Jer	Epistle of Jeremiah (= Vulg. Bar 6)
Ezek	Ezekiel
Dn	Daniel
Theod. Dan.	The Greek translation of the book of Dn attributed to Theodotion
Sus	Susannah (= Vulg. Dn 13)
Bel	Bel and the Dragon (= Vulg. Dn 14)
Hos	Hosea
Jl	Joel
Am	Amos
Ob	Obadiah
Jon	Jonah
Mi	Micah
Na	Nahum
Hab	Habakkuk
Zep	Zephaniah
Hag	Haggai
Zec	Zechariah
Mal	Malachi
NT	New Testament
Mt	Matthew
Mk	Mark
Lk	Luke
Jn	John
Acts	Acts
Rom	The Epistle to the Romans
1–2Cor	The first and second Epistles to the Corinthians
Gal	The Epistle to the Galatians

List of Abbreviations

Eph	The Epistle to the Ephesians
Phil	The Epistle to the Philippians
Col	The Epistle to the Colossians
1–2Thes	The first and second Epistles to the Thessalonians
1–2Tm	The first and second Epistles to Timothy
Ti	The Epistle to Titus
Phlm	The Epistle to Philemon
Heb	The Epistle to the Hebrews
Jas	The Epistle of St. James
1–2Pt	The first and second Epistles of St. Peter
1–3Jn	The first through third Epistles of St. John
Jude	The Epistle of St. Jude
Rv	Apocalypse, Revelation

ANCIENT AUTHORS AND WORKS

Acac. mel.	Cyr. *ep. ad Acacium melitensem*
ad Apoll.	Plu., *Consolatio ad Apollonium*
ad archim. aelienses	Marc., *epistula ad archimandritas aelienses*
ad Ath.	Iul. imp., *Epistula ad athenienses*
ad constan.	Cael., *ep. ad constantinopolitanos*
ad imp.	*ad imperatorem*
ad monach. alex.	Marc., *epistula ad monachos alexandrinos*
ad syn. ephes.	Cael., *ep. ad synodum ephesinam*
Ad Theoph.	Gr. nyss., *ad Theophilum aduersus Apollinaristas*
Adloc. ad Marc.	*Adlocutio synodi chalcedonensis ad Marcianum imperatorem*
Adult. libr. Or.	Ruf., *De adulteratione librorum Origenis*
Adu. tria cap.	Vig., *Epistula aduersus tria capitula*
Aegr.	Procl. cp., *Homilia consolatoria ad aegrotum*
Ael.	Claudius Aelianus
Affect.	Thdt., *Graecarum affectionum curatio*
Ambr.	Ambrosius mediolanensis

List of Abbreviations

Amph.	Amphilochius iconiensis
An recte	Plu., *An recte dictum sit latenter esse uiuendum*
Antir.	Gr. nyss., *Antirrheticus aduersus Apollinarem*
Ap.	Pl., *Apologia*
ap. Leonem ep.	*apud Leonem epistula* (for letters sent to Leo but included in the corpus of his correspondence)
Apoll.	Leont. Byz., *Aduersus fraudes apollinaristarum* (*CPG* #6817)
Apol. orient.	Cyr., *Duodecim capitum defensio aduersus orientales episcopos*
Apol. Thds.	Cyr., *Apologeticus ad imperatorem Theodosium*
Apol. Thdt.	Cyr., *Apologeticus contra Theodoretum*
Apoph. lac.	Ps.-Plu., *Apophthegmata laconica*
App.	*Appendix*
Ar.	Aristophanes
Arcad.	Cyr., *De recta fide ad Arcadiam et Marinam*
Ath.	Athanasius alexandrinus
Aug.	Augustinus hipponensis
Bas.	Basilius caesariensis Cappadociae
Bibl.	Phot., *Bibliotheca*
Breu.	Liberatus, *Breuiarium causae nestorianorum et eutychianorum*
C.	*Carmen, -ina*
Cael.	Caelestinus romanus (Pope Celestine I)
C. Anom.	Chrys., *Homiliae 1–5 Contra Anomaeos*
Cant. cant.	Thdt., *Explanatio in Canticum canticorum*
Cap. ex Nest.	Cyr., *Capitula ex Nestorio excerpta*
Catal.	*Carmen Ebediesu Metropolitae Sobae et Armeniae continens catalogum librorum omnium ecclesiasticorum; v.* ʿAbdishoʿ bar Brikha
Chron.	*Chronicon*
Chron. int.	Prosp. Aquit., *Chronicon integrum*
Chronog.	*Chronographia*

List of Abbreviations

Chron. pasch.	*Chronicon paschale*
Chr. un.	Cyr., *Quod unus sit Christus*
Chrys.	Iohannes Chrysostomus
C. Iul.	Cyr., *Contra Iulianum*
Clem.	Clemens Alexandrinus
C Nic.	*Concilium nicaenum (anno 325)*
CNis.	Ephr(a)em Syrus, *Carmina nisibena*
Coll. ante gesta	*Epistularum ante gesta collectio*
Coll. athen.	*Collectio atheniensis*
Coll. B	*Epistularum collectio B*
Coll. cas.	*Collectio casinensis*
Coll. H	*Epistularum collectio H*
Coll. M	*Epistularum collectio M*
Coll. pal.	*Collectio palatina*
Coll. pat.	*Collectio patmensis*
Coll. sich.	*Collectio sichardiana*
Coll. sirm.	*Collectio sirmondiana*
Coll. uat.	*Collectio uaticana*
Coll. uer.	*Collectio ueronensis*
Com. in Io.	Or., *Commentarii in euangelium Iohannis*
Comm. Coel.	Merc., *Commonitorium super nomine Coelestii*
Comm. Pel. et Coel.	Merc., *Commonitorium aduersum haeresim Pelagii, et Coelestii, uel etiam scripta Iuliani*
Comp. hist.	G. Cedr., *Compendium historiarum*
Conc. chalc.	*Concilium chalcedonense*
Conc. chalc., Act. 1, etc.	*Concilium chalcedonense, Gesta actionis primae, etc.*
Conc. chalc., Rust.	*Gestorum chalcedonensium Versio a Rustico edita*
Conc. constan.	*Concilium constantinopolitanum sub Iustiniano habitum*
Conc. ephes.	*Concilium ephesinum*
Confut.	Euth., *Confutationes quarundam propositionum*

List of Abbreviations

Const. apost.	*Constitutiones apostolorum*
Const. c. Eutych.	*Constitutio Marciani imperatoris contra Eutychen*
Const. de Flau.	*Constitutio Marciani imperatoris de Flauiani memoria*
Const. Marc.	*Constitutio Marciani imperatoris de actis synodi*
Contest.	*Contestatio*
Cor.	D., *De corona*
C.Th.	*Codex theodosianus*
Cyr.	Cyrillus alexandrinus
Cyr. S.	Cyrillus Scythopolitanus
D.	Demosthenes
Dam.	Damasus I
Dan.	Thdt., *Interpretatio in Danielem*
Declin.	ps.-Hdn., *De declinatione nominum* (*Περὶ κλίσεως ὀνομάτων*)
Decr.	Ath., *De decretis nicaenae synodi*
Def. cap.	*Definitio capitulorum quintae synodi que congregata est sub Iustiniano Constantinopoli*
Def. tr. cap.	Fac. herm., *Pro defensione trium capitulorum libri xii*
Demonstr.	Thdt., *Demonstratio per syllogismos*
dial.	*dialogus*
Diod.	Diodorus tarsensis
Ed. Marc. ad Const.	*Edictum Marciani imperatoris ad Constantinopolitanos*
Enn.	Plot., *Enneades*
ep(p).	*epistula(e)*
ep. ad Olymp.	Chrys., *Epistulae ad Olympiadem*
ep. dogm.	*epistula dogmatica*
ep. Epict.	Ath., *epistula ad Epictetum*
ep. Mar.	Ibas edesenus, *epistula ad Marim Persam*
ep. Ruf.	Thdt., *Epistula ad Rufum*
ep(p). theol.	Gr. naz., *epistula(e) theologica(e)*

Epicur.	Epicurus
Epiph.	Epiphanius constantiensis (Epiphanius of Salamis)
Epit. hist.	Io. Zon., *Epitomae historiarum*
Eran.	Thdt., *Eranistes*
Etym. gud.	*Etymologicum gudianum*
Euag. Schol.	Euagrius Scholasticus
Eus.	Eusebius caesariensis
Eus. dor.	Eusebius dorylaeensis
Euth.	Eutherius tyanaeus
Expl. fidei	Dam., *De explanatione fidei*
Fac. herm.	Facundus hermianensis
Falsa leg.	D., *De falsa legatione*
Fid.	Ambr., *De fide ad Gratianum* (*CPL* #150); Cyr., *De recta fide ad Theodosium* (*CPG* #5218); Dam., *Tomus seu Fides* (*CPL* #1633); Flau. cp., *De recta fide ad Theodosium* (*CPG* #5934); Thdt., *Expositio de recta fide* (*CPG* #6218)
Flau. cp.	Flauianus constantinopolitanus
flor.	*florilegium* (Thdt., *Eran.*)
frag(g).	*fragmentum (-ta)*
Gal.	Iul., *Contra Galilaeos*
G. Cedr.	Georgius Cedrenus (or Kedrenos)
Gennad.	Gennadius Presbyter
Gr. Mag.	Gregorius romanus (Pope Gregory I)
Gr. naz.	Gregorius Nazianzenus
Gr. nyss.	Gregorius nyssenus
Haer.	Iren., *Aduersus haereses* or Epiph, *Panarion* or *Aduersus lxxx haereses*
Haer. com.	Thdt., *Haereticarum fabularum compendium*
H. ar.	Ath., *Historia arianorum ad monachos*
Hdn.	Aelius Herodianus
H. e.	*Historia ecclesiastica*
Hebr.	Thdt., *in Ep. S. Pauli ad Hebraeos*

List of Abbreviations

Heracl.	Nest., *Liber Heraclidis*
Hex.	Bas., *Homiliae in Hexaemeron*
Hier.	Hieronymus Presbyter (Jerome)
Hil.	Hilarius pictauiensis (Hilary of Poitiers) or Hilarius diaconus romanus (Pope Hilary I)
H. Laus.	*Historia lausiaca*
Hom.	Homerus
hom.	*homiliae (-ias)*
Hom. 1–88 in Io.	Chrys., *Homiliae 1–88 in Iohannem*
Hom. catech.	Thdr. mops., *Homiliae catecheticae*
Hom. diu.	Cyr., *Homiliae diuersae*
Hom. in ps.	Bas., *Homiliae in Psalmos*
Hom. pasch.	Cyr., *Homilia paschalis*
H. rel.	Thdt., *Historia religiosa*
imp.	*imperator*
Inc.	Thdt. or Ath., *De incarnatione domini*
in Eph.	Thdt., *in Ep. S. Pauli ad Ephesios*
in Ezech.	Thdt., *Interpretatio in Ezechielem*
in Hebr.	Thdt., *in Ep. S. Pauli ad Hebraeos*
in Ier.	Thdt., *Interpretatio in Ieremiam*
in Is.	Cyr. or Thdt., *Commentarii in Isaiam prophetam*
in Mal.	Thdt., *Interpretatio in Malachiam*
in Ps.	Thdt., *Interpretatio in Psalmos*
Inst.	Io. Cass., *De institutis coenobiorum*
Inst. or.	Quint., *Institutio oratoria*
Intr.	Porph., *Isagoge siue quinque uoces*
in Zach.	Cyr., *Commentarii in Zachariam prophetam*
Io. ant.	Iohannes antiochenus
Io. Cass.	Iohannes Cassianus
Io. Dam.	Iohannes Damascenus
Io. Mal.	Iohannes Malalas
Io. Zon.	Iohannes Zonaras

List of Abbreviations

Iren.	Irenaeus lugdunensis
Isid. Pel.	Isidorus Pelusiota
Iul.	Iulius romanus (Pope Julius I) or Iulianus imperator
Iust. Mar.	Iustinus Martyr
keph.	*kephalaion* (κεφάλαιον)
Lam.	Thdt., *Commentarii in Lamentationes Ieremiae*
Leo	Leo romanus (Pope Leo I)
Leont. Byz.	Leontius Byzantinus
Lib.	Libanius
Libel. apel.	Flau. cp., *Libellus appellationis Flauiani ad papam Leonen*
Marc.	Marcianus imperator
Marcel. Com.	Marcellinus Comes
Mart. palaest.	Eus., *De martyribus palaestinae*
Mem.	X., *Memorabilia*
Merc.	Marius Mercator
Mor.	Plu., *Moralia*
N. a.	Ael., *De natura animalium*
Nem.	Pi., *Nemean Odes*
Nest.	Nestorius constantinopolitanus
Nest.	Cyr., *Contra Nestorium*
Nest. et Eut.	Leont. Byz., *Contra Nestorianos et Eutychianos*
Nest. serm.	Merc., *Contra haeresim Pelagii seu Caelestii Sermones I-IV*
Niceph.	Nicephorus Callistus Xanthopulus
Od.	Hom., *Odyssey*
Or.	Origenes
or(r).	*oratio (-iones)*
Or. catech.	Gr. nyss., *Oratio catechetica*
Or. in Const.	Them., *In Imperatorem Constantium oratio*
Or. laud. BMV	*Oratio de laudibus beatae Mariae uirginis*
O.T.	S., *Oedipus Tyrannus*

List of Abbreviations

Pac. form.	*Pacis formula* (*v.* Intro., sec. 3.11)
Pall.	Palladius Monachus
patm.	Thdt., *Epistulae, Collectio patmensis*
Pe.	Prud., *Peristephanon*
Phdr.	Pl., *Phaedrus*
Phot.	Photius constantinopolitanus
Pi.	Pindarus
Pl.	Plato
Plot.	Plotinus
Plu.	Plutarchus
Po.	Aristotle, *Poetics*
Porph.	Porphyrius Tyrius
praef.	*praefatio*
Prec. alt. sept. episc.	*Precatio altera septem episcoporum orientalium ad imperatorem orient.*
Procl. cp.	Proclus constantinopolitanus
Proph. min.	Thdt., *Interpretatio in xii prophetas minores*
Pros. cat.	Hdn., *De prosodia catholica*
Prosp. Aquit.	Prosper Aquitanus
Prouid.	Thdt., *Orationes de prouidentia*
Prud.	Prudentius
Ps.	Thdt., *Interpretatio in Psalmos*
ps.-	pseudo-
ps.-Hdn.	pseudo-Herodian
Pulch.	Cyr., *De recta fide ad Pulcheriam et Eudociam*
Q. in Gen. (Ex., Leu., Num., Deut.,	Thdt., *Quaestiones in Genesim (Exodum, Leuiticum, Numeros, Deuteronomium, Iosuam, Iudices, Ruth) Ios., Iud., Ruth)*
Quaest. in Oct.	Thdt., *Quaestiones in Octateuchum*
Quaest. in Reg. et Par.	Diod. or Thdt., *Quaestiones in Reges et Paralipomena*

Quint.	M. Fabius Quintilianus
Quod unicus filius	Thdt., *Quod unicus filius sit dominus noster Iesus Christus*
Ref. conf. Eun.	Gr. nyss., *Refutatio confessionis Eunomii*
rel.	*relatio*
Rel. ad imp. per Pallad.,	Io. ant., *Relatio ad imperatorem per Palladium*
Rel. syn. ad Leo.	*Relatio synodi chalcedonensis ad Leonem romanum*
Rep.	Pl., *De republica*
Repr.	Thdt., *Reprehensio xii anathematismorum Cyrilli*
Rerum chalc. coll.	*Rerum chalcedonensium collectio uaticana*
Ruf.	Rufinus Aquileiensis
S.	Sophocles
Sen.	Seneca
Sent.	Porph., *Sententiae ad intelligibilia ducentes*
serm.	*sermo, sermones*
Serm. fid.	ps.-Ath., *Sermo maior de fide*
sirm.	Thdt., *Epistulae, Collectio sirmondiana*
Socr.	Socrates Scholasticus
Soz.	Sozomenus
Spir.	Bas., *Liber de spiritu sancto*
Str.	Clem., *Stromata* or *Stromateis*
Symb. nic.-cp.	*Symbolum nicaenum (325) constantinopolitanum (381)*
Symb. Thdri. mops.	Merc., *Symbolum Theodori Mopsuesteni et eius refutatio*
Syn.	Ath., *Epistula de synodis Arimini et Seleuciae* or Hil., *De synodis*
Th.	Thucydides
Thdr. Lect.	Theodorus Lector
Thdr. mops.	Theodorus mopsuestenus
Thdt.	Theodoretus cyrrhensis
Them.	Themistius

Theod.	Theodosius II
Theod. Anag.	Theodorus Anagnostes
Theog.	Theognostos
Theophn.	Theophanes Confessor
Theophyl.	Theophylactus achridensis
Thes.	Theog., *Thesaurus*
Tom.	Ath., *Tomus ad antiochenos* or Leo, *Tomus ad Flauianum*
Tran.	Plu., *De tranquilitate animi*
Trin.	Cyr., *De sancta trinitate dialogi 1-vii* (*CPG* #5432) or Thdt., *De trinitate*
V. Euthym.	Cyr. S., *Vita Euthymii*
VH	Ael., *Varia historia*
Vig.	Vigilius romanus (Pope Vigilius)
Virg.	Gr. nyss., *De uirginitate*
Vir. ill.	Hier. or Gennad. *De uiris illustribus*
V. Sab.	Cyr. S., *Vita Sabae*
V. Sol.	Plu., *Vita Solonis*
X.	Xenophon

MODERN REFERENCE WORKS, SERIES, PERIODICALS

AAH	*Acta antiqua Academiae scientiarum hungaricae*
AAS	*Acta apostolicae sedis*
ABAW.PPH	*Abhandlungen der Bayerischen Akademie der Wissenschaften. philosophisch-philologische und historische Klasse*
ABla	*Analekta Blatadon*
ACO	Schwartz, E., *Acta conciliorum oecumenicorum*
ACW	Ancient Christian Writers
ADB	*Allgemeine Deutsche Biographie*
AGWG.PH	*Abhandlungen der Gesellschaft der Wissenschaften zu Göttingen, philologisch-historische Klasse, ns*

List of Abbreviations

AKG	*Arbeiten zur Kirchengeschichte*
AnBoll	*Analecta bollandiana*
Aug.	*Augustinianum*
BAH	*Bibliothèque archéologique et historique, Institut français d'Archéologie de Beyrouth*
BALAC	*Bulletin d'ancienne littérature et d'archéologie chrétienne*
BCl.S	*Bolletino dei classici, Supplemento*
BEthL	*Bibiotheca ephemeridum theologicarum lovaniensium*
BHG	*Bibliotheca hagiographica graeca*, 3rd ed., 2 voll. (Brussels 1957) + *Supplément, Appendices et Tables* = *SHG*, vol. 8a
Bijdr.	*Bijdragen: Tijdschrift voor philosophie en theologie*
BNP.A	Cancik, H., H. Schneider, C.F. Salazar, *Brill's New Pauly, Antiquity*, 15 voll. + index (Leiden/Boston 2002–10)
BOCV	Assemanus (Assemani), J.S., Bibliotheca orientalis clementino-vaticana
BVP	Bibliotheca veterum patrum antiquorumque scriptorum ecclesiasticorum graeco-latina
ByA	*Byzantinisches Archiv*
ByZ	*Byzantinische Zeitschrift*
Byz.	*Byzantion*
CACSS	Corpus apologetarum christianorum saeculi secundi
CChr.SG	Corpus christianorum: Series graeca
CChr.SL	Corpus christianorum: Series latina
CE	Herbermann, C.G., E.A. Pace, C.B. Pallen, T.J. Shahan, J.J. Wynne, *The Catholic Encyclopedia*, 15 voll. + index (New York 1907–14)
CFHB.Th	Corpus Fontium Historiae Byzantinae, Series Thessalonicensis
CistSS	*Cistercian Studies*
CLA	*Codices Latini Antiquiores: A Palaeographical Guide to Latin Manuscripts Prior to the Ninth Century*

List of Abbreviations

CPG	Geerard, M., F. Winkelmann, *Clavis patrum graecorum,* voll. 1, 2, 4, 5 (Turnhout 1974–87); Geerard, M., and J. Noret, vol. 3, 2nd ed. (Turnhout 2003); Geerard, M., J. Noret, F. Glorie, and J. Desmet, *Supplementum* (Turnhout 1998)
CPL	Dekkers, E., and A. Gaar, *Clavis patrum latinorum* (Steenbrugge 1995)
CRE	*Christian Roman Empire Series*
CSCO	Corpus scriptorum christianorum orientalium
CSCO.S	Corpus scriptorum christianorum orientalium: Scriptores Syri
CSCO.Sub	*Corpus scriptorum christianorum orientalium: Subsidia*
CSEL	Corpus scriptorum ecclesiasticorum latinorum
CUA	The Catholic University of America
DACL	Cabrol, F., and H. Leclercq, *Dictionnaire d'archéologie chrétienne et de liturgie,* 15 voll. (Paris 1907–53)
DCB	Smith, W., and H. Wace, *A Dictionary of Christian Biography,* 4 voll. (London 1877–87)
DGE	*Diccionario Griego-Español*
DHGE	Baudrillart, A., A. Vogt, U. Rouziès, R. Aubert, *et al., Dictionnaire d'histoire et de géographie ecclésiastiques,* voll. 1–26 (Paris 1912–97)
DOP	*Dumbarton Oaks Papers*
DOS	*Dumbarton Oaks Studies*
DThC	Vacant, A., E. Mangenot, and É. Amann, *Dictionnaire de théologie catholique,* voll. 1–15 (Paris 1930–50) + *Tables Générales,* voll. 1–3 (Paris 1951–72)
EC	Paschini, P., *Enciclopedia cattolica,* 12 voll. + supplement (Vatican City 1948–69)
EEC	Ferguson, E., M.P. McHugh, F.W. Norris, *Encyclopedia of Early Christianity,* 2nd ed., 2 voll. (London/New York 1997)

List of Abbreviations

Elec.	*Electrum*
EOMJA	*Ecclesiae occidentalis monumenta iuris antiquissima: Canonum et conciliorum graecorum interpretationes latinae* (Oxford 1899–1939)
EThL	*Ephemerides theologicae lovanienses*
FHG	Fragmenta historicorum graecorum
FilMed	*Filologia mediolatina*
Forcellini	Forcellini, A., I. Furlanetto, F. Corradini, and I. Perin, *Lexicon Totius Latinititis,* 6 voll., 4th ed. (Padua 1965)
FOTC	Fathers of the Church
GCS	Die griechischen christlichen Schriftsteller der ersten drei Jahrhunderte
GEDSH	Brock, S.P., A.M. Butts, G.A. Kiraz, and L. Van Rompay, *Gorgias Encyclopedic Dictionary of the Syriac Heritage* (Piscataway, N.J. 2011)
GRBS	*Greek, Roman, and Byzantine Studies*
Hahn	Hahn, A., G.L. Hahn, and A. von Harnack, *Bibliothek der Symbole und Glaubensregeln der alten Kirche*
HCO	*Histoire des conciles œcuméniques*
Hefele-Leclercq	*Histoire des conciles d'après les documents originaux*
Hist.	*Historia: Zeitschrift für alte Geschichte*
HThR	*Harvard Theological Review*
ILCV	*Inscriptiones latinae christianae veteres*
IThQ	*Irish Theological Quarterly*
JECS	*Journal of Early Christian Studies*
JETS	*Journal of the Evangelical Theological Society*
JHS	*Journal of Hellenic Studies*
JRS	*Journal of Roman Studies*
JThS	*Journal of Theological Studies*
Kl.	*Kleronomia*
LEC	The Library of Early Christianity

List of Abbreviations

LSJ	Liddell, H.G., R. Scott, H.S. Jones, and R. McKenzie, *A Greek-English Lexicon,* 9th ed. (Oxford 1968)
LTP	*Laval théologique et philosophique*
MBAV	*Miscellanea Bibiliothecae Apostolicae Vaticanae*
MGH.AA	Monumenta Germaniae historica, Auctores antiquissimi
MSR	*Mélanges de science religeuse*
NCE	W.J. McDonald, *et al., New Catholic Encyclopedia,* 2nd ed., 14 voll. + Index (New York, *etc.* 1967)
NEBrit.Mic	*The New Encyclopedia Britannica,* 15th ed., *Micropaedia,* voll. 1–29 (Chicago, *etc.* 1995)
NJBC	Brown, R.E., J.A. Fitzmyer, R.E. Murphy, *New Jerome Biblical Commentary* (Englewood Cliffs, N.J. 1990)
NPNF	A Select Library of Nicene and Post-Nicene Fathers of the Christian Church
NTG	*Novum testamentum graece*
OCD	Hornblower, S., and A. Spawforth, *The Oxford Classical Dictionary,* 3rd ed. (Oxford/New York 1996)
ODB	Kazhdan, A., and A.-M. Talbot, *The Oxford Dictionary of Byzantium,* 3 voll. (New York/Oxford 1991)
ODCC	Livingstone, E.A., *The Oxford Dictionary of the Christian Church,* 3rd ed. (Oxford, *etc.* 1997)
Orbis	Stanford Geospatial Network Model of the Roman World (orbis.stanford.edu)
OrChr	*Oriens christianus*
PatMS	*Patristic Monograph Series*
PatSt	*Catholic University of America Patristic Studies*
PCB-E	*Prosopographie chrétienne du bas-empire*
PG	Patrologia graeca
PGL	G.W.H. Lampe, *A Patristic Greek Lexicon* (Oxford 1961)

List of Abbreviations

PL	Patrologia latina
PLRE	*Prosopography of the Later Roman Empire*
PO	Patrologia orientalis
PTS	Patristische Texte und Studien
Quasten	Quasten, J., *Patrology*, 3 voll. (Utrecht 1950); *v.* also Di Berardino, A.
RAC	*Reallexikon für Antike und Christentum* (Stuttgart 1950–)
RB	*Revue biblique*
RE	Wissowa, G., W. Kroll, and K. Witte, *Paulys Real-Encyclopädie der classischen Altertums wissenschaft*
RechAug	*Recherches augustiniennes*
REG	*Revue des études grecques*
RevSR	*Revue des sciences religieuses*
RHE	*Revue d'Histoire Ecclésiastique*
RMab	*Revue Mabillon*
RSPhTh	*Revue des sciences philosophiques et théologiques*
RSR	*Recherches de science religieuse*
RTL	*Revue théologique de Louvain*
SAWW.PH	*Sitzungsberichte der Akademie der Wissenschaften in Wien, philosophisch-historische Klasse*
SBAW.PPH	*Sitzungsberichte der bayerischen Akademie der Wissenschaften in München, philosophisch-philologische und historische Klasse*
SC	Sources chrétiennes
SHG	*Subsidia hagiographica*
SISMEL	Società Internazionale per lo Studio del Medioevo Latino
SJTh	*Scottish Journal of Theology*
SPhTh	*Sciences philosophiques et théologiques*
StAnt	*Studia antoniana*
STG	*Studien zur Theologie und Geschichte*
StPatr	*Studia patristica*

StT	*Studi e Testi*
SupVigChr	*Supplements to Vigiliae christianae*
TD	Textus et Documenta, Series theologica
TECC	Textos y estudios Cardenal Cisneros
Theol.	*Theology: A journal of Historic Christianity*
Theol(A)	*Theologia: Epistēmonikon periodikon*
Theol(P)	*Théologie, Études publiées sous la direction de la faculté de théologie S.J. de Lyon-Fourvière*
ThH	*Theologie historique*
ThQ	*Theologische Quartalschrift*
TLG	*Thesaurus linguae grecae* (stephanus.tlg.uci.edu)
Tr.	*Traditio: Studies in Ancient and Medieval History, Thought and Religion*
TS	*Theological Studies*
TTH	Translated Texts for Historians
TU	*Texte und Untersuchungen zur Geschichte der altchristlichen Literatur*
VigChr	*Vigiliae christianae*
WSA	Works of St. Augustine
ZAC	*Zeitschrift für antikes Christentum*
ZKG	*Zeitschrift für Kirchengeschichte*

MANUSCRIPT ABBREVIATIONS

BAV	Biblioteca Apostolica Vaticana
Bibl.	Biblioteca, Bibliothèque, Bibliothek
BN	Bibliothèque Nationale
Brit.	British
capit.	capitolare
Clar.	*Claromontanus*
expl.	*explicit* (ends)
Genn.	*Gennadius*
gr.	*graecus*

inc. *incipit* (begins)
Kaiserl.-Königl. *Kaiserlich-Königliche*
lat. *latinus*
Libr. Library
Naz. Nazionale
Neap. *Neapolitanus*
Phil. *Phillippicus*
Vat. *vaticanus*

OTHER ABBREVIATIONS

acc. *accusative*
ad loc. *ad locum* (on the aforementioned passage)
ad uoc. *ad uocem* (in the article on that word)
aor. aorist
ap. crit. *apparatus criticus* (the c. nn. on the Greek text)
ap. font. *apparatus fontium* (the apparatus of ancient sources)
art. article
bk(k.) book(s)
Byz. Byzantine
ca. *circa* (approximately)
Calif. California
cf. *confer* (compare)
c. n. critical note (a note of the *ap. crit.*)
cod./codd. codex/codices
d. died
dat. dative
def. definite
demonstr. demonstrative
diss. dissertation
d. o. direct object
e.g. *exempli gratia* (for example)

List of Abbreviations

esp.	especially
ex(x).	example(s)
fasc.	*fasciculus,* fascicle
fem.	feminine
fut.	future
gen.	genitive
Gk.	Greek
ib., ibid.	*ibidem* (in the same work)
i.e.	*id est* (that is)
impf.	imperfect(ive)
indic.	indicative
infin.	infinitive
IRHT	Institut de Recherche et d'Histoire des Textes
Ky.	Kentucky
l(l).	line(s)
LXX	Septuagint (the predominant form of the Greek text of the OT)
LXX var.	*v.* the intro. to the *Index scripturisticus*
masc.	masculine
Mass.	Massachusetts
Mich.	Michigan
ms(s).	manuscript(s)
MT	Masoretic Text (the predominant form of the Hebrew text of the OT)
neg.	negative
neut.	neuter
N.J.	New Jersey
n(n).	note(s)
nom.	nominative
n. s.	new series
N.Y.	New York State
obj.	object

opt.	optative
pass.	passive
per.	person
pl.	plural
p(p).	page(s)
prep.	preposition
pres.	present
pron(n).	pronoun(s)
pt.	part, participle
rel.	relative
rpt.	reprint(ed)
sc.	*scilicet* (signals a word supplied to facilitate comprehension)
sec(c).	section(s)
seq.	*sequitur* (follows)
ser.	series
sg.	singular
sub uoc.	*sub uoce* (indicates a lemma in a lexicon or index)
subj.	subject
subjunc.	subjunctive
tom.	*tomus* (volume or fascicle)
U.K.	United Kingdom
v.	*uide* (see)
vb(b).	verb(s)
viz.	*uidelicet* (namely)
Wisc.	Wisconsin

BIBLIOGRAPHY

Bible: Ancient Texts and Versions

masoretic text (mt)

Kittel, R., K. Elliger, W. Rudolph, *et al., Biblia hebraica stuttgartensia* (Stuttgart 1967–77)

septuagint (lxx)

Wevers, J.W., *Genesis, Septuaginta,* vol. 1 (Göttingen 1974)

Hanhart, R., Esther, 2nd ed., *Septaginta,* vol. 8.3 (Göttingen 1983)

Ziegler, J., *Jeremias, Baruch, Threni, Epistula Jeremiae,* 2nd ed., *Septuaginta,* vol. 15 (Göttingen 1976)

Rahlfs, A., *Psalmi cum odis,* 3rd ed., *Septuaginta,* vol. 10 (Göttingen 1979)

new testament

Nestle, E., B. Aland, *et al., Novum testamentum graece,* 28th ed. (Stuttgart 2012)

vulgate

Weber, R., and R. Gryson, *Biblia sacra iuxta vulgatam versionem,* 4th ed. (Stuttgart 1994)

Bible: Modern Translations and Commentaries

i. translations

The New English Bible: The Old Testament, The New Testament, The Apocrypha (Oxford/Cambridge 1970)

Metzger, B.M., and R.E. Murphy, *The New Oxford Annotated Bible with the Apocryphal / Deuterocanonical Books* (New York 1991)

II. COMMENTARIES

Entire Bible

Brown, R.E., J.A. Fitzmyer, R.E. Murphy, *New Jerome Biblical Commentary* (Englewood Cliffs, N.J. 1990)

2 Corinthians

Murphy-O'Connor, J., "The Second Letter to the Corinthians," *NJBC*, pp. 816–29

Ancient Authors and Works: Texts, Translations, Commentaries[1]

'Abdisho' bar Brikha (Ebedjesus), *Carmen*

Assemanus (Assemani), J.S., *Carmen Ebediesu Metropolitae Sobae et Armeniae continens catalogum librorum omnium ecclesiasticorum,* BOCV, vol. 3.1: *De scriptoribus syris nestorianis* (Rome 1725), pp. 1–362

Acta conciliorum oecumenicorum, *v.* Concilia oecumenica

***Adlocutio synodi chalcedonensis ad Marcianum imperatorem,* *v.* Concilia oecumenica, Concilium chalcedonense (451)**

Aelianus, *De natura animalium*

Scholfield, A.F., *Aelian on the Characteristics of Animals,* 3 voll., vol. 1: *Books I–V* (Cambridge, Mass./London 1958)

Varia Historia

Wilson, N.G., *Aelian, Historical Miscellany* (Cambridge, Mass./London 1997)

Ambrosius mediolanensis, *De fide ad Gratianum*

Faller, O., *Sancti Ambrosii opera,* pt. 8: *De fide,* CSEL, vol. 78 (Vienna 1962)

1. Where the title of a patristic work is followed by two bibliographical entries, the first is that for the ancient text, the second for an English translation.

Bibliography

Amphilochius iconiensis

Datema, C., *Amphilochii iconiensis opera: Orationes, pluraque alia quae supersunt, nonnulla etaim spuria*, CChr.SG, vol. 3 (Turnhout 1978)

Anonymous, *De uita et miraculis Sanctae Theclae libri ii*

Dagron, G., *Vie et miracles de sainte Thècle*, *SHG*, vol. 62 (Brussels 1978)

Apollinaris laodicenus, *Fragmenta*

Lietzmann, H., *Apollinaris von Laodicea und seine Schule* (Tübingen 1904)

Aristophanes, *Pax*

Olson, S.D., *Aristophanes, Peace* (Oxford 1998)

Aristotle, *Poetics*

Kassel, R., *Aristotelis De arte poetica liber* (Oxford 1965)

Athanasius alexandrinus

Opera

Montfaucon, B. de, *Sancti patris nostri Athanasii archiepiscopi alexandrini opera omnia quae extant, etc.*, 2 voll. (Paris 1698); rpt. PG, voll. 25–28 (Paris 1857)

In illud: Omnia mihi tradita sunt

Montfaucon, B. de, *Sancti patris nostri Athanasii archiepiscopi alexandrini opera omnia quae extant, etc.*, vol. 1 (Paris 1698), pp. 103–08; rpt. PG, vol. 25 (Paris 1857), coll. 208–20

Contra gentes

Thomson, R.W., *Athanasius, Contra gentes and De incarnatione* (Oxford 1971)

De decretis nicaenae synodi

Opitz, H.G., *Athanasius Werke*, vol. 2.1 (Berlin 1940), pp. 1–45

De incarnatione

Thomson, R.W., *Athanasius, Contra gentes and De incarnatione* (Oxford 1971)

Epistula ad Epictetum

Ludwig, G., "Athanasii Epistula ad Epictetum" (doctoral diss., University of Jena 1911)

Epistula de synodis Arimini et Seleuciae

Opitz, H.G., *Athanasius Werke*, vol. 2.1–7 (Berlin/Leipzig 1935–40), pp. 231–78

Historia arianorum ad monachos

Opitz, H.G., *Athanasius Werke*, vol. 2.1–7 (Berlin/Leipzig 1935–40), pp. 181–230

Tomus ad antiochenos

Brennecke, H.C., U. Heil, and A. von Stockhausen, *Athanasius Werke*, vol. 2.8: *Die "Apologien,"* (New York/Berlin 2006), pp. 341–51

Atticus constantinopolitanus, *Homiliae in natiuitatem*

Lebon, J., "Discours d'Atticus de Constantinople 'Sur la Sainte Mère de Dieu,'" *Muséon* 46 (1933), pp. 167–202

Augustinus hipponensis, *Epistulae*

Divjak, J., *Epistulae ex duobus codicibus nuper in lucem prolatae*, CSEL, vol. 88 (Vienna 1981)

Teske, R.J., *Letters 156–210*, WSA, vol. 2.3 (New York 2004)

Barhadbeshabba halvaniensis

Causa fundationis scholarum

Scher, A., *La cause de la fondation des écoles*, PO, vol. 4 (Paris 1908), pp. 315–413

Historia

Nau, F., *Barhadbeshabba, Histoire*, PO, vol. 9 (Paris 1913)

Basilius caesariensis Cappadociae

Homiliae in psalmos

Garnier, J., and P. Maran, *Basilii Caesareae archiepiscopi opera omnia*, vol. 1 (Paris 1721), pp. 90–204; rpt. PG, vol. 29 (Paris 1886), coll. 209–494

De spiritu sancto

Pruche, B., *Basile de Césarée, Sur le Saint-Esprit,* 2nd ed., SC, vol. 17bis (Paris 1968)

Epistulae

Courtonne, Y., *Saint Basile, Lettres*, 3 voll. (Paris 1957–66)

Deferrari, R.J., *Saint Basil, The Letters,* 4 voll. (Cambridge, Mass./ London 1926–34)

Homiliae in Hexameron

Giet, S., *Basile de Césarée, Homélies sur l'hexaéméron*, 2nd edn., SC, vol. 26 bis (Paris 1968)

Catenae Graecorum patrum in Novum Testamentum, in 1Cor.

Cramer, J.A., *Catenae graecorum patrum in Novum Testamentum*, vol. 5 (Oxford 1841; rpt. Hildesheim 1967), pp. 1–344

Chronicon Paschale

Dindorf, L., *Chronicon Paschale* (Bonn 1832)

Clemens Alexandrinus, *Stromata*

Stählin, O., L. Früchtel, and U. Treu, *Clemens alexandrinus*, vol. 2, 4th ed., GCS, vol. 52: *Stromata, bkk.* 1–6 (Berlin 1985); *Clemens alexandrinus*, vol. 3, 2nd ed., GCS, vol. 17^2 (Berlin 1968), pp. 3–102

Ferguson, J., *Clement of Alexandria, Stromateis,* Bkk. 1–3, FOTC, vol. 85 (Washington 1991)

Codex theodosianus

Mommsen, T., and P.M. Meyer, *Theodosiani libri XVI cum consitutionibus sirmondianis,* 2nd ed., voll. 1f. (Berlin 1954)

Collectio atheniensis

Schwartz, E., *Concilium vniversale ephesenum, Acta graeca, ACO,* vol. 1.1.7: *Collectio segvierana, Collectio atheniensis, Collectiones minores* (Berlin/Leipzig 1929)

Collectio casinensis

Schwartz, E., *ACO,* vol. 1.3: *Collectionis casinensis sive synodici a Rustico diacono compositi pars prior* (Berlin/Leipzig 1929); vol. 1.4: *Collectionis casinensis sive synodici a Rustico diacono compositi pars altera* (Berlin/Leipzig 1922–23)

Bibliography

Collectio palatina

Schwartz, E., *ACO*, vol. 1.5.1: *Collectio palatina sive qui fertur Marius Mercator* (Berlin/Leipzig 1924–25)

Collectio sichardiana

Schwartz, E., *Concilium vniversale ephesenum*, *ACO*, vol. 1.5.2: *Cyrilli epistula synodica, etc.*; *Collectio sichardiana*; *etc.* (Berlin/Leipzig 1924–26), pp. 245–318

Collectio uaticana

Schwartz, E., *Concilium vniversale ephesenum, Acta graeca, ACO*, vol. 1.1.1: *Collectio vaticana 1–32* (Berlin/Leipzig 1927)

________, *ibid.*, vol. 1.1.2: *Collectio vaticana 33–80* (Berlin/Leipzig 1927)

________, *ibid.*, vol. 1.1.3: *Collectio vaticana 81–119* (Berlin/Leipzig 1927)

________, *ibid.*, vol. 1.1.4: *Collectio vaticana 120–139* (Berlin/Leipzig 1928)

________, *ibid.*, vol. 1.1.5: *Collectio vaticana 140–164* (Berlin/Leipzig 1927)

Collectio ueronensis

Schwartz, E., *Concilium vniversale ephesenum, Acta graeca, ACO*, vol. 1.2: *Collectio veronensis* (Berlin/Leipzig 1925–26)

Concilium laodicense (sometime between 343 and 381?)

Hefele, K.J., and H. Leclercq, *Histoire des Conciles*, vol. 1.2 (Paris 1907), pp. 989–1028

Concilia oecumenica (nicaena, ephesinum I, ephesinum II, chalcedonense, constantinopolitanum II)

Concilia nicaena (325 and 787)

Alberigo, G. *et al.*, *Conciliorum oecumenicorum generaliumque decreta*, vol. 1: *The Oecumenical Councils from Nicaea I to Nicaea II (325–787)* (Turnhout 2006), pp. 19–34

Concilium ephesinum I (431)

Contestatio directa beato Cyrillo

Schwartz, E., *ACO*, vol. 1.4: *Collectionis casinensis sive synodici a Rustico diacono compositi pars altera* (Berlin/Leipzig 1922–23), pp. 27–30 = #82

Precatio altera septem episcoporum orientalium ad imperatorem

Schwartz, E., *Concilium vniversale ephesenum, Acta graeca, ACO*, vol. 1.1.7: *Collectio atheniensis* (Berlin/Leipzig 1929), pp. 74f. = #63

Relatio synodi ad Caelestinum

Schwartz, E., *Concilium vniversale ephesenum, Acta graeca, ACO*, vol. 1.1.3: *Collectio vaticana 81–119* (Berlin/Leipzig 1927), pp. 5–9 = #82

Relatio synodi ad imperatores

Schwartz, E., *Concilium vniversale ephesenum, Acta graeca, ACO*, vol. 1.1.3: *Collectio vaticana 81–119* (Berlin/Leipzig 1927), pp. 3–5 = #81

Concilium ephesinum II (449)

Acta syra

Flemming, J., and G. Hoffman, *Akten der ephesinischen Synode vom Jahre 449: Syrisch, AGWG.PH* 15 (Berlin 1917)[2]

Perry, S.G.F., *The Second Synod of Ephesus Together with Certain Extracts Relating to It* (Dartford, U.K. 1881)

Concilium chalcedonense (451)

Gesta actionis 1

Schwartz, E., *Concilium vniversale chalcedonense, ACO*, vol. 2.1.1: *Epistularum collectiones, Actio prima* (Berlin/Leipzig 1933), pp. 55–196

Gesta actionum 2–7

Schwartz, E., *Concilium vniversale chalcedonense, ACO*, vol. 2.1.2: *Actio secunda, Epistularum collectio B, Actiones 3–7* (Berlin/Leipzig 1933), pp. 3–42, 69–163

Gesta actionum 8–17

Schwartz, E., *Concilium vniversale chalcedonense, ACO*, vol. 2.1.3: *Actiones VIII–XVII. 18–31* (Berlin/Leipzig 1935), pp. 3–99

Price, R.M., and J.M. Gaddis, *The Acts of the Council of Chalcedon*, TTH, vol. 45.1–3 (Liverpool 2005)

2. Flemming offers both the Syriac and a German translation.

Gestorum chalcedonensium Versio a Rustico edita **(= The Latin Translation of the Acts)**

Schwartz, E., *Concilium vniversale chalcedonense, ACO,* vol. 2.3.1: *Gesta actionis primae* (Berlin/Leipzig 1935)

Schwartz, E., *Concilium vniversale chalcedonense, ACO,* vol. 2.3.2: *Gestorum chalcedonensium Versio a Rustico edita,* pt. 2: *Actiones II–VI* (Berlin/Leipzig 1936)

Adlocutio synodi chalcedonensis ad Marcianum imperatorem

Schwartz, E., *Concilium vniversale chalcedonense, ACO,* vol. 2.1.3: *Actiones VIII–XVII. 18–31* (Berlin/Leipzig 1935), pp. 110–16 = #20

Prosopographia et topographia actorum chalcedonensium et encycliorum Indices

Schwartz, E., *Concilium vniversale chalcedonense, ACO,* vol. 2.5 (Berlin/Leipzig 1938)

Relatio synodi chalcedonensis ad Leonem romanum

Schwartz, E., *Concilium vniversale chalcedonense, ACO,* vol. 2.1.3: *Actiones VIII–XVII. 18–31* (Berlin/Leipzig 1935), pp. 116–18 = #21

Concilium constantinopolitanum II sub Iustiniano habitum (553)

Straub, J., *Concilium vniversale constantinopolitanum sub Iustiniano habitum, ACO,* vol. 4.1: *Concilii actiones VIII, etc.* (Berlin 1971)

Price, R.M., *The Acts of the Council of Constantinople of 553* (Liverpool 2009)

Definitio capitulorum quintae synodi quae congregata est sub Iustiniano Constantinopoli

Riedinger, R., *ACO,* ser. 2, vol. 1: *Concilium lateranense a. 649 celebratum* (Berlin 1984), pp. 224–34

Constitutiones apostolorum

Metzger, B.M., *Les Constitutions apostoliques,* SC, voll. 320, 329, 336 (Paris 1985–87)

Creeds, *v.* Symbola

Bibliography

Cyrillus alexandrinus

Opera omnia

Aubertus (Aubert), J., *Sancti patris nostri Cyrilli Alexandriae archiepiscopi opera,* 6 voll. (Paris 1636–38)

Commentarii in Isaiam prophetam

Aubertus (Aubert), J., *Sancti patris nostri Cyrilli Alexandriae archiepiscopi opera,* vol. 2 (Paris 1638), pp. 1–920; rpt. PG, vol. 70 (Paris 1864), coll. 9–1449

Commentarii in Zachariam prophetam

Pusey, P.E., *Sancti patris nostri Cyrilli archiepiscopi alexandrini opera,* vol. 2 (Oxford 1868; rpt. Brussels 1965), pp. 282–544

Commentarii in euangelium Lucae

Payne Smith, R., *A Commentary upon the Gospel According to S. Luke by S. Cyril, Patriarch of Alexandria; now first translated into English from an ancient Syriac version,* 2 voll. (Oxford 1859)

Apologeticus ad imperatorem Theodosium

Schwartz, E., *Concilium vniversale ephesenum, Acta graeca, ACO,* vol. 1.1.3: *Collectio vaticana 81–119* (Berlin/Leipzig 1927), pp. 75–90 = #118

Apologeticus contra Theodoretum

Schwartz, E., *Concilium vniversale ephesenum, Acta graeca, ACO,* vol. 1.1.6: *Collectio vaticana 165–172* (Berlin/Leipzig 1928), pp. 107–46 = ##167–69

Capitula ex Nestorio excerpta

Schwartz, E., *Concilium vniversale ephesenum, Acta graeca, ACO,* vol. 1.1.6: *Collectio vaticana 165–172* (Berlin/Leipzig 1928), pp. 3–13 = #165; *cf. Marius Mercator, Nestorii Capitula excerpta a Cyrillo*

Contra Iulianum imperatorem

Riedweg, C. *et al.*, *Kyrill von Alexandrien,* vol. 1: *Gegen Julian,* pt. 1: *Buch 1–5,* GCS, n. s. vol. 20 (Berlin/Boston 2016)

Kinzig, W., T. Brüggemann, *et al.*, *Kyrill von Alexandrien,* vol. 1: *Gegen Julian,* pt. 2: *Buch 6–10 und Fragmente,* GCS, n. s. vol. 21 (Berlin/Boston 2017)

Contra Nestorium

Schwartz, E., *Concilium vniversale ephesenum, Acta graeca, ACO,* vol. 1.1.6: *Collectio vaticana 165–172* (Berlin/Leipzig 1928), pp. 13–106 = #166

De recta fide ad Arcadiam et Marinam

Schwartz, E., *Concilium vniversale ephesenum, Acta graeca, ACO,* vol. 1.1.5: *Collectio vaticana 140–164* (Berlin/Leipzig 1927), pp. 62–118 = #150

De recta fide ad Pulcheriam et Eudociam

Schwartz, E., *Concilium vniversale ephesenum, Acta graeca, ACO,* vol. 1.1.5: *Collectio vaticana 140–164* (Berlin/Leipzig 1927), pp. 26–61 = #149

De recta fide ad Theodosium

Schwartz, E., *Concilium vniversale ephesenum, Acta graeca, ACO,* vol. 1.1.1: *Collectio vaticana 1–32* (Berlin/Leipzig 1927), pp. 42–72 = #7

De sancta trinitate dialogi i–vii

Durand, G.-M. de, *Cyrille d'Alexandrie, Dialogues sur la Trinité,* SC, voll. 231, 237, 246 (Paris 1976–78)

Duodecim capitum defensio aduersus orientales epsicopos

Schwartz, E., *Concilium vniversale ephesenum, Acta graeca, ACO,* vol. 1.1.5: *Collectio vaticana 140–164* (Berlin/Leipzig 1927), pp. 15–25 = #148

Epistulae

Aubertus (Aubert), J., *Sancti patris nostri Cyrilli Alexandriae archiepiscopi opera,* vol. 5.2 (Paris 1638); rpt. PG, vol. 77 (Paris 1859), coll. 9–390

Schwartz, E., *Codex vaticanus gr. 1431: Eine antichalkedonische Sammlung aus der Zeit Kaiser Zenos* (Munich 1927)[3]

McEnerney, J.I., *St. Cyril of Alexandria, Letters,* FOTC, voll. 76f. (Washington 1987)

3. This volume contains critical editions of Cyr., *epp.* 69, 72, 76.

Epistulae festales

Meunier, B., W. Burns, and M.O. Boulnois, *Cyrille d'Alexandrie, Lettres festales,* voll. 1–3, SC, voll. 372, 392, 434 (Paris 1991–98)

Wickham, L.R., *Cyril of Alexandria, Select Letters* (Oxford 1983)

Homilia diuersa 4: De Maria deipara in Nestorium

Schwartz, E., *Concilium vniversale ephesenum, Acta graeca, ACO,* vol. 1.1.2: *Collectio vaticana 33–80* (Berlin/Leipzig 1927), pp. 102–04 = #80

Quod unus sit Christus

Pusey, P.E., *Sancti patris nostri Cyrilli archiepiscopi alexandrini opera,* vol. 7 (Oxford 1877; rpt. Brussels 1965), pp. 334–424

Cyrillus Scythopolitanus

Vita Euthymii

Schwartz, E., *Kyrillos von Skythopolis, TU* 49.2 (Leipzig 1939), pp. 3–85

Vita Sabae

Schwartz, E., *Kyrillos von Skythopolis, TU* 49.2 (Leipzig 1939), pp. 85–200

Damasus, *Tomus seu Fides Damasi*

Turner, C.H., *EOMJA,* vol. 1, fasc. 2, pt. 1: *Nicaenum concilium, Appendices et Supplementa* (Oxford 1913), pp. 281–94

Definitio capitulorum, etc.; *v.* **Concilia oecumenica, Concilium constantinopolitanum sub Iustiniano habitum (553)**

Demosthenes

De corona

Butcher, S.H., *Demosthenis orationes,* vol. 1 (Oxford 1903)

De falsa legatione

Shilleto, R., *Demosthenis De falsa legatione,* 7th ed. (Cambridge/London 1890)

Ephraem Syrus, *Carmina nisibena*

Beck, E., *Des heiligen Ephraem des Syrers Carmina Nisibena,* vol. 1, CSCO, voll. 218f. (Leuven 1961)

Epicurus, *fragmenta*

Usener, H., *Epicurea* (Leipzig 1887)

Epiphanius, *Panarion*

Holl, K., *Epiphanius,* vol. 1, GCS, vol. 25: *Panarion Haer.* 1–33 (Leipzig 1915), pp. 153–464; *Epiphanius,* vol. 2, GCS, vol. 31: *Panarion Haer.* 34–64 (Leipzig 1922); *Epiphanius,* vol. 3, GCS, vol. 37: *Panarion Haer.* 65–80 (Leipzig 1933), pp. 1–496

Epistula ad Cosmam

Nau, F., *La lettre à Cosme*, PO, vol. 13 (Paris 1916), pp. 271–86

Epistularum ante gesta collectio

Schwartz, E., *Concilium vniversale chalcedonense, ACO,* vol. 2.3.1: *Epistularum ante gesta collectio* (Berlin/Leipzig 1935), pp. 1–23

Epistularum collectio B

Schwartz, E., *Concilium vniversale chalcedonense, ACO,* vol. 2.1.2: *Collectio B* (Berlin/Leipzig 1933), pp. 45–65

Epistularum collectio H

Schwartz, E., *Concilium vniversale chalcedonense, ACO,* vol. 2.1.1: *Epistularum collectiones* (Berlin/Leipzig 1933), pp. 35–52

Epistularum collectio M

Schwartz, E., *Concilium vniversale chalcedonense, ACO,* vol. 2.1.1: *Epistularum collectiones* (Berlin/Leipzig 1933), pp. 3–32

Etymologicum gudianum

Sturz, F.W., *Etymologicum graecae linguae gudianum et alia grammaticorum scripta, etc.* (Leipzig 1818; rpt. Hildesheim 1973)

Euagrius Scholasticus, *Historia ecclesiastica*

Bidez, J., and L. Parmentier, *The Ecclesiastical History of Evagrius* (London 1898)

Euripides, *Troades*

Kovacs, D., *Euripides, Trojan Women, Iphigenia among the Taurians, Ion* (Cambridge, Mass./London 1999)

Eusebius caesariensis, *De martyribus palaestinae*

Schwartz, E., *Eusebius über die Märtyrer in Palaestina, Eusebius Werke,* vol. 2.2, GCS, vol. 6.2 (Berlin 1907; rpt. 1999), pp. 907–50

Eusebius dorylaeensis, *Contestatio*

Schwartz, E., *Concilium vniversale ephesenum, Acta graeca, ACO,* vol. 1.1.1: *Collectio vaticana 1–32* (Berlin/Leipzig 1927), pp. 101f. = #18

Facundus hermianensis, *Pro defensione trium capitulorum libri xii*

Clément, J.-M., and R. Vander Plaetse, *Facundi episcopi ecclesiae hermianensis opera omnia,* CChr.SL, vol. 90A (Brepols 1974), pp. 4–398

Flauianus constantinopolitanus

De recta fide ad Theodosium

Schwartz, E., *Concilium vniversale chalcedonense, ACO,* vol. 2.1.1: *Epistularum collectiones, Actio prima* (Berlin/Leipzig 1933), pp. 35f. = #1

Libellus appellationis ad papam Leonem

Schwartz, E., *Concilium vniversale chalcedonense, ACO,* vol. 2.2.1: *Collectio nouariensis de re Eutychis* (Berlin/Leipzig 1932), pp. 77–79 = #11

Galenus, *De sectis*

Helmreich, G., J. Marquardt, and I. Müller, *Claudii Galeni Pergameni scripta minora,* vol. 3: Περὶ αἱρέσεων τοῖς εἰσαγομένοις (Leipzig 1893)

Gennadius Presbyter, *De uiris illustribus*

Richardson, E.C., *Hieronymus, Liber de viris inlustribus*; *Gennadius, Liber de viris inlustribus, TU* 14 (Leipzig 1896)

Georgius Cedrenus, *Compendium historiarum*

Bekker, I., *Georgius Cedrenus,* 2 voll. (Bonn 1838–39)

Gregorius Magnus, *Registrum epistolarum*

Norberg, D., *Sancti Gregorii Magni Registrum epistularum,* CChr.SL, 2 voll., voll. 140, 140a (Turnhout 1982)

Gregorius Nazianzenus

Carmina de se ipso

Caillau, A.B., *Sancti patris nostri Gregorii Theologi vulgo nazianzeni archiepiscopi constantinopolitani opera omnia ... post operam et studium monachorum ordinis Sancti Benedicti e Congregatione Sancti Mauri,* vol. 2 (Paris 1842), pp. 631–995; rpt. PG, vol. 37, coll. 969–1452 (Paris 1862)

Epistulae

Gallay, P., *Saint Grégoire de Nazianze, Lettres,* 2 voll. (Paris 1964–67)

Browne, C.G., and J.E. Swallow, *Select Letters*, NPNF, ser. 2, vol. 7 (Oxford 1894), pp. 437–82

Epistulae theologicae

Gallay, P., *Grégoire de Nazianze, Lettres théologiques,* SC, vol. 208 (Paris 1974)

Orationes

Barbel, J., *Gregor von Nazianz, Die fünf theologischen Reden* (Düsseldorf 1963)

Gregorius nyssenus

Ad Theophilum aduersus Apollinaristas

Müller, F., *Gregorii nysseni opera,* vol. 3.1 (Leiden 1958), pp. 119–28

Antirrheticus aduersus Apollinarem

Müller, F., *Gregorii nysseni opera,* vol. 3.1 (Leiden 1958), pp. 129–233

De uirginitate

Aubineau, M., *Grégoire de Nysse, Traité de la Virginité,* SC, vol. 119 (Paris 1966)

Epistulae

Pasquali, G., *Gregorii nysseni opera,* vol. 8.2: *Epistulae* (Leiden 1959)

Silvas, A.M., *Gregory of Nyssa: The Letters* (Leiden 2007)

Oratio catechetica

Mühlenberg, E., and R. Windling, *Grégoire de Nysse, Discours catéchétique,* SC, vol. 453 (Paris 2000)

Refutatio confessionis Eunomii

Jaeger, W., *Gregorii nysseni opera,* vol. 2.2 (Leiden 1960), pp. 312–410

Aelius Herodianus, *De prosodia catholica*

Lentz, A., *Herodiani Technici–Reliquiae,* vol. 3.1.1 (Leipzig 1867; rpt. Hildesheim 1965), pp. 1-547

Hieronymus Presbyter (Jerome), *De uiris illustribus*

Richardson, E.C., *Hieronymus, Liber de viris inlustribus; Gennadius, Liber de viris inlustribus, TU* 14 (Leipzig 1896)

Hilarius diaconus romanus (Pope Hilary I), *Epistulae*

Thiel, A., *Epistulae romanorum pontificum genuinae et quae ad eos scriptae sunt,* vol. 1: *A S. Hilaro usque ad Pelagium II* (Braunsberg 1868), pp. 126–70

Hilarius pictauiensis (Hilary of Poitiers), *De synodis*

Coustant, P., *Sancti Hilarii Pictavorum episcopi opera* (Paris 1693); rpt. PL, vol. 10 (Paris 1844), coll. 479–546

Homerus

Ilias

West, M., *Homerus, Ilias,* 2 voll. (Leipzig 1998)

Lattimore, R., *The Iliad of Homer* (Chicago/London 1951)

Graziosi, B., and J. Haubold, *Homer, Iliad, Book VI* (Cambridge 2010)

Odyssea

Mühll, P. von der, *Homeri Odyssea* (Basel 1962)

Ibas edessenus

Epistula ad Marim persam

Concilium vniversale chalcedonense, ACO, vol. 2.1.3: *Actiones VIII–XVII. 18–31* (Berlin/Leipzig 1935), pp. 32–34 = #138

Inscriptiones graecae christianae Asiae Minoris

Grégoire, H., *Recueil des inscriptions grecques-chrétiennes d'Asie Mineure, fasc.* 1 (Paris 1922; rpt. Chicago 1980)

Inscriptiones latinae christianae

Diehl, E., *ILCV,* vol. 1 (Berlin 1925)

Iohannes Antiochenus

Müller, C., *FHG,* vol. 4: *Fragmenta Praxagorae Atheniensis … Joannis Anthiocheni, etc.* (Paris 1851), pp. 535–622

Iohannes Cassianus

De incarnatione

Petschenig, M., and G. Kreuz, *Cassiani opera,* 2nd ed., CSEL, vol. 17 (Vienna 2004), pp. 235–391

De institutis coenobiorum

Petschenig, M., and G. Kreuz, *Cassiani opera,* 2nd ed., CSEL, vol. 17 (Vienna 2004), pp. 3–231

Iohannes Chrysostomus

Opera omnia

Montfaucon, B. de, *Sancti patris nostri Joannis Chrysostomi archiepiscopi constantinopolitani opera omnia,* 13 voll. (Paris 1718–38); rpt. PG, voll. 47–64 (Paris 1859–63)

Homiliae 1–88 in Iohannem

Montfaucon, B. de, *Sancti patris nostri Joannis Chrysostomi archiepiscopi constantinopolitani opera omnia,* vol. 8 (Paris 1728), pp. 1–530; rpt. PG, vol. 59 (Paris 1862), coll. 23–482

Homiliae 1–30 in epistulam II ad Corinthios

Field, F., *Sancti patris nostri Joannis Chrysostomi … in epistulam ad Corinthios homiliae XXX* (Oxford 1845), pp. 1–316

Homiliae 1–24 in epistulam ad Ephesios

Field, F., *Sancti patris nostri Joannis Chrysostomi … in epistulam ad Ephesios homiliae XXIV* (Oxford 1852), pp. 104–365

Homiliae 1–10 in epistulam II ad Timotheum

Field, F., *Sancti patris nostri Joannis Chrysostomi … in epistulas ad Timotheum, Titum et Philemonem homiliae* (Oxford 1861), pp. 162–263

De baptismo Christi

Montfaucon, B. de, *Sancti patris nostri Joannis Chrysostomi archiepiscopi constantinopolitani opera omnia*, vol. 2 (Paris 1718), pp. 367–75; rpt. PG, vol. 49 (Paris 1862), coll. 363–72

Epistulae

Montfaucon, B. de, *Sancti patris nostri Joannis Chrysostomi archiepiscopi constantinopolitani opera omnia,* vol. 3 (Paris 1721), pp. 514–746; rpt. PG, vol. 52 (Paris 1859), coll. 529–760

Epistulae ad Olympiadem

Malingrey, A.-M., *Jean Chrysostome, Lettres à Olympias,* 2nd ed., SC, vol. 13bis (Paris 1968)

Homilia 2 in Sanctum Stephanum

Savile, H., Τοῦ ἐν ἁγίοις πατρὸς ἡμῶν Ἰωάννου ἀρχιεπισκόπου Κωνσταντινουπόλεως τοῦ Χρυσοστόμου τῶν εὑρισκομένων τόμος ἕβδομος (vol. 7, Eton 1612), p. 581; *cf.* PG, vol. 63 (Paris 1858), coll. 931–34

Homiliae Contra Anomoeos, 1–5

Malingrey, A.-M., *Jean Chrysostome, Sur l'incompréhensibilité de Dieu*, SC, vol. 28 bis (Paris 1970), pp. 92–322

Iohannes Damascenus, *Oratio secunda in dormitionem Sanctae dei genetricis Mariae*

Kotter, P., *Die schriften des Johannes von Damaskos,* vol. 5: *Opera homiletica et hagiographica,* PTS, vol. 29 (Berlin/New York 1988), pp. 516–40

Iohannes Malalas, *Chronographia*

Thurn, J., *Ioannis Malalae Chronographia* (Berlin 2000)

Iohannes Zonaras, *Epitomae historiarum*

Büttner-Wobst, T., *Iohannis Zonarae epitomae historiarum libri xviii,* vol. 3: *Libri 13–18* (Bonn 1897)

Irenaeus lugdunensis, *Aduersus haereses*

Rousseau, A., and L. Doutreleau, *Irénée de Lyon, Contre les hérésies, livre III,* vol. 2: *Édition critique, Texte et Traduction,* SC, vol. 211 (Paris 2002)

Isidorus Pelusiota[4]

Possinus (Poussines), P., *Sancti Isidori, pelusiotae, epistularum libri quinque* (Rome 1670); rpt. PG, vol. 78 (Paris 1864), coll. 178–1678

Évieux, P., *Isidore de Péluse, Lettres,* SC, voll. 422, 454 (Paris 1997–2000)

Iulianus imperator

Contra Galilaeos

Wright, W.C., *The Works of Julian with an English Translation,* vol. 3 (Cambridge, Mass./London 1923), pp. 318–427

Epistula ad Athenienses

Wright, W.C., *The Works of Julian with an English Translation,* vol. 2 (Cambridge, Mass./London 1923), pp. 239–91

Iulius romanus (Pope Julius I)

Thompson, G.L., *The Correspondence of Pope Julius I,* LEC, vol. 3 (Washington 2014)

Iustinus Martyr, *v.* **ps.-Iustinus Martyr**

4. Isidore is cited according to the traditional numeration by book and letter followed by Possinus; in addition, Évieux' continuous numeration is cited for those letters he has published so far.

Leo romanus (Pope Leo I)

Epistulae

Schwartz, E., *Concilium vniversale chalcedonense, ACO,* vol. 2.4: *Leonis papae I epistularum collectiones*

Hunt, E., *St. Leo the Great, Letters* (New York 1957)

ad Flauianum (Tomus Leonis)

Schwartz, E., *ACO,* vol. 2.2.1: *Collectio novariensis de re eutychis* (Berlin/Leipzig 1932), pp. 24–33 = #5

Silva-Tarouca, C., *Sancti Leonis Magni, Epistulae contra Eutychis haeresim,* vol. 2, *Epistulae post chalcedonense concilium missae* (452–458) = TD, vol. 20 (Rome 1935)

Feltoe, C.L., *The Letters and Sermons of Leo the Great, Bishop of Rome,* NPNF, ser. 2, vol. 12 (Oxford 1895), pp. 38–43

ad Theodoretum

Schwartz, E., *ACO,* vol. 2.4: *Leonis papae I epistularum collectiones* (Berlin/Leipzig 1932), pp. 78–81 = #71

Leontius byzantinus

Aduersus fraudes apollinaristarum

Daley, B.E., "Leontius of Byzantium: A critical edition of his works with prolegomena" (Ph.D. diss., Oxford University 1978), pp. 201–23

Contra Nestorianos et Eutychianos

Daley, B.E., "Leontius of Byzantium: A critical edition of his works with prolegomena" (Ph.D. diss., Oxford University 1978), pp. 1–74

Libanius, *epistulae*

Foerster, R., *Libanius, opera*, voll. 10f. (Leipzig 1921–22)

Liberatus, *Breuiarium causae nestorianorum et eutychianorum*

Schwartz, E., *ACO,* vol. 2.5: *Collectio sangermanensis* (Berlin/Leipzig 1936), pp. 98–141

Marcellus Comes, *Chronicon*

Mommsen, T., *Chronica minora saec. IV–VII,* MGH.AA, vol. 11 (Berlin 1894; rpt. Munich 1981), pp. 37–108

Bibliography

Croke, B., *The Chronicle of Marcellinus, A Translation and Commentary* (Sydney 1995)

Marcianus imperator

Constitutio Marciani imperatoris contra Eutychen

Schwartz, E., *Concilium vniversale chalcedonense, ACO,* vol. 2.1.3: *Actiones VIII–XVII. 18–31* (Berlin/Leipzig 1935), pp. 122–24 = #25

Constitutio Marciani imperatoris de Flauiani memoria

Schwartz, E., *Concilium vniversale chalcedonense, ACO,* vol. 2.1.3: *Actiones VIII–XVII. 18–31* (Berlin/Leipzig 1935), pp. 121f. = #24

Constitutio Marciani imperatoris de actis synodi

Schwartz, E., *Concilium vniversale chalcedonense, ACO,* vol. 2.1.3: *Actiones VIII–XVII. 18–31* (Berlin/Leipzig 1935), pp. 119f. = #22

Edictum Marciani imperatoris ad Constantinopolitanos

Schwartz, E., *Concilium vniversale chalcedonense, ACO,* vol. 2.1.3: *Actiones VIII–XVII. 18–31* (Berlin/Leipzig 1935), pp. 120f. = #23

Epistulae

ad archimandritas aelienses

Schwartz, E., *Concilium vniversale chalcedonense, ACO,* vol. 2.1.3: *Actiones VIII–XVII. 18–31* (Berlin/Leipzig 1935), pp. 124–27 = #26

ad monachos alexandrinos

Schwartz, E., *Concilium vniversale chalcedonense, ACO,* vol. 2.1.3: *Actiones VIII–XVII. 18–31* (Berlin/Leipzig 1935), pp. 129f. = #28

Marius Mercator

Commonitorium super nomine Coelestii

Schwartz, E., *ACO,* vol. 1.5.1: *Collectio palatina sive qui fertur Marius Mercator* (Berlin/Leipzig 1924–25), pp. 65–70 = #36

Commonitorium aduersum haeresim Pelagii, et Coelestii, uel etiam scripta Iuliani

Schwartz, E., *ACO,* vol. 1.5.1: *Collectio palatina sive qui fertur Marius Mercator* (Berlin/Leipzig 1924–25), pp. 5–23 = ##3–14

Nestorii Capitula excerpta a Cyrillo et a Mario Mercatore translata

Schwartz, E., *ACO,* vol. 1.5.1: *Collectio palatina sive qui fertur Marius Mercator* (Berlin/Leipzig 1924–25), pp. 55–62 = #29; *cf.* Cyrillus alexandrinus, *Capitula ex Nestorio excerpta*

Nestorii Contra haeresim Pelagii seu Caelestii Sermones I–IV

Schwartz, E., *ACO,* vol. 1.5.1: *Collectio palatina sive qui fertur Marius Mercator* (Berlin/Leipzig 1924–25), pp. 60–65 = ##31–34

Symbolum Theodori mopsuesteni et eius refutatio

Schwartz, E., *ACO,* vol. 1.5.1: *Collectio palatina sive qui fertur Marius Mercator* (Berlin/Leipzig 1924–25), pp. 23–28 = ##15–18

Menaea Junii

Spanos, A., *Codex Lesbiacus Leimonos 11, Annotated Critical Edition of an Unpublished Byzantine Menaion for June, ByA,* vol. 23 (Berlin/New York 2010)

Nestorius

Epistula altera ad Caelestinum

Loofs, F., *Nestoriana*: *Die Fragmente des Nestorius* (Halle 1905), pp. 169–72

DelCogliano, M., "The Second Letter of Nestorius to Celestine of Rome," (2005); available at tertullian.org/fathers/nestorius_two_letters_01.htm

Fragmenta

Loofs, F., *Nestoriana*: *Die Fragmente des Nestorius* (Halle 1905)

Liber Heraclidis

Bedjan, P., *Nestorius, Le Livre d'Héraclide* (Paris 1910)

Nau, F., *Nestorius, Le livre d'Héraclide de Damas* (Paris 1910)

Driver, G.R., and L. Hodgson, *The Bazaar of Heracleides* (Oxford 1925)

Sermo 18

Loofs, F., *Nestoriana*: *Die Fragmente des Nestorius* (Halle 1905), pp. 297–313

Nicephorus Callistus, *Historia ecclesiastica*

Ducaeus (du Duc), F., *Nicephori Callisti filii Xanthopuli ecclesiasticae historiae libri XVIII,* 2 voll. (Paris 1630); rpt. PG, voll. 145f. (Paris 1865)

Bibliography

Origenes, *Commentarii in Iohannem*

Blanc, C., *Origène, Commentaire sur Saint Jean,* SC, voll. 120, 157, 222, 290, 385 (Paris 1966–92)

Palladius, *Historia lausiaca*

Bartelink, G.J.M., and M. Barchiesi, *Palladio, La storia lausiaca, Vite dei santi,* vol. 2 (Milan 1974)

Photius, *Bibliotheca*

Henry, R., *Photios, Bibliothèque,* vol. 2: *Codices 84–185* (Paris 1960)

Pindarus

Snell, B., and H. Maehler, *Pindarus,* vol. 1: *Epinicia* (Leipzig 1980)

Farnell, L.R., *The Works of Pindar translated, with Literary and Critical Commentaries* (London 1932)

Race, W.H., *Pindar,* vol. 2: *Nemean Odes, Isthmian Odes, Fragments* (Cambridge, Mass./London 1997)

Pius XI romanus, *Lux ueritatis*

AAS 23 (1931), pp. 493–517; rpt. *The Light of Truth*, translated by Vatican Press (Washington 1932)

Plato

Apologia

Nicoll, W.S.M., *Platonis opera,* vol. 1 (Oxford 1995), pp. 29–63

De Republica

Adam, J., and D.A. Rees, *The Republic of Plato,* 2 voll. (Cambridge 1965)

Leges

Burnet, J., *Platonis opera,* vol. 5: *Tetralogiam nonam, Definitiones et spuria continens* (Oxford 1907)

Phaedrus

Burnet, J., *Platonis opera,* vol. 2: *Tetralogias tertiam et quartam continens* (Oxford 1901)

Plotinus, *Enneades*

Henry, P., and H.-R. Schwyzer, *Plotini opera,* 3 voll. (Oxford 1964–82)

Bibliography

Plutarchus

Moralia

An recte dictum sit latenter esse uiuendum

Einarson, B., and P.H. DeLacy, *Plutarch's Moralia in fifteen volumes*, vol. 14: *1086C–1147A* (Cambridge, Mass./London 1967), pp. 317–41

Consolatio ad Apollonium

Babbit, F.C., *Plutarch's Moralia in fifteen volumes*, vol. 2: *86B–171F* (Cambridge, Mass./London 1928), pp. 108–211

De Tranquilitate Animi

Paton, W.R., M. Pohlenz, and W. Sieveking, *Plutarchi Moralia*, vol. 3 (Leipzig 1972), pp. 187–220

Vita Solonis

Perrin, B., *Plutarch's Lives in eleven volumes*, vol. 1: *Theseus and Romulus, Lycyrgus and Numa, Solon and Publicola* (London/New York 1914)

Porphyrius Tyrius

Isagoge siue quinque uoces

Busse, A., *Porphyrii isagoge et in Aristotelis categorias commentarium* in *Commentaria in Aristotelem Graeca*, vol. 4.1 (Berlin 1887), pp. 1–22

Sententiae ad intelligibilia ducentes

Lamberz, E., *Porphyrii sententiae ad intelligibilia ducentes* (Leipzig 1975), pp. 1–59

Priscus Panites, *Fragmenta*

Bornmann, F., *Prisci panitae fragmenta* (Florence 1979)

Given, J., *The Fragmentary History of Priscus: Attila, the Huns and the Roman Empire, AD 430–476, CRE*, vol. 11 (Merchantville, N.J. 2014)

Proclus constantinopolitanus

Homilia consolatoria ad aegrotum

Rudberg, S.Y., "L'homélie pseudo-basilienne 'consolatoria ad aegrotum,'" *Muséon* 72 (1959), pp. 310–22

Oratio de laudibus beatae Mariae uirginis

Schwartz, E., *Concilium vniversale ephesenum, Acta graeca, ACO,* vol. 1.1.1: *Collectio vaticana 1–32* (Berlin/Leipzig 1927), pp. 103–07 = #19

Prosper Aquitanus, *Chronicon integrum*

Mommsen, T., *Chronica minora saec. IV–VII,* MGH.AA, vol. 9.1 (Berlin 1892), pp. 341–500

***Prosopographia et topographia actorum chalcedonensium et encycliorum Indices, v.* Concilia oecumenica, Concilium chalcedonense (451)**

Prudentius, *Peristephanon*

Cunningham, M., *Aurelii Prudentii Clementis Carmina,* CChr.SL, vol. 126 (Turnhout 1966), pp. 251–389

ps.-Athanasius alexandrinus, *Sermo maior de fide*

Schwartz, E., "Der sogenannte *Sermo maior de fide* des Athanasius," *SBAW.PPH* 6 (1925), pp. 5–37

ps.-Herodian, *De declinatione nominum*

Lentz, A., *Grammatici Graeci*, vol. 3.2.2 (Leipzig 1868–70; rpt. Hildesheim 1965), pp. 634–777

ps.-Iustinus Martyr, *Expositio de recta fide, v.* Theodoretus cyrrhensis

ps.-Plutarchus, *Apophthegmata Laconica*

Nachstädt, W., W. Sieveking, and J.B. Titchener, *Plutarchi Moralia*, vol. 2 (Leipzig 1971), pp. 110–215

Quintilianus, *Institutio oratoria*

Winterbottom, M., *M. Fabi Quintiliani*: *Institutionis oratoriae libri duodecim,* 2 voll. (Oxford 1970; published online 2017)

Russell, D.A., *Quintilian*: *The Orator's Education,* 5 voll. (Cambridge, Mass./London 2001)

***Relatio synodi chalcedonensis ad Leonem romanum, v.* Concilia oecumenica, Concilium chalcedonense (451)**

Rerum chalcedonensium collectio uaticana

Schwartz, E., *Concilium vniversale chalcedonense, ACO,* vol. 2.2.2: *Rerum chalcedonensium collectio uaticana,* pp. 1–27

Rufinus Aquileiensis, *De adulteratione librorum Origenis*

Simonetti, M., *Tyrannii Rufini opera,* CChr.SL, vol. 20 (Turnhout 1961), pp. 3–17

Seneca, *Epistulae morales*

Reynolds, L.D., *L. Annaei Senecae ad Lucilium epistulae morales*, 2 voll. (Oxford 1965)

Seuerus antiochenus, *Liber contra impium grammaticum*

Lebon, J., *Severi antiocheni liber contra impium grammaticum, Orationes III,* CSCO, voll. 93 (CSCO.S tom. 45; Syriac) 94 (CSCO.S tom. 46; Latin transl.) (Louvain 1929)

Socrates Scholasticus, *Historia ecclesiastica*

Bright, W., *Socrates' Ecclesiastical History*, 2nd ed. (Oxford 1893)

Zenos, A.C., *The Ecclesiastical History of Socrates Scholasticus,* NPNF, ser. 2, vol. 2 (Oxford 1892), pp. 1–178

Sophocles, *Oedipus Tyrannus*

Dain, A., and P. Mazon, *Sophocle,* vol. 2: *Ajax, Œdipe Roi, Électre* (Paris 1958)

Sozomenus, *Historia ecclesiastica*

Bidez, J., and G.C. Hansen, *Sozomenus, Kirchengeschichte*, GCS, vol. 50 (Berlin 1960)

Hartranft, C.D., *The Ecclesiastical History of Sozomen*, NPNF, ser. 2, vol. 2 (Oxford 1892), pp. 179–427

Suidae lexicon

Adler, A., *Suidae lexicon* (Leipzig 1928–35)

Symbola (Creeds)

Hahn, A., G.L. Hahn, and A. von Harnack, *Bibliothek der Symbole und Glaubensregeln der alten Kirche,* 3rd ed. (Wroclaw 1897; rpt. Hildesheim 1962)

Symbolum nicaenum (325) constantinopolitanum (381)

Dossetti, G.L., *Il simbolo di Nicea e di Costantiniopoli* (Rome 1967)

Symmachus, *Epistulae*

Callu, J.-P., *Symmaque, Lettres,* vol. 3: *Livres VI–VIII* (Paris 1995)

Themistius, *In Imperatorem Constantium oratio*

Schenkl, H., and G. Downey, *Themistii Orationes quae supersunt,* vol. 1 (Leipzig 1965), pp. 69–89

Theodoretus cyrrhensis

Opera omnia

Schulze, J.L., and A. Nösselt, *Theodoreti episocopi Cyri, opera omnia,* 5 voll. (Halle 1769–74); rpt. PG, voll. 80–84 (Paris 1859–64)[5]

Sirmond, J., *Theodoreti episcopi Cyri opera omnia in quatuor tomos distributa* (Paris 1642) + Garnier (Garnerius), J., *Beati Theodoreti episcopi Cyri operum tomus quintus* (Paris 1684)

Quaestiones in octateuchum

Petruccione, J.F., and R.C. Hill, *Theodoret of Cyrus, Questions on the Octateuch,* LEC, voll. 1f. (Washington 2007)

Quaestiones in reges et paralipomena

Marcos, N.F., and A. Sáenz-Badillos, *Theodoreti Cyrensis Quaestiones in Reges et Paralipomena,* TECC, vol. 32 (Madrid 1984)

Interpretatio in Psalmos

Schulze, J.L., and A. Nösselt, *Theodoreti episocopi Cyri, opera omnia,* vol. 2.2 (Halle 1769); rpt. PG, vol. 80 (Paris 1860), coll. 857–2002

Hill, R.C., *Theodoret of Cyrus, Commentary on the Psalms,* FOTC, voll. 101f. (Washington 2001–02)

Explanatio in Canticum canticorum

Schulze, J.L., and A. Nösselt, *Theodoreti episocopi Cyri, opera omnia,* vol. 2.1 (Halle 1770), pp. 1–164; rpt. PG, vol. 81 (Paris 1859), coll. 28–213

5. References to and quotations from the works of Theodoret follow this edition unless a more recent critical edition is listed below.

Commentarii in Isaiam

Guinot, J.N., *Théodoret de Cyr, Commentaire sur Isaïe,* SC, voll. 276, 295, 315 (Paris 1980–84)

Interpretatio in Ieremiam

Schulze, J.L., and A. Nösselt, *Theodoreti episocopi Cyri, opera omnia,* vol. 2 (Halle 1770), pp. 405–629; rpt. PG, vol. 81 (Paris 1864), coll. 495–760

Commentarii in Lamentationes Ieremiae

Schulze, J.L., and A. Nösselt, *Theodoreti episocopi Cyri, opera omnia,* vol. 2 (Halle 1770), pp. 647–68; rpt. PG, vol. 81 (Paris 1864), coll. 779–806

Interpretatio in Ezechielem

Schulze, J.L., and A. Nösselt, *Theodoreti episocopi Cyri, opera omnia,* vol. 2 (Halle 1770), pp. 669–1052; rpt. PG, vol. 81 (Paris 1864), coll. 807–1256

Interpretatio in Danielem

Schulze, J.L., and A. Nösselt, *Theodoreti episocopi Cyri, opera omnia,* vol. 2 (Halle 1770), pp. 1053–1304; rpt. PG, vol. 81 (Paris 1864), coll. 1256–1546

Interpretatio in xii prophetas minores

Schulze, J.L., and A. Nösselt, *Theodoreti episcopi Cyri, opera omnia,* vol. 2 (Halle 1770), pp. 1305–1694; rpt. PG, vol. 81 (Paris 1864), coll. 1545–1988

Interpretatio in xiv epistulas sancti Pauli

Schulze, J.L., and A. Nösselt, *Theodoreti episocopi Cyri, opera omnia,* vol. 3 (Halle 1771), pp. 11–718, rpt. PG, vol. 82 (Paris 1864), coll. 35–878

Hill, R.C., *Theodoret of Cyrus, Commentary on the Letters of St. Paul,* 2 voll. (Brookline, Mass. 2001)

De incarnatione domini

Guinot, J.N., *Théodoret de Cyr, La Trinité et L'Incarnation,* pt. 2: *L'Incarnation,* SC, vol. 575 (Paris 2015), pp. 10–163

Pásztori-Kupán, I., *Theodoret of Cyrus* (London/New York 2006), pp. 138–71

Demonstratio per syllogismos

Ettlinger, G.H., *Theodoret of Cyrus, Eranistes* (Oxford 1975), pp. 254–65

Ettlinger, G.H., *Theodoret of Cyrus, Eranistes,* FOTC, vol. 106 (Washington 2003), pp. 253–65

De prouidentia

Halton, T.P., *Theodoret of Cyrus on Divine Providence,* ACW, vol. 49 (New York/Mahwah, N.J. 1988)[6]

De trinitate

Guinot, J.N., *Théodoret de Cyr, La Trinité et L'Incarnation,* pt. 1: *La Trinité,* SC, vol. 574 (Paris 2015), pp. 230–365

Pásztori-Kupán, I., *Theodoret of Cyrus* (London/New York 2006), pp. 109–37

Epistula ad Rufum

Schwartz, E., *Concilium vniversale ephesenum, Acta graeca, ACO,* vol. 1.1.3: *Collectio vaticana 81–119* (Berlin/Leipzig 1927), pp. 39–42 = #97

Epistulae

Azéma, Y., *Théodoret de Cyr, Correspondance,* SC, voll. 40, 98, 111, 429 (Paris 1955–98)[7]

Jackson, B., *The Ecclesiastical History, Dialogues, and Letters of Theodoret,* NPNF, ser. 2, vol. 3 (Oxford 1892), pp. 250–348

Eranistes

Ettlinger, G.H., *Theodoret of Cyrus, Eranistes* (Oxford 1975)

Ettlinger, G.H., *Theodoret of Cyrus, Eranistes,* FOTC, vol. 106 (Washington 2003)

6. The subdivisions of the ten discourses *Prouid.* follow those established in this translation.

7. Letters belonging to the Patmos collection are cited by Roman, those belonging to Sirmond's collection by arabic, numerals; the letters preserved in conciliar collections are cited by "vol. 4" (SC, vol. 429) + the arabic numeral assigned to it by Azéma. As Azéma did not introduce subdivisions, passages in the *patmenses* and the letters preserved in conciliar collections are identified by the page and line numbers of his edition.

Bibliography

Expositio de recta fide

Otto, J.C.T. de, *Iustini philosophi et martyris opera quae feruntur omnia,* 3rd ed., CACSS, vol. 4 (Iena 1880), pp. 1–66

Graecarum affectionum curatio

Canivet, P., *Théodoret de Cyr, Thérapeutique des maladies helléniques,* SC, voll. 57.1f., 2nd ed. (Paris 2000–2001)

Haereticarum fabularum compendium

Schulze, J.L., and A. Nösselt, *Theodoreti episocopi Cyri, opera omnia,* vol. 3 (Halle 1772), pp. 280–481; rpt. PG, vol. 83 (Paris 1859), coll. 336–556

Historia ecclesiastica

Martin, A., P. Canivet, *et al., Théodoret de Cyr, Histoire ecclésiastique,* SC, voll. 501, 530 (Paris 2006–09)

Parmentier, L., and G.C. Hansen, *Theodoret, Kirchengeschichte,* 3rd ed., GCS, n. s., vol. 5 (Berlin 1998)[8]

Valois (Valesius), H., *Theodoriti episcopi Cyri et Euagrii scholastici Historia Ecclesiastica item Excerpta ex Historiis Philostorgii et Theodori Lectoris* (Turin 1748)

Jackson, B., *The Ecclesiastical History, Dialogues, and Letters of Theodoret,* NPNF, ser. 2, vol. 3 (Oxford 1892), pp. 33–159

Historia religiosa

Canivet, P., and A. Leroy-Molinghen, *Théodoret de Cyr, Histoire des moines de Syrie,* 2 voll., SC, voll. 234, 257 (Paris 1977–79)

Price, R.M., *A History of the Monks of Syria, CistSS,* vol. 88 (Kalamazoo, Mich. 1985)

Quod unicus filius sit dominus noster Iesus Christus

Guinot, J.N., *Théodoret de Cyr, La Trinité et L'Incarnation,* annexe 3: *Un unique Fils après l'Incarnation,* SC, vol. 575 (Paris 2015), pp. 331–59

Pásztori-Kupán, I., *Theodoret of Cyrus* (London/New York 2006), pp. 188–92

8. Quotations of the *H. e.* follow this edition.

Reprehensio xii anathematismorum Cyrilli

Schwartz, E., *Concilium vniversale ephesenum, Acta graeca, ACO,* vol. 1.1.6: *Collectio vaticana 165–72* (Berlin/Leipzig 1928), pp. 107–46 = #169

Theodorus Anagnostes, *Historia ecclesiastica*

Hansen, G.C., *Theodoros Anagnostes, Kirchengeschichte,* GCS, vol. 54 (Berlin 1971)

Theodorus mopsuestenus

Fragmenta in Matthaeum

Reuss, J., *Matthäus-Kommentare aus der griechischen Kirche, TU* 61 (Berlin 1957), pp. 96–135

Commentarii in epistolas Pauli

Swete, H.B., *Theodori episcopi mopsuesteni in epistolas Beati Pauli commentarii,* 2 voll. (Cambridge 1880–82)

Homiliae catecheticae

Tonneau, R., and R. Devreesse, *Les Homélies catéchétiques de Théodore de Mopsueste* (Vatican City 1949)

Theognostus, *Thesaurus*

Munitiz, J.A., *Theognosti Thesaurus,* CChr.SG, vol. 5 (Turnhout 1979)

Theophanes Confessor, *Chronographia*

Boor, C.G. de, *Theophanis Chronographia,* 2 voll. (Leipzig 1883–85; rpt. Hildesheim 1963, 1980)

Theophylactus achridensis, *Epistulae*

Gautier, P., *Théophylacte D'Achrida, Lettres,* CFHB.Th, vol. 16.2 (Thessalonica 1986)

Thucydides, Historiae

Jones, H.S., and J.E. Powell, *Thucydidis Historiae,* 2 voll., 2nd ed. (Oxford 1942)

Vigilius romanus (Pope Vigilius), *Epistula aduersus tria capitula*

Schwartz, E., *Concilium uniuersale Constantinopolitanum ACO,* vol. 4.2: *Iohannis Maxentii libelli, etc.* (Berlin 1914), pp. 138–68

Xenophon, ***Memorabilia***

Marchant, E.C., *Xenophontis opera omnia,* vol. 2: *Commentarii, Oeconomicus, Convivium, Apologia Socratis*, 2nd ed. (Oxford 1921; rpt. 1971)

Secondary Works: Reference Works, Monographs, Essays, Articles

Abramowski, L., "Der Streit um Diodor und Theodor zwischen den beiden ephesinischen Konzilien," *ZKG* 67 (1955–56), pp. 252–87

_______, "Reste von Theodorets Apologie für Diodor und Theodor bei Facundus," *TU* 63 = *StPatr* 1 (1957), pp. 61–69

_______, *Untersuchungen zum Liber Heraclidis des Nestorius, CSCO. Sub,* vol. 242.22 (Louvain 1963)

_______, "Συνάφεια und ἀσύγχυτος ἕνωσις als Bezeichnung für trinitarische und christologische Einheit," *Drei christologische Untersuchungen* (Berlin 1981), pp. 63–109

_______, "Über die Fragmente des Theodor von Mopsuestia in Brit. Libr. *add 12.516* und das doppelt überlieferte christologische Fragment," *OrChr* 79 (1995), pp. 1–8

Acerbi, S., "Intolerancia dogmática en el siglo V: Un estudio de la legislación imperial anti-herética (CTh. XVI, 5, 66-C. I. I, I, 3-ACO II, III, 3)," *'Ilu. Revista de Ciencias de las Religiones* 18 (2007), pp. 127–44

Adrados, F.R., *DGE,* vol. 2: *ἄλλᾳ-ἀποκοινώνητος* (Madrid 1986)

Agati, M.L., *Giovanni Onorio da Maglie, Copista Greco (1535–1563),* BCl.S, vol. 20 (Rome 2001)

Alberigo, G. *et al.*; *v.* **Concilia oecumenica, Concilium nicaenum (325)**

Allen, P., "The Syrian Church through bishops' eyes: The letters of Theodoret of Cyrrhus and Severus of Antioch," *StPatr* 42 (Leuven 2006), pp. 3–22

Aly, W., "Praylios. 1," *RE,* vol. 22: *Pontarches-Priscianus* (Stuttgart 1954), coll. 1812f.

Amann, E., "L'affaire Nestorius vue de Rome," *RevSR* 23 (1949), pp. 5–37, 207–44; 24 (1950), pp. 28–52, 235–65

Anastos, M.V., "The Immutability of Christ and Justinian's Condemnation of Theodore of Mopsuestia," *DOP* 6 (1951), pp. 125–60

Ashby, G.W., "Theodoret of Cyrrhus on Marriage," *Theol.* 72 (1969), pp. 482–91

Bibliography

Atiya, A.S., *A History of Eastern Christianity* (Millwood, N.Y. 1980)

Azéma, Y., "Sur la chronologie de trois lettres de Théodoret de Cyr," *REG* 67 (1954), pp. 82–94

_______, "Citations d'auteurs et allusions profanes dans la *Correspondance* de Théodoret," *TU* 125 (1981), pp. 5–13

_______, "Sur la date de la mort de Théodoret," *Pallas* 31 (1984), pp. 137–55

Baldwin, B., "A Bishop and His Lady: *AP* 16.19," *VigChr* 35 (1981), pp. 377f.

_______, "Akakios," *ODB*, vol. 1, p. 43

_______, "Amphilochios of Ikonion," *ODB*, vol. 1, p. 80

_______, "Book Titles in the Suda," *JHS* 103 (1983), pp. 136f.

_______, "Chronicon Paschale," *ODB*, vol. 1, p. 447

_______, "Ignatius, Pseudo-," *ODB*, vol. 2, p. 984

_______, "Isidore of Pelusium," *ODB*, vol. 2, p. 1016

_______, "Malalas, John," *ODB*, vol. 3, p. 1275

_______, "Priskos," *ODB*, vol. 3, p. 1721

_______, "Proklos," *ODB*, vol. 3, p. 1729

_______, "Sozomenos," *ODB*, vol. 3, pp. 1932f.

_______, "Theodore of Mopsuestia," *ODB*, vol. 3, p. 2044

_______, and A. Kazhdan, "Diodoros," *ODB*, vol. 1, pp. 626f.

_______, A. Kazhdan, and R.S. Nelson, "John Chrysostom," *ODB*, vol. 2, pp. 1057f.

_______, A. Kazhdan, and N.P. Ševčenko, "Athanasius," *ODB*, vol. 1, p. 217

_______, A. Kazhdan, and N.P. Ševčenko, "Basil the Great," *ODB*, vol. 1, p. 269

_______, A. Kazhdan, and N.P. Ševčenko, "Gregory of Nyssa," *ODB*, vol. 2, p. 882

_______, A. Kazhdan, R.S. Nelson, and N.P. Ševčenko, "Gregory of Nazianzos," *ODB*, vol. 2, pp. 880–82

_______, and N.P. Ševčenko, "Ephrem the Syrian," *ODB*, vol. 1, pp. 708f.

Bardy, G., "Acace de Bérée et son rôle dans la controverse nestorienne," *RevSR* 18 (1938), pp. 20–44

Barrington Atlas: *v.* Talbert, R.J.A.

Baronius, C. (Baronio), *Annales ecclesiastici*, vol. 6: *Incipiens ab anno Domini CCCC.XL. perueniens vsque ad D.XVIII, etc.* (Cologne 1609)

Battifol, P., "Les présents de Saint Cyrille à la cour de Constantinople," *BALAC* 1 (1911), pp. 247–64; rpt. in *Études de liturgie et d'archéologie chrétienne* (Paris 1919), pp. 154–79

Bellini, E., "L'opera sociale di Teodoreto di Ciro alla luce del suo epistolario,"
Aug. 17 (1977), pp. 227–36

Bergjan, S.-P., *Theodoret von Cyrus und der Neunizänismus: Aspekte der altkirchlichen Trinitätslehre, AKG* 60 (Berlin 1994)

Bernard, P., "Garnier, Jean," *DthC,* vol. 6.1: *Flacius Illyricus-Gezon* (Paris 1947), coll. 1160–62

Bignami Odier, J., and J. Ruysschaert, *La Bibliothèque Vaticane de Sixte IV a Pie XI: Recherches sur L'Histoire des Collections de Manuscrits, StT,* vol. 272 (Vatican City 1973)

Bolotov, V.V., *Lektsii po istorii drevnei tserkvi* (*Lectures concerning the history of the Early Church*), vol. 4 (St. Petersburg 1917)

Böhm, T., *Die Christologie des Arius, dogmengeschichtliche Überlegungen unter besonderer Berücksichtigung der Hellenisierungsfrage, STG,* vol. 7 (St. Ottilien 1991)

Bossina, L., "Preistoria di un' *editio princeps*: Teodoreto dal Concilio di Trento alla guerra dei Trent' anni" = pp. 231–91 in Editiones principes *delle opere dei padri greci e latini: Atti del Convegno di studi per lo SISMEL, Certosa del Galluzzo, Millenio Medievale,* vol. 62, Atti di Convegni, vol. 19, ed. Cortesi, M. (Florence 2006)

Bright, W., "Petrus of Alexandria," *DCB,* vol. 4: *N-Z* (London 1887), pp. 333f.

Brok, M.F.A., "A Propos des lettres festales," *VigChr* 5 (1951), pp. 101–10

_______, "The Date of Theodoret's *Expositio rectae fidei*," *JThS* 2 (1951), pp. 178–83

Brown, P.R.L., *Power and Persuasion in Late Antiquity: Towards a Christian Empire* (Madison, Wisc. 1992)

Burgess, R.W., "The Accession of Marcian in the Light of Chalcedonian Apologetic and Monophysite Polemic," *ByZ* 86 (1994), pp. 47–68

Bury, J.B., *A History of the Later Roman Empire from Arcadius to Irene (395 A.D. to 800 A.D.),* 2 voll. (London/New York 1889)

_______, "Justa Grata Honoria," *JRS* 9 (1919), pp. 1–13

Bibliography

Camelot, P.-Th., *Éphèse et Chalcédoine, HCO,* vol. 2 (Paris 1962)

Cameron, A., "Wandering Poets: A Literary Movement in Byzantine Egypt," *Hist.* 14 (1965), pp. 470–509

Canivet, P., *Histoire d'une entreprise apologétique au Vè siècle* (Paris 1957)

_______, "Théodoret et le Messalianisme," *RMab* 51 (1961), pp. 26–34

_______, "Théodoret et le monachisme syrien avant le concile de Chalcédoine," in *Théologie de la vie monastique: Études sur la tradition patristique, Theol(P),* vol. 49 (Vienne 1961), pp. 241–82

_______, "Theodoret of Cyr," *NCE,* vol. 14: *Tha to Zwi,* pp. 20–22

_______, "Catégories sociales et titulature laïque et ecclésiastique dans L'*Histoire Philothée* de Théodoret de Cyr," *Byz.* 39 (1969), pp. 209–50

_______, "L'Apôtre Pierre dans les écrits de Théodoret de Cyr," pp. 29–46 in *Épektasis: Mélanges patristiques offerts au Cardinal Jean Daniélou,* ed. Fontaine, J. and C. Kannengiesser (Beauchesne 1972)

_______, *Le monachisme Syrien selon Théodoret de Cyr, ThH,* vol. 42 (Paris 1977)

Caspari, C.P., *Alte und neue Quellen zur Geschichte des Taufsymbols und der Glaubensregel,* 3 voll. (Malling 1879)

Cataldi Palau, A., *A Catalogue of Greek Manuscripts from the Meerman Collection in the Bodleian Library* (Oxford 2011)

Cave, W., *Scriptorum ecclesiasticorum historia literaria a Christo nato usque ad saeculum decimum quartum* (London 1688)

Cerbu, T., "Tra servizio e ambizione: Allacci studioso e bibliotecario nella corrispondenza con Antonio Caracciolo," pp. 175–97 of *Storia della Biblioteca Apostolica Vaticana,* vol. 3: *La Vaticana nel seicento (1590–1700), Una biblioteca di biblioteche,* ed. Montuschi, C. (Vatican City 2014)

Chadwick, H., "Eucharist and Christology in the Nestorian controversy," *JThS* 2 (1951), pp. 145-64

_______, "The Exile and Death of Flavian of Constantinople: A Prologue to the Council of Chalcedon," *JThS* 6 (1955), pp. 17–34

_______, Preface to A.-J. Festugière, *Actes du Concile de Chalcédoine, Sessions III–VI* (Geneva 1983), pp. 3–12; rpt. as "The Chalcedonian Definition," in *Heresy and Orthodoxy in the Early Church* (Aldershot, U.K. 1991), #18

_______, *The Church in Ancient Society: From Galilee to Gregory the Great* (Oxford 2001)

Chapman, H.P., "Paul of Samosata," *CE,* vol. 11: *New Mexico-Philip* (New York 1913), pp. 589f.

_______, "Photinus," *CE,* vol. 12: *Philip-Revalidation* (New York 1911), p. 43

Chew, K., "Virgins and Eunuchs: Pulcheria, Politics, and the Death of Emperor Theodosius II," *Hist.* 55 (2006), pp. 207–27

Childers, J.W., "'Abdisho' bar Brikha, Ebedjesus (d. 1318)," *GEDSH,* pp. 3f.

Christensen, A., *L'Iran sous les Sassanides,* 2nd ed. (Copenhagen 1944)

Clark, M.T., "Hilary of Poitiers," *EEC,* vol. 1: *A-K,* 2nd ed. (New York 1997), pp. 527f.

Clayton, P.B., "Theodoret, Bishop of Cyrus, and the Mystery of the Incarnation in Late Antiochene Christology" (Ph.D. diss., Union Theological Seminary, New York 1985)

_______, *The Christology of Theodoret of Cyrus: Antiochene Christology from the Council of Ephesus (431) to the Council of Chalcedon (451)* (Oxford 2007)

Constantinides, C.N., and R. Browning, *Greek Manuscripts from Cyprus to the Year 1570, DOS,* vol. 30; *Texts and Studies of the History of Cyprus,* vol. 18 (Washington/Nicosia 1993)

Constas, N., *Proclus of Constantinople and the Cult of the Virgin in Late Antiquity* (Leiden 2003)

Cope, G.M., "An Analysis of the Heresiological Method of Theodoret of Cyrus in the *Haereticarum fabularum compendium*" (Ph.D. diss., CUA, Washington 1990)

Cramer, J.A., *v.* ***Catenae Graecorum patrum in Novum Testamentum, in 1Cor.***

D'Agostino, E., *Da Locri a Gerace: Storia di una diocesi della Calabria bizantina dalle origni al 1480* (Catanzaro 2004)

Dagron, G., *v.* **Anonymous, *De uita et miraculis Sanctae Theclae libri ii***

Davids, T.W., "Galla (5) Placidia," *DCB,* vol. 2: *Eaba - Hermocrates* (London 1880), pp. 594f.

Davis, R.P., "Constantine I," *OCD,* pp. 378–80

Delehaye, H., *Les origines du culte des martyrs,* 2nd ed. (Brussels 1933)

_______, "Quelques dates du Martyrologe Hiéronymien," *AnBoll* 49 (1931), pp. 22–50

Delmaire, R., "Cités et Fiscalité au Bas-Empire: À propos du Rôle des Curiales dans la Levée des Impôts" in C. Lepelley, *La fin de la cité antique e le début de la cité médiévale de la fin du IIIè siècle à l'avènement de Charlemagne,* pp. 59–70

_______, *Les institutions du bas-empire romain de Constantin à Justinien,* vol. 1: *Les institutions civiles palatines* (Paris 1995)

Devreesse, R., *Codices vaticani graeci,* vol. 3: *Codd. 604–866* (Vatican City 1950)

_______, *Le patriarcat d'Antioche depuis la paix de l'Église jusqu'à la conquête arabe* (Paris 1945)

Di Berardino, A., *Patrology,* vol. 4: *The Golden Age of Latin Patristic Literature from the Council of Nicea to the Council of Chalcedon,* translated by P. Solari (Westminster, Md. 1986); *v.* **List of Abbreviations: Modern Reference Works, Series, Periodicals**: Quasten

Diepen, H.M., *Les trois chapitres au concile de Chalcédoine: Une étude de la christologie de l'Anatolie ancienne* (Oosterhout 1953)

_______, "Théodoret et le dogme d'Éphèse," *RSR* 44 (1956), pp. 243–47

Dineen, L., *Titles of Address in Christian Greek Epistolography to 527 A.D., PatSt,* vol. 18 (Ph.D. diss., CUA, Washington 1929)

Duckett, E., *Medieval portraits from East and West* (Ann Arbor, Mich. 1972)

Edelstein, L., and V. Nutton, "Galen, " *OCD,* pp. 600f.

Ehrhard, A., "Die Cyrill von Alexandrien zugeschriebene Schrift Περὶ τῆς τοῦ Κυρίου ἐνανθρωπήσεως, ein Werk Theodorets von Cyrus," *ThQ* 70 (1888), pp. 179–243, 406–50, 623–53

Ermoni, V., *De Leontio Byzantino et de eius doctrina christologica* (Paris 1895)

Évieux, P., *Isidore de Péluse, ThH,* vol. 99 (Paris 1995)

Ferguson, J., *v.* ***Clement of Alexandria, Stromateis***

Fives, D.C., "The Use of the Optative Mood in the Works of Theodoret, Bishop of Cyrus," *PatSt*, vol. 50 (Ph.D. diss., CUA, Washington 1937)

Flemming, J., and G. Hoffman, *v.* **Concilia oecumenica, Concilium ephesinum (449), *Acta syra***

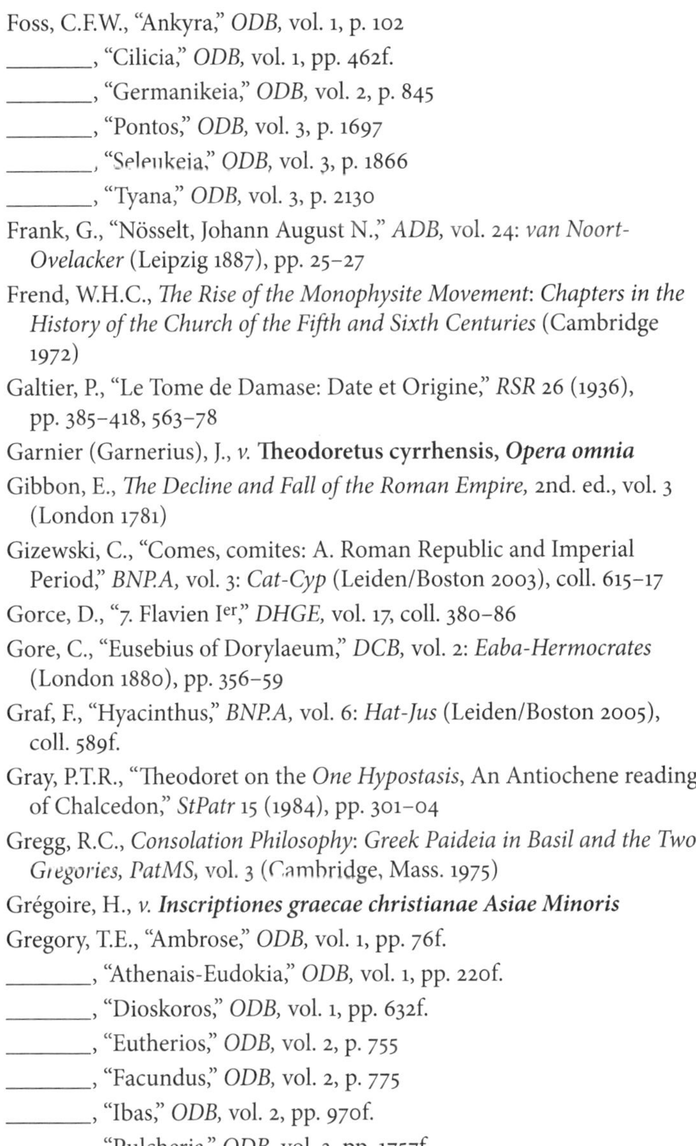

Foss, C.F.W., "Ankyra," *ODB*, vol. 1, p. 102

_______, "Cilicia," *ODB*, vol. 1, pp. 462f.

_______, "Germanikeia," *ODB*, vol. 2, p. 845

_______, "Pontos," *ODB*, vol. 3, p. 1697

_______, "Seleukeia," *ODB*, vol. 3, p. 1866

_______, "Tyana," *ODB*, vol. 3, p. 2130

Frank, G., "Nösselt, Johann August N.," *ADB*, vol. 24: *van Noort-Ovelacker* (Leipzig 1887), pp. 25–27

Frend, W.H.C., *The Rise of the Monophysite Movement: Chapters in the History of the Church of the Fifth and Sixth Centuries* (Cambridge 1972)

Galtier, P., "Le Tome de Damase: Date et Origine," *RSR* 26 (1936), pp. 385–418, 563–78

Garnier (Garnerius), J., *v.* **Theodoretus cyrrhensis, *Opera omnia***

Gibbon, E., *The Decline and Fall of the Roman Empire,* 2nd. ed., vol. 3 (London 1781)

Gizewski, C., "Comes, comites: A. Roman Republic and Imperial Period," *BNP.A,* vol. 3: *Cat-Cyp* (Leiden/Boston 2003), coll. 615–17

Gorce, D., "7. Flavien I[er]," *DHGE,* vol. 17, coll. 380–86

Gore, C., "Eusebius of Dorylaeum," *DCB*, vol. 2: *Eaba-Hermocrates* (London 1880), pp. 356–59

Graf, F., "Hyacinthus," *BNP.A*, vol. 6: *Hat-Jus* (Leiden/Boston 2005), coll. 589f.

Gray, P.T.R., "Theodoret on the *One Hypostasis*, An Antiochene reading of Chalcedon," *StPatr* 15 (1984), pp. 301–04

Gregg, R.C., *Consolation Philosophy: Greek Paideia in Basil and the Two Gregories*, *PatMS*, vol. 3 (Cambridge, Mass. 1975)

Grégoire, H., *v.* ***Inscriptiones graecae christianae Asiae Minoris***

Gregory, T.E., "Ambrose," *ODB*, vol. 1, pp. 76f.

_______, "Athenais-Eudokia," *ODB*, vol. 1, pp. 220f.

_______, "Dioskoros," *ODB*, vol. 1, pp. 632f.

_______, "Eutherios," *ODB*, vol. 2, p. 755

_______, "Facundus," *ODB*, vol. 2, p. 775

_______, "Ibas," *ODB*, vol. 2, pp. 970f.

_______, "Pulcheria," *ODB*, vol. 3, pp. 1757f.

_______, “Timothy Ailouros,” *ODB*, vol. 3, pp. 2086f.

_______, *Vox populi: Popular Opinion and Violence in the Religious Controversies of the Fifth Century A.D.* (Columbus, Oh. 1979)

_______, and A. Kazhdan, “Meletian Schism in Syria,” *ODB*, vol. 2, p. 1333

Grillmeier, A., *Christ in Christian Tradition, From the Apostolic Age to Chalcedon (451)*, translated by J.S. Bowden, 2nd ed. (London/Oxford 1975)

_______, “Jesus Christ the Kyriakos Anthropos,” *TS* 38 (1977), pp. 275–93

_______, “Ὁ κυριακὸς ἄνθρωπος: Eine Studie zu einer christologischen Bezeichnung der Väterzeit,” *Tr.* 33 (1977), pp. 1–63

Grimanis, S., Unpublished description of Athens, Gennadios Library, *ms.* 250 (*v.* “Introduction to the Greek Text,” sec. I.A.)

Guinot, J.-N., *L’Exégèse de Théodoret de Cyr*, *ThH*, vol. 100 (Paris 1995)

_______, “L’*Expositio rectae fidei* et le traité *Sur la Trinité et l’Incarnation* de Théodoret de Cyr: Deux types d’argumentation pour un même propos?,” *RechAug* 32 (2001), pp. 39–74

Hahn, I., “Theodoretus Cyrus und die Frühbyzantinische Besteuerung,” *AAH*, vol. 10 (1962), pp. 123–30

Halleux, A. de, “Actualité du néochalcédonisme,” *RTL* 21 (1990), pp. 32–54

_______, “La définition christologique à Chalcédoine,” *RTL* 7 (1976), pp. 3–23, 155–70 = *Patrologie et œcuménisme: Recueil d’études, BEThL*, vol. 93 (Louvain 1990), pp. 445–80

_______, “Les douze chapitres cyrilliens au concile d’Ephèse (430–433),” *RTL* 23 (1992), pp. 425–58

Hardy, R., “The Further Education of Cyril of Alexandria (412–444): Questions and Problems,” *StPatr* 17 (1982), pp. 116–22

Hefele, K.J., *Consiliengeschichte nach den Quellen bearbeitet*, 2nd. ed., vol. 2 (Freiburg im Breisgau 1875)

Hefele, K.J., and W.R. Clark, *A History of the Councils of the Church*, 5 voll. (Edinburgh 1871–96)

Holum, K.G., “Family Life in the Theodosian House,” *Kl.* 8 (1976), pp. 280–92

_______, *Theodosian Empresses: Women and Imperial Dominion in Late Antiquity* (Berkeley, Calif. 1982)

Honigmann, E., *Patristic Studies*, *StT*, vol. 173 (Vatican City 1953)

Hoskin, M.J.J., "The Recensions of Leo the Great, *Ep.* 12," *FilMed* 25 (2018), pp. 1–21

Hübner, R.M., "Gregor von Nyssa als Verfasser der sog. *Ep.* 38 des Basilius," pp. 463–91 in *Epektasis*: *Mélanges patristiques offerts au Cardinal Jean Daniélou*, ed. Fontaine, J., and C. Kannengiesser (Paris 1972)

Hunger, H., *Katalog der griechischen Handschriften der Österreichischen Nationalbibliothek*, vol. 1: *Codices historici, etc.* (Vienna 1961)

Hunt, E., *v.* **Leo romanus (Pope Leo I), *Epistulae***

Jackson, B., *v.* **Theodoretus cyrrhensis, *Epistulae, Historia ecclesiastica***

Jedin, H.D., "Seripando, Girolamo," *NCE*, vol. 13: *Scu-Tex*, p. 115

Jones, A.H.M., *The Later Roman Empire 284–602*: *A Social, Economic, and Administrative Survey*, 2 voll. (Oxford/Norman, Okla. 1964)

_______, J.R. Martindale, and J. Morris, *PLRE*, vol. 1: *AD 260–396* (Cambridge 1971)

Kazhdan, A., "Attikos," *ODB*, vol. 1, p. 230

_______, "Eutyches," *ODB*, vol. 2, p. 759

_______, "Flavian," *ODB*, vol. 2, pp. 789f.

_______, "Souda," *ODB*, vol. 3, pp. 1930f.

_______, B. Baldwin, and T.E. Gregory, "Eustathios of Antioch," *ODB*, vol. 2, p. 753

Keating, D.A., *The Appropriation of Divine Life in Cyril of Alexandria* (Oxford 2004)

Kelly, J.N.D., *Early Christian Doctrines*, 5th ed. (London 1978)

Klotz, A., "Sergius Plautus. 37," *RE*, 2nd series (*R–Z*), vol. 2.2: *Sclinuntia-Sila* (Stuttgart 1923), col. 1719

Koch, G., *Strukturen und Geschichte des Heils in der Theologie des Theodoret von Kyros*: *Eine dogmen-und theologiegeschichtliche Untersuchung* (Frankfurt am Main 1974)

Kollar, A.F., *Adami Francisci Kollarii ad Petri Lambecii Commentariorum de augusta bibliotheca caes. vindobonensi libros viii supplementorum liber primus*: *Codices graeci, theologici argumenti* (Vienna 1790)

Korolevskij, C., "Beyrouth," *DHGE*, vol. 8: *Benoit-Biscioni* (Paris 1935), pp. 1300–1340

Kosiński, R., "The Life of Nestorius as Seen in Greek and Oriental Sources," *Elec.* 13 (2007), pp. 155–70

Kötting, B., "Digamus," *RAC*, vol. 3: *Christusbild-Dogma I* (Stuttgart 1957), coll. 1016–24

Kyle, R., "Nestorius: The Partial Rehabilitation of a Heretic," *JETS* 32 (1989), pp. 73–83

Laporte, J., "Models from Philo in Origen's Teaching on Original Sin," *LTP* 44 (1988), pp. 191–203

Le Bohec, Y., "Ensigns," *BNP.A*, vol. 4: *Cyr-Epy* (Leiden/Boston 2004), col. 995

Leclercq, H., "Diaconesse," *DACL*, vol. 4: *D-Domestici* (Paris 1920), coll. 725–33

Lepelley, C., *La fin de la cité antique e le début de la cité médiévale de la fin du IIIè siècle à l'avènement de Charlemagne* (Bari 1996)

Liebeschütz, J.H. W.G., *The Decline and Fall of the Roman City* (Oxford 2001)

Limberis, V., *Divine Heiress: The Virgin Mary and the Creation of Christian Constantinople* (London 1994)

Livingstone, E.A., "Cyprian, St," *ODCC*, p. 441

_______, "Damasus, St," *ODCC*, pp. 448f.

_______, "deaconess," *ODCC*, pp. 455f.

_______, "Hippolytus, St," *ODCC*, pp. 773f.

_______, "Irenaeus, St," *ODCC*, pp. 846f.

_______, "Justin Martyr, St," *ODCC*, p. 915

_______, "Phillipps Manuscripts," *ODCC*, pp. 1278f.

_______, "Polycarp, St," *ODCC*, pp. 1305f.

Loofs, F., *Leitfaden zum Studium der Dogmengeschichte* (Halle 1906)

_______, and I. Southhall, *Nestorius and His Place in the History of Christian Doctrine* (Cambridge 1914)

Loon, H. van, *The Dyophysite Christology of Cyril of Alexandria* (Leiden 2009)

Lowe, E.A., *CLA*, part 4: *Italy*: *Perugia-Verona* (Oxford 1947)

MacDowell, D.M., *The Law in Classical Athens* (London 1978)

MacMullen, R., "Roman Bureaucratese," *Tr.* 18 (1962), pp. 364–78

Maffei, S., *Istoria teologica* (Trent 1742)

Magdalino, P., and A.-M. Talbot, "Oikonomos," *ODB*, vol. 3, p. 1517

Mandac, M., "L' union christologique dans les œuvres de Théodoret antérieures au Concile d' Éphèse," *EThL* 47 (1971), pp. 64–96

Mandouze, A., *PCB-E,* vol. 1: *Prosopographie de l'afrique chrétienne (303–533)* (Paris 1982)

Mango, M.M., "Amida," *ODB,* vol. 1, p. 77

_______, "Chalkis Ad Belum," *ODB,* vol. 1, p. 406

_______, "Emesa," *ODB,* vol. 1, p. 690

_______, "Sidon," *ODB,* vol. 3, pp. 1892f.

_______, and A. Cutler, "Apameia," *ODB,* vol. 1, p. 127

Markschies, C., "Isidore of Pelusium," *BNP.A,* vol. 6: *Hat-Jus* (Leiden/ Boston 2005), coll. 961f.

Martindale, J.R., *PLRE,* vol. 2: *A.D. 395–527* (Cambridge, *etc.* 1980)

_______, *PLRE,* vol. 3A-B: *A.D. 527–641* (Cambridge, *etc.* 1992)

Mayer, A., "Monotelismo," *EC* 8: *Mara-NZ* (Florence 1952), coll. 1319–24

McLeod, F., *The Roles of Christ's Humanity in Salvation: Insights from Theodore of Mopsuestia* (Washington 2005)

_______, *Theodore of Mopsuestia* (London 2008)

McGuckin, J.A., *The Westminster Handbook to Patristic Theology* (Louisville, Ky. 2004)

McNamara, K., "Theodoret of Cyrus and the Unity of Person in Christ," *IThQ* 22 (1955), pp. 313–28

Mercier, J., "Sirleto, Guillaume," *DThC,* vol. 14.2: *Scholarios-Szczaniecki* (Paris 1941), coll. 2174f.

Metzger, B.M., *A Textual Commentary on the Greek New Testament,* 3rd ed. (Stuttgart 1975)

Millar, F., "Theodoret of Cyrrhus: A Syrian in Greek Dress?" pp. 105–25 in *From Rome to Constantinople,* ed. Amirav, H., and B. ter Haar Romeny (Leuven *etc.* 2007)

Miola, M.P., "Basile de Séleucie," in Histoire de la littérature chrétienne (forthcoming)

Mioni, E., *Catalogus codicum graecorum Bibliothecae nationalis neapolitanae,* vol. 1.1 (Rome 1992)

Montalverne, P.J., *Theodoreti cyrensis doctrina antiquior de verbo 'inhumanato' (a circiter 423–435)* (Rome 1948)

Murphy, F.X., "Sirmond, Jacques," *NCE,* vol. 13: *Scu-Tex,* pp. 260f.

Newman, J.H., "Trials of Theodoret," in *Historical Sketches* (London 1873), pp. 307–62

Nilsson, M.P., and M.H. Jameson, "Thesmophoria," *OCD*, p. 1509

Norris, F.W., "Libanius," *EEC*, vol. 2: *L-Z* (London 1997), p. 679

Norris, R.A., *Manhood and Christ: A Study in the Christology of Theodore of Mopsuestia* (Oxford 1963)

O'Keefe, J.J., "Kenosis or Impassibility: Cyril of Alexandria and Theodoret of Cyrus on the Problem of Divine Pathos," *StPatr* 32 (1997), pp. 358–65

Orbis, v. **Modern Reference Works, Series, Periodicals**

O'Sullivan, N., "The Future Optative in Greek Documentary and Grammatical Papyri, *JHS* 133 (2013), pp. 93–111

The Oxford Classical Dictionary, v. Hornblower, S., and A. Spawforth

The Oxford Dictionary of Byzantium, v. Kazhdan, A., and A.-M. Talbot

The Oxford Dictionary of the Christian Church, v. Livingstone, E.A.

Papadakis, A., "Alexander," *ODB*, vol. 1, p. 56

_______, "Chorepiskopos," *ODB*, vol. 1, p. 430

_______, "John I, Patriarch of Antioch," *ODB*, vol. 2, pp. 1043f.

_______, "Juvenal," *ODB*, vol. 2, p. 1086

Papadogiannakis, Y., *Christianity and Hellenism in the Fifth Century Greek East: Theodoret's Apologetic Against the Greeks in Context*, Hellenic Studies, vol. 49 (Washington 2012)

Parker, R.C.T., "Panathenaea," *OCD*, p. 1104

Parmentier, M., "A Letter from Theodoret of Cyrus to the Exiled Nestorius (*CPG* #6270) in a Syriac Version," *Bijdr.* 51 (1990), 234–45

Paschalides, S.A., Ὁ Εὐγένιος Βούλγαρης ὡς ἐκδότης πατερικῶν κειμένων = pp. 613–35 of Εὐγένιος Βούλγαρης, Ὁ *homo universalis* τοῦ Νέου Ἑλληνισμοῦ, 300 χρόνια ἀπὸ τὴ Γέννησή τοῦ (1716–2016), ed. Karanasios, X. (Athens 2018)

Pásztori-Kupán, I., "An Unnoticed Title in Theodoret of Cyrus' Περὶ τῆς τοῦ Κυρίου ἐνανθρωπήσεως," *JThS* 53 (2002), pp. 102–11

_______, "The Formation and Ecumenical Importance of the so-called *Nicaeno-Constantinopolitanum*," *Revista Ecumenică Sibiu* 3 (2011), pp. 25–54; available at proteo.hu/dok/PKI/PKI_2011_RES1_Nicaeno-Constantinopolitanum.pdf

_______, "Quotations of Theodoret's *De sancta et vivifica Trinitate* in Euthymius Zigabenus' *Panoplia Dogmatica*," *Aug.* 42 (2002), pp. 481–87

_______, *Theodoret of Cyrus* (London/New York 2006)

_______, *Theodoret of Cyrus' Double Treatise On the Trinity and On the Incarnation: The Antiochene Pathway to Chalcedon* (Kolozsvár/Cluj 2007); available at proteo.hu/dok/PKI/PKI_PhD_Full_text.pdf

_______, Review of Clayton, P.B., Jr., *The Christology of Theodoret of Cyrus: Antiochene Christology from the Council of Ephesus (431) to the Council of Chalcedon (451)* (Oxford 2007), in *SJTh* 64 (2011), pp. 490f.

_______, "Cyril and Theodoret on the Temptation of Christ: An Imaginary Dialogue between Alexandrian and Antiochene Christological Positions," *Perichoresis* 20 (2022), pp. 103–22

_______, "The Number and Authority of the Ecumenical Councils in the Second Helvetic Confession," *Perichoresis* 21 (2023), pp. 40–54

Perry, S.G.F., *v.* **Concilia oecumenica, Concilium ephesinum (449), *Acta syra***

Petit, P., *Libanius et la vie municipale à Antioche au IVè siècle après J.-C., BAH,* vol. 11 (Paris 1955)

Petruccione, J., "The Audience of Theodoret's *Questions on the Octateuch,*" pp. 215–39 in *La littérature des questions et réponses dans l'antiquité profane et chrétienne: De l'enseignement à l'exégèse,* ed. Bussières, M.-P., *Instrumenta patristica et medievalia,* vol. 64 (Turnhout 2013)

Plant, I.M., *Women Writers of Ancient Greece and Rome: An Anthology* (London 2004)

Poulos, A., "Gennadius *250* and the Textual Tradition of the Letters of Theodoret of Cyrus," *MBAV,* vol. 23, *StT*, vol. 516 (Vatican City 2017)

Prestige, G.L., *God in Patristic Thought* (London 1952)

Price, R.M., "Marian Piety and the Nestorian Controversy," in *The Church and Mary: Papers Read at the 2001 Summer Meeting and the 2002 Winter Meeting of the Ecclesiastical History Society*, ed. Swanson, R.N. (New York 2004), pp. 31–38

Quasten, J., *Patrology,* vol. 3: *The Golden Age of Greek Patristic Literature* (Utrecht 1950)

Rammelt, C., *Ibas von Edessa. Rekonstruktion einer Biographie und dogmatischen Position zwischen den Fronten*, *AKG,* vol. 106 (Berlin 2008)

Richard, M., "La tradition des fragments du traité Περὶ τῆς ἀνθρωπήσεως de Théodore de Mopsueste," *Muséon* 55 (1943), pp. 55–75 = *Opera minora,* vol. 2 (Turnhout 1977), #41

_______, "L'introduction du mot *hypostase* dans la théologie de l'Incarnation," *MSR* 2 (1945), pp. 5–32, 243–70 = *Opera minora,* vol. 2 (Turnhout 1977), #42

_______, "Les citations de Théodoret conservées dans la chaîne de Nicétas sur l'Évangile selon Saint Luc," *RB* 43 (1934), pp. 88–96 = *Opera minora,* vol. 2 (Turnhout 1977), #43

_______, "Un écrit de Théodoret sur l'unité du Christ après l'incarnation," *RevSR* 24 (1935), pp. 34–61 = *Opera minora,* vol. 2 (Turnhout 1977), #44

_______, "L'activité littéraire de Théodoret avant le concile d'Éphèse," *RSPhTh* 24 (1935), pp. 83–106 = *Opera minora,* vol. 2 (Turnhout 1977), #45

_______, "Notes sur l'évolution doctrinale de Théodoret," *RSPhTh* 25 (1936), pp. 459–81 = *Opera minora,* vol. 2 (Turnhout 1977), #46

_______, "Théodoret, Jean d'Antioche et les moines d'Orient," *MSR* 3 (1946), pp. 147–56 = *Opera minora,* vol. 2 (Turnhout 1977), #47

_______, "La lettre de Théodoret à Jean d'Égées," *SPhTh* 2 (1941–42), pp. 415–23 = *Opera minora,* vol. 2 (Turnhout 1977), #48

_______, "Proclus de Constantinople et le Théopaschisme," *RHE* 38 (1942), pp. 303–31 = *Opera minora,* vol. 2 (Turnhout 1977), #52

Richardson, N.J., "Olympian Games," *OCD,* p. 1066

_______, "Pythian Games," *OCD,* p. 1285

Rist, J., "Eutyches 3," *BNP.A,* vol. 5: *Equ-Has* (Leiden/Boston 2004), col. 239

_______, "Uranius 1," *BNP.A,* vol. 15: *Tuc-Zyt* (Leiden/Boston 2010), col. 119

Romanides, J.S., "Leo and Theodoret, Dioscorus and Eutyches"; available at orthodoxjointcommission.wordpress.com/2013/12/14/leo-and-theodoret-dioscorus-and-eutyches/

_______, "Highlights in the Debate over Theodore of Mopsuestia's Christology and Some Suggestions for a Fresh Approach," *GOTR* 5 (1959–60), pp. 140–85

_______, "Leo of Rome's Support of Theodoret, Dioscorus of Alexandria's support of Eutyches and the Lifting of the Anathemas," *Theol(A)* 65 (1994), pp. 479–93

Rudolph, K., "Mani, Manichaeans," *BNP.A,* vol. 8: *Lyd-Mine* (Leiden/Boston 2006), coll. 234f.

Russell, N., *Cyril of Alexandria* (London 2000)

_______, *Theophilus of Alexandria* (London 2007)

Sakkelion, I., Πατμιακὴ Βιβλιοθήκη ἤτοι Ἀναγραφὴ τῶν ἐν τῇ Βιβλιοθήκῃ τῆς κατὰ τὴν Νῆσον Πάτμον Μονῆς … τοῦ Ιωάννου τοῦ Θεολόγου Τεθαυρισμένων Χειρογράφων Τευχῶν (Athens 1890)

Schaff, P., *History of the Christian Church*, 7 voll. (New York 1889)

Schieffer, R., "Der Brief Papst Leos d.gr. an Theodoret von Kyros (*CPG* 9053) – pp. 81–87 of ΑΝΤΙΔΩΡΟΝ: *Hulde aan Dr. Maurits Geerard bij de voltooiing van de* Clavis Patrum Graecorum, *etc.*, vol. 1 (Brussels 1984)

Schor, A.M., "Theodoret on the 'School of Antioch': A Network Approach," *JECS* 15 (2007), pp. 517–62

_______, "The Letter Collection of Theodoret of Cyrrus," pp. 269–86 of Sogno, C., B.K. Storin, and E.J. Watts (Oakland, Calif. 2017)

Schwartz, D.L., *Paideia and Cult: Christian Initiation in Theodore of Mopsuestia, Hellenic Studies,* vol. 57 (Washington 2013)

Schwartz, E., "Zur Schriftstellerei Theodorets," *SBAW.PPH* 1 (1922), pp. 30–40

_______, "Codex Vaticanus gr. 1431, Eine antichalkedonische Sammlung aus der Zeit Kaiser Zenos," *ABAW.PPH* 32.6 (1927)

_______, "Cyrill und der Mönch Viktor," *SAWW.PH* 208.4 (1928), pp. 1–51

_______, "Der Prozess des Eutyches," *SBAW.PH* 5 (1929), pp. 1–93

Seaford, R.A.S., "Dionysia," *OCD,* p. 476

Sellers, R.V., "Pseudo-Justin's *Expositio rectae fidei*: A Work of Theodoret of Cyrus," *JThS* 46 (1945), pp. 145–60

_______, *The Council of Chalcedon, A Historical and Doctrinal Survey* (London 1961)

Shay, M.L., "Farnese," *NCE,* vol. 5: *Ead-Foy,* pp. 840f.

Sickenberger, J., *Die Lukaskatene des Niketas von Herakleia*, *TU* 22.4 (1902), pp. 1–118

Singer, M., "Azéma, Yvan, Emile, Louis, Joseph"; available at maitron.fr/spip.php?article10602

Siniossoglou, N., *Plato and Theodoret: The Christian Appropriation of Platonic Philosophy and the Hellenic Intellectual Resistance* (Cambridge 2008)

Slusser, M., "The Scope of Patripassianism," *StPatr* 17 (1982), pp. 169–75

Smyth, H.W., and G.M. Messing, *Greek Grammar* (Cambridge, Mass. 1956)

Spagnolo, A., and S. Marchi, *I manoscritti della Biblioteca Capitolare di Verona* (Verona 1996)

Spanneut, M., "La position théologique d'Eustathe d'Antioche," *JThS* 5 (1954), pp. 220–24

Stewart, J., *Nestorian Missionary Enterprise: The Story of a Church on Fire* (Edinburgh 1928)

Strobel, K., "Cappadocia II. Roman Province," *BNP.A*, vol. 2: *Ark-Cas* (Leiden/Boston 2003), coll. 1076f.

Studemund, W., and L. Cohn, *Verzeichnis der griechischen Handschriften der Königlichen Bibliothek zu Berlin*, vol. 1: *Codices ex bibliotheca meermanniana, phillippici graeci, nunc berolinenses* (Berlin 1890)

Sullivan, F.A., *The Christology of Theodore of Mopsuestia* (Rome 1956)

Swete, H.B., "Theodore of Mopsuestia," *DCB*, vol. 4: *N-Z* (London 1887), pp. 934–48

Talbert, R.J.A., *Barrington Atlas of the Greek and Roman World* (Princeton, N.J./Oxford 2000)

Talbot, A.-M., "Archimandrite," *ODB*, vol. 1, p. 156

_______, "Xanthopoulos, Nikephoros Kallistos," *ODB*, vol. 3, p. 2207

_______, and R.F. Taft, "Akoimetoi, Monastery of," *ODB*, vol. 1, p. 46

Thompson, E.A., *The Huns* (Oxford 1999)

Tillemont, Lenain de, *Mémoires pour servir à l'histoire ecclésiastique des six premiers siècles*, vol. 15 (Venice 1732)

Tompkins, I.G., "Problems of Dating and Pertinence in Some Letters of Theodoret of Cyrrhus," *Byz.* 65 (1995), pp. 176–95

Tsirpanlis, Z.N., Τὸ Ελληνικό κολλέγιο τῆς Ρώμης και οι μαθητές τοῦ (1576-1700), Συμβολὴ στὴ μελέτη τῆς μορφωτικῆς πολιτικῆς τοῦ Βατικανοῦ = *The Greek College in Rome and its alumni (1576–1700): A Study of the Cultural Policy of the Vatican*, *ABla*, vol. 32 (Thessalonica 1980)

Turner, C.H., "Latin Lists of the Canonical Books I: The Roman Council under Damasus, A.D. 382," *JThS* 1 (1899), pp. 554–60

Urbainczyk, T., *Theodoret of Cyrus: The Bishop and the Holy Man* (Ann Arbor, Mich. 2002)

Venables, E., "Ibas," *DCB*, vol. 3: *Hermogenes-Myensis* (London 1882), pp. 192–96

_______, "Irenaeus (7)," *DCB*, vol. 3: *Hermogenes-Myensis* (London 1882), pp. 280–82

_______, "Joannes (31)," *DCB*, vol. 3: *Hermogenes-Myensis* (London 1882), pp. 349–56

_______, "Photius (3)," *DCB*, vol. 4: *N-Z* (London 1887), pp. 395f.

_______, "Rabbulas," *DCB*, vol. 4: *N-Z* (London 1887), pp. 532–34

_______, "Theodoretus (2)," *DCB*, vol. 4: *N-Z* (London 1887), pp. 904–19

Wade-Gery, H.T., "Thucydides," *OCD*, pp. 1516–19

Wagner, J., "Germanicaea," *BNP.A*, vol. 5: *Equ-Has* (Leiden/Boston 2004), coll. 803f.

Wagner, M.M., "A Chapter in Byzantine Epistolography: The Letters of Theodoret of Cyrus," *DOP* 4 (1948), pp. 120–81

Weinandy, T.G., "Cyril and the Mystery of the Incarnation," in Weinandy, T.G., and D.A. Keating, *The Theology of St. Cyril of Alexandria: A Critical Appreciation* (London 2003), pp. 23–54

Wessel, S., "Literary Forgery and the Monothelete Controversy: Some Scrupulous Uses of Deception," *GRBS* 42 (2001), pp. 201–20

Whitmer, K.J., *The Halle Orphanage as Scientific Community: Observation, Eclecticism, and Pietism in the Early Enlightenment* (Chicago/London 2015)

Wickham, L.R., "Pelagianism in the East," pp. 200–213 in *The Making of Orthodoxy: Essays in Honour of Henry Chadwick*, ed. Williams, R. (Cambridge 1989)

Winkler, R., "*Ousia*, Substance, Essence: On the Roman Understanding of Being," *Phronimon* 14 (2013), pp. 101–17

Wright, D.F., "At What Ages Were People Baptized in the Early Centuries?," *StPatr* 30 (1997), pp. 189–94

_______, "Infant Dedication in the Early Church," pp. 352–78 in *Baptism, the New Testament and the Church: Historical and Contemporary Studies in Honour of R.E.O. White*, ed. Porter, S.E., and A.R. Cross (Sheffield, U.K. 1999)

Wright, W., *Catalogue of Syriac Manuscripts in the British Museum Acquired since the Year 1838*, part 2 (London/Berlin 1871)

Yarnold, E., *The Awe-Inspiring Rites of Initiation: Baptismal Homilies of the Fourth Century* (Slough, U.K. 1972)

Zachhuber, J., "Nochmals: Der 38. Brief des Basilius von Caesarea als Werk des Gregor von Nyssa," *ZACh* 7 (2003), pp. 73–90

MAP OF THE ROMAN EMPIRE, 400 AD

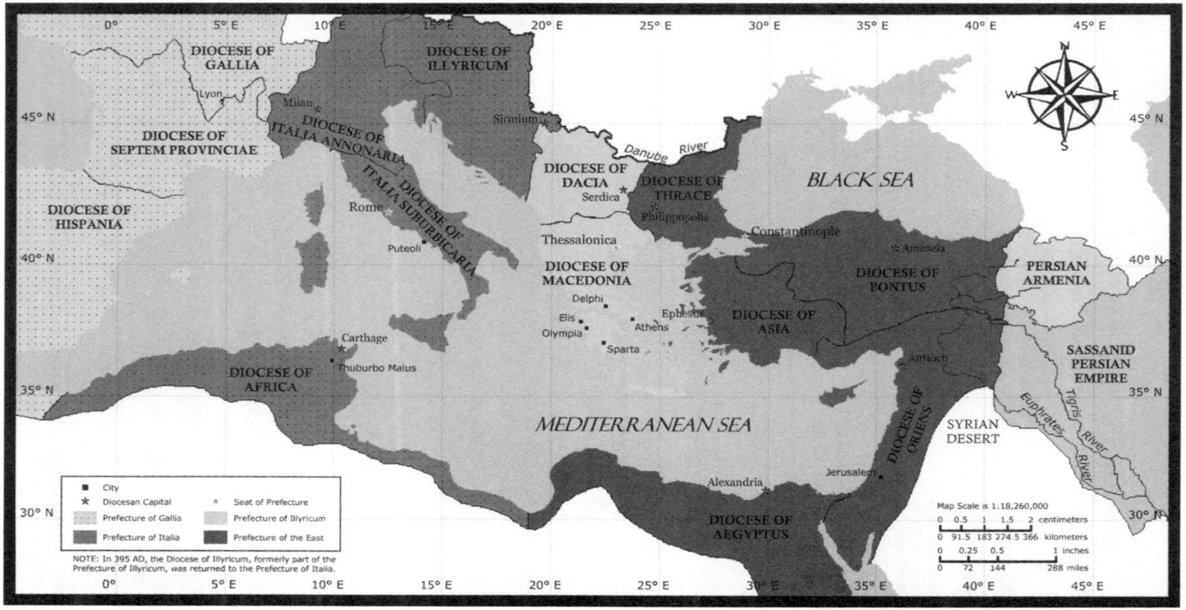

PREFECTURE OF THE EAST, 400 AD

CONSPECTUS SIGLORUM

Manuscripts

N	Naples, Bibl. Naz., gr. 6 (Suppl. gr. 54)
Z	Vatican, BAV, *vat. gr.* 630
A	Berlin, Staatsbibl., *gr.* 41
P	Patmos, Monastery of St. John the Theologian

Additional Witnesses for *Ep.* 83

B	Vienna, Öst. Nationalbibl., gr. 27
V	Vatican, BAV, *vat. gr.* 1455
Λ	Verona, Bibl. capit., 59
Σ	London, Brit. Libr., *Add.* 12156

Editorial Abbreviations

ac	*ante correctionem* = before correction
ar	*ante rasuram* = before erasure
codd.	agreement of *NZA*
coni.	*conieci, -it* = a conjectural reading
corr.	*correxit* = a scribal or editorial correction
edd.	agreement of Sirmond, Nösselt, and Azéma
def.	*deficit* = a manuscript lacks the passage in question
fort.	*fortasse* = perhaps
i.l.	*in linea* = in the text of the ms.; *cf. s.l.*
lect. diff.	*lectio difficilior* = the harder reading
mg.	*margine* = a marginal notation
pr	*post rasuram* = after erasure

scr. — *scripsit, -erunt* = an editor has introduced a reading not transmitted by *N*[1]

scripsi — an emendation introduced by J.P.

seq. — *sequitur* = follows

s.l. — *super lineam* = above the line; *cf. i.l.*

Tit. — *titulus, in titulo* = the designation of the addressee(s) of a letter

u. l. — *uaria lectio* = variant reading

<> — a necessary supplement

| — the beginning of a passage contained in a fragmentary witness

|| — the conclusion of a passage contained in a fragmentary witness

Manuscripts + Editorial Abbreviations: *N* and *P*

* — Before the number of an ep. = attested in *P* as well as in *N*

N or *P* — the clear reading of *N* or *P* (no correction, no doubt)

N? or *P?* — The reading of *N* or *P* is not clear

N^{ac} or P^{ac} — the reading of *N* or *P* before correction

$N^{ac?}$ or $P^{ac?}$ — The reading of *N* or *P* which may or may not have been corrected

$N^{ac}?$ or $P^{ac}?$ — The reading of *N* or *P* before correction is not clear

N^{pcm1} or P^{pcm1} — a correction of *N* or *P* by the scribe of the text

N^{pc} or P^{pc} — the reading of *N* or *P* after correction; corrector cannot be identified

1. Thus, the note "*corr. Cir., scr. edd.*" or "*coni. Cir., scr. edd.*," signifies that the scribe of *A*, corrected a word he had found in *Z* or conjectured a replacement, and that Sirmond, Nösselt, and Azéma adopted his correction or conjecture; similarly, "*scr. Cir., edd.*" indicates that the scribe of *A* wrote into the text a conjecture that subsequent editors have adopted. In these notes, the comma is meant to remind the reader that Ciriaco and Cariofilo recorded their corrections and emendations in a manuscript (*A*), not in a printed book. A notation such as "*scr. Sir. Nös.*" indicates with *scr.* the editor who printed a conjecture of his own (here Sirmond); the following abbreviation(s) list(s) the editor(s) who has/have adopted that conjecture (here Nösselt).

Manuscripts + Editorial Abbreviations: *Z* and *A*

Z	*Z* carries the reading of *N*
A	*A* carries the reading of *Z*[2]
Z?	not used
A?	not used
Z^{ac} or A^{ac}	the reading of *Z* or *A* before correction, *i.e.*, Z^{ac} normally = the reading of *N*, A^{ac} normally = the reading of *Z*
$Z^{ac?}$ or $A^{ac?}$	the reading of *Z* or *A* which may or may not have been corrected; the reading = that of *N*
Z^{ac}? or A^{ac}?	The reading of *Z* or *A* before correction is not clear
Z^{pcm1}	not used
A^{pcm1}	not used[3]
Z^{pc} or A^{pc}	a correction of *Z* or *A*, which ≠ the reading of *N*; corrector cannot be securely identified[4]
$A^{mg.}$	a marginal suggestion in *A* of uncertain authorship
$A^{mg.?}$	a marginal suggestion in *A* that is both of uncertain authorship and not clearly legible
$A^{s.l.}$	a supralineal suggestion in *A* of uncertain authorship

2. As I have pointed out in the Introduction to the Greek Text, whatever *Z* offers that is different from *N*, and whatever *A* offers that is different from *Z* must be regarded as an editorial choice. I use *Onor.* to indicate a reading Onorio has introduced into *Z*, and *Cir.* to indicate a reading Ciriaco has introduced into *A*.

3. Instead, I use *corr. Onor.* to indicate a correction of *N* introduced into *Z* by Onorio and *corr. Cir.* to indicate a correction of *Z* introduced by Ciriaco into *A*.

4. I do not use A^{pc} to record additions in the margins or within the text of *A* that simply restate the reading of *N*. These notes, the work of Sirmond, add nothing to our knowledge of the medieval tradition.

Conspectus siglorum

Editors and Authors of Emendations

Az.	Y. Azéma
Brok	M.F.A. Brok
Car.	G.M. Cariofilo
Cir.	M. Ciriaco
Gar.	J. Garnier (Garnerius)
Gilb.	G. Gilbert
J.P.	J. Petruccione
Nös.	J.A. Nösselt
Onor.	G. Onorio da Maglie
Sir.	J. Sirmond

In constituting the notes, I cite the manuscripts according to the following rules: (1) *N* without *ZA* when *ZA* carry the reading of *N*, since their witness is not independent. (2) *NZ* and the relevant reading conveyed in *A* (*Cir.*, rather than *A*; *corr. Cir.*, rather than A^{pcm1}; *coni. Car.*; $A^{mg.}$ = *a suggestion of uncertain authorship*) when Azéma and I agree in adopting a reading conveyed in *A*, and when Azéma adopts a reading that I reject. In these cases, one must cite *Z* to show that the reading is to be credited to one of the hands of *A* rather than to Onorio, the scribe of *Z*, from which *A* was copied. (3) *Z*, where I print a reading first introduced by Onorio, *i.e.* readings in *Z* that are not in *N*. (4) *P* where I prefer its reading to that of *N*. I do not, however, normally cite *P*, when I reject a reading that differs from the reading of *N*.[5] (5) *NZA*, where Azéma prints, or I print something that is not in the manuscripts; *i.e.*, not passed down by *N* or suggested by correction or conjecture by the scribes of *ZA* or by an annotator of *A*.

I cite the modern editors according to the following rules: (1) Azéma, where I disagree with him, or where I agree with him in adopting a reading of *P* or *BV*, or a reading contained in *A* that differs from the reading of *N*; (2) Sirmond, Garnier, Nösselt, Sakkelion, Schwartz, where one or more agree(s) with a reading adopted by Azéma that I reject or agrees with me in adopting something Azéma rejected; (3) where I introduce a conjecture of my own or accept or reject a conjecture of an earlier editor.

5. Though *P* is an independent witness, it carries much that has little or no claim to serious discussion; *v.*, *e.g.*, *ep.* 23 τὸν μὲν πόνον εἰσενεγκόντας *N* : τ. μ. σπόρον εἰ. *P.*

The Correspondence of Theodoret of Cyrus

The Collectio Sirmondiana

LETTERS 81–147

Letters

Letters

81. ΝΟΜΩΙ ΥΠΑΤΩΙ

(1) Ἐν βραχεῖ μὲν ἡμέρας μορίῳ Τῆς Ὑμετέρας Μεγαλοφυΐας ἀπέλαυσα, βιαίας ἀνάγκης με στερησάσης τοῦ ποθουμένου, ἤλπισα δὲ καὶ τὴν μικρὰν συνουσίαν ζώπυρον εὐνοίας καὶ θερμῆς ἔσεσθαι διαθέσεως. ἐψεύσθην δὲ τῆς ἐλπίδος· δὶς μὲν γὰρ ἤδη γεγραφώς, ἀντιγράφων οὐκ ἔτυχον, βασιλικῇ δὲ ψήφῳ τῆς κυρρεστῶν χώρας τοὺς ὅρους ὑπερβαίνειν κεκώλυμαι.

Αἰτία δὲ οὐδεμία τῇ δοκούσῃ πρόσκειται τιμωρίᾳ, ἀλλ᾽ ὅτι συνόδους ἐπισκοπικὰς συναθροίζω, καί, οὔτε γραφῆς δεικνυμένης, οὔτε τοῦ διώκοντος φαινομένου, οὔτε τοῦ φεύγοντος ἐλεγχθέντος, ἡ ψῆφος ἐξηνέχθη, καὶ στέργομεν ταύτην, τῶν ἀδικουμένων τὰς ἀντιδόσεις εἰδότες.[a] οἶδα μέντοι τὸν Φῆστον· ῥωμαίων δὲ οὗτος ἦν ἡγεμών, τὴν ἰουδαίων εὐταξίαν πεπιστευμένος· ᾐτηκότων τῶν Ἰουδαίων τὴν τοῦ θεσπεσίου Παύλου σφαγήν, ἄντικρυς εἰρηκότα, *Οὐκ* ἔξεστιν ἡμῖν *ῥωμαίοις* οὖσι *χαρίζεσθαι … ἄνθρωπον πρὶν* ἂν *ὁ κατηγορούμενος κατὰ πρόσωπον* σχοίη *τοὺς κατηγόρους τόπον τε ἀπολογίας λάβοι περὶ τοῦ ἐγκλήματος.*[b] καὶ ταῦτα ἔλεγεν ἄνθρωπος οὐ πεπιστευκὼς τῷ Δεσπότῃ Χριστῷ, ἀλλὰ τῇ πολυθέῳ πλάνῃ δουλεύων. ἐγὼ δέ, ουδὲ ἐρωτηθεὶς εἴτε συνάγω συνόδους

l. 19 οὐδὲ ἐρωτηθεὶς *scripsi* : οὔτε ἐ. *codd., edd. The sense requires* οὐδὲ; *i.e. Thdt. was "not so much as even asked." In contrast, οὔτε, in the classicizing usage of Thdt. remains a correlative neg. In a Textual Proximity Search of the authentic works of Thdt. for exx. of οὔτε + οὔτε, the TLG finds 911 in which one οὔτε is connected to at least a second within five words and 537 in which one οὔτε is not connected to at least a second within five words. Eighteen exx. (##167-84) of the latter phenomenon occur in the Coll. sirm. In eleven of these, the οὔτε is correlated to at least one other οὔτε, but at a distance of six or more words; in five places the οὔτε was correlated with a different neg.* (*οὐ, οὐκ, ουδείς*). *Only here and in ep. 136.2 (cf. c. n. ad loc.), are there exx. of οὔτε not correlated with οὔτε or some other neg. In the Coll. pat., there are five exx. of οὔτε correlated with another οὔτε within five words, no ex. of an οὔτε not so correlated. In this passage, the scribe of N or of his exemplar may have mistakenly written οὔτε under the influence of the οὐ that negates the pt.* πεπιστευκὼς, *eleven words back.*

a. *Cf.* Mt 5.11f. b. Acts 25.16 (NT var.)

81. To Nomus, the Consul[1]

(1) I was able to enjoy the presence of Your Eminence for only a brief bit of a day when an obligation that could not be ignored deprived me of that pleasure.[2] Yet, I had hoped that even our short time together would kindle the brand of a positive regard that would flare into a warm friendship. I was disappointed of my hope, for, though I have already written you twice, I have received no reply, and, by a decision taken by the emperor, I am now forbidden to set foot beyond the region of Cyrus.

No reason has been assigned for this apparent punishment, except that I am in the habit of summoning councils of bishops, and, though no indictment has been issued, no prosecutor has stepped forward, and the defendant has not been shown guilty, a verdict has been handed down. We have resigned ourselves to accept this decision, as we know the recompense in store for those who suffer injustice.[a] Nonetheless, I am aware that Festus (a Roman governor, who had been appointed to administer Judea) when asked by the Jews to put St. Paul to death, refused in no uncertain terms: "It is not allowable for us Romans to hand someone over before the accused meet his accusers face-to-face and have an opportunity to defend himself against the charge."[b] And these were the words of a man who was no follower of our Master Christ, but a slave to the error of polytheism. But, in my case, though never asked whether I assemble councils or

1. On Nomus, *v. ep.* 58 n. 1; for the date, *v. ep.* 79 n. 1.

2. Theodoret apparently refers to the death of a close kinsman or friend of his correspondent; *cf. ep.* 58 n. 3.

εἴτε μή, καὶ ἐπὶ τίσι συνάγω, καὶ τί τοῦτο λυμαίνεται ἢ τοῖς ἐκκλησιαστικοῖς ἢ τοῖς κοινοῖς, τοῖς τὰ μέγιστα παρανομήσασι παραπλησίως, τῶν ἄλλων εἴργομαι πόλεων. μᾶλλον δὲ τοῖς μὲν ἄλλοις ἅπασι πᾶσα πόλις ἀνέῳκται· οὐ μόνον τοῖς τὰ Ἀρείου καὶ Εὐνομίου φρονοῦσιν, ἀλλὰ καὶ μανιχαίοις, καὶ μαρκιωνισταῖς, καὶ τοῖς τὰ Βαλεντίνου καὶ Μοντανοῦ νοσοῦσι, καὶ μέντοι καὶ ἕλλησι καὶ ἰουδαίοις· ἐγὼ δέ, τῶν εὐαγγελικῶν ὑπεραγωνιζόμενος δογμάτων, πάσης εἴργομαι πόλεως. ἀλλ᾽ ἐναντία φρονεῖν ἡμᾶς φασί τινες· οὐκοῦν γενέσθω συνέδριον, παρέστωσαν τῶν θεοφιλεστάτων ἐπισκόπων οἱ κρίνειν εἰδότες, παρέστωσαν τῶν ἐν τέλει καὶ ἀξιωμάτων οἱ τὰ θεῖα πεπαιδευμένοι, εἴπωμεν ἃ φρονοῦμεν, εἰπάτωσαν οἱ κρίνοντες ποῖον φρόνημα συμβαίνει τῇ τῶν ἀποστόλων διδασκαλίᾳ.

(2) Ἀλλά γε ταῦτα γέγραφα, οὔτε τὴν μεγίστην πόλιν ἰδεῖν ἐφιέμενος, οὔτε εἰς ἄλλην ἀπᾶραι γλιχόμενος· τῷ ὄντι γὰρ μᾶλλον ἀσπάζομαι τὴν ἡσυχίαν τῶν ἐν μοναχικῷ προσχήματι τὰς ἐκκλησίας οἰκονομεῖν βουλομένων· ἴστω γὰρ Ὑμῶν

not, or why I assemble them, or what harm this causes either Church or state, like a criminal of the worst sort, I am barred from all other cities. Or, as I should say, while every city in the world is open to all the rest, not only to the partisans of Arius and Eunomius, but even to Manicheans and Marcionites, to those infected with Valentinianism and Montanism, even to pagans and Jews,[3] here I am, a man contending on behalf of gospel teachings, barred from every city! Oh, there are some who say that I hold heterodox views.[4] Well then, convene a council, summon bishops beloved of God capable of passing a judgment, summon the magistrates and men of rank who are schooled in religion, have us speak our views, and let the judges tell us which agrees with the teaching of the apostles.

(2) I write this, not that I am eager to see the capital or bent on setting off for some other city, since, in actual fact, I am much happier to enjoy the peace and quiet of those who prefer to direct the affairs of their churches while clad in the monk's habit.[5] In fact, Your Lordship should know that, never during the days of Theodotus,

3. Theodoret is building upon a long-traditional heresiology; Clement (*Str.* 3.102.3) had already linked the names of Marcion and Valentinus in a list of docetic teachers. The grouping of Marcion, Valentinus, and Mani will recur in *epp.* 82.1 (*v. ep.* 82 n. 2), 104.2 (*v. ep.* 104 n. 5), and 126.1, in all three cases as part of a longer catalogue. Theodoret had already presented these heretics as precursors of Eutyches and the monophysites in the *Eran. dial.* 2 (p. 117, ll. 25–27). In that passage, in addition to these three, he lists Simon Magus, Menander, Cerdo, Basilides, and Bardaisan, all of whom "explicitly denied the humanity of Christ" (ἠρνήθησαν ἄντικρυς τὴν ἀνθρωπότητα τοῦ Χριστοῦ).

4. Theodoret's opponents accused him of Nestorianism; *v.* Intro., sec. 4.4.

5. In sec. 2 (τῷ ὄντι γὰρ μᾶλλον ἀσπάζομαι), the adverb μᾶλλον (= "more than") establishes a comparison. I agree with Jackson in understanding the comparison to be between Theodoret's slight or non-existent desire to visit other cities and his happiness to remain at home in Cyrus. Azéma, however construes μᾶλλον with the following genitive τῶν ἐν μοναχικῷ . . . βουλομένων = "I am a greater lover of peace and quiet than those who, though clad in the habit of monks, would like to direct the affairs of the churches." In that case, Theodoret would be establishing a contrast between himself and presumptuous monks, such as Eutyches and his partisans (*v. ep.* 11 nn. 1f. and Intro., sec. 4–4.2), who are not bishops but wish to exercise the power of bishops. But, *cf.* the parallel passage in *ep.* 82.1 (πρῶτον μὲν γὰρ τὴν τριπόθητον ἀπέλαβον ἡσυχίαν = "First of all, because I got back the peace and quiet I yearn for"), where Theodoret seems to be contrasting his earlier, more distracted, with his present, more peaceful, circumstances.

Τὸ Μέγεθος ὡς οὔτε ἐπὶ τοῦ μακαριωτάτου καὶ ἐν ἁγίοις Θεοδότου, οὔτε ἐπὶ τοῦ τῆς μακαρίας μνήμης Ἰωάννου, οὔτε ἐπὶ τοῦ ἁγιωτάτου ἐπισκόπου, τοῦ Κυρίου Δόμνου, ἑκὼν εἰς τὴν Ἀντιόχειαν εἰσῄειν, ἀλλά, καὶ πεντάκις καὶ ἑξάκις καλούμενος, μόλις ὑπήκουον, καὶ ὑπήκουον, τῷ ἐκκλησιαστικῷ κανόνι πειθόμενος ὃς κινδυνεύειν παρακελεύεται τὸν καλούμενον εἰς σύνοδον καὶ παραγίγνεσθαι μὴ βουλόμενον. εἰσιόντες δέ, τί τῶν ἀπαρεσκόντων Θεῷ πεποιήκαμεν; ὅτι τὸν δεῖνα καὶ τὸν δεῖνα σιγῆς ἀξίας παρανομίας τετολμηκότας τῶν ἱερῶν ἐχωρίσαμεν καταλόγων; ὅτι τοὺς ἐπαινουμένους καὶ βίῳ κοσμουμένους τῇ τῆς ἱερωσύνης χειροτονίᾳ προσάγομεν; ὅτι τοῖς λαοῖς τὴν εὐαγγελικὴν διδασκαλίαν προσφέρομεν; εἰ ταῦτα γραφῆς ἄξια καὶ τιμωρίας, καὶ τὰς μείζους ὑπὲρ τούτων ἥδιστα τιμωρίας δεχόμεθα.

Ἀλλὰ γὰρ ἀναγκάζουσί με οἱ συκοφάνται·[c] καὶ πρὸ αὐτῆς τῆς συλλήψεως ὑπέσχοντό με τῷ Θεῷ προσφέρειν οἱ φύσαντες καὶ ἐκ σπαργάνων κατὰ τὰς ἐπαγγελίας ἀνέθηκαν, τροφῆς τοιαύτης ἠξίωσαν. ἐν μοναστηρίῳ τὸν πρὸ τῆς ἐπισκοπῆς διατελέσας

c. *Cf.* 2Cor 12.11.

now in blessed repose among the saints, nor in those of John of blessed memory, nor in these of the holy bishop, My Lord Domnus, have I ever gone of my own choice to Antioch;[6] even when I had been summoned for the fifth or sixth time, I would only grudgingly obey, and I obeyed in compliance with the church canon that imposes legal liability on anyone who refuses to present himself when summoned to a synod.[7] And when I did go, what actions did I take that could be displeasing to God? Seeing to it that this or that man guilty of crimes better left unmentioned be removed from the diptychs? Nominating for the priesthood men of repute whose very life was their commendation? Presenting gospel teaching to the laity? If these are acts worthy of indictment and punishment, I am more than happy to suffer far worse for them!

I would not speak further, but I am forced to it by my lying accusers.[c] Even before my conception, my parents had promised to consecrate me to God, and, while I was still in diapers, they did offer me as they had promised and gave me the appropriate upbringing. I spent the time before my episcopacy in a monastery, and, only with

6. Theodotus (d. 429), the patriarch of Antioch at the time of Theodoret's accession to the see of Cyrus in 423, was the recipient of *epp.* XXXII and XLV. John, patriarch of Antioch from 429–41/42 had been a student along with Nestorius at Antioch. His repudiation of the condemnation of Nestorius at the Council of Ephesus in 431 resulted in the brief schism with Alexandria that was resolved by the accord of 433; *v.* Intro., secc. 3.4, 7; and Papadakis, "John I." For Domnus, *v. ep.* 31 n. 1.

7. Here and in his comments on Col 2.18 and 3.17, Theodoret refers to a collection known as the "Canons of Laodicea," which consists of fifty-nine regulations, most of which are reported only in summary form; a number of them seem likely derived from the canons of Nicaea and other early councils. If, as Theodoret believed, there was actually a Council of Laodicea that issued all or some of these canons, it must have taken place some time between the Councils of Sardica (343) and Constantinople (381); *v.* Hefele-Leclercq, p. 995. The fortieth canon reads, "That bishops must not scorn a summons to council but should go to give and receive teaching for the edification of the Church and the rest. Whoever scorns the summons will be witness against himself, unless his failure to appear be due to indisposition" (Ὅτι οὐ δεῖ ἐπισκόπους καλουμένους εἰς σύνοδον καταφρονεῖν, ἀλλ' ἀπιέναι καὶ διδάσκειν ἢ διδάσκεσθαι, εἰς κατόρθωσιν τῆς Εκκλησίας καὶ τῶν λοιπῶν. Εἰ δὲ καταφρονήσειεν ὁ τοιοῦτος, ἑαυτὸν αἰτιάσεται, παρεκτὸς εἰ μὴ δι' ἀνωμαλίαν ἀπολιμπάνοιτο).

χρόνον, ἄκων τὴν τῆς ἐπισκοπῆς ἐδεξάμην χειροτονίαν. πέντε καὶ εἴκοσι διετέλεσα ἔτη, οὔτε κατεντευχθεὶς ὑπό τινος οὔτε αἰτιασάμενος ἕτερον, οὐ προσήδρευσέν τις δικαστηρίῳ τῶν ὑπ᾿ ἐμὲ εὐλαβεστάτων κληρικῶν ἐν τοσούτοις ἔτεσιν. οὐκ ὀβολόν, οὐχ ἱμάτιον παρά τινος ἐδεξάμην, ἕνα ἄρτον ἢ ᾠὸν οὐδεὶς τῶν ἐμῶν συνοίκων ἐδέξατο πώποτε, πλὴν τῶν ῥακίων ὧν περιβέβλημαι, οὐδὲν κτήσασθαι ἠνεσχόμην. δημοσίας στοὰς ἐκ τῶν ἐκκλησιαστικῶν προσόδων ἀνέστησα, γεφύρας δύο μεγίστας ᾠκοδόμησα, λουτρῶν ἐπεμελήθην κοινῶν. ἐκ τοῦ παραρρέοντος ποταμοῦ τὴν πόλιν ὑδρευομένην εὑρών, τὸν ἀγωγὸν κατεσκεύασα καὶ τὴν ἄνυδρον πόλιν ὑδάτων ἐπλήρωσα.

(3) Καί, ἵνα ταῦτα καταλίπω, κώμας ὀκτὼ τὴν Μαρκίωνος <νόσον νοσούσας> καὶ τὰς πέριξ κειμένας ἀσμένως πρὸς τὴν ἀλήθειαν ἐποδήγησα. ἄλλην κώμην εὐνομιανῶν πεπληρωμένην καὶ ἄλλην ἀρειανῶν τῷ φωτὶ τῆς θεογνωσίας προσήγαγον, καὶ

l. 64 τὴν πόλιν ὑδρευομένην *codd., Sir.* : τ. π. <μὴ> ὑ. *scr. Nös. Az.* = *"When I found that the city was not drawing its water from the river running by it." The middle of* ὑδρεύω *regularly signifies "to fetch water for oneself" and is frequently complemented by a prepositional phrase, introduced by* ἐκ *or* ἀπό, *indicating the source; v. LSJ, ad voc. and cf. Ael. N. a. 5.23.1: Ἐλλοχῶσιν οἱ κροκόδειλοι τοὺς ὑδρευομένους ἐκ τοῦ Νείλου τὸν τρόπον τοῦτον. Thdt. does not mean to say that the citizens of Cyrrus were not drawing water, but that they had to draw it at the riverbank. Furthermore, Nösselt (col. 1261, n. 72) wrongly imagined that Z carried the negative, and that such a reading could have any weight in criticism based on stemmatic considerations.* **ll. 66f.** τὴν Μαρκίωνος <νόσον νοσούσας> *scripsi e.g.* : τὴν Μ. *codd.* : τῆς Μ. *scr. Sir. Nös. Az. As there is no fem. noun to respond to the article, Az. rightly indicates a lacuna following the name "Marcion." My suggested supplement is based on Eran. dial. 2 (p. 128, ll. 26f.): μαρκιωνιστάς φημι, καὶ μανιχαίους, καὶ τοὺς ἄλλους ὅσοι ταύτην νοσοῦσι τὴν νόσον. Cf. also sec. 1 of this letter: τοῖς τὰ Βαλεντίνου καὶ Μοντανοῦ νοσοῦσι. Other possibilities for the abstract noun include* βλασφημίαν *(cf. ep. 112.1),* ἀσέβειαν *(cf. Haer. com. 5.5),* ἀναισχυντίαν *(cf. Trin. 23),* λύτταν *(cf. ep. 82.2),* λύμην *(cf. ep. 146.7). All of these require the acc. of the art. rather than the gen. conjectured by Sir.*

reluctance, accepted my appointment as bishop. I passed twenty-five years without accusation by another or myself bringing accusation against anyone else; in all these years, none of the right reverend clerics under me has ever attended a court hearing. I have never accepted a cent or a shirt from anyone; no member of my household has ever accepted so much as a loaf of bread or an egg; except for the rags I wear, I never permitted myself to purchase a thing.[8] From the proceeds of the diocese, I have raised porticos for general use, built two enormous bridges, provided for the upkeep of the public baths. When I saw that the city drew its water from the river that flows by it, I had a conduit built and filled with water a city that had been waterless.[9]

(3) Furthermore, to put all that aside, I showed zeal in guiding to the truth eight villages and others in their vicinity infected with the malady of Marcionism.[10] And there was another village teeming with Eunomians and another with Arians that I led to the light of the knowledge of God, and, through the grace of God, there is not a

8. Canivet remarks ("Théodoret et le Messalianisme," pp. 30–33) that Theodoret's insistence on his self-sufficiency echoes a contemporary debate regarding the practical expression of monastic poverty: was it better for monks to support themselves by their own labor or to abstain from work and depend on the charity of the faithful? Here Theodoret affirms that, throughout his episcopacy, he has remained faithful to the discipline of work he had observed in his earlier monastic life; *cf.* also, *id.*, "Théodoret et le monachisme," p. 280.

9. Azéma (*v.* his *ap. crit.* and translation *ad loc.*), perhaps following Jackson ("On finding that the city was not watered by the river running by it"), supposes that, before Theodoret's intervention, the city of Cyrus received no water from the river. Theodoret, however, clearly means that, by constructing a conduit into the city, he made it possible for the citizens to get their water closer to home without the need for frequent trips to the riverside; *v.* my c. n.

10. The text of this sentence is lacunose; *v.* the c. n. *Cf. ep.* 113.4, where Theodoret reports that he had won over to orthodoxy more than a thousand Marcionites. Marcion, a Greek-speaking theologian from Sinope on the Black Sea, formed at Rome a Christian community that by the 140s was separate from the great Church and propagating itself throughout the Mediterranean basin. Rejecting allegorical interpretation and relying on a strictly historical reading of the Jewish Scriptures, he preached a dualistic theology, in which he opposed the God of the OT to the Father revealed in the NT; *v.* Kelly, pp. 57f., 67, 142; and Canivet, "Théodoret et le Messalianisme," n. 11. Theodoret provides a brief exposé of his teaching in *Haer. com.* 1.24.

διὰ τὴν θείαν χάριν οὐδὲ ἓν παρ᾽ ἡμῖν αἱρετικῶν ὑπελείφθη ζιζάνιον.[d] καὶ ταῦτα οὐκ ἀκινδύνως πεποίηκα, ἀλλὰ τὸ αἷμά μου πολλάκις ἐκχύσας, πολλάκις καταλευσθεὶς ὑπ᾽ αὐτῶν, καὶ εἰς αὐτὰς φθάσας τοῦ ᾅδου τὰς πύλας.[e]

Ἀλλὰ γὰρ ἄφρων ἐγενόμην καυχώμενος, τῆς δὲ ἀνάγκης, οὐ τῆς γνώμης, τὰ εἰρημένα. τοῦτο δὲ καὶ ὁ τρισμακάριος Παῦλος ἠναγκάσθη δρᾶσαί ποτε, τῶν κατηγορούντων ἐμφράττων τὸ στόμα.[f] στέργω δὲ ὅμως τὴν δοκοῦσαν ἀτιμίαν καὶ τιμὴν ἄκραν ὑπολαμβάνω· ἀκούω γὰρ τῆς ἀποστολικῆς βοώσης φωνῆς· *Πάντες … οἱ θέλοντες ζῆν εὐσεβῶς ἐν Χριστῷ Ἰησοῦ διωχθήσονται.*[g]

Τὴν δὲ Ὑμετέραν Μεγαλοπρέπειαν παρακαλῶ φροντίσαι τῶν ἐκκλησιαστικῶν πραγμάτων καὶ τὴν ἐπαναστᾶσαν κατευνάσαι ζάλην· τῷ ὄντι γὰρ οὐδὲ ἐν ἀρχῇ τῆς διαστάσεως τοιαύτη τὴν Ἐκκλησίαν κατέλαβε σύγχυσις. οὐδεὶς ὑμᾶς διδάσκει τῶν κινδύνων τὸ μέγεθος, τῶν ἐν Φοινίκῃ χριστιανῶν τοὺς θρήνους, τῶν παρ᾽ ἡμῖν ἁγιωτάτων μοναζόντων τοὺς ὀδυρμούς· οὗ δὴ χάριν καὶ πλείοσιν ἐχρησάμην λόγοις ἵνα, μαθοῦσα Ὑμῶν Ἡ Μεγαλοφυΐα τῶν ἐκκλησιῶν τὸν κλύδωνα, καταπαύσῃ τοῦτον καὶ τὴν ἐντεῦθεν ὠφέλειαν καρπώσηται.

ll. 72f. εἰς αὐτὰς … τὰς πύλας *scr.* $A^{s.l.}$ *(Car.?), edd.* : αὐ…. τ. π. *NZ. The loss of a preposition is clear.* εἰς, *conjectured perhaps by Cariofilo, is a plausible supplement (v. Chrys., Hom. 2.5 in 2Tm:* *Ἴσως γὰρ μετὰ τὸ ἐλθεῖν εἰς αὐτὰς τοῦ ᾅδου τὰς πύλας, …*); πρός *is equally possible (id., in 2Cor, hom. 2.3:* *Ὅταν γὰρ ἄνθρωπον ἀπογνωσθέντα, καὶ πρὸς αὐτὰς ἐλθόντα τοῦ ᾅδου τὰς πύλας ἀνελκύσῃ, …*). **l. 77** στέργω *scripsi* : στέγω *codd., edd.* = *"I put up with seeming ignominy." Thdt. is probably employing the device of ring-composition and repeating, with the same verb, the sentiment of resignation to mistreatment and misrepresentation expressed at the beginning of this letter; cf.* *οὔτε γραφῆς δεικνυμένης … καὶ στέργομεν ταύτην* *(sec. 1). Elsewhere, he uses forms of the verb* *στέγω* *only six times, always in quotations of the Pauline epistles; cf. his notes ad 1Cor 9.12, 13.7; 1Thes 3.1–3, 5.*

d. *Cf.* Mt 13.24–30. e. *Cf.* 2Cor 11.25. f. *Cf.* 2Cor 11.16f.; 12.11. g. 2Tm 3.12

single heretical tare left in our region.[d] It was not without personal risk that I achieved this, but frequently shedding my own blood, frequently enduring stoning at their hands, and being brought down to the very gates of death.[e]

But I was mad to boast; I have said this much, because I was forced to, not because I wanted to. Even the most blessed Apostle Paul was once forced to this to stop up the mouths of his accusers.[f] Yet I have resigned myself to accept this apparent disgrace and regard it as the highest possible commendation, for I can hear the voice of the Apostle crying out, "Everyone who intends to live a godly life in Christ Jesus will suffer persecution."[g]

I implore Your Excellency to take thought for church affairs and to quell the tempest that has arisen. Indeed, even at the start of this controversy, the Church was not in the grip of such terrible disturbance. No one informs you of the extent of the danger, of the dirges of the Christians of Phoenicia, of the laments of the holy monks of our region; I have gone on at such length, so that, once apprised of the storm that is threatening the churches, Your Eminence might put it to rest and reap the benefit accruing therefrom.

82. ΕΥΣΕΒΙΩΙ ΕΠΙΣΚΟΠΩΙ ΑΓΚΥΡΑΣ

(1)Ἤλπισα συχνὰς ἐν τῷ παρόντι καιρῷ δέξασθαι Τῆς Σῆς Ἁγιωσύνης ἐπιστολάς· προδηλοτάτην γὰρ ὑπομεμενηκότες συκοφαντίαν, παραψυχῆς ἀδελφικῆς ἐδεόμεθα. οἱ γὰρ τὴν Μαρκίωνος, καὶ Βαλεντίνου, καὶ Μάνητος, καὶ τῶν ἄλλων δοκητῶν αἵρεσιν ἐπὶ τοῦ παρόντος ἀνανεούμενοι, δυσχεραίνοντες ὅτι τὴν αἵρεσιν αὐτῶν ἄντικρυς στηλιτεύομεν, ἐξαπατῆσαι τὰς βασιλικὰς ἐπειράθησαν ἀκοάς, *αἱρετικοὺς* ἡμᾶς ἀποκαλοῦντες καὶ εἰς δύο μερίζειν υἱοὺς συκοφαντοῦντες τὸν ἕνα Κύριον ἡμῶν Ἰησοῦν Χριστόν, τὸν ἐνανθρωπήσαντα Θεὸν Λόγον, ἀλλ᾽ οὐκ ἔπεισαν ὥσπερ ἤλπισαν λέγοντες. οὗ δὴ χάριν ὑπομνηστικὸν ἐγράφη τῷ μεγαλοπρεπεστάτῳ καὶ ἐνδοξοτάτῳ στρατηγῷ καὶ ὑπάτῳ, αἱρέσεως μὲν κατηγορίαν οὐδεμίαν ἔχον, ἄλλας δέ τινας αἰτίας, καὶ ταύτας ψευδεῖς· συνόδους γὰρ ἔλεγόν με συχνὰς εἰς τὴν Ἀντιόχειαν συναγείρειν, καὶ τοῦτό τινας λυπεῖν, καὶ διὰ τοῦτο χρῆναί με ἡσυχίαν ἄγειν καὶ τὰς ἐγκεχειρισμένας οἰκονομεῖν ἐκκλησίας.

Τούτου μοι τοίνυν τοῦ ὑπομνηστικοῦ δειχθέντος, ἥρπασα τὴν ψῆφον, ὡς πρόξενον ἀγαθῶν· πρῶτον μὲν γὰρ τὴν τριπόθητον

82. To Eusebius, Bishop of Ancyra[1]

(1) Given the present circumstances, I had hoped to receive frequent letters from Your Holiness, as, being the victim of a patently false accusation, we were in need of brotherly encouragement. Those people who are right now bent on renewing the heresy of the Marcionites, Valentinians, Manicheans, and all the other docetists,[2] full of resentment at our public denunciation of their heresy, have tried to work a deception on the emperor; they have been calling us "heretics" and unjustly accusing us of dividing into two sons our one Lord Jesus Christ, God the Word, who became man.[3] But, for all their talk, they have failed to convince him as they had hoped. Therefore, an order was written to His Excellency, our glorious commander and consul, which contained no accusation of heresy, just several other charges, all of them false.[4] For example, they alleged that I was summoning many councils to Antioch, that this caused distress among some people, and that, because of this, I should keep silent and administer the churches entrusted to my care.

So, when this order was shown me, I eagerly grasped it as a source of blessings. First of all, I got back the peace and quiet I yearn

1. As bishop of Ancyra (now Ankara, in north-central Anatolia, the capital of Turkey), Eusebius was the metropolitan of the province of Galatia; *v.* Foss, "Ankyra." A churchman who adapted his views to those of the party most powerful at the moment, he subscribed to the condemnation of Eutyches at the Council of Constantinople in November 448 (*v.* Intro., sec. 4.2), then agreed to the reinstatement of Eutyches and the deposition of Theodoret at the Robber Council of August 449 (*v. ib.*, sec. 4.7), and then signed the explicitly anti-monophysite declaration of faith approved at the sixth session of the Council of Chalcedon in October 451; *v. ib.*, sec. 5.10, 13. Azéma (vol. 2, pp. 198f.) dates this letter to late 448, somewhat later than *epp.* 79–81. He notes that, in *ep.* 82, Theodoret had become the target of attacks by the Alexandrians, a new development not mentioned in the three previous. Furthermore, as he points out, *ep.* 109 also addressed to Eusebius during the same crisis, must be prior to *ep.* 82, for, in *ep.* 109, Theodoret had requested the confirmation of his views that, as he here complains, Eusebius had as yet failed to supply.

2. *V. ep.* 81 n. 3.

3. On these theological issues, *v. ep.* 21 n. 2.

4. "His Excellency, our glorious commander and consul" is Zeno; *v. epp.* 65, 71, 79.1.

ἀπέλαβον ἡσυχίαν, εἶτα δὲ πολλὰς ἐλπίζω τῶν ὑπ᾽ ἐμοῦ πλημμεληθέντων ἐξαλειφθῆναι κηλῖδας διὰ τὴν τυρευθεῖσαν καθ᾽ ἡμῶν ἀδικίαν ὑπὸ τῶν τῆς ἀληθείας ἐχθρῶν. ἔδειξεν δὲ καὶ λίαν ἐναργῶς κἀν τῷ παρόντι βίῳ τῶν ὅλων ὁ Πρύτανις ὅσην τῶν ἀδικουμένων ποιεῖται κηδεμονίαν· ἡμῶν γὰρ ἡσυχίαν ἀγόντων καὶ εἴσω τῶν τῆς πατρίδος ὅρων εἰργομένων, καὶ τῶν κατὰ τὴν Ἀνατολὴν πάντων ἀνιωμένων μὲν καὶ πικρῶς ὀδυρομένων, σιγᾶν δὲ διὰ τὸ προσπεσὸν δέος ἠναγκασμένων· τὰ γὰρ καθ᾽ ἡμῶν γεγενημένα τὸ τῆς δειλίας πᾶσιν ἐνέθηκε δέος· αὐτὸς ὁ Κύριος ἐκ τοῦ οὐρανοῦ διέκυψεν, καὶ τῶν τὴν συκοφαντίαν ὑφηνάντων τὴν συκοφαντίαν διήλεγξε, καὶ τὸ δυσσεβὲς αὐτῶν ἐγύμνωσε φρόνημα.

(2) Οὗτοι καὶ τὴν Ἀλεξάνδρειαν ἐξώπλισαν καθ᾽ ἡμῶν καὶ τὰς πάντων ἀκοὰς περιβομβοῦσι διὰ τῶν ἀξίων αὐτῶν ὑπουργῶν ὡς ἡμεῖς, ἀνθ᾽ ἑνός, δύο κηρύττομεν υἱούς. ἐγὼ δὲ τοσοῦτον ἀπέχω τοῦ μυσαροῦ τούτου φρονήματος ὅτι, καί τινας τῶν ἁγίων πατέρων τῶν ἐν Νικαίᾳ συνεληλυθότων εὑρηκὼς πρὸς τὴν Ἀρείου μανίαν ἐν συντάγμασιν ἀποτεινομένους καὶ ἀναγκαζομένους διὰ τὸν πρὸς ἐκείνους ἀγῶνα πλείονι διαιρέσει κεχρῆσθαι, δυσχεραίνω καὶ οὐ προσίεμαι τὴν τοιαύτην διαίρεσιν· οἶδα γὰρ ὡς ἡ ἀνάγκη τῆς διαιρέσεως ἀμετρίαν εἰργάζετο.

Καί, ἵνα με μή τις ὑπολάβοι δεδιότα νῦν ταῦτα λέγειν, ἔξεστιν τῷ βουλομένῳ τοῖς παλαιοῖς μου συγγράμμασιν ἐντυχεῖν, τοῖς πρὸ τῆς συνόδου τῆς ἐν Ἐφέσῳ καὶ τοῖς μετ᾽ ἐκείνην, τοῖς πάλιν πρὸ δυοκαίδεκα ἐτῶν· διὰ γὰρ τὴν τοῦ Θεοῦ χάριν, καὶ τοὺς προφήτας ἅπαντας ἡρμηνεύσαμεν, καὶ τὸ ψαλτήριον, καὶ τὸν Ἀπόστολον, καὶ πρὸς τοὺς τὰ Ἀρείου φρονοῦντας, καὶ πρὸς

l. 31 ἐξώπλισαν *coni. Car., scr. edd.* : ἐξετόκησαν *codd. The reading carried by N is a non-existent word. Cariofilo's ingenious conjecture gives excellent sense and is supported by Q. in Iud. 27.1: δικαίῳ γὰρ χρησάμενοι κατὰ τῶν ἐν τῇ Γαβαὼν παρανενομηκότων θυμῷ, τὰς τετρακοσίας ἐξώπλισαν χιλιάδας.*

for; second, thanks to this unjust plot that the enemies of the truth are cooking up against us, I have hopes that the stain of many a sin will be wiped clean. The Ruler of the universe has given abundant proof, and even in the present life, of the depth of his concern for those who suffer injustice, for, while we are living in peace and quiet, confined within the bounds of our homeland, and all the easterners, though grieving and bitterly mourning, have been compelled to keep silent by the fear that has fallen upon them—our case having struck a cowardly fear into them all—the Lord has himself bent down from heaven to expose the web of false accusation woven by my accusers and to lay bare their impiety.

(2) The same people have even raised Alexandria in arms against us and, with the aid of others no better than themselves, drone into the ears of all the world that we preach two, rather than one, son. In fact, I am far from holding this irreligious position, and, while I'm aware that some of the holy fathers who met in Nicaea, in their strenuous opposition to the delirium of Arius, wrote treatises in which, for the purposes of the debate, they were forced to make too much of the distinction in Christ, I do not tolerate, I refuse to admit such a distinction. Of course, I realize that the exaggeration of the distinction was due to force of circumstances.[5]

And, so that no one will suspect I'm speaking out of fear, whoever wishes may consult my previous treatises, ones written prior to the Council of Ephesus and others in its aftermath, twelve years back. Through the grace of God, we have written commentaries on all the prophets, on the psalms, and on the Apostle Paul; in addition, long ago, we wrote treatises against the Arians, and those suffering from

5. As Azéma (vol. 2, p. 202, n. 1) indicates, Theodoret seems to have in mind the christological dualism of Eustathius of Antioch, confirmed by Spanneut, who concedes (p. 223), "La tendance exagérément dualiste est évidente chez Eustathe." But, underlining Eustathius' insistence on the unity of person of Christ, Spanneut concludes, like Theodoret, that Eustathius was drawn to explicitly dualist statements by a concern to disallow Arian positions that diminished both the divinity and humanity of Christ ("Contre ceux qui diminuaient tour à tour dans le Christ l'humain et le divin, il eut à montrer la perfection réciproque de l'homme et du Verbe").

τοὺς τὰ Μακεδονίου νοσοῦντας, καὶ πρὸς τὴν Ἀπολιναρίου τερθρείαν, καὶ πρὸς τὴν Μαρκίωνος λύτταν συνεγράψαμεν πάλαι, καὶ ἐν ἑκάστῳ τῶν συγγραμμάτων, διὰ τὴν τοῦ Θεοῦ μου χάριν, τὸ ἐκκλησιαστικὸν φρόνημα διαλάμπει. καὶ μυστικὴ δὲ ἡμῖν συγγέγραπται βίβλος, καὶ περὶ προνοίας ἑτέρα, καὶ πρὸς τὰς πεύσεις τῶν μάγων ἄλλη, καὶ τῶν ἁγίων οἱ βίοι, καὶ πρὸς τούτοις ἕτερα πολλά, ἵνα μὴ καθ' ἕκαστον λέγω. ἀπηρίθμησα δὲ ταῦτα, οὐ φιλοτιμίᾳ χρώμενος, ἀλλὰ πρόκλησιν προσφέρων καὶ τοῖς κατηγόροις καὶ τοῖς κρίνειν ἐθέλουσιν ὁποῖα ἂν ἐθέλωσι βασανίσαι τῶν συγγραμμάτων· οὐ γὰρ εὑρήσουσιν ἡμᾶς, διὰ τὴν τοῦ Θεοῦ μου χάριν, ἄλλο τι φρονοῦντας ἢ ἅπερ παρὰ τῆς ἁγίας Γραφῆς παρειλήφαμεν.

(3) Ταῦτα τοίνυν μαθοῦσα παρ' ἡμῶν Ἡ Ἁγιότης Σου, διδαξάτω τοὺς ἀγνοοῦντας καὶ τὰς λοιδορούσας ἡμᾶς ἀχαλινώτους γλώττας καὶ τοὺς ἐξηπατημένους πειθέτω μὴ τοιαῦτα περὶ ἡμῶν δοξάζειν οἷα παρὰ τῶν συκοφαντούντων ἔμαθον, ἀλλὰ πείθεσθαι τῷ νομοθέτῃ βοῶντι, *Ἀκοὴν ματαίαν οὐ παραδέξῃ,*[a] καὶ ἀναμένειν τὴν τῶν πραγμάτων ἐξέτασιν. ἐγὼ δὲ εὔχομαι μὲν γαλήνης ἀπολαῦσαι τὰς ἐκκλησίας, καὶ τὸν

a. Ex 23.1

the malady of Macedonius, against the subtleties of Apollinaris, and the ravings of Marcion. And in every one of these treatises, thanks to the grace of God, it is the mind of the Church that shines through for all to see. I have written as well a book regarding the sacraments, another regarding providence, another against the inquiries of the Magi, biographies of the saints, and, so as not to list them all, many other works besides.[6] The point of this catalogue is not to praise myself, but to challenge my accusers—and any others who may wish to pass judgment—to examine whichever of my works they choose. Thanks to the grace of my God, they will find us holding no doctrine that we have not received from holy Scripture.

(3) Now that we have provided this information, we ask Your Holiness to instruct the ignorant and to persuade those who are reviling us with unchecked tongue as well as those who have been deceived to reject opinions regarding us that they have received from slanderers, and, in obedience to the Lawgiver who cries out, "You shall not take up a false rumor,"[a] to await an examination of the facts. My prayer is for the tranquility of the churches and the end of this long

6. Theodoret provides a similar bibliography of his own works in *ep.* 113.4, written to Leo I in autumn 449 and in *Q. in Leu.* 1.1. Richard ("L'activité littéraire") dates the anti-heretical treatises against the Arians, the Macedonians, and Marcion to before the Council of Ephesus; the *On Providence* to 435 or later, the commentaries on the Psalms, the prophets, and the epistles of St. Paul to the period subsequent to the *On Providence.* He finds the evidence insufficient to place the works against Apollinaris and the Magi or the μυστικὴ ... βίβλος. The most probable date for the biographies of the saints (*H. rel.*) is 440; *v.* Azéma ("Chronologie") and Price, pp. xiii–xv. Jackson's (*v.* p. 278, n. 1, γ) identification of the μυστικὴ ... βίβλος as "XII Books on the Mysteries of the Faith" is probably drawn from Venables' list of Theodoret's lost works (p. 918), which itself depends on a list compiled by the seventeenth-century scholar William Cave. Cave speaks of an "*Opus Mysticum, seu de Mysteriorum fidei expositione libri xii,*" but cites no ancient source for either the number twelve or the supposed contents (*v.* p. 318). My translation, "a book regarding the sacraments," is meant to suggest that this was a catechetical work, like, *e.g.*, the works for the newly baptised by Ambrose and Cyril of Jerusalem; *v.* Lampe, *sub voc.* μυστικός, sec. B.2. It is not clear, however, just what sort of work Theodoret has in mind. For a succinct discussion of the lost work on the Persian Magi and of other lost works mentioned elsewhere, *v.* Koch, pp. 38f.

μακρὸν τοῦτον καὶ χαλεπὸν διαλυθῆναι χειμῶνα, εἰ δὲ οὐκ ἐᾷ τῶν ἡμετέρων ἁμαρτημάτων τὸ πλῆθος, ἀλλ᾽ ἐξεδόθημεν διὰ ταῦτα τῷ σινιάζοντι,[b] εὐχόμεθα τῶν ὑπὲρ τῆς πίστεως κινδύνων μεταλαχεῖν ἵν᾽, ἐπειδὴ τὴν ἀπὸ τοῦ βίου παρρησίαν οὐκ ἔχομεν,[c] ἀπό γε τοῦ φυλάξαι τὴν πίστιν ἀκίβδηλον οἴκτου τύχωμεν καὶ συγγνώμης ἐν τῇ τῆς δεσποτικῆς ἐπιφανείας ἡμέρᾳ.[d] ταῦτα δὲ ἡμῖν συνεύξασθαι καὶ Τὴν Σὴν παρακαλοῦμεν Ἁγιωσύνην.

b. Lk 22.31 c. *Cf.* 1Jn 3.21f. d. *Cf.* 1Jn 4.17.

and violent tempest, but if this is not to be because of the multitude of our sins, and, because of these, we have been turned over to him who will pass us through the sieve,[b] we pray for a share of perils in defense of the faith. As the quality of our life gives us no claim to be heard,[c] on the day of the Lord's second coming, may we meet with pity and forgiveness for having preserved the faith pure and unadulterated.[d] We implore Your Holiness to join us in this prayer.

83. ΔΙΟΣΚΟΡΩΙ ΕΠΙΣΚΟΠΩΙ ΑΛΕΞΑΝΔΡΕΙΑΣ

(1) Τῷ εὐλαβεστάτῳ καὶ θεοφιλεστάτῳ Διοσκόρῳ Θεοδώρητος χαίρειν. |μεγίστην φέρει τοῖς συκοφαντουμένοις παραψυχὴν τὰ τῆς θείας Γραφῆς διηγήματα·|| ὅταν γάρ τις ὑπὸ γλώττης ἀχαλινώτου ψευδηγορίαις βληθεὶς τὰς ὀξείας δέξηται τῆς ἀθυμίας ἀκίδας, ἀναμιμνήσκεται τῆς κατὰ τὸν ἀξιάγαστον Ἰωσὴφ ἱστορίας καί, ὁρῶν τῆς σωφροσύνης τὸ ἄγαλμα καὶ τῆς παντοδαπῆς ἀρετῆς τὸν διδάσκαλον συκοφαντίας γραφὴν ὑπομείναντα καὶ ὡς γάμον ἀλλότριον διορύξαντα καθειρχθέντα, καὶ πεδηθέντα,[a] καὶ πλεῖστον ὅσον ἐν εἱρκτῇ διατρίψαντα χρόνον,[b] τῷ τούτου τοῦ διηγήματος φαρμάκῳ θεραπεύει τὴν ἀλγηδόνα. οὕτω πάλιν, εὑρίσκων τὸν πραότατον Δαυὶδ ὡς τύραννον ὑπὸ τοῦ Σαοὺλ ἐλαυνόμενον,[c] δὶς τὸν πολέμιον καὶ θηρεύσαντα καὶ ἀλώβητον ἀπολύσαντα,[d] ἀλεξιφάρμακον πάλιν ἐντεῦθεν τῆς ἀθυμίας λαμβάνει. |ὅταν δὲ καὶ αὐτὸν ἴδῃ τὸν Δεσπότην Χριστόν, τῶν αἰώνων τὸν Ποιητήν,[e] τὸν τῶν ἁπάντων Δημιουργόν,[f] τὸν *ἀληθινὸν θεὸν* καὶ τοῦ *ἀληθινοῦ Θεοῦ* υἱόν,[g] *πλάνον* ὑπὸ τῶν ἀλιτηρίων ἰουδαίων

ll. 1f. Τῷ εὐλαβεστάτῳ καὶ θεοφιλεστάτῳ Διοσκόρῳ Θεοδώρητος χαίρειν *BV, cf. Λ* (Domino meo uere deoamantissimo archiepiscopo Dioscoro Theodoritus in domino gaudere = *"Joy in the Lord to my lord Dioscorus, archbishop most beloved of God, from Theodoret"*), *Sch.* : *om. N, Σ, Sir. Gar. Nös. Az. For this letter and this alone, one branch of the ms. tradition (BVΛ) preserves not only a title giving the name and rank of the addressee but also a greeting. In the other branch of the direct tradition of ep. 83 (N) and in the tradition of the other letters of the* corpus *(N and, where available, P), the title takes the place of the greeting. Perhaps that substitution reflects the set-up of the register in which Thdt. retained copies of his correspondence.*

a. Gn 39.6–20 b. Gn 41.1 c. 1Sm 19.11–17
d. 1Sm 24; 26 e. Heb 1.2 f. *Cf.* Prv 8.22–31; Jn 1.3; 1Cor 8.6.
g. *Symb. nic.-cp.*

83. To Dioscorus, Bishop of Alexandria[1]

(1) Greetings from Theodoret to Dioscorus, right reverend and beloved of God. It is a deep consolation that the stories of sacred Scripture bring to those who are the butt of false accusation. As he suffers the pricks of sore distress, the victim of the lying tales of an unbridled tongue will call to mind the story of that excellent man Joseph and observe how the very exemplar of chastity and master of every virtue was falsely charged with trying to steal another man's wife, thrown into prison, bound with shackles,[a] and confined for ever so long,[b] and will then make use of this story as though it were a medicine, to soothe his pain. Likewise, when he learns how David, that meekest of men, exiled by Saul on a charge of insurrection,[c] twice captured his enemy and then released him unharmed,[d] he finds in this story another cure for his distress. But when he sees how our Master Christ, Maker of the ages,[e] Creator of the universe,[f] true God and Son of the true God[g] was called "a deceiver" by the

1. On Dioscorus, *v. ep.* 60 n. 1. Azéma (vol. 2, pp. 204f.) dates this letter to early summer 448, somewhat after the deposition of Irenaeus of Tyre (*v. ep.* 3 n. 1 and *ep.* 79 n. 8).

ὠνομασμένον,[h] οὐκέτι μόνον ψυχαγωγίαν, ἀλλὰ καὶ εὐθυμίαν καρποῦται μεγίστην, ἅτε δὴ τῆς δεσποτικῆς ἀξιούμενος κοινωνίας.[i]

(2) Ταῦτα δὲ γράψαι νῦν ἠναγκάσθην, ἐντυχὼν τοῖς παρὰ Τῆς Σῆς Ἁγιότητος γραφεῖσι τῷ θεοφιλεστάτῳ καὶ ἁγιωτάτῳ ἀρχιεπισκόπῳ τῷ Κυρίῳ Δόμνῳ· προσέκειτο γὰρ αὐτοῖς καὶ τόδε, ὥς τινες, τὴν μεγίστην πόλιν τὴν ὑπὸ Τῆς Σῆς Ὁσιότητος ἰθυνομένην κατειληφότες, ἐγράψαντο ἡμᾶς, ὡς εἰς δύο υἱοὺς μερίζοντας τὸν ἕνα Κύριον ἡμῶν Ἰησοῦν Χριστόν, καὶ ταῦτα ἐν Ἀντιοχείᾳ διαλεγομένους, ἔνθα πολλαὶ μυριάδες τῶν ||Σ ἀκροατῶν πληροῦσι τὸν σύλλογον.|| καὶ ἐκείνους μὲν ἐθρήνησα προφανῆ συκοφαντίαν ὑφᾶναι τετολμηκότας, ἤλγησα

l. 22 Ἁγιότητος *N, Az.* : Ὁσιότ- *BVΣ. In the four places in this letter (two more exx. in sec. 2 and one in sec. 4), where N carries an honorific form of address containing either ὁσιότης or ἁγιότης, BV offer a different formulation. Here, and in the second ex. in sec. 2 (v. c. n. ad* Ὁσιότητος), *BV present the alternative abstract; in the third ex. (v. c. n. ad* Ἡ Σὴ Ὁσιότης), *both the alternative abstract and a different placement of the possessive adjective; in sec. 4, the same abstract but with a possessive adjective preceding, rather than a pron. following, the noun. I regard these variations, except for the third in sec. 2* (Ἡ Σὴ Ὁσιότης) *as indicative of deliberate editing. On the general issue of the reliability / unreliability of BV, v. Intro. to the Greek Text, sec. III.E.* **ll. 22f.** γραφεῖσι τῷ θεοφιλεστάτῳ καὶ ἁγιωτάτῳ ἀρχιεπισκόπῳ τῷ Κυρίῳ Δόμνῳ *N, Az.* : γ. τῷ δεσπότῃ μου τῷ θ. κ. ἁγ. ἀρ. Δ. *BVΛΣ = "the letter of Your Holiness to my lord, the most holy archbishop, beloved of God, Domnus." The formulation carried by N (superlative epithet + a form of ἀρχιεπίσκοπος + a form of κύριος or δεσπότης + name) is securely attested in other places; v. ep. 92: ὁ ὁσιώτατος ἀρχιεπίσκοπος ὁ κύριος Δομνος; also epp. 43, 116.2, 121. In the five occurences elsewhere in the works of Thdt., a form of δεσπότης + μου always precedes a personal name, both in the four places where he is quoting a letter written by someone else (H. e. 1.6.1, p. 27, l. 20 and 1.6.8, p. 29, l. 15) and in the one case where he uses the phrase himself (ep. 116.2).* **l. 24** Ὁσιότητος *N, Az.* : Ἁγιότ- *BVΣ; v. c. n. ad l. 22* (Ἁγιότητος) **l. 29** προφανῆ συκοφαντίαν ὑφᾶναι τετολμηκότας *N, Sir.* : ὡς π. σ. ὑ. τ. *BVΛ, Gar. Nös. Sch. Az. When Thdt. uses the pf. pt. τετολμηκό- to express cause, he sometimes introduces the non-finite clause with ὡς, sometimes not. For a cause stated without ὡς, v. ep. 81.2: ὅτι τὸν δεῖνα καὶ τὸν δεῖνα σιγῆς ἀξίας παρανομίας τετολμηκότας τῶν ἱερῶν ἐχωρίσαμεν καταλόγων. For a cause stated with ὡς, v. ad Am 4.3: Ὑπομενεῖτε δέ, φησί, ταῦτα, ὡς … καὶ τριημέρους ἑορτὰς τοῖς εἰδώλοις πανηγυρίζειν τετολμηκότες.*

h. Mt 27.63 i. Acts 5.41

wicked Jews,[h] he reaps not just a consolation, but a deep joy, since he has been deemed worthy of companionship with the Lord.[i]

(2) I have felt compelled to write this, after I saw what Your Holiness had written to His Holiness, Archbishop Lord Domnus, beloved of God. Your letter included the statement that some people who had come to that great city governed by Your Holiness had accused us of dividing into two sons our one Lord Jesus Christ—and this while preaching in Antioch, where there is a packed congregation of thousands of hearers. First, I wept for them for having the shameless audacity to fabricate a patently false accusation; then I felt

δέ· καί μοι σύγγνωθι, Δέσποτα, ὑπ᾽ ὀδύνης λέγειν βιαζομένῳ· ὅτι μοι θατέραν ταῖν ἀκοαῖν Ἡ κατὰ Θεόν Σου Τελειότης οὐκ ἐφύλαξεν ἀκεραίαν, ἀλλὰ τοῖς ψευδῶς παρ᾽ ἐκείνων εἰρημένοις ἐπίστευσεν. καίτοι ἐκεῖνοι μὲν τρεῖς εἰσιν, ἢ τέσσαρες, ἢ πεντεκαίδεκα, ἐγὼ δὲ πολλὰς ἔχω μυριάδας ἀνθρώπων τῇ τῆς διδασκαλίας ὀρθότητι μαρτυρούσας. ἓξ μὲν γὰρ ἔτη διετέλεσα διδάσκων ἐπὶ τοῦ τῆς μακαρίας καὶ ὁσίας μνήμης Θεοδότου, τοῦ τῆς ἀντιοχέων ἐπισκόπου, ὃς καὶ βίῳ λαμπρῷ καὶ τῇ τῶν θείων δογμάτων ἐκεκόσμητο γνώσει, τριακαίδεκα δὲ πάλιν ἕτερα ἐπὶ τοῦ μακαρίου Ἰωάννου, ὃς τοσοῦτον ἐγάννυτο, διαλεγομένων ἡμῶν, ὡς ἄμφω τὼ χεῖρε κινεῖν καὶ διανίστασθαι πολλάκις· ὅτι δέ, παιδόθεν τοῖς θείοις λογίοις ἐντεθραμμένος,[j]

l. 31 θατέραν ταῖν ἀκοαῖν *scripsi* : θ. τῶν -οῶν *codd., edd. The phrase,* θατέραν ταῖν ἀκοαῖν, *used by Thdt. alone, is attested in the ms. tradition in two other places* (*H. e. 1.33.3; ep. 91*) *and should probably be printed also in ep. 146.11. The form of the phrase with the pl. art. + noun is attested only here in the works of Thdt. and in two passages of late Byz. authors* (*Theophyl. ep. 98, l. 86; Theog., Thes. ch. 19, sec. 6, ll. 74f.*). *Quite likely, the more common pl. has driven out the rare dual, thus banalizing a typically Theodoretean turn of phrase.* **l. 39** τρία καὶ δέκα δὲ πάλιν *N, Λ, Sir. Sch.* : τ. κ. δέκα π. *BV, Nös. Az. Cf. H. rel., Vita 21.17: τρεῖς δὲ εὐχὰς ἐξανύσας … ὀκτὼ δὲ πάλιν προσευχὰς συμπεράνας.* **ll. 39f.** ἐγάννυτο διαλεγομένων ἡμῶν *BVΛ* (exultabat disputantibus nobis), *Az.* : ἰαίνετο ὑποδ- ἡ. *N. The reading of BV is entirely in agreement with Thdt.'s usage, that carried by N and the mss. dependent on it obviously inappropriate. While the works of Thdt. contain twenty-five examples of the imperfective stem* (*middle voice*) *of γάννυμαι, this would be his sole use of any form of ἰαίνομαι, an archaic verb, used primarily in epic poetry* (*e.g. Hom., Od.*) *though also in the hexameters of Gr. naz.* (*e.g., C. de se ipso, 45.75, 331*). *While διαλέγομαι is very common in the works of Thdt.* (*including eight examples of the pt. gen. pl.; cf. ep. 99: Πολλάκις γὰρ ἡμῶν ἐν ἐκκλησίᾳ διαλεγομένων ἀκήκοεν καὶ τὸν ἕνα Κύριον Ἰησοῦν κηρυττόντων*) *a vb. ὑποδιαλέγομαι is unattested anywhere. While a scribe who imagined that ἐγάννυτο was passive might insert the preposition ὑπό to govern what he took to be an expression of agent, it is difficult to see how ἐγάννυτο could give rise to ἰαίνετο. The latter, however, is not the more difficult, but an almost impossible, reading.* **l. 41** τοῖς θείοις λογίοις *BV* (λόγοις), *Gar.* (λόγοις) : τοῖς λ. τοῖς θ. *N, Sir. Sch. Az. The TLG attributes to Thdt. 107 uses of this pl. phrase in which the attributive placement of the adjective is achieved by means of a single article; it offers no other example of his use of the doubled construction in which the article is repeated before this adjective; cf. the following c. n.* (Ἡ Σὴ Ὁσιότης).

j. *Cf.* 2Tm 3.14.

aggrieved—here I must beg your pardon, my Master, for what I am about to say under the constraint of my distress—that Your Godly Perfection did not keep one unbiased ear for me but gave credence to the false declarations made by those men. Yet they were no more than three, or four, or a dozen, but I have thousands who can testify to the orthodoxy of my teaching. I exercised the office of teacher for six years during the time of Theodotus of blessed and holy memory, bishop of the Antiochenes—distinguished by the luster of his life and his knowledge of religious doctrine—then for thirteen more under the blessed John—who took such delight at my preaching that he would clap his hands and leap up from his seat time and again (In your letter, Your Holiness bears witness to the fact that, raised as he was on the sacred Scriptures,[j] he had a most accurate

ἀκριβῆ λίαν εἶχεν τῶν θείων δογμάτων τὴν εἴδησιν, ἐμαρτύρησεν ἐν τοῖς γράμμασιν Ἡ Σὴ Ὁσιότης· πρὸς δὲ τούτοις ἕβδομόν ἐστιν ἔτος τοῦ θεοφιλεστάτου ἀρχιεπισκόπου τοῦ Κυρίου Δόμνου, καὶ μέχρι τῆς σήμερον ἡμέρας, τοσούτου διεληλυθότος χρόνου, οὐδεὶς οὔτε τῶν θεοφιλεστάτων ἐπισκόπων οὔτε τῶν εὐλαβεστάτων κληρικῶν τοῖς παρ' ἡμῶν εἰρημένοις ἐμέμψατο πώποτε. μεθ' ὅσης δὲ θυμηδίας καὶ οἱ φιλόχριστοι λαοὶ τῶν ἡμετέρων ἐπακούουσι λόγων, ῥᾴδιόν Σου Τῇ κατὰ Θεὸν Τελειότητι παρὰ τῶν ἐκεῖθεν αὐτόσε παραγιγνομένων καὶ μέντοι καὶ παρὰ τῶν ἐντεῦθεν ἐκεῖσε ἀφικνουμένων μαθεῖν.

Καὶ ταῦτα λέγω, οὐ σεμνυνόμενος, ἀλλ' ἀπολογεῖσθαι βιαζόμενος, οὔτε μὴν λαμπρότητα, ἀλλὰ ὀρθότητα μόνην τοῖς ἐμαυτοῦ λόγοις μαρτυρῶν. καὶ ὁ μέγας δὲ τῆς οἰκουμένης

l. 43 Ἡ Σὴ Ὁσιότης *BV, Gar. Nös.* : Ἡ Ἁγιότης Ἡ Σή *N, Sir. Sch. Az. V. c. n. ad l. 22* (Ἁγιότητος). *For* Ἡ Σὴ Ὁσιότης (*the reading of BV also at p. 218, l. 6*), *there is only one entirely reliable parallel relevant to Thdt.'s usage; v. ep. XLI and cf. the quotation of Constantine in H. e. 1.17.8, p. 63, l. 14. Thdt. normally joins the gen. of the pron. to the nom. ἡ ὁσιότης* (*σου preceding in seven places, following in three more*). *The doubled construction with art. + ὁσιότης + art. + possessive adj. is not attested in his works. The TLG offers from Thdt.'s works no other example of ἁγιότης + σή in either the construction with one article or the doubled construction with two, though the phrase ἡ ἁγιότης σου occurs once; v. ep. 82.2. Perhaps the odd and labored ἡ ἁγιότης ἡ σή is conceivable as an attempt at ironic effect* (*cf. the insistence on Dioscorus' humility in ep. 60 and the descriptive δικαιότατος applied to Dioscorus in ep. 113.3*), *but cf. the preceding c. n.* (τοῖς θείοις λογίοις). **l. 53** μόνην *N, Sir.* : -νον *BVΛ* (solummodo), *Gar. Nös. Sch. Az. The fem. acc. sg., though not uncommon, is the lect. diff. For οὔτε μὴν + ἀλλὰ + μόνην + noun v. Affect. 9.7, l. 5: Μίνως οὐκ ἔπεισε δὲ οὔτε σικελιώτας οὔτε καρχηδονίους οὔτε μὴν τοὺς ἕλληνας κατὰ τοὺς αὐτοῦ πολιτεύεσθαι νόμους, ἀλλὰ μόνην τὴν νῆσον ἐκείνην, ἧς ἐβασίλευσε. Cf. also Q. in 1Par., intro.* (*p. 251, ll. 17–19*) *and Q. 1* (*p. 252, ll. 16f.*). **l. 54** μαρτυρῶν *BV* : προσμ- *N, Sir. Gar. Nös. Sch. Az. = "my testimony is not to the brilliance, but also the orthodoxy, of my preaching." The uncompounded nom. sg. masc. pt. occurs five times elsewhere in Thdt.'s own words. V. sec. 4 of this letter: Καὶ ἀντέγραψε πάλιν ἡμῖν καὶ ἀκρίβειαν ἡμῖν καὶ διάθεσιν μαρτυρῶν. The corresponding compounded form occurs in one other place of the works of Thdt., where it is used in a negative / positive antithesis similar to this one; v. Dan. ad 7.4: οὐκ ἰσχὺν αὐτῇ πλείονα προσμαρτυρῶν, ἀλλ' ὡς πρώτην τιμιωτέραν ἀποφαίνων. It is easier to account for a change from the compound to the simplex, and the rarer compound is the lect. diff. Yet, in this sentence of ep. 83, the compound with προσ- would destroy the logic.*

knowledge of religious doctrine)—and this is now the seventh year of Archbishop Lord Domnus, beloved of God, and up to the present day, throughout such a long time, not one of the bishops beloved of God, not one of our right reverend clergy has ever found fault with anything we have said.[2] And, as for the joy with which the Christian laity listen to our preaching—Your Godly Perfection may easily inform yourself from the reports of those who have come here from Alexandria or gone from here to there.

I have said this much, not in self-praise, but because forced to defend myself, and my testimony is not to the brilliance, but just the orthodoxy, of my preaching. Even the great teacher of the world, the

2. For the succession of the bishops of Antioch, *v. ep.* 81 n. 6. We have none of Theodoret's sermons; the passages identified as excerpts in PG, vol. 84, cols. 33–60 are not authentic. Nonetheless, at least his *Quaest. in Oct.* likely contain material that was first presented in sermons before being reworked for a clerical audience; *v.* Petruccione, esp. p. 237.

διδάσκαλος, ὁ θεσπέσιος Παῦλος, *ἔσχατον* ἑαυτὸν τῶν ἁγίων[k] καὶ πρῶτον τῶν ἁμαρτωλῶν[l] ὀνομάζων ἀεί, ἠναγκάσθη, τῶν ψευδηγόρων ἐμφράττων τὰ στόματα, τὸν τῶν οἰκείων πόνων ἐνθεῖναι κατάλογον καί, δεικνὺς ὡς τῆς ἀνάγκης ἦν, ἀλλ᾽ οὐ τῆς γνώμης, ἡ τῶν παθημάτων διήγησις, ἐπήγαγεν, *Ἄφρων* ἐγενόμην καυχώμενος· *ὑμεῖς με ἠναγκάσατε.*[m]

|Σ (3) |Ἐγὼ δὲ ἄθλιον ἐμαυτὸν καὶ τρισάθλιον οἶδα· πολλοῖς γὰρ ὑπόκειμαι πλημμελήμασι,[n] διὰ μόνης δὲ πίστεως[o] ἐν τῇ τῆς θείας ἐπιφανείας ἡμέρᾳ φειδοῦς τινος ἀπολαύσεσθαι προσδοκῶ·τοῖς γὰρ τῶν ἁγίων πατέρων ἀκολουθεῖν ἴχνεσιν καὶ προθυμοῦμαι καὶ προσεύχομαι καὶ τὴν εὐαγγελικὴν διδασκαλίαν, ἣν ἐν κεφαλαίῳ παρέδοσαν ἡμῖν οἱ ἐν Νικαίᾳ τῆς Βιθυνίας συνεληλυθότες ἁγιώτατοι πατέρες, σπουδάζω

l. 62 διὰ μόνης δὲ πίστεως *scripsi* : διὰ δὲ μ. π. *BVΛ* (per solam uero fidem) *Gar. Nös.* : διὰ -νην δὲ -τιν *N, Sir. Sch. Az. I have followed the morphology of BVΛ, but the word order of N. The* per of *Λ supports the gen. of the Greek; διὰ + acc. would be better rendered with propter. In the works of Thdt., διὰ + the gen. of πίστις appears dozens of times, διὰ + acc. of πίστις in only four other places. In all of these four, the noun is modified by the definite article. For close parallels to this passage, v. Affect. 7, sec. 33, l. 1: Οὐ γὰρ δὴ δι᾽ ἔργων ἀξιεπαίνων, ἀλλὰ διὰ μόνης πίστεως τῶν μυστικῶν τετυχήκαμεν ἀγαθῶν; Q. in Ruth 1 (ll. 9f.), and Haer. com. 5.28 (PG, vol. 83, col. 552, l. 50). The usage διὰ + anarthrous gen. is probably due to the influence of Gal. 2.16. For the word order of N, cf. in Hebr. 10.19–22 (PG, vol. 82, col. 752, ll. 29–31): ἐπειδὴ πάντα ἀθέατα, καὶ τὰ ἄδυτα τῆς σκηνῆς, καὶ ἡ θυσία, καὶ ὁ ἀρχιερεὺς, διὰ μόνης δὲ τῆς πίστεως θεωρεῖται.*
l. 67 συνεληλυθότες *N, Az.* : συναχθέντες *BVΛ* (congregati). *In the works of Thdt., the formula συνεληλυθότ- + ἐν + name of city is common (eight cases in his own words, all of these referring to the Council of Nicaea). In contrast, the juncture συναχθέν- + ἐν + name of city occurs in only one other place in his own words (v. ep. 121: τῶν ἐν Νικαίᾳ συναχθέντων ἁγίων πατέρων), three times in quotations. While συναχθέντες might be regarded as the lect. diff., it may also be no more than an attempt to improve Thdt.'s prose.* **l. 67** πατέρες *N, Az.* : π. ἣν καὶ ἡ ἐν Ἐφέσῳ ἁγία σύνοδος κρατεῖν διηγόρευσεν *BVΛΣ* = *"the gospel teaching that the holy fathers gathered in Nicaea of Bithynia handed down to us in their creedal statement, and whose continued validity was confirmed by the holy synod of Ephesus." Each reading has the support of a single independent*

k. 1Cor 15.8 (NT var.) l. 1Tm 1.15 m. 2Cor 12.11 (NT var.)
n. *Cf.* 1Cor 4.4. o. *Cf.* Gal 2.16.

divinely-inspired Paul, who always called himself the "last among saints"[k] and "first among sinners,"[l] was forced to produce a catalogue of his own labors in order to stop up the mouths of his calumniators, and, to show that this list of his sufferings came of necessity, not of his own choice, he added, "I have bragged like a fool, but you gave me no choice."[m]

(3) I realize I am no more than a wretch, a most pitiable wretch, weighed down by many transgressions,[n] and, thus, I expect that, on the day of the second coming, it will be only through my faith that I shall receive any mercy at all.[o] It is my zeal and my prayer to follow in the footsteps of the holy fathers, my aim to defend from blemish the gospel teaching that the holy fathers gathered in Nicaea of Bithynia handed down to us in their creedal statement. And, just as

φυλάττειν ἀκήρατον. καὶ ὥσπερ ἕνα πιστεύω εἶναι *Θεὸν Πατέρα* καὶ ἓν *Πνεῦμα Ἅγιον … ἐκ τοῦ Πατρὸς ἐκπορευόμενον* οὕτως ἕνα *Κύριον, Ἰησοῦν Χριστόν, … Υἱὸν τοῦ Θεοῦ … μονογενῆ … πρὸ … τῶν αἰώνων ἐκ τοῦ Πατρὸς γεγεννημένον,*[p] *Ἀπαύγασμα τῆς δόξης καὶ χαρακτῆρα τῆς* τοῦ Πατρὸς *ὑποστάσεως,*[q] *διὰ τὴν* τῶν ἀνθρώπων *σωτηρίαν … σαρκωθέντα … καὶ ἐνανθρωπήσαντα* καὶ κατὰ σάρκα *ἐκ … Μαρίας τῆς Παρθένου* τεχθέντα.[r] οὕτω γὰρ ἡμᾶς καὶ ὁ πάνσοφος ἐδίδαξε Παῦλος· *Ὧν οἱ πατέρες*, φησί, *καὶ ἐξ ὧν ὁ Χριστός, τὸ κατὰ σάρκα, ὁ ὢν ἐπὶ πάντων Θεὸς εὐλογητὸς εἰς τοὺς αἰῶνας* τῶν αἰώνων. *ἀμήν*·[s] καὶ πάλιν, *Περὶ τοῦ Υἱοῦ αὐτοῦ τοῦ γενομένου ἐκ σπέρματος Δαυὶδ κατὰ σάρκα, τοῦ ὁρισθέντος Υἱοῦ Θεοῦ ἐν δυνάμει κατὰ πνεῦμα ἁγιωσύνης.*[t] διὰ γάρ τοι τοῦτο καὶ *Θεοτόκον* ἀποκαλοῦμεν τὴν ἁγίαν Παρθένον καὶ τοὺς τὴν προσηγορίαν ταύτην παραιτουμένους ἀλλοτρίους τῆς εὐσεβείας ἡγούμεθα.

---

witness. As Nös. remarked (n. 11, col. 1270), it is Thdt.'s practice in his apologetic letters to cite only the authority of the Council of Nicaea. In the other passages of the correspondence where Thdt. refers to this Council or to its creed (epp. 82.2, 84, 88–90, 94, 121, 144, 146.3, 147.11), he never appends an appeal to the confirmation of the work of Nicaea by the Council of Ephesus. Indeed, Thdt. had consistently rejected the acts of Cyril's council, and his Pac. form. constituted just the sort of theological statement Cyril had tried to forestall by forbidding all formularies conceived as clarifications of the Nicene Creed; v. Intro., secc. 3.6, 10f. Thus, the clause that appears in BVΛΣ after πατέρες *must have been added by an editor committed to defending the ecumenicity of the first Council of Ephesus, and the agreement of BVΛΣ in this interpolation constitutes a conjunctive error indicating their descent from a single hyparchetype.* **l. 77** εἰς τοὺς αἰῶνας τῶν αἰώνων *N, Sir.* : ε. τ. αἰ. *BVΛΣ, Gar. Nös. Sch. Az. = "God blessed forever." The reading of BVΛΣ reproduces the text of the NTG, which offers no variant; N inserts an extra gen. Thdt. quotes the doxology of Rom 9.5 in seven other places. The longer form appears once in ep. 147.5 and in one of the two places where the verse is quoted in the commentary on the epp. of St. Paul (ad Phil 4.20). In addition, Ettlinger notes the longer form as a uar. lect. in Eran. dial. 1 (p. 72, l. 13). Thus, the longer reading has multiple attestations and is clearly the lect. diff.; it is far more likely that an editor has corrected what he took to be a slight error of quotation than that he deliberately introduced a form at variance with the most widely accepted text of this verse.*

p. *Symb. nic.-cp.* q. Heb 1.3 (NT var.) r. *Symb. nic.-cp.*
s. Rom 9.5 (NT var.) t. Rom 1.3f.

I believe that there is one "God the Father" and one "Holy Spirit proceeding from the Father," so also, that there is "one Lord, Jesus Christ, the only-begotten Son of God, begotten of the Father before all ages,"[p] the "radiance of the glory and the exact representation of the Father's being,"[q] "who for the salvation of mankind was made flesh and became man and was born, according to the flesh, from the Virgin Mary."[r] This is just what the all-wise Paul has taught us: "Theirs are the patriarchs," he says, "from them, according to the flesh, is the Christ, who is over all, God blessed forever and ever. Amen";[s] and again, "Regarding his Son, born from the seed of David, according to the flesh, who has been declared to be the Son of God in power according to the spirit of holiness."[t] It is because of this that we call the holy Virgin "Mother of God" and regard those who reject this title as alien to our religion.

Ὡσαύτως δὲ καὶ τοὺς εἰς δύο πρόσωπα, ἢ δύο υἱούς, ἢ δύο κυρίους μερίζοντας τὸν ἕνα Κύριον ἡμῶν Ἰησοῦν Χριστὸν *κιβδήλους* ὀνομάζομεν καὶ τῆς τῶν φιλοχρίστων ἀποκρίνομεν μοίρας· ἠκούσαμεν γὰρ τοῦ θειοτάτου Παύλου λέγοντος, *Εἷς Κύριος, μία πίστις, ἓν βάπτισμα·*[u] καὶ πάλιν, *Εἷς Κύριος Ἰησοῦς Χριστός, δι᾽ οὗ τὰ πάντα·*[v] καὶ αὖθις, *Ἰησοῦς Χριστὸς* χθὲς *καὶ σήμερον ὁ αὐτὸς καὶ εἰς τοὺς αἰῶνας·*[w] καὶ ἑτέρωθι, ||Σ *Ὁ καταβὰς αὐτός ἐστιν καὶ ὁ ἀναβὰς ὑπεράνω*|| *πάντων τῶν οὐρανῶν,*[x] καὶ μυρίας δὲ τοιαύτας ἑτέρας ἔστιν εὑρεῖν παρ᾽ |Σ αὐτῷ φωνὰς τὸν ἕνα Κύριον κηρυττούσας. |οὕτω καὶ ὁ θεῖος εὐαγγελιστὴς βοᾷ, *Καὶ ὁ Λόγος σὰρξ ἐγένετο καὶ ἐσκήνωσεν ἐν ἡμῖν, καὶ ἐθεασάμεθα τὴν δόξαν αὐτοῦ, δόξαν ὡς μονογενοῦς παρὰ πατρός, πλήρης χάριτος καὶ ἀληθείας.*[y] καὶ ὁ τούτου γε ὁμώνυμος, ὁ βαπτιστὴς φημί, βοᾷ λέγων, *Ὀπίσω μου ἔρχεται ἀνὴρ ὃς ἔμπροσθέν μου γέγονεν, ὅτι πρῶτός μου ἦν.*[z] καί, τὸ ἓν πρόσωπον δείξας, ἀμφότερα τέθεικεν καὶ τὰ θεῖα καὶ τὰ ἀνθρώπεια· ἀνθρώπειον μὲν γὰρ καὶ τὸ *ἀνὴρ* καὶ τὸ *ἔρχεται*, θεῖον δὲ τὸ *ὅτι πρῶτός μου ἦν*. ἀλλ᾽ ὅμως οὐκ ἄλλον οἶδεν τὸν ὀπίσω ἐρχόμενον καὶ ἄλλον τὸν πρὸ αὐτοῦ ὄντα, ἀλλὰ τὸν αὐτὸν οἶδεν, προαιώνιον μὲν ὡς θεόν, ἄνθρωπον δὲ μετ᾽ αὐτὸν ||Σ ἐκ τῆς Παρθένου τεχθέντα.|| οὕτω καὶ ὁ τρισμακάριος Θωμᾶς, τῇ τοῦ Κυρίου σαρκὶ τὴν χεῖρα προσενεγκών, *Κύριον* ὠνόμασεν καὶ *Θεόν,*[ba] διὰ τῆς ὁρωμένης φύσεως καταμαθὼν τὴν ἀόρατον· οὕτω καὶ ἡμεῖς τῆς μὲν αὐτοῦ σαρκὸς καὶ τῆς θεότητος τὴν

l. 95 γε *NB, Sir.* : δὲ *VΣ, Gar. Nös. Sch. Az. Either formulation would be consonant with Thdt.'s usage. Yet the reading of N, confirmed by B, is the lect. diff. Cf. H. e. 4.28.3:* (*A list of famous mountain-dwelling ascetics*) *καὶ γὰρ ἐν τούτῳ Πέτρος ὁ Γαλάτης διέλαμπε, καὶ ὁ τούτου γε ὁμώνυμος ὁ Αἰγύπτιος.*
l. 106 τῆς θεότητος *BV, Az.* : θ. *N. We find the gen. sg. of σάρξ joined by καὶ to that of θεότης* (*always in this order*) *in ten other passages of the works of Thdt. In all of these, both nouns are treated the same, i.e. both are anarthous* (*eight times*) *or both are preceded by the article* (*two times*)*. V. sec. 4 of this letter: Τοὺς γὰρ τῆς δεσποτικῆς σαρκὸς καὶ τῆς θεότητος τὴν διαφορὰν ἀρνουμένους.*

u. Eph 4.5 v. 1Cor 8.6 w. Heb 13.8 (NT var.) x. Eph 4.10
y. Jn 1.14 z. Jn 1.30 ba. Jn 20.28

In the same way, we call "counterfeiters" any who divide our one Lord Jesus Christ into two persons, or two sons, or two lords and expel them from the Christian people. We have listened to the god-like Paul who says, "One Lord, one faith, one baptism";[u] and again, "One Lord Jesus Christ, through whom are all things";[v] and once more, "Jesus Christ the same yesterday, today, and forever";[w] and in another place, "He who came down is he who has gone up above all the heavens."[x] And we could find in his letters thousands more declarations of this sort proclaiming the one Lord. Likewise, the holy evangelist cries out, "And the Word became flesh and dwelt among us, and we have seen his glory, the glory as of the Only-begotten of the Father, full of grace and truth."[y] And his namesake, I mean the Baptist, cries out, "After me comes a man who is before me, because he was prior to me."[z] Indicating just a single person, he has set out both the divine and the human: the human, in the words "man" and "comes," the divine, in "was prior to me." It is not as if he recognizes one who comes after him and another who existed before him; rather he recognizes the same, both preëxisting the ages as God and born after himself from the Virgin as man. Thus, Thomas, thrice-blest, laying his hand on the body of the Lord, called him "Lord" and "God,"[ba] as, through the seen, he grasped the unseen. In the same way, we also understand the difference between the flesh and the godhead but recognize one Son, God the Word, who became man.

διαφορὰν ἐπιστάμεθα, ἕνα δὲ ἴσμεν Υἱόν, τὸν ἐνανθρωπήσαντα Θεὸν Λόγον.

|Σ (4) |Ταῦτα γὰρ καὶ παρὰ τῆς θείας Γραφῆς ἐδιδάχθημεν καὶ παρὰ τῶν ταύτην ἡρμηνευκότων πατέρων, Ἀλεξάνδρου καὶ Ἀθανασίου, τῶν μεγαλοφώνων κηρύκων τῆς ἀληθείας, οἳ τὸν ἀποστολικὸν ὑμῶν διεκόσμησαν θρόνον, καὶ Βασιλείου, καὶ Γρηγορίου, καὶ τῶν ἄλλων τῆς οἰκουμένης φωστήρων.[bb] ὅτι δέ, καὶ τοῖς τῶν μακαρίων Θεοφίλου καὶ Κυρίλλου συγγράμμασιν κεχρημένοι, τοὺς ἀντιλέγειν τολμῶντας καὶ διὰ ||Σ τούτων ἐπιστομίζομεν, αὐτὰ μαρτυρεῖ τὰ πράγματα·|| τοὺς γὰρ τῆς δεσποτικῆς σαρκὸς καὶ τῆς θεότητος τὴν διαφορὰν ἀρνουμένους καὶ ποτὲ μὲν τὴν θείαν φύσιν εἰς σάρκα τετράφθαι λέγοντας, ποτὲ δὲ τὴν σάρκα εἰς θεότητος μεταβεβλῆσθαι φύσιν,

l. 114 μακαρίων *N, Az.* : -ωτάτων *BVΛ* (beatissimorum). *While Thdt. makes frequent use of the phrase τῶν ἁγίων καὶ μακαρίων πατέρων, no other passage presents the gen. pl. of the basic form modifying personal names. Still, the gen. sg. appears in honorific reference to deceased authoritative teachers; v. sec. 2 of this letter: ἐπὶ τοῦ μακαρίου Ἰωάννου. The superlative gen. pl. is elsewhere completely unattested in the works of Thdt., but in the sg., this form is also used to refer to a deceased teacher: v., e.g., ep. 86.1: τοῦ μακαριωτάτου καὶ ἐν ἁγίοις Ἀθανασίου. I suspect that the superlative attributed to Thdt. in this passage represents a further effort to exaggerate his deference toward the Alexandrians; v. c. n. ad l. 67* (πατέρες). *Indeed, the annotator of V thought it worthwhile to point out to the reader that Thdt. had used the superlative with regard to Cyril: σημ(είωσαι) πῶς γράφει μακαριώτατον τὸν Κύριλλον ὁ Θεοδώρητος; v. Schwartz, ad loc.*
l. 116 πράγματα *BVΛ* (causae) *Σ, Gar. Sch.* : γράμμ- *N, Sir. Nös. Az.* = *"Our letters bear witness." As Az. (vol. 2, p. 215, n. 5) points out, Thdt. is probably referring to his quotation of these fathers in his Eran. But this work. is a treatise* (*σύγγραμα*), *not a letter. Some lines further down, Thdt. refers to letters from Cyril: καὶ ἀντέγραψε πάλιν ἡμῖν …, καὶ σώζεται παρ' ἡμῖν ταῦτα τὰ γράμματα. Among the sixty-five uses of this form in the H. e. and the epp.,* γράμματα = *"treatise" only in two places of ep. 113 to Leo of Rome (v. sec. 2), but there the reference is to the* Tome, *which was sent as a letter to Flavian of Constantinople. The emendation of* γράμματα *to* συγγράμματα *seems precluded by the use of συγγράμμασιν in a previous clause. The competing reading* πράγματα *could well refer to the action suggested by θεραπεύειν σπουδάζομεν in the next sentence. The variation between BVΛΣ and N in this passage, is very like that between N and A* (λόγοις / ἔργοις) *in ep. 2, l. 10. There someone (Sirmond?) was clearly emending N, and here* πράγματα *may be no more than an editor's attempt at improving the text. Yet it might be genuine tradition, since, in a capital text,* πράγματα *might easily be misread as* γράμματα.
l. 118 τετράφθαι *BV, Az.* : -τρέφ- *N*

bb. Phil 2.15

(4) This is what we have learned from sacred Scripture and from the fathers who have expounded it: Alexander and Athanasius, the great-voiced heralds of the truth, who held your apostolic throne with distinction, and Basil and Gregory, and the other luminaries of the world.[3bb] Our deeds bear witness that we also make use of the writings of Theophilus and Cyril of blessed memory to shut up the mouths of those who dare to contradict these teachings.[4] We lose no time in applying the works of these eminent men, as though they were so many medicines, to the healing of those who deny the difference between the Master's flesh and his godhead and sometimes claim that the divine nature was changed into flesh, at others that the flesh was transformed into the divine nature. Their teaching on the

3. As Azéma (*ad loc.*) had suggested, the Gregory in question is probably Basil's brother, Gregory of Nyssa. Theodoret's insistence on the unity of the one Christ and the propriety of using divine names to refer to Jesus is fully in accord with, *e.g.*, Gr. Nyss., *Ad Theoph.* (*CPG* #3143), p. 127, l. 11 to p. 128, l. 15. On Theodoret's use of the Pauline metaphor (Phil 2.15), *v. ep.* 125 n. 7.

4. Both Jackson ("our own writings testify") and Azéma ("mes ouvrages eux-mêmes l'attestent") translated the reading of the *neapolitanus* (γράμματα). As the c. n. indicates, I have preferred the alternative πράγματα. Theodoret seems to be developing the traditional contrast between words and deeds by affirming that he not only praises Alexandrian teachers, but actually follows their doctrine.

τοῖς τῶν θαυμασίων τούτων ἀνδρῶν φαρμάκοις θεραπεύειν σπουδάζομεν. σαφῶς γὰρ καὶ τῶν δύο φύσεων ἡμᾶς τὴν διαφορὰν ἐκπαιδεύουσι· καὶ τὸ ἄτρεπτον τῆς θείας κηρύττουσι φύσεως καὶ τὴν δεσποτικὴν σάρκα *θείαν* μὲν ἀποκαλοῦσιν, ὡς τοῦ Θεοῦ Λόγου σάρκα γεγενημένην, τὸ δὲ εἰς θεότητος αὐτὴν μεταβεβλῆσθαι φύσιν ὡς ἀσεβὲς ἀποκηρύττουσιν.

|Σ |Ὅτι δὲ καὶ ὁ τῆς μακαρίας μνήμης Κύριλλος πολλάκις ἡμῖν ἐπέστειλεν, οἶμαι καὶ Τὴν Σὴν εἰδέναι σαφῶς Ἁγιότητα. καὶ ἡνίκα δὲ τὰ κατὰ Ἰουλιανοῦ συγγράμματα εἰς τὴν Ἀντιόχειαν πέπομφεν, ὡσαύτως δὲ καὶ τὰ εἰς τὸν ἀποπομπαῖον γραφέντα, τὸν μακάριον ᾔτησεν Ἰωάννην, τὸν τῆς ἀντιοχέων ἐπίσκοπον, ἐπιδεῖξαι αὖτα τοῖς κατὰ τὴν ἑῴαν διαπρέπουσι διδασκάλοις. καὶ δή, τοῖς γράμμασιν εἴξας, ὁ μακάριος Ἰωάννης πέπομφεν ἡμῖν τὰς βίβλους, καὶ ἀναγνόντες ἐθαυμάσαμεν καὶ ἐπεστείλαμεν τῷ ||Σ τῆς μακαρίας μνήμης Κυρίλλῳ,|| καὶ ἀντέγραψεν πάλιν ἡμῖν,

l. 125 ἀποκηρύττουσιν *BVΛ* (abdicant), *Az.* : ἀπεκήρυξαν *N* = *"they rejected as contrary to right religion." The reading of BVΛ is consonant with the use of the pres. impf. throughout this passage and preserves the homoeoteleuton emphasizing the antithesis between* ἀποκηρύττουσιν *at the end of the period and* κηρύττουσι *in the second finite clause.* **l. 126** ὁ τῆς μακαρίας μνήμης *N, Sir. Nös.* : ὁ τ. μα. καὶ ὁσίας μν. *BVΛ* (beatae sanctaeque memoriae) *Σ, Gar. Sch. Az. = "Cyril of blessed and holy memory." While the shorter formula is quite frequent in the works of Thdt.* (*nine other exx.*)*, the longer occurs only twice elsewhere. V. sec. 2 of this letter* (*τοῦ τῆς μακαρίας καὶ ὁσίας μνήμης Θεοδότου*) *and the reference to Alexander of Antioch in ep. 110.2. The shorter is twice applied to Cyril, both later in this letter and in letter 86. While the longer formula might seem the lect. diff., it might better be regarded as an editorial change, meant to emphasize Thdt.'s respect for the Alexandrians; cf. the c. n. on l. 114* (μακαρίων). **l. 130** ἀντιοχέων *BVΛ, Gar. Nös. Sch.* : Ἀντιοχείας *N, Sir. Az. The masc. gen. pl. is both the lect. diff. and better attested in the works of Thdt. This combination in which a masc. art. precedes, and a form of the noun ἐπίσκοπος follows,* τῆς ἀντιοχέων *appears in five other passages* (*H. e. 1.7.18, p. 33, l. 17; Haer. com. 1.19, 25; 2.8; and sec. 1 of this letter*)*: Θεοδότου τοῦ τῆς ἀντιοχέων ἐπισκόπου. Cf. H. e. 4.11.5, p. 230, ll. 10f. and the analogous usage with Ἀλεξανδρέων in ep. 113.3. In contrast, there are only two cases in which a masc. art. precedes, and a form of the noun ἐπίσκοπος follows, τῆς Ἀντιοχείας, and both appear in the chapter summaries of H. e.* (*keph. 1.21 and 5.24*) *that cannot be securely attributed to Thdt.; v. Martin's remarks in Théodoret de Cyr, Histoire ecclésiastique, vol. 1, pp. 102–05.*

difference between the two natures is entirely explicit, for they declare the immutability of the divine nature and apply the term "divine" to the Master's flesh in so far as the flesh has become that of God the Word, but they reject as contrary to right religion the proposition that the flesh has been transformed into the nature of the godhead.

I take it that Your Holiness is well aware that Cyril of blessed memory wrote many letters to us. And when he sent to Antioch his treatise against Julian and his work on the scapegoat, he asked John of blessed memory, the bishop of Antioch, to show them to the preëminent teachers of the East.[5] Bowing to this request, John of blessed memory sent these books to us. We read them with admiration and wrote to Cyril of blessed memory, and, in his reply, he attested to our perspicuity and kindliness, and this letter remains in our possession.

5. Theodoret is referring to *Against Julian*, dedicated to the emperor, Theodosius, and intended to refute Julian's *Gal. On the Scapegoat*, (Περὶ τοῦ ἀποπομπαίου) = Cyr, *ep.* 41, to Acacius (*FOTC*, vol. 76, pp. 168–82).

καὶ ἀκρίβειαν ἡμῖν καὶ διάθεσιν μαρτυρῶν, καὶ σῴζεται παρ᾽ ἡμῖν ταῦτα τὰ γράμματα.

|Ὅτι δὲ καὶ τοῖς περὶ Νεστορίου ὑπαγορευθεῖσι τόμοις ὑπὸ τοῦ τῆς μακαρίας μνήμης Ἰωάννου δὶς ὑπεγράψαμεν, μαρτυροῦσιν ἡμῶν αἱ χεῖρες,|| ἀλλ᾽ οὗτοι ταῦτα περὶ ἡμῶν θρυλοῦσι, τὴν οἰκείαν νόσον τῇ καθ᾽ ἡμῶν συκοφαντίᾳ συσκιάζειν πειρώμενοι. ἀποστραφήτω τοίνυν Ἡ Ὁσιότης Σου *τοὺς λαλοῦντας τὸ ψεῦδος*,[bc] καὶ τῆς ἐκκλησιαστικῆς φροντισάτω γαλήνης, καὶ τοὺς διαφθείρειν τολμῶντας τῆς ἀληθείας τὰ δόγματα ἢ τοῖς ἀλεξικάκοις θεραπευέτω φαρμάκοις ἢ τὴν θεραπείαν μὴ δεχομένους, ὡς ἀνηκέστως διακειμένους, τῶν ποιμνίων ἐξελασάτω ἵνα μὴ τῆς ἐκείνων λώβης μεταλάχῃ τὰ πρόβατα, ἡμᾶς δὲ τῆς συνήθους ἀξιούτω προσρήσεως.

(5) |Ὅτι γὰρ ἃ φρονοῦμεν γεγράφαμεν, μαρτυρεῖ καὶ τὰ παρ᾽ ἡμῶν συγγραφέντα εἴς τε τὰς θείας Γραφὰς καὶ κατὰ τῶν τὰ Ἀρείου καὶ Εὐνομίου φρονούντων. πρὸς δὲ τούτοις καὶ σύντομον ἀκροτελεύτιον τίθημι· εἴ τις οὐ λέγει τὴν ἁγίαν Παρθένον *Θεοτόκον*, ἢ *ψιλὸν ἄνθρωπον* καλεῖ τὸν Κύριον ἡμῶν Ἰησοῦν Χριστόν, ἢ εἰς δύο υἱοὺς μερίζει τὸν ἕνα Μονογενῆ καὶ Πρωτότοκον *πάσης κτίσεως*,[bd] ἐκπέσοι τῆς εἰς Χριστὸν ἐλπίδος, *καὶ ἐρεῖ πᾶς ὁ λαός, Γένοιτο, γένοιτο.*[be]||

ll. 135f. παρ᾽ ἡμῖν ταῦτα τὰ γράμματα *N, Az.* : ταῦτα τὰ γ. παρ᾽ ἡ. *BVΛ* (et seruantur haec litterae apud nos) **ll. 137–41** Ὅτι δὲ … πειρώμενοι *BVΛ* (*om.* δὶς) *Σ* (*om.* Ἰωάννου), *Az.* : *om. N* **l. 152** καλεῖ *N, Λ?* (uocat), *Sir.* : ἀποκ- *BV, Gar. Nös. Sch. Az. Perhaps Λ supports the simplex of N, since the compound might have been rendered by appellat. Thdt. elsewhere uses both the simplex and the compound in this factitive and theological sense. For a close parallel, v. Eran. dial. 2 (p. 113, l. 34): Ἰησοῦν τὸν Χριστὸν τί χρὴ καλεῖν; ἄνθρωπον ἢ θεόν; For the compound, v. sec. 3 of this letter: διὰ γάρ τοι τοῦτο καὶ Θεοτόκον ἀποκαλοῦμεν τὴν ἁγίαν Παρθένον.*

bc. Ps 5.6 bd. Col 1.15 (NT var.) be. Ps 106.48

That we have twice subscribed to the decrees regarding Nestorius issued by John of blessed memory, our own hands are witness.[6] But these men are spreading such reports about us in an attempt to cover up their own unsoundness by bringing false accusation against us. Therefore, I ask Your Holiness to turn your back on "the speakers of falsehood,"[bc] take thought for the tranquility of the Church, and, as for those who dare to corrupt true doctrine, either treat them with healing medicines or, should they refuse treatment, drive them, as beyond cure, from their flocks to protect the sheep from contagion, but regard us as worthy of the customary salutation.

(5) For proof that this letter conveys our true sentiments, we refer to the witness of our commentaries on sacred Scripture and our works against the Arians and Eunomians. In addition to these, I append a succinct final word: If anyone refuses to call the holy Virgin "Mother of God" or terms our Lord Jesus Christ "mere man," or divides the one Only-begotten and "Firstborn of all creation"[bd] into two sons, let him be excluded from hope in Christ, and "all the people will say, 'So be it, so be it.'"[be]

6. On John's two writings *v.* Richard, "Théodoret, Jean d'Antioch."

Τούτων δὲ παρ᾽ ἡμῶν οὕτως εἰρημένων, τὰς ἱεράς σου εὐχὰς παρασχεῖν μοι, Δέσποτα, καταξίωσον καὶ ἀντιγράφοις εὐφρᾶναι δηλοῦσιν ὡς ἀπεστράφη Σοῦ Ἡ Ἁγιωσύνη τοὺς συκοφάντας.
|Σ |πᾶσαν τὴν σὺν Τῇ Σῇ Θεοσεβείᾳ ἐν Χριστῷ ἀδελφότητα ἐγώ
||Σ τε καὶ οἱ σὺν ἐμοὶ προσαγορεύομεν.||

ll. 156–60 Τούτων δὲ … προσαγορεύομεν *BV* (πᾶσαν τὴν σῇ) *Λ*, *Az.* : *om.* *N*

Now that I have made this declaration, be so kind, my Lord, as to offer your holy prayers on my behalf and to gladden me with a response indicating that Your Sanctity has turned away my malicious accusers. I send greetings, as do those with me, to all the brethren joined to your Reverence in Christ.

84. ΤΟΙΣ ΕΝ ΚΙΛΙΚΙΑΙ ΕΠΙΣΚΟΠΟΙΣ

Τὰς καθ᾽ ἡμῶν γεγενημένας συκοφαντίας μεμάθηκεν πάντως Ἡ Ὑμετέρα Φιλοθεΐα· οἱ γὰρ τἀναντία τῇ ἀληθείᾳ φρονοῦντες εἰς δύο μερίζειν ἡμᾶς υἱούς φασι τὸν ἕνα Κύριον ἡμῶν, Ἰησοῦν Χριστόν, τὸν μονογενῆ τοῦ Θεοῦ Υἱόν. λέγουσι δέ τινες τῆς συκοφαντίας αὐτοὺς λαμβάνειν τὰς ἀφορμὰς ἔκ τινων εὐαριθμήτων παρ᾽ ὑμῖν ταῦτα φρονούντων καὶ εἰς δύο πρόσωπα διαιρούντων τὸν ἐνανθρωπήσαντα Θεὸν Λόγον, οὓς δεῖ τῆς ἀποστολικῆς ἐπακοῦσαι φωνῆς διαρρήδην βοώσης, *Εἷς Κύριος Ἰησοῦς Χριστός, δι᾽ οὗ τὰ πάντα·*[a] καὶ πάλιν, *Εἷς Κύριος, μία πίστις, ἓν βάπτισμα.*[b] ἔδει δὲ αὐτοὺς καὶ ταῖς δεσποτικαῖς ἀκολουθῆσαι διδασκαλίαις· καὶ γὰρ αὐτὸς ὁ Κύριος οὕτω φησίν· *Οὐδεὶς ἀναβέβηκεν εἰς τὸν οὐρανὸν εἰ μὴ ὁ ἐκ τοῦ οὐρανοῦ καταβάς, ὁ Υἱὸς τοῦ ἀνθρώπου,* ὁ ὢν ἐν τῷ οὐρανῷ·[c] καὶ πάλιν, *Ἐὰν οὖν* ἴδητε *τὸν Υἱὸν τοῦ ἀνθρώπου ἀναβαίνοντα ὅπου ἦν τὸ πρότερον.*[d] καὶ ἡ παράδοσις δὲ τοῦ ἁγίου βαπτίσματος ἕνα Υἱὸν ἡμᾶς εἶναι διδάσκει, ὡς ἕνα Πατέρα, καὶ ἓν Ἅγιον Πνεῦμα.[e]

Καταξιωσάτω τοίνυν Ἡ Ὑμετέρα Φιλοθεΐα, εἴπερ ἄρα τινὲς ὅλως εἰσὶν· ἐγὼ γὰρ οὐ πείθομαι· τοῖς ἀποστολικοῖς δόγμασιν ἀπειθοῦντες, καὶ ἐπιστομίσαι αὐτούς, καὶ ἐκκλησιαστικῶς σωφρονίσαι, καὶ διδάξαι τοῖς τῶν ἁγίων πατέρων ἀκολουθεῖν ἴχνεσιν καὶ τὴν ἐν Νικαίᾳ τῆς Βιθυνίας ἐκτεθεῖσαν πίστιν ὑπὸ τῶν ἁγίων καὶ μακαρίων πατέρων ἀκήρατον φυλάττειν, ἅτε δὴ τὴν εὐαγγελικὴν καὶ ἀποστολικὴν διδασκαλίαν ἐν κεφαλαίῳ διδάσκουσαν. πρέπει γὰρ ὑμῖν, θεοφιλέστατοι, καὶ τῆς τοῦ Θεοῦ δόξης καὶ τῆς κοινῆς εὐκλείας φροντίσαι καὶ μὴ περιιδεῖν

a. 1Cor 8.6 b. Eph 4.5 c. Jn 3.13 (NT var.)
d. Jn 6.62 (NT var.) e. Mt 28.19

84. To the Bishops of Cilicia[1]

Reverend Fathers, Your Piety is well informed regarding the false accusations that have been brought against us, that people who think the very opposite of the truth are claiming that we divide into two our one Lord Jesus Christ, the only-begotten Son of God. Some say they find grounds for their false accusation among a very few of you who hold that position and separate into two persons God the Word who became man. Such men should pay attention to the voice of the Apostle who cries out in no uncertain terms, "One Lord, Jesus Christ, through whom are all things";[a] and again, "One Lord, one faith, one baptism."[b] And they ought to have followed the Master's own teachings, for it is the Lord himself who says, "No one has gone up to heaven except for him who has come down from heaven, the Son of Man, who is in heaven";[c] and again, "What if you were to see the Son of Man going back up to where he was before?"[d] The traditional rite of holy baptism also teaches us that there is one Son just as there is one Father and one Holy Spirit.[e]

And so, I urge you, if there are any at all—though I find it hard to believe that there are—who reject the tenets of the apostles, to stop up their mouths, discipline them according to church usage, and teach them to follow in the footsteps of the holy fathers and to defend from blemish the creedal statement set out in Nicaea of Bithynia by our holy fathers of blessed memory, as this constitutes a summary of the evangelical and apostolic doctrine. It is for you, beloved of God, to take thought for the glory of God and the good reputa-

1. This letter is evidently an encyclical meant for all the bishops of the two provinces of Cilicia (I–II). These administrative units were created under Diocletian. The metropolis of Cilicia I was Tarsus, that of Cilicia II Anazarbus; in civil administration, both formed part of the Diocese of Oriens (*v. ep.* 42 n. 1 and *ep.* 76 n. 1), and, in ecclesiastical administration, both sees were subject to the Patriarch of Antioch (*v.* Foss, "Cilicia"). Of the bishops of Cilicia, Eustathius of Aegae is the only one named in Theodoret's correspondence (*ep.* 70). Azéma (vol. 2, p. 220, n. 1) places this letter in the spring of 448.

τὴν κατὰ τοῦ κοινοῦ χωροῦσαν λοιδορίαν διὰ τὴν τῶν ὀλίγων τούτων ἀνθρώπων ἀμαθίαν ἢ φιλονεικίαν, εἴπερ τινὲς ὅλως εἰσίν, εἰ καὶ μὴ κατὰ τούτων, ὥσπεροῦν καὶ καθ' ἡμῶν, παρέθηξαν *τὰς γλώσσας*[f] οἱ συκοφάνται. καταξιοῦτε δὲ μνημονεύειν ἡμῶν ἐν ταῖς πρὸς τὸν Κύριον προσευχαῖς· τοῦτο γὰρ ὁ τῆς ἀγάπης παρακελεύεται νόμος.[g]

f. Ps 64.3 g. *Cf.* Gal. 6.2; Eph 6.18; Jas 5.16.

tion of us all; do not overlook the defamatory report that is spreading against all of us because of the ignorance or contentiousness of just a few—if there really are any—unless our false accusers have sharpened "their tongues"[f] against them as they have against us. Please remember us in your prayers to the Lord; that is what the law of love enjoins.[g]

85. ΒΑΣΙΛΕΙΩΙ ΕΠΙΣΚΟΠΩΙ

Κεφάλαιον τῶν ἀγαθῶν τὴν ἀγάπην ὁ θεσπέσιος προσηγόρευσε Παῦλος[a] καὶ ταύτῃ τρέφεσθαι τῆς πίστεως τοὺς τροφίμους παρεκελεύσατο.[b] ταύτης ἔχουσα τὸν πλοῦτον, Ἡ Σὴ Θεοσέβεια καὶ ἅπερ ἐχρῆν εἰσηγήσατο καὶ τὰ θυμήρη μεμήνυκεν· τί γὰρ θυμηρέστερον τοῖς φοβουμένοις τὸν Κύριον τῆς τῶν ὀρθῶν δογμάτων ὑγιείας τε καὶ συμφωνίας; εὖ ἴσθι τοίνυν, θεοφιλέστατε, ὡς ἄγαν ἥσθημεν τὰ περὶ τοῦ κοινοῦ φίλου μεμαθηκότες, καί, ὅσον πρώην ἠλγήσαμεν ἀκούσαντες ὡς μίαν εἶναι φύσιν σαρκὸς καὶ θεότητος λέγει καὶ ὡς ἄντικρυς τῇ ἀπαθεῖ θεότητι τὸ σωτήριον πάθος προσάπτει, οὕτως ηὐφράνθημεν τοῖς Τῆς Σῆς Ὁσιότητος γράμμασιν ἐντυχόντες καὶ μεμαθηκότες ὡς ἀκεραίους φυλάττει τὰς τῶν φύσεων ἰδιότητας,

a. 1Cor 13.13 b. *Cf.* 1Cor 16.14; Gal 5.13; Eph 4.1f.; 1Tm 4.12.

85. To Bishop Basil[1]

The divinely inspired Paul named love as the most important of all goods[a] and enjoined that the nurslings of the faith should be fed on love.[b] Your Reverence richly provided as you are with love, has given the necessary instruction and reported joyful news. What, indeed, could be a greater source of joy to those who fear the Lord than to learn that orthodoxy has been maintained in its integrity and endorsed in concord? You may be well-assured, beloved of God, that we were delighted to receive the news regarding our common friend, and, just as we were earlier pained to hear he was saying that there was one nature of the flesh and the godhead and was explicitly assigning the saving passion to the impassible divinity, so we were glad to receive Your Holiness' letter and to learn that he keeps intact the

1. Basil, bishop of Seleucia (modern Silifke in south-central Turkey close to the Mediterranean coast; *v.* Foss, "Seleukeia"), was the metropolitan of the province of Isauria. His see was renowned as the guardian of the tomb of St. Thecla. For a brief description of Basil's christology and his ecclesiastical career and a full accounting of works attributed to him and the editions available for each, *v.* Miola. He first enters the historical record in November 448, when he attended the council convened by Flavian in Constantinople at which he voted for the deposition of the archimandrite Eutyches (*v.* Intro., sec. 4.2); indeed, Basil's christology was of a decidedly Antiochene type. Yet, like Eusebius of Ancyra (*v. ep.* 82 n. 1), he was wary of controversy. Not even a year later, he joined the majority in subscribing to the rehabilitation of Eutyches and the deposition of Theodoret at the Robber Council of Ephesus in 449 (*v.* Intro. sec. 4.7). At the end of the first session the Council of Chalcedon, Basil and others who had been supporters of Dioscorus at Ephesus II were excluded from the proceedings, though they were re-admitted in the fourth session (*v.* Intro. sec. 5.5). Disassociating himself from Dioscorus, he endorsed the council's christological definition, of which he remained a strong defender to the end of his career. Basil was a scriptural scholar, and a considerable body of his sermons on both the Old and the New Testaments is extant (*v.* PG, vol. 85), though some of those ascribed to him in the medieval tradition belong to Athanasius. He is also identified as the author of a prose work on the life and miracles of St. Thecla in the headings of most of the manuscripts (*CPG* #6675), but Dagron (pp. 12–16), the editor of that work, shows the impossibility of this attribution. Honigmann (pp. 181–83) argues that Basil, whose death has frequently been placed in 458, must have lived at least until late in 468. As the reference toward the end of this letter to a letter sent to Dioscorus of Alexandria indicates, *ep.* 85 is subsequent to 83; Azéma (vol. 2, p. 222, n. 1) suggests that it was written sometime in September 448.

καὶ οὔτε τὸν Θεὸν Λόγον εἰς σάρκα τετράφθαι φησὶν οὔτε τὴν σάρκα εἰς θεότητος μεταβεβλῆσθαι φύσιν, ἀλλ᾽ ἐν τῷ ἑνὶ Υἱῷ, τῷ Κυρίῳ ἡμῶν, Ἰησοῦ Χριστῷ, τῷ ἐνανθρωπήσαντι Θεῷ Λόγῳ, ἀσυγχύτους μεμενηκέναι φησὶν τὰς ἑκατέρας φύσεως ἰδιότητας, καὶ τὸν τῶν ὅλων Θεὸν ἀνυμνήσαμεν ἐπὶ τῇ τῆς θείας πίστεως συμφωνίᾳ.[c]

Εἰς μέντοι Κιλικίαν ἑκατέραν γεγράφαμεν, καίτοι σαφῶς οὐκ εἰδότες εἴπερ τινές εἰσιν ἐναντία τῇ ἀληθείᾳ φρονοῦντες, καὶ παρηγγυήσαμεν τοῖς θεοφιλεστάτοις ἐπισκόποις ἰχνεῦσαι καὶ ζητῆσαι εἴπερ ἄρα τινές εἰσιν εἰς δύο υἱοὺς διαιροῦντες τὸν ἕνα Κύριον, Ἰησοῦν Χριστόν, καὶ ἢ παραινετικῶς σωφρονίσαι ἢ τοῦ καταλόγου χωρίσαι τῶν ἀδελφῶν· τῷ ὄντι γὰρ ὁμοίως ἀποστρεφόμεθα καὶ τοὺς μίαν φύσιν σαρκὸς καὶ θεότητος εἶναι λέγειν τολμῶντας καὶ τοὺς εἰς δύο υἱοὺς μερίζοντας τὸν ἕνα Κύριον ἡμῶν, Ἰησοῦν Χριστόν, καὶ τῶν ἀποστολικῶν ὅρων ἔξω βαίνειν ἐπιχειροῦντας.

Ὅτι δὲ καὶ πρὸς εἰρήνην ἐσμὲν εὐτρεπεῖς, θαρρείτω Σοῦ Ἡ Ὁσιότης· εἰ γὰρ ὁ προφήτης φησίν, *Μετὰ τῶν μισούντων τὴν εἰρήνην ἤμην εἰρηνικός,*[d] πολλῷ μᾶλλον ἡμεῖς τὴν κατὰ Θεὸν εἰρήνην ἀσπαστῶς προσδεχόμεθα. ἐπειδὴ δὲ καὶ εἰς τὴν Ἀλεξάνδρειάν τινες ἔδραμον τῶν τῷ ψεύδει συντεθραμμένων[e] καὶ συκοφαντίας ἔρραψαν καθ᾽ ἡμῶν, καί, τοῖς τοιούτοις λόγοις ὑπαχθείς, ὁ θεοφιλέστατος τῆς πόλεως ἐκείνης ἐπίσκοπος, καίτοι πληροφορηθεὶς δι᾽ ἡμετέρων γραμμάτων, τινὰ τῶν θεοσεβεστάτων ἐπισκόπων εἰς τὴν βασιλεύουσαν ἀπέστειλε πόλιν, καταξιωσάτω Σοῦ Ἡ Θεοσέβεια τὴν οἰκείαν εὔνοιαν δεῖξαι συνήθως καὶ ἀντιτάξαι τῷ ψεύδει τὴν ἀλήθειαν.

c. 1Cor 12.24–26 d. Ps 120.6f. e. *Cf.* Jn. 8.44.

distinctive attributes of the natures and denies both the change of God the Word into flesh and the transformation of the flesh into the nature of the godhead while affirming that, in the one Son our Lord Jesus Christ, God the Word, who became man, the special attributes of each nature remained unconfused. And so, we sang praise to the God of the universe for concord in our God-given faith.[c]

We have sent letters to both provinces of Cilicia,[2] although uncertain whether there are any who hold positions contrary to the truth, and urged the bishops beloved of God to conduct a thorough search to determine if there really are any who separate the one Lord Jesus Christ into two sons and either set them right with counsel or strike them from the roll of the brethren. Indeed, we oppose with equal firmness those who recklessly declare that there is just one nature of the flesh and the godhead and those who attempt to divide into two sons our one Lord Jesus Christ and thus step outside the bounds laid down by the apostles.

Your Holiness can be quite assured of our preference for peace; after all, if the prophet says, "I was peaceable with those who hate peace,"[d] we are all-the-more inclined to welcome a godly peace. Now, as some people, children of falsehood,[e] have run off to Alexandria and stitched together false accusations against us, and the bishop of that city, beloved of God, has been misled by this talk, and, though previously informed by our letter, has sent one of his right reverend bishops to the capital city, I beg Your Reverence to give proof of the kindliness that is yours and set truth against falsehood.[3]

2. On the two Cilicias, *cf. ep.* 84 n. 1.

3. The first section of this letter, dealing with Theodoret's fears regarding the possible heterodoxy of an unnamed ecclesiastic, is completed by the last in which Theodoret reveals that he is now under suspicion of heresy. While the unnamed mutual friend was suspected of monophysitic positions (confounding the two natures of Christ into one), Theodoret is suspected of dividing the one Son into two. As Basil had set out the truth regarding his cleric and, in consequence, was able to allay Theodoret's fears of disunity in the faith, so, as Theodoret hopes, Basil will set out the truth regarding Theodoret and set to rest any concerns regarding his orthodoxy. In both cases Basil is imagined to act from love; to ἀγάπην in the first sentence, corresponds εὔνοιαν in the last.

86. ΦΛΑΒΙΑΝΩΙ ΕΠΙΣΚΟΠΩΙ ΚΩΝΣΤΑΝΤΙΝΟΥΠΟΛΕΩΣ

(1) Πολλὰς μὲν ἐν τῷ παρόντι καιρῷ, τὰ πάντα θεοφιλέστατε, τρικυμιῶν ἐδεξάμεθα προσβολὰς καί, τὸν τοῦ παντὸς ἐπικαλεσάμενοι Κυβερνήτην, ἀντισχεῖν ἠδυνήθημεν πρὸς τὸν κλύδωνα, τὰ δὲ νῦν καθ᾽ ἡμῶν ἐπιχειρηθέντα πᾶσαν τραγικὴν ὑπερβαίνει διήγησιν. νομίσαντες γὰρ σύμμαχον σχήσειν καὶ συνεργὸν εἰς τὰ κατὰ τῆς ἀποστολικῆς πίστεως τυρευόμενα τὸν θεοφιλέστατον τῆς Ἀλεξανδρείας ἐπίσκοπον, τὸν Κύριον Διόσκορον, ἀπεστείλαμεν ἕνα τῶν παρ᾽ ἡμῖν εὐλαβεστάτων πρεσβυτέρων συνέσει κοσμούμενον μετὰ συνοδικῶν γραμμάτων, διδάξαντες Αὐτοῦ Τὴν Θεοσέβειαν ὡς ταῖς γεγενημέναις ἐπὶ τοῦ τῆς μακαρίας μνήμης Κυρίλλου συνθήκαις ἐμμένομεν· καὶ τήν τε παρ᾽ αὐτοῦ γραφεῖσαν στέργομεν ἐπιστολήν, τήν τε τοῦ μακαριωτάτου καὶ ἐν ἁγίοις Ἀθανασίου ἣν πρὸς τὸν μακάριον Ἐπίκτητον ἔγραψεν ἀσπασίως δεχόμεθα καί, πρό γε τούτων, τὴν ἐν Νικαίᾳ τῆς Βιθυνίας ἐκτεθεῖσαν πίστιν ὑπὸ τῶν ἁγίων καὶ

Title ΦΛΑΒΙΑΝΩΙ ΕΠΙΣΚΟΠΩΙ ΚΩΝΣΤΑΝΤΙΝΟΥΠΟΛΕΩΣ = *"To Flavian, Bishop of Constantinople"* : ܠܡܪܝ ܩܕܝܫܐ ܘܪܚܡ ܐܠܗܐ: ܐܚܘܢ ܘܒܪ ܫܘܬܦܘܬܢ ܦܠܒܝܢܐ: ܕܘܡܢܘܣ ܒܡܪܢ ܫܠܡ = *"To the holy lord Flavian, our brother and colleague, beloved of God, from Domnus, greetings in our Lord"* **ll. 2f.** τὸν τοῦ παντὸς … Κυβερνήτην = *"the Helmsman of the universe"* : ܠܡܕܒܪܢܘܬܐ ܕܟܘܠܐ = *"the Helmsman of the ark"* **l. 8** ἀπεστείλαμεν = *"we dispatched"* : ܫܕܪܢ ܐܦ ܚܢܢ ܐܠܝܨܝ ܐܝܬ = *"we had no choice but to dispatch"* **l. 11** ἐμμένομεν = *"we stand by"* : ܐܦ ܚܢܢ ܠܗ ܕܠܐ ܟܡܠܝܘܬܐ ܫܠܡܝܢ ܚܢܢ = *"we regard it as appropriate to accept"* **l. 12** τήν … ἐπιστολήν = *"the letter he wrote"* : ܐܓܪܬܐ ܕܠܐ ܟܝ ܡܢܐ ܟܬܝܒ ܡܢ ܟܠܗܝܢ ܐܫܠܡ ܕܫܠܡ ܠܡܠܦܢܘܬܐ ܕܥܕܬܐ = *"letter, which is entirely in agreement with the teachings of the Church"*

86. To Flavian, Bishop of Constantinople[1]

(1) On many an occasion during the present crisis, most beloved of God, we have been tossed about by the turbulent sea, but, calling upon the aid of the Helmsman of the universe,[2] we have managed to defy the rough water. Yet the attacks now mounted against us go beyond anything you might find in the plot of a tragedy. You see, imagining that we could recruit Lord Dioscorus, bishop beloved of God of the city of Alexandria,[3] as an ally to help us against intrigues that have been stirred up against the faith of the apostles, we dispatched one of our right reverend priests, a man of understanding, with a synodical letter, in which we informed His Reverence that we stand by the terms of the agreement made during the time of Cyril of blessed memory—that we accept the letter he wrote[4] and gladly approve that written by the right blessed and sainted Athanasius to Epictetus of blessed memory[5] and prior to these, the creed set out by the holy fathers of blessed memory in Nicaea of Bithynia—and

1. On Flavian *v. ep.* 11 n. 1. This letter is preserved not only in Greek but also in a Syriac translation embedded in the acts of the *Latrocinium* of 449, where the author is identified as Domnus of Antioch (on Domnus, *v. ep.* 31 n. 1). Most likely, Theodoret wrote a draft for his metropolitan that Domnus then revised. The original Greek of that revised and final form is no longer extant, but the Syriac may be a witness to it. In the critical notes, we provide those passages of the Syriac that differ in sense from, or make additions to, the Greek. As Azéma (vol. 2, p. 226, n. 1) indicates, this letter was probably sent by Domnus in September 448, a date suggested by the last section of the Syriac, in which Domnus apprises Flavian of the consecration of Photius of Tyre on the previous September ninth. Perhaps Theodoret wrote the original form of *ep.* 86 in late August or early September.

2. The Syriac version reads "Helmsman of the ark." This locution has a long lineage in Syriac literature (*v., e.g.*, Ephraem, *CNis.* 1.3, albeit with a different word for "Helmsman," *mallāḥā*); thus, this usage of the Syriac may not reflect the Greek of Domnus' revision.

3. On Dioscorus, *v. ep.* 60 n. 1.

4. On the letter of Cyril to Acacius (*Coll. athen.* 107), *v.* Intro., sec. 3.10; that letter bears the number 33 in McEnerney's translations of the letters of Cyril.

5. On Athanasius, *ep. Epict.* (*CPG* #2095), *v.* Quasten, vol. 3, pp. 59f.; *cf. epp.* 144 n. 3 and 145 n. 3.

μακαρίων πατέρων· καὶ παρεκαλέσαμεν τοὺς τούτοις ἐμμένειν οὐ βουλομένους ἐμμεῖναι παρασκευάσαι, ἀλλά τις ἐντεῦθεν δραμὼν τῶν τἀναντία φρονούντων καὶ τοὺς θορύβους τούτους ἐργαζομένων, ἐξαπατήσας τῶν αὐτόθι τινάς, καὶ μυρίας καθ' ἡμῶν συκοφαντίας ὑφήνας, παρεσκεύασεν ἀθέσμους καθ' ἡμῶν ἐκβοήσεις γενέσθαι.

Ὁ δὲ θεοφιλέστατος ἐπίσκοπος Διόσκορος γέγραφεν ἡμῖν ἐπιστολὴν ἣν οὐκ ἔδει γράψαι τὸν παρὰ τοῦ τῶν ὅλων Θεοῦ μεμαθηκότα *ἀκοὴν ματαίαν* οὐ παραδέχεσθαι·[a] πιστεύσας γὰρ τοῖς καθ' ἡμῶν εἰρημένοις ὡς ἀκριβῶς τούτων ἕκαστον ἐξετάσας καὶ ἐκ τῆς βασάνου μεμαθηκὼς τἀληθές, οὕτως ἡμῶν κατεψηφίσατο. ἀλλ' ἡμεῖς γενναίως τὴν συκοφαντίαν ἠνέγκαμεν καὶ χρηστοῖς γράμμασιν ἠμειψάμεθα· καὶ πεπείκαμεν Αὐτοῦ Τὴν Θεοσέβειαν ὡς πάντα ταῦτα ψευδῆ, καὶ ὡς οὐδεὶς τῶν τῆς Ἀνατολῆς θεοφιλεστάτων ἐπισκόπων ἐναντία τοῖς ἀποστολικοῖς φρονεῖ δόγμασιν. ἐπείσθησαν δὲ καὶ δι' αὐτῆς τῶν πραγμάτων τῆς πείρας καὶ οἱ ἀποσταλέντες παρ' αὐτοῦ εὐλαβέστατοι κληρικοί, ὁ δέ, πᾶσιν ἐρρῶσθαι φράσας καὶ τοῖς συκοφαντοῦσιν τὰς ἀκοὰς ἐκδούς, πρᾶγμα πεποίηκεν οὐδαμῶς πιστευθῆναι δυνάμενον εἰ μὴ πᾶσαν εἶχεν μαρτυροῦσαν τὴν ἐκκλησίαν· ἠνέσχετο μὲν γὰρ τῶν ἀναθεματιζόντων ἡμᾶς, ἀναστὰς δὲ καὶ προσφωνήσας, τὰς ἐκείνων φωνὰς ἐπεβεβαίωσεν. πρὸς δὲ τούτοις, καί τινας τῶν θεοφιλεστάτων ἐπισκόπων εἰς τὴν βασιλεύουσαν ἀπέστειλεν, ὡς ἔγνωμεν, πόλιν, αὐξῆσαι τοὺς καθ' ἡμῶν θορύβους ἐλπίζων.

l. 20 καθ' ἡμῶν = "*against us*" : ܥܠ ܪ̈ܚܡܝ ܐܠܗܐ ܐܦܝܣ̈ܩܘܦܐ ܕܡܕܢܚܐ = "*against the bishops of the east, beloved of God*" **ll. 22f.** Ὁ δὲ θεοφιλέστατος ἐπίσκοπος Διόσκορος γέγραφεν ἡμῖν ἐπιστολὴν = "*Then, Dioscorus, bishop beloved of God, wrote us a letter*" : ܠܗܠܝܢ ܕܝܢ ܟܕ ܫܦܝܪܐܝܬ ܨܒܐ ܗܘܐ ܡܪܝ ܕܝܘܣܩܘܪܘܣ ܐܦܝܣܩܘܦܐ ܕܢܫܠܐ ܝܓܒ ܟܕ ܐܫܬܘܕܝ ܕܢܟܬܘܒ ܠܢ. ܘܢܫܕܪ ܢܟܦ̈ܐ ܡܝܩܪ̈ܐ ܠܘܬܢ. ܘܗܠܝܢ ܕܥܠܝܢ ܡܬܐܡܪ̈ܢ ܢܘܕܥ ܠܢ. ܐܝܟ ܕܐܦ ܥܒܕ. ܐܠܐ ܟܬܒ ܐܓܪܬܐ = "*As Dioscorus, bishop beloved of God, expressed a commendable wish to lay these issues to rest, he promised to write us, to send us venerable priests, and to inform us about the rumors concerning us—all this he did—but he wrote a letter*" **l. 26** τ'ἀληθὲς *scr. Nös. Az.* : ἀ- *codd., Sir.*

a. Ex 23.1

we urged him to compel those who do not wish to abide by these to abide by them. Nonetheless, one of those who are opposed to us in doctrine, one of the authors of this uproar, ran off from here, misled some people over there, and, weaving together myriad false accusations, has raised this shameful outcry against us.

Then, Dioscorus, bishop beloved of God, wrote us a letter that should not have been written by a man who has learned from the God of the universe not to give heed to "false rumor."[a] Putting full faith in the reports attacking us, as though he had carefully examined each heading and determined the truth by careful analysis, he has passed sentence of condemnation against us. We, on our side, bore this false accusation with fortitude and wrote a gentle response to persuade His Reverence that all these reports are false and that not a single one of the eastern bishops beloved of God holds positions contrary to the apostolic doctrine. An acquaintance with the actual situation was all that was needed to convince even those right reverend clerics who had been sent by him, but he, paying no attention, gave full credence to our accusers, and proceeded to do something that would be impossible to believe except for the fact that he had the entire Church as his witness: he joined sides with those who were pronouncing anathemas against us, and, rising up from his seat and adding his voice to theirs, seconded their outcry! What is more, as we have learned, he has also sent several of his bishops beloved of God to the capital city in the hope of intensifying the turbulence against us.

(2) Ἡμεῖς δὲ πρῶτον μὲν *τὸν* τῶν ὅλων *Ἐπόπτην*[b] πρόμαχον ἔχομεν· ὑπὲρ γὰρ τῶν θείων αὐτοῦ δογμάτων ἀγωνιζόμεθα. ἔπειτα δὲ καὶ Τὴν Σὴν Ἁγιωσύνην παρακαλοῦμεν τῆς πολεμουμένης πίστεως ὑπερμαχῆσαι καὶ τῶν πατηθέντων ὑπεραγωνίσασθαι κανόνων· ἐν ἐκείνῃ γὰρ τῇ βασιλευούσῃ πόλει συνελθόντες, οἱ μακάριοι πατέρες συμφώνως τοῖς ἐν Νικαίᾳ συναθροισθεῖσι τὰς διοικήσεις διέκριναν καὶ ἑκάστῃ διοικήσει τὰ ἑαυτῆς ἀπένειμαν, ἄντικρυς ἀπαγορεύσαντες ἐξ ἑτέρας τινὰς διοικήσεως ἑτέρᾳ μὴ ἐπιέναι, ἀλλὰ τὸν Ἀλεξανδρείας ἐπίσκοπον τὰ τῆς Αἰγύπτου μόνα διοικεῖν, καὶ ἑκάστην διοίκησιν τὰ οἰκεῖα. ὁ δὲ τούτοις ἐμμένειν τοῖς ὅροις οὐ βούλεται, ἀλλ᾽ ἄνω καὶ κάτω τοῦ μακαρίου Μάρκου τὸν θρόνον προβάλλεται, καὶ ταῦτα, σαφῶς εἰδὼς ὡς τοῦ μεγάλου Πέτρου τὸν θρόνον ἡ ἀντιοχέων μεγαλόπολις ἔχει, ὃς καὶ τοῦ μακαρίου Μάρκου διδάσκαλος ἦν καὶ τοῦ χοροῦ τῶν ἀποστόλων πρῶτος καὶ κορυφαῖος. ἀλλ᾽ ἡμεῖς τοῦ μὲν θρόνου τὸ ὕψος ἐπιστάμεθα, ἑαυτοὺς δὲ καὶ γινώσκομεν καὶ μετροῦμεν· τὴν γὰρ ἀποστολικὴν ταπεινοφροσύνην ἄνωθεν μεμαθήκαμεν.[c] Τὴν δὲ Σὴν Ὁσιότητα παρακαλοῦμεν μήτε τοὺς ἁγίους κανόνας πατουμένους παριδεῖν καὶ τῆς θείας πίστεως ὑπερμαχῆσαι προθύμως· εἰς ταύτην γὰρ ἔχομεν τὴν ἐλπίδα τῆς σωτηρίας καὶ διὰ ταύτης τυχεῖν προσδοκῶμεν φιλανθρωπίας.

l. 51 ὁ δὲ … βούλεται = *"Yet he will not abide by these boundaries"* : ܐܝܟ ܕܣܘܥܪ̈ܢܐ ܚܘܘ = *"As these matters have shown, he …"* **l. 60** εἰς ταύτην γὰρ ἔχομεν τὴν ἐλπίδα = *"it is with regard to the faith that we have any hope for salvation"* : ܐܝܟ ܕܐܦ ܡܗܝܡܢܝܢ ܐܢܬܘܢ = *"It is with regard to the faith that we have any hope for salvation, as you are also convinced"* **l. 61** τυχεῖν προσδοκῶμεν φιλανθρωπίας = *"we hope to encounter mercy"* : ܠܚ̈ܢܢܐ ܘܠܛܝܒܘܬܐ ܕܢܬܦܓܥ ܡܣܟܝܢ ܚܢܢ. ܘܕܢܩܘܡ ܩܕܡ ܒܐܡܐ ܕܚܝܠܬܐ ܕܐܠܗܐ ܘܦܪܘܩܢ ܡܪܢ ܝܫܘܥ ܡܫܝܚܐ ܣܝܡܝܢ ܚܢܢ = *"we hope to encounter mercy and grace, and we resolve to stand before the dreadful judgement seat 'of … God and our Savior, our Lord, Jesus Christ'"* (Ti 2.13)

b. Est D.2 (LXX; LXX var.) (*Cf.* 3Macc 2.21.)
c. *Cf.* Mt 23.6–12; Lk 14.7–11; Jas 4.10.

(2) But, to begin with, we have "the One who watches over the universe"[b] for the champion of our cause; after all, it is on behalf of his holy doctrine that we are contending. And, next, we implore Your Holiness to take up the defense of the embattled faith and the fight for the canons that have been trampled underfoot. In that very capital city, the fathers of blessed memory coming together in council, in agreement with those who had gathered in Nicaea, delimited the dioceses and left to each the administration of its own affairs. They expressly forbade anyone from one diocese from encroaching on another, thus limiting the bishop of Alexandria to the administration of Egypt alone and each diocese to the administration of its own affairs. Yet he will not abide by these boundaries but alleges the authority of the throne of the blessed Mark on this side and that,[6] and he does this, although knowing full well that it is the metropolis of the Antiochenes that possesses the throne of the great Peter, who was not only the teacher of the blessed Mark, but also the first and leader of the chorus of the apostles. Of course, while understanding the grandeur of our throne, we know our own measure, for we have learned apostolic humility from above.[c] We implore Your Holiness, do not ignore the trampling of the holy canons, and take up with a good will the fight for the faith that comes from God. Indeed, it is with regard to the faith that we have any hope for salvation, and through this faith we have our expectation of mercy.[7]

6. Jackson marks the end of a paragraph at "thus limiting … its own affairs" (ἄντικρυς ἀπαγορεύσαντες … διοικεῖν) and takes ἄνω καὶ κάτω τοῦ μακαρίου Μάρκου τὸν θρόνον προβάλλεται as referring to disorder or confusion: Dioscorus "is turning the see of the blessed Mark upside down"; *v.* also Frend, p. 27. But, as Azéma's paragraphing indicates, this remark is a continuation of Domnus' complaint regarding Dioscorus' deliberate and presumptuous assertion of authority outside the boundaries of his see. For προβάλλομαι = "bring forward," "use as an excuse or pretext," *v. LSJ, sub uoc.* προβάλλω, B.III.2.b. This interpretation is corroborated by the Syriac translation, which has "show" or "indicate" (ܚܘܝ).

7. Theodoret sounds a theme that recurs throughout his correspondence: the bishop, though guilty of many sins, may still derive hope for salvation from his efforts to preserve the integrity of the faith; *cf. epp.* 83.3, 89.

(3) Ἵνα δὲ μηδὲ τοῦτο ἀγνοήσῃ Σοῦ Ἡ Ὁσιότης, ἴσθι, Δέσποτα, ὡς τὴν πρὸς ἡμᾶς ἔσχεν μικροψυχίαν ἐξ οὗ τοῖς παρ᾽ ὑμῖν γεγενημένοις συνοδικοῖς ἐπὶ τοῦ τῆς μακαρίας μνήμης Πρόκλου συνεθέμεθα, τοῖς τῶν ἁγίων πατέρων κανόσιν ἀκολουθήσαντες, καὶ περὶ τούτου καὶ ἅπαξ ἡμῖν καὶ δὶς ἐνεκάλεσεν ὡς *προδεδωκόσιν καὶ τῆς ἀντιοχέων*, ὡς λέγει, *καὶ τῆς ἀλεξανδρέων ἐκκλησίας τὰ δίκαια*. τούτων μεμνημένος καὶ καιρὸν εὑρών, ὡς ὑπέλαβεν, τὴν δυσμένειαν ἔδειξεν, ἀλλὰ τῆς ἀληθείας οὐδὲν ἰσχυρότερον· οἶδεν γὰρ αὕτη καὶ δι᾽ ὀλίγων νικᾶν. παρακαλῶ δέ Σου Τὴν Ἁγιότητα καὶ μνημονεύειν ἡμῶν ἐν ταῖς πρὸς τὸν Κύριον προσευχαῖς ἵνα ἀντισχεῖν δυνηθῶμεν πρὸς τὰ διάφορα κύματα.

ll. 62–73 Ἵνα δὲ … κύματα = *"So that Your Holiness may have full information … this turbulent sea"* : ܕܬܪܬܝܢ ܠܟ ܕܝܢ ܘܬܗܘܐ ܠܟ ܟܠܡ. ܐܬܦܢܝܗ ܡܪܝ، ܕܟܠ ܡܕܡ ܩܕܝܫܐ. ܕܡܠܟܗ̇ ܐܣܝܘܬܐ ܕܚܝܟ: ܐܢܐ ܘܕܥܡܝ ܗܟܢ ܒܫܠܡܐ ܫܐܠܝܢ ܣܓܝ. ܬܘܒ ܕܝܢ ܢܣܒܬ ܐܠܗܐ ܕܚܝܟ: ܕܠܝ ܗܘ ܡܬܟܬܒܘܬܟ: ܗܘܐ ܐܦܣܩܘܦܐ ܠܡܕܝܢܬܐ ܥܠܬܐ ܗܘܐ ܕܨܘܪ: ܢܚܡܐ ܦܘܛܝܘܣ ܩܫܝܫܐ. ܒܝ ܠܗ ܗܟܝܠ ܡܦܝܣ ܐܢܐ: ܕܬܬܠܝܢ ܘܬܬܦܫܛ ܫܝܢܐ ܫܠܝܚܝܐ ܒܥܕܬܐ ܩܕܝܫܬܐ ܕܒܟܠ ܥܠܡܐ. ܕܗܘܝܢ. ܕܢܫܬܠܡ ܒܟܘܢ. ܒܝ ܠܗ ܡܪܝ، ܕܟܫܝܪܐ ܪܚܡ ܐܠܗܐ܀ = *"My most-holy lord, we implore you to follow and pray for us. My brethren and I extend warm greetings to you and your brethren. I take this opportunity to inform your Reverence that the venerable priest Photius was consecrated bishop of the metropolis of Tyre on the ninth of this past September. In conclusion, I beg you to pray that the apostolic peace grow strong and spread in the holy churches throughout the world. Pray, my lord, truly beloved of God, that we may receive healing from our Lord."*

(3) So that Your Holiness may not lack full information on this point, I would have you know, my Master, that he took up this quarrel from the moment that, following in the footsteps of our holy fathers, we subscribed to the acts of the council issued in your city in the time of Proclus of blessed memory. And he has reproached us once and then again for "being traitors," as he says, "of the rights of both the Antiochene and the Alexandrian church."[8] Bearing a grudge for this and finding what he takes to be a good opportunity, he has revealed his hostility. Yet there is nothing more powerful than the truth, which knows how to gain the victory with the support of no more than a few. I beg Your Holiness to make mention of us in your prayers to the Lord, that we may have the strength to confront this turbulent sea.

8. It is not clear to which synodical document Theodoret/Domnus is referring. Most likely, the issue somehow involved Theodoret, Domnus, Proclus, and Cyril, the bishop of Alexandria, contemporary with Proclus in Constantinople. As Proclus would have known about the decision taken at Antioch in 445 with regard to Athanasius of Perrhe, the synodical acts to which the author refers may have contained a confirmation by Proclus of the validity of that deposition; *v. ep.* 42 n. 3. If, in obedience to canon 3 of the First Council of Constantinople (*v.* Intro., sec. 1.4), Domnus had recognized Proclus' jurisdiction over the eastern church and, thus, submitted the decision of his Antiochene council to the confirmation of Proclus, Dioscorus would have regarded this act as prejudicial to the ancient order of precedence placing Alexandria and Antioch directly after Rome. The author of *ep.* 86, however, would understand this compliance as a case of "following in the footsteps of our holy fathers," *i.e.* the fathers of the second ecumenical council.

87. ΔΟΜΝΩΙ ΕΠΙΣΚΟΠΩΙ ΑΠΑΜΕΙΑΣ

Ὁ μὲν τῆς φιλαδελφίας ἀπῄτει νόμος πολλὰς ἡμᾶς ἐν τῷ παρόντι καιρῷ δέξασθαι παρὰ Τῆς Σῆς Φιλοθεΐας ἐπιστολάς· παρεγγυᾷ γὰρ ὁ θεῖος Ἀπόστολος *κλαίειν μετὰ κλαιόντων* καὶ *χαίρειν μετὰ χαιρόντων*·[a] ἐδεξάμην δὲ οὐδεμίαν, καίτοι παραγενομένων ἔναγχος πρὸς ἡμᾶς τῶν τε θεοσεβεστάτων μοναζόντων τῆς ὑμετέρας μονῆς καὶ τοῦ θεοσεβεστάτου Ἡλίου τοῦ πρεσβυτέρου. ἐγὼ δὲ γράφω, καὶ προσφθέγγομαί Σου Τὴν Ὁσιότητα καὶ γνωρίζω ὡς ἤρκεσεν ἡμῖν ἀντὶ πάντων ἡ τοῦ Δεσπότου ψυχαγωγία· τῷ ὄντι γάρ, οὐδ᾿ εἰ ἰσάριθμα τῶν ἡμετέρων τριχῶν σχοίημεν στόματα, ὑμνῆσαι αὐτὸν ἀξίως ἰσχύομεν, διὰ τὴν εἰς αὐτὸν ὁμολογίαν τῆς δοκούσης ἀτιμίας ἀξιωθέντες,[b] ἣν πάσης τιμῆς σεβασμιωτέραν ἡγούμεθα, εἰ δὲ καὶ τὰς ἐσχατιὰς τῆς οἰκουμένης οἰκῆσαι κατακριθείημεν, πλέον αὐτὸν ἀνυμνήσομεν ὅσῳ μειζόνων ἀγαθῶν ἀξιούμεθα.[c]

Εὐξάσθω δὲ ὅμως Ἡ Ὁσιότης Σου καὶ αἰτησάτω ταῖς ἁγίαις ἐκκλησίαις γαλήνην· τῆς γὰρ τούτων ἕνεκα ζάλης καὶ ἡμεῖς

a. Rom 12.15 b. Acts 5.41 c. Mt 5.11f.

87. To Domnus, Bishop of Apamea[1]

According to the law of brotherly love, in the midst of this present crisis, I should have received many a letter from Your Piety—indeed, the holy Apostle charges us "to weep with those that weep" and "to rejoice with those that rejoice"[a]—yet I have received not a single one, although just recently the right reverend monks of your monastery and the right reverend priest Elijah have paid us a call. So, now I write; I greet Your Holiness and inform you that I have found in the consolation afforded by our Master one outweighing everything else. Had we so many mouths as hairs on our head, we could never sing his praises adequately now that, on account of our confession of him, we have been deemed worthy of this apparent disgrace,[b] which we regard as more honorable than any dignity of office, and should we be condemned to live in exile on the farthest shores of the world, we shall praise him all the more for being judged worthy of even greater blessings.[2c]

All the same, I implore Your Holiness to offer up prayers for the tranquility of the holy churches; it is for this tempest they are en-

1. We know little about Domnus of Apamea. At the Second Council of Ephesus, his suffragan, Meletius of Larissa, would subscribe in his name to the deposition of Domnus of Antioch; *v.* Flemming and Hoffman, pp. 148f. Apamea was the metropolitan see of the province of Syria II, formed in the early fifth century; *v.* Mango and Cutler. As the last paragraph indicates, this letter reflects a moment during a controversy within the church of Edessa. In spring 447, Ibas of Edessa, the metropolitan of Osrhoëne, had excommunicated four of his priests, who, in an effort to depose Ibas and win their own reinstatement, enlisted the support of one of Ibas' suffragans, Uranius, bishop of Himeria and a supporter of Eutyches. In February 449, after a series of hearings in which Ibas' doctrine and episcopal conduct were investigated and declared unexceptionable, a compromise was reached; Ibas kept his see and was reconciled to the four priests. As the implication is that the priests are still under ban of excommunication, the letter must precede that date; *v.* Intro., sec. 4.4. Furthermore, as Theodoret mentions that he did not attend the synod in Antioch that considered this case, he had probably already received the order of Theodosius II confining him to his diocese; *v. ep.* 79 n. 1. Thus, Azéma (vol. 2, p. 232, n. 1) assigns this letter to the early summer of 448.

2. Exile to a far-off land would represent an aggravation of the obloquy under which Theodoret now labors; as that obloquy is actually a badge of honor, exile would signify an increase in distinction.

θρηνοῦμεν, καὶ στένομεν, καὶ ὀλοφυρόμεθα· καὶ γὰρ ἐξῶσαν, ὥς ἔγνωμεν, ταύτην οἱ ἀπὸ Ὀσροηνῆς κληρικοί, μυρία πάντων ἡμῶν καταχέαντες, καίτοι ἐμοῦ οὐδὲ συνδικάσαντος οὐδὲ τῆς ἐπ᾽ αὐτοῖς κοινωνήσαντος ψήφου, ἀλλ᾽, ὡς οἶδεν Σοῦ Ἡ Ὁσιότης, καὶ τὴν κοινωνίαν αὐτοῖς δοθῆναι τὸ Πάσχα παρακαλέσαντος, ἀλλὰ ῥᾴδιον τοῖς συκοφάνταις λέγειν ἃ βούλονται. ἡμᾶς δὲ ὁ τοῦ Δεσπότου παραμυθεῖται μακαρισμός· *Μακάριοι* γάρ *ἐστε*, φησίν, *ὅταν ὀνειδίσωσιν ὑμᾶς, καὶ διώξωσιν, καὶ εἴπωσι πᾶν πονηρὸν* ῥῆμα *καθ᾽ ὑμῶν ἕνεκεν ἐμοῦ ψευδόμενοι· χαίρετε καὶ ἀγαλλιᾶσθε, ὅτι ὁ μισθὸς ὑμῶν πολὺς ἐν τοῖς οὐρανοῖς.*[d]

d. Mt 5.11f. (NT var.)

during that we lament, we groan, we grieve. As we have learned, the clergy of Osrhoëne have repudiated this church and poured out a thousand complaints against us all,[3] although I was not among the judges who heard their case and had no share in the sentence passed on them, but, as Your Holiness is aware, urged that they be admitted to communion for Easter; yet false accusers will not hesitate to say whatever they like. We, for our part, draw consolation from the Master's beatitude that goes, "Blessed are you when people revile and persecute you and falsely utter every kind of evil against you on my account; rejoice and be glad, because your reward is great in heaven."[d]

3. Taking the referent of the demonstrative ταύτην as referring to the tranquility (γαλήνην) mentioned several lines previous, both Jackson and Azéma understand that the clergy of Osrhoëne are taxed with rejecting peace. Nonetheless, it seems more natural to interpret ταύτην in relation to the preceding τούτων (the churches unsettled by controversy) and to understand the accusative as referring to the church of Cyrus, *i.e.* Theodoret and his clergy. Theodoret, following the usage of the LXX, elsewhere uses the verb ἐξωθέω only of casting off a person or a people.

88. ΤΑΥΡΩΙ ΠΑΤΡΙΚΙΩΙ

Ὑπερβαίνειν με τοὺς ὅρους οἱ συκοφάνται βιάζονται καὶ γράφειν ὑμῖν, τοῖς τὰς μεγίστας κεκοσμηκόσιν ἀρχὰς καὶ τὰς ὑπερτάτας εἰληχόσι τιμάς, ἀναγκάζουσιν· οὗ δὴ χάριν παρακαλῶ συγγνώμης μεταλαχεῖν. γράφω γάρ, οὐκ αὐθαδείᾳ χρώμενος, ἀλλ᾽ ὑπὸ τῆς χρείας ὠθούμενος, οὐδὲ τὸ σκυθρωποῖς τισιν ἀδίκως περιπεσεῖν ὑφορώμενος· τοῦτο γὰρ ὡς ἐπίπαν πεπόνθασιν ἅπαντες οἱ τῷ Θεῷ γνησίως δεδουλευκότες·[a] ἀλλὰ Τὴν Ὑμετέραν Μεγαλοφυΐαν πεῖσαι βουλόμενος ὡς ψευδεῖς καθ᾽ ἡμῶν ὠδίνουσι λόγους οἱ τῶν ἡμετέρων κατηγοροῦντες δογμάτων. ἡμεῖς μὲν γάρ, μετὰ τὴν μητρῴαν θηλήν, τὴν ἀποστολικὴν τροφὴν ἐδεξάμεθα, καὶ τὴν ἐκτεθεῖσαν ἐν Νικαίᾳ πίστιν ὑπὸ τῶν ἁγίων καὶ μακαρίων πατέρων καὶ μεμαθήκαμεν καὶ διδάσκομεν, καὶ τοὺς ἄλλο τι παρὰ ταύτην φρονοῦντας δυσσεβείας γραφόμεθα. εἰ δέ τις ἕτερα διδάσκειν ἡμᾶς παρὰ ταύτην ἰσχυρίζεται, μὴ ἐρήμην κατηγορείτω, ἀλλὰ παρόντας ἐλεγξάτω· τοῦτο γὰρ καὶ τοῖς θείοις νόμοις[b] καὶ τοῖς ἀνθρωπείοις δοκεῖ. τίνι δὲ οὕτω προσήκει τῶν ἀδικουμένων ὑπερμαχεῖν ὡς ὑμῖν, ὦ φιλόχριστοι, οἷς καὶ τοῦ γένους ἡ περιφάνεια, καὶ τῶν ἀξιωμάτων τὸ ὕψος, καὶ μέντοι καὶ τὸ τῶν νομίμων πρωτεύειν παρέχει τὴν παρρησίαν;

l. 16 ἐλεγξάτω *NZ* : ἐξε- *scr. Cir., edd. There is no need for Ciriaco's emendation. The TLG attributes to Thdt. seventy-nine uses of the uncompounded form, and this governs a personal d. o. in a dozen places. In five of these, the d. o. consists of, or contains, a participle. Cf. ep. 146.8: ἵνα καὶ τοὺς ἀρνουμένους τοῦ σώματος τὴν ἀνάληψιν … ἐλέγξῃ.*

a. *Cf.* 2Tm 3.12. b. Dt 19.16f.

88. To Taurus, the Patrician[1]

False accusers force me to overstep my bounds and compel me to write a letter to you, a man distinguished for commands of the upmost importance and the highest dignities of office, and for this I must beg your pardon. In writing this, I am not indulging in arrogance, but yielding to the pressure of necessity, nor am I concerned that I have fallen into trouble I don't deserve—that, after all, is what has happened to just about everyone who has served God with true devotion[a]—but I do wish to convince Your Eminence that the people bringing forth complaints against our doctrine are giving birth to nothing but lying words. Indeed, we were weaned on apostolic teaching, and we are disciples of the faith set forth in Nicaea by the holy fathers of blessed memory; this we teach, and those who hold opinions contrary to this we charge with impiety. If anyone insists that we teach something other than this faith, he must not bring charges in the absence of the defendant but accuse him in his presence; that is the requirement of divine[b] and human law alike. Now, who has the duty to champion the victims of injustice, if not you, a lover of Christ, who, by reason of your distinguished family, the preëminence of your distinctions, and, most of all, your direction of justice, have a claim to be heard?

1. The addressee, Flavius Taurus, was of a noble family. His father, Aurelianus, had served in 400 as the eastern consul alongside Stilicho, Consul of the West (*v.* "Aurelianus 3," *PLRE*, vol. 1, pp. 128f.). He was himself the eastern consul in 428 and the Praetorian Prefect of the East from early 433 to late 434 and possibly once more in 445 (*v.* "Fl. Taurus 4," *PLRE*, vol. 2, pp. 1056f.). On the duties of the praetorian prefects, *v. ep.* 42 nn. 4f.; on the title "patrician," *v. ep.* 23 n. 1. *Epp.* 88–91 form a group; all were addressed to highly placed officials or former officials, and all were occasioned by the accusations raised against Theodoret's christological doctrine. They probably reflect the same ecclesiastical / political situation described in *ep.* 87; Azéma (vol. 2, p. 234, n. 1) assigns them to the fall of 448. Taurus died in 449.

89. ΦΛΩΡΕΝΤΙΩΙ ΠΑΤΡΙΚΙΩΙ

Μείζονι μὲν ἢ κατ' ἐμαυτὸν ἐγχειρῶ πράγματι, Τῷ Ὑμετέρῳ Μεγέθει πέμπων ἐπιστολάς, ἀλλ' οὐ θρασύτης αἰτία τῆς τόλμης, ἀλλ' οἱ ταῖς καθ' ἡμῶν λοιδορίαις χρησάμενοι· προὔργου γὰρ ὑπελάβομεν διδάξαι τὰς ἀκλινεῖς ὑμῶν ἀκοὰς ὡς ἄντικρυς ἡμᾶς συκοφαντοῦσιν οἱ τῶν ἡμετέρων κατηγοροῦντες δογμάτων.

Ἡμεῖς δὲ ἕτερα μὲν πλεῖστα πεπλημμεληκέναι φαμέν, τὴν δέ γε δογματικὴν τῶν ἀποστόλων διδασκαλίαν μέχρι τοῦ παρόντος ἀλώβητον ἐφυλάξαμεν καὶ διὰ ταύτην μόνην οἴκτου τυχεῖν καὶ φιλανθρωπίας ἐν τῇ τῆς δεσποτικῆς ἐπιφανείας ἐλπίζομεν ἡμέρᾳ· ὑπὲρ γὰρ ταύτης πρὸς τὰς παντοδαπὰς αἱρέσεις διατελοῦμεν ἀγωνιζόμενοι, ταύτην διηνεκῶς τοῖς τροφίμοις τῆς εὐσεβείας προσφέρομεν, διὰ ταύτης λύκους μυρίους εἰς πρόβατα μεταβαλόντες, τῷ πάντων ἡμῶν *Ἀρχιποιμένι*[a] καὶ Σωτῆρι προσενηνόχαμεν. ταῦτα δὲ ἡμῖν παρέδοσαν οὐ μόνον ἀπόστολοι καὶ προφῆται,[b] ἀλλὰ καὶ οἱ τὰ τούτων ἡρμηνευκότες συγγράμματα· Ἰγνάτιος, Εὐστάθιος, Ἀθανάσιος, Βασίλειος, Γρηγόριος, Ἰωάννης, καὶ οἱ ἄλλοι τῆς οἰκουμένης *φωστῆρες*,[c] καί, πρὸ τούτων, οἱ ἐν Νικαίᾳ συνεληλυθότες ἅγιοι πατέρες, ὧν τὴν ὁμολογίαν τῆς πίστεως ὡς πατρῷον κλῆρον φυλάττομεν ἄσυλον

l. 1 Μείζονι μὲν ἢ κατ' ἐμαυτὸν *corr. A*$^{s.l.}$ *(Car.?), scr. edd.* : Μ. μ. κατ' ἐ. *NZ. The supralinear addition of the* ἢ *in A, perhaps the work of Cariofilo, is necessary for the sense and conforms precisely to Thdt.'s usage. Cf. H. e. 1.1.3: ἐγὼ δὲ τῇ μὲν ἐμαυτοῦ δυνάμει τόδε τὸ ἔργον σταθμώμενος, τὴν ἐγχείρησιν ὀρρωδῶ, θαρρῶν δὲ τῷ φιλοτίμῳ δοτῆρι τῶν ἀγαθῶν, μείζοσιν ἢ κατ' ἐμαυτὸν ἐγχειρῶ.*
ll. 14f. οὐ μόνον ἀπόστολοι καὶ προφῆται *NZ* : οὐ μ. οἱ ἀ. κ. π. *scr. Cir., edd. Ciriaco's emendation is not consonant with Thdt.'s usage. There are just a half dozen places where he pairs the plural nominatives* ἀπόστολοι *and* προφῆται *without qualifying either by a descriptive adjective or genitive. In all but one (Eran. p. 110, l. 29), he omits the article. Note esp. Affect. 4.72 (Ταῦτα οὐ μόνον ἡμᾶς εὐαγγελισταὶ παιδεύουσι καὶ ἀπόστολοι, ἀλλὰ καὶ προφῆται καὶ τῶν προφητῶν ὁ κορυφαῖος), where the neut. demonstr. acc. again precedes the first per. pl. pron.*

a. 1Pt 5.4 b. *Cf.* Eph 2.20; 3.5; 4.11. c. Phil 2.15

89. To Florentius, the Patrician[1]

In sending letters to Your Lordship I am daring a deed too great for one of my position, yet it is not arrogance, but the defamatory reports about us that account for this boldness; we have thought it worthwhile to explain to your unbiased ears that the people raising objections against our teaching are engaging in boldfaced calumny.

While we are ready to admit to countless sins of other sorts, when it comes to the authoritative teaching of the apostles, that, at least, we have defended in its integrity up to this present moment, and it is on this doctrine alone that we base our hopes of receiving compassion and forgiveness on the day of the second coming of the Lord. It is on account of this doctrine that we continue our fight against heresies of every description; this is the doctrine we set before the nurslings of religion; it is through this doctrine that we have converted thousands of wolves into sheep and set them before the Chief Shepherd[a] and Savior of us all. We have received this tradition not only from the apostles and the prophets,[b] but also from the commentators on their writings—Ignatius, Eustathius, Athanasius, Basil, Gregory, John,[2] and all the other luminaries of the world[c]—and, before these, from the holy fathers who came together in Nicaea, whose confession of

1. By the time he received this letter (*v. ep.* 88 n. 1), Florentius had served at least two terms as Praetorian Prefect of the East; *v. ep.* 44 n. 3. On his title, "patrician," *v. ep.* 23 n. 1. On November 22, 448, Florentius presided over the session of the Home Council (*v.* Intro., n. 281), at which Eutyches was deposed and deprived of his priestly status; *v.* Intro., secc. 4.1f. It is not certain if this letter precedes or follows that date.

2. Theodoret regards the exposition of Scripture as the special province of the bishop. Ignatius (d. *ca.* 107; *v.* Baldwin, "Ignatius, Pseudo-") and Eustathius (d. *ca.* 337; *v.* Kazhdan, Baldwin, and Gregory, "Eustathios of Antioch") were bishops of Antioch; Athanasius (*ca.* 295–373; *v.* Baldwin, Kazhdan, and Ševčenko, "Athanasius") was bishop of Alexandria, Basil of Caesarea (*ca.* 329–79; *v.* Baldwin, Kazhdan, and Ševčenko, "Basil the Great"), and John Chrysostom of Constantinople (*ca.* 340–407; *v.* Baldwin, Kazhdan, and Nelson, "John Chrysostom"). Though Theodoret does not specify which Gregory he has in mind, Gregory of Nyssa (*ca.* 335–94; *v.* Baldwin, Kazhdan, and Ševčenko, "Gregory of Nyssa") or Gregory of Nazianzus (329/30–ca. 390; Baldwin, Kazhdan, Nelson, and Ševčenko, "Gregory of

καὶ τοὺς ταῦτα παραβαίνειν τολμῶντας τὰ δόγματα *κιβδήλους* ἀποκαλοῦμεν καὶ *τῆς ἀληθείας ἐχθρούς*.

Παρακαλῶ τοίνυν Τὴν Ὑμετέραν Μεγαλοφυΐαν, ταῦτα παρ᾽ ἡμῶν διδαχθεῖσαν, ἐπιστομίσαι τοὺς λοιδορίαις καθ᾽ ἡμῶν χρησαμένους· ἄτοπον γὰρ οἶμαι τοῖς κατὰ τῶν ἀπόντων λεγομένοις ὡς ἀληθέσι πιστεύειν, ἔννομον δὲ καὶ δίκαιον τοὺς βουλομένους διώκειν παρόντων κατηγορεῖν τῶν φευγόντων καὶ τοὺς ἐλέγχους παράγειν· οὕτω γὰρ οἱ δικάζοντες εὑρεῖν τἀληθὲς ῥᾳδίως δυνήσονται.

faith we preserve intact like an inheritance received from a father. Any who dare to stray from these teachings we call "counterfeit" and "enemies of the truth."

Now that I have informed you, I implore Your Eminence to stop up the mouths of those defaming us. As I see it, it is out of place to accept as true anything said against people who are not present, but lawful and just for those wishing to bring a prosecution to make their accusations and present their evidence in the presence of the defendants; in this way, judges will be able to come to an expeditious determination of the truth.

Nazianzos"), he is probably referring to the former; *v. ep.* 83 n. 3. In the *florilegia* of the *Eran.*, he had cited Ignatius, Eustathius, Athanasius, Basil, John, and both Gregories as authoritative exponents of the orthodox faith. *Cf. ep.* 146.7, where Theodoret much extends this catalogue. If this letter postdates the Home Synod (*v.* n. 1 above), it may be meant as a reply to the catalogue of authoritative testimonies that Florentius had heard Eutyches present in his defense; *cf.* Frend, p. 33. On Theodoret's adaptation of Paul's metaphor (Phil 2.15), *v. ep.* 125 n. 7.

90. ΛΟΥΠΠΙΚΙΝΩΙ ΜΑΓΙΣΤΡΩΙ

Τοὺς τῆς νεότητος διεξελθόντες ἀγῶνας, καὶ τῶν τοῦ γήρως ὅρων εἴσω γενόμενοι, καὶ πλείονος τιμῆς, ὡς γεγηρακότες, ἀπολαύσεσθαι προσδοκήσαντες, τοῖς τῆς συκοφαντίας βαλλόμεθα βέλεσιν καὶ πρὸς τὰς γεγενημένας κατηγορίας ἀπολογίαν προσφέρειν ἀναγκαζόμεθα. οὗ δὴ χάριν καὶ Τὴν Ὑμετέραν παρακαλοῦμεν Μεγαλοπρέπειαν ταῖς τῶν κατηγορούντων ἡμᾶς μὴ πιστεῦσαι ψευδολογίαις· εἰ μὲν γὰρ τῶν σιωπὴν ἀσπαζομένων ἐτύγχανον ὤν, ἴσως ἂν εἶχε χώραν τῆς κακοδοξίας ἡ ὑποψία, ἐπειδὴ δὲ διηνεκῶς ἐν ταῖς ἐκκλησίαις διαλεγόμεθα, πολλὰς διὰ τὴν θείαν χάριν ἔχομεν μυριάδας τῇ τῶν δογμάτων ὀρθότητι μαρτυρούσας. τοῖς γὰρ ἀποστολικοῖς ὅροις καὶ νόμοις ἀκολουθοῦμεν καί, τὴν ἐκτεθεῖσαν ἐν Νικαίᾳ πίστιν ὑπὸ τῶν ἁγίων καὶ μακαρίων πατέρων οἷόν τινα κανόνα καὶ γνώμονα τοῖς λόγοις προσφέροντες, τὴν διδασκαλίαν εὐθύνομεν.

Εἰ δέ τις ἕτερά τινα παρὰ ταῦτα φρονεῖν ἡμᾶς ἰσχυρίζεται, παρόντων κατηγορείτω, μὴ ἀπόντας συκοφαντείτω· δίκαιον γὰρ λόγου μεταλαχεῖν καὶ τὸν φεύγοντα καὶ πρὸς τὴν γεγενημένην κατηγορίαν τὴν ἀπολογίαν ποιήσασθαι, καὶ τηνικαῦτα τοὺς δικάζοντας κατὰ τοὺς νόμους τὴν ψῆφον ἐξενεγκεῖν. τούτων ἀπολαῦσαι κἀγὼ διὰ Τῆς Ὑμετέρας Μεγαλοπρεπείας παρακαλῶ, εἰ δ᾽ ἐρήμην τινὲς ἡμῶν καταψηφίσασθαι βούλονται, ἀσπαστῶς

Title Λουππικίνῳ *codd.* : -υπι- *scr. Sir. Gar.* (*p. 224*) *Nös. Az. Λουππικῖνος, the form of this name presupposed by the reading of N, is attested elsewhere*; *v. Iul. imp. ad Ath. secc. 5.8*; *5.10. I am unsure whether Sirmond deliberately or inadvertently reduced the two π's to one.* **l. 8** ἐτύγχανον ὤν *scripsi* : *ἐ. codd., edd.* When τυγχάνω signifies "to happen to be" rather than "to meet with" or "obtain," Thdt. normally uses it in conjunction with a complementary pt. *Cf., e.g., H. rel., Vita 21.33: Εἰ γὰρ οἰκέτης ἀνθρώπου ὁμοφυοῦς ἐτύγχανον ὤν, etc. An haplography after either* ἐτύγχανον *or* ἀσπαζομένων *would be an easy mistake.* **l. 18** λόγου *NZ* : -γων *scr. Cir., edd. The combination of* λόγου + *the impf. or aor. stem of* μεταλαγχάνω *here signifies "a chance to speak." Cf. Ael., VH 1.21* (*referring to an embassy to the king of Persia*): *νόμος ἐστὶν ἐπιχώριος Πέρσαις, τὸν ἐς ὀφθαλμοὺς ἐλθόντα βασιλέως μὴ πρότερον λόγου μεταλαγχάνειν πρὶν ἢ προσκυνῆσαι αὐτόν. Cf. ep. 141, c. n.* (λόγου). *Thdt. elsewhere uses the pl.* λόγων + *μεταλαχ- to refer to the ability to read or the opportunity to study literature*; *v. Affect. 7.6f.*

90. To Luppicinus, Master of the Offices[1]

After passing through the contests of youth and stepping across the threshold of old age, we imagined we would be treated with the greater honor due to the elderly; instead, we are made a target for the darts of calumny and are constrained to offer a defense against the accusations brought against us. Therefore, I implore Your Excellency not to place any trust in the lies of the accusers. After all, if I were one to keep silent, there might perhaps be some room for suspicion of heresy, but as I am continually preaching in the churches,[2] I have (thanks to the grace of God!) thousands of witnesses to the orthodoxy of my doctrine. We follow the definitions and the laws laid down by the apostles and, applying the creed set out by the holy fathers of blessed memory at Nicaea like a guiding rule or principle, we direct our teaching aright.

If anyone insists that we hold views contrary to this, let him bring his accusation face-to-face, not slander us behind our backs. It is only right that even the defendant should have an opportunity to speak and defend himself against the accusations, and that the judges then, and only then, give their verdict according to the laws. In my case as well, I ask to have the enjoyment of this right through the intervention of Your Excellency, but if there are those who want

1. Garnier (p. 231) identified the addressee of this letter with that of *ep.* 120; *v.* c. n. *ad tit.* Tillemont (vol. 15, p. 300), Azéma (vol. 1, p. 51), and Martindale (*v.* "Lupicinus 2," *PLRE*, vol. 2, p. 693), have all agreed that the identification is likely or at least possible. In addition, Canivet ("Catégories sociales," p. 221, n. 1) has suggested that this Luppicinus is perhaps to be identified with a highly placed Christian official mentioned in the life of the hermit Macedonius (*H. rel.* 13.15). The modern scholars have unnecessarily adopted a form of the name with a single "p"; this is not, as Canivet asserted, that carried by *N* or its descendants. *V.* c. n. (Λουππικίνῳ). It is not known how long Luppicinus held the key office of *Magister Officiorum*—perhaps until 451 (*v.* "Ioannes Vincomalus," *PLRE*, vol. 2, p. 1169). On the *Magister Officiorum, v. ep.* 58 n. 1. For the date of this letter, *ep.* 88 n. 1.

2. On Theodoret's sermons, *v. ep.* 83 n. 2.

καὶ τὴν ἄδικον δεχόμεθα ψῆφον· ἀναμένομεν γὰρ τὸ τοῦ Δεσπότου κριτήριον, ἔνθα οὔτε μαρτύρων οὔτε κατηγόρων δεόμεθα· *πάντα* γὰρ *γυμνὰ καὶ τετραχηλισμένα* ἐνώπιον αὐτοῦ,[a] κατὰ τὸν θεῖον Ἀπόστολον.

a. Heb 4.13 (NT var.)

to see us condemned in our absence, we shall receive even that verdict, unjust as it is, with joy. You see, we await our appearance before the tribunal of our Master, where there is no need for witnesses or accusers, since, in the words of the holy Apostle, "Before him, everything lies naked and exposed to sight."[a]

91. ΕΝΤΡΕΧΙΩΙ ΥΠΑΡΧΩΙ

Τὴν περὶ ἡμᾶς διάθεσιν Τῆς Ὑμετέρας Μεγαλοπρεπείας οἶδα σαφῶς καὶ λόγων οὐ δέομαι ταύτην με διδασκόντων· σαφέστερον γὰρ διδάσκει τῶν λόγων τὰ πράγματα. τῆς δὲ γεγενημένης εἰς ἡμᾶς ἀδικίας ἐβουλόμην τὴν αἰτίαν μαθεῖν· καινότατον γὰρ ὑπομένομεν πρᾶγμα, κατὰ ταὐτὸν ἄγαμοι καὶ δίγαμοι πολεμούμενοι.

Εἰ δὲ οἱ νῦν τὰς καθ᾽ ἡμῶν συκοφαντίας ὑφήναντες παραχαράττειν ἡμᾶς τὴν εὐαγγελικὴν διδασκαλίαν φασίν, τί δήποτε μὴ παρόντας ἐλέγχουσιν, ἀλλ᾽ ἀπόντων κατηγοροῦσιν; τοῦτο γὰρ αὐτῶν μάλιστα διελέγχει τὸ ψεῦδος· εἰδότες γὰρ ὡς πολλὰς ἕξομεν μυριάδας τοῖς ἀποστολικοῖς ἡμῶν δόγμασιν μαρτυρούσας, ἐρήμην ἐποιήσαντο τὴν γραφήν, ἀλλὰ χρὴ τοὺς ἐννόμως δικάζοντας τῷ κατηγορουμένῳ θατέραν ταῖν ἀκοαῖν ἀκεραίαν φυλάξαι. εἰ δὲ τοῖς τῶν ἀντιδίκων λόγοις ἑκατέραν προσφέρουσιν καὶ τὴν ἐκείνοις δοκοῦσαν ἐκφέρουσι ψῆφον, στέρξομεν τὴν ἀδικίαν, ὡς τῆς τῶν οὐρανῶν πρόξενον βασιλείας, καὶ τὸ ἀκλινὲς ἐκεῖνο δικαστήριον προσμενοῦμεν, ἔνθα οὔτε κατήγορος, οὔτε συνήγορος, οὔτε μάρτυς, οὔτε ἀξιωμάτων διαφορά, ἀλλ᾽ ἔργων καὶ λόγων κρίσις καὶ ἡ κατ᾽ ἀξίαν ἀντίδοσις· *Πάντες γάρ*, φησίν, *παραστησόμεθα τῷ βήματι τοῦ* Χριστοῦ[a] *ἵνα κομίσηται ἕκαστος τὰ διὰ τοῦ σώματος πρὸς ἃ ἔπραξεν, εἴτε ἀγαθὸν εἴτε* κακόν.[b]

Title Ἐντρεχίῳ *codd* : Εὐ- *scr. Sir. Az. Nös.*; *v. c. n. ad tit. ep. 57.*

a. Rom 14.10 (NT var.) b. 2Cor 5.10 (NT var.)

91. To Entrechius, the Prefect[1]

I am well aware of Your Excellency's regard for us and have no need of words to tell me this—actions, of course, speak louder than words—but I was desirous of learning the cause of the injustice that has been perpetrated against us; after all, there is no precedent for the treatment to which we are now subjected, under attack at one and the same time for entirely contradictory reasons.[2]

If the people who have woven this tissue of false accusations against us make the claim that we are counterfeiting the gospel teaching, why in the world don't they submit us to cross examination face-to-face, rather than accusing us behind our backs? This is the best proof of their mendacity; since they know we can call on thousands to attest to the apostolic character of our doctrine, they have entered an indictment in the absence of the defendant, but law-abiding judges must keep one unbiased ear for the accused. Yet, even if they give both ears to the accusations of our opponents and hand down a verdict to their liking, we shall accept the injustice as opening the door to the kingdom of heaven and await our appearance at that impartial tribunal where there is no accuser, no counsel, no witness, no distinction of rank, only judgment of deeds and words and a fitting requital. As Scripture has it, "We shall all of us stand before the judgment seat of Christ"[a] "so that each may receive either good or evil according to his works in the flesh."[3b]

1. On Entrechius and his prefecture, *v. ep.* 57 n. 1; for the date, *ep.* 88 n. 1.

2. Theodoret actually says, "under attack at one and the same time for being bachelor and bigamist" (κατὰ ταὐτὸν ἄγαμοι καὶ δίγαμοι πολεμούμενοι).

3. As Azéma (vol. 2, p. 242, n. 1) points out, Theodoret juxtaposes these two texts in this same form also at the end of *Prouid.* 9 (PG, vol. 83, col. 740, ll. 15–17).

92. ΑΝΑΤΟΛΙΩΙ ΠΑΤΡΙΚΙΩΙ

Τοὺς μὲν θεοσεβεστάτους ἐπισκόπους εἰς τὴν βασιλεύουσαν ἀνελθεῖν παρεσκεύασε πόλιν ὁ ὁσιώτατος ἀρχιεπίσκοπος ὁ Κύριος Δόμνος ὥστε τὴν κατὰ πάντων ἡμῶν γεγενημένην διελέγξαι συκοφαντίαν. Τῆς δὲ Ὑμετέρας Μεγαλοφυΐας διαφερόντως ἐπὶ τοῦ παρόντος δεόμεθα, ἐπειδὴ τῶν ὅλων ὁ Κύριος καὶ πίστιν ὑμῖν εἰλικρινῆ δέδωκεν, καὶ ζῆλον ὑπὲρ ταύτης θερμόν, καὶ φρένας συνέσει κεκοσμημένας, καί, πρὸς τούτοις, δύναμιν τοῖς ἀγαθοῖς ὑμῶν ὑπουργοῦσαν βουλεύμασιν. ἐπαμύνατε τοιγαροῦν τοῖς ἀδικουμένοις· καὶ τὸ ψεῦδος καταγωνίσασθε καὶ τῆς ἀποστολικῆς διδασκαλίας πολεμουμένης ὑπερμαχήσατε. συνεργήσει γὰρ δήπουθεν τῶν ἐκκλησιῶν ὁ Δεσπότης καὶ Κυβερνήτης τῇ Τῆς Ὑμετέρας Μεγαλοπρεπείας σπουδῇ· καὶ διαλύσει τὸ νέφος τὸ σκυθρωπὸν καὶ καθαρὰν αἰθρίαν χαριεῖται τοῖς τροφίμοις τῆς πίστεως. εἰ δὲ καὶ συγχωρήσοι τὸν χειμῶνα νικῆσαι, Τὸ μὲν Ὑμέτερον Μέγεθος τέλειον ἀπολήψεται τὸν μισθόν, ἡμεῖς δὲ τὸν κλύδωνα στέρξομεν καί, ἔνθα ἂν ἡμᾶς ἐξώσῃ, μετὰ ψυχαγωγίας διάξομεν, τὸ θεῖον κριτήριον ἀναμένοντες καὶ τὴν ὀρθὴν ἐκείνην καὶ δικαίαν προσμένοντες ψῆφον.

92. To Anatolius, the Patrician[1]

His Holiness, the archbishop, Lord Domnus[2] has arranged for these right reverend bishops to travel up to the capital city with the charge of confuting the false accusations raised against us all. At this moment we apply for help to you above all, since the Lord has given you a pure faith, a warm zeal for that faith, a mind well-endowed with understanding, and, in addition, power to further the good you purpose. So then, protect the victims of injustice by putting falsehood to flight and championing the apostolic teaching now under attack. The Master and Captain of the churches will second Your Excellency's efforts: scattering the menacing clouds and granting clear bright skies to the nurslings of the faith. But, even if he permit the storm to rage on, Your Lordship will receive all the recompense you deserve, and we shall make no complaint about the rough seas, but dwell wherever they drive us, taking comfort in our expectation of the judgment of God and his true and righteous sentence.

1. On Anatolius *v. ep.* 45 n. 1, and for the title "Patrician," *v. ep.* 23 n. 1. *Epp.* 92–96, 99–101, 103f., 106 are all addressed to people in Constantinople. As these all refer to a delegation of Syrian bishops that was setting out to the capital to defend the orthodoxy of Antiochene christological views, they must have been carried by the bishops themselves. Azéma, noting the sad tone of this letter, places their composition in November 448, before Theodoret had received the news of the condemnation of Eutyches; *v.* Intro., sec. 4.2. Richard plausibly suggests that the Antiochenes took along with them the short christological treatise *Quod unicus filius*; *v. ep.* 16 n. 4. Richard dates the composition of the latter to after the condemnation of Eutyches, but, if Azéma's dating of these letters is correct, the treatise was probably written before the judgment itself, or before Theodoret had heard of it.

2. On Domnus, *v. ep.* 31 n. 1.

93. ΣΕΝΑΤΟΡΙ ΠΑΤΡΙΚΙΩΙ

Καὶ διὰ τῶν θεοφιλεστάτων καὶ ὁσιωτάτων ἐπισκόπων προσφθέγγομαι Τὴν Ὑμετέραν Μεγαλοπρέπειαν, ἧς τὴν μνήμην ἄσβεστον περιφέρω. καταλαβεῖν δὲ αὐτοὺς τὴν βασιλίδα παρεσκεύασε πόλιν ὁ ὁσιώτατος ἐπίσκοπος ὁ Κύριος Δόμνος ἵνα τὸ καθ' ἡμῶν συντεθὲν διαλύσωσι ψεῦδος· προφανῆ γάρ τινες καθ' ἡμῶν συκοφαντίαν ἐξύφηναν καὶ ζάλης τὰς ἐκκλησίας ἐνέπλησαν, ὑπὲρ ὧν ὁ Δεσπότης Χριστὸς *σταυρὸν ὑπέμεινεν, αἰσχύνης καταφρονήσας,*[a] ὑπὲρ ὧν ὁ τῶν θείων ἀποστόλων χορὸς καὶ τῶν νικηφόρων μαρτύρων οἱ δῆμοι ταῖς παντοδαπαῖς τοῦ θανάτου παρεδόθησαν ἰδέαις. ὑπὲρ τῆς τούτων εἰρήνης Τὴν Ὑμετέραν ἀγωνίσασθαι Μεγαλοφυΐαν παρακαλῶ· ῥᾴδιον μὲν γὰρ ἦν τῷ τῶν ὅλων Θεῷ νεῦσαι καὶ λῦσαι τὰ σκυθρωπά, ἀλλ' ἀναβάλλεται, καὶ τῶν πολεμουμένων τὴν ἀνδρείαν ἐπιδεικνὺς καὶ ὑμῖν ἀφορμὰς εἰς ὠφέλειαν παρέχων.

Title Σενάτορι *scripsi* : -τορίῳ *codd.* : -τωρίῳ *edd. V. c. n.* (Σενάτορι) *ep. 44.*

a. Heb 12.2

93. To Senator, the Patrician[1]

Now, through the intermediary of Their Holinesses, bishops beloved of God, I address myself to Your Excellency, a man whose unfading memory I carry about with me wherever I go. His Holiness, the Lord bishop Domnus, has arranged for them to travel to the capital city to undo this tissue of lies that has been put together against us. You see, some people have woven against us a fabric of patently false accusation and started a tempest within the churches, the churches on whose behalf the Master Christ "endured the cross, making light of its disgrace,"[a] on whose behalf the chorus of the holy apostles and the masses of triumphant martyrs were handed over to death in all its shapes. I call upon Your Eminence to contend for peace within them. It would be an easy matter for the God of the universe to nod his head and disperse the turbulence, but he holds off to put on display the valor of those who are under attack and to provide you with an opportunity to come to their aid.

1. On Senator, *v. ep.* 44 n. 1; for the title "Patrician," *v. ep.* 23 n. 1; for the date and circumstances of this letter, *v. ep.* 92 n. 1.

94. ΠΡΩΤΟΓΕΝΕΙ ΥΠΑΡΧΩΙ

Πάλαι μὲν δέδωκεν ὑμῖν ὁ φιλάνθρωπος Δεσπότης δύναμιν ἀρκοῦσαν ὑπουργῆσαι τῇ γνώμῃ, ηὔξησεν δὲ ταύτην ἐπὶ τοῦ παρόντος ἵνα ῥᾷον καὶ τῆς ἀληθείας πολεμουμένης ὑπερμαχήσῃ Τὸ Ὑμέτερον Μέγεθος, καὶ καταλύσῃ τὸ ψεῦδος, καὶ ταῖς ἐκκλησίαις τὴν ποθουμένην πρυτανεύσῃ γαλήνην· ὁπόσης γὰρ ἐνεπλήσθησαν ζάλης τῆς ἑῴας αἱ ἐκκλησίαι, παρὰ πολλῶν μὲν καὶ ἄλλων Ἡ Ὑμετέρα Μεγαλοφυΐα μεμάθηκεν, ἀκριβέστερον δὲ παρὰ τῶν θεοφιλεστάτων ἐπισκόπων μαθήσῃ οἳ τῆς μακρᾶς ταύτης ἀποδημίας ἐν ὥρᾳ χειμῶνος τούτου χάριν ἠνέσχοντο, μετὰ τὴν θείαν χάριν τῇ Τῆς Ὑμετέρας Ἐξουσίας προμηθείᾳ θαρροῦντες. λύσατε τοίνυν ἡμῖν, ὦ φιλόχριστοι, τὸν χειμῶνα, καὶ τὴν σκοτομήνην εἰς αἰθρίαν καθαρὰν μεταβάλετε, καὶ τὰς καθ᾽ ἡμῶν κινηθείσας χαλινώσατε γλώττας· ἡμεῖς γὰρ διὰ τὴν θείαν χάριν τῶν ἀποστολικῶν διηνεκῶς ὑπερμαχοῦμεν δογμάτων, καὶ τὴν ἐκτεθεῖσαν ἐν Νικαίᾳ πίστιν φυλάττομεν ἄσυλον, καὶ τοὺς ταῦτα παραχαράττειν τολμῶντας τὰ δόγματα *ἀσεβεῖς* ὀνομάζομεν, καὶ τούτων μάρτυρες οἱ παρ᾽ ἡμῶν κατηχούμενοι, οἱ παρ᾽ ἡμῶν βαπτιζόμενοι, οἱ τῶν ἐν ταῖς ἐκκλησίαις διαλέξεων ἐπαΐοντες. εἰ δὲ κατηγορεῖν ἐννόμως ἐθέλουσι, χρὴ παρόντας ἐλέγχειν, οὐκ ἀπόντας συκοφαντεῖν· οὕτω γὰρ καὶ τοῖς ἄλλοις Ἡ Ὑμετέρα Μεγαλοφυΐα δικάζουσα πράγμασιν ἐκφέρει τὰς ψήφους, ἐκ τῶν τῆς κατηγορίας καὶ ἀπολογίας λόγων συνορῶσα τὸ δίκαιον.

94. To Protogenes, the Prefect[1]

It is now long since that our kindly Master has granted you power sufficient to further your purposes, and, in the present crisis, he has increased it to make it easier for Your Lordship to undertake the defense of the embattled truth, scatter this falsehood, and restore to the churches the tranquility they yearn for. Your Eminence has been informed by others of the gravity of the storm that has filled the churches of the East and now will receive a more detailed account from the bishops beloved of God, who, heartened first by the grace of God, then by your wise exercise of authority, have been willing to undertake for this very purpose such a long winter journey.[2] So then, friend of Christ, put an end to the wintry storm, and change the dark of a moonless night to bright sunshine, and put a bridle on the mouths that have been set in motion against us. On our side, through the grace of God, we fight without rest in defense of the apostolic teachings, we preserve inviolate the creed set out at Nicaea, and those who dare to counterfeit these teachings we call "enemies of religion"; the witnesses for these claims are those we instruct, those we baptize, those who hear our sermons in the churches. Now, if they wish to press lawful charges, they must accuse us in our presence, not just slander us in our absence. After all, in the adjudication of other cases, this is how Your Eminence passes judgment; by listening to the pleadings for the prosecution and the defense, you come to your understanding of what is just.

1. *V.* "Fl. Flor(entius?) Romanus Protogenes," *PLRE*, vol. 2, pp. 927f. Protogenes succeeded Antiochus, the recipient of *ep.* 95, as Praetorian Prefect of the East (on the duties of this official, *v. ep.* 42 and *ep.* 42 nn. 4f.). He attended several sessions of the Council of Chalcedon, including the sixth, at which the definition was promulgated; *v.* Intro., sec. 5.13. He became *consul designatus* in 449 and *patricius* between 449–51. Flemming and Hoffman (p. 21), followed by Frend (p. 37), mistakenly divide this one official into three different people. For the date and circumstances of this letter, *v. ep.* 92 n. 1.

2. The words I have rendered with "by your wise exercise of authority" (τῇ τῆς Ὑμετέρας Ἐξουσίας προμηθείᾳ) actually contain an abstract noun used as an honorific form of address. A more literal translation would be "by the foresight of Your Authority."

95. ΑΝΤΙΟΧΩΙ ΥΠΑΡΧΩΙ

Τῆς μεγίστης ἀρχῆς τὰς μὲν φροντίδας ἀπέθεσθε, τὸ δὲ κλέος ὑμῶν παρὰ πᾶσιν ἀνθεῖ· οἱ γὰρ τὰς ὑμετέρας εὐεργεσίας τρυγήσαντες ᾄδουσι ταύτας ἐνδελεχῶς· πλεῖστοι δὲ οὗτοι καὶ πανταχοῦ· καὶ πολλοῖς τὰς εὐφημίας προσφέροντες καὶ τὰς ἐκείνων γλώττας πάλιν εἰς ἐπαίνους κινοῦντες, ἐγὼ δὲ γάννυμαι, θεωρῶν τὸν ἀξιέραστον καρπὸν τὴν πολυθρύλητον ὡραΐζοντα ῥίζαν. οὗ δὴ χάριν ἐπὶ τὰ μείζω καὶ τελειότερα Τὴν Ὑμετέραν Μεγαλοφυΐαν παρακαλῶ καὶ τῆς τῶν ἐκκλησιῶν ἀξιῶ φροντίσαι γαλήνης· πολλοῦ γὰρ ταύτας χειμῶνος ἐνέπλησαν οἱ τὰς καθ' ἡμῶν συκοφαντίας ὑφήναντες. διά τοι τοῦτο καὶ οἱ θεοφιλέστατοι ἐπίσκοποι, καὶ μακρᾶς ὁδοιπορίας, καὶ ἀσθενείας, καὶ γήρως καταφρονήσαντες καὶ τὰ σφέτερα ποίμνια καταλιπόντες ἀποίμαντα, τὴν μακρὰν ταύτην πορείαν ἐστείλαντο, διελέγξαι τὸ κατὰ πάντων ἡμῶν συντεθὲν ἐπειγόμενοι ψεῦδος. ἐπαμυνάτω τοίνυν αὐτοῖς Τὸ Ὑμέτερον Μέγεθος, καὶ τῆς συκοφαντουμένης ἑῴας κηδόμενον καὶ τῆς ἀποστολικῆς προμηθούμενον πίστεως· πρέπει γὰρ ὑμῖν τοῖς ἄλλοις κατορθώμασι καὶ τόδε προσθεῖναι τὸ κλέος.

95. To Antiochus, the Prefect[1]

You have laid aside the concerns of high office, but your renown is in flower throughout the world; the people who have reaped the benefit of your good deeds sing their praises unceasingly—there are throngs of such people everywhere—and, as they spread these glowing reports to others, they make them also take up your praise, and it is my delight to see the stock renowned among all now decked with this lovely fruit. And so, I urge Your Eminence to what is even greater and more sublime and beseech you to take thought for the tranquility of the churches. These have been filled with a violent storm raised by people who have woven a web of false accusations against us. Therefore, these bishops beloved of God, setting at naught the road to be travelled and the infirmity of old age and leaving behind their flocks unshepherded, have set off on this long journey in their zeal to expose the falsehood that has been fabricated against us. So then, my Lordship, place them under your protection; show your consideration for the eastern church that is now the object of slander and your concern for the faith of the apostles; indeed, it is only fitting that you should add to so many others this glorious deed as well.

1. *V.* "Antiochus (Chuzon II) 10," *PLRE*, vol. 2, p. 104. As Martindale points out, at the date of writing, Antiochus had already retired from the position of Praetorian Prefect of the East; *v. ep.* 94 n. 1. Between 448 and 451, he was granted the title *patricius*; *v. ep.* 23 n. 1. Like Protogenes (*v. ep.* 94 n. 1), he attended the sixth session of the Council of Chalcedon. For the date and circumstances of this letter, *v. ep.* 92 n. 1.

96. ΝΟΜΩΙ ΠΑΤΡΙΚΙΩΙ

Δὶς μὲν ἤδη γράψας, οἶμαι δ᾽ ὅτι καὶ τρίς, ἀντιγράφων οὐκ ἔτυχον καί, σιγῆσαι λοιπὸν βουληθεὶς καὶ νῦν γοῦν ἐμαυτόν τε γνῶναι καὶ τῶν ἐξουσιῶν τὸ μέγεθος ἐπιγνῶναι, ἄμεινον ᾠήθην αὖθις γράψαι καὶ παρακαλέσαι μαθεῖν τὴν αἰτίαν τῆς σιωπῆς· τῷ ὄντι γὰρ οὐκ οἶδά τι πλημμελήσας εἰς Τὴν Ὑμετέραν Μεγαλοπρέπειαν. ἐπειδὴ δὲ οὐ μόνον ἑκόντες, ἀλλὰ καὶ ἄκοντες πταίομεν καὶ ἀγνοοῦμεν ἔστιν ὅτε ἃ πλημμελοῦμεν, Ἡ Ὑμετέρα Μεγαλοφυΐα, τῶν θείων νόμων ἀναμνησθεῖσα οἳ διαρρήδην παρεγγυῶσιν, Ἐὰν ἁμάρτῃ *ὁ ἀδελφός σου εἰς σέ, ... ἔλεγξον αὐτὸν μεταξὺ σοῦ μόνου καὶ αὐτοῦ,*[a] δήλην μοι τῆς λύπης ποιῆσαι καταξιωσάτω τὴν ἀφορμὴν ἵνα ἢ ἀθῷον ἐμαυτὸν ἐπιδείξω ἤ, γνοὺς τὸ πλημμέλημα, συγγνώμην αἰτήσω· ἐλπίζω δὲ τὸ πρότερον ἔσεσθαι, τῇ τοῦ συνειδότος μαρτυρίᾳ θαρρῶν. πάντας μὲν οὖν ἀνθρώπους ἡ μεγαλοψυχία κοσμεῖ, οὐχ ἥκιστα δὲ τούς, κατὰ Τὴν Ὑμετέραν Μεγαλοφυΐαν, καὶ διὰ τῆς θύραθεν παιδείας ἠγμένους, καὶ τὰ θεῖα πεπαιδευμένους, καὶ τῶν ἀποστολικῶν ἐπαΐοντας νόμων ἄντικρυς βοώντων, *Μὴ ἐπιδυέτω ὁ ἥλιος ἐπὶ τῷ παροργισμῷ ὑμῶν,*[b] καὶ τῶν ὁμηρικῶν μεμνημένους ἐπῶν, *Σὺ δέ, μεγαλήτορα θυμόν / ἴσχειν ἐνὶ στήθεσσι· φιλοφροσύνη γὰρ ἀμείνων.*[c]

Ταῦτα δέ, οὐ διδάσκων, ἔφην, ἀλλ᾽ ἀναμιμνήσκων[d] ἐν πολλοῖς οὖσαν Τὴν Ὑμετέραν Μεγαλοπρέπειαν καὶ μέντοι καὶ τῶν τοῦ

l. 10 μόνου *codd.* (*cf. NTG*) : -ον *scr. Sir. Nös. Az. Perhaps Sirmond simply misread NA; cf. ep. 90, c. n.* (Λουππικίνῳ). **l. 22** καὶ μέντοι καὶ *scr. Sir. Nös. Az.* : κ. μ. *codd. Sirmond's emendation is felicitous. In the works of Thdt., the longer form of the phrase is attested with far greater frequency. The form with the repeated* καὶ *is also more appropriate to mark the logical crescendo in the transition from the concerns of the high official to the law of the Lord; cf. Quaest. in Reg. et Par. ad 2Chr 16.1f.:* [*Asa of Judah*] *τὸν βασιλέα τῆς Συρίας εἰς*

a. Mt 18.15 b. Eph 4.26 c. Hom., *Il.* 9.255f.
d. *Cf.* Rom 15.15.

96. To Nomus, the Patrician[1]

Having already written you twice—or three times, so I think—I have yet to receive a reply.[2] And though I had decided to maintain silence from now on, recognizing at this late hour my own place and taking stock of the importance of high officials, I decided it would be better to write yet again and urge you to let me know the cause of your silence. In fact, I just do not know what offence I have given Your Excellency. Given that we commit faults not only willfully, but sometimes even against our will, and sometimes have no realization of a trespass we have committed, I implore Your Eminence to recall the words of the divine law that explicitly enjoins, "If your brother sin against you, call him to account, just the two of you together,"[a] and to be good enough to inform me of the cause of your resentment so I may either demonstrate my innocence or, recognizing my trespass, beg your pardon; encouraged by the testimony of conscience, I expect it will be the former. Magnanimity, of course, is an adornment for everyone, but especially for men, like Your Eminence, brought up with both a secular and a religious education, and thus at once attentive to the apostolic law that explicitly proclaims, "Let not the sun set on your anger,"[b] and mindful of the Homeric verses, "But be it yours to hold fast in your bosom / the anger of the proud heart, for kindliness is better."[3c]

I have said so much not to instruct, but to remind Your Excellency,[d] immersed as you are in so many concerns, and I recall as well the

1. On Nomus, *v. ep.* 58 n. 1; for the title "Patrician," *v. ep.* 23 n. 1; and for the date and circumstances of this letter, *v. ep.* 92 n. 1.

2. Nomus, a supporter of Chrysaphius, was sympathetic to the Eutychian cause; *v.* introduction, sec. 4.10.

3. The translation of the Homeric verses is, with slight adaptation, that of Lattimore.

Κυρίου μεμνημένος νόμων οἳ ταῦτα διαγορεύουσιν· *Ἐὰν· … προσφέρῃς τὸ δῶρόν σου ἐπὶ τὸ θυσιαστήριον κἀκεῖ μνησθῇς ὅτι ἔχει τι ὁ ἀδελφός σου κατὰ σοῦ, ἄφες ἐκεῖ τὸ δῶρόν σου ἔμπροσθεν τοῦ θυσιαστηρίου καὶ ὕπαγε, πρῶτον διαλλάγηθι τῷ ἀδελφῷ σου, καί, τότε ἐλθών,* προσφέρεις *τὸ δῶρόν σου.*[e] τούτοις ἑπόμενος, ἀναγκαῖον ᾠήθην καὶ διὰ τῶν θεοφιλεστάτων ἐπισκόπων προσειπεῖν Ὑμῶν Τὸ Μέγεθος καὶ παρακαλέσαι φροντίσαι τῆς τῶν ἐκκλησιῶν γαλήνης· παμπόλλης γὰρ ἐνεπλήσθησαν ζάλης.[f]

συμμαχίαν ἐκάλεσεν, ἐκ τῶν βασιλικῶν θησαυρῶν καὶ μέντοι καὶ τῶν θείων, χρυσὸν αὐτῷ πέμψας ὅτι μάλιστα πλεῖστον.

e. Mt 5.23f. (NT var.)

f. *Cf.* Mk 4.35–39.

prescription of the law of the Lord, "If you bring your gift to the altar and remember that your brother has something against you, leave your gift before the altar, and go, be reconciled to your brother, and then come and offer your gift."[e] Guided by these words, I thought I should greet your Lordship through these bishops beloved of God and urge you to take thought for the tranquility of the churches, as they have been filled with a mighty storm.[f]

97. ΣΦΩΡΑΚΙΩΙ ΚΟΜΗΤΙ

Ἐψυχαγώγησέν με Τῆς Ὑμετέρας Μεγαλοπρεπείας τὰ γράμματα, ηὔξησεν δέ μου τὴν θυμηδίαν καὶ ὁ θεοφιλέστατος πρεσβύτερος καὶ μονάζων Ἰάμβλιχος, τὸν θερμὸν ὑμῶν διηγησάμενος ζῆλον· καὶ τὴν περὶ τὰ θεῖα σπουδήν, καὶ τὴν περὶ ἡμᾶς γνησίαν διάθεσιν. ἐγὼ δέ, καὶ ταῦτα μαθὼν καὶ τοῦ ἐνδοξοτάτου καὶ φιλοχρίστου τοῦ Κυρίου τοῦ πατρικίου τοὺς ὑπὲρ ἡμῶν ἀγῶνας ἀκούων, τὴν ἀποστολικὴν ὑμῖν εὐλογίαν προσφέρω ἣν ὁ μακάριος Ὀνησιφόρος ἐκ τῆς ἁγίας ἐκείνης ἐκαρπώσατο γλώττης· *Δῴη ἔλεος.... Κύριος τῷ* ὑμετέρῳ *οἴκῳ, ὅτι πολλάκις με ἀνέψυξεν καὶ τὴν ἅλυσίν μου οὐκ ἐπῃσχύνθη*·[a] *δῴη* ὑμῖν *ὁ Κύριος ἔλεος εὑρεῖν παρὰ Κυρίου ἐν ἐκείνῃ τῇ ἡμέρᾳ*.[b] ταῦτα ὑμῖν ἐπεύχομαι κἂν μείζοσιν οἱ τῆς ἀληθείας ἐχθροὶ περιβάλωσί με λυπηροῖς, ὡς νομίζουσιν· εἰς γὰρ τὴν πρόθεσιν ἀφορᾶν ἐδιδάχθημεν. καὶ τοῦτο δὲ ἴστω Ὑμῶν Τὸ Μέγεθος· ὡς μετὰ τῆς εὐσεβείας καὶ ὁ θάνατος ἡμῖν ἥδιστος καὶ αἱ τῆς οἰκουμένης ἐσχατιαί· ἀνιᾷ δὲ ὅμως ἡμᾶς τῶν ἐκκλησιῶν ὁ χειμών, ὃν δυνατὸς λῦσαι τῶν ὅλων ὁ Κύριος.

Title Σφωρακίῳ *codd., Sir.* : Σπο- *scr. Nös. Az. In the Acts of the Council of Chalcedon, the name appears several times* (Conc. chalc., Act. 1, *sec. 2, #6*; Act. 3, *sec. 1, #6*; Act. 4, *sec. 1, #6*), *and in each place the mss. are split between Σφ- and Σπ-. The spelling preferred by Nösselt is that adopted by Schwartz and that which Schulze printed in the dedication of the Haer. com.*

a. 2Tm 1.16 b. 2Tm 1.18

97. To Count Sporacius[1]

I received encouragement from Your Excellency's letter, and my joy was increased at the report of the monk Iamblichus, priest beloved of God, regarding the ardent zeal of your devotion to religion and of the true friendship you bear us. Now that I know this and hearing as well of the efforts that renowned and Christian gentleman, my Lord the patrician, is making on our behalf,[2] I offer you the Apostle's blessing, once reaped from that holy mouth by the blessed Onesiphorus: "May the Lord grant mercy to your household, which has so often given me respite and has never disavowed me in my imprisonment";[a] "may the Lord grant that you find mercy from the Lord on that day."[b] This is my prayer for you. But even if the enemies of the truth hem me round with what they take to be troubles worse than these—for, as we have been taught, it is their intention we consider—I would have your Lordship know this: that for me even death or banishment to the ends of the world, if accompanied by orthodoxy, will be the sweetest of pleasures; nonetheless, we are distressed by the tempest in the churches, which the Lord of the universe can scatter in his might.

1. The addressee is known to have served as *Comes domesticorum Peditum* for the East in 450–51; on the various levels of officialdom distinguished by the designation *comes* and on this particular office, *v. ep.* 22 n. 1. In that position, he attended several sessions of the Council of Chalcedon, including that of October 25; *cf.* Intro., 5.13. In 452, he was Consul for the East; *v.* "Fl. Sporacius 3," *PLRE,* vol. 2, pp. 1026f. Azéma suggests that both this and the following letter may have been written toward the end of 448 and carried to Constantinople by the delegation of Syrian bishops, to which Theodoret refers in *epp.* 92–96, 99–101, 103f., 106; *v. ep.* 92 n. 1. If that is so, this letter would have been written prior to the earliest date for which we can document Sporacius' tenure of the position of *Comes domesticorum Peditum.* A devout Christian, Sporacius received the dedication of Theodoret's last large work, the *Haer. com.,* probably composed shortly after Chalcedon; *v.* Intro., sec. 6.6.

2. The word πατρίκιος could be read as an honorific title (*v. ep.* 23 n. 1) or as a man's name. Azéma (vol. 3, p. 13, n. 5) rejects the possibility that Theodoret could be referring to Patricius, the son of the general Aspar (*v. epp.* 34 and 140), since that Patricius, an Arian, could not be termed φιλόχριστος. He makes the very plausible suggestion that here πατρίκιος is an honorific referring to Anatolius, the nephew of Sporacius and Theodoret's great friend; *v. ep.* 45 n. 1.

98. ΠΑΓΧΑΡΙΩΙ

Ἡμεῖς μὲν ἀνιώμεθα, τῶν ἐκκλησιῶν τὸν κλύδωνα βλέποντες, ὁ δὲ τούτων Δεσπότης καὶ Κυβερνήτης ἀεὶ διὰ τρικυμιῶν ἔδειξεν τοῖς ἀνθρώποις τὴν οἰκείαν σοφίαν καὶ δύναμιν· ἐξαίφνης γὰρ ἐπιτιμᾷ τοῖς ἀνέμοις καὶ τὴν γαλήνην ἐργάζεται, τοῦτο δὲ καὶ ἐπὶ τοῦ σκάφους τῶν ἀποστόλων πεποίηκεν.[a] ἀλλ᾽ ὅμως καὶ ταύτην τοῦ Σωτῆρος ἡμῶν τὴν δύναμιν ἐπιστάμενοι καὶ τὰς ἄλλας αὐτοῦ πάλιν οἰκονομίας εἰδότες, κἂν τι τῶν ἐναντίων ἐκβῇ, χάριν ὁμολογοῦμεν καὶ ὡς θεόσδοτον δεχόμεθα δῶρον· τῶν γὰρ παρόντων καταφρονεῖν, τὰ δὲ προσδοκώμενα προσμένειν ἐδιδάχθημεν ἀγαθά. Τὴν δὲ Σὴν Μεγαλοπρέπειαν τὴν ὑπὲρ τῆς ἀποστολικῆς πίστεως εἰσενεγκεῖν προσήκει σπουδὴν ἵνα τὴν ὑπὲρ ταύτης ἀντίδοσιν παρὰ τοῦ Θεοῦ τῶν ὅλων κομίσηται.

l. 12 παρὰ τοῦ Θεοῦ *N* : π. Θ. *scr. Onor. A, edd.*

a. *Cf.* Mk 4.35–39.

98. To Pancharius[1]

We are distressed at the sight of the churches on the rough sea, but it has always been the way of their Master and Helmsman to make use of towering waves to display among men the wisdom and might that belong to him alone. In a single moment, he rebukes the winds and makes all calm as he did when he was on the boat with the apostles.[a] Nonetheless, while we appreciate the might of our Savior and know about his other miracles, even when adversity befalls us, we express our gratitude and receive this as a gift sent from God, for we have been taught to make light of our present goods and to await those of the future. It is incumbent on Your Excellency to bring to bear your zeal for the faith of the apostles and thus win the reward it will bring from the God of the universe.

1. The addressee, otherwise unknown, must have been "a person of rank"; *v.* "Pancharius 2," *PLRE*, vol. 2, p. 828. On the form of address, "Your Excellency," *v. ep.* 5 n. 1; for the date and circumstances of this letter, *v. ep.* 92 n. 1 and *ep.* 97 n. 1.

99. ΚΛΑΥΔΙΑΝΩΙ ΑΝΤΙΓΡΑΦΕΙ

Οἶμαι καὶ Τὴν Σὴν εἰδέναι Μεγαλοπρέπειαν, καίτοι μηδέπω συναφθεῖσαν ἡμῖν, τῆς καθ' ἡμῶν γεγενημένης συκοφαντίας τὸ προφανές· πολλάκις γὰρ ἡμῶν ἐν ἐκκλησίᾳ διαλεγομένων ἀκήκοεν καὶ τὸν ἕνα Κύριον Ἰησοῦν κηρυττόντων καὶ δεικνύντων τά τε τῆς θεότητος τά τε τῆς ἀνθρωπότητος ἴδια· οὐ γὰρ εἰς δύο υἱοὺς τὸν ἕνα διαιροῦμεν, ἀλλ', ἕνα Μονογενῆ προσκυνοῦντες, σαρκὸς καὶ θεότητος δείκνυμεν τὸ διάφορον· τοῦτο δέ, ὡς οἶμαι, καὶ οἱ τὰ Ἀρείου φρονοῦντες ὁμολογοῦσιν, καὶ οὐ καλοῦσι τὴν σάρκα *θεότητα* οὔτε μὴν τὴν θεότητα *σάρκα* προσαγορεύουσιν, σαφῶς γὰρ ἡμᾶς ἡ θεία Γραφὴ καὶ ταύτην κἀκείνην διδάσκει τὴν φύσιν· ἀλλ' ὅμως, τούτων οὕτω παρ' ἡμῶν εἰρημένων ἀεί, ψευδεῖς τινες καθ' ἡμῶν ὑφαίνουσι λόγους. ἡμεῖς δέ, τῷ συνειδότι θαρροῦντες καὶ μάρτυρα τῆς διδασκαλίας ἔχοντες τῶν ἐννοιῶν *τὸν … Ἐπόπτην*,[a] *ἱστὸν ἀράχνης*,[b] κατὰ τὸν προφήτην, ὑπολαμβάνομεν τὰ τῆς συκοφαντίας ὑφάσματα· ἐκεῖνο γὰρ προσμένομεν τὸ κριτήριον τὸ μὴ δεόμενον λόγων, ἀλλὰ δῆλα ποιοῦν τὰ τέως λανθάνοντα.[c]

Ταῦτα διὰ τῶν θεοφιλεστάτων ἐπισκόπων γράφω, προὔργου νομίσας προσειπεῖν Τὴν Σὴν δι' αὐτῶν Μεγαλοπρέπειαν καὶ τῆς ὑποσχέσεως ἀναμνῆσαι· οὐδὲ γὰρ πολεμούμενος τοῦ θηρεύειν ἀπέχομαι· οἶδα γὰρ καὶ τοὺς ἱεροὺς ἀποστόλους μετὰ τοῦ βάλλεσθαι τῇ πνευματικῇ σαγήνῃ χρησαμένους ἀεί.[d]

a. Est D.2 (LXX) (*Cf.* 3Macc 2.21.) b. Is 59.5 c. *Cf.* 1Cor 4.5. d. *Cf.* Mt 13.47.

99. To Claudian, the Bureau Chief[1]

I suppose that even Your Excellency, though not yet one of us,[2] perceives the blatant lie in the accusation that has been brought against us. On many occasions you have heard us preach in church, proclaiming the one Lord Jesus and pointing out the properties peculiar to the godhead and the humanity. We do not, in fact, divide the one Son into two, but, while adoring the one Only-begotten, point out the difference between flesh and godhead—that much I suppose even the Arians confess; they don't call the flesh "godhead" or the godhead "flesh," for there is no ambiguity in the teaching of the holy Scripture regarding each of these two natures—nonetheless, though we have always said this, some people have been weaving a tissue of lies against us. On our side, buoyed by conscience and having the One who sees our thoughts[a] to bear witness to our teaching, we dismiss this fabric of false accusation as, to use the word of the prophet, "a spider's web,"[b] since we await that tribunal that has no need of words, but makes manifest things till then hidden.[c]

I am sending this letter by the hands of the bishops beloved of God, as I thought it worthwhile to greet Your Excellency through them and to remind you of your promise. You see, embattled as I am, I shall not give up my hunting, as I know how the holy apostles continued to ply their spiritual net[d] even while under assault.

1. On Claudian, *v. ep.* 41 n. 1; for the date and circumstances of this letter, *v. ep.* 92 n. 1.

2. Jackson, followed by Azéma, renders the participial clause καίτοι μηδέπω συναφθεῖσαν ἡμῖν as though it referred to a face-face encounter ("although you have not yet met me" / "bien qu'elle ne nous ait pas encore rencontré"). Yet, Theodoret here mentions that Claudian had often heard him preach, so it would seem likely that they had already met. As Azéma notes, in the conclusion of this letter and in that of *ep.* 59, Theodoret refers to a promise that Claudian has made him; this Azéma takes to be a promise to convert to Christianity ("sa promesse de se convertir"; *v.* vol. 2, pp. 136f., n. 4). But the promise is more probably that of receiving baptism. Claudian is a catechumen, but has yet to take the step of becoming a member of the Christian community.

100. ΑΛΕΞΑΝΔΡΑΙ

Ἐδεξάμην πρώην Τῆς Ὑμετέρας Σεμνοπρεπείας τὰ γράμματα καί, μαθὼν τὴν γεγενημένην ὑμῖν ὑπὲρ ἡμῶν σπουδήν, χάριν ὡμολόγησα καὶ τὸν τῶν ὅλων Δεσπότην ἱκέτευσα καὶ τὰ παρόντα ὑμῖν ἀγαθὰ φυλάξαι, καὶ ταῖς προσθήκαις αὐξῆσαι, καὶ τῶν μελλόντων καὶ αἰωνίων χαρίσασθαι τὴν ἀπόλαυσιν. πιστεύομεν δὲ αὐτὸν καὶ τῶν περιωρισμένων ἀκούειν, μᾶλλον δὲ πολλῷ πλέον τούτων, ἐπειδὴ διὰ τὴν θείαν αὐτοῦ διδασκαλίαν τὴν δοκοῦσαν ὑπομένουσιν αἰτίαν. ταῦτα διὰ τῶν θεοφιλεστάτων ἐπισκόπων γράφω, παρακαλῶν τῆς ὑμετέρας αὐτοὺς ἀπολαῦσαι κηδεμονίας· τῆς γὰρ εὐαγγελικῆς ἕνεκα πίστεως καὶ τῆς τῶν ἐκκλησιῶν χάριν εἰρήνης τὴν μακρὰν ταύτην ἀποδημίαν εἵλοντο.

Title Ἀλεξάνδρᾳ *Cir., edd.* : -ρα *NZ; cf. c. n. ad tit. ep. 14.*

100. To Alexandra[1]

When I just lately received Your Ladyship's letter and learned of your effort on our behalf, I prayed a prayer of thanksgiving and begged the Master of the universe to keep secure the blessings you now possess, to add to these new ones, and to grant you the enjoyment of eternal blessings to come. We are confident that he listens to the prayers of those who have been subjected to relegation, indeed that he pays them special heed, since it is because of his divine teaching that they are laboring under what looks like a charge of misconduct. I am sending this letter by the hands of the bishops beloved of God, to beg you to put them under your care, as they have chosen to undertake this long journey for the sake of the gospel faith and for the peace of the churches.

1. As *N* identifies the recipient of *ep.* 14 as "Alexandria" and the recipient of this letter as "-dra," Theodoret may well have written two different women with very similar names. Even if Garnier's emendation of the inscription of *ep.* 14 (*v.* c. n. *ad loc.*) be correct, it would still be hazardous to identify the two. For the date and circumstances of this letter, *v. ep.* 92 n. 1.

101. ΚΕΛΕΡΙΝΗΙ ΔΙΑΚΟΝΩΙ

Ἐξήφθη πάλιν ὁ καθ' ἡμῶν πόλεμος, καί, σμικρὸν ἐνδούς, ὁ τῶν ἀνθρώπων ἀλάστωρ πάλιν ὥπλικεν καθ' ἡμῶν τοὺς τῷ ψεύδει συντεθραμμένους,[a] οἵ, προφανῶς ἡμᾶς συκοφαντοῦντες, εἰς δύο λέγουσιν μερίζειν ἡμᾶς υἱοὺς τὸν ἕνα Κύριον ἡμῶν Ἰησοῦν Χριστόν. ἡμεῖς δὲ θεότητος μὲν καὶ ἀνθρωπότητος τὸ διάφορον ἐπιστάμεθα, ἕνα δὲ ὁμολογοῦμεν Υἱόν, τὸν ἐνανθρωπήσαντα Θεὸν Λόγον, καὶ αὐτὸν εἶναί φαμεν Θεὸν προαιώνιον καὶ ἄνθρωπον *ἐπ' ἐσχάτου τῶν ἡμερῶν*[b] γενόμενον οὐ τῇ τροπῇ τῆς θεότητος, ἀλλὰ τῇ προσλήψει τῆς ἀνθρωπότητος. ἀλλὰ γὰρ περιττὸν ποιῶ, Τὴν Σὴν διδάσκων Φιλοθεΐαν ἅπερ φρονῶ, τὴν ἀκριβῶς εἰδυῖαν ἅπερ κηρύττομεν καὶ τοὺς ἀγνοοῦντας διδάσκομεν.

Παρακαλῶ τοίνυν, ἐπειδὴ πάντων ὁμοῦ τῶν τῆς Ἀνατολῆς θεοφιλεστάτων ἐπισκόπων κατέχεαν τὴν λοιδορίαν οἱ τοῦ ψεύδους ἐργάται καὶ τὰς ἐκκλησίας ζάλης ἐνέπλησαν, τὴν δυνατὴν ὑπὲρ τῶν εὐαγγελικῶν δογμάτων καὶ τῆς τῶν ἐκκλησιῶν εἰρήνης εἰσενεγκεῖν σπουδὴν Τὴν Σὴν Θεοσέβειαν. διὰ γὰρ δὴ ταῦτα καὶ οἱ θεοφιλέστατοι ἐπίσκοποι καὶ τὰς ὑπ' αὐτῶν ποιμαινομένας κατέλιπον ἐκκλησίας, καὶ τῆς τοῦ χειμῶνος κατεφρόνησαν ὥρας, καὶ τῶν τῆς ὁδοιπορίας ἠνέσχοντο πόνων ἵνα τὸν ἐπαναστάντα καταπαύσωσιν χειμῶνα, οὓς εὖ οἶδ' ὅτι ὄψεταί Σου Ἡ κατὰ Θεὸν Τελειότης εὐσεβείας προμάχους καὶ τῶν ἐκκλησιῶν κυβερνήτας.

l. 12 διδάσκομεν *codd., edd.* : -ουσαν *coni. J.P.* = *"Your Piety, who is well informed of what we preach and explains that to the uninformed." I think it likely that in this passsage Thdt. is presenting Celerina as well informed in doctrinal matters and capable of explaining his true positions to those who imagine he is teaching heresy; i.e. that she is doing precisely what he asks* (*ep.* 83.2) *of Eusebius of Ancyra: Ταῦτα τοίνυν μαθοῦσα παρ' ἡμῶν Ἡ Ἁγιότης Σου, διδαξάτω τοὺς ἀγνοοῦντας. This reading would give particular point to the preceding ἀλλὰ γὰρ περιττὸν ποιῶ. Cf. also in Ps. 106.21f.* (*PG, vol. 80, col. 1744, ll. 12–14*)*: Χρὴ δὲ μὴ μόνους εἰδέναι τὰς θείας θαυματουργίας, ἀλλὰ καὶ τοὺς ἀγνοοῦντας διδάσκειν. For the act. pt. fem. sg., v. H. rel., Vita 30.1:* [*Δομνίνα*] *παντὸς ἑτέρου χωρίου τὸν ἀφιερωμένον τῷ θεῷ χῶρον σεβασμιώτερον εἶναι καὶ ὑπολαμβάνουσα καὶ τοὺς ἄλλους διδάσκουσα. The change to the indic. first pl. would be an easy banalization. Yet the reading of N is clear and gives acceptable sense.*

a. *Cf.* Jn 8.44. b. Heb 1.2 (*Cf.* Nm 24.14; Jer 23.20; 25.19.)

101. To Celerina, the Deaconess[1]

The war against us has burst into flame again, and the destroyer of mankind,[2] after a brief retreat, has once more armed against us the offspring of the liar,[a] and these, making blatantly false accusations, go around saying that we divide our one Lord Jesus Christ into two sons. Now, we perceive the difference between godhead and humanity, but we confess one Son, God the Word who became man, and we declare that he is both God before all ages and a man born "at the end of days"[b] not by changing his godhead, but by assuming humanity. But I waste time explaining my positions to Your Piety, who is well informed of what we preach, and what we teach to the uninformed.

So, as the workers of falsehood, defaming all the bishops of the East beloved of God with the same accusation, have filled the churches with a violent storm, I entreat Your Reverence to bring to bear all possible zeal on behalf of the gospel teaching and the peace of the churches. Indeed, these bishops, beloved of God, have left behind the churches they shepherd, and, without so much as a thought for the wintry weather, undertaken the travails of this journey for this very reason—to put an end to the storm that has swept down on us. These, I feel sure, Your Godly Perfection will regard as champions of orthodoxy and helmsmen of the churches.

1. We know of the deaconess Celerina only from this letter. On the office of deaconess, *v. ep.* 17 n. 1; for the date and circumstances of this letter, *v. ep.* 92 n. 1.

2. Theodoret makes frequent use of this phrase ("the destroyer of mankind" = ὁ τῶν ἀνθρώπων ἀλάστωρ) and variations of it to refer to the devil. For the theme here developed, that of the devil rousing his human allies to make an assault on truth, *v.* also his comment on 2Tm 3.13.

102. ΒΑΣΙΛΕΙΩΙ ΕΠΙΣΚΟΠΩΙ

Τὸ μὲν τοὺς ἀγνοοῦντας ἡμᾶς σιγῇ τῶν καθ' ἡμῶν ἀκούειν λοιδοριῶν οὐδὲν ἀπεικός, τὸ δὲ Τὴν Σὴν Ὁσιότητα τῶν λοιδορουμένων μὴ διελέγχειν τὸ ψεῦδος ἢ μετρίως τοῦτο ποιεῖν καὶ μὴ λίαν ἐκθύμως, οὐκ ἄν τις πιστεύσαι τὴν ἡμετέραν συνήθειαν ἐπιστάμενος, οὐκ ἐπειδὴ τῆς ἀληθείας δεῖ τὴν φιλίαν προκρίνειν, ἀλλ' ὅτι τῇ φιλίᾳ καὶ ἡ τῆς ἀληθείας πρόσεστιν μαρτυρία· καὶ γὰρ ἐπ' ἐκκλησίας λεγόντων ἡμῶν πολλάκις ἀκήκοεν Ἡ Σὴ Θεοσέβεια καί, ἐν συλλόγοις ἑτέροις δογματικῶν ἡμῖν κινηθέντων λόγων, τοὺς παρ' ἡμῶν εἰρημένους ἐπήκουσεν, καὶ οὐκ οἶδα πώποτε μεμψαμένην ἡμῖν, ὡς οὐκ ὀρθοῖς δόγμασιν κέχρημαι, Τὴν Σὴν Θεοσέβειαν.

Τί τοίνυν ἐπὶ τοῦ παρόντος γεγένηται; τί δήποτε μὴ κινεῖς, ὦ φίλη κεφαλή, κατὰ τοῦ ψεύδους τὴν γλῶτταν, ἀλλὰ καὶ φίλον συκοφαντούμενον, καὶ τὴν ἀλήθειαν πολεμουμένην ὑπερορᾷς; εἰ μὲν ὡς ἀπόρων καὶ λίαν σμικρῶν ἀμελῶν, τῆς δεσποτικῆς ἐντολῆς ἐπακοῦσαι προσήκει διαρρήδην βοώσης, *Ὁρᾶτε μὴ καταφρονήσητε ἑνὸς τῶν μικρῶν τούτων*[a] τῶν ἐλαχίστων *τῶν πιστευόντων εἰς ἐμέ·*[b] ἀμὴν *γὰρ λέγω ὑμῖν … οἱ ἄγγελοι αὐτῶν* … καθ' ἡμέραν ὁρῶσιν *τὸ πρόσωπον τοῦ πατρὸς* ὑμῶν *τοῦ ἐν*

l. 4 πιστεύσαι *scripsi* : -σοι *codd., edd. Thdt. is unlikely to have employed a fut. opt. with* ἄν *in an apodosis of an unexpressed condition, i.e. to express the idea of potentiality; v. the entirely classical formulation in Affect. 1.86 (l. 8): Πῶς δ' ἂν πιστεύσαι,* (*i.e. a pagan receiving instruction in Christianity*) *μὴ πρότερον ἐξορίσας τῆς διανοίας τὰ κακῶς προεντεθέντα μαθήματα; For further exx., v. Eran. dial. 3* (*p. 219, ll. 10–12 and p. 214, ll. 27f.*). **l. 19** ὑμῶν *NZ* : μου *scr. Cir., edd.* = "'*their angels every day behold the face of my Father who is in heaven.*'" *Ciriaco has probably made a deliberate correction of the reading he found in Z, but it must be admitted that the choice of pronoun is not certain. Thdt. quoted this dominical word in five other places; in two* (*Cant. cant. ad 1.8 and Eran. dial. 1, p. 74, l. 12*) *editors have printed the gen. of the pl. second per., in three* (*Q. in Gen. 3, 20.2; Haer. com. 5.7*) *the gen. of the first per. sg. It is impossible to argue that one or the other would come more naturally to Thdt.; he quoted other passages of this gospel in which both forms occur* (*e.g., Mt 5.45: τοῦ πατρὸς ὑμῶν*

a. Mt 18.10 b. Mt 18.6

102. To Bishop Basil[1]

There would be no reason to be surprised if people unacquainted with us were to listen to the abuse that is heaped on us without saying a word, but no one who knew of our friendship could possibly believe that Your Holiness would not be refuting the lie circulated by my abusers, or even that you would refute it in measured words rather than heated vehemence—not that friendship is to be given priority to truth, but because friendship is supported by the witness of the truth. After all, Your Reverence has often listened to us preaching in church and has heard what we have said in other gatherings where issues of doctrine have been discussed among us, and I cannot think of a single occasion on which Your Reverence has rebuked us for holding unsound doctrine. So, what is to explain this present situation? For what conceivable reason, dear friend, aren't you speaking out against this lie, but looking the other way when a friend is under false accusation, and the truth under attack? If your lack of concern is due to our weakness and insignificance, you ought to pay attention to the commandment of our Master enjoining in no uncertain terms, "See that you not look down on one of these little ones,"[a] "the least of those who believe in me";[b] "amen, I say unto you, their angels every day behold the face of your Father, who is in

1. On Basil, *v. ep.* 85 n. 1.

οὐρανοῖς,[c] εἰ δὲ τῶν κατηγορούντων ἡμᾶς ἡ δύναμις Τῇ Σῇ Φιλοθεΐᾳ τὴν σιωπὴν πραγματεύεται, χρὴ τῆς ἑτέρας ἀκοῦσαι νομοθεσίας λεγούσης, *Οὐ* λήψῃ *πρόσωπον … δυνάστου*·[d] καί, *Δικαίαν κρίσιν* κρίνατε·[e] καί, *Οὐκ ἔσῃ μετὰ* πολλῶν *ἐπὶ κακίᾳ*·[f] καί, *Καμμύων τοὺς ὀφθαλμοὺς* αὐτοῦ, *ἵνα μὴ ἴδῃ ἀδικίαν*, καὶ κλείων *τὰ ὦτα* αὐτοῦ *ἵνα μὴ ἀκούσῃ κρίσιν αἵματος* ἀδίκου.[g] καὶ ἕτερα δὲ μυρία τοιαῦτα ἔστιν εὑρεῖν παρὰ τῇ θείᾳ Γραφῇ, ἃ περιττὸν ὑπέλαβον συλλέξαι, πρὸς ἄνδρα γράφων τοῖς θείοις ἐντεθραμμένον λογίοις καὶ τὴν διδασκαλικὴν ἀρδείαν προσφέροντα τοῖς φιλοχρίστοις λαοῖς. τοῦτο τοίνυν μόνον ἐρῶ· ὅτι πάντες παραστησόμεθα τῷ βήματι τοῦ Χριστοῦ καὶ τῶν λόγων καὶ τῶν ἔργων τὰς εὐθύνας ὑφέξομεν.[h] ἐγὼ δέ, τῶν ἄλλων ἕνεκα πάντων τοῦτο δεδιὼς τὸ κριτήριον,[i] ἐν τοῖς καθ' ἡμῶν λεγομένοις ἐκ τῆς τούτου μνήμης λαμβάνω τῆς ψυχαγωγίας τὰς ἀφορμάς.

τοῦ ἐν οὐρανοῖς; 7.21 and 10.33: τοῦ πατρός μου τοῦ ἐν οὐρανοῖς), and it is not clear that one makes better sense in this context. Yet, ὑμῶν *may possibly have a claim to be the lect. diff., since, the formulation with the first person sg. pron. is the predominant tradition of Mt 18.10; the editors of the NTG list no witnesses for* ὑμῶν.

c. Mt 18.10 (NT var.)
d. Lv 19.15 (LXX var.)
e. Jn 7.24 (NT var.)
f. Ex 23.2 (LXX var.)
g. Is 33.15 (LXX var.)
h. *Cf.* 2Cor 5.10.
i. *Cf.* 1Cor 4.4.

heaven."[c] But if the influence wielded by our accusers is the cause of Your Piety's silence, you must give heed to the law of the Old Testament, which says, "You will not defer to the great,"[d] and "Judge righteous judgment,"[e] and "You will not join a mob to do evil,"[f] and "Shutting his eyes so as not to contemplate injustice and closing his ears tight so as not to hear the unjust sentence of death."[g] One could find thousands of passages like these in the holy Scripture, but I thought it unnecessary to collect them all in a letter to a man who was raised on the divine oracles and himself pours the waters of instruction into the ears of the Christian laity. I shall say only this: that all of us will stand before the bench of Christ to give an account of our words and deeds.[h] As for me, though I dread that tribunal for every other reason,[i] I find good grounds for consolation when I call it to mind in the midst of this talk that has been raised against us.

103. ΑΠΟΛΛΩΝΙΩΙ ΚΟΜΗΤΙ

Τοὺς μὲν θεοφιλεστάτους ἐπισκόπους εἰς τὴν βασιλεύουσαν εἵλκυσε πόλιν ἡ κατὰ πάντων ἡμῶν γεγενημένη συκοφαντία, ἐγὼ δὲ διὰ Τῆς Αὐτῶν Ὁσιότητος Τῇ Σῇ Μεγαλοπρεπείᾳ προσφέρω τὴν πρόσρησιν. καὶ τῆς φιλίας ἐκτίνω τὸ χρέος, οὐχ ἵνα τὸ τριπόθητον ὄφλημα διαλύσω, ἀλλ᾽ ἵνα πλέον ἐργάσωμαι· τὰ γὰρ τῆς φιλίας ὀφλήματα διὰ τῆς ἐκτίσεως αὔξεται. τὸ μέντοι καὶ ἡμᾶς τῶν τῆς συκοφαντίας ἀπολαῦσαι καρπῶν οὐδὲν ἀπεικός· ἄνθρωπον γὰρ ὄντα πάντα δεῖ προσδοκᾶν. τούτου δὴ χάριν τοῖς φιλοσοφεῖν δεδιδαγμένοις τὰ τοιαῦτα πάντα ἐστὶν φορητά, ἓν δὲ μόνον ἀνιαρόν, τὸ λώβης τινὸς μεταλαχεῖν τὴν ψυχήν.

103. To Count Apollonius[1]

The bishops beloved of God have been dragged all the way to the capital city by the false accusation raised against all of us, and, through the intermediary of Their Holinesses, I dispatch a greeting to Your Excellency. Thus, I make full payment on my debt of friendship—not to eliminate a debt so dear to my heart, but to make it even greater, as debts of friendship increase as they're paid off. Of course, there's no reason for surprise in the fact that even we're reaping a harvest of false accusation,[2] since, human as we are, we must expect everything. For those who have learned their philosophy, all such troubles are bearable, and one thing only is a real cause of distress: to suffer some harm to one's soul.

1. For Apollonius, *cf. ep.* 73 n. 1, and for the date and circumstances of this letter, *v. ep.* 92 n. 1.

2. Given the popular derivation of the term συκοφαντία (*v. ep.* 21 n. 6), there is a coherence in Theodoret's metaphor of harvesting (τῆς συκοφαντίας ἀπολαῦσαι καρπῶν) that cannot be reproduced in the English.

104. ΦΛΑΒΙΑΝΩΙ ΕΠΙΣΚΟΠΩΙ ΚΩΝΣΤΑΝΤΙΝΟΥΠΟΛΕΩΣ

(1) Καὶ ἤδη Σου Τὴν Ἁγιότητα δι᾽ ἑτέρων ἐδίδαξα γραμμάτων ὡς ἄντικρυς ἡμᾶς συκοφαντοῦσιν οἱ τῆς ἡμετέρας κατηγοροῦντες διδασκαλίας, καὶ νῦν δὲ ὡσαύτως διὰ τῶν θεοφιλεστάτων ἐπισκόπων τοῦτο ποιῶ, καὶ αὐτοὺς μάρτυρας ἔχων τῆς τῶν δογμάτων ὀρθότητος, καὶ ἑτέρας πολλὰς μυριάδας ἀνθρώπων οἳ τῶν ἡμετέρων ἐν ταῖς κατὰ τὴν ἑῴαν ἐκκλησίαις ἐπαΐουσι λόγων, καί, πρὸ τούτων, τὸ συνειδὸς καὶ *τὸν* τοῦ συνειδότος *Ἐπόπτην.*[a] οἶδα δὲ καὶ τὸν θεῖον Ἀπόστολον πολλάκις τῇ τοῦ συνειδότος μαρτυρίᾳ χρησάμενον· *Ἡ γὰρ καύχησις ἡμῶν αὕτη ἐστίν, τὸ μαρτύριον τῆς συνειδήσεως ἡμῶν*·[b] καὶ πάλιν, *Ἀλήθειαν λέγω ἐν Χριστῷ, οὐ ψεύδομαι, συμμαρτυρούσης μοι τῆς συνειδήσεώς μου ἐν Πνεύματι Ἁγίῳ.*[c]

Ἴστω τοίνυν ἡ ἱερά σου καὶ θεοφιλὴς κεφαλὴ ὡς οὐδεὶς ἡμῶν ἀκήκοεν πώποτε δύο κηρυττόντων υἱούς· τῷ ὄντι γάρ μοι μυσαρὸν καὶ δυσσεβὲς τόδε τὸ δόγμα δοκεῖ· *εἷς* γὰρ *Κύριος Ἰησοῦς Χριστός, δι᾽ οὗ τὰ πάντα.*[d] τοῦτον ἐγὼ καὶ Θεὸν προαιώνιον οἶδα καὶ ἄνθρωπον *ἐπ᾽ ἐσχάτου τῶν ἡμερῶν*[e] καὶ μίαν, ὡς Μονογενεῖ, προσφέρω προσκύνησιν. σαρκὸς μέντοι καὶ θεότητος τὸ διάφορον ἐδιδάχθην· ἀσύγχυτος γὰρ ἡ ἕνωσις. οὕτω κατὰ τῆς Ἀρείου καὶ Εὐνομίου παρατεταττόμενοι λύττης, ῥᾷστα τὴν κατὰ τοῦ Μονογενοῦς παρ᾽ αὐτῶν τολμωμένην διελέγχομεν βλασφημίαν, τὰ ταπεινῶς εἰρημένα παρὰ τοῦ Δεσπότου καὶ τῇ ληφθείσῃ φύσει προσφόρως ὡς ἀνθρώπῳ προσάπτοντες, καὶ αὖ

l. 20 παρατατтόμενοι *Onor. A, Az.* : -ραττό- *N* **l. 20** λύττης $N^{s.l.m1}$, *Az.* : λύτταις $N^{i.l.}$

a. Est D.2 (LXX; LXX var.) (*Cf.* 3Macc 2.21.)
b. 2Cor 1.12
c. Rom 9.1
d. 1Cor 8.6
e. Heb 1.2 (*Cf.* Nm 24.14; Jer 23.20; 25.19.)

104. To Flavian, Bishop of Constantinople[1]

(1) I have indicated to Your Sanctity in a previous letter that those bringing charges against our teaching are engaging in a blatantly false accusation,[2] and I am now doing this once more through the intermediary of these bishops beloved of God. I can call on them as witnesses to the orthodoxy of my teaching, on many thousands of others who hear my addresses in the churches of the East, and more importantly, on my own conscience and the One who sees into the conscience.[a] I know that the holy Apostle also made frequent appeal to the witness of his conscience: "For our boast consists in just this, the witness of our conscience";[b] and again, "I speak the truth in Christ—I do not lie—and my conscience bears me witness in the Holy Spirit."[c]

I would have you know, man holy and beloved of God, that no one has ever heard me preaching two sons. Indeed, that teaching seems to me a piece of loathsome irreligion, "for there is one Lord Jesus Christ, through whom are all things."[d] I know that he is both God before all ages and man "at the end of the days,"[e] and to him as Only-begotten I offer a single act of worship. Yet I have been taught to see the difference between the flesh and the godhead, for theirs is an unmingled union.[3] When we take our stand against the madness of Arius and Eunomius, it is an easy matter to confute the blasphemy of their reckless utterance against the Only-begotten; we apply to our Master as man those declarations of his that are humble and appropriate to the nature that was assumed and then apply to him

1. On Flavian, *v. ep.* 11 n. 1, and for the date and circumstances of this letter, *v. ep.* 92 n. 1.

2. This previous letter has been lost, unless, perhaps, Theodoret is referring to *ep.* 86, a draft of which he most likely composed for his metropolitan Domnus (*v. ep.* 86 n. 1).

3. Theodoret is here citing the "Formula of Reunion," in which he had made use of the adjective ἀσύγχυτος; the adverbial form will figure among the four key adverbs of the definition of Chalcedon; *v.* Intro., sec. 5.11.

πάλιν ὡς Θεῷ τὰ θεοπρεπῆ καὶ τῆς φύσεως ἐκείνης δηλωτικά, οὐκ εἰς δύο πρόσωπα διαιροῦντες, ἀλλὰ τῷ ἑνὶ Μονογενεῖ καὶ ταῦτα κἀκεῖνα προσήκειν διδάσκοντες· τὰ μὲν ὡς Θεῷ καὶ Ποιητῇ καὶ Δεσπότῃ τῶν ὅλων, τὰ δὲ ὡς ἀνθρώπῳ δι᾽ ἡμᾶς γενομένῳ.[f] ἄνθρωπον δὲ αὐτὸν ἡ θεία λέγει γεγενῆσθαι Γραφή,[g] οὐ τῆς θεότητος τραπείσης, ἀλλὰ τῆς ἀνθρωπίνης φύσεως ἐκ σπέρματος Ἀβραὰμ ληφθείσης· τοῦτο γὰρ ὁ θεῖος Ἀπόστολος ἄντικρυς βοᾷ, λέγων, *Οὐ γὰρ δήπου ἀγγέλων ἐπιλαμβάνεται, ἀλλὰ σπέρματος Ἀβραὰμ ἐπιλαμβάνεται, ὅθεν ὤφειλεν κατὰ πάντα τοῖς ἀδελφοῖς ὁμοιωθῆναι·*[h] καὶ πάλιν, *Τῷ δὲ Ἀβραὰμ ἐρρέθησαν αἱ ἐπαγγελίαι καὶ τῷ σπέρματι αὐτοῦ. οὐ λέγει, Καὶ τοῖς σπέρμασιν, ὡς ἐπὶ πολλῶν, ἀλλ᾽ ὡς ἐφ᾽ ἑνός, Καὶ τῷ σπέρματί σου, ὅς ἐστι Χριστός.*[i]

(2) Ταῦτα καὶ τὰ τοιαῦτα τῆς θείας Γραφῆς περικόψαντες, Σίμων, καὶ Βασιλείδης, καὶ Βαλεντῖνος, καὶ Βαρδησάνης, καὶ Μαρκίων, καὶ ὁ τῆς μανίας ἐπώνυμος μόνον *Θεὸν* ἀποκαλοῦσι τὸν Δεσπότην Χριστὸν οὐδὲν ἀνθρώπειον ἔχοντα, ἀλλὰ φαντασίᾳ καὶ δοκήσει φανέντα τοῖς ἀνθρώποις ὡς ἄνθρωπον. οἱ δὲ τὰ Ἀρείου καὶ Εὐνομίου φρονοῦντες σῶμα μόνον ἀνειληφέναι τὸν Θεὸν Λόγον φασίν, αὐτὸν δὲ τῆς ψυχῆς ἐν τῷ σώματι πληρῶσαι τὴν χρείαν. Ἀπολινάριος δὲ *ἔμψυχον*[j] μὲν τὸ Δεσποτικὸν σῶμα καλεῖ, τὸν δὲ νοῦν τῆς γεγενημένης σωτηρίας ἀποστερεῖ, οὐκ οἶδα πόθεν μαθὼν ψυχῆς καὶ νοῦ τὴν διαίρεσιν, ἡ δὲ τῶν θείων ἀποστόλων διδασκαλία ψυχὴν λογικήν τε καὶ νοερὰν μετὰ σαρκὸς προσειλῆφθαι διδάσκει καὶ τελείαν τοῖς πιστεύουσιν ὑπισχνεῖται τὴν σωτηρίαν.

f. *Cf. Pac. form.* g. Jn 1.14; Phil 2.6f. h. Heb 2.16f. i. Gal 3.16
j. *V., e.g.,* Gr. nyss., *Antir.* vol. 3.1, p. 140, l. 20 - p. 141, l. 7; p. 208, ll. 23–27; p. 210, ll. 7f.; p. 213, ll. 1–3; p. 215, ll. 14–17.

as God those that are worthy of divinity and indicative of the divine nature. We do not divide him into two persons, but teach that the former and the latter pertain to the sole Only-begotten, some as God and Creator and Master of the universe, others as man born on our account.[f] Holy Scripture declares that he became man,[g] not as though the divinity underwent a change, but by the assumption of the human nature from the seed of Abraham. This is what the holy Apostle cries out: "For, of course, it is not the angels that he takes to himself, but the seed of Abraham. Thus, he had to be made like his brethren in all things";[h] and again, "The promises were spoken to Abraham and to his seed. Scripture does not say 'and to your seeds' with reference to many, but with reference to one 'and to your seed,' and that is Christ."[i]

(2) Trimming away these passages of holy Scripture and others like them, Simon, Basilides, Valentinus, Bardaisan, Marcion, and the one whose very name has become a word for manic insanity,[4] refer to our Master Christ only as "God," as though he had nothing of humanity but manifested himself to men as man in nothing but an image without substance.[5] Then the Arians and Eunomians declare that God the Word assumed a body but no more, and that he himself performed the function of soul in that body. Next, Apollinaris applies the term "ensouled" to the body of our Master,[j] but excludes our mind from the benefit of salvation with his distinction of soul and mind that he picked up who knows where. The teaching of the holy apostles holds that a rational intelligent mind was also assumed and thus promises those who believe a salvation that is complete.[6]

4. Theodoret is referring to Mani (216–76), the founder of a dualistic religion based on gnostic Christian and Zoroastrian ideas; *v.* Rudolph, "Mani, Manichaeans." In a pun that is certainly more than a jest, he derives the common noun "mania" (μανία) from the proper noun "Mani" (Μάνης).

5. Theodoret places these six very various early Christian figures in the category of docetics; *v. ep.* 81 n. 3. He devotes a short discussion to each in book one of his *Haer. com.*: Simon (sec. 1); Basilides (sec. 4); Valentinus (sec. 7); Bardaisan (sec. 22); Marcion (sec. 24); Mani (sec. 26).

6. Theodoret's persistent criticism of the incomplete acknowledgment of the

Ἔστιν δὲ καὶ ἕτερον στῖφος αἱρετικῶν, τἀναντία τούτοις θρησκεῦον· Φωτεινὸς γάρ, καὶ Μάρκελλος, καὶ ὁ ἐκ Σαμοσάτων Παῦλος ἄνθρωπον μόνον εἶναι λέγουσιν τὸν Κύριον ἡμῶν καὶ Θεόν. ἀνάγκη δέ, πρὸς τούτους μὲν διαλεγομένους ἡμᾶς, τὰς περὶ θεότητος μαρτυρίας προσφέρειν καὶ δεικνύναι ὡς καὶ Θεὸς προαιώνιος ὁ Δεσπότης Χριστός, πρὸς δὲ τὴν ἑτέραν ἀγωνιζομένους συμμορίαν ἣ *Θεὸν* μόνον ἀποκαλεῖ τὸν Κύριον ἡμῶν Ἰησοῦν Χριστόν, τὴν θείαν αὐτοῖς ἀντιτάττειν Γραφὴν καὶ τὰς περὶ τῆς ληφθείσης ἀνθρωπότητος ἐκεῖθεν μαρτυρίας συλλέγειν· χρὴ γὰρ τὸν ἰατρὸν ἁρμοδίοις πρὸς τὰ πάθη κεχρῆσθαι φαρμάκοις καὶ ἑκάστῳ προσφέρειν τὸ πρόσφορον.

Παρακαλῶ τοίνυν Τὴν Σὴν Ἁγιωσύνην τὴν καθ' ἡμῶν συντεθεῖσαν διαλῦσαι συκοφαντίαν καὶ τὰς μάτην ἡμῖν λοιδορουμένας χαλινῶσαι γλώττας· ἡμεῖς γάρ, καὶ μετὰ τὴν ἐνανθρώπησιν, ἕνα προσκυνοῦμεν Υἱὸν τοῦ Θεοῦ, τὸν Κύριον ἡμῶν Ἰησοῦν Χριστόν, καὶ τοὺς ἄλλο τι φρονοῦντας *δυσσεβεῖς* ὀνομάζομεν. παρασχεῖν δὲ ἡμῖν καὶ τὰς ἁγίας σου προσευχάς, Δέσποτα, καταξίωσον ἵνα, τῆς θείας ἀπολαύοντες εὐμενείας, τὸ κινδύνων μεστὸν διαπεράσωμεν πέλαγος καὶ εἰς τοὺς ἀπηνέμους τοῦ Σωτῆρος μεθορμισθῶμεν λιμένας.

l. 55 ἑτέραν *corr. Car.?, scr. edd.* : ἡμετέραν *NZ*, A^{ac}*?* = *"when contending with our own faction," etc.* **l. 66** ἡμῖν *corr. Car., scr. edd.* : ἡμᾶς *NZ*, A^{ac} = *"Deign also, my Lord, that we give your holy prayers"*

There is a second troop of heretics, who take the opposite position. Photinus, Marcellus, and Paul of Samosata assert that our Lord and God was no more than a man.[7] So, when we are preaching against these, the task is to present the proof texts regarding the divinity and to demonstrate that our Master Christ is also God before all ages, and when contending against that other group, the one that uses only the designation "God" for our Lord Jesus Christ, we must confront them with a collection of proof texts from holy Scripture regarding the assumed humanity. A doctor must use remedies appropriate to the diseases and apply to each the one that suits the case.

So then, I urge Your Holiness to refute the false accusation that has been fabricated against us and to bridle the mouths that are slandering us with lies. As for us—even after the incarnation, we adore one Son of God, our Lord Jesus Christ[8] and term those who hold any other position "enemies of religion." I beseech you, Master, to grant us your holy prayers that, with the aid of God's favor, we may make our way across the perilous sea and find refuge in the tranquil harbors of our Savior.

---

humanity of Christ by Arius and Apollinaris is motivated by his soteriology, *i.e.* the conviction that any aspect of humanity not taken up in the incarnation will not have participated in the salvation effected by Christ; *v.* Koch, pp. 72f.; *cf. ep.* 144 n. 4.

7. For Paul of Samosata, *v.* Intro., sec. 2.4, esp. n. 134; for Marcellus of Ancyra, *v. ib.*, sec. 1.2, esp. n. 12; and for Photinus of Sirmium, *ib.*, esp. n. 15.

8. Theodoret likely refers to the apologia in defense of his own christological orthodoxy (Ὅτι καὶ μετὰ τὴν ἐνανθρώπησιν εἷς Υἱὸς ὁ Κύριος ἡμῶν Ἰησοῦς Χριστός = "That our Lord Jesus Christ is one Son even after the Incarnation"); *v. ep.* 16 n. 3 and *ep.* 92 n. 1.

105. ΕΥΛΟΓΙΩΙ ΟΙΚΟΝΟΜΙ

Τοὺς μὲν ὑπὲρ τῆς εὐσεβείας ἀγῶνας Τῆς Σῆς Φιλοθεΐας παρὰ πολλῶν μεμαθήκαμεν, δίκαιον δὲ καὶ τῷ διὰ ταύτην συκοφαντουμένῳ προθύμως συνηγορεῖν καὶ διελέγχειν τῶν λοιδορουμένων τὸ ψεῦδος· ἀκριβῶς γὰρ οἶσθα, θεοφιλέστατε, καὶ τίνα φρονοῦμεν, καὶ τίνα διδάσκομεν, καὶ ὅτι δύο κηρυττόντων υἱοὺς οὐδεὶς ἡμῶν ἀκήκοεν πώποτε. χρησάσθω[a] τοίνυν Ἡ Σὴ Θεοσέβεια κἀνταῦθα τῷ ζήλῳ καὶ ἐμφραξάτω στόματα *λαλούντων ἄδικα*· ἐν γὰρ τοῖς τοιούτοις ἀγῶσιν οὐ μόνον προσήκει τῶν φίλων, ἀλλὰ καὶ τῶν λελυπηκότων, ὑπερμαχεῖν.

l. 6 χρησάσθω *corr. Cir., scr. edd.* : -άτω *NZ*, A^{ac}. *Ciriaco's correction should be adopted. The TLG offers nineteen other attestations of the middle form (v., e.g., Est 1.19; Bas., ep. 240.2, and Ath., Inc. 48, l. 8), but the act. is attested only four times in late sources.*

a. Ps 63.11

105. To Eulogius, the Steward[1]

We have learned from many sources of Your Piety's contests on behalf of religion. And now it would be right for you to exert yourself in the defense of one under false accusation for his devotion to religion and to show up the lies of those who are covering him with abuse. You, of course, beloved of God, know very well our thoughts and our teachings, and that no one has ever heard us preaching two sons. Therefore, I beg Your Reverence to put your zeal to work in this case as well by shutting up the mouths "of those who speak injustice."[a] Indeed, in this sort of contest, it is our duty to take up the part not just of friends, but even of those who have done us harm.

1. Given the placement of *ep.* 105, Azéma (vol. 2, pp. 30f. n. 1) plausibly suggests that this was among the letters committed to the delegation of Syrian bishops; *v. ep.* 92 n. 1. If so, Eulogius was probably a priest of the capital. It is not chronologically impossible that he might be identified with the Eulogius who figures among twelve Constantinopolitan clerics who had sent a letter (*Coll. uat.* 86) to the Cyrillian faction at Ephesus to inform the council that they agreed to the deposition of Nestorius, and that they had announced his deposition to the laity; *cf.* Azéma, vol. 1, p. 40. A steward (οἰκονόμος) was a cleric whose duties might include the management of properties (especially land-holdings), the collection of revenues and the payment of expenses, and the maintenance of buildings for a diocese, a church, or a monastery; *v.* Magdalino and Talbot.

106. ΑΒΡΑΑΜΗΙ ΟΙΚΟΝΟΜΩΙ

Καὶ διὰ τῶν θεοφιλεστάτων ἐπισκόπων προσφθέγγομαί Σου Τὴν Θεοσέβειαν καὶ παρακαλῶ τῆς τῶν ἐκκλησιῶν φροντίσαι γαλήνης καὶ τῆς συκοφαντίας διαλῦσαι τὰ κύματα·[a] *Ὃ γὰρ ἂν σπείρῃ ἄνθρωπος, τοῦτο καὶ θερίσει,*[b] κατὰ τὸν θεῖον Ἀπόστολον. ὁ τοίνυν τῶν ἀποστολικῶν ὑπερμαχῶν δογμάτων δῆλον ὅτι τὴν ἀποστολικὴν εὐλογίαν τρυγήσει καὶ τῆς ἐκείνων ἀπολαύσεται κοινωνίας.

Title ἀβραάμῃ *scr. Cir.* : -μη *NZ* : -μῳ *scr. Sir. Nös. Az. The name of Thdt.'s addressee is unclear. If, as previous editors have assumed, his name is Ἀβραάμ (Abraham), one would not expect the form of the dat. first printed by Sirmond. Thdt. treats the name of the patriarch as invariable; indeed, the entirety of the TLG contains only five other exx. of a dat. of this name ending in -ῳ. If, however, the name of the recipient is Ἀβραάμης, a graecisized version of Ἀβραάμ (v. H. rel., ed. Canivet and Leroy-Molinghen, vol. 2, p. 35, n. 2), the expected form of the dat., though not elsewhere attested, would be that written by Ciriaco, i.e. only a very slight adjustment of the reading of NZ.*

a. *Cf.* Mk 4.35–39. b. Gal 6.7 (NT var.)

106. To Abrahames, the Steward[1]

I greet Your Reverence through these bishops beloved of God and urge you to take thought for the tranquility of the churches and to quell the waves of false accusation.[a] As the holy Apostle says, "As a man sows, so shall he reap."[b] Thus, we can be sure that the champion of the teachings of the apostles will gather for himself the blessing of the apostles and have the joy of their fellowship.

1. Abrahames must have been a cleric resident in the capital. On the date and circumstances of this letter, *v. ep.* 92 n. 1, and for the office of "steward," *ep.* 105 n. 1.

107. ΘΕΟΔΟΤΩΙ ΠΡΕΣΒΥΤΕΡΩΙ

Οὐκ ἔλαθον οἱ Τῆς Σῆς Φιλοθεΐας ἀγῶνες οὓς ὑπὲρ τῶν ἀποστολικῶν ἀνεδέξω δογμάτων, ἀλλ᾽ ᾄδουσι τούτους οὐ μόνον οἱ πείρᾳ μεμαθηκότες, ἀλλὰ καὶ οἱ παρὰ τούτων ἀκηκοότες. ἔχου τοίνυν, ὦ φίλη κεφαλή, τῶν ἀγώνων καὶ τῶν πατρῴων ὑπεράθλησον δογμάτων, ὑπὲρ ὧν καὶ ἡμεῖς πολλαχόθεν βαλλόμεθα καί, τὰς τρικυμίας δεχόμενοι, τὸν Κυβερνήτην ἀντιβολοῦμεν ἢ νεῦσαι καὶ τὸν κλύδωνα λῦσαι[a] ἢ τοῖς κλυδωνιζομένοις[b] ἀνδρείαν χαρίσασθαι.

a. *Cf.* Mk 4.35–39. b. *Cf.* Eph 4.14.

107. To Theodotus, the Priest[1]

The contests Your Piety has taken upon yourself on behalf of the apostolic teachings have not gone unnoticed. These are celebrated not only by the witnesses to the fact but also by those who have heard their reports. So, dear friend, continue to fight, and step forward to champion the teachings we have received from the fathers. For these we are also under attack from every quarter, and, battered by the waves, we entreat the Helmsman to nod his head and quell the raging sea[a] or grant us the grace to face it like men.[b]

1. The recipient is otherwise unknown. Possibly this letter belongs among those brought to Constantinople by the embassy of eastern bishops in late 448; *v. ep.* 92 n. 1.

108. ΑΚΑΚΙΩΙ ΠΡΕΣΒΥΤΕΡΩΙ

Ἀληθὴς ἄρα ἡ τῆς δαυϊτικῆς μελῳδίας ὑπόσχεσις· *τὸ γὰρ πνεῦμα τῆς ἀληθείας*[a] δι᾽ ἐκείνου ταύτην προσενήνοχεν τοῖς πιστεύουσιν· *Ἀποκάλυψον πρὸς Κύριον τὴν ὁδόν σου καὶ ἔλπισον ἐπ᾽ αὐτόν, καὶ αὐτὸς ποιήσει καὶ ἐξοίσει ὡς φῶς τὴν δικαιοσύνην σου καὶ τὸ κρῖμά σου ὡς μεσημβρίαν.*[b] τοῦτο καὶ ἐπὶ Τῆς Σῆς Θεοσεβείας γεγενημένον εὑρίσκομεν· ὁπόσην γὰρ τῶν ὀρφανίαν ὀδυρομένων ποιεῖται κηδεμονίαν Ἡ Σὴ Θεοσέβεια καὶ ὅπως ὑπὲρ τῶν ἀποστολικῶν ἀγωνίζῃ δογμάτων, ᾄδουσι πάντες, δήλων, κατὰ τὴν προφητείαν, τῶν κεκρυμμένων γεγενημένων.[c] τούτου δὴ χάριν κἀγώ, τοὺς ἀξιεπαίνους πόνους Τῆς Σῆς Φιλοθεΐας μεμαθηκώς, γράφω, καὶ προσφθεγγόμενός σε, θεοφιλέστατε, καὶ παρακαλῶν αὐξῆσαι τὸ κλέος τῇ προσθήκῃ τῶν πόνων καὶ τῆς εὐαγγελικῆς ὑπερμαχῆσαι διδασκαλίας ἵνα καὶ τὸν πατρῷον κλῆρον φυλάξωμεν ἄσυλον καὶ τὸ τάλαντον τῷ Δεσπότῃ μετὰ τῆς καλῆς προσενέγκωμεν ἐργασίας[d].

l. 1 Ἀληθὴς ἄρα *codd., Sir. Nös.* : Ἀ. γὰρ *Az.*

a. *Cf.* Jn 14.17; 15.26; 16.13; 1Jn 4.6. b. Ps 37.5f. c. *Cf.* Mt 10.26; Lk 8.17. d. Mt 25.27

108. To Acacius, the Priest[1]

So, the promise of David's song has come true! As you know, speaking through him, "the Spirit of truth"[a] has made this promise to those who believe: "Make known your path before the Lord, and put your hope in him, and he will bring it to pass, and he will bring forth like light your righteousness and your justice like high noon."[b] And, as we see, this is what has taken place in the case of Your Reverence: Your Reverence's great attention to the woes of orphans and your contests on behalf of the apostolic teachings are celebrated by all, as, in accordance with the prophecy, what was hidden is now manifest.[2c] Since I too am informed of Your Piety's praiseworthy labors, I write to send you my greeting, beloved of God, and to urge you to increase your fame by adding yet another to your labors and stepping forward to champion the gospel teaching so we may preserve inviolate the inheritance passed down from our fathers and set before our Master his talent with the interest of our good works.[d]

1. Acacius is not otherwise known. Possibly this letter belongs among those brought to Constantinople by the embassy of eastern bishops in late 448; *v. ep.* 92 n. 1.

2. Theodoret here presents David as a prophet (*cf. ep.* 85 n. d) and Ps 37.5f. as a prophecy that has been fulfilled in the case of Acacius. As the inspired psalmist had promised ("in accordance with the prophecy"), Acacius now enjoys an excellent reputation, because his good deeds have been made manifest before the Lord (note the imperative Ἀποκάλυψον = make known, uncover, reveal).

109. ΕΥΣΕΒΙΩΙ ΕΠΙΣΚΟΠΩΙ ΑΓΚΥΡΑΣ

(1) Πολλὰ μὲν τὰ καθ᾽ ἡμῶν τυρευόμενα καὶ δι᾽ ἡμῶν κατὰ τῆς ἀποστολικῆς καττυόμενα πίστεως, ψυχαγωγεῖ δὲ ἡμᾶς τὰ τῶν ἁγίων παθήματα προφητῶν, ἀποστόλων, μαρτύρων, καὶ τῶν ἐν ταῖς ἐκκλησίαις διαπρεψάντων ἐν τῷ λόγῳ τῆς χάριτος, πρὸς δὲ τούτοις καὶ αἱ *τοῦ … Θεοῦ καὶ Σωτῆρος ἡμῶν*[a] ἐπαγγελίαι. οὐδὲν γὰρ ἡμῖν ἐν τῷ παρόντι βίῳ τερπνὸν οὐδὲ θυμῆρες ὑπέσχετο, ἀλλὰ θλίψεις, καὶ πόνους, καὶ κινδύνους, καὶ πολεμίων ἐπαναστάσεις· *Ἐν τῷ κόσμῳ*, γάρ φησιν, *θλίψιν ἔχετε·*[b] καί, *Εἰ ἐμὲ ἐδίωξαν, καὶ ὑμᾶς διώξουσιν·*[c] καί, *Εἰ τὸν οἰκοδεσπότην Βεελζεβοὺλ* ἐκάλεσαν, *πόσῳ μᾶλλον τοὺς οἰκειακοὺς αὐτοῦ;*[d] καί, *Ἔρχεται ὥρα ἵνα πᾶς ὁ ἀποκτείνας ὑμᾶς δόξῃ λατρείαν προσφέρειν τῷ Θεῷ·*[e] καί, *Στενὴ ἡ πύλη καὶ τεθλιμμένη ἡ ὁδὸς ἡ ἀπάγουσα εἰς τὴν ζωήν·*[f] καί, *Ὅταν … διώκωσιν ὑμᾶς ἐν τῇ πόλει ταύτῃ, φεύγετε εἰς τὴν ἑτέραν,*[g] καὶ ὅσα τούτοις ἐστὶν παραπλήσια. Συνῳδὰ δέ φησιν καὶ ὁ θεῖος Ἀπόστολος, *Πάντες … οἱ θέλοντες ζῆν εὐσεβῶς ἐν Χριστῷ Ἰησοῦ διωχθήσονται, πονηροὶ δὲ ἄνθρωποι καὶ γόητες προκόψουσιν ἐπὶ τὸ χεῖρον, πλανῶντες καὶ πλανώμενοι.*[h] ταῦτα μὲν οὖν ἡμῖν παραψυχὴν ἐν τῇδε τῇ ζάλῃ παρέσχε μεγίστην.

Ἐπειδὴ δὲ εἰκὸς καὶ μέχρι Τῆς Σῆς Ἁγιωσύνης τὰς καθ᾽ ἡμῶν διαβῆναι συκοφαντίας, παρακαλῶ Σου Τὴν Ὁσιότητα μηδ᾽ ὅλως ὑποσχεῖν ταῖς τῶν συκοφαντῶν ψευδολογίαις τὰς ἀκοάς· ἐγὼ γὰρ οὐκ οἶδα μέχρι τοῦ παρόντος διδάξας εἰς δύο πιστεύειν υἱούς· εἰς ἕνα γὰρ ἐδιδάχθην πιστεύειν Μονογενῆ, τὸν Κύριον ἡμῶν Ἰησοῦν Χριστόν, τὸν ἐνανθρωπήσαντα Θεὸν Λόγον. σαρκὸς μέντοι καὶ θεότητος ἐπίσταμαι τὸ διάφορον,

a. Ti 2.13 b. Jn 16.33 c. Jn 15.20 d. Mt 10.25 (NT var.)
e. Jn 16.2 f. Mt 7.14 g. Mt 10.23 h. 2Tm 3.12f.

109. To Eusebius, Bishop of Ancyra[1]

(1) People are concocting all sorts of mischief against us, and, through us, against the apostolic faith. Nonetheless, we draw comfort from the sufferings of the holy prophets, apostles, martyrs, and those who have stood out in the churches for preaching the word of grace, and, what is more, from the promises "of our . . . God and Savior."[a] As you know, he promised us no pleasure or joy in this present life, just persecution, toil, danger, and the assaults of our enemies. As he said, "In the world, you will have persecution";[b] and, "If they persecuted me, they will persecute you as well";[c] and, "If they called the head of the house 'Beelzebul,' how much more all the members of his household!";[d] and, "The hour is coming when everyone who kills you will think he is performing a service to God";[e] and, "Narrow is the gate and straightened the way that leads to life";[2f] and, "Whenever they persecute you in this city, flee to another";[g] and other words of similar import. And the holy Apostle speaks in the same strain: "Everyone who desires to live a pious life in Christ Jesus will be persecuted; evil men and cheats will go from bad to worse, deceiving and themselves deceived."[h] These are the passages that have given us great comfort in the midst of this storm.

Since it is likely that these false accusations have traveled even as far as Your Sanctity, I implore Your Holiness to give no hearing to the lies of my accusers. As far as I know, up to this very day, I have never taught anyone to believe in two sons; I was taught to believe in one Only-begotten, our Lord Jesus Christ, God the Word who became man. Of course, I can also see the difference between the flesh and

1. On Eusebius, *v. ep.* 82 n. 1, and for the date and circumstances of this letter, *ep.* 92 n. 1.

2. This interpretation of Mt 7.14 as a reference to persecution rests on the derivation of the participle τεθλιμμένη (τεθλιμμένη ἡ ὁδός = "straightened / narrow is the way") from the noun θλίψις (tribulation). John Cassian may have been thinking of the same etymological interpretation in *Inst.* 4.38, where he prefixes a quotation of Acts 14.22 to that of Mt 7.14 (*per multas . . . tribulationes oportet nos introire in regnum dei: angusta namque est porta et arta uia*).

καὶ δυσσεβεῖν μοι δοκοῦσιν οἱ εἰς δύο υἱοὺς μερίζοντες τὸν ἕνα Κύριον ἡμῶν Ἰησοῦν Χριστόν, καὶ οἱ τὴν ἐναντίαν τούτοις ὁδεύοντες καὶ *μίαν φύσιν* ἀποκαλοῦντες τὴν θεότητα τοῦ Δεσπότου Χριστοῦ καὶ τὴν ἀνθρωπότητα· ἐναντίοι γὰρ ἀλλήλοις οὗτοι κρημνοί, μέση δὲ ἡ τῶν εὐαγγελικῶν δογμάτων ὁδός, τοῖς τῶν ἁγίων προφητῶν καὶ ἀποστόλων ἴχνεσι κοσμουμένη καὶ τῶν μετὰ τούτους ἐν τῷ διδασκαλικῷ διαπρεψάντων χαρίσματι. ἐβουλόμην δὲ καὶ τὰς τούτων παραθεῖναι χρήσεις καὶ δεῖξαι τῷ ἡμετέρῳ μαρτυρούσας φρονήματι, ἀλλὰ πλειόνων δεῖ μοι λόγων ἢ κατὰ μέτρον ἐπιστολῆς, οὗ δὴ χάριν ἐν κεφαλαίῳ γράψας, ἃ περὶ τῆς τοῦ Μονογενοῦς ἐνανθρωπήσεως μεμαθήκαμεν ἀπέστειλά Σου Τῇ κατὰ Θεὸν Τελειότητι. ἔγραψα δέ, οὐκ ἄλλοις προσφέρων διδασκαλίαν, ἀλλὰ πρὸς τὴν γεγενημένην συκοφαντίαν ἀπολογίαν ποιούμενος καὶ τὸ ἐμαυτοῦ φρόνημα τοῖς ἀγνοοῦσιν τοῦτο δεικνύς.

(2) Ἀναγνοῦσα τοίνυν Ἡ Ἁγιωσύνη Σου, εἰ μὲν εὕροι τὰ γεγραμμένα τοῖς ἀποστολικοῖς συμβαίνοντα δόγμασιν, τοῖς πρὸς ἡμᾶς ἀντιγράφοις βεβαιωσάτω τὸ φρόνημα. εἰ δέ τι τῶν ἐγκειμένων τῇ διδασκαλίᾳ τῇ θείᾳ μὴ συμφωνεῖ, καὶ τοῦτο μαθεῖν παρὰ Τῆς Σῆς Ὁσιότητος ἀξιῶ. καὶ γὰρ πολὺν ἐν τῇ διδασκαλίᾳ καταναλώσαντες χρόνον, ἔτι δεόμεθα τοῦ διδάσκοντος· *Ἐκ μέρους γάρ*, φησὶν ὁ θεῖος Ἀπόστολος, *γινώσκομεν*,[i] ἠκούσαμεν δὲ αὐτοῦ πάλιν λέγοντος, *Εἰ δέ τις δοκεῖ ἐγνωκέναι τι, οὐδέπω ἔγνω καθὼς δεῖ γνῶναι.*[j] καὶ τἀληθὲς τοίνυν παρὰ Τῆς Σῆς Ὁσιότητος παρακαλοῦμεν μαθεῖν, καὶ τῆς ἐκκλησιαστικῆς φροντίσαι γαλήνης καὶ τῶν θείων ὑπερμαχῆσαι δογμάτων· τούτων γὰρ δὴ χάριν καὶ οἱ θεοφιλέστατοι

l. 49 οὐδέπω ἔγνω *scr. Onor. A, Az.* (*Cf. NTG*: οὔπω ἔ.) : ἔ. ο. *N. Onorio reversed the order of the negative and the vb. to produce what he took to be the proper form of 1Cor 8.2, that printed in the NTG and recorded in the thirteen other quotations of this verse listed in the TLG. Only Thdt. provides witness for the negative οὐδέπω* (*Cf. Prouid. 10, PG, vol. 83, col. 741, l. 4: οὐδέπω οὐδὲν ε.*), *the reading of some uncials and what the NTG terms the "Majority Text."*

i. 1Cor 13.9 j. 1Cor 8.2 (NT var.)

the godhead, and it seems to me that heresy is being espoused not only by those who divide our one Lord Jesus Christ into two sons, but also by those who take the opposite path and refer to the godhead and the humanity of our Master Christ as "one nature." These two cliffs stand opposite each other, and between them passes the path of the gospel teachings, the path honored by the footsteps of the holy prophets and apostles, and of those who have stood out in later times for the spiritual gift of teaching. I would have liked to include passages from their writings as well and to show how their witness agrees with mine, but that is a task requiring more words than appropriate to a letter. Therefore, I have enclosed for Your godly Perfection a summary statement of what we have learned regarding the incarnation of the Only-begotten.[3] I have written not to instruct others, but to rebut the false accusation that has arisen against me and to present my position to those who do not yet know it.

(2) I ask Your Sanctity to read this, and if you find that what I have written accords with the apostolic teachings, please confirm this understanding by writing us a reply.[4] But if anything herein does not agree with the instruction we have received from God, I ask to hear of this also from Your Holiness. Though having spent so much time teaching, we still stand in need of a teacher, for, as the holy Apostle says, "Our knowledge is but partial,"[i] and we have also heard him declare, "Whoever thinks he knows something has not yet known as he ought to know."[j] We, therefore, implore Your Holiness to teach us the truth and to take thought for the tranquility of the Church and step forward as a champion of the teachings of God. It is on account of

3. On this brief treatise, *v. ep.* 16 n. 3; *ep.* 92 n. 1; *ep.* 104 n. 8.

4. In *ep.* 82.1 (*v.* n. 1), Theodoret apparently refers to Eusebius' failure to comply with this request and send a letter of confirmation.

ἐπίσκοποι, καὶ τῶν τῆς ὁδοιπορίας πόνων καὶ τῆς χειμερινῆς καταφρονήσαντες ὥρας, ἐπὶ τὴν βασιλεύουσαν ὥρμησαν πόλιν, λύσιν τινὰ πορίσαι τῷ κλύδωνι μηχανώμενοι. καὶ αὐτοὺς τοίνυν ἐφοδιάσαι ταῖς προσευχαῖς καὶ ἡμᾶς ταύταις ἐρεῖσαι παρακλήθητι, Δέσποτα.

these teachings that these bishops beloved of God, without so much as a thought for the discomforts of the journey and the wintry weather, have set off for the capital in an effort to find some way of quelling the stormy sea. So, please be so kind, My Lord, as to send them on their way with your prayers, and, with your prayers, to support us as well.

110. ΔΟΜΝΩΙ ΕΠΙΣΚΟΠΩΙ ΑΝΤΙΟΧΕΙΑΣ

(1) Ἀναγνοὺς τὰ γράμματα, τῆς μακαριωτάτης ἀνεμνήσθην Σουσάννας, ἥ, τοὺς ἀλάστορας ἐκείνους ὁρῶσα καὶ τὸν τῶν ὅλων Θεὸν παρεῖναι πιστεύουσα, τὴν θαυμασίαν ἐκείνην ἀφῆκε φωνήν· *Στενά μοι πάντοθεν.*[a] ἀλλ' ὅμως εἵλετο μᾶλλον ταῖς τῆς συκοφαντίας πάγαις περιπεσεῖν ἢ τοῦ δικαίου καταφρονῆσαι Κριτοῦ. καὶ νῦν, Δέσποτα, δύο πρόκειται· τοῦτο δὲ πολλάκις εἰρήκαμεν· ἢ Θεῷ προσκροῦσαι καὶ βλάψαι τὸ συνειδός, ἢ ταῖς ἀδίκοις τῶν ἀνθρώπων ψήφοις περιπεσεῖν.

Ἐμοὶ δὲ οὐδὲ δοκεῖ τούτων εἰδέναι τι τὸν εὐσεβέστατον βασιλέα· τί γὰρ ἐκώλυσεν αὐτὸν γράψαι καὶ ἐπιτρέψαι τὴν χειροτονίαν γενέσθαι εἴπερ ἀληθῶς αὐτὸν ἐθεράπευεν τοῦτο; τί δήποτε δὲ ἔξωθεν ἀπειλοῦσιν καὶ δεδίττονται, γράμματα δὲ προφανῶς τοῦτο κελεύοντα οὐ πέμπουσιν; δυοῖν γὰρ θάτερον· ἢ οὐ πείθεται γράψαι ὁ εὐσεβέστατος βασιλεύς, ἢ κατασκευάζουσι παρανομῆσαι ἡμᾶς καὶ δίκας ὑπ' αὐτῶν ὕστερον τῆς παρανομίας ἀπαιτηθῆναι. πρόκειται γὰρ ἡμῖν τὸ κατὰ τὸν μακάριον Πριγκίπιον ὑπόδειγμα· ἐκεῖ γάρ, καὶ ἐγγράφως κελεύσαντες, δίκας ἀπῄτουν τὸν ὑπακούσαντα.

Ἃ δὲ ἀνέγνων κατ' αὐτὴν τὴν ἡμέραν καθ' ἣν ὁ λεκτικάριος ἀφίκετο γράμματα ἐναντία τούτοις ἐστίν· ἅγιος γάρ τις μονάζων τῶν ἐπισήμων ἔγραψεν πρός τινα ὡς ἐδέξατο γράμματα καὶ τοῦ μεγαλοπρεπεστάτου σπαθαρίου καὶ τοῦ ἐνδοξοτάτου ἀπὸ μαγίστρων σημαίνοντα ὡς διορθώσεως τεύξεται τὰ κατὰ τὸν

a. Dn 13.22 (Theod.; = Sus 22) (*Cf.* 2Sm 24.14.)

110. To Domnus, Bishop of Antioch[1]

(1) When I had finished reading your letter, I thought of Susannah most blessed, when, face-to-face with those villains but confident in the protection of the God of the universe, she made that wonderful declaration, "I am hemmed in on every side!"[a] And yet, she preferred to allow herself to fall into the snare of false accusation rather than disregard the righteous Judge. Now we too, my Master, (as we have frequently remarked) are faced with two options: either offend God and do violence to our conscience or allow ourselves to be ensnared in unjust judgments passed by men.

As far as I can see, the most-Christian emperor must be quite uninformed about this matter. After all, what is to prevent him, if that is really what he wants, from sending a letter to require that an election be held? Why do they try to raise fear with vague threats but send no letters explicitly enjoining this?[2] There are two possible answers: Either the most-Christian emperor is not agreeing to issue an order, or they are trying to force us to commit a transgression so they can punish us for this at some future date. We have before us the example of the blessed Principius. In that case, they issued an order in writing and, after he had obeyed, had him punished.[3]

Now the letter I read on the day the bearer arrived was entirely at odds with this. A certain holy monk had written to a certain prominent gentleman that he had received letters from both the right honorable guardsman and the distinguished former official indicat-

1. On Domnus of Antioch, *v. ep.* 31 n. 1. The date must be subsequent to the deposition of Irenaeus of Tyre in April of 448; *v.* Azéma, vol. 2, p. 38, n. 1.

2. My translation of τί δήποτε δὲ ἔξωθεν ἀπειλοῦσι καὶ δεδίττονται ("Why do they try to raise fear with their vague threats") is only tentative. I take the adverb ἔξωθεν in a sense used by grammarians, *i.e.* that unexpressed words must be supplied from the context for the completion of a thought (*v. LSJ, sub uoc. III*); the threats would be suggested or implied but not spelled out. In an attempt to give ἔξωθεν a meaning it frequently bears, an annotator of the *Berolinensis* inserted an article before it (οἱ ἔξωθεν = non-Christians).

3. We have no information regarding Principius or the intrigue to which he fell victim.

θεοφιλέστατον ἐπίσκοπον τὸν Κύριον Εἰρηναῖον, καὶ ταύτης γε τῆς σπουδῆς ἀντιδόσεις ἀπῄτουν τὰς ὑπὲρ αὐτῶν προσευχάς.

(2) Ἐγὼ τοίνυν νομίζω χρῆναι γραφῆναι πρὸς τοὺς γεγραφότας ἀπὸ τῆς βασιλευούσης πόλεως κληρικούς, ὅτι *Ψήφῳ μὲν τῶν τῆς Φοινίκης θεοφιλεστάτων ἐπισκόπων πεισθείς, ἐχειροτόνησα τὸν θεοφιλέστατον ἐπίσκοπον Εἰρηναῖον, τόν τε ζῆλον, καὶ τὴν μεγαλοψυχίαν, καὶ τὴν φιλοπτωχείαν, καὶ τὰς ἄλλας αὐτῷ συνειδὼς ἀρετάς, καί, πρὸς τούτοις, τὴν τῶν δογμάτων ὀρθότητα· οὐκ οἴδαμεν γὰρ αὐτὸν παραιτησάμενον πώποτε* Θεοτόκον *καλέσαι τὴν ἁγίαν Παρθένον ἢ ἄλλο τι ἐναντίον φρονήσαντα τοῖς εὐαγγελικοῖς δόγμασιν. εἰς δὲ τὸ τῆς διγαμίας, τοῖς πρὸ ἡμῶν ἠκολουθήσαμεν· καὶ γὰρ ὁ τῆς μακαρίας καὶ ὁσίας μνήμης Ἀλέξανδρος, ὁ τὸν ἀποστολικὸν τοῦτον διακοσμήσας θρόνον, σὺν τῷ μακαριωτάτῳ Ἀκακίῳ τῷ Βεροίας ἐπισκόπῳ τὸν τῆς μακαρίας μνήμης Διογένην ἐχειροτόνησαν, δίγαμον ὄντα, ὡσαύτως δὲ καὶ ὁ μακάριος Πραΰλιος Δομνῖνον,*

l. 28 μὲν *coni.* $A^{mg.}$, *scr. Az.* : μετὰ *codd.*

ing that the case of Lord Irenaeus, bishop beloved of God, would be resolved favorably, and as recompense for their good offices they asked him to pray for them.[4]

(2) So then, as I see it, the answer to the clergy of the capital city should be "In agreement with the vote of the bishops of Phoenicia beloved of God, I consecrated Irenaeus, bishop beloved of God, as I have full knowledge of his virtues, including his zeal, his generosity, his concern for the poor, and, in addition to these, the orthodoxy of his beliefs.[5] We are not aware that he has ever refused to apply the title 'Mother of God' to the holy Virgin or adopted any other position at odds with gospel doctrine.[6] With regard to his having been twice married, we followed in the steps of our predecessors. Alexander of blessed and holy memory, who governed this apostolic see, in concert with the most blessed Acacius, bishop of Beroea, consecrated Diogenes of blessed memory though he had been twice married. Likewise, the blessed Praylius consecrated Domninus of Caesarea though he had been twice married.[7] Thus, we have followed

4. The identities of most of the personages mentioned in this paragraph are unknown to us. The term "bearer" represents λεκτικάριος, which is itself a transcription of the Latin *lecticarius* = a servant who helped bear a *lectica* (a sedan chair). The Greek term was used not only of chair-men but also of those who transported the indigent dead for burial; a synonymous term was δεκανός. Though not themselves clerics, these bearers served in a corporation under clerical supervision and were entitled to a small recompense for the performance of this act of mercy; *v.* Grégoire, #108. Jackson's "letter-bearer" ("The letters which I read on the very day of the letter-bearer's arrival") is, thus, a mistranslation. "Guardsman" represents σπαθάριος, a eunuch entrusted with bearing the emperor's sword (σπάθη; *v.* Delmaire, pp. 167f.); at this time that title was held by Theodosius' powerful counselor, Chrysaphius (*v.* Intro., sec. 4). The "former official" may have served as the head of one of the bureaux of the civil service or as a military chief; *v.* Delmaire, p. 179, *sub. uoc., Magister, -tri.*

5. On Irenaeus of Tyre, his friendship with Theodoret, his ecclesiastical career, and his deposition on charge of heresy, *v. ep.* 3 n. 1.

6. For the christological controversy arising from the application of this title to the Virgin, *v.* Intro., sec. 2.4, and *cf. ep.* 16.2.

7. Opposition to the episcopal ordination of men who had been twice married was supported by reference to 1Tm 3.2, which describes a suitable candidate with the words μιᾶς γυναικὸς ἄνδρα ("a husband of one wife" or "married only once"). In his commentary on this verse, Theodoret understands μιᾶς γυναικὸς ἄνδρα to mean that the bishop should live in chastity with his wife, without mistress or

τὸν Καισαρείας, δίγαμον ὄντα· ἔθει τοίνυν ἠκολουθήσαμεν καὶ ἀνδράσιν ἐπισήμοις καὶ ἐπὶ γνώσει καὶ βίῳ πολυθρυλήτοις. πολλὰ δὲ καὶ ἄλλα τοιαῦτα δεδιδαγμένος, ὁ τῆς μακαρίας μνήμης Πρόκλος, ὁ τῆς Κωνσταντινουπολιτῶν ἐπίσκοπος, καὶ αὐτὸς τὴν χειροτονίαν ἐδέξατο καὶ ἔγραψεν ἐπαινῶν καὶ θαυμάζων, ὡσαύτως δὲ καὶ οἱ πρωτεύοντες τῆς ποντικῆς διοικήσεως θεοφιλέστατοι ἐπίσκοποι καὶ οἱ παλαιστῖνοι πάντες, καὶ οὐδεμία ἀμφιβολία περὶ τούτου γεγένηται, καὶ δυσσεβὲς νομίζομεν τὸ κατακρῖναι ἄνδρα πολλοῖς καὶ παντοδαποῖς κατορθώμασι λαμπρυνόμενον.

Ταῦτα καὶ τὰ τοιαῦτα κατὰ τὴν ἐμὴν γνώμην δεῖ γράψαι, εἰ δὲ ἄλλο τι συνορᾷ Σου Ἡ Ἁγιότης, τὸ δοκοῦν γιγνέσθω. ἐγὼ γὰρ καὶ τὴν μίαν, ὡς νομίζουσιν, τιμωρίαν δεξάμενος, ἕτοιμός εἰμι, τοῦ Θεοῦ μοι βοηθοῦντος, δέξασθαι καὶ τὴν ἄλλην, εἰ δὲ καὶ τρίτην βούλονται καὶ τετάρτην, τῆς θείας χάριτος ἐπερειδούσης, οἴσομεν, τὸν Δεσπότην ὑμνοῦντες. εἰ δὲ δοκιμάζει Σου Ἡ Ὁσιότης, ἴδωμεν καὶ τὰς ἀπὸ Παλαιστίνης ἀποκρίσεις, καί, ἀκριβέστερον τὸ πρακτέον σκοπήσαντες, οὕτω γράψομεν εἰς Κωνσταντινούπολιν.

l. 56 οὕτω *N* : οὐ. καὶ *scr. Sir. Nös. Az.* **l. 56** γράψομεν *N* : -ψωμ- *A, edd.*

precedent and the example of prominent men held in the highest regard for both their learning and way of life.[8] Furthermore, Proclus, bishop of Constantinople,[9] himself aware of many other such cases, also accepted this consecration and wrote a letter full of praise and admiration—likewise the leading bishops beloved of God of the diocese of Pontus[10] and all the bishops of Palestine—and, as there has been no disagreement in this matter, we reject as a piece of irreligion the condemnation of a man who shines with the luster of such abundant, such manifold merit."

(3) In my opinion, the reply should say these and other things of the same tenor, but if Your Sanctity should think differently, do as you see fit. For my part, having received what they take to be one punishment, I am ready, with the help of God, for the next, and if they want to inflict a third or a fourth, I shall bear that also with the support of God's grace and sing the praises of our Master. But, if Your Holiness thinks it best, let's wait to see the replies from Palestine, and then we'll write to Constantinople when we have a clearer idea of how to proceed.

---

concubine; he expressly denies that it should be understood to exclude those who had been married twice (οὐ γὰρ τὸν δεύτερον … ἐξέβαλε γάμον ὅγε πολλάκις τοῦτο γενέσθαι κελεύσας). Yet, in a letter (*ep.* 12; for the complex textual history of this letter, *v.* Hoskin) to the bishops of Mauritania, Leo I remarks (sec. 3) that this passage has been traditionally understood to mean that both the bishop and his wife should have had no previous marriage. Their union must reflect the mystical marriage of Christ and the Church. Indeed, Leo extends the rule of a single marriage also to the aspirants to the deaconship and the priesthood and to their wives. Kotting (coll. 1022f.) regards the prohibition against the episcopal ordination of men married more than once as the position predominant in antiquity.

8. Alexander was the predecessor of Theodotus as Patriarch of Antioch; *cf. ep.* 81 n. 6. For Acacius of Beroea, *v. ep.* 75 n. 2. The see of Diogenes has not been identified. Praylius, bishop of Jerusalem from 416–25, was the successor of John (*v.* Thdt., *H. e.* 5.37 and Aly).

9. For Proclus of Constantinople, *v. epp.* 47 n. 1 and 86 n. 8.

10. The diocese of Pontus comprised eight provinces, including Galatia, Cappadocia, and Armenia, situated in central and northern Asia Minor; its vicar had his headquarters in Amaseia; *v.* Foss, "Pontos," and *cf. ep.* 42 n. 1.

111. ΑΝΑΤΟΛΙΩΙ ΠΑΤΡΙΚΙΩΙ

Ἡ μὲν Ὑμετέρα Μεγαλοφυΐα τῶν εἰς ἡμᾶς εὐεργεσιῶν παρὰ τοῦ Θεοῦ τῶν ὅλων κομιεῖται τὰς ἀντιδόσεις· πᾶν γὰρ ὁτιοῦν αὐτοῦ χάριν γιγνόμενον μισθὸν ἔχει συνεζευγμένον. ἐγὼ μέντοι τῶν συκοφαντιῶν τὸ πλῆθος γελῶ· καὶ γὰρ τὰ σφοδρότερον αἰκιζόμενα σώματα τῆς ὀδύνης οὐκ ἐπαισθάνεται, νεκρωθείσης λοιπὸν τῆς αἰκιζομένης σαρκός· θρηνῶ δὲ ὅμως τὰ ἀθυρώτατα στόματα ψευδολογίας προφέροντα.

Τί γὰρ παρ᾽ ἡμῶν ἀδικηθέντες, οἱ τοῦ θεοφιλεστάτου ἐπισκόπου Ἴβα κατήγοροι ταύταις καθ᾽ ἡμῶν ταῖς ψευδολογίαις ἐχρήσαντο; πρῶτον μὲν γὰρ οὐδὲ τῶν κριτῶν ἤμην ἐγώ· κατὰ γὰρ τὴν βασιλικὴν ψῆφον ἐν τῇ Κύρρῳ διῆγον. ἔπειτα δέ, ὡς παρὰ πολλῶν ἀκήκοα, καὶ δυσχεραίνοντες διετέλουν τὴν ἡμετέραν ἀπόλειψιν· καὶ γὰρ τῆς μυστικῆς αὐτοὺς ἐν τῷ σωτηρίῳ Πάσχα μεταλαχεῖν κοινωνίας ἐγὼ παρεσκεύασα, καί, πολλάκις ἡμῖν συντυχεῖν ἐθελήσαντας, εὐμενῶς ἐδεξάμην, καὶ εἰσηγησάμην ἅπερ ἐχρῆν. ἵνα δὲ καὶ ὑπὲρ τοῦ θεοφιλεστάτου ἐπισκόπου τοῦ Κυρίου Δόμνου ἀπολογήσωμαι, τί ἔδει πρᾶξαι τὸν οὕτως φανερῶς πολεμούμενον καὶ θεώμενον τοὺς ψήφῳ συνοδικῇ καθαιρουμένους εἰς ἑτέραν διοίκησιν πεμπομένους καί, παρὰ τοὺς ἐκκλησιαστικοὺς θεσμούς, τὴν ἱερωσύνην ἀπολαμβάνοντας, καὶ τὰ σεπτὰ καὶ θεῖα παρὰ τῶν ἐχθρῶν τῆς ἀληθείας γελώμενά τε καὶ κωμῳδούμενα; τούτου χάριν, ὡς ἔγνω, τὴν κρίσιν ἑτέροις παρέπεμψεν, καὶ οὐ μόνον τῷ θεοφιλεστάτῳ τῷ Κυρίῳ Ἴβᾳ, ἀλλὰ καὶ τῷ ἁγιωτάτῳ ἐπισκόπῳ τῷ Κυρίῳ Συμεῶνι τῷ Ἀμίδης ὥστε τῶν δύο ἐπαρχιῶν τοὺς μητροπολίτας διακοῦσαι τῶν ὑποθέσεων. πῶς δὲ δίκαιον τοὺς αὐτοὺς ὠμότητα καὶ φιλανθρωπίαν κατηγορεῖσθαι· καὶ

111. To Anatolius, the Patrician[1]

Your Eminence will receive the recompense for your acts of kindness toward us from the God of the universe, for every and any action undertaken on his behalf is coupled to a reward. As far as I'm concerned, I just laugh at my false accusers, the whole bunch of them. After all, a body subjected to severe torture loses all sensation of pain once the tortured flesh has been mortified. Yet, I can't help lamenting for those uncontrolled mouths, who are spouting falsehoods.

What injustice have the accusers of Ibas, bishop beloved of God, suffered at our hands that they should deploy all these lies against us?[2] First of all, I was not even one of the judges, since I was keeping to Cyrus in obedience to the decision of the emperor. Second, as I've heard from a number of people, they went on angrily about my abandoning them, and yet I was the one who had arranged for them to take Holy Communion on Easter, the feast of our salvation, and, on numerous occasions, when they made requests to meet us, I received them graciously and advised them on the proper course of action. And, to say something in defense of Lord Domnus, bishop beloved of God, what was he to do in the midst of those brazen attacks, when he could see men being deposed by vote of the synod, then being sent to another diocese, and, in defiance of ecclesiastical norms, getting reinstated in their priesthood, and all that is holy and godly being turned into a laughing stock and derision by the enemies of the truth? It was because of this that, as soon as he knew it, he had the judgment sent along to others, not only to Lord Ibas, most beloved of God, but also to Lord Symeon, the holy bishop of Amida, so that the metropolitans of the two provinces might inform themselves from the proceedings.[3] How is it fair to blame the same

1. On Anatolius, *v. ep.* 45 n. 1.

2. Theodoret is referring to the schism between Ibas of Edessa and some of his clergy and the hearing of this case before Domnus of Antioch; *v. ep.* 87 n. 1.

3. Ibas, as bishop of Edessa, was the metropolitan of the province of Osrhoëne

γάρ, ἐκβάλλοντες, κινδυνεύομεν καί, μὴ ἐκβάλλοντες, τοὺς κινδύνους οὐ διαφεύγομεν; καὶ μόνοι πολεμούμεθα παρὰ πᾶσαν τὴν οἰκουμένην, καὶ αἱ μὲν ἄλλαι διοικήσεις ἐν ἡσυχίᾳ διάγουσιν, ἡμεῖς δὲ μόνοι τοῖς συκοφάνταις προκείμεθα, ἐγὼ δὲ διαφερόντως, καίτοι μήτε συνδικάσας καὶ παντελῶς ἀνεύθυνος ὤν.

Ταῦτα ἠναγκάσθην γράψαι, τοῖς Τοῦ Ὑμετέρου Μεγέθους γράμμασιν ἐντυχὼν καὶ μαθὼν δι᾽ αὐτῶν ὡς καὶ διὰ ταῦτα κίνησις μεγίστη γέγονεν καθ᾽ ἡμῶν, ἀνδρῶν περιορισθέντων, καὶ ἡσυχίαν ἀγόντων, καὶ οὐδὲ τοῖς τῆς ἐπαρχίας θεοφιλεστάτοις ἐπισκόποις συνεδρευόντων· τῷ ὄντι γὰρ δὶς ἤδη χειροτονίας ἐπισκοπικῆς ἐν τῇ ἐπαρχίᾳ τῇ ἡμετέρᾳ γεγενημένης, οὐδεμιᾶς ἐκοινώνησα. εἰ δὲ μὴ τῷ βασιλικῷ κατειχόμην νόμῳ, ἄρα ἂν ἀπέστην καί, τινὰ καταλαβὼν ἐσχατιάν, ἐκεῖ τὰς λειπομένας ἡμέρας διήγαγον· ἀπείρηκα γὰρ πρὸς τὰ κατ᾽ ἐμοῦ τυρευόμενα· καὶ γὰρ τούτους αὐτοὺς τοὺς ἐδεσηνοὺς οὐκ οἶμαι αὐτομάτους ταύτην καθ᾽ ἡμῶν τὴν συκοφαντίαν ὑφῆναι, ἀλλ᾽ ὑπὸ τῶν αὐτόθι φιλαλήθων ἀνθρώπων ταῦτα καθ᾽ ἡμῶν διδαχθῆναι. καὶ χάρις τῷ Σωτῆρι τῶν ὅλων, ὅτι με, ἀνάξιον ὄντα, τῶν εὐαγγελικῶν ἠξίωσεν μακαρισμῶν.[a] διά τοι τοῦτο, καὶ τὸν περιορισμὸν μεθ᾽ ἡδονῆς ἐδεξάμην, καὶ τὴν ἐξορίαν προσδέχομαι, καὶ πᾶν ὅπερ ἂν ἐπαγαγεῖν ἐθέλωσιν ἀσπαστῶς δέχομαι *διὰ τὴν ἀποκειμένην ἐλπίδα.*[b] Τῆς δὲ Ὑμετέρας Μεγαλοφυΐας διηνεκῶς ὑπερεύχομαι καὶ τοὺς ἁγίους ἅπαντας κοινωνεῖν μοι τῶν εὐχῶν ἱκετεύω.

a. Mt 5.11f. b. Col 1.5

men for cruelty and for kindness? The truth is, if we excommunicate them, there are risks for us, and if we don't, we don't escape those risks. We alone in all the world are subjected to attack; while other dioceses are living in tranquility, we alone are exposed to these false accusations, and I more than anyone else although I took no part in the case and have nothing to give an accounting for.

I felt I had to make this reply after receiving Your Lordship's letter and learning of the great outcry this affair has occasioned against us, though under order of relegation and living quietly and not even meeting with the bishops beloved of God in our own province; indeed, two episcopal ordinations have already taken place in our province, and I took no part in either. If it weren't for the imperial decree, I would have left this place and gone off to some far-off corner of the world and spent my remaining days there, as I can no longer stand up against all these intrigues that are being concocted against me. I don't suppose that it was the Edesenes all by themselves who've spun this false accusation against us; they were prompted to make these charges against us by those people there, those lovers of truth. And thanks be to the Savior of the universe who has deemed me, though unworthy, worthy of the beatitudes of the gospel![a] This is the reason I have received my relegation with delight and look forward to exile. Whatever they might wish to inflict on me I shall be glad to receive "for the sake of that hope that is laid up for us."[b] I pray unceasingly for Your Eminence and beg all the saints to join in my prayers.[4]

(*v. ep.* 52 n. 1 and Intro., sec. 4.4), and Symeon, as bishop of Amida, metropolitan of the province of Mesopotamia. For Amida, a stronghold of the empire on the Tigris in southeastern Anatolia, *v.* Mango. The city is now Dijarbakir in Turkey.

4. By "the saints" (τοὺς ἁγίους), Theodoret means the practitioners of the ascetic life, such as the holy man Jacob, who lived in his diocese; *cf. epp.* 42 n. 10 and 44 n. 7.

112. ΔΟΜΝΩΙ ΕΠΙΣΚΟΠΩΙ ΑΝΤΙΟΧΕΙΑΣ

(1) Ἠλπίσαμεν πεπαῦσθαι τὰ σκυθρωπά· τινῶν ἡμῖν μεμηνυκότων ὡς ἐσβέσθη μὲν ἡ τοῦ καλλινίκου βασιλέως μικροψυχία, καταλλαγαὶ δὲ μεταξὺ αὐτοῦ καὶ τοῦ θεοφιλεστάτου ἐπισκόπου γεγένηνται, καὶ πέπαυται μὲν ἡ τῆς συνόδου κλῆσις, ἡ δὲ τῶν ἐκκλησιῶν ἐπανῆλθεν εἰρήνη· τὰ δὲ νῦν παρὰ Τῆς Σῆς Ὁσιότητος γραφέντα σφόδρα ἡμᾶς ἠνίασεν.

Οὐδὲν γὰρ ἔστιν ἐκ τῆς θρυλουμένης συνόδου προσδοκῆσαι χρηστὸν εἰ μὴ ἄρα ὁ φιλάνθρωπος Δεσπότης, τῇ συνήθει κηδεμονίᾳ χρησάμενος, τῶν ταραχωδῶν δαιμόνων διαλύσει τὰς μηχανάς. καὶ γὰρ ἐν τῇ μεγάλῃ συνόδῳ, τῇ ἐν Νικαίᾳ συναθροισθείσῃ φημί, συνεψηφίσαντο μὲν τοῖς ὀρθοδόξοις οἱ τῆς Ἀρείου συμμορίας καὶ τῇ ἀποστολικῇ διὰ τῶν χειρῶν ἐκθέσει συνέθεντο, διετέλεσαν δὲ τῇ ἀληθείᾳ πολεμοῦντες ἕως τὸ σῶμα τῆς Ἐκκλησίας διέρρηξαν. καὶ τριάκοντα μὲν ἔτη διετέλεσαν κοινωνοῦντες ἀλλήλοις οἵ τε τῶν ἀποστολικῶν ἀντεχόμενοι δογμάτων καὶ οἱ τὴν Ἀρείου βλασφημίαν νοσοῦντες, ἐν Ἀντιοχείᾳ δέ, τῆς ἐσχάτης συνόδου γεγενημένης, ὅτε τὸν τοῦ Θεοῦ ἄνθρωπον τὸν μέγαν Μελέτιον τοῖς ἀποστολικοῖς ἐκείνοις ἐνίδρυσαν θώκοις εἶτα μετ᾽ ὀλίγας αὐτὸν ἡμέρας διὰ τῆς βασιλικῆς ἐξέβαλον δυναστείας, προεβλήθη μὲν Εὐζώιος, προφανῆ τὴν Ἀρείου περικείμενος λύμην, ἀπέστησαν δὲ παραυτίκα οἱ τῶν εὐαγγελικῶν δογμάτων ὑπερασπίζοντες, καὶ ἐξ ἐκείνου μεμένηκεν ἡ διαίρεσις. εἰς ἐκεῖνα ἀφορῶσα καὶ τὰ

112. To Domnus, Bishop of Antioch[1]

(1) It was our hope that our troubles were over—we had received reports that the animosity of our glorious emperor had been assuaged, a reconciliation had been effected between him and the bishop beloved of God, that an end had been made of the plan for convening a council, and peace had returned to the churches[2]—but now we have been deeply troubled by the news in Your Holiness' letter.

We cannot expect any good to come out of this synod everyone's talking about, unless, that is, our kindly Master, with the care that belongs to him, foil the trickery of these rioting demons. As you recall, at the great Council, I mean the one that assembled in Nicaea, the sectaries of Arius cast their votes along with the orthodox and subscribed at least with their hands to that apostolic creed, yet they continued warring against the truth until they had torn asunder the body of the Church. For the next thirty years, the supporters of the apostolic teachings and those infected with the Arian blasphemy continued in communion with each other. Then, at the last council in Antioch, when Meletius, that great man of God, was seated on this apostolic throne and just a few days later driven into exile by the imperial power, and Euzoius, a man patently corrupted with Arianism was put in his place, the champions of the gospel doctrines immediately seceded, and that was the beginning of the schism.[3] When I look back to those events of the past and forward to more of

1. On Domnus, *v. ep.* 31 n. 1. This letter presupposes Domnus' receipt of the summons to the Second Council of Ephesus issued by Theodosius II on March 30, 449; *v.* Intro., sec. 4.4. As Azéma (vol. 3, p. 55 n. 4) suggests, the very intensity of the tone in which Theodoret offers his advice may betray his lack of confidence in Domnus' steadfastness; some months later, the patriarch of Antioch would acquiesce in Theodoret's deposition; *v.* Intro., sec. 4.8.

2. The bishop reconciled to the emperor was most probably Irenaeus of Tyre; *v. ep.* 3 n. 1.

3. The council to which Theodoret refers was held in Antioch in 361; the emperor was Constantius II. Theodoret recounts the events of the council and its aftermath in *H. e.* 2.27; *v.* also Gregory and Kazhdan, "Meletian Schism in Syria"; and Intro., sec. 1.4.

ὅμοια προορῶσα, ἡ ἀθλία ψυχή μου στένει καὶ ὀδύρεται, οὐδὲν καραδοκοῦσα χρηστόν.

Οὐδὲ γὰρ ἴσασιν οἱ ἐκ τῶν ἄλλων διοικήσεων τὸν ἐγκείμενον *τοῖς δώδεκα κεφαλαίοις* ἰόν, ἀλλά, τῇ περιφανείᾳ τοῦ ταῦτα γεγραφότος προσέχοντες, οὐδὲν ὑποπτεύουσι φλαῦρον. καὶ οἶμαι ὡς ὁ τὸν ἐκείνου διαδεξάμενος θρόνον πάντα πραγματεύεται ὥστε δευτέρᾳ ταῦτα κρατῦναι συνόδῳ· ὁ γὰρ ἐξ ἐπιτάγματος τοιαῦτα πρώην γράψας καὶ ἀναθεματίσας τοὺς τούτοις ἐμμένειν οὐ βουλομένους τί οὐκ ἂν πράξαι ἐν οἰκουμενικῇ προκαθίσας συνόδῳ; καὶ εὖ ἴσθι, Δέσποτα, ὡς οὐδεὶς τῶν τὴν ἐγκειμένην αὐτοῖς αἵρεσιν ἐγνωκότων ἀνέξεται αὐτὰ δέξασθαι κἂν δὶς τοσοῦτοι ψηφίσωνται· καὶ γὰρ ἤδη καὶ πλειόνων, ὡς ἔτυχεν, ταῦτα βεβαιωσάντων, ἀντέστημεν ἐν Ἐφέσῳ καὶ οὐ πρότερον ἐκοινωνήσαμεν τῷ ταῦτα γεγραφότι ἕως, τοῖς παρ᾽ ἡμῶν ἐκτεθεῖσι συνθέμενος, σύμφωνον αὐτοῖς διδασκαλίαν προσήρμοσεν, οὐδεμίαν τῶν *κεφαλαίων* ἐκείνων ποιησάμενος μνήμην.

(2) Καὶ τοῦτο ῥᾴδιον γνῶναι Τὴν Σὴν Ὁσιότητα, κελεύσασαν ζητηθῆναι τὰ πεπραγμένα· ἀπόκειται γὰρ πάντως, κατὰ τὸ παρακολουθῆσαν ἔθος· τῆς συνόδου τὰς ὑπογραφὰς ἔχοντα. ἔστιν δὲ πλείονα ἢ πεντήκοντα συνοδικὰ τὴν κατηγορίαν *τῶν δώδεκα κεφαλαίων* δεικνύντα· πρὸ μὲν γὰρ τῆς εἰς Ἔφεσον ἀποδημίας, ὁ μακάριος γέγραφεν Ἰωάννης τοῖς περὶ τὸν θεοφιλέστατον ἐπίσκοπον Εὐθήριον τῶν Τυάνων, καὶ Φίλμον τὸν Καισαρείας, καὶ Θεόδοτον τὸν Ἀγκύρας, *Ἀπολιναρίου διδασκαλίαν* τὰ κεφάλαια ταῦτα καλέσας, καί ἐν Ἐφέσῳ δὲ ἡ

l. 42 ἀπόκειται *scripsi* : -ειντ- *codd., edd. The TLG offers numerous exx. of* ἀπόκειται + *neut. pl. subj., many from patristic authors. V., e.g., Euag. schol., H. e. 2.3: Εἴσω δὲ τοῦ θόλου … εὐπρεπὴς ἐστι σηκός, ἔνθα τὰ πανάγια τῆς μάρτυρος ἀπόκειται λείψανα. For the same combination of ἀπόκειται + λείψανα, v. Them., Or. in Const., p. 85, ll. 3f. In the two other places in the works of Thdt. where* τὰ πρεπραγμένα *functions as the subj. of a vb., the vb. is sg.* (*no pl. variant attested*)*; v. H. e. 2.23.5 (δεδήλωκε δὲ τὴν ἐκείνου γνώμην τὰ πεπραγμένα); also ib. 2.29.12. For the same morphological issue with a related vb., v. c. n. ep. 145* (κατάκειται).

the same, my heart is downcast, and groans in pain, and can expect no good.

The bishops of the other dioceses have no idea what poison lies in those *Twelve Chapters*. As they consider nothing but the preëminence of the author, they have no suspicion of anything bad and, as far as I can see, his successor in the see is making every effort to get them confirmed in a second council.[4] This man, who just recently, in compliance with a command, wrote letters of that tenor and anathematized all who refused to abide by them—imagine what he would be able to accomplish as president of an ecumenical council! You can be quite certain, my Master, that nobody who recognizes the heresy contained in them will approve them even if twice as many should endorse them. Previously, though a great number unthinkingly agreed with them, we refused to concur at Ephesus and would not join in communion with their author until he had acceded to the points we had laid down and brought his teaching into agreement with them and without any mention of those *Chapters*.

(2) To confirm this Your Holiness need do no more than order a search for the acts—they have certainly been preserved according to the normal practice—containing the signatures of the Council. But there are more than fifty conciliar letters setting out objections to the *Twelve Chapters*. Indeed, before departing for Ephesus, John of blessed memory wrote a letter to Eutherius of Tyana, Firmus of Caesarea, and Theodotus of Ancyra, bishops beloved of God, and their suffragans in which he referred to those *Chapters* as "the teaching of Apollinaris."[5] Then, in Ephesus, our deposition of the bishops

4. On the *Twelve Chapters* or the twelve anathemas that Cyril of Alexandria attached to his third letter to Nestorius, *v.* Intro., sec. 2.7. Cyril's successor was Dioscorus; *v. ep.* 60 n. 1.

5. Eutherius and Firmus were the metropolitans of the provinces of Cappadocia I and II. Cappadocia, now a region of south-central Turkey, was divided into two provinces in 371–72; *v.* Strobel. Tyana (modern Kemerhisar) was located to the south and the west of the larger and more important Caesarea (modern Kayseri); *v.* Foss, "Tyana" and "Caesarea." For Ancyra, *v. ep.* 82 n. 1. Eutherius was a supporter of Nestorius and a critic of Cyril, against whose *Twelve Chapters* he composed a treatise sometimes attributed in the manuscript tradition to Athanasius or Theodoret

παρ᾽ ἡμῶν γεγενημένη καθαίρεσις τοῦ τε τῆς ἀλεξανδρέων καὶ τοῦ τῆς ἐφεσίων αἰτίαν ἔχει τὴν τῶν *κεφαλαίων* τούτων ἔκθεσιν καὶ βεβαίωσιν, καὶ συνοδικὰ δὲ πολλὰ ἐν Ἐφέσῳ πρός τε τὸν καλλίνικον βασιλέα καὶ πρὸς τοὺς μεγάλους ἄρχοντας περὶ τούτων ἐγράφη, ὡσαύτως δὲ καὶ πρὸς τὸν ἐν Κωνσταντινουπόλει λαὸν καὶ πρὸς τὸν εὐλαβέστατον κλῆρον, καὶ μὲν δή, καὶ εἰς τὴν Κωνσταντινούπολιν κληθέντες, πέντε διαγνώσεις ἐπ᾽ αὐτοῦ τοῦ βασιλέως ἐσχήκαμεν καὶ τρεῖς ὕστερον αὐτῷ διαμαρτυρίας ἐπέμψαμεν, καὶ τοῖς θεοφιλεστάτοις δὲ τῆς δύσεως ἐπισκόποις· τῷ Μεδιολάνου φημί, καὶ τῷ Ἀκυλείας, καὶ τῷ Ῥαβέννης· περὶ τούτων ἐγράψαμεν, διαμαρτυρόμενοι ὡς τῆς Ἀπολιναρίου ταῦτα καινοτομίας πεπλήρωται, καὶ αὐτῷ δὲ τῷ ταῦτα γράψαντι ὁ μακάριος ἐπιστέλλων Ἰωάννης διὰ τοῦ μακαρίου Παύλου, προφανῶς αὐτοῖς ἐπεμέμψατο, ὡσαύτως δὲ καὶ ὁ τῆς μακαρίας μνήμης Ἀκάκιος. καί, ἵνα συντόμως μάθῃ Σοῦ Ἡ Ἁγιότης, ἀπέστειλα τῆς τε τοῦ μακαρίου Ἀκακίου ἐπιστολῆς καὶ τῆς τοῦ μακαρίου Ἰωάννου πρὸς τὸν μακαρίτην Κύριλλον γραφείσης τὸ ἴσον ἵνα γνῷς ὡς, καὶ περὶ συμβάσεως αὐτῷ γράφοντες, τὴν τῶν *κεφαλαίων* τούτων κατηγορίαν ἐποιήσαντο. καὶ αὐτὸς δὲ ὁ μακαρίτης Κύριλλος, γράφων τῷ μακαρίῳ Ἀκακίῳ, τὸν τῶν *κεφαλαίων* τούτων παρεδήλωσε σκοπόν, εἰρηκώς, ὅτι *Ἐκεῖνα πρὸς τὰς τοῦδε καινοτομίας ἐγράψαμεν,* καί, ὅτι *Τῆς εἰρήνης γενομένης, ἐκλευκανθήσεται,* καὶ αὕτη τοίνυν ἡ ἀπολογία βεβαιοῖ τὴν κατηγορίαν.

of Alexandria and Ephesus was based on their presentation of and insistence on the *Chapters*.[6] And while we were in Ephesus, many conciliar letters were sent to the invincible emperor and high officials regarding them, as well as to the laity and the right reverend clergy of Constantinople. Furthermore, we were summoned to Constantinople and had five discussions in the presence of the emperor himself and afterward sent him three appeals. And then we wrote a letter about the *Chapters* to the bishops of the West, beloved of God—I mean the bishops of Milan, Aquileia, and Ravenna—protesting that they were full of Apollinaris' inventions. What is more, by the intermediary of Paul of blessed memory, John of blessed memory sent a letter to their author in which he expressly censured them, and Acacius of blessed memory did the very same thing.[7] So that Your Sanctity may inform yourself from a summary of the material, I have sent copies of the letters written to the blessed Cyril, by Acacius of blessed memory and by John of blessed memory; you will note that even at the moment they were writing him regarding a reconciliation, they objected to the *Chapters*. As for blessed Cyril himself—in a letter to Acacius of blessed memory, he gave the following explanation of the purpose of the *Chapters*: "We wrote these in answer to the inventions of that man," and "As soon as peace is established, they will be whitewashed."[8] So, this very defense of his supports our accusation!

(*Confut.* = *CPG* #6147); *v.* Quasten, vol. 3, pp. 519–21. In addition, we possess Latin translations of five of his letters, including one written to John of Antioch (*CPG* #6152), one to Alexander of Hierapolis (*CPG* #6150), and one to Alexander and Theodoret (*CPG* #6149); *v.* also Gregory, "Eutherios."

6. On John of Antioch's absence from the opening session of the First Council of Ephesus and the depositions of Cyril of Alexandria and Memnon of Ephesus decreed by John's assembly, *v.* Intro., secc. 3.2–4.

7. On the negotiations for a reconciliation between the Alexandrians and the Antiochenes and for the part played in these by Paul of Emesa and Acacius of Beroea, *v.* Intro., sec. 3.10.

8. "As soon as peace is established, they will be whitewashed" corresponds to τῆς εἰρήνης γενομένης, ἐκλευκανθήσεται. In this, I follow Azéma ("la paix faite, ils seront blanchis"). The image seems to be that of an album, a whitewashed plank, on which outdated announcements, written in black, are covered over with white-

(3) Ἀπέστειλα δὲ καὶ τῶν παρ᾽ αὐτοῦ γραφέντων ἐν τῷ τῆς συμβάσεως καιρῷ τὸ ἀντίγραφον ἵνα γνῷς, Δέσποτα, ὡς οὐδεμίαν τούτων ἐποιήσατο μνήμην, καὶ ὡς χρὴ τοὺς ἀπιόντας εἰς τὴν σύνοδον τὰ ἐν τῷ καιρῷ τῆς συμβάσεως γραφέντα προσενεγκεῖν καὶ σαφῶς εἰπεῖν τίνα μὲν εἰργάσατο τὴν διάστασιν, ἐπὶ τίσιν δὲ τὰ διεστῶτα συνήφθη· τοὺς γὰρ εἰς τὸν ὑπὲρ τῆς εὐσεβείας καλουμένους ἀγῶνα πάντα πόνον ἀναδέξασθαι χρὴ καὶ τὴν θείαν ἐπικαλέσασθαι συμμαχίαν ἵνα τὸν παρὰ τῶν προγόνων ἡμῖν καταλειφθέντα κλῆρον διατηρήσωμεν ἄσυλον. χρὴ δὲ σκοπῆσαι Σοῦ Τὴν Ἁγιωσύνην καὶ τῶν θεοφιλεστάτων ἐπισκόπων τοὺς ὁμογνώμονας καὶ κοινωνοὺς τῆς ἀποδημίας ποιήσασθαι καὶ τῶν εὐλαβεστάτων κληρικῶν τοὺς τὸν ὑπὲρ τῆς εὐσεβείας ἔχοντας ζῆλον ἵνα μή, καὶ παρὰ τῶν οἰκείων προδοθέντες, ἢ ἀναγκασθῶμέν τι πρᾶξαι τῶν ἀπαρεσκόντων τῷ τῶν ὅλων Θεῷ ἤ, μονωθέντες, εὐεπιχείρητοι τοῖς πολεμοῦσιν γενώμεθα. πίστις ἐστί, παρακαλῶ, ἐν ᾗ τὰς ἐλπίδας ἔχομεν τῆς σωτηρίας, καὶ χρὴ πάντα κινῆσαι πόρον ὥστε μηδὲν αὐτῇ νόθον ἐπεισαχθῆναι, μηδὲ τὴν ἀποστολικὴν παραφθαρῆναι διδασκαλίαν. ταῦτα ἐγώ, καὶ πόρρωθεν ὤν, στένων καὶ θρηνῶν γράφω καὶ τὸν κοινὸν Δεσπότην ἀντιβολῶ τὸ στυγνὸν τοῦτο διαλῦσαι νέφος καὶ καθαρὰν ἡμῖν αἰθρίαν χαρίσασθαι.

(3) I have sent a copy of his letters from the time of the reconciliation so you may see, my Master, that in these he made no mention of the *Chapters*, and realize how important it is that those who will be going to the council present these letters from the time of the reconciliation and state plainly the causes of the disagreement and the grounds on which the opposing parties were reunited. After all, when called upon to contend for the faith, every one of us is obliged to undertake any toil and call upon the aid of God in our effort to preserve inviolate the inheritance bequeathed us by our forebears. And Your Sanctity must select like-minded bishops beloved of God and take them as companions on this journey—as well as right reverend clergymen possessed of a zeal for the faith—to forestall the possibility that we could be betrayed by our own side and forced to do something displeasing to the God of the universe, or, for lack of allies, fall an easy prey to our enemies. I urge you to consider that our faith is the source of our hope of salvation, and we are obliged to do everything possible to preserve the apostolic teaching from the introduction of falsehood or from any perversion. From far away, I write you this letter amidst sorrow and lamentation and beseech the Master of us all to scatter this dark cloud and bless us with bright clear skies.

---

wash to make room for something new. The verb ἐκλευκαίνω is rare, and the forms derived from the stem ἐκλευκαν- number only fifteen; *v. TLG*. Of these fifteen, one is Dn 12.10 (ἐκλευκανθῶσιν), and almost all the others explicitly refer to this verse, where the meaning is that of "purifying" or "cleansing." Theodoret and his readers probably saw the scriptural allusion and understood Cyril to be conceding that his *Chapters* were only a roughly expressed polemic written to meet the needs of the moment. Thus, Theodoret protests that Cyril himself saw their inadequacies.

113. ΛΕΟΝΤΙ ΕΠΙΣΚΟΠΩΙ ΡΩΜΗΣ

(1) Εἰ Παῦλος, τῆς ἀληθείας ὁ κῆρυξ, ἡ τοῦ Παναγίου Πνεύματος σάλπιγξ, πρὸς τὸν μέγαν ἔδραμε Πέτρον ὥστε τοῖς ἐν Ἀντιοχείᾳ περὶ τῆς κατὰ νόμον πολιτείας ἀμφισβητοῦσι παρ᾽ αὐτοῦ κομίσαι τὴν λύσιν,[a] πολλῷ μᾶλλον ἡμεῖς, οἱ εὐτελεῖς καὶ σμικροί, πρὸς τὸν ἀποστολικὸν ὑμῶν τρέχομεν θρόνον ὥστε παρ᾽ ὑμῶν λαβεῖν τοῖς τῶν ἐκκλησιῶν ἕλκεσι θεραπείαν· διὰ πάντα γὰρ ὑμῖν τὸ πρωτεύειν ἁρμόττει. πολλοῖς γὰρ ὁ ὑμέτερος θρόνος κοσμεῖται πλεονεκτήμασιν· τὰς μὲν γὰρ ἄλλας πόλεις ἢ μέγεθος, ἢ κάλλος, ἢ τὸ πλῆθος τῶν οἰκητόρων κοσμεῖ, ἐνίας δέ, τούτων ἐστερημένας, πνευματικά τινα λαμπρύνει χαρίσματα, τῇ δὲ ὑμετέρᾳ φορὰν ἔδωκεν ἀγαθῶν ὁ τῶν ἀγαθῶν Χορηγός· ἡ γὰρ αὐτὴ πασῶν μεγίστη, καὶ λαμπροτάτη, καὶ τῆς οἰκουμένης προκαθημένη, καὶ τῷ πλήθει τῶν οἰκητόρων κυμαίνουσα, πρὸς δὲ τούτοις, καὶ τὴν νῦν κρατοῦσαν ἡγεμονίαν ἐβλάστησεν καὶ τῆς οἰκείας προσηγορίας τοῖς ἀρχομένοις μετέδωκεν. κοσμεῖ δὲ αὐτὴν διαφερόντως ἡ πίστις, καὶ μάρτυς ἀξιόχρεως ὁ θεῖος Ἀπόστολος βοῶν, ὅτι *Ἡ πίστις ὑμῶν καταγγέλλεται ἐν ὅλῳ τῷ κόσμῳ.*[b] εἰ δέ, εὐθὺς δεξαμένη τὰ τοῦ σωτηρίου κηρύγματος σπέρματα, τοῖς ἀξιαγάστοις τούτοις ἐβεβρίθει καρποῖς, τίς ἀπόχρη λόγος τὴν νῦν ἐν αὐτῇ πολιτευομένην εὐσέβειαν εὐφημῆσαι;

Ἔχει δὲ καὶ τῶν κοινῶν πατέρων καὶ διδασκάλων τῆς ἀληθείας Πέτρου καὶ Παύλου τὰς θήκας, τῶν πιστῶν τὰς ψυχὰς φωτιζούσας. ἡ δὲ τρισμακαρία τούτων καὶ θεία ξυνωρὶς ἀνέτειλεν μὲν ἐν τῇ ἑῴᾳ καὶ πάντοσε τὰς ἀκτῖνας ἐξέπεμψεν, ἐν δὲ τῇ δύσει προθύμως ἐδέξατο τὰς τοῦ βίου δυσμάς, κἀκεῖθεν νῦν καταυγάζει τὴν οἰκουμένην. οὗτοι τὸν ὑμέτερον περιφανέστερον ἀπέφηναν θρόνον, οὗτος τῶν ἀγαθῶν τῶν

a. Acts 15.1–35 b. Rom 1.8

113. To Leo, Bishop of Rome[1]

(1) If Paul, that herald of the truth, that trumpet of the most Holy Spirit, ran to the great Peter to get from him an answer for those in Antioch who were debating the question of living in accordance with the law,[a] we, of no account, insignificant as we are, have all the more reason to run to your apostolic see to receive from your hand a cure for the wounds of the churches. Indeed, every consideration joins in support of your preëminence, for your see is distinguished by so many advantages. Other cities may be distinguished by their size, their beauty, or their population, while others with no such claims derive splendor from spiritual gifts, but the great Provider has bestowed on your city an abundance of good things: she is at once the biggest, the most splendid; she presides over the world, overflows with a sea of inhabitants, and, what is more, having given birth to the empire that now rules the world, she has shared her own name with those she governs. But her principal distinction is that of her faith, of which the holy Apostle is a trustworthy witness, exclaiming, "Your faith is proclaimed in all the world."[b] As her boughs were covered with these wondrous fruits so soon after receiving the seeds of the salvific proclamation, what words could suffice to praise the devotion to religion now typical of life within her? She contains the sepulchers of Peter and Paul—the fathers and teachers of truth to all the world—which enlighten the souls of the faithful. This holy, thrice-blessed pair was like a star that rose in the east, that sent forth its rays in all directions, and then received with no hesitation the sunset of life in the west, and it is from there that they shine down on the world. It is these who have conferred on your see a brilliance seen far and wide; this is the blessing that crowns all your blessings.

1. This letter which refers to Theodoret's deposition by Dioscorus of Alexandria ("the leader of the Alexandrian church," sec. 3 below) and his allies must have been written after the end of the Second Council of Ephesus in August 449. Azéma (vol. 3, p. 56, n. 1) dates it to September or October. On Leo's (bishop of Rome, 440–61; *v.* Livingstone, "Leo I, St.") preparations for, and reaction to, this Council, *v.* Intro., secc. 4.6–9.

ὑμετέρων ὁ κολοφών. ὁ δ᾽ ἐκείνων Θεὸς καὶ νῦν τὸν ἐκείνων ἐλάμπρυνε θρόνον, Τὴν Ὑμετέραν Ἁγιωσύνην ἱδρύσας ἐν τούτῳ τῆς ὀρθοδοξίας τὰς ἀκτῖνας ἀφιεῖσαν.

(2) Καὶ τούτου πολλὰ μὲν ἔστιν εὑρεῖν καὶ ἄλλα τεκμήρια, ἀρκεῖ δὲ ὑμῶν καὶ ὁ κατὰ τῶν δυσωνύμων μανιχαίων ζῆλος, ὃν πρώην Ὑμῶν Ἡ Ὁσιότης ἐγύμνωσεν, δείξασα τὴν περὶ τὰ θεῖα Τῆς Ὑμετέρας Φιλοθεΐας σπουδήν. ἀπόχρη καὶ τὰ νῦν παρ᾽ ὑμῶν γραφέντα τὸν ἀποστολικὸν ὑμῶν χαρακτῆρα δηλῶσαι· ἐντετυχήκαμεν γὰρ τοῖς παρὰ Τῆς Σῆς γραφεῖσι Ὁσιότητος περὶ τῆς *τοῦ … Θεοῦ καὶ Σωτῆρος ἡμῶν*[c] ἐνανθρωπήσεως καὶ ἐθαυμάσαμεν τὴν τῶν γεγραμμένων ἀκρίβειαν. ἀμφότερα γὰρ κατὰ ταὐτὸν ἐδήλου· καὶ τὴν ἐκ τοῦ ἀϊδίου Πατρὸς ἀΐδιον θεότητα τοῦ Μονογενοῦς καὶ τὴν ἐκ σπέρματος Ἀβραὰμ καὶ Δαυὶδ ἀνθρωπότητα, καὶ ὅτι κατὰ πάντα ἡμῖν ἡ ληφθεῖσα φύσις ἐῴκει, μόνον δὲ ἀνόμοιος ἦν τῷ πάσης ἁμαρτίας ἀμύητος διαμεῖναι, ἐπειδήπερ οὐκ ἐκ φύσεως, ἀλλ᾽ ἐκ προαιρέσεως αὕτη φύεται. εἶχεν δὲ καὶ τοῦτο τὰ γράμματα· ὡς εἷς μὲν ὁ μονογενὴς τοῦ Θεοῦ Υἱός, ἀπαθὴς δὲ αὐτοῦ ἡ θεότης, καὶ ἄτρεπτος, καὶ ἀναλλοίωτος[d] καθάπερ ὁ γεννήσας αὐτὸν Πατὴρ καὶ τὸ Πανάγιον Πνεῦμα, καὶ διὰ τοῦτο τὴν παθητὴν ἔλαβε φύσιν· ἐπειδήπερ ἡ θεία φύσις οὐκ ἐδέχετο πάθος· ἵνα, τῷ πάθει τῆς ἰδίας σαρκὸς τὴν ἀπάθειαν τοῖς εἰς αὐτὸν πεπιστευκόσι χαρίσηται. ταῦτα, καὶ ὅσα τούτοις ἐστὶ συγγενῆ, περιεῖχεν τὰ

l. 36 ὑμῶν *corr. Cir., scr. edd.* : ἡμ- *NZ* = *"what we have just now written"*

c. Ti 2.13 d. *Cf. Pac. form.*

And even in our own time, their God has continued to glorify their throne by seating upon it Your Sanctity, a radiant source of orthodox instruction.

(2) And among the many proofs of this, it is sufficient to mention the concern for religion Your Piety has lately demonstrated in the zeal Your Holiness has shown in the struggle against the Manichees, those bearers of that name of ill omen.[2] Indeed, what you have just now written is enough to show your genuine apostlic character. We have read, and with admiration for the precision with which you express yourself, what Your Holiness has written regarding "our … God and Savior"[c] made man.[3] There is a clear exposition of the two aspects to be found in one and the same subject—namely the eternal godhead of the Only-begotten of the eternal Father and his humanity derived from the seed of Abraham and David—and of the fact that the nature he assumed was like our own in all respects, except that he remained free from all sin, since sin comes not from nature, but from choice. And your letter also states that the only-begotten Son of God is one; that his godhead is impassible, immutable, unchangeable,[4d] as are the Father who begat him and the Holy Spirit; that he assumed a passible nature, since the divine nature admitted no passion, so that, by the suffering of his own flesh, he might confer the gift of freedom from suffering on those who put their faith in him. Your letter included these points and others related to them.

2. On the Manichees and the evil omen suggested by their name, *cf. ep.* 104 n. 4.

3. I understand τοῖς παρὰ Τῆς Σῆς γραφεῖσι Ὁσιότητος to refer to a single letter of Leo, *ep.* 28, the *Tomus ad Flauianum* (*v.* Intro., sec. 4.6). According to Theodoret, in the *Tome,* Leo made two closely related points (ἀμφότερα … ἐδήλου), *i.e.* regarding the divinity and the humanity of the Son. The plural participle γραφεῖσι, like the plural noun γράμματα may refer to a single letter, and the subject of the finite verb is the nominative Ὁσιότης easily supplied from the genitive a few words above. Jackson and Azéma have seen in the plural participle γραφεῖσι a reference to a plurality of works, and Jackson, making ἀμφότερα the subject of ἐδήλου translates "both writings agreed in setting forth." Azéma ("Car ils mettaient en lumière les deux éléments à la fois") agrees with me in taking ἀμφότερα as direct object, but makes the supposed plural writings (écrits) the subject of ἐδήλου. For the text of the *Tome*, v. Bibliography, **Leo romanus (Pope Leo I), *Epistulae, ad Flauianum,* (*Tomus Leonis*)**; for a translation, *v.* Hunt, pp. 92–105; for analysis of the *Tome*, *v.* Intro., sec. 4.6.

4. Theodoret had used two of these adjectives (ἀπαθής = "impassible" and ἄτρεπτος = "immutable") as the titles of two of the three books of the *Eranistes,* composed in 447; *v.* Intro., sec. 4.1.

γράμματα, ἡμεῖς δὲ τὴν πνευματικήν σου σοφίαν θαυμάσαντες, τὴν δι᾽ ὑμῶν φθεγξαμένην τοῦ Παναγίου Πνεύματος ἀνυμνήσαμεν χάριν, καὶ παρακαλοῦμεν, καὶ ἀντιβολοῦμεν, καὶ δεόμεθα, καὶ ἱκετεύομεν Σοῦ Τὴν Ἁγιωσύνην ἐπαμῦναι ταῖς τοῦ Θεοῦ ἐκκλησίαις χειμαζομέναις.

(3) Λύσιν γὰρ ἔσεσθαι τοῦ κλύδωνος προσδοκήσαντες διὰ τῶν παρὰ Τῆς Ὑμετέρας Ἁγιωσύνης εἰς τὴν Ἔφεσον ἀποσταλέντων, χαλεπωτέρᾳ περιπεπτώκαμεν ζάλῃ· ὁ γὰρ τῆς Ἀλεξανδρέων δικαιότατος πρόεδρος οὐκ ἠρκέσθη τῇ ἀνόμῳ ταύτῃ καὶ ἀδικωτάτῃ καθαιρέσει τοῦ ἁγιωτάτου καὶ θεοφιλεστάτου τῆς Κωνσταντινουπολιτῶν ἐπισκόπου τοῦ Κυρίου Φλαβιανοῦ, οὐδὲ ἐνέπλησεν αὐτοῦ τὸν θυμὸν τῶν ἄλλων ἐπισκόπων ἡ παραπλησία σφαγή, ἀλλὰ κἀμέ, τὸν ἀπόντα, ὁμοίως καλάμῳ κατέσφαξεν, οὔτε καλέσας εἰς κριτήριον οὔτε παρόντα κρίνας, οὐκ ἐρωτήσας τίνα φρονῶ περὶ τῆς *τοῦ … Θεοῦ καὶ Σωτῆρος ἡμῶν*[e] ἐνανθρωπήσεως. καὶ τοὺς μὲν ἀνδροφόνους, καὶ τυμβωρύχους, καὶ τοὺς τὰς ἀλλοτρίας συλήσαντας εὐνὰς οὐ πρότερον κατακρίνουσιν οἱ δικάζοντες ἕως ἂν ἢ αὐτοὶ τὰς κατηγορίας ταῖς ὁμολογίαις κυρώσωσιν ἢ παρ᾽ ἑτέρων ἐναργῶς ἐλεγχθῶσιν, ἡμᾶς δὲ ὁ τοῖς θείοις νόμοις ἐντεθραμμένος, πέντε καὶ τριάκοντα σταθμοῖς ἀφεστηκότας, κατέκρινεν ὡς ἠθέλησεν. καὶ τοῦτο οὐ νῦν μόνον πεποίηκεν, ἀλλὰ καὶ πέρυσι δύο ἄνδρας τῶν τὴν Ἀπολιναρίου νόσον εἰσδεξαμένων ἐκεῖσε δραμόντας καὶ συκοφαντίας καθ᾽ ἡμῶν ὑφήναντας δεξάμενος, ἀναστὰς ἐπ᾽ ἐκκλησίας, ἡμᾶς ἀνεθεμάτισεν, καὶ ταῦτα, ἐμοῦ γράψαντος πρὸς αὐτὸν καὶ ἃ φρονῶ διὰ γραμμάτων δηλώσαντος.

ll. 59f. ὁ … τῆς Ἀλεξανδρέων … πρόεδρος *codd.* : Ὁ … τ. -είας … π. *scr. Sir. Nös.* : Ὁ … τ. Ἀ. <πόλεως> … π. *scr. Az. V. c. n. ad ep. 83, l. 130* (ἀντιοχέων). **ll. 73–75** δύο ἄνδρας … δραμόντας καὶ συκοφαντίας καθ᾽ ἡμῶν ὑφήναντας δεξάμενος *scripsi* : *deest* δεξάμενος *N* : μετὰ δυο ἄ.… δρ. κ. σ. καθ᾽ ἡ. ὑ. *coni. Car., scr. edd.* = *"Last year, after two men infected with the Apollinarian disease ran off to Alexandria with a web of false accusations, he stood up," etc. It seems clear that, following the second of the participles, there is a lacuna of perhaps a word, perhaps more. My proposed supplement presupposes an haplography due to the similar appearance of* εἰσδεξαμένων *and* δεξάμενος. *Thdt. several times uses*

e. Ti 2.13

Filled with admiration for your spiritual wisdom, we sang a hymn of thanksgiving to the grace of the most Holy Spirit, who has spoken through you, and we urge, entreat, beg, and supplicate Your Sanctity to champion the churches of God that are now being tossed about in this storm.[5]

(3) In fact, though in expectation that the envoys sent by Your Sanctity to Ephesus would rescue us from the waves, we have been engulfed by an even more violent storm.[6] The leader of the Alexandrian church, in that great justice for which he is known, not content with the lawless and grossly unjust deposition of my lord Flavian, most holy bishop of Constantinople, beloved of God, nor having sated his rage by bringing other bishops likewise to slaughter, has also cut me down with a stroke of his pen, without a summons to a hearing, without passing judgment on me while I was myself present, never having put a question to me regarding my position regarding the incarnation "of our … God and Savior!"[e] Even murderers, grave-robbers, those who plunder other men's beds are not condemned by their judges until they confirm the truth of the charges by their own confession, or their guilt is proven by the prosecution. But in my case, while I was at a distance of thirty-five days' journey, this man—this man devoted, as he is, to the laws of religion—passed sentence on me just as he pleased. And this is not the only time he has done this. Last year, after taking in two men infected with the Apollinarian disease, who had run off to Alexandria with a web of false accusations, he stood up before the congregation and pronounced us anathema—and that even though I had written him a letter setting out my position!

5. Wagner points out that this sentence marks the end of the most elaborate of Theodoret's *prooemia* contrasting the lowliness of the author with the preëminence of the recipient, a strategy deployed also in *epp.* 42–44, 88f.

6. Leo had sent the four legates, Julius, bishop of Pozzuoli, the priest Renatus, and the deacons Hilary and Dulcitius, to serve as his representatives at the Second Council of Ephesus; *v.* Intro., sec. 4.5.

(4) Ἐγὼ δὲ ὀδύρομαι μὲν τῆς Ἐκκλησίας τὸν κλύδωνα, τὴν δὲ ἡσυχίαν ἀσπάζομαι· ἓξ γὰρ καὶ εἴκοσι ἔτη τὴν ἐγχειρισθεῖσάν μοι παρὰ τοῦ Θεοῦ τῶν ὅλων ἐκκλησίαν ἰθύνας διὰ τὰς ὑμετέρας εὐχάς, οὐκ ἐπὶ τοῦ μακαριωτάτου Θεοδότου, τοῦ τῆς Ἀνατολῆς προέδρου, οὐκ ἐπὶ τῶν μετ᾽ ἐκεῖνον, τῶν τὸν ἀντιοχέων διαδεξαμένων θρόνον, τὴν τυχοῦσαν μέμψιν ὑπέμεινα, ἀλλά, τῆς θείας μοι χάριτος συνεργησάσης, πλείους μὲν ἢ χιλίας ψυχὰς ἠλευθέρωσα τῆς Μαρκίωνος νόσου, πολλοὺς δὲ ἄλλους ἐκ τῆς Ἀρείου καὶ Εὐνομίου συμμορίας προσήγαγον τῷ Δεσπότῃ Χριστῷ. καὶ ἐν ὀκτακοσίαις ἐκκλησίαις ἔλαχον ποιμαίνειν· τοσαύτας γὰρ ἡ Κύρρος παροικίας ἔχει· ἐν αἷς οὐδὲ ἓν διὰ τὰς ὑμετέρας εὐχὰς μεμένηκε ζιζάνιον,[f] ἀλλὰ πάσης αἱρετικῆς ἠλευθέρωται πλάνης τὸ ἡμέτερον ποίμνιον. οἶδεν ὁ πάντα Ἐφορῶν[g] πόσους ἐδεξάμην λίθους ὑπὸ τῶν δυσωνύμων κατ᾽ ἐμοῦ πεμφθέντας αἱρετικῶν, πόσους ἐν ταῖς πλείοσι τῆς Ἀνατολῆς πόλεσιν ἔσχον ἀγῶνας πρὸς ἕλληνας, πρὸς ἰουδαίους, πρὸς πᾶσαν πλάνην αἱρετικήν, καὶ μετὰ τοσούτους ἱδρῶτας καὶ πόνους, μὴ δικασάμενος, κατεκρίθην.

Ἐγὼ δὲ τοῦ ἀποστολικοῦ ὑμῶν θρόνου περιμένω τὴν ψῆφον· καὶ ἱκετεύω καὶ ἀντιβολῶ Τὴν Σὴν Ἁγιότητα ἐπαμῦναί μοι τὸ ὀρθὸν ὑμῶν καὶ δίκαιον ἐπικαλουμένῳ κριτήριον καὶ κελεῦσαι δραμεῖν παρ᾽ ὑμᾶς καὶ ἐπιδεῖξαί μου τὴν διδασκαλίαν τοῖς ἀποστολικοῖς ἴχνεσιν ἑπομένην· ἔστιν γάρ μοι τὰ μὲν πρὸ εἴκοσι ἐτῶν συγγεγραμμένα, τὰ δὲ πρὸ ὀκτωκαίδεκα, τὰ δὲ πρὸ πεντεκαίδεκα, τὰ δὲ πρὸ δυοκαίδεκα· τὰ μὲν πρὸς ἀρειανοὺς καὶ εὐνομιανούς, τὰ δὲ πρὸς ἰουδαίους καὶ ἕλληνας, τὰ δὲ πρὸς τοὺς

---

the simplex pt. to refer to the reception of an inferior by a superior (or seeming superior); v. in Cant. cant., 1.1 (PG, vol. 81, col. 57, ll. 1f., of Symeon taking into his hands the baby Jesus): Τεχθέντα τοίνυν, καὶ εἰς τὸν ναὸν ἀνενεχθέντα, δεξάμενός … ἐν χερσὶν; also Q. in Num. 14 (of Joshua receiving the Gibeonites into his protection); Eran. flor. 2.63 (p. 174, l. 18, of God rescuing fallen man). Though Thdt. uses the prep. μετά thousands of times, the construction suggested by Cariofilo seems to me more typical of Latin than Greek.

f. Mt 13.24–30 g. *Cf.* 2Macc 12.22; 15.2; Sir 15.18.

(4) I mourn for the churches on these rough seas, as I am a lover of peace. In the twenty-six years I have been guiding, with the help of your prayers, this church entrusted to my care by the God of the universe, I have never incurred any complaint, even of a minor sort, not under the blessed Theodotus, Patriarch of the East, nor under any of his successors, who have followed him on the see of Antioch.[7] To the contrary, with the assistance of the grace of God, I have freed more than a thousand souls from the disease of Marcionism; many others I have guided from the sect of Arius and Eunomius to the Lord Christ.[8] It has been my lot to shepherd eight hundred churches—that is the number of parishes Cyrus contains—in which, thanks to your prayers, there remains not a single tare;[f] our flock stands freed from all heretical deceit. He who sees all[g] knows how many times I have been struck by stones cast by baneful heretics, how many contests in so many of the cities of the East I have endured with Hellenes, with Jews, with every sort of heretical deceit. And after all that sweat and toil, I was condemned without a trial!

Now I await the verdict of your apostolic see. Making my appeal to your upright and just tribunal, I supplicate and entreat Your Sanctity to champion my cause, to command me to run to you and demonstrate how my teaching follows in the footsteps of the apostles. I can produce treatises I composed twenty, eighteen, fifteen, and twelve years ago, against the Arians and the Eunomians, against the Jews and the Hellenes, against the Persian magi, and others regard-

7. On the succession of Antioch, *v. ep.* 81 n. 6.

8. On Marcion and his teaching, *v. ep.* 81 n. 10; on Arius, Intro., sec. 1.2; on Eunomius, Intro., sec. 1.7 and n. 68.

ἐν Περσίδι μάγους, ἄλλα περὶ τῆς καθόλου Προνοίας, ἕτερα δὲ περὶ θεολογίας καὶ τῆς θείας ἐνανθρωπήσεως, ἡρμήνευταί μοι διὰ τὴν θείαν χάριν καὶ τὰ ἀποστολικὰ συγγράμματα καὶ τὰ προφητικὰ θεσπίσματα, καὶ ῥᾴδιον ἐκ τούτων καταμαθεῖν εἴτε ἀκλινῆ τὸν κανόνα τῆς πίστεως διετήρησα εἴτε τὴν τούτου παρέβην εὐθύτητα. ἀλλὰ μὴ διαπτύσητέ μου τὴν ἱκετείαν, παρακαλῶ, μηδὲ τὴν ἀθλίαν μου παρίδητε πολιὰν μετὰ πολλοὺς ὑβρισμένην καμάτους.

(5) Πρὸ δὲ πάντων μαθεῖν ἀντιβολῶ παρ᾽ ὑμῶν εἴτε χρή με στέρξαι τὴν ἄδικον ταύτην καθαίρεσιν εἴτε μή· τὴν γὰρ ὑμετέραν προσμένω ψῆφον, κἂν κελεύσητε τοῖς καταψηφισαμένοις ἐμμεῖναι, ἐμμενῶ καὶ οὐδενὶ ἀνθρώπων ἐνοχλήσω λοιπόν, ἀλλὰ μενῶ τὸ ἀκλινὲς *τοῦ … Θεοῦ καὶ Σωτῆρος ἡμῶν*[h] κριτήριον. ἐμοὶ δέ, ὡς ὁ Δεσπότης μαρτυρεῖ Θεός, οὐ τιμῆς μέλει καὶ δόξης, ἀλλὰ μόνον τοῦ γεγενημένου σκανδάλου, ὅτι πολλοὶ τῶν ἁπλουστέρων, καὶ μάλιστα οἱ ἐκ διαφόρων αἱρέσεων παρ᾽ ἡμῶν ζωγρηθέντες, τῷ θρόνῳ τῶν κατακρινάντων προσέχοντες, αἱρετικοὺς ἴσως ἡμᾶς ὑπολήψονται, τὴν τοῦ δόγματος ἀκρίβειαν κατιδεῖν οὐ δυνάμενοι. ὅτι δέ, τοσοῦτον χρόνον ἐπισκοπεύσας, οὐκ οἰκίαν ἐκτησάμην, οὐκ ἀγρόν, οὐκ ὀβολόν, οὐ τάφον, ἀλλὰ τὴν αὐθαίρετον ἠσπασάμην πενίαν, καὶ τὰ παρὰ τῶν πατέρων εἰς ἡμᾶς ἐλθόντα μετὰ τὴν ἐκείνων τελευτὴν εὐθὺς διανείμας, ἴσασιν ἅπαντες οἱ τὴν ἑῴαν οἰκοῦντες.

Πρὸ δὲ πάντων ἱκετεύω τὴν ἱερὰν ὑμῶν καὶ τῷ Θεῷ φίλην κεφαλὴν παρασχεῖν μοι τῶν προσευχῶν τὴν βοήθειαν. ταῦτα διὰ τῶν εὐλαβεστάτων καὶ θεοφιλεστάτων πρεσβυτέρων Ὑπατίου καὶ Ἀβραμίου, τῶν χωρεπισκόπων, καὶ Ἀλυπίου, τοῦ ἐξάρχου

h. Ti 2.13

ing the universal providence, the doctrine of the Trinity, and the doctrine of the incarnation of God. I have also, thanks to the grace of God, written commentaries on the writings of the Apostle and the oracles of the prophets.[9] From these it is an easy matter to determine whether I have kept to the straight rule of faith or transgressed against its rectitude. I beg you not to reject my supplication; I urge you not to disregard my pitiable white hairs that have been subjected to such wanton outrage after so many toils.

(5) Above all, I request to learn from you whether or not I must resign myself to this unjust deposition, for it is your verdict that I await. Should you command me to abide by the decisions that have already been rendered, I shall abide by them and never afterward give annoyance to any man alive; instead, I shall await that unbiased tribunal "of our ... God and Savior."[h] As our Master God is my witness, I am not one to be concerned with honor and glory. My only concern is with the scandal that has been raised: that many of the simple, especially those we have rescued from one heresy or another, in their respect for the see that has issued this condemnation and lacking as they are in the ability to make clear distinctions of doctrine, may imagine that I am a heretic. As to the fact that, after such a long time as bishop, I have acquired no home, no farmland, not a cent, no tomb, but have gladly chosen a life of poverty, even distributing what I received from my parents right after their death—so much is common knowledge among those who live in the East.[10]

Above all, I beg you, holy and dear to God, to grant me the support of your prayers. I have informed Your Sanctity on these matters through the intermediary of the right reverend priests, beloved of God, Hypatius and Abramius, my co-adjutor bishops,[11] and Alypius,

9. Theodoret provides a similar catalogue of his works in *ep.* 82.2 (*v.* n. 6) and in *Q.* 1 *in Leu.* (*v.* n. 1).

10. *Cf. ep.* 81.2, where Theodoret similarly emphasizes his voluntary embrace of apostolic poverty.

11. The term "co-adjutor bishop" is a rendering of χωρεπίσκοπος, a title whose first syllable (χωρ-) refers to the country (χώρα). Hypatius and Abramius must have presided over some of the numerous country churches comprised within the

τῶν παρ᾽ ἡμῖν μοναζόντων, Τὴν Ὑμετέραν Ἁγιωσύνην ἐδίδαξα, ἐπειδήπερ ἐμὲ δραμεῖν πρὸς ὑμᾶς τὰ τῶν βασιλικῶν γραμμάτων ἐπέσχε δεσμά, ὥσπεροῦν καὶ τοὺς ἄλλους. καὶ παρακαλῶ Τὴν Ὑμετέραν Ὁσιότητα καὶ ἰδεῖν αὐτοὺς πατρικῶς, καὶ τὰς ἀκλινεῖς ὑμῶν ἀκοὰς εὐμενεῖς αὐτοῖς παρασχεῖν, καὶ τὸ συκοφαντούμενον καὶ μάτην πολεμούμενόν μου γῆρας τῆς ὑμετέρας ἀξιῶσαι κηδεμονίας, καί, πρὸ πάντων, τῆς ἐπιβουλευομένης πίστεως παντὶ σθένει φροντίσαι καὶ φυλάξαι ταῖς ἐκκλησίαις τὸν πατρῷον κλῆρον ἀκήρατον ἵνα καὶ τὰς ἀντὶ τούτων ἀντιδόσεις δέξηται Ὑμῶν Ἡ Ἁγιότης παρὰ τοῦ μεγαλοδώρου Δεσπότου.

superior of the monks of our diocese, since I, like others, am prevented by the restraint laid upon me by the emperor's letter from running to your protection. Finally, I entreat Your Holiness to look upon them with the eyes of a father and to give them a kindly hearing with unprejudiced ears, to deign my gray hairs, now falsely accused and wrongly embattled, worthy of your concern, but, above all, to exert all your strength on behalf of the faith now being subverted by conspirators and to preserve for the churches free from all blemish our inheritance from the fathers so that Your Sanctity may receive from our munificent Master the recompense due to such deeds.[12]

---

diocese of Cyrus. On the historical development and gradual elimination of this office. *v.* Papadakis, "Chorepiskopos." Hypatius is the addressee of the *Quaest. in Oct.* and the *Quaest. in Reg. et Par.*, works that must post-date the Council of Chalcedon; *v. Quaest. in Oct.*, pp. xix–xxi.

12. Theodoret received no reply from Leo until June 453, about a year and a half after the close of the Council of Chalcedon. In that letter (*ep.* 71), Leo expressed his gratitude for Theodoret's support of the christological teaching of the *Tome*; *v.* Intro., sec. 6.5 and n. 508.

114. ΑΝΔΙΒΕΡΙ

Ὁ εὐλαβέστατος πρεσβύτερος Πέτρος κοσμεῖται μὲν τῇ τῆς ἱερωσύνης ἀξίᾳ, κοσμεῖται δὲ καὶ τῇ τῶν σωμάτων λογικῇ θεραπείᾳ. συχνὸν δὲ παρ᾽ ἡμῖν οἰκήσας χρόνον, εἷλεν ἅπαντας τῇ τῶν ἠθῶν εὐαρμοστίᾳ, οὗτος νῦν τὴν Κύρρον καταλιπεῖν ἐδοκίμασεν, τὴν ἐμὴν ἐκδημίαν μεμαθηκώς. οὗ δὴ χάριν αὐτὸν Τῇ Ὑμετέρᾳ Μεγαλοπρεπείᾳ συνίστημι καὶ παρακαλῶ τῆς ὑμετέρας αὐτὸν προμηθείας τυχεῖν, χρήσιμον αὐτὸν τῇ πόλει γενέσθαι δυνάμενον· τὴν γὰρ Ἀλεξάνδρειαν οἰκήσας, τὴν τοιαύτην ἤσκησε τέχνην.

114. To Andiber[1]

Peter, the right reverend priest, is a man doubly distinguished: alike for the dignity of the priesthood and the scientific care of the body.[2] During his lengthy residence among us, he has won everyone over with his excellence of character,[3] but, now that he has learned of my departure, he has decided to leave Cyrus. Therefore, I recommend him to your Excellency and request that he have the benefit of your consideration. He is a man who can make himself useful to your city; indeed, he practiced the same profession in Alexandria, where he once lived.

1. This, like the following, is a letter of recommendation for the priest and doctor Peter ("Petrus 9," *PLRE*, vol. 2, p. 866). Given the form of address "Your Excellency" (Ἡ Ὑμετέρα Μεγαλοπρέπεια), we can conclude that Andiber was a layman of high rank; *cf. ep.* 5 n. 1. Martindale (p. 87) remarks that the name "suggests Germanic origin." Azéma (vol. 3, p. 68, n. 1) points out that letters 114–19 were all composed in 449 during the interval between Theodoret's deposition (in August) and his departure for his former monastery in Apamea; *v. ep.* 119.2 and Intro., sec. 4.8.

2. It is difficult to know what Theodoret intends with the adjective λογικός. Perhaps as my translation and those of my predecessors suggest (*cf.* Jackson, "wise practice in medicine"; and Azéma, "la science qui soigne les corps") he means no more than that Peter has acquired specialised knowledge through study. Yet, the second/third-century medical authority Galen (*v.* Edelstein and Nutton) distinguishes two schools of medicine, the empirical and the logical (ὀνόματά γε ταῖς αἱρέσεσιν ἔθεντο ἐμπειρικήν τε καὶ λογικήν; *De sectis,* ch. 1), the former being concerned only with the observable effects of phenomena, and the latter seeking knowledge also of underlying causes.

3. Peter exemplifies in his character and conduct the proper internal balance (τῇ τῶν ἠθῶν εὐαρμοστίᾳ) on which good health depends; *cf. ep.* 22 n. 2.

115. ΑΠΕΛΛΗΙ

Τὴν Κύρρον ἰθύνειν λαχών, τὰς ἀναγκαίας αὐτῇ πάντοθεν ἐπόρισα τέχνας, πρὸς δὲ τούτοις καὶ τοὺς τῆς ἰατρικῆς ἐπιστήμονας οἰκῆσαι ταύτην προέτρεψα. εἷς τούτων ἐστὶν ὁ εὐλαβέστατος πρεσβύτερος Πέτρος, λογικῶς μὲν μεταχειρίζων τὴν τέχνην, κοσμῶν δὲ ταύτην τοῖς ἤθεσιν, ἀλλὰ νῦν, ἐκδημούντων ἡμῶν, πολλοὶ μὲν καὶ ἄλλοι ταύτην ἀπέλιπον, ἐκδημῆσαι δὲ καὶ αὐτὸς ἐδοκίμασεν. διά τοι τοῦτο Τὴν Σὴν παρακαλῶ Μεγαλοπρέπειαν κηδεμονίας αὐτὸν ἀξιῶσαι· ἱκανὸς γάρ ἐστιν ἐπικουρῆσαι τοῖς κάμνουσι καὶ πολεμῆσαι ταῖς νόσοις.

115. To Apelles[1]

When it fell to my lot to govern Cyrus, I not only supplied the city from every possible source with all the necessary craftsmen, but also persuaded men endowed with medical knowledge to take up residence here. One of the latter is Peter, the right reverend priest, who practices his craft with scientific skill and does it honor with his virtue.[2] But, now that we are departing, many others have already left the city, and he has also decided to depart. Therefore, I pray Your Excellency to bestow your care on him, for he is well equipped to come to the aid of the sick and to wage war on their ailments.

1. On the purpose and date of this letter, *v. ep.* 114 n. 1. Apelles is the addressee also of *ep.* LI (of unknown date). Martindale ("Apelles 2," *PLRE*, vol. 2, p. 109) suggests that he is possibly to be identified with the *scholasticus* Apelles who served on the first commission charged with the compilation of the *C.Th.* If so, Apelles, unlike many a *scholasticus*, must have been learned in the law; *cf. ep.* 10 n. 1.

2. The adverb λογικῶς (here rendered "with scientific skill") may perhaps bear a more technical sense; *cf. ep.* 114 n. 2.

116. ΡΕΝΑΤΩΙ ΠΡΕΣΒΥΤΕΡΩΙ

(1)Ἔγνωμεν τὸν θερμὸν καὶ δίκαιον Τῆς Σῆς Ὁσιότητος ζῆλον καὶ τὴν δικαιοτάτην καὶ ἔννομον παρρησίαν, ᾗ χρησάμενος, Δέσποτα, τὰ ἐν Ἐφέσῳ τολμηθέντα ἤλεγξας. οὐχ ἡμεῖς δὲ μόνοι μεμαθήκαμεν ταῦτα, ἀλλ᾽ *εἰς πᾶσαν τὴν γῆν* τῆς σῆς ὀρθότητος *ἐξῆλθεν ὁ φθόγγος,*[a] καὶ πάντες ᾄδουσι τὴν δικαιοσύνην, τὸν ζῆλον, τὴν παρρησίαν, τὰς κατὰ τῆς παρανομίας παρ᾽ ὑμῶν γεγενημένας ἀπειλάς. καὶ ταῦτα ἔδρασεν Σοῦ Ἡ Ὁσιότης, τὴν μίαν θεασαμένη σφαγήν· εἰ δὲ καὶ τὰς ἄλλας ἑωράκεις τὰς μετὰ τὴν σὴν ἐκδημίαν γεγενημένας, τάχα ἂν τὸν Φινεὲς ἐκεῖνον ἐζήλωσας.[b]

Εἷς δὲ τῶν μετὰ ταῦτα κατακριθέντων ἐγώ, δραμεῖν μὲν αὐτόθι κωλυθεὶς διὰ γραμμάτων βασιλικῶν, ἀπὼν δὲ κατακριθείς· μετὰ γὰρ ἓξ καὶ εἴκοσι ἔτη τῆς ἐπισκοπῆς, μετὰ τοὺς πολλοὺς καὶ μυρίους πόνους, μετὰ τοὺς ὑπὲρ τῆς εὐσεβείας ἀγῶνας, μετὰ τὸ προσενέγκαι τῷ Σωτῆρι τῶν ὅλων πολλὰς αἱρετικῶν μυριάδας τῆς προτέρας πλάνης ἀπηλλαγμένας, ἐγύμνωσαν μὲν ἱερωσύνης, ἐξελαύνουσι δὲ καὶ πόλεων, οὐδὲ τὸ γῆρας αἰδεσθέντες οὐδὲ τὴν πολιὰν τὴν ἐν εὐσεβείᾳ τραφεῖσαν.

Διά τοι τοῦτο Τὴν Ὑμετέραν Ἁγιωσύνην παρακαλῶ πεῖσαι τὸν ἁγιώτατον καὶ ὁσιώτατον ἀρχιεπίσκοπον τῇ ἀποστολικῇ χρήσασθαι ἐξουσίᾳ καὶ εἰς τὸ ὑμέτερον ἀναδραμεῖν κελεῦσαι συνέδριον· ἔχει γὰρ ὁ πανάγιος θρόνος ἐκεῖνος τῶν κατὰ τὴν οἰκουμένην ἐκκλησιῶν τὴν ἡγεμονίαν διὰ πολλά, καὶ πρὸ τῶν ἄλλων ἁπάντων, ὅτι αἱρετικῆς μεμένηκεν δυσωδίας ἀμύητος καὶ οὐδεὶς τἀναντία φρονῶν εἰς ἐκεῖνον ἐκάθισεν, ἀλλὰ τὴν

l. **17** πόλεων *NZ* : -εως *scr. Cir., edd. The pl. is in conformity with the practice of banning deposed bishops from the cities; v. H. e. 1.20.11 (regarding the depositions of Eusebius of Nicomendia and Theognis of Nicaea), where the pl. gen. is coupled with a passive form of the vb. ἐξελαύνω: Τότε μὲν οὖν οὗτοι καὶ καθῃρέθησαν καὶ τῶν πόλεων ἐξηλάθησαν. Cf. also ep. 81.1 where Thdt. complains of the restrictions placed on his own movements by the order of relegation: τοῖς τὰ μέγιστα παρανομήσασι παραπλησίως τῶν ἄλλων εἴργομαι πόλεων.*

a. Ps 19.4 (LXX var.)   b. Nm 25.1–13

116. To Renatus, the Priest[1]

(1) We have learned, my Master, of the warmth and righteousness of Your Holiness' zeal and the regard for justice and legal procedure with which you spoke out against those outrageous proceedings in Ephesus. We are not the only ones who know about this; indeed "the fame" of your rectitude "has gone out over all the earth,"[a] and there is a universal chorus of praise for your justice and zeal and the threats with which you confronted that lawlessness. Such were Your Holiness' deeds after seeing only a single murderous act of violence; if you had witnessed those others that took place after your departure, you might well have imitated the zeal of Phineus of old.[2b]

Of those condemned afterward, I, and I alone, was prevented from hastening to the council by a letter of the emperor and then condemned in my absence. Yes, after my twenty-six years in the episcopacy, my countless labors, my struggles on behalf of orthodoxy, my delivering over to the Savior of the world tens of thousands that I had rescued from the error of their former belief, they have stripped me of my priesthood and are even driving me out of the cities, with no regard for my old age or for my hair grown gray in devotion to orthodoxy! Therefore, I appeal to Your Sanctity to move your archbishop, most godly and most holy, to exercise his apostolic authority and command me to have recourse to your judgment seat. For that all-holy see holds the position of leadership of all the churches in the world for many reasons, but, above all, because it has remained untainted by the bad odor of heresy; those who have succeeded to that chair have never espoused unorthodox views, but have defended

1. Renatus was one of Leo's representatives to the Second Council of Ephesus (*v. ep.* 113 n. 6). As his name does not appear in the conciliar acts, he may have died during the journey across the Mediterranean; *v.* Intro., sec. 4.5. If so, Theodoret would not have been informed; *v.* n. 2 below. On the date of this letter, *v. ep.* 114 n. 1.

2. It is generally assumed that Theodoret was ill-informed about who said what at the Council. At least, there is no doubt that the Roman deacon Hilary interposed a veto to the deposition of Flavian of Constantinople and left Ephesus before the session at which Theodoret, Ibas, and Domnus were deposed; *v.* Hefele, vol. 3 (English translation, pp. 260–62), and Intro., sec. 4.8.

ἀποστολικὴν χάριν ἀκήρατον διεφύλαξεν· τὰ γὰρ παρ᾽ ὑμῶν κριθησόμενα στέρξομεν, ὁποῖα ἂν ᾖ, τῇ ὑμετέρᾳ δικαιοκρισίᾳ θαρροῦντες.

(2) Καὶ ἀξιοῦμεν ἀπὸ τῶν ἐγγράφων κριθῆναι· πλείους γὰρ ἢ τριάκοντα συνέγραψα βίβλους κατὰ Ἀρείου καὶ Εὐνομίου, κατὰ Μαρκίωνος, κατὰ Μακεδονίου, κατὰ ἑλλήνων, κατὰ ἰουδαίων, ἡρμήνευσα δὲ καὶ τὴν θείαν Γραφήν. καὶ ῥᾴδιον τῷ βουλομένῳ καταμαθεῖν ὡς τοῖς ἀποστολικοῖς ἴχνεσιν ἠκολούθησα, ἕνα κηρύττων Υἱόν, ὡς ἕνα Πατέρα καὶ ἓν Ἅγιον Πνεῦμα, μίαν τῆς Τριάδος θεότητα, μίαν βασιλείαν, μίαν ἐξουσίαν, ἀϊδιότητα, ἀτρεπτότητα, ἀπάθειαν, ἓν θέλημα· τελείαν τοῦ Κυρίου ἡμῶν Ἰησοῦ Χριστοῦ τὴν θεότητα, τελείαν τὴν ἀνθρωπότητα, τὴν *διὰ τὴν ἡμετέραν σωτηρίαν*[c] ληφθεῖσαν καὶ ὑπὲρ ἡμῶν τῷ θανάτῳ παραδοθεῖσαν. Οὐκ ἄλλον οἶδα τὸν Υἱὸν τοῦ ἀνθρώπου καὶ ἄλλον τὸν Υἱὸν τοῦ Θεοῦ, ἀλλὰ τὸν αὐτόν· *Υἱὸν* μὲν *τοῦ Θεοῦ* καὶ *Θεὸν … ἐκ Θεοῦ* γεγενημένον,[d] Υἱὸν δὲ ἀνθρώπου διὰ τὴν ἐκ σπέρματος Ἀβραὰμ καὶ Δαυὶδ ληφθεῖσαν τοῦ *δούλου μορφήν*.[e] ταῦτα καὶ τὰ τούτοις παραπλήσια διατελῶ διδάσκων, ταῦτα καὶ ἐν τοῖς γράμμασιν τοῦ ἁγιωτάτου καὶ ὁσιωτάτου ἀρχιεπισκόπου, τοῦ Δεσπότου μου Λέοντος, εὗρον ἐγκείμενα καὶ τὸν τῶν ὅλων ὕμνησα Δεσπότην, ὅτι τοῖς ἀποστολικοῖς αὐτοῦ δόγμασιν συμφωνῶ.

Δέξασθέ μου τοίνυν, παρακαλῶ, τὴν ἱκεσίαν καὶ μὴ παρίδητε ἠδικημένον· τούτου γὰρ δὴ χάριν καὶ τοὺς θεοφιλεστάτους πρεσβυτέρους Ὑπάτιον καὶ Ἀβράμιον, τοὺς χωρεπισκόπους, καὶ Ἀλύπιον, τὸν τῶν παρ᾽ ἡμῖν μοναζόντων ἔξαρχον, πρὸς Τὴν

l. 51 Ἀλύπιον τὸν τῶν παρ᾽ ἡμῖν μοναζόντων ἔξαρχον *scripsi* : Ἀ. τὸν παρ᾽ ἡ. μ. ἔ. *codd.* : Ἀ. τῶν παρ᾽ ἡ. μ. τὸν ἔ. *scr. Sir. Nös. Az. Adding the gen. pl. art. for μοναζόντων and moving the acc. art. τὸν, Sirmond reproduces the phraseology of the corresponding passage in ep. 117. Yet the loss of the gen. art. is easier to explain if Thdt. had placed it between τὸν and the prep. phrase. The TLG offers 11 exx. of the phrase τὸν τῶν … ἔξαρχον. Cf. Chrys. (?), hom. 2 in Sanctum Stephanon (CPG #4692): Ἡμεῖς δὲ ἔχομεν αὐτὸν ὑπὲρ ἡμῶν πρεσβεύοντα, … τὸν τοῦ Χριστοῦ μαθητήν, τὸν τῶν Ἰουδαίων ἔλεγχον, τὸν τῶν μαρτύρων ἔξαρχον.*

c. *Symb. Nic-CP; Pac. form.* d. *Symb. Nic-CP* e. Phil 2.7

from blemish the grace they received from the apostles. Relying on your justice, we shall resign ourselves to your judgment, whatever it may be.

(2) And I demand to be judged by my writings. I have written more than thirty books against Arius and Eunomius, against Marcion, against Macedonius, against the Hellenes, against the Jews, and I have also commented upon the holy Scripture,[3] and anyone who wants to can easily determine that I have followed in the footsteps of the apostles: I preach one Son, just as one Father, and one Holy Spirit—one godhead of the Trinity, one kingship, one power, one eternity, immutability, impassibility,[4] one will—the full divinity of our Lord Jesus Christ, the full humanity he assumed "for our salvation"[c] and which, for our sake, he handed over to death. I do not know of one who is Son of man and another who is son of God, but one and the same who is "Son of God and God ... begotten of God"[d] as well as Son of man through the "form of the slave"[e] assumed through the seed of Abraham and David. This and what agrees with this is what I have been teaching. It is just these teachings that I have found also in the letter of the archbishop, my master Leo, most godly and most holy, and I hymned the praises of the Master of the universe, since I find myself in agreement with his apostolic teachings.[5]

So then, I pray you, receive my supplication, and do not ignore the victim of injustice. I have sent to Your Piety the priests beloved of God, Hypatius and Abramius, my co-adjutor bishops, and

3. On Marcion, Arius, and Eunomius, *v. ep.* 113 n. 8. For Macedonius, who denied the divinity of the Holy Spirit, *v.* Intro., sec. 1.1. On this catalogue of Theodoret's works, *v. ep.* 113 n. 9.

4. On the terms ἀπαθής (= "impassible") and ἄτρεπτος (= "immutable"), *v. ep.* 113 n. 4.

5. Theodoret is referring to Leo's *Tome*; *v. ep.* 113 n. 3.

Ὑμετέραν Φιλοθεΐαν ἀπέστειλα, βίῳ μὲν λαμπρῷ κοσμουμένους, δυναμένους δὲ καὶ διὰ τῆς γλώττης ἀκριβῶς ὑμᾶς διδάξαι τὰ κατὰ Τὴν Ἡμετέραν Εὐτέλειαν.

l. 53 διὰ τῆς γλώττης *scr. Sir. Nös. Az.* : δ. γ. *codd.* = *"they will be capable of providing a full explanation aloud." Sirmond's correction is probably correct. In the works of Thdt., the phrase with the article is much more common than that without. Furthermore, the few exx. of the anarthrous construction seem restricted to contexts where the contrast is not between the written and the spoken word, but between silence and speech; v. Haer. com. 13* (*PG, vol. 83, col. 364, l. 30, regarding the rites of certain gnostics*): *Τὰς δὲ μυστικὰς αὐτῶν τελετὰς τίς οὕτω τρισάθλιος ὥστε διὰ γλώττης προενεγκεῖν τὰ τελούμενα;*

Alypius, superior of the monks of our diocese, men distinguished by the excellence of their conduct; they will be capable of providing a full explanation in person of the situation of Our Insignificance.[6]

6. On Hypatius, Abramius, and Alypius, *v. ep.* 113 n. 11.

117. ΦΛΩΡΕΝΤΙΩΙ ΕΠΙΣΚΟΠΩΙ

Οὐ παντελῶς ἄρα τῶν ἀνθρώπων τὸ γένος ἡ *τοῦ … Θεοῦ καὶ Σωτῆρος ἡμῶν*[a] ἐπιλέλοιπεν χάρις, ἀλλ᾽ *ἐγκατέλιπεν ἡμῖν σπέρμα* Τὴν Ὑμετέραν Ἁγιωσύνην ἵνα μὴ *ὡς Σόδομα* γενηθῶμεν *καὶ …* Γομόρροις ὁμοιωθῶμεν.[b] τοῦτο ἡμᾶς ἀπαγορεύειν παντάπασιν οὐκ ἐᾷ, ἀλλὰ τοῦ χαλεποῦ χειμῶνος προσμένειν τὴν λύσιν παρεγγυᾷ, τοῦτο ἡμᾶς εὐέλπιδας ἀπεργάζεται. διά τοι τοῦτο καὶ τοὺς θεοφιλεστάτους πρεσβυτέρους Ὑπάτιον καὶ Ἀβράμιον, τοὺς χωρεπισκόπους, καὶ Ἀλύπιον, τῶν παρ᾽ ἡμῖν μοναζόντων τὸν ἔξαρχον, πρὸς Τὴν Ὑμετέραν ἀπεστείλαμεν Ἁγιότητα ἵνα τὴν ἐπισκήψασαν ταῖς τῆς Ἀνατολῆς ἐκκλησίαις διαλύσητε συμφοράν.

Καὶ πρῶτον μὲν τὴν ἄνωθεν παρὰ τῶν ἱερῶν ἀποστόλων παραδοθεῖσαν ἡμῖν κρατύνητε πίστιν, καὶ τὴν ἐπαναστᾶσαν αἵρεσιν στηλιτεύσητε, καὶ τοὺς παραχαράττειν τολμῶντας τῆς οἰκονομίας τὸ κήρυγμα προφανῶς ἐξελέγξητε, ἔπειτα δὲ καὶ τῶν ὑπὲρ τῆς εὐσεβείας πολεμουμένων ὑπερμαχήσητε· ὑπὲρ γὰρ τῆς ἀποστολικῆς πίστεως, Ἁγιώτατοι, τὴν ἄδικον ταύτην σφαγὴν ὑπεμείναμεν, ὡς τῶν εὐαγγελικῶν δογμάτων οὐ προϊέμενοι τὴν ἀλήθειαν. πρέπει δὲ Ὑμῶν Τῇ Ὁσιότητι μὴ παριδεῖν τοὺς ὁμόφρονας ἀδίκως ἐλαυνομένους, ἀλλὰ παῦσαι τῇ δικαίᾳ βοηθείᾳ τὴν ἀδικίαν καὶ διδάξαι τοὺς κατὰ τῆς ἀληθείας θρασυνομένους ὡς οὐ *πάντα* δρᾶν *ἔξεστιν*[c] τοῖς πᾶν ὁτιοῦν ἀδεῶς ποιεῖν πειρωμένοις.

a. Ti 2.13 b. Rom 9.29 (NT var.) (*Cf.* Mt 10.15.) c. 1Cor 10.23 (NT var.)

117. To Bishop Florentius[1]

So, it seems that the grace "of our ... God and Savior"[a] has not entirely failed the human race. No, for he has left us Your Sanctity as a seed, "to prevent us from becoming another Sodom, from being likened to Gomorrah."[b] It is this seed that keeps us from giving up, that encourages us to weather the harshness of the storm, that gives us good grounds for hope. And so, we have sent to Your Sanctity the priests beloved of God, Hypatius and Abramius, my co-adjutor bishops, and Alypius, superior of the monks of our diocese,[2] so that you will put an end to the trouble that has stricken the churches of the East.

First and foremost, confirm the faith that, from the very beginning, has been handed down to us by the holy apostles, decrying the heresy that has risen up, and publicly refuting those who have the audacity to counterfeit the proclamation of the incarnation. Then step forward to shield those who are fighting on behalf of orthodoxy. Indeed, Your Sanctity, it is on account of that apostolic faith that we have been unjustly sent to our slaughter, because we have refused to discard gospel teaching. It is Your Holiness' duty not to allow men of like mind to be driven unjustly into exile, but to come to our aid with justice to stop this injustice and to teach those who have the temerity to attack the truth that not "everything is permitted"[c] to those who set themselves to do whatever they like with no fear of consequences.

1. As Theodoret's use of honorifics such as "Your Sanctity" (Τὴν Ὑμετέραν Ἁγιωσύνην) indicate, the Florentius addressed in this letter must have been a bishop, not the former Praetorian Prefect of the East, addressed in *ep.* 89. Azéma (vol. 1, p. 37) suggests that this bishop is possibly to be identified with the African Florentius, a refugee of the Vandal invasion, for whom Theodoret composed a letter of introduction (*ep.* XXII) to Eusebius of Ancyra while Florentius was making his way westward from Cyrus to Constantinople (*v.* Azéma, vol. 1, p. 92, n. 7). It might be that, some time after reaching the eastern capital, he took refuge with Leo in Rome. On the date of this letter, *v. ep.* 114 n. 1.

2. On Hypatius, Abramius, and Alypius, who were the bearers also of letters 113 and 116, *v. ep.* 113 n. 11.

118. ΤΩΙ ΑΡΧΙΔΙΑΚΟΝΩΙ ΡΩΜΗΣ

Παγχάλεπος χειμὼν ταῖς παρ' ἡμῖν ἐκκλησίαις ἐπέσκηψεν, οἱ δὲ τῆς ἀποστολικῆς ἀντεχόμενοι πίστεως Τὴν Ὑμετέραν Ἁγιωσύνην εὔστομον ἔχουσι λιμένα καὶ εὔδιον· οὐ γὰρ τῶν εὐαγγελικῶν ὑπερμαχεῖτε δογμάτων μόνον, ἀλλὰ καὶ τὴν καθ' ἡμῶν γεγενημένην ἀδικίαν πάντως μυσάττεσθε. πόρρω γὰρ ἡμᾶς διάγοντας καὶ πέντε καὶ τριάκοντα σταθμοῖς ἀφεστηκότας κατέκριναν, ὡς ἠθέλησαν, οἱ δικαιότατοι δικασταί, καί, τὴν ἐκ τῆς τοῦ Θεοῦ Σωτῆρος[a] παρουσίας μέχρι καὶ τήμερον ἐν ταῖς ἐκκλησίαις κρατήσασαν διδασκαλίαν παραλιπόντες, καινήν τινα, καὶ νόθον, καὶ ἄντικρυς ἐναντίαν τῇ παραδόσει τῶν ἀποστόλων εἰσήγαγον, καὶ τοῖς τὰ παλαιὰ κρατοῦσι κηρύγματα προφανῶς πολεμοῦσιν.

Καταξίωσον τοίνυν, θεοφιλέστατε, πυρσεῦσαι τὸν ζῆλον τοῦ πάντα ἁγιωτάτου καὶ ὁσιωτάτου ἀρχιεπισκόπου ὥστε καὶ τὰς τῆς Ἀνατολῆς ἐκκλησίας τῆς ὑμετέρας ἀπολαῦσαι κηδεμονίας, καὶ διαφερόντως τῆς ἄνωθεν παρὰ τῶν ἱερῶν ἀποστόλων παραδοθείσης ὑπερμαχῆσαι πίστεως καὶ ἄσυλον τὸν πατρῷον κλῆρον διαφυλάξαι, καὶ τὴν ἐπικειμένην ὀμίχλην ἀποσκεδάσαι καί, ἀντὶ τῆς σκοτομήνης, καθαρὰν αἰθρίαν ἐργάσασθαι, καὶ τὴν καθ' ἡμῶν ἀδίκως γεγενημένην ἐξελέγξαι σφαγήν. πρέπει γὰρ Σοῦ Τῇ Ὁσιότητι τοῖς ἄλλοις αὐτῆς κατορθώμασιν καὶ τοῦτον προσθεῖναι τὸν ζῆλον.

a. *Cf.* Ti 2.13.

118. To the Archdeacon of Rome[1]

Such a dire storm has come down on the churches of our parts, but those who hold to the apostolic faith have in Your Sanctity a haven, both wide and calm; not only do you step forward to defend the gospel teachings, but you also express your disgust for the injustice that has been committed against us. And with good reason: Those most righteous of judges have indulged their whim and condemned us, though so far off, indeed thirty-five days' journey away, and, abandoning the teaching current in the churches from the coming of God the Savior[a] up to today, they have introduced this new teaching of theirs, one that is spurious and entirely opposed to the apostolic tradition, and openly wage war against those who hold fast to the ancient teachings!

Therefore, beloved of God, I beg you to kindle the zeal of the archbishop, most godly and most holy, so that even the churches of the East may enjoy the benefit of your kindly care. First and foremost, make yourself a champion of the faith that, from the very beginning, has been passed down by the holy apostles and keep inviolate our inheritance from the fathers, scatter the gloom that lies upon us and change the dark of a moonless night to bright sunshine, and show up the injustice with which we were sent to our slaughter. It is only fitting that Your Holiness should add this act of zeal to your other fine deeds.

1. It is unclear who bore this title at this date, or whether Theodoret himself knew. The deacon Hilary (*v.* Intro. n. 313) succeeded Leo, but he is not given the title of "archdeacon" in the acts of Ephesus II. On the date, *v. ep.* 114 n. 1.

119. ΑΝΑΤΟΛΙΩΙ ΠΑΤΡΙΚΙΩΙ

(1)Ἔγνω πάντως Τὸ Ὑμέτερον Μέγεθος τὰ παρὰ τῶν δικαιοτάτων ἐν Ἐφέσῳ γενόμενα δικαστῶν· *εἰς πᾶσαν* γὰρ *τὴν γῆν ἐξῆλθεν ὁ φθόγγος αὐτῶν, καὶ εἰς τὰ πέρατα τῆς οἰκουμένης* ἡ ὀρθοτάτη ψῆφος *αὐτῶν*·[a] ποία γὰρ ἐκκλησία τὴν ἐντεῦθεν ἐπαναστᾶσαν οὐκ ἐδέξατο ζάλην; οἱ μὲν γὰρ ἠδίκησαν, οἱ δὲ ἠδικήθησαν, οἱ δέ, τοῦτο μήτε ὑπομείναντες μήτε δράσαντες, τοῖς μὲν ἠδικημένοις συναλγοῦσιν, τοὺς δὲ ἠδικηκότας θρηνοῦσιν, ὡς ὠμῶς ἄγαν καὶ παρὰ πάντας τοὺς νόμους, τούς τε θείους τούς τε ἀνθρωπίνους, τὰ οἰκεῖα κατασφάξαντας μέλη.

Τοὺς μὲν γὰρ τοιχωρύχους ἁλισκομένους ἐπ' αὐτοφώρῳ κρίνουσιν πρῶτον, εἶθ' οὕτω κολάζουσιν οἱ δικάζοντες· καὶ μέντοι καὶ τοὺς ἀνδροφόνους, καὶ τοὺς τυμβωρύχους, καὶ τοὺς τὰς ἀλλοτρίας ἀποσυλῶντας εὐνὰς εἰσάγουσι πρότερον εἰς τὸ κριτήριον, καὶ τοῖς κατηγόροις ποιεῖσθαι κελεύουσι τὰς γραφάς, καὶ τὸν τῶν μαρτύρων σκοπὸν ἐξετάζουσιν, εἰ μὴ πρὸς χάριν μαρτυροῦσι τῶν διωκόντων, εἰ μὴ τῶν φευγόντων εἰσὶν δυσμενεῖς, καί, πρὸς τούτοις, ἀπολογεῖσθαι τοῖς κατηγόροις κελεύουσιν· καὶ τοῦτο δὶς γίγνεται, καὶ τρίς, ἔστιν δὲ ὅτε καὶ τετράκις, καὶ τότε λοιπόν, ἐν τοῖς τούτων κἀκείνων λόγοις ζητήσαντες τὴν ἀλήθειαν, τὴν ψῆφον ἐκφέρουσιν.

Οὗτοι δὲ ὅπως μὲν τοῖς ἄλλοις ἐδίκασαν, οὐδὲν ἐρῶ ἵνα μὴ δόξω περιττός τις εἶναι καὶ πολυπραγμονεῖν τὰ ἀλλότρια, ὑπὲρ ἐμαυτοῦ δὲ λέγειν μόνον βιάζομαι, τῆς ἀδίκου με καταναγκαζούσης σφαγῆς· οἴκοι γάρ με τοῦ βασιλικοῦ καθείργοντος νόμου καὶ περαιτέρω τῶν ὅρων τῆς ὑπ' ἐμοῦ ποιμαινομένης πόλεως προβαίνειν κωλύοντος, ἐκάθισαν μὲν

a. Ps 19.4 (LXX var.)

119. To Anatolius, the Patrician[1]

(1) Your Lordship is well aware of the decisions taken by those most just judges in Ephesus; "their voice has gone out to all the earth," the righteousness of their verdict "to the ends of the world."[2a] Indeed, is there any church that has not been visited by the storm that rose up in that place? There were those who committed injustice, and those that suffered injustice while those who neither endured nor inflicted injustice sympathize with the victims and lament for the guilty, who, acting with such savagery and in contravention of all law, both divine and human, have cut off members of their own body.

In the case of burglars caught in the very act, their judges never punish them without first putting them on trial. Even murderers, grave-robbers, those who plunder other men's beds are first hauled into court, and their accusers are instructed to set forth the charges; then the motivations of the witnesses are examined to determine if they are influenced in favor of the prosecution or have a grudge against the defendants, and the defendants are instructed to make their reply to their accusers. This is done twice, three times, sometimes even four until, at last, when the truth has been elicited from the testimony of both sides, the verdict is pronounced.

Now, as I have no wish to seem to be dealing with things that don't concern me or meddling in the affairs of others, I won't say anything about the way the Council has passed judgment on other men, but, as I have been unjustly sent to slaughter, I'm constrained to speak at least about my own case. There I was at home, because the emperor's edict forbade me to step beyond the limits of the city under

1. On Anatolius, *v. ep.* 45 n. 1, and for the date of this letter, *v. ep.* 114 n. 1.

2. *V.* Rom 10.18, where St. Paul applies Ps 19.4 to the preaching of the gospel by the apostles. Theodoret further develops the ironical note he had sounded with the reference to his "most just judges." As they are not just, but unjust, they are no true apostles of the word, but heretics; *cf.* sec. 2 below.

κατ᾽ ἐμοῦ τὸ συνέδριον, τὸν δὲ πέντε καὶ τριάκοντα σταθμοῖς ἀφεστηκότα κατέκριναν. καὶ ὁ μὲν τῶν ὅλων Θεὸς πρὸς τὸν πατριάρχην Ἀβραὰμ περὶ Σοδόμων ἔφη καὶ Γομόρρων, *Κραυγὴ Σοδόμων καὶ* Γομόρρων *πεπλήθυνται* πρός με, *καὶ αἱ ἁμαρτίαι αὐτῶν μεγάλαι σφόδρα· καταβὰς οὖν ὄψομαι εἰ κατὰ τὴν κραυγὴν αὐτῶν, τὴν ἐρχομένην* ταύτην *πρός με, συντελοῦνται, εἰ δὲ μή, ἵνα γνῶ.*[b] καίτοι σαφῶς ᾔδει τῶν ἀνθρώπων ἐκείνων τὴν πονηρίαν, ἀλλ᾽ ὅμως ἔφη, *Καταβὰς … ὄψομαι,* διδάσκων ἡμᾶς ἀναμένειν τῶν πραγμάτων τὴν πεῖραν. οὗτοι δέ, οὐκ εἰς δικαστήριον ἡμᾶς καλέσαντες, οὐ φωνῆς ἡμῶν ἐπακούσαντες, οὐ τί φρονοῦμεν μαθεῖν παρ᾽ ἡμῶν ἐθελήσαντες, τῷ θυμῷ τῶν τῆς ἀληθείας ἐχθρῶν τὴν ἡμετέραν σφαγὴν ἐχαρίσαντο.

(2) Ἐγὼ δὲ τὴν μὲν ἡσυχίαν ἀσπάζομαι, καὶ διαφερόντως ἐν τῷ παρόντι καιρῷ, τῶν ἀποστολικῶν παρὰ πολλοῖς διαφθαρέντων δογμάτων, καὶ τῆς καινῆς κρατυνθείσης αἱρέσεως. ἵνα δὲ μή τις τῶν ἀγνοούντων ἡμᾶς ἀληθεῖς εἶναι πιστεύσῃ τὰς καθ᾽ ἡμῶν γεγενημένας διαβολὰς καὶ σκανδαλισθῇ, νομίσας ἕτερα παρὰ τὴν εὐαγγελικὴν διδασκαλίαν φρονεῖν, ἀντιβολῶ Τὴν Ὑμετέραν Μεγαλοπρέπειαν ταύτην αἰτῆσαι τὴν χάριν τὴν καλλίνικον κορυφὴν ὥστε με τὴν Ἑσπέραν καταλαβεῖν, καὶ παρὰ τοῖς ἐν ἐκείνῃ θεοφιλεστάτοις καὶ ἁγιωτάτοις ἐπισκόποις δικάσασθαι, καί, εἰ ὀφθείην βραχὺ γοῦν τι παρεκβαίνων τοῦ κανόνος τῆς πίστεως, αὐτῷ με παραδοθῆναι τῷ μεσαιτάτῳ τῆς θαλάττης βυθῷ. εἰ δὲ οὐδὲ ταύτην ὑμῶν τὴν δέησιν δέχεται, οἰκῆσαι γοῦν με κελευσάτω τὸ ἡμέτερον μοναστήριον, ὃ τῆς μὲν Κυρρεστῶν εἴκοσι καὶ ἑκατὸν μιλίοις ἀφέστηκεν, τῆς δὲ Ἀντιόχου πέντε καὶ ἑβδομήκοντα, ἀπὸ δὲ τριῶν μιλίων τῆς Ἀπαμέων διάκειται πόλεως. τούτων, εἰ μὲν δυνατόν, τὸ πρότερον, εἰ δὲ μή, τὸ γοῦν δεύτερον παρασχεθῆναί μοι διὰ Τοῦ Ὑμετέρου Μεγέθους παρακαλῶ, οὗ τὴν μνήμην κἂν τῇ διανοίᾳ κἂν τῇ

l. 42 ἀληθεῖς *codd.* : -θὲς *edd.*

b. Gn 18.20f. (LXX var.)

my pastoral care, when they assembled their court and passed judgment against me, a man thirty-five days' journey away![3] And yet, in the case of Sodom and Gomorrah the God of the universe said to the patriarch Abraham, "The whole world cries out to me against Sodom and Gomorrah, and their sins are very great. Therefore, I shall go down to see if, according to the outcry against them that is coming to me, the number of their sins is complete, or, if not, I intend to find out."[b] Though he already knew quite well the evil behavior of those men, he still said, "I shall go down to see," thus teaching us to wait for proof of the facts. But these people, without summoning us to court, or so much as hearing us speak, unwilling to receive a statement of our position, have made our slaughter a gift to gratify the rage of the enemies of the truth.

(2) I, for one, am a lover of quiet retreat, especially in the present situation, when the apostolic teachings are being corrupted by many, and this new heresy is gaining ground.[4] Yet, for fear that some who don't know us may believe that the slanders raised against us are actually true and take scandal in the belief that we hold opinions at variance with gospel doctrine, I entreat Your Excellency to request this grace from our glorious commander: that I be permitted to travel to the West to receive judgment before the bishops there, beloved of God and most holy, and that, should I be seen to diverge even in the slightest from the rule of faith, I be cast into the depths of the sea. And if he refuse to grant you that prayer, let him give command for me to go live in our monastery, 120 miles from Cyrus, seventy-five from Antioch, three miles from the city of Apamea.[5] Of these, I urge Your Lordship, if possible, to get me the grant of the first, but if not, of the second. We always carry about with us, in

3. On the confinement of Theodoret to his diocese, part of a larger strategy to prevent the defense of Antiochene christology at the Second Council of Ephesus, *v.* Intro., sec. 4.4, esp. n. 307.

4. Theodoret refers to the reinstatement of Eutyches and the favorable hearing accorded to Cyril's Apollinarian formula, "one incarnate nature of the Word" (μίαν φύσιν τοῦ Λόγου σεσαρκωμένην); *v.* Intro., sec. 4.7.

5. It is the second of these alternatives that will be granted; *v.* *epp.* 123, 126.

γλώττῃ διηνεκῶς περιφέρομεν, ἱκετεύοντες τὸν τῶν δυνάμεων Κύριον ἀμείψασθαι Τὴν Ὑμετέραν Μεγαλοπρέπειαν καὶ τοῖς παροῦσι καὶ τοῖς μέλλουσιν ἀγαθοῖς. ταῦτα δὲ γράψαι νῦν ἠναγκάσθην, μαθὼν ὥς τινες καὶ τὴν ἐντεῦθέν μοι καττύουσι μετανάστασιν.

thought and in word, the remembrance of Your Lordship, begging the Lord of hosts to requite Your Excellency with blessings both in the present and in the time to come. I had no choice but to write this letter after learning that some people were patching together a plot to have me removed from here.

120. ΛΟΥΠΠΙΚΙΝΩΙ

Οἶμαι καὶ τοὺς τῆς ἀληθείας σχετλιάζειν ἐχθροὺς ἐπὶ ταῖς ἀδίκοις ἡμῶν καὶ παρανόμοις σφαγαῖς· πολλῷ δὲ πλέον, ὡς εἰκός, ἀνιᾷ τοὺς τροφίμους τῆς εὐσεβείας ἡ καινὴ αὕτη καὶ παράδοξος τραγῳδία, ὧν Ἡ Ὑμετέρα πρωτεύει Μεγαλοπρέπεια. προσήκει δὲ τοὺς πλεῖον ἀλγοῦντας πλείονα σπουδήν τε καὶ προθυμίαν εἰσενεγκεῖν ὥστε τὰ δυσσεβῶς καὶ παρανόμως γεγενημένα λύσιν λαβεῖν, τὸ δὲ διασπασθῆναι κινδυνεῦον σῶμα τῆς Ἐκκλησίας εἰς τὴν προτέραν συμφωνίαν ἐπανελθεῖν. τούτου δὴ χάριν παρακαλῶ Τὸ Ὑμέτερον Μέγεθος πνευματικῆς ἐμπορίας ἀφορμὴν νομίσαι τὸν παρόντα καιρόν, καὶ τὴν μὲν ὑπὲρ τῆς εὐσεβείας εἰσενεγκεῖν προθυμίαν, ἀντιλαβεῖν δὲ παρὰ τοῦ μεγαλοδώρου Δεσπότου, κἀν τῷ παρόντι βίῳ, τὴν μεγίστην κηδεμονίαν, κἀν τῷ μέλλοντι, τὴν τῶν οὐρανῶν βασιλείαν.

Title Λουππικίνῳ *scripsi* : -ίῳ *codd.* : -υπι- *Gar.* (*p. 231*) : Λουπικίῳ *scr. Sir. Nös. Az. V. c. n. ad tit. ep. 90.*

120. To Luppicinus[1]

I imagine that even the enemies of the truth must be indignant over the unjust and illegal way we were sent to our slaughter. Yet, as you would expect, this strange tragedy, in which we never know what to expect next, is far more vexatious to the nurslings of religion, among whom Your Excellency holds the place of honor. Now, the more aggrieved one feels, the more zeal he should bring to bear to put a stop to these irreligious and illegal proceedings and to see that the body of the Church, now in danger of being rent asunder, be restored to its former state of concord.[2] Thus, I urge Your Lordship to regard this crisis as an opportunity for a transaction in spiritual goods: bring zealous support to the cause of religion, and receive in return from our munificent Master not only his kindliest care in this present life, but also the kingdom of heaven in the life to come.

1. The name of the addressee of this letter is not quite certain; *v.* the c. n. and *ep.* 90 n. 1. Azéma dates *epp.* 120–32 to the period between October 449 (*i.e.* after the promulgation of the edict confirming the acts of the Second Council of Ephesus; *v.* Leo, *epp.* 43–45, 47–51; Intro., sec. 4.9) and August 450 (*i.e.* before the death of Theodosius II).

2. Theodoret has referred to the story of the depositions, his own and those of his allies, as a "tragedy." In this sentence, he uses the term λύσις (here rendered "end") to refer to the effect of Luppicinus' hoped-for intervention. While Theodoret employs this term elsewhere to mean little more than a deliverance from evil (*epp.* 5, 109.2, 113.3, 117), in this context, he may have coupled this ordinary usage with a reference to Aristotle's use of the term to designate the dénouement of a tragedy. The philosopher had commended plots in which one situation arose necessarily or plausibly from those that preceded it (*Po.* 1455b24) and insisted that the dénouement should seem a natural outcome, not the result of some extrinsic force (1454a37). Theodoret, however, emphasizes that, in his own tragedy, he has no idea of what to expect next (παράδοξος τραγῳδία).

121. ΑΝΑΤΟΛΙΩΙ ΠΑΤΡΙΚΙΩΙ

Ἔδειξεν ὁ πάντ᾽ ἐφορῶν καὶ πρυτανεύων Δεσπότης καὶ τὴν ἀποστολικὴν τῶν ἡμετέρων δογμάτων ἀλήθειαν καὶ τῆς καθ᾽ ἡμῶν γεγενημένης συκοφαντίας τὸ ψεῦδος· τὰ γὰρ παρὰ τοῦ θεοφιλεστάτου καὶ ἁγιωτάτου τῆς μεγάλης Ῥώμης ἀρχιεπισκόπου, τοῦ Κυρίου Λέοντος, τὰ πρὸς τὸν τῆς ὁσίας μνήμης Φλαβιανὸν καὶ πρὸς τοὺς ἄλλους τοὺς ἐν Ἐφέσῳ συναθροισθέντας γραφέντα ἄγαν συμφωνεῖ τοῖς παρ᾽ ἡμῶν καὶ συγγραφεῖσι καὶ ἐπ᾽ ἐκκλησίας κηρυχθεῖσιν ἀεί. οὗ δὴ χάριν, εὐθὺς ἐντυχών, ὕμνησα τὸν φιλάνθρωπον Κύριον, ὅτι οὐ τὰς ἐκκλησίας παντελῶς καταλέλοιπεν, ἀλλ᾽ ἐφύλαξεν τὸν τῆς ὀρθοδοξίας σπινθῆρα, μᾶλλον δὲ οὐ σπινθῆρα, ἀλλὰ πυρσὸν μέγιστον ἱκανὸν ἐξάψαι καὶ φωτίσαι τὴν οἰκουμένην. ἀληθῶς γὰρ τὸν ἀποστολικὸν ἐν οἷς ἔγραψεν διεφύλαξεν χαρακτῆρα, καὶ ἃ παρειλήφαμεν παρὰ τῶν ἁγίων καὶ μακαρίων προφητῶν καὶ ἀποστόλων, καὶ τῶν μετ᾽ ἐκείνους κηρυξάντων τὸ εὐαγγέλιον, καὶ μέντοι καὶ τῶν ἐν Νικαίᾳ συναχθέντων ἁγίων πατέρων εὕρομεν ἐν τοῖς γράμμασιν· τούτοις ἐμμένειν ὁμολογοῦμεν

l. 11 μᾶλλον δὲ *scr. Car., edd.* : μ. *N. The emendation is all but certain. In cases where Thdt. uses ἀλλὰ and μᾶλλον and omits δέ after μᾶλλον, ἀλλὰ always begins the phrase (twenty-five exx. in the TLG); ἀλλὰ πολλῷ μᾶλλον and ἀλλὰ μᾶλλον are common. For the word order re-established by Cariofilo, cf. in Ps. 8.1 (PG, vol. 80, col. 913, ll. 19–21): Πλῆθος γὰρ ληνῶν ἀκούοντες [οἱ ἰουδαῖοι], καὶ σαφῶς εἰδότες ὡς μία τις ἐδόθη ληνός, μᾶλλον δὲ οὐδὲ ληνός, ἀλλὰ προλήνιον … νοεῖν οὐκ ἐθέλουσιν, ὡς ἐπαύσατο μὲν τὰ παλαιά, etc.* **ll. 13f.** καὶ ἃ παρειλήφαμεν παρὰ τῶν ἁγίων *scripsi* : καὶ ἃ παρὰ τ. ἁ. *codd.* : καὶ τὰ παρὰ τ. ἁ. *coni. Car., scr. Sir., Nös, Az. The emendation conjectured by Cariofilo and accepted by Azéma, leaves the reader in expectation of a noun or a participle. Furthermore, it is the defective text of N that must provide the starting point for emendation. As the prep. phrase begins with* παρὰ, *and, in N,* παρὰ *stands at the end of its line, it might well be that the scribe missed a preceding form of* παραλαμβάνω. *Cf. Haer. com. (vol. 83, col. 532, l. 29), where the same idea (the tradition of the faith) is expressed in very similar phraseology: Ταῦτα παρὰ τῶν θεοφόρων ἀνδρῶν, προφητῶν, φημὶ, καὶ ἀποστόλων, καὶ τῶν ἐκείνους διαδεξαμενων, παρείληφεν ἡ Ἐκκλησία τὰ δόγματα; v. also in Ps. 48.13 (PG, vol. 80, col. 1217, ll. 8–10): Χρὴ γὰρ γενεὰν ἑκάστην τῇ μετ᾽ αὐτὴν παραδιδόναι, ἃ παρὰ τῆς προτέρας παρειλήφαμεν.*

121. To Anatolius, the Patrician[1]

The Master who watches over and directs all things has made known the apostolic truth of our teaching and shown up the lie behind the false accusation that has been raised against us. There is, you see, complete agreement in what the archbishop of mighty Rome, Leo, beloved of God and most holy, had written to Flavian of holy memory and the other bishops gathered in Ephesus and what we have all along written in our treatises and preached in church.[2] As soon as I read the letter, I sang the praises of our kindly Lord for not entirely abandoning the churches, but preserving a spark of orthodoxy, indeed no mere spark, but a bright torch to set aflame and illuminate all the world! Without a doubt, in this letter, he has kept incorrupt the hallmark of apostolic character, and the teachings we find in this letter are those we have received from the holy and blessed prophets and apostles, those who have preached the gospel after them, and, of course, the holy fathers of the Council of Nicaea;

1. On Anatolius, *v. ep.* 45 n. 1, and, for the date of this letter, *v. ep.* 120 n. 1.

2. Theodoret now knows of the death of Flavian, which had occurred after the Latrocinium; *v.* Intro., sec. 4.8. This indicates that *ep.* 121 must be somewhat later than *ep.* 113, where only Flavian's deposition is mentioned (sec. 3).

καὶ τοὺς ἄλλο τι παρὰ ταῦτα φρονοῦντας ἀσεβείας γραφόμεθα. συνέταξα δὲ τοῖσδέ μου τοῖς γράμμασιν μίαν τῶν εἰς τὴν Ἔφεσον παρ᾽ αὐτοῦ πεμφθεισῶν ἐπιστολῶν ἵν᾽, ἐντυχοῦσα Ὑμῶν Ἡ Μεγαλοφυΐα, τῶν παρ᾽ ἡμῶν πολλάκις ἐπ᾽ ἐκκλησίας εἰρημένων ἀναμνησθῇ, καὶ γνῷ τῶν δογμάτων τὴν συμφωνίαν, καὶ μισήσῃ *τοὺς λαλοῦντας τὸ ψεῦδος*[a] καὶ τοὺς τὴν καινὴν αἵρεσιν κατὰ τῶν ἀποστολικῶν συντεθεικότας δογμάτων.

a. Ps 5.6

based on these we make our confession of faith, and we charge with irreligion any who hold opinions at variance with them. I have attached to this letter of mine one of the letters he sent to Ephesus,[3] so that when Your Eminence receives it, you may remember what we have often preached in church, note the agreement between Leo's teaching and my own, and conceive abhorrence for those "speaking falsehood"[a] and those concocting this new heresy in opposition to the apostolic teachings.

3. Theodoret is referring to Leo's *ep.* 28 (to Flavian), the *Tome*; *v. ep.* 113, n. 3.

122. ΟΥΡΑΝΙΩΙ ΕΠΙΣΚΟΠΩΙ ΕΜΕΣΗΣ

Ὅτι μὲν συνεζεύχθημεν ἐν τοῖς γράμμασιν οἱ τῇ διαθέσει συνεζευγμένοι, λίαν ἥσθημεν· οὐ νενοήκαμεν δὲ τό, ὅτι *Οὐχ οὗτοι οἱ λόγοι μου;*[a] εἰ μὲν γὰρ προσρήσεως χάριν εἴρηται μόνης, οὐκ ἀνιᾷ τὸ λεχθέν, εἰ δὲ συμβουλῆς ἀναμιμνήσκει σιγὴν παραινεσάσης καὶ τὴν καλουμένην *οἰκονομίαν*, χάριν ὁμολογοῦμεν, μὴ δεξάμενοι τὴν εἰσήγησιν· ὁ γὰρ θεῖος Ἀπόστολος τἀναντία παρεγγυᾷ· *Ἐπίστηθι εὐκαίρως, ἀκαίρως*,[b] καὶ ὁ Δεσπότης αὐτῷ γε τούτῳ τῷ κήρυκι· *Λάλει καὶ μὴ σιωπήσῃς*,[c] καὶ τῷ Ἡσαΐᾳ· *Ἀναβόησον* τῇ *ἰσχύϊ* σου *καὶ μὴ φείσῃ*,[d] καὶ τῷ Μωϋσῇ· *Καταβὰς διαμάρτυραι τῷ λαῷ* τούτῳ,[e] καὶ μέντοι καὶ τῷ Ἰεζεκιήλ· *Σκοπὸν δέδωκά σε τῷ οἴκῳ Ἰσραήλ*,[f] καὶ ἔσται *ἐὰν* μὴ *διαστείλῃ τῷ ἀνόμῳ*,[g] καὶ τὰ τούτοις ἀκόλουθα· περιττὸν γὰρ πρὸς εἰδότα μηκύνειν. οὐ μόνον τοίνυν οὐκ ἀλύομεν, παρρησίᾳ χρησάμενοι, ἀλλὰ καὶ γαννύμεθα καὶ γεγήθαμεν, καὶ τὸν τούτων ἡμᾶς ἀξιώσαντα τῶν παθημάτων ὑμνοῦμεν,[h] καὶ μὲν δὴ καὶ τοὺς συνήθεις ἐπὶ τοὺς αὐτοὺς ἀγῶνας παρακαλοῦμεν. εἰ μὲν γὰρ ἴσασιν ἡμᾶς τὸν ἀποστολικὸν κανόνα τῆς πίστεως μὴ φυλάττοντας, ἀλλ᾽ ἐκκλίνοντας δεξιὰ ἢ ἀριστερά, καὶ μισησάτωσαν, καὶ τῆς ἐναντίας γενέσθωσαν μοίρας, καὶ μετὰ τῶν πολεμούντων τετάχθωσαν, εἰ δὲ τὴν ὀρθὴν τοῦ εὐαγγελικοῦ κηρύγματος προσμαρτυροῦσιν ἡμῖν διδασκαλίαν, βοῶμεν πρὸς αὐτούς, *Στῆτε* καὶ ὑμεῖς *περιζωσάμενοι* τὰς ὀσφύας *ὑμῶν*

Title Ἐμέσης *scr. Sir. Nös. Az.* : -μισ- *codd.*

a. Jon 4.2 b. 2Tm 4.2 c. Acts 18.9
d. Is 58.1 (LXX var.) e. Ex 19.10 (LXX var.) f. Ez 3.17, 33.7
g. Ez 3.19 (LXX var.) h. *Cf.* Phil 1.28f.

122. To Uranius, Bishop of Emesa[1]

I was delighted when, already joined to one another by a bond of esteem, we also established a bond of correspondence. But I remain in doubt regarding the meaning of "Didn't I tell you so?"[a] If this is meant as no more than a way of getting my attention, the expression causes no annoyance, but if it's meant to remind me of advice to remain silent, what people call "prudent discretion," I thank you, but with no intention of following your suggestion. You see, the holy Apostle recommends the opposite, "Insist at the right time, at the wrong time,"[b] and our Master's words to this same herald were, "Speak, and do not fall silent";[c] and to Isaiah, "Shout out with all your strength, and do not hold back";[d] and to Moses, "Go on down, and warn this people";[e] and then to Ezekiel as well, "I have made you a lookout over the house of Israel,"[f] and it shall come to pass that "if you fail to command the lawless,"[g] *etc.*; I need not go on at length with someone so well-informed. It's not just that we feel no regret for speaking out; we are glad and rejoice and sing the praises of him who has deemed us worthy to suffer,[h] and, what is more, we call on our friends to join in the same struggles. Now, if they're aware that we've not kept pure the apostolic rule of faith, that we veer off to one side or the other, let them hold us in abhorrence, join the other side, and take their stand with those who are battling against us, but if they agree that our teaching is the orthodox proclamation of the gospel, we call out to them, "Take your stand, you as well, with your

1. Theodoret had written *ep.* 36 to Pompeianus, the predecessor of Uranius in the see of Emesa; *v. ep.* 36 n. 1. At the death of Pompeianus, the succession to the see was disputed between Uranius and another, previously elected, bishop. Uranius attended the synod of Constantinople in late 448, where he voted for the deposition of Eutyches; *v.* Intro., sec. 4.2 and Rist. His name also appears among the signatories to the Acts of the Council of Chalcedon (*Conc. chalc.*, *Act.* 6, sec. 9, #124). It was during his episcopacy that Marcellus, archimandrite of a local monastery, claimed to have discovered the head of John the Baptist, and this skull was placed in the cathedral of Emesa for the veneration of the faithful. For the earliest account of this invention, *v.* Marcel. Com., *Chron.*, *anno* 453 (*Vincomali et Opilionis*); *cf.* Mango, "Emesa." For the date of this letter, *v. ep.* 120 n. 1.

ἐν ἀληθείᾳ, … καὶ ὑποδησάμενοι τοὺς πόδας ἐν ἑτοιμασίᾳ τοῦ εὐαγγελίου τῆς εἰρήνης,[i] καὶ τὰ ἑξῆς.

Φασὶ γὰρ τὴν ἀρετήν οὐ μόνον σωφροσύνην, καὶ δικαιοσύνην, καὶ φρόνησιν, ἀλλὰ καὶ ἀνδρείαν ἔχειν καί, διὰ ταύτης, κατορθοῦσθαι κἀκείνας· καὶ γὰρ ἡ δικαιοσύνη εἰς τὸν κατὰ τῆς ἀδικίας πόλεμον δεῖται τῆς ἀνδρείας συμμάχου, καὶ ἡ σωφροσύνη, συνεργῷ τῇ ἀνδρείᾳ χρωμένη, τὴν ἀκολασίαν νικᾷ. διά τοι τοῦτο καὶ ὁ τῶν ὅλων Θεὸς πρὸς τὸν προφήτην ἔφη, *Ὁ δὲ δίκαιός μου ἐκ πίστεως ζήσεται καί, ἐὰν ὑποστείληται, οὐκ εὐδοκεῖ ἡ ψυχή μου ἐν αὐτῷ·*[j] *ὑποστολὴν* δὲ τὴν δειλίαν ὠνόμασεν. ἔχου τοίνυν, ὦ φίλη κεφαλή, τῶν ἀποστολικῶν δογμάτων· *ἥξει γὰρ … ὅσον ὅσον ὁ ἐρχόμενος … καὶ οὐ* χρονιεῖ[k] καὶ *ἀποδώσει ἑκάστῳ κατὰ τὰ ἔργα αὐτοῦ·*[l] *παράγει γὰρ τὸ σχῆμα τοῦ κόσμου τούτου,*[m] καὶ φανήσεται ἡ τῶν πραγμάτων ἀλήθεια.

i. Eph 6.14f. (NT var.)
j. Heb 10.38 (*Cf.* Hab 2.4.)
k. Heb 10.37 (NT var.)
l. Rom 2.6
m. 1Cor 7.31

loins girt with the truth, your feet shod in preparation for the gospel of peace,"[i] *etc.*

As you know, it is generally held that virtue consists not solely of temperance, justice, and prudence, but of courage as well, and that it is through courage that the others achieve their ends. In the war against injustice, justice must have courage as her ally, and temperance draws on the support of courage to vanquish licentiousness.[2] Thus, the God of the universe said to the prophet, "My just man shall live by faith, but when he shrinks back, my heart takes no pleasure in him."[j] "Shrinking back" is his term for cowardice. So then, my dear friend, cling to the apostolic teachings; "in just a little, he who is coming will arrive, and he will not delay,"[k] and "he will repay each in accordance with his works,"[l] "for the form of this age is passing away,"[m] and the true nature of our deeds will be made manifest.

2. On the four cardinal virtues, *cf. ep.* 71 n. 2.

123. ΤΩΙ ΑΥΤΩΙ

Καὶ μακρὰ ἡ ἐπιστολή, καὶ χαρίεσσα, καὶ τὸ τῆς ἀγάπης θερμόν τε καὶ γνήσιον ὑποφαίνουσα, καὶ τοσαύτης με θυμηδίας ἐνέπλησεν ὥστε ἥκιστα μεταγνῶναι ὅτι δὴ ἑτέραν ἔχειν ἐτόπασα διάνοιαν τὸ τῆς προτέρας προοίμιον· τοῦ γὰρ νοῦ τῶν γραμμάτων ἡ ἄγνοια τὸν τῆς ἀδελφικῆς φιλοστοργίας ἀπεκάλυψε θησαυρόν, καὶ τὸ τῆς πίστεως ἐδήλωσεν ἀκραιφνές, καὶ τὸν περὶ τὴν εὐσέβειαν ἐγνώρισε ζῆλον. τοῦ μέντοι προφήτου τοὺς λόγους καὶ πειρασμοὺς διενειμάμεθα· καὶ Ἡ μὲν Ὁσιότης Σου τοῖς λόγοις ἐχρήσατο, ἡμεῖς δὲ ταῖς καταιγίσι καὶ τρικυμίαις βαλλόμεθα καὶ κατὰ τῶν τὸ σκάφος ἐρεττόντων μετ᾿ ἐκείνου βοῶμεν, *Φυλασσόμενοι μάταια καὶ ψευδῆ* ἔλεον *αὐτῶν ἐγκατέλιπον.*[a] παρέξει δὲ ἴσως ὁ καὶ ἡμῶν κἀκείνου Δεσπότης καὶ ἡμᾶς ἀναδῦναι καὶ τοῦ κήτους ἀπαλλαγῆναι.[b]

Εἰ δὲ καὶ ζέον ἐπιμείνῃ τὸ ῥόθιον, ἐλπίζομεν καὶ οὕτως τῆς θείας ἀπολαύσεσθαι προμηθείας καὶ τῇ πείρᾳ μαθεῖν ὡς *ἡ . . . δύναμις* αὐτοῦ *ἐν ἀσθενείᾳ τελειοῦται.*[c] καὶ γὰρ αὐτοὺς τοὺς κινδύνους τῇ ἀσθενείᾳ ἡμῶν ἐμέτρησεν·[d] τὸν μὲν γὰρ θεῖον ἐκεῖνον προφήτην ἅπαντες καθῆκαν εἰς τὸ πέλαγος οἱ συμπλέοντες,[e] ἐμοὶ δὲ καὶ τὴν Τῆς Σῆς Ὁσιότητος παρέσχεν παραψυχὴν καὶ μέντοι καὶ ἄλλων θεοφιλῶν ἀνδρῶν, οὓς τῆς Ὀνησιφόρου τοῦ θαυμασίου τυχεῖν εὐλογίας μετὰ Τῆς Σῆς Φιλοθεΐας προσεύχομαι, ὅτι *τὴν ἅλυσιν* ἡμῶν *οὐκ* ἐπησχύνθητε,[f] ἀλλὰ τῶν ὑπὲρ τῆς πίστεως ἡμῖν κεκοινωνήκατε θλίψεων.

Τοῦτο μέντοι εὖ ἴσθι, Δέσποτα, ὡς καὶ ἑτέρων μοι πεμψάντων θεοφιλεστάτων ἐπισκόπων εὐλογίας, οὐκ ἐδεξάμην, οὐχ ὡς ὑβρίζων τοὺς πεπομφότας· μὴ γένοιτο· ἀλλ᾿ ὡς τὴν ἀναγκαίαν

a. Jon 2.8 (LXX var.) b. Jon 2.10 c. 2Cor 12.9 (NT var.)
d. *Cf.* 1Cor 10.13. e. Jon 1.15 f. 2Tm 1.16

123. To the Same[1]

Your letter was long and delightful, and let me glimpse the warmth of your unfeigned friendship. It filled me with such joy that I had no reason to regret imagining that the beginning of your previous letter had a different meaning; as it happened, my inability to grasp the meaning of your words has led to the revelation of your brotherly love, shown forth the purity of your faith, and made known your zeal for true religion. Indeed, we had divided between us that prophet's words and trials: Your Holiness taking his words, and we, all the time buffeted by the high seas of this tempest, calling out against the oarsmen of the boat, "Those who cherish empty lies have forsaken their mercy!"[a] But it may be that Jonah's master and mine will make me rise up from the depths and get free of the whale.[b]

But even if the swirling deep awaits us, we expect that even so, with the help of God's providential care, we shall learn by experience how his "might is fully revealed through weakness,"[c] for, as we know, he limits our temptations according to our weakness.[d] In the case of that holy prophet, all the crew joined in casting him into the sea,[e] but in my case, God has granted me the encouragement of Your Holiness and of other godly men as well, and it is my prayer that they, along with Your Piety, will attain to the blessing of that excellent Onesiphorus, for you have shown "no shame at" our "bonds,"[f] but have accepted a share in our tribulations on account of the faith.

I would have you know, my Master, that I have refused the gifts sent me by other bishops beloved of God—not to show disrespect to the senders (Heaven forbid!), but because I get what is necessary for

1. For the addressee and date of this letter, *v. ep.* 122 n. 1. The reference to the gifts at the conclusion of this letter suggests that Theodoret is already in exile.

τροφὴν τέως ποριζόμενος παρὰ τοῦ καὶ τοῖς κόραξι ταύτην ἀφθόνως παρέχοντος.[g] ἐπὶ δὲ Τῆς Σῆς Φιλοθεΐας οὐδὲν τοιοῦτο πεποίηκα· τῷ ὄντι γὰρ ἐνίκησεν ἡ τῆς ἀγάπης θερμότης τὸν ἐγγενόμενόν μοι τέως σκοπόν· ὅτι γάρ, ἐξ οὗ τὰ τῆς συνηθείας ἡμῖν ηὐξήθη, καὶ τὸ φίλτρον σφοδρότερον ἐξήφθη πειθέσθω ἡ θεοφιλής σου ψυχή.

g. Lk 12.24

my sustenance from him who makes such bountiful provision even for the crows.[2g] Yet, in the case of Your Piety, I have done no such thing, for the warmth of your charity has quite overwhelmed the resolution I was maintaining up to now; indeed, you may be certain, soul beloved of God, that, as our acquaintance has grown, the flame of my love for you has burned all the brighter.

2. Theodoret refers to blessings or gifts (εὐλογίας) that have been sent to him by Uranius and other bishops. Most likely, he is now in exile in his monastery near Apamea, and the gifts are meant as demonstrations of solidarity. Lampe points out (*sub uoc.* sec. F.2) that this term may refer to a gift of edibles, an interpretation that seems confirmed by Theodoret's allusion to his own sustenance and to God's gracious sustenance of the crows (Lk 12.24; *cf.* Ps 146.9, Jb 38.41).

124. ΜΑΡΑΝΑΙ ΣΧΟΛΑΣΤΙΚΩΙ

Τὰς μὲν ἐκκλησιαστικὰς ὀλοφύρομαι κἀγὼ συμφορὰς καὶ τὸν ἐπικείμενον ὀδύρομαι κλύδωνα, ἐμαυτῷ μέντοι συνήδομαι, θορύβων ἀπηλλαγμένῳ καὶ γαλήνης ἀπολαύοντι τῆς ἐρασμίας μοι.[a] οὓς δὲ νῦν ἀδικεῖν Ἡ Σὴ Παίδευσις εἴρηκεν οὐκ εἰς μακρὰν τίσουσι δίκας ὧν νῦν παρανόμων τολμῶσιν· σταθμῷ γὰρ ἅπαντα καὶ μέτρῳ πρυτανεύει τῶν ὅλων ὁ Κύριος, καί, ὅταν τινὲς εἰς ἀμετρίαν παρανομίας ἐκπέσωσιν, μακροθυμεῖ μὲν οὐκέτι, δικαστικῶς δὲ λοιπὸν ἐπιφέρει τὴν τιμωρίαν.[b] ταῦτα προορῶντες, ἡμεῖς παύσασθαι αὐτοὺς τῆς ἀμετρίας εὐχόμεθα ἵνα μή, κολαζομένους ὁρῶντες, πάλιν αὐτοὺς θρηνεῖν βιαζώμεθα. Τῆς δὲ Ὑμετέρας Θαυμασιότητος διηνεκῶς μνημονεύομεν καὶ τὸν κοινὸν Δεσπότην ἀντιβολοῦμεν τὴν ὑμετέραν οἰκίαν εὐλογίας ἐμπλῆσαι.

Title Μαράνᾳ *scr. qui codicem A resarcivit* (*v.* "*Intro. to the Gk. Text,*" *n.* 13), *Sir. Nös.* : -άνα N^{ac} (-ανα N^{pr}), *Az. Cf. ep.* 67, *n.* 1. **l. 4** νῦν *NZ* : καὶ ν. *scr. qui codicem A resarcivit* (*v.* "*Intro. to the Gk. Text,*" *n.* 13), *edd. Earlier editors have followed the hand that supplied lost portions of the codex in this needless insertion.* **l. 4** μακρὰν *codd.* : -ρὸν *scr. Sir. Nös. Az. The phrase οὐκ εἰς μακρὰν occurs in twenty-three other places of the works of Thdt., all in his own words; v. e.g.: H. e.* 3.13.1: *Ἀλλὰ τῶν δυσσεβῶν τούτων καὶ μανικῶν τολμημάτων οὐκ εἰς μακρὰν ἔτισαν δίκας. Editors have printed οὐκ εἰς -ρὸν only here and in Dan.* 7.17*f.* (*PG, vol.* 81, *col.* 1428, *l.* 39). **l. 5** παρανόμων *NZ* : -μως *corr. qui codicem A resarcivit* (*v.* "*Intro. to the Gk. Text,*" *n.* 13), *scr. Sir. Nös. Az. The correction made by the hand that supplied lost portions of the codex and followed by earlier editors is entirely unnecessary. Thdt. makes frequent use of the substantive παράνομα, and the assimilated gen. is both idiomatic and the lect. diff.* **ll. 5f.** σταθμῷ … μέτρῳ *corr. qui codicem A resarcivit* (*v.* "*Intro. to the Gk. Text,*" *n.* 13), *scr. Sir. Nös. Az.* : -μον (N^{pc}; *-μοιν* N^{ac}?) … -ρον *N. This correction by the supplementer of A restores sense to the meaningless phraseology of N. Cf. in Jos. Q.* 15: *διδάσκει τοίνυν ἡμᾶς ὁ λόγος, ὡς σταθμῷ καὶ μέτρῳ πάντα πρυτανεύων, Θεὸς συνεχώρει τούτοις ἀντιπαρατάττεσθαι τῷ λαῷ.*

a. *Cf.* Mk 4.35–39. b. *Cf.* 1Thes 2.16.

124. To Maranas, the Advocate[1]

I also lament for the troubles of the Church and groan at the rough water now engulfing it, and yet, for myself, I'm delighted to escape the turbulence and enjoy this tranquility dear to my heart.[a] As for those men you mention, those now committing injustice—it won't be long, Councilor, before they pay for their reckless transgressions. In his governance of the universe, the Lord weighs and measures all things, and when people indulge in a lawlessness that exceeds that measure, he puts aside his forbearance, and like a judge, pronounces the penalty.[b] As we can foresee what will happen, we pray for them to desist from their excess and spare us the need of weeping for them a second time when we see them in the midst of their punishments. We always make mention of Your Honor to our common Master and beg him to fill your home with his blessing.

1. On Maranas, *v. ep.* 67 n. 1, and on the title "advocate," *v. ep.* 10 n. 1. This letter must have been written during the period of Theodoret's exile from Cyrus; *v. ep.* 120 n. 1.

125. ΙΩΑΝΝΗΙ ΕΠΙΣΚΟΠΩΙ ΓΕΡΜΑΝΙΚΕΙΑΣ

(1) Τὰ μὲν πρότερα γράμματα Τῆς Σῆς Ὁσιότητος εὐθὺς δεξάμενος, ἀντιγέγραφα, περὶ δὲ τῶν προκειμένων οὐδέν ἐστιν ἐλπίσαι χρηστόν· τῆς γὰρ παντελοῦς ἀποστασίας ὑπολαμβάνω ταῦτα εἶναι προοίμια.[a] τὸ γὰρ τοὺς θρηνοῦντας τὰ κατὰ βίαν, ὥς φασιν, ἐν Ἐφέσῳ γεγενημένα μὴ μεταμέλεσθαι, ἀλλ᾽ ἐπιμένειν τοῖς παρανόμως παρ᾽ αὐτῶν τολμηθεῖσιν καὶ ἐποικοδομεῖν κατὰ ταὐτὸν τήν τε ἀδικίαν καὶ τὴν ἀσέβειαν, καὶ τὸ τοὺς ἄλλους μήτε συμβουλεύειν αὐτοῖς ἐξαρνηθῆναι τὰ τολμηθέντα, μήτε ἐπιμενόντων οἷς παρανόμως ἔδρασαν φεύγειν τὴν κοινωνίαν τί τῶν χρηστῶν ἐλπίζειν ἐᾷ; εἰ μὲν γὰρ ἐπῄνουν τὰ γεγενημένα, ὡς εὖ καὶ καλῶς ἔχοντα, εἰκότως τοῖς παρὰ σφῶν ἐπαινουμένοις ἐπέμενον, εἰ δὲ θρηνοῦσιν, ὡς λέγουσιν, καὶ ἀνάγκῃ καὶ βίᾳ ταῦτα πεπραχέναι φασίν, τί δήποτε μὴ ἐξαρνοῦνται ἃ παρανόμως δεδράκασιν, ἀλλὰ τὸ παρόν, καὶ σφόδρα ὂν ὀλιγοχρόνιον, τοῦ μέλλοντος προτετίμηται; τί δήποτε δὲ καὶ προφανῶς ψεύδονται καί φασι μηδεμίαν γεγενῆσθαι περὶ τὸ δόγμα καινοτομίαν;

Διὰ ποίους φόνους καὶ γοητείας ἐξηλάθην ἐγώ; ὁ δεῖνα τίνας μοιχείας ἐτόλμησεν; ποίους ὁ δεῖνα διώρυξεν τάφους; δῆλόν ἐστι καὶ τοῖς βαρβάροις ὡς δογμάτων χάριν κἀμὲ καὶ τοὺς ἄλλους ἐξήλασαν. καὶ γὰρ τὸν Κύριον Δόμνον, ὡς τὰ

l. 8 συμβουλεύειν αὐτοῖς ἐξαρνηθῆναι τὰ τολμηθέντα *coni. Gilb., scripsi* : σ. ἵνα αὐ. ἐξαρνηθῇ τὰ τ. *NZ* (*A def.*), *edd. Sirmond* (*alii vero, nec consilium dant vt eiurent quae patrata sunt*) *and Azéma* (*"les autres ne conseillent point aux premiers de désavouer leurs audaces"*) *have elicited Thdt.'s meaning from the unintelligible phraseology of the mss. These carry the vb.* ἐξαρνηθῇ (*disown*) *which would have to be interpreted as passive with the neut. pl. subj.* τὰ τολμηθέντα, *but the vb.* ἐξαρνοῦμαι *is deponent and must be active in meaning;* τὰ τολμηθέντα *is clearly the d.o. As Dr. Gilbert has pointed out to me, the corruption in the medieval tradition is probably to be traced to a dittography of the letters* ιν α (συμβουλεύειν αὐτοῖς), *which then led to the alteration of the inf. to the subjunctive. Such an error could easily occur in the transcription into minuscule of a capital text written without word division.*

a. *Cf.* 2Thes 2.3; 1Tm 4.1.

125. To John, Bishop of Germanicia[1]

I replied to Your Holiness' earlier letter as soon as I received it. As for the situation now before us, we have no ground for hope; indeed, I'm inclined to think that this is the prelude to the general apostasy.[a] The fact that people deplore what they claim to have been accomplished in Ephesus only by force and yet think no better of their behavior, but stand by their criminal recklessness and go on building on this foundation of injustice and irreligion, and the fact that the rest are not advising them to disown their disregard for justice or fleeing the communion of those who stand by their illegal actions—how does this leave hope for good?[2] If they approved of these actions as right and rightly done, they might properly stand by what they approved of; but, if, as they claim, they deplore them and admit that they were accomplished through a show of force, why on earth don't they disavow these illegal actions instead of placing more importance on the present world, momentary as it is, than on what is to come? Why do they go on stating the obvious lie that there has been no innovation in doctrine?

If that's true, why have I been sent into exile? Name the murder or the black magic! And what about this other one? Just what were his shameless acts of adultery? And that one? What tombs did he break into? Even pagans can see that I as well as the others have been sent into exile because of our theological positions. These excellent gen-

1. We follow Azéma in restoring this letter to the place it occupies in the *Neapolitanus, viz.* #125; *v.* the "Introduction to the Greek Text," secc. II.A, C. John would be a prominent bishop at the Council of Chalcedon: one of the three bishops sent to summon Dioscorus to face his accusers (Intro., sec. 5.7), a vocal opponent of the first statement produced by the patriarch Anatolius (*v.* Intro., sec. 5.9), and one of the few bishops required by the Council to pronounce anathema on Nestorius (*v.* Intro., sec 5.15); *v.* Honigmann, p. 179. His see, Germanicia, named in honor of the Roman emperors Caligula and Claudius, is now the southeastern Turkish city of Maras; *v.* Wagner, "Germanicaea." It sits "at the edge of the Mesopotamian plain, on roads connecting Asia Minor and Syria." A city of Euphratensis, Germanicia was dependent upon the metropolitan of Hierapolis; *v.* Foss, "Germanikeia." For the date of this letter, *v. ep.* 120 n. 1.

2. On the violence employed by Dioscorus at the Latrocinium to force compliance with his theological views and ecclesiastical policies, *v.* Intro., secc. 4.7f.

κεφάλαια μὴ δεξάμενον, καθεῖλον οἱ βέλτιστοι, *πανεύφημα* ταῦτα καλέσαντες καὶ ἐμμένειν τούτοις ὁμολογήσαντες· ἐγὼ γὰρ αὐτῶν τὰς καταθέσεις ἀνέγνων. ἐμὲ δὲ ὡς τῆς αἱρέσεως ἔξαρχον ἀπεκήρυξαν καὶ τοὺς ἄλλους ὡσαύτως διὰ τὴν αὐτὴν αἰτίαν ἐξέβαλον. ὅτι γὰρ τὴν πρακτικὴν ἀρετὴν τοῖς ἁμαξοβίοις μᾶλλον ἢ αὐτοῖς νενομοθετῆσθαι παρὰ τοῦ Σωτῆρος ὑπέλαβον, αὐτὰ βοᾷ τὰ πράγματα· κατὰ γὰρ Κανδιδιανοῦ τοῦ Πισίδου λιβέλλους ἐπέδοσάν τινες, μοιχείας αὐτοῦ κατηγοροῦντες πολλὰς καὶ ἑτέρας παρανομίας, καί φασιν εἰρηκέναι τῆς συνόδου τὸν ἔξαρχον, *Εἰ δογμάτων κατηγορεῖτε, δεχόμεθα τοὺς λιβέλλους· οὐ γὰρ ἤλθομεν μοιχείαις δικάσαι.* διά τοι τοῦτο καὶ Ἀθήνιον καὶ Ἀθανάσιον ὑπὸ τῆς ἀνατολικῆς ἐκβληθέντας συνόδου τὰς οἰκείας ἀπολαβεῖν ἐκκλησίας ἐκέλευσαν, ὡς οὐδὲν μὲν περὶ βίου τοῦ Σωτῆρος ἡμῶν νομοθετήσαντος, μόνα δὲ τὰ δόγματα φυλάττειν κελεύσαντος, ἃ πρὸ τῶν ἄλλων διέφθειραν οἱ σοφώτατοι.

(2) Μὴ τοίνυν παιζέτωσαν, μηδὲ κρυπτέτωσαν τὴν ἀσέβειαν ἣν καὶ ταῖς γλώτταις καὶ ταῖς χερσὶν ἐβεβαίωσαν. εἰ δὲ μὴ ταῦθ' οὕτως ἔχει, εἰπάτωσαν τῶν σφαγῶν τὰς αἰτίας, ὁμολογησάτωσαν ἐγγράφως τῶν τοῦ Σωτῆρος ἡμῶν φύσεων τὸ διάφορον, τῆς ἑνώσεως τὸ ἀσύγχυτον,[b] εἰπάτωσαν ὡς, καὶ μετὰ τὴν ἕνωσιν,

b. *Pac. form.*

tlemen deposed my Lord Domnus on the grounds that he refused to accept the *Chapters*, which they praised to the skies, and which they all agreed to endorse.[3] You see, I've read their determinations: they've banished me as though the founder of a heresy; they've excommunicated the others for the very same reason. As their acts proclaim, they take it that our Savior enjoined virtuous behavior on the Scythians in their wagon trains, not on them! In the case of Candidianus of Pisidia, there were those who submitted indictments for multiple acts of adultery as well as other crimes, and the word is that the president of the council declared, "If you are raising objections regarding his dogmatic positions, we shall take up your accusations; as you know, we have not come here to pass judgment on cases of adultery." So it was that they ordered Athenius and Athanasius, though excommunicated by the eastern council, to retake possession of their churches.[4] As if our Savior had never laid down for us any law of conduct, but only commanded us to safeguard the purity of doctrine—which these wise men have done more to corrupt than anyone else!

(2) Enough of this game of theirs and this effort to dissimulate their heresy, which they've sanctioned with words backed up by violence! But, if this isn't the case, have them explain the charges that led to this blood-letting, have them confess in writing the difference between the natures of our Savior, the union without confusion;[b] have them declare that, even after the union, both the divinity and

3. On the doctrine of Cyril's *Twelve Chapters*, *v.* Intro., sec. 2.7; on the rejection of this doctrine by the oriental bishops, *v. ib.*, secc. 3.10f.

4. Candidianus was bishop of Antioch in Pisidia; at the Latrocinium, he voted for the reinstatement of Eutyches (*Conc. chalc.*, *Act. 1*, sec. 884, #30) and the deposition of Flavian of Constantinople (*ib.*, sec. 990, l. 9). On Athanasius of Perrhe and Sabinianus, Athanasius' successor to the see of Perrhe, *v. ep.* 42 n. 3. Sabinianus, the addressee of *ep.* 126, was among those deposed at Ephesus II. The identity of Athenius remains a mystery; this is the only place where he is mentioned in any of the theological authors of the Ephesian-Chalcedonian period. His obscurity indicates that he was probably a bishop of a smaller church, perhaps, as Theodoret's pairing of the two suggests, an associate of Athanasius of Perrhe. Despite obvious moral failings, both he and Athanasius were restored to their sees at the Latrocinium. As his name does not appear in the acts or among the signatories of the Council of Chalcedon, it is conceivable, that, lacking Athanasius' connections at court, he lost the position to which he was restored even before 451.

ἀκραιφνὴς καὶ ἡ θεότης καὶ ἡ ἀνθρωπότης διέμεινεν. *Θεὸς οὐ μυκτηρίζεται.*[c] ἀρνηθῶσιν νῦν *τὰ κεφάλαια,* ἃ πολλάκις μὲν ἀπεκήρυξαν, ἐν Ἐφέσῳ δὲ νῦν ἐβεβαίωσαν.

Μὴ ἐξαπατάτωσαν Σοῦ Τὴν Ὁσιότητα, λόγοις κεχρημένοι ψευδέσιν· ἐπῄνουν τὰ παρ' ἐμοῦ ἐν Ἀντιοχείᾳ λεγόμενα καὶ ἀδελφοὶ ὄντες, καὶ ἀναγνῶσται γενόμενοι, καὶ διάκονοι χειροτονηθέντες, καὶ πρεσβύτεροι, καὶ ἐπίσκοποι, καί, μετὰ τὸ τέλος τῆς διαλέξεως, περιεπτύσσοντο καὶ κατεφίλουν καὶ κεφαλήν, καὶ στήθη, καὶ χεῖρας, τινὲς δὲ αὐτῶν καὶ γονάτων ἥπτοντο, τὴν διδασκαλίαν ἡμῶν *ἀποστολικὴν* ὀνομάζοντες, καὶ ταύτην νῦν ἀπεκήρυξαν, ταύτην ἀνεθεμάτισαν, καὶ ἐγὼ μέν, ὃν *φωστῆρα* ἐκάλουν,[d] οὐ τῆς Ἀνατολῆς μόνης, ἀλλὰ καὶ τῆς οἰκουμένης, ἀπεκηρύχθην καὶ οὐδὲ ἄρτου, τό γε εἰς αὐτοὺς ἧκον, μεταλαγχάνω· καὶ γὰρ τοὺς προσδιαλεγομένους ἡμῖν ἀνεθεμάτισαν. ὃν δὲ πρὸ βραχέος καθεῖλον καὶ τὰ Βαλεντίνου καὶ Ἀπολιναρίου φρονεῖν ἔφασαν, τοῦτον ὡς νικηφόρον περιεῖπον τῆς πίστεως, καὶ τῶν τούτου προεκυλινδοῦντο ποδῶν, καὶ συγγνώμην ἐζήτουν, καὶ *πατέρα πνευματικὸν*

l. 42 Θεὸς *N, cf. NTG* : ὁ Θ. *Onor., edd. In his commentary on Gal, Thdt. quotes the verse (6.7) without the article.*

c. Gal 6.7 d. Phil 2.15

the humanity remained unmixed. "God is not mocked."[5c] Let them disavow the *Chapters*, which they have rejected on numerous occasions but have now sanctioned in Ephesus.

Don't let them try to deceive Your Holiness with their lying words. They heaped praise on my preaching in Antioch when they were just brethren, after they were made readers, when they had been consecrated as deacons, priests, and then bishops. When I had finished preaching, they would wrap their arms around me and kiss me on the head, the chest, and the hands. Why, some of them would even grasp me by the knees as they proclaimed my teaching "apostolic." And this is the teaching that these same people have now rejected, that they have declared anathema![6] Me, the man they once called "a luminary," not of the East alone, but of the entire world,[d] they've declared excommunicate and, for all they care, I could die of starvation.[7] They have pronounced anathema on anyone who associates with me, and yet, that man they just deposed, the partisan, so they declared, of Valentinus[8] and Apollinaris,[9] him they have honored as a champion of the faith: they groveled at his feet, begged his pardon, called him their "spiritual father."[10] Can an octopus change its color

5. Theodoret is referring to the language of the "Formula of Reunion"; *v. ep.* 104 n. 3.

6. Theodoret exclaims that betrayal has come from a totally unexpected direction, from churchmen whose advancement—from layman to bishop—he had himself helped celebrate. Those very churchmen who had praised his doctrine when he had come to Antioch to preach at their consecrations to ever higher positions, having risen to the rank of bishop, have now condemned his teaching at the Second Council of Ephesus. Note the polysyndeton (καὶ appears five times) punctuating the outline of an ecclesiastical career (καὶ ἀδελφοὶ ὄντες, *etc.*) and here indicative of profound indignation.

7. Theodoret regularly applies the Pauline metaphor of "luminary" (φωστήρ; *v.* Phil 2.15) to Christian teachers of authoritative preëminence in the formulation of doctrine; *v. epp.* 11 (Flavian of Constantinople), 83.3 (Alexander and Athanasius of Alexandria; Basil of Caesarea, and Gregory of Nyssa), 89 (Ignatius and Eustathius of Antioch, Athanasius of Alexandria, Basil of Caesarea, Gregory of Nyssa, and John Chrysostom), 144 ("our celebrated fathers"), 146.7 (Eustathius, Meletius, and Flavian of Antioch), 147.9 (Basil of Caesarea).

8. On Valentinus, *v. epp.* 81 n. 3 and 104 n. 5.

9. On Apollinaris, *v.* Intro., sec. 1.5.

10. Theodoret decries the reinstatement of Eutyches; on Eutyches' christology

ἐκάλουν. ποῖοι πολύποδες οὕτως πρὸς τὰς πέτρας τὴν οἰκείαν ἐναλλάττουσι χρόαν, ἢ χαμαιλέοντες πρὸς τὰ φύλλα τὸ χρῶμα, ὡς οὗτοι τὴν γνώμην πρὸς τοὺς καιροὺς μεταβάλλουσιν; ἡμεῖς δὲ αὐτοῖς παραχωροῦμεν καὶ θρόνων, καὶ ἀξιωμάτων, καὶ τῆς προσκαίρου τρυφῆς, μετὰ δὲ τῶν ἀποστολικῶν δογμάτων τὰς χαλεπὰς νομιζομένας προσμένομεν ἐξορίας, ἀρκοῦσαν ἔχοντες παραψυχὴν τὸ τοῦ Δεσπότου κριτήριον· ἐλπίζομεν γὰρ ὡς πολλὰ τῶν ἡμετέρων ἁμαρτημάτων διὰ τήνδε τὴν ἀδικίαν ὁ Δεσπότης ἀφήσει.

(3) Τὴν δὲ Σὴν Ὁσιότητα παρακαλῶ φυλάξασθαι τῆς ἀσεβείας τὴν κοινωνίαν καὶ προτεῖναι μὲν αὐτοῖς ἀρνηθῆναι τὰ πεπραγμένα, εἰ δὲ μὴ θελήσαιεν, φυγεῖν ὡς προδότας τῆς πίστεως. τέως δὲ προσμείνασαν Σοῦ Τὴν Θεοσέβειαν ἰδεῖν εἰ ἄρα τις ἔσται τοῦ χειμῶνος μεταβολή, οὐδαμῶς ἐμεμψάμεθα. μετὰ μέντοι τὴν χειροτονίαν τοῦ τῆς Ἀνατολῆς προέδρου, δήλη πάντως ἡ ἑκάστου γενήσεται γνώμη. εὔξασθαι δὲ ὑπὲρ ἡμῶν, Δέσποτα, καταξίωσον· νῦν γὰρ διαφερόντως τῆσδε τῆς βοηθείας δεόμεθα ἵνα δυνηθῶμεν ἀντισχεῖν πρὸς τὰ καθ' ἡμῶν μελετώμενα.

to match a rock, or a chameleon blend in with the foliage with so much ease as these men, in accordance with the demands of the moment, exchange one set of convictions for another?[11] As far as I'm concerned, they may have their sees, their honors, and the luxuries of the moment, while I, possessed of the teachings of the apostles, await this exile people think so hard to bear; the judgment of our Master is all the consolation I need, for it is my hope that our Master will forgive many a transgression of mine on account of the injustice I'm now suffering.

(3) I urge Your Holiness to hold back from communion with this irreligion, to offer them the opportunity to renounce their works, but, if they refuse, to shun them as traitors to the faith. I have not uttered a word of reproach against Your Reverence, so long as you were waiting for some possible let-up in this tempest. Of course, after the appointment of the archbishop of the eastern church, it will be clear where each man stands.[12] Be so kind as to pray for us, my Master. Now is the moment when we have most need of your assistance, that we may be able to hold our ground amidst the plots that are being laid against us.

---

and its condemnation in 448, *v.* Intro., secc. 4, 4.2, and on his reinstatement at Ephesus in 449, *v. ib.*, sec. 4.7.

11. For the octopus adapting its color to the surrounding rocks, *v.* Ael., *N. a.* 1.32. Gregory Nazianzus compares (*Or.* 36.9) this trick of the octopus to the inconstant behavior of those who remain true to virtue only so long as they expect some profit and then change their conduct to take advantage of new opportunities.

12. For Maximus, the successor of Domnus, *v.* esp. Intro., secc. 4.9; 5.14–16.

126. ΑΦΘΟΝΙΩΙ, ΘΕΟΔΩΡΗΤΩΙ, ΝΟΝΝΩΙ, ΣΚΥΛΑΚΙΩΙ, ΑΦΘΟΝΙΩΙ, ΙΩΑΝΝΗΙ, ΠΟΛΙΤΕΥΟΜΕΝΟΙΣ ΖΕΥΓΜΑΤΟΣ

126. To Aphthonius,[1] Theodoret, Nonnus, Scylacius, Aphthonius, John, Decurions of Zeugma[2]

1. The addressees of *ep.* 126 are identified as "decurions," officials charged with the governance and financial administration of the town; on the tax-gathering responsibilities of the decurions, *v. ep.* 42 n. 5. *Epp.* VIIIf. are likewise addressed to decurions of Zeugma, but there is no overlap between that group of three and this group of six. Perhaps one of the men named Aphthonius may be identified with the *comes* who was praised or blamed in a lost poem by the hexameter poet Panolbius; *v. Suda*, π 204 (Πανόλβιος); *PLRE*, vol. 2, "Aphthonius 4," p. 110; and *cf.* Cameron, pp. 505f. with Baldwin, "Titles." Azéma dates this letter to the first half of 450, when Theodoret was still in exile at his monastery near Apamea. As Azéma points out, the remark (*v.* sec. 3) that the archimandrite Mekimas had made a long journey from Zeugma makes better sense if Theodoret was residing at Apamea rather than Cyrus; *v.* Intro., sec. 4.8. According to the calculation of "Orbis," by the ancient roads indicated in the *Barrington Atlas*, Apamea (68 B3), was located at a distance of some 295 kilometers, Cyrus (67 D3) only about 102, from Zeugma (67 F2); *cf. ep.* 32 n. 1.

2. Azéma (p.104 n. 1) cites this letter and *ep.* 131 as best exemplifying Theodoret's reluctance to accept the doctrine of *communicatio idiomatum.* In fact, this term had not been defined at any ancient council. In this letter, Theodoret rejects the notion that, through the union, the properties of the two natures become interchangeable in the sense that each property becomes relevant to both natures of Christ. In such a mingling of the two natures, God would cease to be God, and the manhood to be manhood. This is what he and the other Antiochenes saw in Cyril's "natural union" (ἕνωσις φυσική), a key expression of his third anathema against Nestorius; *v.* Intro. sec. 2.7. Yet, while rejecting the notion of interchangeability, Theodoret affirms that the qualities of the two natures belong to the one and common person of Christ. According to his human nature, Christ is a passible creature, and, according to his divine nature, the impassible Creator. The union is personal, not natural; *v.* sec. 2 of this letter, and *cf. Inc.* 32: Οὕτως ὁ Θεὸς Λόγος οἰκειοῦται τῆς τοῦ δούλου μορφης τὴν εὐτέλειαν, καὶ Θεὸς ὑπάρχων, ἄνθρωπος ἠθέλησεν ὀνομάζεσθαι (translated by Pásztori-Kupán, *Theodoret of Cyrus,* p. 168). *V.* also Richard's remarks ("Proclus de Constantinople, pp. 327–29) based on the analysis of passages of *Eran.* bk. 3. Theodoret's doctrine is in agreement with that of Leo, who (*Tom.* 3) also locates the union on the level of the person while preserving the properties of both natures. Thus, Frend is quite wrong to assert that, in the *Tome,* Leo emphasized the unity of the two natures "through the mutual sharing of properties, the *communicatio idiomatum*" (p. 38; *cf.* p. 48, n. 5). Indeed, as Frend himself points out (*ib.*, n. 6), at Chalcedon, some Illyrian and Palestinian bishops at first objected to Leo's doctrinal statement as Nestorian; *v.* Intro., sec. 5.6. The views of Theodoret and Leo were, of course, explicitly endorsed in the wording of the Chalcedonian definition; *v.* Intro. sec. 5.11.

To Aphthonius, Theodoret, Nonnus, Scylacius, Aphthonius, John, Decurions of Zeugma

(1) Ἔγνων τῆς ὑμετέρας πίστεως τὸ σταθερόν τε καὶ βέβαιον καὶ θυμηδίας ἐνεπλήσθην ὅτι μάλιστα πλείστης· ἐπειδὴ γὰρ εἰς ἓν σῶμα τελοῦμεν οἱ τῆς ἀϊδίου Τριάδος προσκυνηταί, εἰκότως δήπου τοῖς ὑγιαίνουσι τῶν μελῶν τὰ λοιπὰ συναγάλλεται μέλη· τοῦτό φησιν καὶ ὁ θεῖος Ἀπόστολος· Εἰ *δοξάζεται μέλος, συγχαίρει πάντα τὰ μέλη.*[a] συνήδομαι τοίνυν ὑμῖν τῶν ἀποστολικῶν ὑπεραθλοῦσι δογμάτων καὶ τὸν Ναβουθὲ τὸν πολυθρύλητον ἐκεῖνον ἐν τοῖς ἀμείνοσι μιμουμένοις· ἐκεῖνος γὰρ ὑπὲρ ἀμπελῶνος τὴν ἀδικωτάτην ὑπέστη σφαγήν, τὸν πατρῷον οὐ προέμενος κλῆρον.[b] ὑμεῖς δέ, οὐκ ἀμπελώνων, ἀλλὰ θείων ὑπερμαχεῖτε δογμάτων καὶ τὴν καινὴν ταύτην καὶ κίβδηλον αἵρεσιν ἀποστρέφεσθε, ὡς τὸ καθαρὸν τῆς εὐαγγελικῆς θολοῦσαν διδασκαλίας, καὶ τῆς παναγίας Τριάδος τὸν ἀριθμὸν οὔτε μειοῦν οὔτε αὔξειν ἀνέχεσθε.

Μειοῦσι μὲν γὰρ οἱ τῇ θεότητι τοῦ Μονογενοῦς τὸ πάθος προσάπτοντες, αὔξουσιν δὲ οἱ ἕτερον Υἱὸν ἐπεισάγειν τολμῶντες. ὑμεῖς δὲ εἰς ἕνα Μονογενῆ πιστεύετε καθάπερ εἰς ἕνα Πατέρα καὶ εἰς ἓν Ἅγιον Πνεῦμα, ἐν δὲ τῷ σαρκωθέντι Μονογενεῖ τὴν ληφθεῖσαν θεωρεῖτε φύσιν, ἥν, ἐξ ἡμῶν λαβών, ὑπὲρ ἡμῶν προσενήνοχεν. ἡ γὰρ ταύτης ἄρνησις φροῦδον τὴν ἡμετέραν σωτηρίαν ποιεῖ· εἰ γὰρ ἀπαθὴς ἡ τοῦ Μονογενοῦς θεότης· ἀπαθὴς γὰρ τῆς Τριάδος ἡ φύσις· τὸ δὲ πάσχειν πεφυκὸς μὴ προσομολογηθῇ παρ᾽ ἡμῶν, μάτην θρυλεῖται τὸ μὴ γενόμενον πάθος· τοῦ γὰρ πάσχοντος οὐκ ὄντος, πῶς ἂν γένοιτο πάθος; ἀπαθῆ μὲν γὰρ τὴν θείαν φύσιν κηρύττομεν· συνομολογοῦσι δὲ τοῦτο κἀκεῖνοι παραπλησίως ἡμῖν· πῶς ἂν οὖν γένοιτο πάθος,

l. 2 ἐνεπλήσθην *scr. Sir. Nös. Az.* : ἐπε- *codd. Sirmond's conjecture is to be adopted. The TLG offers just one ex. of the prefix with pi (the 10th c. epic author Diogenes Acritas), over 500 exx. of the prefix with nu.*

a. 1Cor 12.26 (NT var.)   b. 1Kgs 21.1–16 (LXX 20.1–16)

(1) I have received a report of the immovable solidity of your faith, and this has filled me with so much joy; since, as you know, we, the worshippers of the eternal Trinity, all form one body, it is to be expected that the rest of the body will take delight in the members that enjoy good health. For this we have the word of the holy Apostle: "When one member is glorified, the others rejoice along with it."[a] Thus, I am delighted by your contests on behalf of the apostolic teachings and your imitation, yet in more important things, of that Naboth of ancient renown. In defense of his vineyard, he suffered the foulest of murders, because he refused to give up the inheritance he had received from his fathers.[3b] You fight for no vineyard, but for doctrine given by God—shunning, as you do, this recently introduced heresy, this counterfeit and polluted version of the evangelical teaching—and you refuse to reduce or to increase the number of the most Holy Trinity.

Indeed, those who attribute the suffering to the divinity of the Only-begotten do reduce that number while those who recklessly introduce a second Son increase it, but you believe in one Only-begotten, as in one Father and one Holy Spirit, yet in the Only-begotten made flesh you perceive the nature that was assumed, the nature he took to himself and offered up on our behalf. To deny this nature is to do away with our salvation, for given that the godhead of the Only-begotten is impassible—as, of course, the nature of the Trinity is impassible—if we refuse to acknowledge the passible nature, there is no point in proclaiming far and wide a passion that never took place. If there is no one capable of suffering, how could there be a passion? After all, we proclaim that the nature of God is impassible—and even they agree with us in making the same confession—so, how could a passion take place in the absence of one who can suffer? The great

3. Theodoret again and again speaks of the tradition of faith passed down through the apostles and the Church as an inheritance bequeathed to the faithful; *v. epp.* 89, 108, 112.3, 113.5, 118, 132. Here, in a letter to decurions, officials much concerned with assessing the value of farmland and crops, he cites Naboth's literal defense of his ancestral allotment against expropriation by Ahab; *cf. ep.* 9.

οὐχ ὑποκειμένου τοῦ πάσχοντος; δόκησις γὰρ ἀντὶ τῆς ἀληθείας καὶ φαντασία φανήσεται τὸ μέγα τῆς οἰκονομίας μυστήριον· τοῦτον δὲ τὸν μῦθον Βαλεντῖνος, καὶ Βαρδησάνης, καὶ Μαρκίων, καὶ Μάνης ἐγέννησαν.

(2) Ἡ δὲ ἀνέκαθεν ταῖς ἐκκλησίαις παραδοθεῖσα διδασκαλία ἕνα μὲν Υἱὸν καὶ μετὰ τὴν ἐνανθρώπησιν οἶδεν τὸν Κύριον ἡμῶν Ἰησοῦν Χριστὸν καὶ τὸν αὐτὸν ὁμολογεῖ Θεὸν προαιώνιον καὶ ἄνθρωπον *ἐπ᾿ ἐσχάτου τῶν ἡμερῶν* γενόμενον,[c] γενόμενον δὲ ἄνθρωπον τῇ προσλήψει τῆς ἀνθρωπότητος, οὐ τῇ τροπῇ τῆς θεότητος·[d] εἰ γὰρ τὴν εἰς ἀνθρωπείαν φύσιν ἡ θεία φύσις ὑπέστη τροπήν, οὐκ ἔμεινεν ὅπερ ἦν, εἰ δὲ μὴ ἔστιν ὅπερ ἦν, ψευδῶς αὐτὸν καλοῦσι *Θεὸν* οἱ ταῦτα θρησκεύοντες. ἀλλ᾿ ἡμεῖς ἄτρεπτον ἴσμεν τὸν μονογενῆ τοῦ Θεοῦ Υἱόν, ὡς Θεὸν καὶ τοῦ ὄντως Θεοῦ Υἱόν· μεμαθήκαμεν γὰρ παρὰ τῆς θείας Γραφῆς ὡς, *ἐν μορφῇ Θεοῦ ὑπάρχων*, ἔλαβεν τὴν τοῦ *δούλου μορφήν*[e] καὶ *σπέρματος Ἀβραὰμ* ἐπελάβετο,[f] οὐκ εἰς σπέρμα Ἀβραὰμ μετεβλήθη, καὶ *κεκοινώνηκεν … παραπλησίως* ἡμῖν *σαρκός* τε *καὶ αἵματος* καὶ ψυχῆς ἀθανάτου καὶ ἀμώμου.[g] ταῦτα διατηρήσας, ὑπὲρ μὲν τῶν ἡμαρτηκότων σωμάτων τὸ ἀναμάρτητον αὐτοῦ προσενήνοχε σῶμα, ὑπὲρ δὲ τῶν ψυχῶν τὴν πάσης ἐλευθέραν κηλῖδος.

Διά τοι τοῦτο καὶ τῆς κοινῆς ἀναστάσεως ἔχομεν τὴν ἐλπίδα· τῇ γὰρ ἀπαρχῇ δήπουθεν κοινωνήσει τὸ γένος· καθάπερ γὰρ τῷ Ἀδὰμ ἐκοινωνήσαμεν τῆς τελευτῆς, οὕτω δὴ καὶ τῷ Σωτῆρι Χριστῷ κοινωνήσομεν τῆς ζωῆς. καὶ τοῦτο σαφῶς ἡμᾶς ὁ θεῖος Ἀπόστολος ἐξεπαίδευσεν· *Νυνί*, γάρ φησι, *Χριστὸς ἐγήγερται ἐκ νεκρῶν, ἀπαρχὴ τῶν κεκοιμημένων ἐγένετο· ἐπειδὴ γὰρ δι᾿ ἀνθρώπου ὁ θάνατος, καὶ δι᾿ ἀνθρώπου ἀνάστασις νεκρῶν· ὥσπερ γὰρ ἐν τῷ Ἀδὰμ πάντες ἀποθνῄσκουσιν, οὕτως καὶ ἐν τῷ Χριστῷ πάντες ζωοποιηθήσονται.*[h]

c. Heb 1.2 (*Cf.* Nm 24.14; Jer 23.20; 25.19.)
d. *Cf. Pac. form.*
e. Phil 2.6f. (NT var.)
f. Heb 2.16
g. Heb 2.14 (NT var.)
h. 1Cor 15.20–22 (NT var.)

mystery of our salvation will be reduced from historical fact to a false image, a mere appearance! This is the myth originated by Valentinus, Bardaisan, Marcion, and Mani.[4]

(2) The teaching that has been handed down in the churches from the beginning recognizes, even after the incarnation, the one Son, our Lord Jesus Christ, and confesses that he is both God before all ages and man born "at the end of days,"[c] born man by the assumption of the humanity, not by a change in the godhead.[d] For if the divine nature underwent a change into the human, it did not remain what it was, and, if it is no longer what it was, those who are committed to this position are wrong to call it "God." But, as we know, the only-begotten Son of God, as God and Son of the very God, is not subject to change. As we have learned from holy Scripture, he who "was in the form of God" took up "the form of the slave";[e] he took up "the seed of Abraham,"[f] but was not changed into the seed of Abraham, and, along with us, "he took part in flesh and blood," with a deathless soul free of sin. Preserving both his divinity and humanity, he made offer of his sinless body on behalf of the bodies of sinners and of his soul free of all stain on behalf of our souls.[g]

It is precisely because of this that we have reason to hope for a share in his resurrection: Surely the stock will share along with the first fruits. As with Adam we have shared in death, so with our Savior Christ we shall share in life. For this we have the unequivocal teaching of the holy Apostle: "Now," so he says, "Christ is risen from the dead, becoming the first fruits of those who have fallen asleep. As death came through a man, so also through a man the resurrection of the dead. As all die in Adam, so shall all be made alive in Christ."[h]

4. On these four heretical teachers, *v. epp.* 81 n. 3 and 104 n. 5.

(3) Ταῦτα νῦν οὐ διδάσκων, ἀλλ᾽ ἀναμιμνήσκων, γράφω[i] καί, συντεμεῖν σπουδάσας, τῆς ἐπιστολῆς ὑπερέβην, ὡς οἶμαι, τὸν ὅρον. ἐπιστεῖλαί με δὲ προὔτρεψεν ὁ πάντα εὐλαβέστατος καὶ θεοφιλέστατος πρεσβύτερος καὶ ἀρχιμανδρίτης Μεκίμας, διὰ μὲν τὸν τῆς ἀγάπης νόμον ὁδὸν τοσαύτην ἐξανύσας, διδάξας δὲ ἡμᾶς τὸν Τῆς Ὑμετέρας Θαυμασιότητος ζῆλον καὶ αἰτήσας πυρσεῦσαι τοῦτον τοῖς γράμμασιν. ἐγὼ τοίνυν καὶ τὴν αἴτησιν ἐδεξάμην καὶ γέγραφα τὴν ἐπιστολὴν καὶ τὸν τῶν ὅλων ἱκετεύω Δεσπότην φρουρῆσαι ὑμᾶς ἐν τῇ πίστει καὶ κρείττους ἀποφῆναι τοῦ σινιάζοντος.[j]

l. 59 Ἐπιστεῖλαί με δὲ προὔτρεψεν *codd., Az.* : Ἐ. δέ με π. *scr.* (*fort. recte*) *Sir. Nös. Sirmond's emendation would put the particle and the pron. in a more expected order. This is the only passage in the works of Thdt. presenting* με δὲ, *while there are twenty-seven examples in his own words of the reversed order. Yet the structure of this passage* (*inf. + subj. of infin. + particle + fin. vb.*) *is without parallel in those twenty-seven other passages. Cf. in Am 1.5* (*PG. vol. 81, col. 1669, ll. 22f., Πλέον δέ με χαλεπαίνειν κατ᾽ αὐτῶν ἀναγκάζει τὰ … ὑπ᾽ αὐτῶν τολμώμενα*)*, where we find the same syntax and the normal δέ με. Yet, the inf. follows, rather than precedes με. Note also that, as in ep. 126, the pronoun is juxtaposed with the infin. of which it is the subj.*

i. *Cf.* Rom 15.15. j. *Cf.* Lk 22.31.

(3) I have written not to teach you these things, but to remind you of what you already know,[i] and, despite my effort to be brief, I rather think I've exceeded the limits of a letter. It was the right reverend Mekimas, priest beloved of God and archimandrite, who urged me to write to you; in obedience to the law of love, he traveled all this distance, set out for us Your Excellencies' zeal, and begged me to set it aflame with a letter. So now I have complied with his request and written the letter, and I beg the Master of the universe to keep you safe in the faith and give you the strength to prevail over him who sifts us.[j]

127. ΣΑΒΙΝΙΑΝΩΙ ΕΠΙΣΚΟΠΩΙ

Ἐπῄνεσα Σοῦ Τὴν Ὁσιότητα, καταλιποῦσαν τὸν ἐπίφθονον θρόνον· ὁ γὰρ πάλαι σεβάσμιος νῦν γέγονε καταγέλαστος· ὤνιον γὰρ αὐτὸν ἡμεῖς ἐποιήσαμεν. ἐθαύμασα δέ, μαθὼν ὡς πρὸς τοὺς ἐξελάσαντας ἔδραμες· δρᾶσαι γὰρ τοὐναντίον ἐχρῆν καί, παρακαλούμενον ἔχεσθαι τῶν οἰάκων, φυγεῖν τὴν κυβέρνησιν, ὡς τῶν συμπλεόντων πολεμίων γεγενημένων. ἢ οὐκ οἶσθα, θεοφιλέστατε, τίνα μὲν ὁ Σωτὴρ ὁ ἡμέτερος διὰ τῶν ἱερῶν ἀποστόλων κηρύττειν ἡμᾶς ἐδίδαξεν, τίνα δὲ νῦν θρησκεύειν ἐνομοθέτησαν οἱ τῶν ἀποστολικῶν κληρονόμοι δογμάτων; τίς γὰρ τῶν παλαιῶν διδασκάλων, ἐξ οὗπερ κατηγγέλη τὸ κήρυγμα μέχρι τῆς κατεχούσης νῦν σκοτομήνης, ἀκήκοεν σαρκὸς καὶ θεότητος *μίαν φύσιν* κηρύξαντος ἢ ἐτόλμησεν πώποτε *παθητὴν* ὀνομάσαι τοῦ Μονογενοῦς τὴν θεότητα; ταῦτα νῦν παρ᾽ ἐνίων λέγεσθαι προφανῶς τολμᾶται, παρὰ δὲ τῶν ἄλλων περιορᾶται λεγόμενα, καὶ σιγῇ τοῦ μύσους μεταλαγχάνουσιν.

Τί οὖν χρὴ ποιεῖν, εἴποι τις ἄν, *τοὺς ταῦτα μυσαττομένους;* δυοῖν θάτερον εἴποιμ᾽ ἄν· ἢ ὁμόσε χωρεῖν καὶ διελέγχειν τῶν δογμάτων τὸ κίβδηλον ἢ φεύγειν ὡς προφανῶς δυσσεβούντων τὴν κοινωνίαν· καὶ γὰρ ἐγὼ τὴν κατ᾽ ἐμοῦ γεγενημένην ἀδικίαν ὡς θείαν ἐδεξάμην εὐεργεσίαν, οὐ τοῖς ἠδικηκόσι χάριν ὁμολογῶν· πῶς γὰρ τοῖς γε ἀδελφοκτόνοις καὶ τῆς τοῦ

127. To Bishop Sabinianus[1]

I applauded Your Holiness for giving up a see that had become so odious; though in times past an episcopal seat was an object of reverence, in our day it has become an object of ridicule, something we buy and sell. Yet, I was surprised to hear how you had run into the arms of the very men who had run you out. Indeed, you should have done just the opposite and abandoned your captaincy, even though they begged you to keep hold of the rudder, on the ground that your crew had gone over to the enemy. Is it possible, beloved of God, that you could be unaware of the difference between what, our Savior, through apostolic tradition, has taught us to preach, and what these heirs of the apostolic teachings have now instructed us to believe? Name one of our ancient teachers, from the first proclamation of the gospel down to our own dark days, who ever gave heed to anyone preaching "one nature" of the body and the godhead, or who was so reckless as to refer to the Only-begotten as "passible."[2] At this moment, there are people openly making such reckless statements, and their pronouncements are tolerated by the rest, who by their silence, defile themselves with the same heresy.

So if anyone should ask me, "What should we do, those of us who reject these abominable doctrines?" I would suggest one of two alternatives: either join with the enemy at close quarters and show these doctrines up for the counterfeit coin they are, or flee all communion with these people, because they are openly offending against sound religion. In my own case, I have welcomed the injustice committed against me as a gift from God. Not that I feel any gratitude toward those who have perpetrated this wrong—how could I feel grateful

1. For Sabinianus, bishop of Perrhe, a see, like Theodoret's Cyrus, dependent upon the metropolitan of Hierapolis, the capital of the province of Euphratensis, *v. ep.* 42 n. 3. For the date of this letter, *v. ep.* 120 n. 1.

2. *Cf. Eran. dial.* 3 (p. 200, l. 13), where the opponent of orthodoxy declares, "holy Scripture says that the Son of God submitted to suffering" (Η θεία γραφὴ τὸν Υἱὸν τοῦ Θεοὺ τὸ πάθος ὑπομεμενηκέναι φησί).

Κάϊν γεγενημένοις μερίδος·[a] ἀλλὰ τὸν ἐμὸν Δεσπότην ὑμνῶν, ὅτι με καὶ τῆς τῶν ἠδικημένων κατηξίωσεν μοίρας[b] καὶ τῶν ἠδικηκότων καὶ βλασφημούντων ἐχώρισεν καὶ τὴν ἐρασμιωτάτην ἐμοὶ ἔδωκεν ἡσυχίαν.

a. Gn 4.8 b. *Cf.* Mt 5.11f.; 1Pt 2.20.

to men who kill their own brothers and make common cause with Cain?[a]—yet I sing a hymn of praise to my Master, who has deemed me worthy to share the lot of those who suffer injustice,[b] separated me from wrongdoers and blasphemers, and granted me the peace I desire above all else.

128. ΙΩΒΙΩΙ ΠΡΕΣΒΥΤΕΡΩΙ ΚΑΙ ΑΡΧΙΜΑΝΔΡΙΤΗΙ

Ἀβραὰμ ὁ πατριάρχης, καὶ μετὰ γῆρας, ἠρίστευσεν,[a] καὶ Μωϋσῆς ὁ μέγας, πρεσβύτης ἤδη γενόμενος, εἰς προσευχὴν τὰς χεῖρας ἐκτείνων, τὸν Ἀμαλὴκ κατηκόντισεν,[b] καὶ Σαμουὴλ ὁ θεσπέσιος, μετὰ πολιάν, τοὺς ἀλλοφύλους ἐτρέπετο.[c] τούτους τὸ σεβάσμιόν σου γῆρας ζηλοῖ κἀν τοῖς ὑπὲρ εὐσεβείας πολέμοις ἀνδραγαθίζεται, καὶ τῶν εὐαγγελικῶν δογμάτων ὑπερμαχεῖ, καὶ τοὺς νέους ἀποκρύπτει τῇ προθυμίᾳ τῆς γνώμης. ἐγὼ δέ, ταῦτα ἀκούων, γάννυμαι καὶ εὐφραίνομαι καὶ περιπτύξασθαι μὲν ποθῶ τὴν σεπτοτάτην σου πολιάν.

Ἐπειδὴ δὲ τούτου διαμαρτάνω· Τὴν μὲν γὰρ Σὴν Θεοσέβειαν οἴκοι γῆρας ἐπέχει, ἐμὲ δὲ νόμος ἐνθάδε καθείργει βασιλικός· διὰ τῶν γραμμάτων σοφίζομαι τὸ ποθούμενον καὶ προσφέρω Σοῦ Τῇ Φιλοθεΐᾳ τὸν ἐμοὶ πανεπέραστον ἀσπασμόν, καὶ παρακαλῶ εὐχαῖς ἐπαμῦναι ταῖς ἐκκλησίαις ζάλης ἐμπεπλησμέναις, καὶ μέντοι κἀμοὶ τὴν θείαν προξενῆσαι ῥοπήν, ὑπὲρ μὲν τῶν ἀποστολικῶν πολεμουμένῳ δογμάτων, δεομένῳ δὲ τῆς ἄνωθεν ἀντιλήψεως.

a. Gn 22.1–19 b. Ex 17.8–13 c. 1Sm 7.3–17

128. To Job, Priest and Archimandrite[1]

In old age, the patriarch Abraham triumphed in battle;[a] already elderly, the great Moses stretched out his hands in prayer and smote Amalek;[b] gray with years, Samuel, that holy man, would put the Philistines to flight.[c] In venerable age, you now emulate men such as these as you join in heroic combats for right religion, fight on behalf of the gospel teachings, and, in your fervent zeal, put young men in the shade. I rejoice, I'm filled with joy to hear this news, and I feel a deep desire to wrap my arms around your head and its worshipful gray hair.

But as this is quite beyond my reach—Your Reverence kept at home by old age, while I'm confined to this place by the emperor's edict—I make up for what I'm missing by writing a letter. I extend my warmest greeting to Your Piety and urge you to offer prayers on behalf of the churches engulfed in storm and to procure help from God for me as well, embattled as I am in defense of the apostolic teachings and in sore need of support from heaven.

1. The archimandrite Job is known to us as a signatory to the deposition of Eutyches at Flavian's Synod of Constantinople in 448; *v. Conc. chalc., Act. 1,* sec. 552, #36. He is also one of a group of priests and archimandrites from whom Leo (*ep.* 31) sought support for a delegation of clerics sent to Constantinople with a dossier of patristic texts for the instruction of Theodosius II on points of doctrine that Leo expected the newly consecrated Anatolius (*v.* Intro., sec. 4.9) to endorse. On the title "archimandrite," *v. ep.* 27 n. 1; for the date of this letter, *v. ep.* 120 n. 1.

129. ΚΑΝΔΙΔΩΙ ΠΡΕΣΒΥΤΕΡΩΙ ΚΑΙ ΑΡΧΙΜΑΝΔΡΙΤΗΙ

Ἐνίκησεν, ὡς ἔοικεν, τὸ γῆρας τῆς θεοφιλοῦς σου ψυχῆς τὴν προθυμίαν, καὶ τὰς χεῖρας οὐκ ἔχεις συνήθως ἐκτεταμένας· διά τοι τοῦτο καὶ φιλονεικεῖ νικᾶν ὁ Ἀμαλήκ. γενέσθωσαν τοίνυν τινὲς ἐπίκουροι τῆς ἀσθενείας, καθάπερ πάλαι ποτὲ Ὢρ καὶ Ἀαρὼν ὑπεστήριζον τοῦ νομοθέτου τὰς χεῖρας, ἵνα καὶ τὸν Ἀμαλὴκ καταλεύσῃς καὶ τὸν Ἰσραὴλ διασώσῃς.[a] νῦν γὰρ μάλιστα σπουδαιοτέρων δεῖ προσευχῶν, ἑλλήνων μὲν καὶ ἰουδαίων, καὶ πάσης εἰρηνευούσης αἱρέσεως, μόνης δὲ τῆς Ἐκκλησίας χειμαζομένης καὶ παγχαλέπῳ κλύδωνι περιπεσούσης. καὶ ἡμεῖς δὲ διαφερόντως τῆς τῶν ὑμετέρων προσευχῶν δεόμεθα βοηθείας, καὶ τῶν νομισθέντων συναγωνιστῶν ἀνταγωνιζομένων.

a. Ex 17.8–13

129. To Candidus, Priest and Archimandrite[1]

It looks as if old age has defeated the pious zeal of your heart, and, as you cannot continue to hold your arms outstretched, Amalek is pressing on to victory. You need helpers to come to the aid of your weakness—as in ancient times Hur and Aaron supported the Lawgiver's arms—to give you strength to crush Amalek and save Israel from danger.[a] Now is the moment of greatest need for fervent prayer. While the Hellenes, the Jews, and every heretical sect are enjoying calm and quiet, the Church alone is engulfed in high waters and tossed about in the storm. We have especial need for the help of your prayers at this time when even those we thought were fighting on our own side are fighting against us.[2]

1. Candidus is known to us only through this letter. On the title "archimandrite," *v. ep.* 27 n. 1; for the date of this letter, *v. ep.* 120 n. 1.

2. Perhaps, as Azéma (vol. 3, p. 109, n. 5) suggests, Theodoret is referring to his metropolitan Domnus. Of course, Domnus was also deposed and exiled by Dioscorus and his associates at the Second Council of Ephesus; *cf. ep.* 31 n. 1.

130. ΜΑΓΝΩΙ. ΑΝΤΩΝΙΩΙ ΠΡΕΣΒΥΤΕΡΩΙΣ ΚΑΙ ΑΡΧΙΜΑΝΔΡΙΤΗΑΙΣ

Τοὺς μὲν νύκτωρ πλέοντας οἱ τῶν λιμένων ψυχαγωγοῦσι πυρσοί, τοὺς δὲ τῆς ἀποστολικῆς προκινδυνεύοντας πίστεως τῶν ὁμοπίστων ὁ ζῆλος. ἱκανὴν τοίνυν ἔχομεν παραψυχήν, Τῆς Ὑμετέρας Φιλοθεΐας τοὺς ὑπὲρ τῶν θείων δογμάτων ἀγῶνας ἀκούοντες· καὶ γὰρ ταύτην ὑμῖν τὴν γνώμην ὁ Μεγαλόδωρος ἐδωρήσατο, καὶ τῆς τούτων ἕνεκα φυλακῆς πάντα πόνον εἰσφέρετε. ἐγὼ δέ, διὰ τῆς ὑμετέρας ψυχαγωγούμενος προθυμίας, μικρὰν ἀντίδοσιν εἰσφέρω, τῶν ἀγώνων ὑμᾶς τῶν θείων ἔχεσθαι παρακαλῶν καὶ τῶν ἀντιπάλων, ὡς εὐαλώτων, καταφρονεῖν· τί γὰρ ἀσθενέστερον τῶν τῆς ἀληθείας ἐστερημένων· πεποιθέναι δὲ τῷ εἰπόντι, *Οὐ μή σε ἀνῶ οὐδὲ … μή σε ἐγκαταλίπω*·[a] καί, *Ἰδοὺ ἐγὼ μεθ' ὑμῶν εἰμι πάσας τὰς ἡμέρας ἕως τῆς συντελείας τοῦ αἰῶνος.*[b] ἐπαμύνατε δὲ κἀμοὶ ταῖς προσευχαῖς ἵνα θαρρῶν ἐπιλέγω, *Κύριος ἐμοὶ βοηθός*, καὶ *οὐ φοβηθήσομαι τί ποιήσει μοι ἄνθρωπος.*[c]

Title μάγνωι. ἀντωνίω πρεσβυτέροις (πρε πρε) καὶ ἀρχιμανδρίταις (-ριτ) *N* : μάγνῳ -νίῳ -ρῳ καὶ -ριτῃ *scr. Onor.* (-ριτ), *A*^{ac} (-ριτ) = *"To Magnus Antonius, Priest and Archimandrite"* : μ. - νίνῳ -ρῳ καὶ -ριτῃ (-ριτ) *corr. Onor., A*^{pc}, *edd. = "To Magnus Antoninus, Priest and Archimandrite." I take it that, in the title of N, the point following* μάγνωι *and the repated syllable* πρε *indicate a plurality of recipients; cf. c. n. ad tit. ep. 1 regarding* διαφοφο = διαφόρους. *Thus, Onorio's inscription, insofar as it presupposes a single recipient, may be due to a misunderstanding of N, rather than to deliberate change. Still, he did take the step of changing the form of the second name by adding the nu; one cannot help wondering why. In the second sentence of this letter, the use of the pronominal adj. of the sec. per. pl. (ἡ ὑμετέρα) to modify the abstract honorific Φιλοθεΐα is further evidence of a plurality of recipients; cf. ep. 75 (to the clergy of Beroea). Of course, decorum, both ecclesiastical and courtly, frequently dictates the use of pl. pron. and vb. forms in reference to individuals, and ἡ ὑμετέρα does appear alongside honorifics applied to a single person (v., e.g., epp. 45, 71, 92, 111, 119, 139 to Anatolius). Yet, it is notable that, in the two preceding letters, addressed each to a single abbot, forms clearly referring to the recipient alone are sg., while, in this letter, the pronn. are invariably pl. Cf. ep. 132, where some of the pl. vbb. may be due to the association of the archimandrite Longinus with his deacons Matthew and Isaac.*

a. Heb 13.5 b. Mt 28.20 c. Ps 118.6 (LXX var.) (*Cf.* Heb 13.6.)

130. To Magnus and Antonius, Priests and Archimandrites[1]

Men sailing at night are cheered by the signal fires in the harbors, and the champions of the apostolic faith by the zeal of others who share that faith. We have been much encouraged to learn of your contests, Reverend Fathers, on behalf of the teachings we have received from God. Indeed, your determination is a gift from the Giver of bounty, and there is no toil you will not undertake on their behalf. In thanks for the encouragement I receive from your zeal, I can offer only a small return, by urging you to remain steadfast in your defense of religion, to look down in contempt on opponents you can easily defeat—after all, what can be weaker than that which is destitute of truth?—and to trust in the one who said, "I shall never leave you, nor shall I ever desert you,"[a] and "Behold, I am with you all days, even until the end of the world."[b] Now hasten to my aid with your prayers, so I may confidently declare, "The Lord is on my side, and I shall not fear. What can man do to me?"[c]

1. It is a question whether this letter is addressed to one person named Magnus Antoni(n)us or to two: Magnus and Antoni(n)us. Jackson (p. 301, n. 1) had opted for the former alternative, though, without ruling out the second; Azéma, citing the *Vaticanus* (*Z*) and the *Berolinensis* (*A*), chose more definitely for the first. He believed he could identify the Magnus Antoninus he took to be the recipient of this letter with one of the archimandrites addressed by Leo in *ep.* 24, but Schwartz (*ad loc.*, ll. 8f.) prints "Emmanuhel" in place of the two names *magno heliae* found in some manuscripts. *V.* my c. n. *ad tit.* On the title "archimandrite," *v. ep.* 27 n. 1; for the date of this letter, *v. ep.* 120 n. 1.

131. ΤΙΜΟΘΕΩΙ ΕΠΙΣΚΟΠΩΙ

(1) Οὐ μάτην ἄρα τῶν ὅλων ὁ Κυβερνήτης συγχωρεῖ τοῖς πνεύμασιν τοῖς ἐναντίοις διεγεῖραι τῆς ἀσεβείας τὰ κύματα, ἀλλ᾽ ἵνα τῶν πλεόντων βασανίσῃ τὰς γνώμας, καὶ τῶν μὲν τὴν ἀνδρείαν γυμνώσῃ, τῶν δὲ τὴν δειλίαν ἐλέγξῃ, καὶ τοὺς μὲν τὴν τῆς εὐσεβείας ἔξωθεν περικειμένους μορφὴν γυμνοὺς δείξῃ τῶν προσωπείων,[a] τοὺς δὲ τῆς ἀληθείας ἀνακηρύξῃ προμάχους. τοῦτο καὶ νῦν γεγενημένον ἐθεασάμεθα· τοῦ γὰρ χειμῶνος ἐπαναστάντος, οἱ μὲν ἐγύμνωσαν τὴν κεκρυμμένην ἀσέβειαν, οἱ δὲ προὔδοσαν ἣν εἶχον ἀλήθειαν καὶ τῆς τῶν ἀντιπάλων ἐγένοντο φάλαγγος καὶ μετ᾽ ἐκείνων βάλλουσιν οὓς *ἀριστέας* ὠνόμαζον. Οἱ δέ, ταῦτα ὁρῶντες, τοὺς μὲν πολεμίους μισοῦσι, τοὺς δὲ αὐτομόλους θρηνοῦσιν, τοῖς δ᾽ ὑπὲρ τῶν ἀποστολικῶν πολεμουμένοις δογμάτων ἐπαρκεῖν ὀρρωδοῦσιν, εἰ δὲ καὶ βιαιότερον αὐτοῖς οἱ προδεδωκότες ἐπίθοιντο, τάχα δὴ καὶ αὐτοὶ τῶν τοξευόντων γενήσονται καὶ τῶν ὁμοπίστων οὐ φείσονται, ἀλλὰ κατὰ τούτων τοὺς καλάμους μετὰ τῶν ὑπὸ σφῶν κατηγορουμένων ὠθήσουσιν, καὶ ταῦτα παρὰ τῆς θείας δεδιδαγμένοι Γραφῆς ὡς τὸ μὲν ἀδικῆσαι τὸν πέλας τιμωρίας ὑπεύθυνον, τὸ δέ γε ἀδικηθῆναι τῶν μεγάλων καὶ διαρκῶν ἀντιδόσεων πρόξενον.[b]

Τῆς δὲ Σῆς Θεοσεβείας καὶ τὸν ὑπὲρ τῆς πίστεως ζῆλον καὶ τὴν περὶ ἡμᾶς εὔνοιαν οὗτος ὁ κλύδων ἐπέδειξεν· καὶ γὰρ δὶς ἡμῖν ἐπέστειλας, τῶν δεδιττομένων καταφρονήσας, καὶ τὴν ἀδελφικὴν φιλοστοργίαν διὰ τῶν γραμμάτων ἐδήλωσας, καὶ οὓς ἔχεις ἀγῶνας ὑπὲρ τῶν ἀποστολικῶν δογμάτων ἐμήνυσας· γράψαι γὰρ ἡμᾶς ἐπέστειλας ἅπερ χρὴ περὶ τοῦ σωτηρίου

a. *Cf.* Mt 7.15. b. *Cf.* Mt 5.11f.; 1Pt 4.12–14.

131. To Bishop Timothy[1]

(1) As we can now see, the Helmsman of the universe has his reasons for allowing contrary winds to stir up the storms of godlessness.[2] Indeed, his purpose is to test the spirits of the sailors: to reveal the courage of some and put to shame the cowardice of others, to strip the masks off those who put on an outward display of religion[a] and to proclaim the champions of the true faith. This is just what we have witnessed today: As this storm has risen up, some have laid bare the heresy they had concealed within, while others, relinquishing the truth they once possessed and going over to the enemy, now join them in shooting arrows at men they used to call "heroes."[3] Then there are those who see all this and hate the enemy and deplore the deserters, but are too frightened to offer support to those under siege for their defense of the apostolic teachings. And— who knows?—if the traitors put enough pressure on them, the onlookers may well go over to the archers and, with no thought of mercy for their co-religionists, attack them alongside the very people they condemn—all this despite the teaching of holy Scripture that he who wrongs his neighbor will be called to account while the suffering of injustice is a means to gain great, eternal rewards![b]

But the same tempest has revealed Your Reverence's zeal for the faith and your good will toward us. Dismissing those who tried to deter you, you have written us two letters expressing your brotherly love and describing the contests you have endured for the apostolic teachings. You have asked me to set out in writing how we should

1. Timothy was bishop of Doliche, a see of Euphratensis about a hundred kilometers to the north of Cyrus; it is now the Turkish town of Dülük. Timothy had attended the Council of Antioch in 445 at which Athanasius of Perrhe was deposed (*Conc. chalc. Act. 14*, secc. 15, 56; *v. ep.* 42 n. 3) and would attend also the Council of Chalcedon (*Conc. chalc. Act. 17*, sec. 9, list of signatures, no. 161). For the date, *v. ep.* 120 n. 1.

2. Theodoret's nautical metaphor may be understood on two levels: πνεύμασι τοῖς ἐναντίοις = "contrary winds" or "perverse spirits," "spirits opposed to the truth."

3. *Cf. ep.* 125 n. 6.

πάθους καὶ φρονεῖν καὶ κηρύττειν. ἐγὼ δὲ τὴν αἴτησιν ἀσπαστῶς ἐδεξάμην καὶ ἃ παρὰ τῆς θείας ἐδιδάχθην Γραφῆς καὶ παρὰ τῶν ταύτην ἡρμηνευκότων πατέρων προθύμως ἐρῶ, οὐχ ἵνα διδάξω, ἀλλ᾽ ἵνα τὴν τῷ Θεῷ φίλην ὑπομνήσω κεφαλήν.[c]

(2)Ἴσθι τοίνυν, θεοφιλέστατε, ὡς χρὴ πρὸ τῶν ἄλλων ἁπάντων εἰδέναι τὴν τῶν ὀνομάτων διαφορὰν καί, πρὸς τούτῳ, τῆς θείας ἐνανθρωπήσεως τὴν αἰτίαν· τούτων γὰρ εὐκρινῶν γενομένων, οὐδεμία περὶ τοῦ πάθους ἀμφιβολία καταλειφθήσεται. οὐκοῦν τοὺς ἀντιλέγειν πειρωμένους ἐρωτήσομεν πρότερον τίνα μὲν τῆς ἐνανθρωπήσεως πρεσβύτερα τῶν ὀνομάτων τοῦ μονογενοῦς Υἱοῦ τοῦ Θεοῦ, τίνα δὲ αὖ νεώτερα, μᾶλλον δὲ τῷ τῆς οἰκονομίας ἔργῳ συνεζευγμένα. ἐροῦσι δε πάντως ὡς τὸ *Θεὸς Λόγος*[d] καὶ *μονογενὴς Υἱός*,[e] καὶ *Παντοκράτωρ*[f] καὶ *Κύριος τῆς κτίσεως ἁπάσης* ἐστὶ πρεσβύτερα, τὸ δὲ *Ἰησοῦς, Χριστὸς* τῆς ἐνανθρωπήσεως ἴδια· ἐνανθρωπήσας γὰρ ὁ Θεὸς Λόγος, ὁ μονογενὴς Υἱὸς τοῦ Θεοῦ *Ἰησοῦς Χριστὸς* ὠνομάσθη· Ἰδού, γάρ φησιν, τίκτεται *ὑμῖν σήμερον … Χριστὸς Κύριος*.[g] ἐπειδὴ γὰρ *χριστοὶ* καὶ ἄλλοι προσηγορεύθησαν· καὶ ἱερεῖς,[h] καὶ βασιλεῖς,[i] καὶ προφῆται·[j] ἵνα μή τις αὐτὸν ὑπολάβοι ἐκείνοις προσόμοιον, συνέζευξαν οἱ ἄγγελοι τὸ *Κύριος* ὄνομα τῷ *Χριστῷ*, τὸ δεσποτικὸν ἀξίωμα τοῦ τικτομένου δεικνύντες. καὶ τῇ πανευφήμῳ δὲ Παρθένῳ πάλιν ὁ Γαβριήλ, *Ἰδοὺ σὺ ἐν γαστρὶ ἕξεις*,[k] *καὶ τέξῃ υἱόν*,[l] *καὶ καλέσεις τὸ ὄνομα αὐτοῦ Ἰησοῦν*,[m] ὅτι

l. 43 τίκτεται ὑμῖν *corr. Cir., scr. edd.* : τ. ἡμ- *NZ. Thdt. quotes this verse with the 2nd per. pron. in two other places (ep. 147.5 and Eran., dial. 2, p. 114, l. 4). In the first, this is the reading of ZA (N is here lacunose); in the second, Ettlinger reports no var.*

c. *Cf.* Rom 15.15.
d. *Cf.* Jn 1.1; Ti 2.13.
e. Jn 1.14
f. *V., e.g.*, 2Cor 6.18; Rv 1.8
g. Lk 2.11 (NT var.)
h. *V., e.g.*, Lv 4.5; 2Mac 1.10.
i. *V., e.g.*, 1Sm 24.10 (LXX 24.11); 2Sm 22.51 (= Ps 18.50); Is 45.1.
j. *V., e.g.*, 1Chr 16.22 (LXX = Ps 104.5).
k. Jgs 13.5 (A)
l. Lk 1.31
m. Lk 1.31; Mt 1.21
n. Mt 1.21 (NT var.)

understand and preach the passion of our Savior. Yours is a welcome request, and I shall be glad to tell you what I have learned from holy Scripture and from the fathers who have interpreted it—to be your prompter, not your teacher, friend of God.[c]

(2) So then, beloved of God, the most important point is to take cognizance of the different sorts of names and then the reason for the incarnation of God. Clear discernment on these points will leave no room for uncertainty regarding the passion. We should begin by asking our would-be opponents which names belong to the only-begotten Son of God prior to the incarnation, which after, that is to say, which are associated with the work of salvation. Without a doubt they will answer that "God the Word"[d] and "only-begotten Son,"[e] and "Almighty" and "Lord of all Creation,"[f] refer to the prior state while "Jesus" and "Christ" belong to the incarnation. It was in the incarnation that God the Word, the only-begotten Son of God, received the name Jesus Christ. As Scripture says, "Behold! today is born to you Christ the Lord."[g] As there were others who had been given the title "Christ, Messiah"—priests,[h] kings,[i] and prophets[j]—to make sure that no one would imagine that he was just like them, the angels joined to "Christ" the name "Lord" and thus set in evidence the sovereign dignity of the newborn. Likewise, Gabriel announced to the blessed Virgin, "Behold! You will conceive"[k] "and bring forth a son,"[l] and "you will name him 'Jesus,'"[m] because "he will save his people from their

αὐτὸς … σώσει τὸν λαὸν αὐτοῦ ἀπὸ τῶν ἁμαρτιῶν αὐτοῦ.[n] πρὸ δέ γε τῆς ἐνανθρωπήσεως, οὔτε *Χριστὸς* οὔτε *Ἰησοῦς* ὠνομάζετο· καὶ γὰρ οἱ θεῖοι προφῆται, τὰ ἐσόμενα προθεσπίζοντες, ἐχρήσαντο ταῖς φωναῖς ὥσπερ καὶ τὰ περὶ τῆς γεννήσεως καὶ τοῦ σταυροῦ καὶ τοῦ πάθους προηγόρευσαν, μηδέπω τῶν πραγμάτων γεγενημένων. καλεῖται δὲ ὅμως, καὶ μετὰ τὴν ἐνανθρώπησιν, καὶ *Θεὸς Λόγος*, καὶ *Κύριος*, καὶ *Παντοκράτωρ*, καὶ *μονογενὴς Υἱός*, καὶ *Ποιητής*, καὶ *Δημιουργός*. Οὐ γὰρ τραπεὶς γέγονεν ἄνθρωπος, ἀλλά, μένων ὅπερ ἦν, ἔλαβεν ὅπερ ἐσμέν· *Ἐν μορφῇ* γὰρ *Θεοῦ ὑπάρχων*, κατὰ τὸν θεῖον Ἀπόστολον, ἔλαβεν τὴν τοῦ *δούλου μορφήν*.[o] τούτου δὴ χάριν, καὶ μετὰ τὴν ἐνανθρώπησιν, καὶ ταῖς πρὸ τῆς ἐνανθρωπήσεως ὀνομάζεται κλήσεσιν, ἐπειδήπερ ἀναλλοίωτον ἔχει τὴν φύσιν καὶ ἄτρεπτον.

(3) Τὸ μέντοι πάθος ἡ θεία διηγουμένη Γραφή, οὐδαμοῦ τὸ *Θεὸς* τέθεικεν ὄνομα, ἐπειδὴ τῆς ἁπλῆς ἐστι φύσεως ὄνομα· οὐδεὶς γὰρ ἀκούσας, *Ἐν ἀρχῇ ἦν ὁ Λόγος, καὶ ὁ Λόγος ἦν πρὸς τὸν Θεόν, καὶ Θεὸς ἦν ὁ Λόγος*[p] καὶ ὅσα τούτοις προσόμοια, τὴν σάρκα φαίη ἂν πρὸ τῶν αἰώνων ὑπάρχειν, ἢ ὁμοουσίαν εἶναι τῷ τῶν ὅλων Θεῷ, ἢ δημιουργὸν γεγονέναι τῆς κτίσεως, ἀλλ᾽ οἶδεν ὅτι ταῦτα τῆς θεότητος ἴδια. οὔτε μὴν τοῦ Ματθαίου τις γενεαλογοῦντος ἀκούσας,[q] τὸν Δαυὶδ καὶ τὸν Ἀβραὰμ κατὰ φύσιν ἂν ὑπολάβοι τοῦ Θεοῦ προγόνους· ἡ γὰρ προσληφθεῖσα φύσις ἐξ ἐκείνων κατάγεται.

Ὥσπερ τοίνυν εὐκρινῆ ταῦτα καὶ ἀναμφίλεκτα καὶ τοῖς ἄγαν αἱρετικοῖς, καὶ ἴσμεν τὴν μὲν προαιώνιον, τὴν δὲ πρόσφατον φύσιν, οὕτως εἰδέναι χρὴ τό τε τῆς σαρκὸς παθητὸν καὶ τὸ τῆς θεότητος ἀπαθές, οὐ διαιροῦντας τὴν ἕνωσιν οὐδὲ εἰς δύο μερίζοντας πρόσωπα τὸν Μονογενῆ, ἀλλ᾽ ἐν τῷ ἑνὶ θεωροῦντας Υἱῷ τὰ τῶν φύσεων ἴδια. εἰ γὰρ ἐπὶ ψυχῆς καὶ σώματος, τῶν

n. Mt 1.21 (NT var.) o. Phil 2.6f. (NT var.) p. Jn 1.1 q. Mt 1.1–17

sins."[n] Now, before the incarnation, he was not called either "Christ" or "Jesus"—though, of course, the holy prophets, pronouncing oracles regarding the future, as when they foretold his birth, cross, and passion, made use of these appellations before the events had taken place—and yet, he is called "God the Word," "Lord," "Almighty," "only-begotten Son," "Maker," and "Creator" even after the incarnation. It was not that he underwent a change and became man, but remaining what he already was, he took on what we are. As the holy Apostle has it, "Though being in the form of God, he took on the form of a slave."[o] Precisely because of this, even after becoming man, he is called by the titles belonging to him before the incarnation, since his nature is unchangeable and immutable.

(3) In the account of the passion, holy Scripture never makes use of the name "God," a term used to designate the uncompounded nature. Of course, no one who hears, "In the beginning was the Word, and the Word was with God, and the Word was God,"[p] and statements similar to these could conclude that the flesh existed before the ages, that it was of the same substance as the God of the universe, or that it was the maker of the created world. Everyone knows that these are attributes belonging solely to the divinity. Nor would anyone who had heard Matthew's genealogy[q] imagine that David and Abraham were progenitors of God according to their nature; they are the sources of the nature that was assumed.

Now, as we distinguish the nature that exists before the ages from that which is of recent origin, a distinction accepted without demur even among heretics of extreme views, we must distinguish also between the passibility of the flesh and the impassibility of the godhead, not separating the union or dividing the Only-begotten into two persons, but beholding in the one Son the properties belonging to the two natures. If this distinction is a matter of course in the case of the soul and the body, natures belonging to the same time

ὁμοχρόνων φύσεων καὶ φυσικῶς ἡνωμένων, τοῦτο ποιεῖν εἰώθαμεν καὶ τὴν μὲν ψυχὴν καλοῦμεν *ἁπλῆν*, καὶ *λογικήν*, καὶ *ἀθάνατον*, καὶ *ἀόρατον*, τὸ δὲ σῶμα *σύνθετον* ὀνομάζομεν, καὶ *παθητόν*, καὶ *θνητόν*, καὶ τὴν ἕνωσιν οὐ διαιροῦμεν οὐδὲ διχῇ τὸν ἕνα τέμνομεν ἄνθρωπον, πολλῷ μᾶλλον ἐπὶ τῆς πρὸ αἰώνων ἐκ τοῦ Πατρὸς γεννηθείσης θεότητος καὶ τῆς ληφθείσης ἐκ σπέρματος τοῦ Δαυὶδ ἀνθρωπότητος τοῦτο προσήκει ποιεῖν καὶ σαφῶς εἰδέναι τῆς μὲν τὸ αἰώνιον καὶ ἀΐδιον, ἁπλοῦν τε καὶ ἀπερίγραφον, ἀθάνατον καὶ ἀναλλοίωτον, τῆς δὲ τὸ πρόσφατόν τε καὶ σύνθετον, καὶ περιγεγραμμένον, καὶ ῥευστὸν καὶ θνητόν. εἰ γὰρ καὶ τὴν σάρκα νῦν ἀθάνατον ἴσμεν καὶ ἄφθαρτον, ἀλλ᾽ οὖν πρὸ τῆς ἀναστάσεως καὶ θανάτου καὶ πάθους ἦν δεκτική· πῶς γὰρ ἄλλως προσηλώθη τῷ ξύλῳ καὶ παρεδόθη τῷ τάφῳ; εἰδότας δὲ ὅμως τῶν φύσεων τὸ διάφορον, τὸν ἕνα χρὴ προσκυνεῖν Υἱὸν καὶ τὸν αὐτὸν εἰδέναι Υἱὸν Θεοῦ καὶ Υἱὸν ἀνθρώπου, μορφὴν Θεοῦ καὶ μορφὴν δούλου, υἱὸν Δαυὶδ καὶ Κύριον τοῦ Δαυὶδ, σπέρμα Ἀβραὰμ καὶ ποιητὴν Ἀβραάμ.

(4) Ἡ γὰρ ἕνωσις κοινὰ ποιεῖ τὰ ὀνόματα, ἀλλ᾽ οὐ συγχεῖ ταύτας τό τῶν ὀνομάτων κοινόν· δῆλον γὰρ τοῖς εὖ φρονοῦσιν ὅτι τὰ μὲν ὡς Θεῷ, τὰ δὲ ὡς ἀνθρώπῳ προσήκει. οὕτω καὶ τὸ παθητὸν καὶ τὸ ἀπαθὲς ἁρμόττει τῷ Δεσπότῃ Χριστῷ· πέπονθε μὲν γὰρ κατὰ τὸ ἀνθρώπειον, ἀπαθὴς δὲ μεμένηκεν ὡς Θεός. εἰ δέ, κατὰ τὸν τῶν δυσσεβῶν λόγον, κατὰ τὴν θεότητα πέπονθεν, περιττὴ δήπουθεν τῆς σαρκὸς ἡ ἀνάληψις· οὐ γὰρ ἔχρηζεν τῆς παθητῆς ἀνθρωπότητος, τῆς θείας φύσεως δέξασθαι δυναμένης τὸ πάθος. εἰ δέ, καὶ κατὰ τὸν αὐτῶν λόγον, ἀπαθὴς ἡ θεότης, καὶ ἀληθὲς τὸ πάθος, μὴ ἀρνείσθωσαν τὸ πεπονθὸς ἵνα μὴ ἀρνηθῶσι

and joined in a natural union,[4] and we refer to the soul as "uncompounded," "rational," "immortal," and "invisible," and to the body as "compounded," "passible," and "mortal," but without separating the union or dividing the one man into two, it is all the more appropriate to proceed in the same manner in the case of the godhead begotten of the Father before time and the humanity assumed from the seed of David and to take clear cognizance of the fact that the one is timeless, eternal, uncompounded and uncircumscribed, deathless and unchangeable, while the other is time-bound and compounded, circumscribed, ever-changing, and mortal. Even if we recognize that his flesh is now immortal and incorruptible, nonetheless, before the resurrection, it was susceptible of both death and suffering. How else could it have been nailed to the wood of the cross and laid to rest in a tomb? Although we make this distinction between the natures, we are bound to worship one Son and recognize the same as Son of God and Son of man, form of God and form of the slave, son of David and Lord of David, seed of Abraham and maker of Abraham.

(4) The union causes the names to be common, but the community of names does not confound the natures.[5] As is apparent to all right-thinkers, some terms are applied to him as God, others as man. Thus, both terms "passible" and "impassible" are fittingly used of the Master Christ; according to his humanity, he suffered, but, as God, he remained impassible. If, as heretics have it, he suffered according to his divinity, we can only conclude that the assumption of the flesh was pointless; after all, he had no need for the passible humanity if the divine nature was susceptible of suffering. If, as even they admit, the godhead is impassible, and the passion a real passion, they must

4. The union of the body and the soul (τῶν ὁμοχρόνων φύσεων) may truly be termed "a natural union" (φυσικῶς ἡνωμένων) because body and soul belong to the same category of created realities. Their union takes place within the bounds of human nature; *cf. Eran. dial.* 3, p. 200, ll. 3–7. Theodoret could not, however, countenance Cyril's use of this language (*e.g.*, in his third anathema against Nestorius; *v.* Intro. sec. 2.7) to speak of the union of the divine and the human (*i.e.* two different realities: a creating and a created nature) in the person of Christ.

5. I have taken over Jackson's excellent translation of this key sentence.

καὶ τὴν τοῦ πάθους ἀλήθειαν· ψευδὲς γὰρ τὸ πάθος, οὐκ ὄντος τοῦ πάσχοντος.

Ὅτι δὲ καὶ ἡ θεία Γραφὴ προφανῶς τοῦ σώματος κηρύττει τὸ πάθος, ῥᾴδιον τῷ βουλομένῳ τῶν ἱερῶν εὐαγγελίων ἀναπτύξαι τὴν τετρακτὺν καὶ μαθεῖν ἐκεῖθεν ὅπως Ἰωσὴφ ὁ ἀπὸ Ἀριμαθίας προσῆλθεν τῷ Πιλάτῳ καὶ ᾔτησεν τὸ σῶμα τοῦ Ἰησοῦ, καὶ ὡς ὁ Πιλάτος προσέταξεν δοθῆναι τὸ σῶμα τοῦ Ἰησοῦ, καὶ ὡς ὁ Ἰωσὴφ καθεῖλεν ἀπὸ τοῦ ξύλου τὸ σῶμα τοῦ Ἰησοῦ, καὶ ὡς ἐνείλησεν τῇ σινδόνι τὸ σῶμα τοῦ Ἰησοῦ, καὶ ὡς τοῦτο κατέθηκεν ἐν τῷ καινῷ μνημείῳ.[r] ταῦτα οἱ τέσσαρες εὐαγγελισταὶ συνέγραψαν, πολλάκις τοῦ σώματος μνημονεύσαντες.

Εἰ δὲ τὰ παρὰ τοῦ ἀγγέλου πρὸς τὰς περὶ Μαρίαν εἰρημένα προφέρουσιν· *Δεῦτε* βλέπετε … *ὅπου ἔκειτο* ὁ Κύριος,[s] ἀκουσάτωσαν τῆς τῶν Πράξεων ἱστορίας λεγούσης, ὅτι *Συνεκόμισαν … τὸν Στέφανον ἄνδρες εὐλαβεῖς,*[t] καὶ σκοπείτωσαν ὡς οὐ τὴν ψυχὴν τοῦ νικηφόρου Στεφάνου, ἀλλὰ τὸ σῶμα τῶν νομιζομένων ἠξίωσαν. καὶ μέχρι δὲ τοῦ παρόντος, εἰς τοὺς τῶν καλλινίκων μαρτύρων εἰσιόντες σηκούς, ἐρωτᾶν εἰώθαμεν, *Τίς ὁ ἐν τῇ θήκῃ καλεῖται;* οἱ δὲ τἀληθὲς εἰδότες ἀποκρίνονται, ἢ *Ἰουλιανόν,* τυχόν, *τὸν μάρτυρα,* ἢ *Ῥωμανόν,* ἢ *Τιμόθεον·* καίτοι πολλάκις οὐδὲ τελείων τῶν σωμάτων κειμένων, ἀλλὰ σμικροτάτων λειψάνων, ἀλλ᾽ ὅμως τῷ κοινῷ ὀνόματι καὶ τὸ

ll. 123f. εἰς τοὺς τῶν … μαρτύρων εἰσιόντες σηκούς *scripsi* : ἐν τοῖς τῶν … μ. εἰ. -οῖς *codd., edd. Though N and the mss. descended from N agree in combining εἰσιόντες with the prep.* ἐν + *dat., elsewhere Thdt. construes the finite and non-finite forms of this verb of motion with the prep.* εἰς + *acc. V., e.g., Q. in Leu. 18: ἀκάθαρτοι οὖν οἱ εἰς τὰς τούτων συναγωγὰς εἰσιόντες, ὡς εἰς λεπρῶσαν οἰκίαν εἰσιόντες.*

r. Mt 27.57–60; Mk 15.42–46; Lk 23.50–53; Jn 19.38–42
s. Mt 28.6 (NT var.) t. Acts 8.2

not go on denying that which suffered; otherwise they end up denying the reality of the passion, as there is no real passion if there is no one to suffer.

As to the fact that holy Scripture explicitly proclaims the passion of the body—all anyone has to do is open up the fourfold gospel-book[6] to learn how Joseph of Arimathea approached Pilate to ask for the body of Jesus, how Pilate commanded that Jesus' body be handed over, how Joseph took Jesus' body down from the cross, "wrapped" the body of Jesus "in a sheet," and laid it in the freshly hewn tomb.[r] This is all described—and with frequent mention of the body—by the four evangelists.

But if any should cite the speech of the angel to Mary Magdalen and her friends, "Come and see the place where the Lord lay,"[s] they should also pay attention to that passage in Acts relating how "pious men carried Stephen out for burial,"[t] and take note that it wasn't the soul, but the body of the victorious Stephen to which they accorded the customary rites. Even nowadays, when we enter the shrines of the glorious martyrs, we normally ask the name of the person in the tomb, and those who are well-informed might reply "the martyr Julian" or "Romanus," or "Timothy"[7] —though it is often the case that not even their whole bodies are buried there, but just tiny fragments, still, we apply to the body the name that belongs to the body

6. As Jackson had pointed out, Theodoret's use of the term τετρακτύς for "fourfold" is surprising. This term had been used by Pythagoreans and theorists of music to refer to mathematical relationships fundamental to observed realities. He suggests that Theodoret's usage amounts to an endorsement "of the theory of the mystic and necessary number of the gospels" formulated by Iren., *Haer.* 3.11.8.

7. Julian, Romanus, and Timothy were especially honored in Antioch. For Julian, born in Anazarbus in Cilicia and martyred as a youth at Aegeae, our earliest source is Chrysostom's eulogy (*BHG* #967 = PG, vol. 50, coll. 665–76). His relics were venerated in a church outside the city of Antioch; *v.* Delehaye (*Origines*), pp. 166, 200. For the earliest account of Romanus, deacon and exorcist of Caesarea, martyred at Antioch during the persecution of Diocletian, *v.* Eus., *Mart. palaest.* 2; for a fifth-century passion in Latin verse, *v.* Prud., *Pe.* 10. Of the life and death of Timothy of Antioch nothing certain is known. Delehaye ("Quelques dates," pp. 38–41) identified April 8 as the probable date of his feast, and thus, of his death.

σῶμα προσαγορεύομεν· οὕτως ὁ ἄγγελος τοῦ Κυρίου τὸ σῶμα *Κύριον* προσηγόρευσεν, ἐπειδὴ σῶμα ἦν τοῦ τῶν ὅλων Κυρίου. καὶ αὐτὸς δὲ ὁ Κύριος οὐ τὴν ἀόρατον φύσιν, ἀλλὰ τὸ σῶμα δώσειν ὑπέσχετο *ὑπὲρ τῆς τοῦ κόσμου ζωῆς*· Ὁ γὰρ ἄρτος, φησίν, *ὃν ἐγὼ δώσω ἡ σάρξ μου ἐστίν*, ἣν ἐγὼ δώσω *ὑπὲρ τῆς τοῦ κόσμου ζωῆς*·[u] κἀν τῇ τῶν θείων μυστηρίων παραδόσει, λαβὼν τὸ σύμβολον, ἔφη, *Τοῦτό ἐστιν τὸ σῶμά μου, τὸ ὑπὲρ ὑμῶν διδόμενον*,[v] ἢ *κλώμενον*,[w] κατὰ τὸν Ἀπόστολον, καί, οὐδαμοῦ, περὶ πάθους διαλεχθείς, τῆς ἀπαθοῦς ἐμνήσθη θεότητος. χρὴ δὲ πρὸ τῶν ἄλλων ἁπάντων τοὺς ἀντιλέγειν ἐπιχειροῦντας

l. 133 ἣν $A^{s.l.}$, *Az.* : ὃν *NZ*, $A^{i.l.}$ *The supralinear note in A* (*Car.?*) *offers the necessary correction to the reading of the mss. Thdt. cites this verse in seven other places, all of which have the fem. pronoun referring to* σάρξ. *V., e.g., ep. 146.6, where N carries* ἣν; *also Eran. dial. 1, p. 79, ll. 15f.; dial. 3, p. 221, ll. 2f.; Demonstr. γ, p. 261, ll. 17f., in all of which, according to Ettlinger, the fem. is the sole reading. Cf. also flor. 3, p. 249, l. 32 - p. 250, l. 1.*

u. Jn 6.51 (NT var.) v. Lk 22.19 w. 1Cor 11.24 (NT var.)

as a whole—in the same way, the angel of the Lord, applied to the body the name "Lord," because the body was that of the Lord of the universe.[8] Moreover, the Lord himself promised that he would offer not his invisible nature, but his body, for the life of the world. As he declared, "The bread that I shall give is my body, which I shall offer for the life of the world."[u] And, in the transmission of the sacred mysteries, he picked up the token[9] and said, "This is my body, which is handed over for you"[v] or, according to the Apostle, "broken for you."[10w] Nowhere, in anything he said about the passion did he make

8. Theodoret's argument depends on the analogy he has drawn between the union of the divine and the human natures in Christ and the union of the soul and the body in a human being; insofar as each element is a part of the whole, reference to one may be a loose way of referring to the other. Thus, in Mt 28.6, "Lord" (Κύριος) must be understood as a reference to the body of Christ in the same way that in Acts 8.2 "Stephen" clearly designates the body, not the soul, of the protomartyr. Mt 28.6, thus, cannot be cited to support the idea that the divinity of Christ suffered in the passion; *cf. ep.* 126 n. 2. The remarks regarding the partition of relics add a complicating and secondary consideration: we refer even to a particle of a body as though it were the entire body. Thus, in the clause ἀλλ' ὅμως τῷ κοινῷ ὀνόματι καὶ τὸ σῶμα προσαγορεύομεν the adjective κοινῷ means "the name that belongs to the body as a whole"; *cf.* Azéma, "nous les désignons par le nom général de corps." On the practice of partitioning and distributing to different churches the physical remains of the martyrs, at this time more frequent in the East than in the West, *v.* Delehaye (*Origines*), pp. 59–68.

9. Theodoret's use of the term σύμβολον ("token") to refer to the bread of the Eucharist is in accord with what modern scholarship has termed the *disciplina arcani,* the studied avoidance of explicit description of that part of the sacramental liturgy that was celebrated only by the fully initiated, *i.e.* the baptized, and deliberately concealed from catechumens and those outside the Church; *v., e.g.,* Yarnold (pp. 50–54), who dates the full development of this practice to the fourth and early fifth centuries. On the use of σύμβολον to refer to the elements of the eucharist, *cf. ep.* 74 n. 2 and *ep.* 147.3 ("the mystery of the divine service").

10. Theodoret compares Jesus' words over the bread as reported by Luke (22.19) and Paul (1Cor 11.24). In fact, in the ancient tradition of the latter passage, there are witnesses for διδόμενον (handed over) as well as for κλώμενον (broken): διδόμενον is attested by the Latin vulgate, the Coptic, and the Ethiopic versions, while κλώμενον is the reading of the majority Greek text and the Syriac translations and was inserted into the *Sinaiticus* by a corrector of the seventh century. The *NTG* prints the shorter text (τὸ σῶμά τὸ ὑπὲρ ὑμῶν) attested by a papyrus of the early third century (#46), the *Vaticanus* (fourth century), the *Alexandrinus* (fifth century), and the first hand of the *Sinaiticus* (fourth century). Metzger (*A Textual* Commentary) argues (*ad loc.*) that both participles should be understood as ex-

ἐρωτᾶσθαι εἰ συνομολογοῦσιν τελείαν ὑπὸ τοῦ Θεοῦ Λόγου προσειλῆφθαι τὴν ἀνθρωπείαν φύσιν καὶ εἰ τὴν ἕνωσιν ἀσύγχυτον γεγενῆσθαί φασιν· εἰ γὰρ ταῦτα συνομολογηθείη, καὶ τἄλλα κατὰ τάξιν προβήσεται, καὶ τὸ πάθος τῇ παθητῇ προσαρμοσθήσεται φύσει.

(5) Ταῦτα ἐν κεφαλαίῳ νῦν ὑπηγόρευσα καὶ τῆς ἐπιστολῆς ὑπερέβην τὸ μέτρον, ἀπέστειλα δὲ καὶ ἣν πρώην ἔγραψα, προτραπεὶς ὑπὸ τοῦ θεοφιλεστάτου καὶ ἁγιωτάτου ἀνθρώπου τοῦ Θεοῦ τοῦ Κυρίου < ..... >, σύντομον διδασκαλίαν, ἱκανὴν οὖσαν καὶ αὐτὴν διδάξαι τὴν τῶν ἀποστολικῶν δογμάτων ἀλήθειαν. εἰ δὲ εὕροιμι καλλιγράφον, πέμψω Σοῦ Τῇ Ὁσιότητι καὶ ἃ διαλογικῶς συνέγραψα, τουτέστιν κατʼ ἐρώτησιν καὶ ἀπόκρισιν, καὶ τὸν λόγον εὐρύνας καὶ ὀχυρώσας τὰ ἡμέτερα ταῖς τῶν πατέρων διδασκαλίαις, ἀπέστειλα δέ νῦν καὶ ὀλίγας τῶν ἀρχαίων διδασκάλων χρήσεις, ἱκανὰς οὔσας δεῖξαι τὸν τῆς ἐκείνων διδασκαλίας σκοπόν. ἀντιδοῦναι τοίνυν ἡμῖν, θεοφιλέστατε, καταξίωσον τὴν ἐπικουρίαν τῶν προσευχῶν ἵνα τὸν χαλεπὸν διαπεράσωμεν κλύδωνα καὶ τῶν εὐστόμων τοῦ Σωτῆρος ἐπιτύχωμεν λιμένων.

l. 147 τοῦ Κυρίου < ..... > *uacat spatium quinque uel sex litterarum N*

mention of his impassible divinity. So then, the most important question to put to our opponents is whether they agree that it was human nature in its totality that was assumed by God the Word, and if they are willing to say that the union occurred without confusion. If they concede these points, all the rest will fall into order, and the passion will be attributed to the nature that is capable of suffering.

(5) I dictated these points in summary form, but even so have gone beyond the limit of a letter, yet I have enclosed with this a brief exposition I recently composed in answer to the request of my Lord < ..... > that holy man beloved of God,[11] which can also be used in teaching the true apostolic doctrine. Should I be able to find a copyist, I'll send Your Holiness as well a work I composed as a dialogue, *i.e.*, proceeding by question and answer, which provides a fuller treatment of the argument, and in which my own teaching is reinforced with that of the fathers.[12] For now, I've sent you some well-known passages of early teachers: just a few, but adequate to make the point those fathers intended to convey. So then, beloved of God, be so kind as to offer us the recompense of your prayers so that we may make our way through these rough seas and reach the welcoming harbors of our Savior.

---

planatory additions, κλώμενον referring back to ἔκλασεν earlier in the verse. In *ep.* 146.6 (*v.* n. 5), Theodoret quotes 1Cor 11.24 according to yet another reading, close in meaning to κλώμενον.

11. The name of the dedicatee is missing in the manuscripts; after τοῦ Κυρίου ("my Lord"), the *Neapolitanus* contains a blank space large enough to accommodate five or six letters. Azéma (vol. 3, p. 37, n. 2, and p. 122, n. 1) identifies the work in question as the *Proof by Syllogisms* (Ἀπόδειξις διὰ συλλογισμῶν = *Demonstr.*), which provides a brief syllogistic recapitulation of the themes set out in the three dialogues of the *Eran.* Ettlinger, however, argues that, as Theodoret mentions the syllogistic appendix at the end of the prologue to the *Eran.*, and most of the earlier manuscripts present it as the conclusion of the *Eran.*, "it must be regarded as "an organic part" of that work. Whether the *Demonstr.* or some other lost tract, this brief, recently composed work (πρωὴν) seems to have been meant to perform a function much like the *Quod unicus filius* (*ep.* 16 n. 3).

12. Theodoret refers to the *Eran.*; *v.* Intro., secc. 4.1 and 2.7. If Azéma's identification of the work discussed in the previous note is correct, this passage would indicate that Theodoret produced a second, supplemented, edition of the *Eran.*

132. ΛΟΓΓΙΝΩΙ ΑΡΧΙΜΑΝΔΡΙΤΗΙ ΔΟΛΙΧΗΣ

Καὶ τὸν ὑπὲρ τῆς εὐσεβείας ζῆλον καὶ τὴν περὶ τὸν πέλας ἀγάπην ἔδειξεν Ὑμῶν Ἡ Θεοσέβεια· ἀμφότερα γὰρ ἐπὶ τοῦ παρόντος συνέζευκται· ὑπὲρ γὰρ τῶν ἀποστολικῶν πολεμούμεθα δογμάτων, ἐπειδὴ τὸν πατρῷον οὐ προϊέμεθα κλῆρον, ἀλλὰ πᾶν ὁτιοῦν παθεῖν αἱρούμεθα μᾶλλον ἢ μίαν κεραίαν[a] ἐκ τῆς εὐαγγελικῆς πίστεως παριδεῖν συλουμένην. κεκοινωνήκατε τοίνυν ἡμῖν τῶν παθημάτων, καὶ διὰ γραμμάτων ψυχαγωγήσαντες καὶ πέμψαντες πρὸς ἡμᾶς τοὺς τιμιωτάτους καὶ εὐλαβεστάτους Ματθαῖον καὶ Ἰσαάκην τοὺς διακόνους, καί, εὖ οἶδα, ἀκούσεσθε παρὰ τοῦ δικαίου Κριτοῦ, *Ἐν φυλακῇ ἤμην, καὶ* ἤλθετε *πρός με.*[b] εἰ γὰρ καὶ ἡμεῖς εὐτελεῖς, καὶ σμικροί, καὶ πολὺν ἁμαρτημάτων φόρτον περικείμενοι, ἀλλ᾽ ὁ Δεσπότης φιλότιμός τε καὶ μεγαλόδωρος· διά τοι τοῦτο οὐ τῶν μεγάλων, ἀλλὰ τῶν σμικρῶν μέμνηται καί φησιν, *Ἐφ᾽ ὅσον ἐποιήσατε ἑνὶ*[c] *τῶν μικρῶν*[d] *τῶν ἐλαχίστων*[e] *τῶν πιστευόντων εἰς ἐμέ,*[f] *ἐμοὶ ἐποιήσατε.*[g] ἐπειδὴ τοίνυν καὶ ἐν τοῖς ὀρθοῖς διαπρέπετε δόγμασιν καὶ τῷ ἀξιεπαίνῳ λάμπετε βίῳ καὶ πολλὴν ἐντεῦθεν πρὸς τὸν Θεὸν ἔχετε παρρησίαν,[h] ἐπαμύνατέ μοι ταῖς προσευχαῖς ἵνα ἀντισχεῖν δυνηθῶ, κατὰ τὴν ἀποστολικὴν φωνήν, *πρὸς τὰς μεθοδείας*[i] *τῆς πλάνης,*[j] καὶ διαφύγω τὰς τοῦ ἀλάστορος πάγας,[k] καὶ μετὰ σμικρᾶς παρρησίας ἐν τῇ τῆς ἐπιφανείας ἡμέρᾳ παραστῶ τῷ δικαίῳ Κριτῇ.[l]

a. Mt 5.18
b. Mt 25.36 (NT var.)
c. Mt 25.40
d. Mt 18.6
e. Mt 25.40
f. Mt 18.6
g. Mt 25.40
h. *Cf.* 1Jn 3.21f.
i. Eph 6.11
j. Eph 4.14
k. *Cf.* 1Tm 3.7; 2Tm 2.26.
l. *Cf.* 1Jn 4.17.

132. To Longinus, Arhimandrite of Doliche[1]

Your Reverence has given proof of both your zeal for orthodoxy and your love of neighbor—at the moment, the two are inseparably joined—for we are under attack because we refuse to give up the inheritance we have received from our forebears and choose to undergo any and all suffering rather than allow the gospel faith to be plundered of a single iota.[a] You have made yourself a partner in our suffering by encouraging us with your letter and sending us the right honorable and reverend deacons Matthew and Isaac, and I know that one day you will hear our righteous Judge declare, "I was in prison, and you came to visit me."[b] We are, it is true, of no account, just little ones, and burdened with a great load of sins, but our Master is generous and a giver of great gifts. Precisely for this reason, he singles out not the great, but the little ones, when he says, "Whenever you have done something for one"[c] "of the little ones,"[d] "the least"[e] "of those who believe in me,"[f] "this you have done for me."[g] So then, as the well-known orthodoxy of your teaching and the shining virtue of your exemplary life allow you to speak to God with great good confidence,[h] come to my aid with your prayers, that I may find the strength to stand up against what the Apostle calls "the wiles[i] of deceit,"[j] avoid the snares of the destroyer,[k] and, with my own little bit of confidence, go to stand before the righteous Judge on the day of his appearance.[l]

1. The archimandrite Longinus is known to us only from this letter. On Doliche, *v. ep.* 131 n. 1; for the date of *ep.* 132, *v. ep.* 120 n. 1; for the title "archimandrite," *v. ep.* 27 n. 1.

133. ΙΒΑΙ ΕΠΙΣΚΟΠΩΙ ΕΔΕΣΗΣ

Τοὺς ἀδικουμένους οὐκ ἀθυμεῖν, ἀλλὰ χαίρειν ὁ Δεσπότης προσέταξεν καὶ ἐκ τῶν παλαιῶν ἕλκειν παραδειγμάτων τῆς ψυχαγωγίας τὰς ἀφορμάς·[a] ἐκ γὰρ τῶν πρῶτον φύντων ἀνθρώπων μέχρι τοῦ παρόντος καιροῦ, τοὺς τὸν ὅλων ἐσπουδακότας σέβειν Θεὸν ἔστιν εὑρεῖν παρὰ τῶν συμβεβιωκότων ἀνθρώπων ἠδικημένους καὶ πλείστοις ἄγαν περιπεπτωκότας ἀνιαροῖς. καὶ τούτων ἂν τὸν κατάλογον ἅπαντα διεξῆλθον εἴπερ ἐπέστελλον ἀνδρὶ τὴν θείαν ἀκριβῶς οὐκ ἐπισταμένῳ Γραφήν· ἐπειδὴ δὲ παιδόθεν τοῖς θείοις ἐνετράφης λογίοις,[b] θεοφιλέστατε, παρέλκον οἶμαι τοῦτο ποιεῖν, εἰς ἐκείνους δὲ μόνον ἀφορᾶν ἀξιῶ καὶ τῶν φιλανθρωποτάτων ἱερέων τοὺς μὲν ἠδικηκότας θρηνεῖν, τοὺς δὲ παρορῶντας ἐλεεῖν, καὶ τὸν μὲν τῆς Ἐκκλησίας ὀδύρεσθαι κλύδωνα, ὅτι δὲ τῶν ὑπὲρ τῆς εὐσεβείας παθημάτων μετέσχομεν, χαίρειν καὶ γάννυσθαι[c] καὶ τὸν ταύτης ἡμᾶς τῆς μερίδος πεποιηκότα διηνεκῶς ἀνυμνεῖν. παραχωρήσωμεν τοῖς ἀπεκτονόσιν καὶ τιμῆς, καὶ τρυφῆς, καὶ προεδρίας, καὶ τῆς δυστήνου δόξης, μόνον δὲ ἡμεῖς τῶν εὐαγγελικῶν δογμάτων ἐχώμεθα, καὶ μετ᾽ ἐκείνων, ἂν δέῃ, πᾶν ὁτιοῦν ἀλγεινὸν ὑπομένωμεν, καὶ τὴν ἀξιόκτητον πενίαν τοῦ πολυφρόντιδος προτιμήσωμεν πλούτου.

Ταῦτα δὲ γράφω, οὐ παραίνεσιν εἰσφέρων· ἔγνων γὰρ Σοῦ Τῆς Ὁσιότητος τὴν ἐν τοῖς ἀλγεινοῖς παρρησίαν· ἀλλὰ τὴν ἐμαυτοῦ γνώμην δήλην Τῇ Σῇ Φιλοθεΐᾳ ποιῶν καὶ διδάσκων ὡς ἔχεις, Δέσποτα, συναγωνιστὰς ἀσμένως τῆς ἀληθείας προκινδυνεύοντας. τοῦτο πάλαι βουληθεὶς ἐπιστεῖλαι, οὐχ εὗρον

l. 27 εὐσεβείας *codd., Sir. Nös.* : θεοσ- *Az.*

a. *Cf.* Mt 5.11f. b. *Cf.* 2Tm 3.15. c. Mt 5.11f.

133. To Ibas, Bishop of Edessa[1]

Our Master commanded those who suffer unjustly not to lose heart, but to rejoice and to look for their consolation to the examples of ancient history.[a] As we know, from the beginnings of the human race up to the present moment, those devoted to the service of God have suffered injustice at the hands of their contemporaries and suffered woes beyond counting, and I might have produced a full catalogue of examples had I been writing to a man little acquainted with holy Scripture. But, as you, beloved of God, were raised from boyhood on the word of God,[b] I know that would be quite unnecessary; I do no more than call on you to consider the examples of the past, and, in regard to the clergy—the most kind-hearted clergy!—to weep for those who commit injustice and pity those who stand by and watch, to mourn for the storm that has engulfed the Church, but rejoice and exult that we have had to suffer on behalf of orthodoxy,[c] and to sing without surcease the praises of him who has granted us this portion. Let our murderers have their honors, luxuries, their seats of honor, and their miserable prestige; our one concern must be to hold fast the teachings of the gospels, and if necessary, with them to endure every suffering no-matter-what, preferring poverty, a precious good, to wealth that brings nothing but care.

If I write in these terms, it is not to offer you encouragement—I know very well the freedom with which Your Holiness speaks your mind even in the midst of these trials—but to make my own determination plain to Your Piety and inform you, my Lord, that you have comrades glad to fight on your side and risk their lives on behalf of the truth. I have been wanting to send this message for a long time but have never been able to find anyone to deliver it. Now that

1. On Ibas, *v. epp.* 52 n. 1 and 87 n. 1. As the letter presupposes the deposition of both Theodoret and Ibas (*v.* Intro., secc. 4.8f.), it must have been written subsequent to August 449. It is unclear whether Theodoret is still in Cyrus or in exile at the monastery near Apamea (*v.* Intro., sec. 4.8).

τὸν κομιοῦντα τὰ γράμματα, ἐπιτυχὼν δὲ νῦν τοῦ τιμιωτάτου καὶ εὐλαβεστάτου πρεσβυτέρου Ὀζζέου, ἀνδρὸς καὶ τῆς εὐσεβείας ὑπερμαχοῦντος καὶ Τῆς Σῆς ἐξηρτημένου Θεοσεβείας, καὶ γράφω, καὶ περιπτύσσομαι Σοῦ Τὴν Ὁσιότητα, καὶ παρακαλῶ ταῖς προσευχαῖς ἡμᾶς ὑπερείδειν καὶ στηρίζειν τοῖς γράμμασιν.

l. 28 θεοσεβείας *codd.* : εὐσ- *edd.*

I have met the right honorable and reverend priest Uzziah, both a courageous champion of religion and a man close to Your Reverence, I write, I embrace Your Holiness, and I urge you to support us with your prayers and strengthen us with your letters.

134. ΙΩΑΝΝΗΙ ΕΠΙΣΚΟΠΩΙ ΓΕΡΜΑΝΙΚΕΙΑΣ

Ὅτι μὲν οὐκ ἀμνημονεῖς, Δέσποτα, τῆς ἡμετέρας φιλίας, καὶ ᾔδειν καὶ οἶδα σαφῶς, ἐβουλόμην δὲ ὅμως καὶ ηὐχόμην Τὴν μὲν Σὴν Θεοσέβειαν τῆς ἀκριβείας φροντίσαι καὶ φυγεῖν τῶν τὴν εὐσέβειαν προδεδωκότων τὴν κοινωνίαν, ἀναθεῖναι δὲ τῷ Κηδεμόνι τῶν ὅλων τὴν ὑπὲρ ἡμῶν καὶ ὑμῶν φροντίδα· καὶ γάρ, σιγώντων ἡμῶν καὶ ἡσυχίαν ἀγόντων, τάς τε πικροτάτας καὶ ὠμοτάτας διέλυσε τιμωρίας καί, ἀντὶ τοῦ χαλεποῦ κλύδωνος, τὴν λευκὴν ταύτην παρέσχεν γαλήνην,[a] καί, ταύτης δὲ ἡμῖν παρὰ τοῦ φιλανθρώπου παρασχεθείσης Δεσπότου, τὴν ἡσυχίαν ἀξιεραστοτάτην νομίζομεν. πεῖσαι μὲν γὰρ τοὺς ταῖς καθ᾽ ἡμῶν ὑπαχθέντας συκοφαντίαις ἀναγκαῖον ὑπολαμβάνομεν καὶ δεῖξαι μὲν τὴν τῶν εὐαγγελικῶν δογμάτων ἀλήθειαν, διελέγξαι δὲ τὸ κατ᾽ αὐτῶν στρατευσάμενον ψεῦδος, μετὰ μέντοι τοὺς ἐλέγχους καὶ τῆς ἀληθείας τὸ κράτος, φυγεῖν ἡμῖν πρόκειται τὴν τῶν κοινῶν ἐπιμέλειαν καὶ πρὸς τὴν τριπόθητον ἡμῖν ἡσυχίαν παλινδρομῆσαι. περὶ δέ γε τῶν τῆς ἀληθείας ἐχθρῶν, μετὰ τοῦ προφήτου βοῶμεν, *Ἀπώλετο τὸ μνημόσυνον αὐτῶν μετ᾽* ἤχου, *καὶ ὁ Κύριος εἰς τὸν αἰῶνα μένει.*[b] περὶ δέ γε ἡμῶν αὐτῶν ἐκεῖνο ψάλλομεν· *Ἐξαπέστειλεν ἐξ ὕψους καὶ ἔλαβέν με· προσελάβετό με ἐξ ὑδάτων πολλῶν* καὶ ἐρρύσατό *με ἐξ ἐχθρῶν μου δυνατῶν.*[c]

Ταῦτα δὲ νῦν γράφω, δύο Τῆς Σῆς Θεοσεβείας δεξάμενος ἐπιστολάς· τὴν μὲν δι᾽ Ἀναστασίου τοῦ βεροιαίου πρεσβυτέρου, τὴν δὲ διὰ Θεοδότου τοῦ δρακωναρίου· τὴν γὰρ ἄλλην οὐδεὶς ἡμῖν ἀπέδωκεν, περὶ ἧς ἐν τοῖς τελευταίοις δεδήλωκας γράμμασιν. περὶ δὲ τῆς αὐτόσε πορείας οὐδὲν γράψαι δύναμαι πρὶν ἂν γνῶ τί περὶ ἡμῶν προσέταξεν ὁ εὐσεβέστατος βασιλεύς· οὐδέπω γὰρ ἦλθεν ὁ ταῦτα κομίζων τὰ γράμματα.

a. *Cf.* Mk 4.35–39. b. Ps 9.6f. (LXX var.) c. Ps 18.16f. (LXX var.)

134. To John, Bishop of Germanicia[1]

I was and remain quite convinced, my Lord, that you are mindful of our friendship, yet it was my wish and my prayer that Your Reverence would have strict regard for correctness and cut off all communion with those who have betrayed the cause of orthodoxy and leave concern for me and yourself in the hands of the Protector of the universe. Indeed, without us having said or done anything ourselves, he has put an end to our punishment, bitter and cruel as it was, and changed that wild tempest to these bright tranquil seas.[a] Now that we have received this gift from the bounty of our Master, we prize our peace and quiet more than anything else in the world. Of course, we understand the importance of winning over those misled by the false charges brought against us, of demonstrating the truth of the gospel teachings and exposing the deception of those who have gone to war against them, but when these refutations and the victory of the truth have been accomplished, we have before us the opportunity to make our escape from the cares of everyday life and rush back to the peace and quiet, which is the object of our yearning. As for the enemies of the truth, we join the prophet in calling out, "All memory of them has perished with a loud noise, and the Lord remains forever."[b] And with regard to ourselves, we chant that verse of the psalm, "He sent from on high and took hold of me; he rescued me from many waters and saved me from the power of my enemies."[c]

As I compose this, I am in receipt of two letters from Your Reverence, the one conveyed by Anastasius the priest of Beroea, the other by the standard-bearer Theodotus,[2] but no one ever delivered to us the third to which you refer in your last. As to any trip back there, I cannot write anything without first learning what decision the right reverend emperor has taken in our regard;[3] the messenger has not yet arrived with the letter.

1. On John of Germanicia, *v. ep.* 125 n. 1. The letter, written from Theodoret's place of exile (*v.* Intro. n. 345), must date to sometime after the death of Theodosius II in late August 450; *v.* Intro., secc. 4.11–5.

2. For the title "standard-bearer," *v. ep.* 59 n. 2.

3. Theodoret refers to Marcian, proclaimed emperor August 24, 450; *v.* Intro., sec. 4.11.

135. ΘΕΟΚΤΙΣΤΩΙ ΕΠΙΣΚΟΠΩΙ ΒΕΡΟΙΑΣ

(1)Ἤρετό τις τὸν Σωτῆρα, καὶ Νομοθέτην, καὶ Κύριον ποία ἐντολὴ πρώτη.[a] ὁ δὲ ἔφησεν, *Ἀγαπήσεις Κύριον τὸν Θεόν σου ἐξ ὅλης τῆς καρδίας σου, καὶ ἐξ ὅλης τῆς ψυχῆς σου, καὶ ἐξ ὅλης τῆς διανοίας σου,*[b] καὶ ἐπήγαγεν, *Αὕτη ἐστὶν … ἐντολὴ πρώτη, δευτέρα δὲ ὁμοία αὐτῇ· Ἀγαπήσεις τὸν πλησίον σου ὡς σεαυτόν,*[c] καὶ προσέθηκεν, *Ἐν ταύταις ταῖς δυσὶν ἐντολαῖς ὅλος ὁ νόμος καὶ οἱ προφῆται* κρέμανται.[d] ὁ τοίνυν ταύτας φυλάττων δῆλον ὅτι πάντα πληροῖ τὸν νόμον κατὰ τὸν δεσποτικὸν ὅρον, ὁ δ᾽ αὖ παραβαίνων, παντὸς τοῦ νόμου παραβάτης ἁλίσκεται.

Σκοπήσωμεν τοίνυν, τοῦ συνειδότος ὀρθῶς καὶ δικαίως δικάζοντος, εἰ τὰς θείας πεπληρώκαμεν ἐντολάς· πληροῖ δὲ τὴν μὲν πρώτην ὁ τὴν θεόσδοτον πίστιν φυλάττων ἀκήρατον, καὶ τοὺς ταύτῃ πολεμοῦντας, ὡς τῆς ἀληθείας ἐχθρούς, μυσαττόμενος, καὶ μισῶν ἐκθύμως τοὺς μισοῦντας τὸν Ἀγαπώμενον, τὴν δὲ δευτέραν ὁ τὴν τοῦ πέλας θεραπείαν περὶ πλείστου ποιούμενος καὶ μὴ μόνον ἐν ταῖς εὐπραξίαις, ἀλλὰ κἀν ταῖς δοκούσαις δυσημερίαις διατηρῶν τῆς φιλίας τοὺς ὅρους, οἱ δὲ τῆς μὲν οἰκείας, ὡς νομίζουσιν, ἀσφαλείας φροντίζοντες, τῶν δὲ τῆς φιλίας νόμων διὰ ταύτην ὀλιγωροῦντες, καὶ πολεμουμένους παρορῶντες τοὺς φίλους τῆς τῶν φαύλων εἰσί, καὶ παρὰ τοῖς ἔξω, μερίδος. ὁ δὲ τῶν ὅλων Δεσπότης τὰ τελεώτερα παρὰ τῶν οἰκείων ἀπαιτεῖ μαθητῶν· *Ἀγαπᾶτε,* γάρ φησιν, *τοὺς ἐχθροὺς ὑμῶν·*[e] *εἰ γὰρ τοὺς ἀγαπῶντας ὑμᾶς ἀγαπᾶτε,*[f] *τί* πλέον *ποιεῖτε;*[g] ἰδοὺ *καὶ οἱ ἁμαρτωλοὶ*[h] *καὶ οἱ τελῶναι* τοῦτο *ποιοῦσιν.*[i]

a. Mk 12.28
b. Mk 12.30
c. Mt 22.38f.
d. Mt 22.40 (NT var.)
e. Lk 6.27
f. Lk 6.32 (NT var.)
g. Mt 5.47 (NT var.)
h. Lk 6.33 (NT var.)
i. Mt 5.46 (NT var.)

135. To Theoctistus, Bishop of Beroea[1]

(1) Someone once asked our Savior, Lawgiver, and Lord which was the most important of the commandments,[a] and he replied, "You will love the Lord your God with all your heart, and all your soul, and all your mind."[b] Then, he went on, "This is the most important commandment, and the second is like it, 'You shall love your neighbor as yourself.'"[c] Then further, "The law as a whole and the prophets depend on these two commandments."[d] We can therefore conclude that, according to our Master's own definition, whoever observes these fulfills the entire law, and whoever transgresses them stands condemned as transgressing the law in its entirety.

Now let's ask ourselves whether, on a right and just judgment of conscience, we've done what is enjoined by these laws of God. The one who fulfills the first law preserves free from blemish the faith we have received from God, turns in loathing from those who battle against it, regarding them as enemies of the truth, and hates with all the ardor of his heart those who hate the One he loves; he who fulfills the second devotes himself to the care of his neighbor and observes the demands of friendship not only in good times, but also in those seemingly bad, but people who take thought for their own safety—or imagine that that's what they're doing—and, to protect themselves, disregard the laws of friendship and look the other way when their friends are under attack—these are an object of scorn even among those outside the Church. The Master of the universe requires better things from his own disciples; "Love your enemies," he says,[e] "for, if you love those who love you,[f] how is your conduct better than others'?[g] Behold, both sinners[h] and tax-collectors do as much."[i]

1. On Theoctistus and Beroea, *v. ep.* 32 n. 1; for the date, *v. ep.* 134 n. 1.

(2) Ἡμεῖς δὲ οὐδὲ τῆς τελωνικῆς ἀπελαύσαμεν ἀγάπης. καὶ τί λέγω *τελωνικῆς;* οὐδὲ ἧς τυγχάνουσιν οἱ ἀνδροφόνοι καὶ γόητες ἐν τοῖς δεσμωτηρίοις παραψυχῆς ἀπελαύσαμεν. εἰ δὲ πάντες ταύτην ἐζήλωσαν τὴν ὠμότητα, οὐδὲν ἕτερον ὑπελείπετο ἢ ζῶντας μὲν ὑπ᾽ ἐνδείας ἀναλωθῆναι, τελευτήσαντας δὲ μηδὲ τάφῳ παραδοθῆναι, ἀλλὰ κυνῶν καὶ θηρῶν γενέσθαι βοράν, ἀλλ᾽ ἤρκεσαν ἡμῖν οἱ τοῦδε τοῦ βίου καταφρονοῦντες καὶ τῶν αἰωνίων ἀγαθῶν προσδεχόμενοι τὴν ἀπόλαυσιν, οἳ παντοδαπῆς ἡμᾶς ψυχαγωγίας ἠξίωσαν. ὁ δὲ φιλάνθρωπος Κύριος *ἐκ τοῦ οὐρανοῦ* ἠκούτισεν *κρίσιν,* ἡ δὲ *γῆ ἐφοβήθη καὶ ἡσύχασεν ἐν τῷ ἀναστῆναι εἰς κρίσιν τὸν Θεόν,*[j] *οἱ δὲ ἐχθροὶ* αὐτοῦ *ἅμα τῷ δοξασθῆναι αὐτοὺς καὶ ὑψωθῆναι,* ἐκλείποντες *ὡσεὶ καπνός, ἐξέλιπον.*[k] ἐστηλίτευται δὲ τὸ τῆς καινῆς αἱρέσεως ψεῦδος, κηρύττεται δὲ προφανῶς ἡ τῶν θείων εὐαγγελίων ἀλήθεια, ἡμεῖς δὲ μετὰ τοῦ μακαρίου βοῶμεν Δαυίδ, *Εὐλογητὸς … ὁ Θεός…, ὁ ποιῶν θαυμάσια* μεγάλα *μόνος, καὶ εὐλογητὸν τὸ ὄνομα τῆς δόξης αὐτοῦ, … καὶ πληρωθήσεται τῆς δόξης αὐτοῦ πᾶσα ἡ γῆ. γένοιτο, γένοιτο.*[l]

j. Ps 76.8f. (LXX var.) k. Ps 37.20 (LXX var.) l. Ps 72.18f. (LXX var.)

(2) Now in our own case, we've had not so much as even the tax-collectors' love. Tax-collectors' love? Not even the comfort permitted to murderers or conjurers behind bars! If everyone had emulated this sort of cruel behavior, here's where we would've ended up: living until taken off by hunger, and then dead, denied even so much as burial, we would've become food for dogs and wild beasts! But my needs were met by men who have little regard for this life, men who expect to possess goods that will not pass away; they have bestowed on me their every attention.[2] "From heaven has" the good Lord "made his judgment heard; the earth shuddered in fear and fell silent as God rose up to judge,"[j] "and, at the moment of their glorification and exaltation, his enemies faded away and vanished like smoke."[k] Now that the falsehood of this new heresy has been exposed, and the truth based on the holy gospels is being publicly proclaimed, we join the blessed David in calling out, "Blessed is God who alone performs great wonders, and blessed his glorious name; the whole earth will be filled with his glory. Amen, Amen!"[l]

2. Theodoret refers to the monks of the monastery near Apamea, where he had lived prior to his appointment as bishop of Cyrus, and to which he returned during the exile from Cyrus following his deposition; *v.* Intro., sec. 4.8.

136. ΡΩΜΥΛΩΙ ΕΠΙΣΚΟΠΩΙ

(1) Ἐπειδὴ τῆς παλαιᾶς ἡμᾶς ἀνέμνησας ἱστορίας καὶ τῶν σύρων ἔφης τὸν βασιλέα, τῶν τοῦ Ἰσραὴλ βασιλέων τὸ φιλάνθρωπον λογισάμενον, ἱκέτου σχῆμα λαβεῖν καὶ μὴ διαμαρτεῖν τῆς αἰτήσεως,[a] ἀναμνήσθητι, Δέσποτα, καὶ τῆς θείας ὀργῆς· τὸν γὰρ Ἀχαάβ, τῷ ἐλέῳ χρησάμενον, πανωλεθρίᾳ παρέδωκεν καὶ διὰ τοῦ προφήτου τὴν ψῆφον ἐξήνεγκεν· *Ἔσται,* γάρ φησιν, *ἡ ψυχή σου ἀντὶ τῆς ψυχῆς αὐτοῦ, καὶ ὁ λαός σου ἀντὶ τοῦ λαοῦ αὐτοῦ.*[b] ἡμεῖς δὲ κελευόμεθα διὰ τούτων κρίσει κεραννύναι τὸν ἔλεον, ὡς οὐ παντὸς ἐλέου ἀρέσκοντος τὸν τῶν ὅλων Κύριον. διαφερόντως δὲ λογισμοῦ δεῖται σώφρονος ἡ παροῦσα ὑπόθεσις· περὶ γὰρ θείων ἀγωνιζόμεθα δογμάτων, ἐν οἷς ἔχομεν τὴν τῆς σωτηρίας ἐλπίδα.

Πολλὴν δὲ ὅμως ἔστιν ἰδεῖν κἀν τούτοις ἀνθρώπων διαφοράν· οἱ μὲν γὰρ ἀληθῶς τὴν κοινὴν νοσοῦσιν ἀσέβειαν, οἱ δὲ ἀδιαφόρως καὶ ταῦτα καὶ τὰ τούτοις ἐναντία προσφέρουσιν, ἕτεροι δέ, τὴν ἀλήθειαν ἐπιστάμενοι, ταύτην μὲν ἐν τοῖς τῆς ψυχῆς κατακρύπτουσι ταμιείοις, τὰ δὲ δυσσεβῆ μετὰ τῶν ἄλλων κηρύττουσιν, ἄλλοι δέ, τοῦ φθόνου τὸ πάθος δεξάμενοι, τὸ οἰκεῖον ἔχθος ἀφορμὴν τοῦ κατὰ τῆς ἀληθείας πολέμου πεποίηνται καὶ πᾶσαν κατὰ τῶν τῆς ἀληθείας κηρύκων εἰσφέρουσιν κακοήθειαν, εἰσὶ δὲ οἳ τῶν μὲν ἀποστολικῶν δογμάτων ἀσπάζονται τὴν ἀλήθειαν, τὴν δὲ τῶν κρατούντων δείσαντες δυναστείαν, δημοσιεῦσαι ταύτην πεφρίκασιν, καὶ στένουσι μὲν καὶ ὀδύρονται τῶν κακῶν τὴν φοράν, σύνεισι δὲ ὅμως τοῖς τὰς τρικυμίας ἐγείρουσι. ταύτης τῆς συμμορίας Τὴν

a. 1Kgs 20.31–34 (LXX 21.31–34) b 1Kgs 20.42 (LXX 21.42)

136. To Bishop Romulus[1]

(1) You have reminded me of that event of ancient history, how the king of Syria, recalling the generosity of the kings of Israel, adopted the posture of a suppliant and succeeded in gaining his petition,[a] yet, my Master, you should also remember the wrath of God. For this display of mercy, God consigned Ahab to perdition and pronounced his sentence through the prophet: "Your life," he said, "will pay for his life, and your people for his people."[b] For us the lesson of this story is that we should temper our mercy with an admixture of judgment, as not every act of mercy is pleasing to the Lord of the universe. The issue now before us is one that requires the most prudent consideration; after all, our contest regards divinely imparted doctrine, the basis of our hope of salvation.

And yet, even in an issue like this, there is much difference among people: There are those who really do labor with the malady of this widespread heresy; others are indifferent and profess first one doctrine and then its opposite; others understand the truth but hide it away in the recesses of their heart and join others in preaching these impious ideas; there are those, who, in prey to spite, are motivated by personal hatred to take up arms against the true religion and bring all their malice to bear against the heralds of the truth; and, last of all, there are those who embrace the true teachings of the apostles, but, in terror of the might of those in power, are afraid to pronounce them in public—moaning and groaning over this great harvest of evil, they go on associating with the very people who are causing the storm to rage. This is the group to which, according to our classifica-

1. Romulus was bishop of Chalcis in Syria I, and thus, like Theodoret, a suffragan of the patriarchal see of Antioch. The ancient Chalcis lay south of Beroea (67 D4) on the road that links Cyrus (67 D3) to Apamea (68 B3; *Barrington Atlas*); *cf. ep.* 32 n. 1. Though it survived until the end of the eleventh century, today it is in ruins; *v.* Mango, "Chalkis Ad Belum." In the second section of this letter, Theodoret alludes to public statements made by ecclesiastics who, now that Theodosius was dead, thought they should disassociate themselves from Dioscorus and his allies and their monophysite doctrine. Thus, the date is subsequent to July 450 and prior to the summoning of the Council of Chalcedon in May 451; *v.* Intro., secc. 4.11–5.

Σὴν εἶναι Θεοσέβειαν ὁριζόμεθα· ὑγιαίνειν μὲν γὰρ αὐτὴν ἐν τοῖς θείοις δόγμασι πεπιστεύκαμεν καὶ τὴν περὶ ἡμᾶς διασώζειν ἀγάπην νομίζομεν, διὰ μόνην δὲ δειλίαν συμπεριφέρεσθαι τῷ καιρῷ. οὗ δὴ χάριν, οὐδενὶ τῶν ἄλλων ἐπιστέλλοντες, Τῇ Σῇ Φιλοθεΐᾳ καὶ γράφομεν καὶ παρ᾽ αὐτῆς δεχόμεθα γράμματα, τὸν μὲν σκοπὸν εἰδότες, τῇ δὲ δειλίᾳ συγγνώμην οὕτω πως νέμοντες.

(2) Ὁ δὲ φιλάνθρωπος Κύριος καὶ τὰς τῆς δειλίας παντελῶς νῦν ἀπέκοψεν ἀφορμάς, τὴν μὲν καινοτομηθεῖσαν δείξας ἀσέβειαν, τὴν δὲ τῶν εὐαγγελίων γυμνὴν ἐπιδείξας ἀλήθειαν. ἡμεῖς δέ, ουδὲ ταῖς θριξὶν ἰσαρίθμων ἡμῖν γενομένων στομάτων, ὑμνῆσαι κατ᾽ ἀξίαν τὸν φιλάνθρωπον δυνάμεθα Κύριον, ὅτι τὰ παρ᾽ ἡμῶν κηρυττόμενα καὶ τοὺς ἐναντιωτάτους προφανῶς κηρύττειν ἠνάγκασεν· ἠκούσαμεν γὰρ ὡς καὶ Τῆς Σῆς Φιλοθεΐας ὁ σύνοικος, γνοὺς τοὺς ἐν ταῖς μεγάλαις πόλεσιν γεγενημένους ἀναθεματισμούς, ἐπαύσατο μὲν τὴν λοξὴν τῶν καρκίνων πορείαν μιμούμενος, ἐβάδισεν δὲ τὴν εὐθεῖαν,[c] περὶ δογμάτων διαλεχθεὶς ἔν τινι πανηγύρει. χρὴ δέ, μὴ τοῖς καιροῖς προσαρμόττειν τοὺς λόγους, ἀλλ᾽ ἀκλινῆ τῆς ἀληθείας τὸν κανόνα διασώζειν ἀεί.

l. 30 γράμματα *N* : τὰ γ. *scr. Onor. A, edd.* = *"we write to Your Piety and receive your letters." Onorio's emendation would point to specific letters received from Romulus. The omission of the article is in accord with canonical usage that forbids contact with heretics, including through the writing and receipt of letters; v. the ep. of the Council of Sardica (343) to the churches of Alexandria, Ancyra, and Gaza quoted in H. e. 2.8.36: καὶ φυλάξασθε, ἀδελφοὶ ἀγαπητοί, μήτε γράφειν πρὸς αὐτοὺς μήτε γράμματα παρ᾽ αὐτῶν δέχεσθαι* **l. 35** οὐδὲ ταῖς θριξὶν ἰσαρίθμων ἡμῖν γενομένων στομάτων *scripsi* : οὔτε, *etc. codd., edd. The sense requires the emphatic* οὐδὲ = *"not even if," not the correlative neg.* οὔτε, usually = *"neither … nor"; cf. ep. 81, c. n.* (οὐδὲ ἐρωτηθεὶς).

c. *Cf.* Ar., *Pax* 1083.

tion, Your Reverence belongs. We are confident that your religious beliefs are sound, and believe your love for us unimpaired, that your temporizing is due to nothing but cowardice. And so, we write to none of the others, but, in the case of Your Piety, both write and receive letters,[2] knowing, as we do, your real sentiments, and making allowances, somehow or other, for your cowardice.

(2) But now all inducements to cowardice have been swept away by the good Lord, who has shown up this heresy for the novelty it is and shown forth to all the world the plain truth of the gospels. Even if we had as many tongues as we have hairs on our head, we still could not praise as we should the goodness of the Lord, who has compelled even our bitterest opponents to preach what we preach. Indeed, we have learned that even that colleague of Your Piety's, hearing of the recantations that have taken place in the principal cities,[3] has stopped walking sideways like a crab and straightened his stride in a doctrinal sermon delivered on a feast day.[4c] Yet, what is really necessary is to refuse to adapt your teaching to the circumstances of the moment and always keep straight the rule of the true faith.

2. Theodoret is not considering the dynamics of a personal relationship (as suggested by Jackson's "I write to your holiness and receive your reply" and Azéma's "nous écrivons à ta Piété et acceptons ses lettres"), but conforming to a general ecclesiastical norm. Thus, the translation should not include a possessive pronoun referring solely to letters received from Romulus; *v.* c. n.

3. "Recantations that have taken place in the principal cities" represents Theodoret's τοὺς ἐν ταῖς μεγάλαις πόλεσι γεγενημένους ἀναθεματισμούς. As Lampe points out (sub. uoc. 2.b.) the noun ἀναθεματισμός can refer to a curse pronounced against heretics as an indication that the speaker is returning to orthodoxy.

4. If this letter was written in spring 451, Theodoret may be referring to a sermon preached on the recently past Easter; *v. PGL, sub uoc.* πανήγυρις 1.iii. He uses the images of walking straight and crooked (ὀρθὰ / λοξὰ βαδίζειν) to contrast good conduct with conduct that is for some reason unsatisfactory. In this context, the adjective / adverb λοξά, referring literally to the sideways walk of the crab, suggests "ambiguous" or "devious" theological language. The transformation of this cleric's behavior is all the more remarkable, because, as the proverb had it, the crab will never learn to walk straight: οὔποτε ποιήσεις τὸν κάρκινον ὀρθὰ βαδίζειν (Ar. *Pax* 1083); *v.* Olson, *ad loc.*

137. ΚΥΡΩΙ ΜΑΓΙΣΤΡΙΑΝΩΙ

(1) Λίαν ἤλγησα, τὴν συμβᾶσαν ὑμῖν ἀθυμίαν μεμαθηκώς· πῶς γὰρ οὐκ ἔμελλον τοῦτο πείσεσθαι, τὰ ὑμέτερα οἰκειούμενος καὶ τῆς ἀποστολικῆς μεμνημένος νομοθεσίας ἣ οὐ μόνον *χαίρειν μετὰ χαιρόντων*, ἀλλὰ καὶ *κλαίειν μετὰ κλαιόντων* παρεγγυᾷ;[a] καὶ αὐτὸ δέ γε τὸ πάθος ἱκανὸν εἰς συμπάθειαν καὶ τοὺς δυσμενεστάτους ἑλκύσαι· τί γὰρ οὕτως ἀνιαρὸν ὡς ὁμοζύγου στερηθῆναι ἐννόμως μὲν ἑλκυσάσης τὸν τοῦ γάμου ζυγόν, τῷ δὲ συνοίκῳ θυμήρη τὸν βίον ἐργασαμένης, καὶ τῆς οἰκίας τὰς φροντίδας μερισαμένης· καὶ τὰ μὲν ἔνδον οἰκουρησάσης, τὰ δ' ἄλλα πάντα συγκυβερνησάσης, καὶ τὸ συνοίσειν μέλλον εἰσηγησαμένης καὶ ταῖς τοῦ ἀνδρὸς ὑποθημοσύναις εἰξάσης; τὸ δὲ καὶ σὺν ταύτῃ τὸν ἐξ αὐτῆς φύντα, καὶ ἐπιμελῶς ἐκτραφέντα, καὶ λόγοις ἐνασκηθέντα, καὶ γηρωκόμον ἐλπισθέντα γενήσεσθαι, ἐν αὐτῷ τῷ ἦρι τῆς ἡλικίας, ἰούλων λοιπὸν καθερπόντων, παραδοῦναι τῷ τάφῳ ποίας ἀχθηδόνος ὑπερβολὴν καταλείπει; εἰ μὲν οὖν εἰς αὐτὴν ἀποβλέψαιμεν μόνην τοῦ πάθους τὴν φύσιν, οὐδεμίαν ψυχαγωγίαν εἰσδέχεται.

Εἰ δὲ τὸ θνητὸν τοῦ γένους εἰς νοῦν λάβοιμεν, καὶ τὴν θείαν ψῆφον, τὴν κατὰ τοῦ γένους ἐξενεχθεῖσαν,[b] καί, πρὸς τούτοις, τὸ τοῦ πάθους κοινόν· πλήρης γὰρ τῶν τοιούτων παθημάτων ὁ βίος· οἴσομεν γενναίως τὸ γεγονός, καὶ τὰς τῆς ἀθυμίας ἀποκρουσόμεθα προσβολάς, καὶ τὴν θαυμασίαν ἐκείνην ᾄσομεν ὑμνῳδίαν· *Ὁ Κύριος ἔδωκεν, ὁ Κύριος ἀφείλετο· ὡς τῷ Κυρίῳ ἔδοξεν, οὕτως καὶ ἐγένετο. εἴη τὸ ὄνομα Κυρίου εὐλογημένον* εἰς τοὺς αἰῶνας.[c]

l. 4 ἀλλὰ καὶ κλαίειν *A*$^{s.l.}$ (*Car.?*), *Az.* : καὶ κλ. *N* (*uerbo* καὶ *et litteris -*αί*- infinitivi in ras. scriptis*) *Z*. *The supplement suggested, probably by Cariofilo, is clearly necessary and correct. The erasure in N suggests confusion over the reading. Perhaps the omission of* ἀλλὰ *was due to haplography; the eye of the scribe passed from one* λα *to another.*

a. Rom 12.15 b. Gn 3.19 c. Jb 1.21 (LXX var.)

137. To Cyrus, Assistant to the Master of the Offices[1]

(1) It was with great pain that I heard of the despondency that has taken hold of you. How could I have felt otherwise, considering anything that concerns you as concerning me and mindful of the Apostle's instruction that we are not just to rejoice with those who are rejoicing, but also weep with those who are weeping?[a] What you have suffered is, in itself, enough to wring sympathy even from your worst enemies. Who could imagine anything more distressing than the loss of your helpmate, the woman who bore with you the yoke of lawful wedlock, brightened with joy the life of her companion, and shared the cares of the household: managing your life at home and helping steer all your affairs, offering advice on what would be useful, but bowing to the decisions of her husband? And, then, to have to bury along with her the son she bore, a son so carefully raised, trained in rhetoric—the one you hoped would be your support in old age dying in the very spring of youth, at the moment his beard was just beginning to sprout on his cheeks! What grief could be heavier to bear? If we fix our attention on nothing but the suffering, no consolation is possible.

Yet, if we recall the mortality of our race due to the judgment God has rendered against it,[b] and, furthermore, that this is an experience common to us all—human life is everywhere beset with such sufferings—we shall bear this experience with fortitude, repelling all the attacks of grief and ourselves singing that grand and ancient song of praise, "The Lord has given, the Lord has taken away; as the Lord has decreed, so has it happened. May the name of the Lord be praised forever."[c]

1. It is unclear whether this Cyrus should be identified with the addressee of *ep.* 13; *v.* "Cyrus 2," *PLRE*, vol. 2, p. 336. The title given to Cyrus (μαγιστριανός) signifies the same rank as that (καθωσιωμένος) given to Euphronius in *ep.* 79.1 (*v.* n. 6); *v.* Delmaire, p. 98. Date: unknown.

(2) Ἡμεῖς δὲ καὶ πλείους ἔχομεν εἰς παραψυχὴν ἀφορμάς· τὰς γὰρ τῆς ἀναστάσεως ἐλπίδας ἐναργῶς ἐδεξάμεθα, καὶ τὴν τῶν τεθνεώτων προσμένομεν ἀναβίωσιν, καὶ πολλάκις ἀκηκόαμεν τοῦ Δεσπότου *ὕπνον* κεκληκότος τὸν θάνατον.[d] εἰ δὲ πιστεύομεν, ὥσπεροῦν πιστεύομεν, ταῖς τοῦ Σωτῆρος φωναῖς, οὐ δεῖ θρηνεῖν τοὺς κοιμηθέντας, κἂν μακρότερος ᾖ τοῦ εἰωθότος ὁ ὕπνος, ἀλλὰ προσδέχεσθαι μὲν χρὴ τὴν ἀνάστασιν,[e] εἰδέναι δὲ ὡς, σοφὸς ὢν τῶν ὅλων ὁ Πρύτανις καὶ οὐ τὰ παρόντα μόνον, ἀλλὰ καὶ τὰ μέλλοντα γιγνώσκων σαφῶς, πρὸς τὸ συμφέρον ἰθύνει τὰ πράγματα. τοῦτό τοι καὶ σοφός τις εἰδώς, περὶ τῶν τοιούτων θανάτων φιλοσοφεῖ καί φησιν, *Ἡρπάγη* πρὶν ἢ *κακία ἀλλάξῃ σύνεσιν αὐτοῦ, ἢ δόλος ἀπατήσῃ ψυχὴν αὐτοῦ.*[f] παραχωρήσωμεν τοίνυν, παρακαλῶ, τῷ σοφῷ τοῦ παντὸς Κυβερνήτῃ καὶ στέρξωμεν τὰ οἰκονομούμενα ὁποῖά ποτ᾽ ἂν ᾖ· κἂν θυμήρη, κἂν λυπηρά· σύμφορα γὰρ ταῦτα, καὶ λυσιτελῆ, καὶ φιλοσοφίας πρόξενα, καὶ στεφάνων τοῖς καρτεροῦσι παρεκτικά.

l. 35 τοῦτό τοι *NZ*, A^{ac} : τοῦτο δὴ A^{pc} (*Car.? tono super littera -ο et uerbo* τοι *cancellatis*, δὴ *s.l. scr.*), *edd. There are three other exx. of* τοῦτό τοι *in the works of Thdt.; all of these occur in a context of aphoristic or philosophical discourse quite similar to this passage. V., e.g. Affect.. 12.7. l. 4: Τοῦτό τοι διδάσκων καὶ ὁ μέγας κῆρυξ τῆς ἀληθείας βοᾷ, Γίνεσθε οὖν μιμηταὶ τοῦ Θεοῦ; v. also Haer. com. 5.1 (PG, vol. 83, col. 444, l. 31).* **l. 36** πρὶν ἢ *coni. Gilb., scripsi* : πρὶν ἡ *codd., edd. Thdt. has accommodated the text of Wis 4.11 (ἡρπάγη μὴ κακία ἀλλάξῃ σύνεσιν αὐτοῦ, etc.) to the context of his sentence by the introduction of the adverbial conjunction* πρὶν. *The Neapolitanus reports just πρὶν followed by the fem. def. art. This makes good sense, and simple πρὶν + subjunc. is found elsewhere in the works of Thdt.: e.g. Affect.. 10.24, l. 4: Πάλαι μὲν γάρ, πρὶν δέξηται τὸ πέρας ἡ προφητεία, etc. It is easier however, to account for the eta if he used the common combination πρὶν ἤ. In his own composition, Thdt. normally combines πρὶν ἤ with an infin. and πρὶν ἂν with a finite mood, but there are two exx. of πρὶν ἤ + subjunc. in scriptural quotations. V. in Ps 57.10, PG, vol. 82, col. 1301, l. 9: Πρὶν ἢ αὐξηθῶσιν αἱ ἄκανθαι ὑμῶν, ὥστε γενέσθαι ῥάμνον.); also in Ier. 47.5, PG, vol. 81, col. 693, ll. 40f. It is very unlikely that he would have introduced an article for κακία, which stands in parallelism with the anarthrous δόλος.* **l. 37** ἀπατήσῃ *corr. Cir., scr. Az.* : -σει *NZ*, A^{ac}? : *deest Sir. Nös.*

d. *V., e.g.,* Mk 5.39; Jn 11.11.
e. *Cf.* Jn 11.11–13, 23–27.
f. Wis 4.11 (LXX var.)

(2) And yet, we are in possession of even stronger reasons to take consolation. After all, we have been given palpable hopes of resurrection and await the restoration to life of those who have died. Indeed, we have often heard our Master referring to death as "sleep."[d] If we put our trust—as of course, we do—in the words of our Savior, there can be no lamenting those who have fallen asleep, though their sleep be somewhat longer than usual. No, we must wait in expectation of the resurrection[e] and realize that, in his wisdom, the Ruler of the universe, who has full knowledge of what is and what is to be, directs all things for our benefit. Well aware of this, a wise man spoke with philosophical resignation of a death such as your son's: "He was snatched away before evil could pervert his understanding, or deceit lead his soul astray."[f] So, I urge you, let us yield to the will of the wise Helmsman of the universe, resign ourselves to his dispositions, whatever they be, whether bringing joy or grief. In the end, they are to our benefit, to our advantage—teaching us the philosopher's self-control[2] and offering the crown of victory to those who patiently endure.

2. On Theodoret's use of the term "philosophy" (φιλοσοφία), *v. ep.* 17 n. 2.

138. Ἰωάννῃ ἀρχιμανδρίτῃ

Ὁ μὲν μακάριος Δαυὶδ ἕτερά τινα πεπλημμέληκεν ἃ καὶ ἀνάγραπτα πεποίηκεν εἰς τὴν τῶν ὕστερον ἐσομένων ὠφέλειαν ὁ σοφῶς ἅπαντα πρυτανεύων Θεός, Ἀβεσαλῶν δέ, ὁ πατραλοίας καὶ μιαιφόνος, καὶ δυσσεβὴς καὶ παμπόνηρος τύραννος, οὐκ ἐκείνων χάριν τὴν κατὰ τοῦ πατρὸς ἀνεδέξατο λύτταν, ἀλλά, τῆς τυραννίδος ἐπιθυμήσας, τὸν ἀδικώτατον ἐκεῖνον προείλετο πόλεμον·[a] ὁ μέντοι θεῖος Δαυίδ, καὶ τούτων οὕτω γιγνομένων, τῆς εἰργασμένης ἀνεμιμνῄσκετο πλημμελείας.[b] κἀγὼ τοίνυν ἕτερα μέν τινα ἐμαυτῷ σύνοιδα πλημμελήματα, τὴν δέ γε δογματικὴν τῶν ἀποστόλων διδασκαλίαν ἀκραιφνῆ διετήρησα, οἱ δέ, καὶ τοὺς θείους καὶ τοὺς ἀνθρωπείους πατήσαντες νόμους καὶ ἀπόντας ἡμᾶς κατακρίναντες, οὐχ ὑπὲρ ὧν ἡμάρτομεν τὴν ψῆφον ἐξήνεγκαν· οὐ γὰρ ἦν αὐτοῖς δῆλα τὰ κεκρυμμένα· ἀλλὰ ψευδολογίαν καὶ συκοφαντίαν ὕφηναν καθ' ἡμῶν, μᾶλλον δέ, τοῖς ἀποστολικοῖς δόγμασι προφανῶς πολεμοῦντες, τὸν ἐκείνοις ἑπόμενον ἀπεκήρυξαν.

Ἀλλ' *ἐξηγέρθη, ὡς ὁ ὑπνῶν, Κύριος, … καὶ* διήλεγξεν *τοὺς ἐχθροὺς αὐτοῦ* … καὶ *ὄνειδος αἰώνιον ἔδωκεν αὐτοῖς,*[c] καὶ τὰ μὲν κίβδηλα καὶ νόθα διεσκέδασεν δόγματα, ἃ δὲ παρέδωκεν ἡμῖν ἐν τοῖς ἱεροῖς εὐαγγελίοις σὺν παρρησίᾳ κηρύττεσθαι παρεσκεύασεν. ἡμῖν δὲ ταῦτα εἰς τελείαν ἀρκεῖ θυμηδίαν· οὐδὲ γὰρ πόλεως ἐπιθυμοῦμεν ἐν ᾗ μοχθοῦντες τὸν ἅπαντα διατετελέκαμεν χρόνον, ἀλλὰ τὴν τῶν εὐαγγελίων ἀλήθειαν ποθοῦμεν κρατυνομένην ὁρᾶν· τοῦτον δὲ ἡμῶν τὸν πόθον ὁ Δεσπότης πεπλήρωκεν. διὰ τοῦτο γαννύμεθα καὶ γεγήθαμεν, καὶ τὸν μεγαλόδωρον Κύριον ὑμνοῦμεν, καὶ Τὴν Ὑμετέραν

a. 2Sm 13–18 b. Ps 51 c. Ps 78.65f. (LXX var.)

138. To John, the Archimandrite[1]

God, the wise Ruler of the universe, caused some of the sins that the blessed David committed to be recorded for the edification of future generations, but it wasn't for these that Absalom, the parricide and murderer, the impious and evil tyrant, began a mad assault against his father; rather, it was for lust of tyranny that he decided to undertake that most unjust war.[a] Even so, David, a god-fearing man, began to think about the sin he had committed.[b] In my case, though there are sins I bear on my conscience, I have maintained the purity of the teaching of the apostles, insofar as it applies to doctrine, and it was not for my sins that I was condemned by those who trampled underfoot the laws of man and pronounced me guilty in my absence—after all, they were in no position to see what was hidden. No, they wove a tissue of lies and false allegations against me, or—what was really the case—they went to war against the teachings of the apostles and excommunicated the man who remained true to them.

"Yet the Lord has arisen, like one who was sleeping, he has exposed his enemies and bestowed on them an everlasting shame."[c] And while he has scattered their counterfeit and spurious teachings, he has seen to the open proclamation of what he handed down to us in the holy gospels. That is enough to make our joy complete; our yearning is not for that city of ours where every moment was drudgery, but to see the establishment of the truth, and this desire our Master has completely satisfied. This is the source of our glad celebrations, and we praise in song the generosity of the Lord and urge Your Reverence to join us and, as we sing the song of praise, to

1. We lack the information necessary to identify the recipient. As Azéma points out, we encounter an archimandrite John among recipients of a letter written by Cyril after the First Council of Ephesus (*Coll. cas.* 229) and the same or a different archimandrite John among the authors of a letter to the emperor Marcian (*Conc. Chalc. Act.* 4, sec. 105); at least in the second case, it seems likely that the cleric is a Constantinopolitan. For the date, *v. ep.* 136 n. 1; for the title "archimandrite," *ep.* 27 n. 1.

Θεοσέβειαν τοῦτο σὺν ἡμῖν παρακαλοῦμεν ποιεῖν, καὶ ὑμνοῦντας ἱκετεῦσαι σπουδαίως ἵνα καὶ τοὺς νῦν μὲν ταῦτα, νῦν δὲ ἐκεῖνα λέγοντας καὶ πρὸς τοὺς καιροὺς μεταβαλλομένους, καθάπερ οἱ χαμαιλέοντες τὴν τῶν φύλλων μεταμφιέσκονται χρόαν, ὁ φιλάνθρωπος βεβαιώσῃ Κύριος καὶ ἐπὶ τῆς πέτρας ἐρείσῃ[d] καὶ δοίη πάντων προτιμᾶν τὴν ἀλήθειαν.

d. *Cf.* Ps 40.2.

make a heartfelt prayer for those who sometimes say this and other times that, people who adjust themselves to the exigencies of the moment like chameleons changing their color to match the foliage: that the good Lord set them upon a rock,[d] give them firm footing, and grant them the gift of putting the truth before all else.[2]

2. For the image of the chameleon, *cf. ep.* 125.2.

139. ΑΝΑΤΟΛΙΩΙ ΠΑΤΡΙΚΙΩΙ

(1) Ἡμεῖς μὲν ἣν ἐλάχομεν ἡσυχίαν ἀσπαστῶς ἐδεξάμεθα καὶ τοὺς ὀνησιφόρους αὐτῆς καὶ ἡδίστους τρυγῶμεν καρπούς, ὁ δὲ φιλόχριστος ἡμῶν βασιλεύς, τῆς εὐσεβείας καρπὸν τὴν βασιλείαν δρεψάμενος, ἀπαρχὰς τῆς βασιλείας τῷ Δοτῆρι τῆς βασιλείας προσήνεγκεν τῶν χειμαζομένων ἐκκλησιῶν τὴν γαλήνην,[a] τὸ τῆς πολεμηθείσης πίστεως κράτος, τῶν εὐαγγελικῶν δογμάτων τὴν νίκην. προστέθεικεν δὲ τούτοις τῆς ἡμετέρας ἀδικίας τὴν ἴασιν.

Τίς γὰρ τοιαύτην ἢ τοσαύτην ἀδικίαν ἀκήκοεν πώποτε; τίς ἀπὼν ἀνδροφόνος κατεδικάσθη; τίς γάμων ἐπίβουλος μὴ παρὼν κατεκρίθη; τίς τοιχωρύχος, ἢ τυμβωρύχος, ἢ γόης, ἢ ἱερόσυλος, ἢ ἄλλο τι τῶν τοῖς νόμοις ἀπειρημένων τολμήσας, δραμεῖν μὲν εἰς τὸ δικαστήριον ἐπειγόμενος ἐκωλύθη, ἀνῃρέθη δέ, πόρρωθεν ὤν, τῇ τοῦ δικάζοντος ψήφῳ; ἀλλ᾽ ἐπ᾽ ἐκείνων μὲν γέγονεν τοιοῦτον οὐδέν· οἱ γὰρ νόμοι κελεύουσι πλησίον ἀλλήλων πρὸ τοῦ δικάζοντος ἑστάναι καὶ τὸν διώκοντα καὶ τὸν φεύγοντα, καὶ τοὺς προφανεῖς ἐλέγχους ἀναμένειν τὸν δικαστὴν καὶ τηνικαῦτα λοιπὸν ἢ ὡς ἀθῷον ἀφιέναι, ἢ κολάζειν ὡς ὑπεύθυνον ταῖς γραφαῖς.

Ἐφ᾽ ἡμῶν δὲ πᾶν τοὐναντίον συνέβη· τὰ βασιλικὰ μὲν γὰρ ἡμᾶς γράμματα καταλαβεῖν τὴν πολυθρύλητον ἐκείνην ἐκώλυσε σύνοδον, οἱ δὲ δικαιότατοι δικασταὶ τὸν ἀπόντα κατέκριναν, οὐ δικάσαντες, μᾶλλον δὲ καὶ λίαν ἐπαινέσαντες τὰ δῆθεν εἰς

a. *Cf.* Mk 4.35–39.

139. To Anatolius, the Patrician[1]

(1) Here we are enjoying a harvest of sweet delights, the fruits of the peace and quiet that, much to our joy, have fallen to our lot, but our emperor, devoted to Christ, has reaped for himself a throne, the fruit of his piety and to the one who bestowed it upon him has made offering of the first fruits of his rule: the calm seas for the churches that were engulfed in storm,[a] the victory of the faith that had been under attack, the triumph of gospel doctrine. To all of this he has added the righting of the wrong done to us.[2]

Who has ever heard of such an injustice, of this sort, of this enormity? What murderer was ever judged guilty in his absence? Was ever any schemer against another man's marriage condemned though not physically present? What burglar, tomb-robber, conjurer, profaner of the sacred, what criminal, what shameless perpetrator of any other act proscribed by law, has ever been prevented, if he so wished, from speedy recourse to the judgment seat or been put to death by sentence of a judge when far from court? Nothing of the sort has ever been done in cases such as these, and that's because the laws prescribe that plaintiff and defendant must stand side-by-side before the judge, and the judge must wait for the presentation of clear proofs, and then, and only then, either dismiss the defendant if innocent, or punish him if guilty as charged.

In my case, it was the complete opposite. First, I was forbidden to attend that most renowned of councils. Then that most just of juries condemned me in my absence, not passing true judgment, but rather voicing loud endorsement of documents submitted in accusation

1. For Anatolius, *v. ep.* 45 n. 1; for the date, *v. ep.* 136 n. 1. As Azéma (vol. 2, pp. 142f., n. 2) points out, *epp.* 139–41 are the latest of the extant letters of Theodoret, since we have nothing but a fragment of a letter (to the Nestorian bishop John of Aegeae) dating to the period following the Council of Chalcedon; *v.* Richard, "La lettre de Théodoret."

2. For the deposition of Theodoret at the Second Council of Ephesus and his consequent exile, *v.* Intro., sec. 4.8.

κατηγορίαν ἡμῶν ἐπιδοθέντα συγγράμματα. καὶ οὔτε θεῖος νόμος οὔτε ἀνθρώπων αἰδὼς διεκώλυσεν τὴν σφαγήν, ἀλλὰ προσέταττε μὲν ὁ πρόεδρος, προέμενος τὴν ἀλήθειαν καὶ τὴν δυναστείαν θεραπεύων τὴν πρόσκαιρον, ὑπήκουον δὲ οἱ ταὐτὰ ἡμῖν φρονοῦντες, καὶ τῶν δογμάτων κοινωνοῦντες, καὶ τὰ ἡμέτερα ἐπὶ πλεῖστον θαυμάσαντες.

(2) Ἀλλ᾽ ὅμως ὁ χαλεπὸς ἐκεῖνος καιρὸς τῶν μὲν τὴν προδοσίαν, τῶν δὲ τὴν δειλίαν διήλεγξεν, ἡμῖν δὲ παρέσχεν ἀφορμὴν παρρησίας τὰ ὑπὲρ τῆς ἀληθείας παθήματα, καὶ κεχάρισται ἡμῖν ὁ Δεσπότης Χριστὸς *οὐ μόνον τὸ εἰς αὐτὸν πιστεύειν, ἀλλὰ καὶ τὸ ὑπὲρ αὐτοῦ πάσχειν·*[b] χάρισμα γάρ ἐστι μέγιστον τὰ ὑπὲρ τοῦ Δεσπότου παθήματα, ὁ δὲ θεῖος Ἀπόστολος καὶ τῶν μεγάλων ταῦτα θαυμάτων προτίθησιν. ἐπὶ τούτοις κἀγὼ σεμνυνόμενος, ὁ χαμαιπετὴς καὶ σμικρός, καὶ μηδεμίαν ἔχων ἄλλην καυχήματος ἀφορμήν, Τὴν Ὑμετέραν Μεγαλοφυΐαν παρακαλῶ τὰς εὐχαριστηρίους φωνὰς ὑπὲρ Τῆς Ἐμῆς Εὐτελείας τῷ φιλοχρίστῳ προσενεγκεῖν βασιλεῖ καὶ τῇ εὐσεβεστάτῃ καὶ θεοφιλεστάτῃ αὐγούστῃ, τῇ τῶν καλῶν διδασκάλῳ, ὅτι τοιούτοις δώροις τὸν μεγαλόδωρον Δεσπότην ἠμείψαντο καὶ τῆς βασιλείας ὑποβάθραν καὶ κρηπῖδα τὸν ὑπὲρ τῆς εὐσεβείας ἐποιήσαντο ζῆλον. πρὸς δὲ τούτοις, καὶ ἱκετεύσατε Αὐτῶν Τὴν Θεοφιλῆ Κορυφὴν τέλος ἐπιθεῖναι τοῖς ὁρισθεῖσι καλῶς καὶ συναγαγεῖν σύνοδον, μὴ πάλιν ταραχοποιῶν καὶ συγκλύδων ἀνθρώπων πεπληρωμένην, ἀλλὰ τούτων μὲν πάντων κεχωρισμένην, κρινόντων δέ, τῶν τὰ θεῖα περὶ πολλοῦ ποιουμένων καὶ πάντων ὁμοῦ τῶν ἀνθρωπίνων τὴν ἀλήθειαν προτιμώντων. εἰ δὲ βούλεται Αὐτῶν Τὸ Κράτος τὴν παλαιὰν πρυτανεῦσαι ταῖς ἐκκλησίαις εἰρήνην· βούλεται δέ· ἀντιβολήσατε Αὐτῶν Τὴν Εὐσέβειαν παρεῖναι τοῖς πραττομένοις ἵνα τοὺς

l. 27 ταὐτὰ *scr. Az.* : τὰ ταυτὰ *NZ*, *A^{pc} (Car.?)* : ταῦτα *corr. Cir.*, *scr. Sir.* : ταυτὰ *Nös.* **l. 43** ἠμείψαντο *scr. Az.* : -ατο *codd.*, *Sir. Nös. Azéma's correction is necessary; the sg. would make no sense in coördination with the following ἐποιήσαντο.*

b. Phil 1.29

against me.[3] Neither the law of God nor regard for human decency stood in the way of this murderous violence, in which the president of the council, disregarding the truth and currying favor with a merely temporal authority, issued his commands, and even those who agreed with my position, who shared my teachings on doctrine, and had the highest opinion of my work did what they were told to do.[4]

(2) That terrible moment laid bare the treachery of some and the cowardice of others, but for us, our suffering in the service of truth provided some grounds to hope that God may hear us. Yes, our Master Christ has granted us "not only the grace to believe in him but also to suffer for his sake."[b] As you know, to suffer for the Master is the very greatest of gifts; indeed, the holy Apostle ranked it higher than great miracles. Priding myself on these sufferings, though lowly and unimportant, and lacking any other ground for boasting, I entreat Your Eminence to offer, on behalf of My Insignificance, expressions of gratitude to the emperor, devoted to Christ, and the right reverend Augusta, beloved of God and counsellor of righteousness, for, in making this sort of return to their munificent Master, they have established zeal for orthodoxy as the support and foundation of their throne.[5] Moreover, please entreat Their Royal Highnesses, devoted to God, to give full effect to their decisions by calling a council—not another mob of rioters, but closed to men of that sort—a council of men who will render judgment, who will regard religion as of the utmost importance and place truth before any and all human considerations. If it is the will of Their Victorious Might to restore to the churches the peace they once enjoyed—and it is their will—request of Their Reverences that they attend the proceedings in person so their very presence may inspire terror in those who are

3. Theodoret may be referring to the imperial letter relegating him to his diocese and forbidding him to attend the Council; *v. ep.* 80.1 and Intro., sec. 4.4.

4. Theodoret is thinking of Domnus of Antioch and other bishops of the Antiochene patriarchy who acquiesced in his deposition; *cf. ep.* 125.2.

5. For Marcian, the successor of Theodosius II, *v. ep.* 134 n. 3; for his consort (the Augusta), Pulcheria, the elder sister and mentor of Theodosius II, *v. ep.* 43 n. 1.

τἀναντία προαιρουμένους τῇ παρουσίᾳ δεδίξηται, καὶ μηδένα ἀντίπαλον ἡ Ἀλήθεια ἔχῃ, ἀλλ᾽ αὐτὴ καθ᾽ αὑτὴν ἐξετάζῃ τῶν πραγμάτων τὴν φύσιν καὶ τὸν τῶν ἀποστολικῶν δογμάτων χαρακτῆρα.

(3) Ταῦτα δὲ ἐξαιτῶ παρὰ Τῆς Ὑμετέρας Μεγαλοφυΐας, οὐχ ὡς τὴν Κύρρον πάλιν ἰδεῖν ποθῶν· οἶδεν γὰρ Ὑμῶν Τὸ Μέγεθος τῆς πολίχνης τὴν ἐρημίαν, ἧς ἀμηγέπη τὸ εἰδεχθὲς κατεκρύψαμεν ταῖς τῶν παντοδαπῶν οἰκοδομημάτων πολυτελείαις· ἀλλ᾽ ἵνα δειχθῇ καὶ τὰ παρ᾽ ἡμῶν κηρυττόμενα τοῖς ἀποστολικοῖς συμβαίνοντα δόγμασιν, καὶ νόθα καὶ κίβδηλα τὰ τῶν ἐναντίων εὑρέματα. τούτου γὰρ γιγνομένου, σὺν Θεῷ δὲ εἰρήσθω, τὰς λειπομένας ἡμέρας σὺν εὐθυμίᾳ βιώσομεν ἔνθα ἂν ἡμᾶς διάγειν ὁ Δεσπότης κελεύσῃ. πρέπει δὲ ὑμῖν, εὐσεβείᾳ συντεθραμμένοις καὶ τῆς ἀρετῆς κεκτημένοις τὸν πλοῦτον, τόνδε τὸν ζῆλον ἀναλαβεῖν καί, προθυμίαν ἔχοντας καὶ τὸν εὐσεβέστατον βασιλέα καὶ τὴν φιλόχριστον αὐγοῦσταν, ταῖς παρακλήσεσι προθυμοτέρους ἐργάσασθαι ἵνα τῷ ἀξιεπαίνῳ ζήλῳ τὴν πανεύφημον αὐτῶν βασιλείαν κρατύνωσιν.

l. 51 εἰρήνην βούλεται δὲ N^{pcm1}, *ZA, Sir. Nös.* : ε. N^{ac}, *Az. Azéma, who reports that only ZA carry* βούλεται δὲ, *must have missed the superscript sign of insertion ad loc. and the two words written in the lefthand margin by the first hand of N. The longer reading is certainly rougher than the shorter and could have originated as a dittography, yet we find such parenthetical and resumptive phraseology elsewhere: v., e.g., ep. 137: εἰ δὲ πιστεύομεν, ὥσπεροῦν πιστεύομεν, etc.* **ll. 53f.** μηδένα ἀντίπαλον *scripsi* : μηδὲν ἀ. *codd., edd.* = *"so that the Truth face no obstacle." It seems likely that Thdt. would have spoken of personal antagonists to the personified Ἀλήθεια (Truth; v. n. 6). The phrase is attested in Apoph. lac., p. 212D. The final* -α *might well have been lost in an haplography.* **l. 63** γινομένου *codd.* : γεν- *Az. V. "Intro. to the Gk. Text," sec. III.B.5.a.* **l. 67** ἔχοντας *scr. Sir. Nös. Az.* : -τα *codd. Sirmond's correction reëstablishes the parallelism between* προθυμίαν ἔχοντας *and the following* προθυμοτέρους.

planning disruption, and there be no enemy to oppose the Truth. Let Truth herself and by herself look deeply into these issues to identify which teachings bear the hallmark of the apostles.[6]

(3) If I make these requests of Your Eminence, it is not because I yearn to see Cyrus again—Your Lordship is well aware of the isolation of that town whose ugliness I did my best to cover up with many building projects and at great cost—but so that my preaching may be shown to be in agreement with the teachings of the apostles, and the inventions of my opponents, doctrines of illegitimate birth, counterfeit coinage.[7] After that has been accomplished—with the help of God!—we shall be glad to live out the rest of our days wherever our Master would have us dwell. But here is a fitting task for you, a man raised in the faith, richly endowed with virtue: arm yourself with zeal, and, applying the force of your counsels, encourage the right reverend emperor and the Augusta, devoted to Christ, already determined as they are, to an even greater determination to make their praiseworthy zeal for religion the firm support of their glorious reign.

6. Like Jackson, I take the feminine demonstrative pronoun (αὕτη) to refer to the just mentioned "Truth" (Ἀλήθεια) and make Truth the subject of the verb ἐξετάζῃ ("look deeply into"). Azéma, however, understanding the demonstrative to refer back to Αὐτῶν τὴν Εὐσέβειαν, makes the royal couple the subject of ἐξετάζῃ ("qu'elles-mêmes examinent la nature des faits," *etc.*). Although Theodoret sometimes attributes considerable theological expertise to laymen, he would certainly have considered the christological debate to be the proper concern of bishops; *v.* Petruccione, "The Audience."

7. Theodoret's use of the term εὑρέματα may involve a double entendre. Given his intention to characterize the doctrines of his opponents as recent innovations in contrast to longstanding Christian tradition, I have translated "inventions." Yet Sophocles (*O.T.* 1106) had used the singular form of a foundling, and Theodoret immediately goes on to contrast doctrines of illegitimate origin (νόθα) with those that can be traced back to the apostles.

140. ΑΣΠΑΡΙ ΥΠΑΤΙΚΩΙ ΚΑΙ ΠΑΤΡΙΚΙΩΙ

Ἔδει καὶ τοῦτο τοῖς ἄλλοις Τῆς Ὑμετέρας Ἀνδρίας κατορθώμασι προστεθῆναι· τὸ τὸν εὐσεβέστατον ἡμῶν καὶ φιλόχριστον βασιλέα, ὃν ἡ θεία χάρις ἐπ' εὐεργεσίᾳ τῶν ἀρχομένων ἀνέδειξεν, διὰ Τῆς Ὑμετέρας Μεγαλοφυΐας μαθεῖν τὴν τῆς καθ' ἡμῶν ἀδικίας ὑπερβολὴν καὶ λῦσαι νόμῳ νόμον, δικαίῳ τὸν οὐ τοιοῦτον. εἰ γὰρ καὶ ἡμεῖς, ὑπὸ τῆς θείας ἐρειδόμενοι προμηθείας, ἀφορμὴν ἀγαθῶν ἐποιήσαμεν τὴν νομισθεῖσαν τιμωρίαν καὶ τὴν ἡσυχίαν ἀσπαστῶς ἐδεξάμεθα, ἀλλ' οὖν ἄδικα πεπόνθαμεν καὶ παράνομα, οὐδὲν μὲν πεπλημμεληκότες ὧν ἐσυκοφάντησαν ἡμᾶς οἱ τῆς ἀληθείας ἐχθροί, τὰ δὲ τῶν τὰ μέγιστα τετολμηκότων πεπονθότες δεινά. μᾶλλον δέ, καὶ τούτων ὑπέστημεν χαλεπώτερα· ἀκρίτως γὰρ καὶ ἐκρίθημεν, καὶ ἀπόντες κατεδικάσθημεν, καί, βασιλικοῖς γράμμασιν κωλυθέντες καταλαβεῖν τὴν Ἔφεσον, τὴν δικαιοτάτην τῶν ἱερῶν δικαστῶν ἐδεξάμεθα ψῆφον. ἀλλὰ ταῦτα πάντα λέλυκεν ὁ γαληνότατος βασιλεὺς διὰ τὴν Τῆς Ὑμετέρας Μεγαλοπρεπείας σπουδήν.

Ἐγὼ δέ, ἀδικεῖν νομίσας, εἰ σι|γήσαιμι καὶ μηδὲ χάριν ὁμολογήσαιμι, ἐπὶ τάδε ἦλθον τὰ γράμματα, δι' ὧν Τὸ Ὑμέτερον παρακαλῶ Μέγεθος τὰς ὑπὲρ ἡμῶν εὐφημίας καὶ τῷ νικηφόρῳ

Title Ασπάρι ὑπατικῷ *Nös. Az.* : Α. -τῷ *codd., Sir.* : Αβιένῳ -τῳ *coni. Gar.*
l. 18 σι|γήσαιμι *In codice N ordo foliorum turbatus est: fol. 173v explicit* σι-, *fol. 184r incipit* -γήσαιμι.

140. To Aspar, Consular and Patrician[1]

That was yet another excellent deed for Your Valor to add to so many others! Thanks to Your Eminence our right reverend emperor, devoted to Christ, chosen by God's grace for the welfare of his subjects, learned of the extraordinary injustice perpetrated against us and, with a just law, undid another most unjust.[2] Relying on the support of God's providential care, we took this supposed punishment as a source of blessings and gladly welcomed the peace and quiet. Yet it remains the case that we were victims of both injustice and illegal procedure, since, despite our innocence of all the accusations fabricated against us by those enemies of the truth, we were made to suffer penalties reserved for the most reckless criminals. Indeed, we have endured far worse than those: brought to trial but given no trial, we were condemned in our absence, and, though the emperor's letter prevented us from going to Ephesus, we still received that most just of sentences passed by our sacerdotal judges.[3] But now, through the good offices of Your Excellency, his Most Serene Highness has undone all of that.

Thinking I would myself be guilty of injustice if I kept silent and gave no expression to my gratitude, I have ventured on this letter and entreat Your Lordship to present our congratulations to the glorious

1. The recipient of this letter is not entirely certain. Garnier (p. 234), noting that Theodoret reserves the title "consul" for the year in which his correspondent actually holds that position, emended the name "Aspar" to "Avienus," the name of the Consul of the East in 450. Nösselt, however, suggested changing "consul" to "consular," and retained the name "Aspar," an expedient accepted by Azéma, whom I have followed. Flavius Aspar had held the position of Consul of the West in 434 and thus served as colleague of Areobindas (*v. ep.* 23 n. 1). He was one of the most important generals of the fifth century and held the rank of *Magister utriusque Militiae* for many years, possibly continuously from 431–71. He was present when the dying Theodosius named Marcian as his successor. He might himself have succeeded to the throne, but for the fact that he was an Arian Christian; *v.* "F. Ardabur Aspar," *PLRE*, vol. 2, pp. 164–69, and *cf. ep.* 97 n. 2. For the title, "patrician," *v. ep.* 23 n. 1. For the date of this letter, *v. epp.* 136 n. 1 and 139 n. 1.

2. For Marcian and his consort Pulcheria, *v. ep.* 139 n. 5.

3. For the deposition of Theodoret at the Second Council of Ephesus and his consequent exile, *v.* Intro., sec. 4.8.

καὶ φιλοχρίστῳ βασιλεῖ προσενεγκεῖν καὶ τῇ θεοφιλεστάτῃ καὶ εὐσεβεστάτῃ Αὐγούστῃ, ὑπὲρ ὧν, εἰς δύναμιν, τὸν ἀγαθὸν ἱκετεύω Δεσπότην ὥστε αὐτῶν βεβαίαν φυλάξαι τὴν βασιλείαν, τῶν μὲν ὑπηκόων φιλανθρώπως προμηθουμένην, τοὺς δὲ πολεμίους δεδιττομένην, καὶ τὴν ἀξιέπαινον εἰρήνην πρυτανεύουσαν ἅπασιν. ἱκετεῦσαι δὲ αὐτοὺς παρακληθήτω Τὸ Ὑμέτερον Μέγεθος δοῦναι λύσιν τελείαν τῷ τῆς Ἐκκλησίας χειμῶνι καὶ κελεῦσαι συναθροισθῆναι σύνοδον· μὴ πάλιν τῶν θορυβεῖν εἰωθότων, τὸ συνέδριον ταραττόντων, ἀλλὰ μεθ' ἡσυχίας τῶν τὰ θεῖα πεπαιδευμένων, τὰ μὲν ἀποστολικὰ δόγματα βεβαιούντων, ἀποκρινόντων δὲ τὰ νόθα καὶ τῆς ἀληθείας ἀλλότρια· ἵνα καὶ τὸ ἐντεῦθεν δρέψηται κέρδος Τὸ Ὑμέτερον Μέγεθος.

emperor, devoted to Christ, and to the right reverend Augusta, beloved of God. With all my heart, I beg our good Master to make their rule secure, generously devoted to the good of their subjects, a terror to their enemies, and, for all, a source of honorable peace. I beseech Your Lordship to hear my plea and entreat them to put an end, once and for all, to the storm within the Church and give order for the summoning of a council, not another council of rioters who disrupt the assemblage, but one conducted in calm deliberation by theological experts who will confirm the apostolic teachings and reject what is spurious and foreign to the truth. I make this request in the hope that it prove yet another source of profit for your Lordship.

141. ΒΙΓΚΟΜΑΛΩΙ ΜΑΓΙΣΤΡΩΙ

Λίαν ἐθαύμασα γνοὺς ὅτι, πάμπαν ἀγνοοῦσα τὰ καθ' ἡμᾶς Ἡ Ὑμετέρα Μεγαλοπρέπεια, μόνην δὲ τὴν καθ' ἡμῶν ἀδικίαν μαθοῦσα, συνήγορος ἡμῶν ἀνεφάνη καὶ πάντα πόρον ἐκίνησεν ὥστε διαλῦσαι τὰ καθ' ἡμῶν τυρευθέντα. ἀλλὰ Τῷ μὲν Ὑμετέρῳ Μεγέθει δώσει πάντως τὰς ἀντιδόσεις ὁ μεγαλόδωρος Κύριος· ὁ γὰρ ὑπὲρ σμικροῦ ὕδατος μισθὸν δώσειν ἐπαγγειλάμενος,[a] μείζους παρέξει δήπουθεν ἀμοιβὰς τοῖς τὰ μείζονα δεδωκόσιν.

Ἡμεῖς δὲ τοιαῦτα πεπόνθαμεν οὐ μόνον παρὰ τῶν προδηλοτάτων ἐχθρῶν, ἀλλὰ καὶ παρὰ τῶν γνησίων, ὡς ὑπελαμβάνομεν, φίλων· ὑπὸ μὲν ἐκείνων πολεμηθέντες, ὑπὸ δὲ τούτων προδοθέντες· οἷα ἢ οὐδεὶς ἢ ἄγαν ὀλίγοι τῶν παλαιῶν ὑπέστησαν. τίς γὰρ τοιαύτης δίκης ἀκήκοεν πώποτε; τίς, τὸν κατηγορούμενον πρὸ πέντε καὶ τριάκοντα πεδήσας σταθμῶν, ἐκέλευσεν δικάσαι τῷ μὴ παρόντι τοὺς δικαστάς; τίς δὲ οὕτως ὠμὸς καὶ θηριώδης γεγένηται δικαστὴς ὥστε δικάσαι ἀνδράσιν ὧν τῆς φωνῆς οὐκ ἐπήκουσεν, καὶ οὐ δικάσαι μόνον, ἀλλὰ καὶ καταδικάσαι, καὶ τοῦτο λίαν ὠμῶς καὶ θηριωδῶς; τοῦ γὰρ Κυρίου προστεταχότος τὸν πλημμελοῦντα τῶν ἀδελφῶν καὶ τῆς συμβουλίας οὐκ ἀνεχόμενον μετὰ πρώτην, καὶ δευτέραν, καὶ τρίτην νουθεσίαν ὕστερον ἔχειν ὡς τὸν ἐθνικὸν καὶ τὸν τελώνην,[b] οἱ ὀρθότατοι καὶ δικαιότατοι κριταὶ οὐδὲ ὧν τοῖς ἐθνικοῖς καὶ τελώναις μεταδιδόασιν τοῖς ὁμοπίστοις μετέδοσαν· ἐκείνους μὲν γὰρ καὶ ὁρῶσιν καὶ ἔστιν ὅτε προσδιαλέγονται καὶ μετὰ πλείστης ὅσης τιμῆς εἴπερ τινὰ ἔχοιεν ἀξιώματος περιφάνειαν· ἡμᾶς δὲ προσέταξαν μὴ στέγης, μὴ ὕδατος, μὴ λόγου μεταλαχεῖν. οὕτως ἐβουλήθησαν μιμηταὶ γενέσθαι *τοῦ*

l. 26 λόγου *N* : ἄρτου *coni.* (*fort. recte*) *Car.* = *"we were to be denied shelter, water, indeed, even sustenance."* : ὅλου *scr. Onor. A, edd.* = *"we were to be denied . . . absolutely everything"* (?). *The reading of N may bear the sense "contact by word." Elsewhere the sequence* μὴ στέγης, μὴ ὕδατος, μὴ λόγου,

a. Mt 10.42 b. Mt 18.17

141. To Vincomalus, Master of the Offices[1]

I was amazed to find out that Your Excellency, though knowing nothing more about our case than the fact of the injustice that was done to us, became our advocate and, leaving no stone unturned, put an end to the intrigues concocted against us. There can be no doubt that the Lord will generously requite Your Lordship for this; after all, if he promised to bestow a reward for just a sip of water,[a] I am certain he will make greater returns to those who have made greater gifts.

Ancient history supplies no, or at least very few, precedents for the sufferings we have endured at the hands of our declared enemies—who made open war against us—and even of those we imagined to be our best friends—who betrayed us.[2] Who has ever even heard of such a travesty of justice? Who has ever tied the defendant up thirty-five days' journey away and then ordered a jury to pass judgment on his case in his absence? Has there ever been a judge of such wild cruelty as to hear the case of men whose voice he has never heard—not just hear their case, but even pass sentence, a sentence of such uncivilized brutality? Though the Lord has laid down the rule that a sinner who disregards the admonitions of the brethren once, twice, and a third time, is then, and only then, to be treated as a gentile or a tax-collector,[b] these most righteous and just of judges have treated their fellows in faith worse than they would have treated even gentiles or tax-collectors. Those they allow into their sight and sometimes even talk to them—and that with oh-so-much deference should they be men of prestige and rank. But, according to their sentence, we were to be denied shelter, water, indeed, any and all interaction. That was how they chose to follow the example of our Father in heaven, "who

1. On Vincomalus, *cf.* SC, vol. 40, p. 51; Vincomalus was Master of the Offices for the East in 451–52 (on this title, *v. ep.* 58 n. 1) and Consul of the East in 453. A Christian, he attended four sessions of the Council of Chalcedon, and in retirement, became a monk; *v.* "Ioannes Vinomalus," *PLRE,* vol. 2, pp. 1169f. This letter must have been written not long prior to the convening of the Council; *v. ep.* 139 n. 1.

2. For the deposition of Theodoret at the Second Council of Ephesus and his consequent exile, *v. ep.* 139 n. 2; for the perfidy of his supposed allies, *v. ep.* 139 n. 4.

Πατρὸς ἡμῶν *τοῦ ἐν οὐρανοῖς, ὃς ἀνατέλλει τὸν ἥλιον αὐτοῦ ἐπὶ πονηροὺς καὶ ἀγαθοὺς καὶ βρέχει ἐπὶ δικαίους καὶ ἀδίκους.*[c] ἀλλὰ τούτους μὲν ἐάσω· ἐγγὺς γὰρ τὸ τοῦ Δεσπότου κριτήριον, ἔνθα οὐ ζητεῖται σχημάτων ὑπόκρισις, ἀλλὰ πραγμάτων ἀλήθεια.

Τὸ δὲ Ὑμέτερον παρακαλῶ Μέγεθος τὴν ὑπὲρ ἡμῶν τῆς χάριτος ὁμολογίαν τῷ φιλοχρίστῳ καὶ νικηφόρῳ προσενεγκεῖν βασιλεῖ καὶ τῇ εὐσεβεστάτῃ καὶ θεοφιλεστάτῃ Αὐγούστῃ, ὅτι τῇ εὐσεβεῖ βασιλείᾳ ῥίζαν ἔδωκαν ἰσχυρὰν τὴν εὐσέβειαν, καὶ ἀντιβολῆσαι Αὐτῶν Τὸ Κράτος βεβαίαν πρυτανεῦσαι ταῖς ἐκκλησίαις τὴν εἰρήνην καὶ σύνοδον ἀθροισθῆναι κελεῦσαι· μὴ τῶν ταραχοποιῶν πάλιν ἀνθρώπων διακυκώντων τὸν σύλλογον, ἀλλὰ τῶν τῆς ἀληθείας ἐραστῶν τὴν ἀποστολικὴν κρατυνόντων διδασκαλίαν καὶ ἀποκηρυττόντων τὴν καινὴν ταύτην καὶ κίβδηλον αἵρεσιν· ἵνα καὶ τῶν ἀξιεράστων τούτων πόνων παρὰ τοῦ φιλανθρώπου Κυρίου κομίσησθε τοὺς καρπούς.

---

would seem weak rhetoric, but λόγου *here completes an antithesis contrasting the interaction allowed with publicans and pagans with the isolation imposed on Thdt.; cf. ep. 90, c. n.* (λόγου). *Cariofilo's conjecture gives good sense and seems stylistically unexceptionable; "bread" goes well with "water" and accords with Thdt.'s complaint in ep. 135.2 that, but for the support given by the monks of his monastery, he might have died of starvation. Furthermore, in his exposition of 1Cor 10.17 (οἱ γὰρ πάντες ἐκ τοῦ ἑνὸς ἄρτου μετέχομεν), Thdt. used the juncture ἄρτου + μεταλαγχ-; v. PG, vol. 82, col. 305, ll. 17f.: ἐπειδὴ πάντες ἐκ τοῦ ἑνὸς ἄρτου μεταλαγχάνομεν. Still, the very plausibility and smoothness of the conjecture raises suspicion. Onorio's emendation seems impossible. TLG proximity searches (within five and ten words) turn up no other attestation of ὅλου with either the impf. or the aor. stem of μεταλαγχάνω.* **ll. 35f.** βεβαίαν πρυτανεῦσαι ταῖς ἐκκλησίαις εἰρήνην *codd.* : β. π. ταῖς ἐ. τὴν εἰ. *scr.* (*fort. recte*) *Sir. Az. = "to make the peace of the churches firm" (Jackson). Sirmond's conjecture, presupposing a factitive construction (like the preceding* ῥίζαν ἔδωκαν ἰσχυρὰν τὴν εὐσέβειαν), *could well be correct, but the clause makes good sense as a simple transitive active; cf. Q. 1 in 2Par., p. 266, ll. 23f.: καὶ βάρβαροι πολλάκις συνεσθίοντες πολεμίοις βεβαίαν εἰρήνην φυλάττουσι.* **l. 39** καινὴν *scr. Cir., edd.* : κεν- *NZ = "cast out from among us this meaningless and spurious heresy." Confusion between forms of καινός and κένος recurs throughout the Thdt. ms. traditon; cf. epp. 143, c. n.* (καινὴν) *and 144, c. n.* (καινῆς); *Eran., flor. 2, p. 187, l. 22 and flor. 3, p. 248, l. 31. For the medieval scribes, the alternatives are, of course, homophone. Thdt., however, attacks heresy not as meaningless, but as of recent, as opposed to apostolic, origin. The same phrase, τὴν καινὴν ταύτην καὶ κίβδηλον αἵρεσιν, occurs in ep. 126.1 without var.*

c. Mt 5.45 (NT var.)

makes the sun rise on the wicked as well as the good and makes the rain fall on just and unjust alike."[c] But I say no more about them; the judgment of God is coming soon, and then there will be no question of hypocritical posturing, just the truth revealed in our actions.

I ask Your Lordship to convey our expression of gratitude to the glorious emperor, devoted to Christ and to the right reverend Augusta, beloved of God,[3] for planting their throne upon the firm roots of orthodoxy, and to beseech their Majesties to confer a secure peace on the churches by giving order for the gathering of a council, not a council of rioters who will disrupt the assemblage, but of lovers of the truth who will confirm the teachings of the apostles and cast out from among us this spurious heresy of recent birth.[4] This I urge in the hope that you will reap from the hand of our good Lord the fruits of your fine deeds.

3. For Marcian and his consort Pulcheria, *v. ep.* 139 n. 5.
4. *Cf. ep.* 139 n. 7.

142. ΜΑΡΚΕΛΛΩΙ ΑΡΧΙΜΑΝΔΡΙΤΗΙ ΤΩΝ ΑΚΟΙΜΗΤΩΝ

Λαμπρύνει μὲν Ὑμῶν Τὴν Θεοσέβειαν ὁ ἀξιέπαινος βίος, τῆς τῶν ἀγγέλων πολιτείας ἐν τῇ γῇ τὴν εἰκόνα δεικνύς, λαμπρότερον δὲ τοῦτον ἀπέφηνεν ὁ ὑπὲρ τῆς ἀποστολικῆς πίστεως ζῆλος· ὅπερ γάρ ἐστιν πλοίῳ μὲν τρόπις, οἰκίᾳ δὲ θεμέλιος, τοῦτο τοῖς εὐσεβεῖν προαιρουμένοις ἡ τῶν εὐαγγελικῶν δογμάτων ἀλήθεια. ταύτης δὲ πολεμηθείσης ἐκθύμως ὑπερηθλήσατε, οὐχ ὡς ἀσθενούσης προκινδυνεύοντες, ἀλλὰ τὴν φιλόθεον ἐπιδεικνύντες διάθεσιν· ἡ γὰρ τοῦ Δεσπότου Χριστοῦ διδασκαλία τὸ σταθερὸν ἔχει καὶ βέβαιον κατὰ τὴν αὐτοῦ τοῦ Σωτῆρος ὑπόσχεσιν· *Πύλαι* γὰρ *ᾅδου*, φησίν, *οὐ κατισχύσουσιν αὐτῆς.*[a]

Ὑπὲρ ταύτης καὶ ἡμᾶς ἀτιμασθῆναι καὶ σφαγῆναι ὁ φιλάνθρωπος καὶ μεγαλόδωρος ἠξίωσεν Κύριος· τὴν γὰρ δὴ ἀτιμίαν τιμήν, καὶ τὴν σφαγὴν ζωὴν ὑπειλήφαμεν· ἠκούσαμεν γὰρ τοῦ Ἀποστόλου λέγοντος, ὅτι Ἡμῖν ἀπὸ Θεοῦ *ἐχαρίσθη οὐ μόνον τὸ εἰς αὐτὸν πιστεύειν, ἀλλὰ καὶ τὸ ὑπὲρ αὐτοῦ πάσχειν.*[b]

a. Mt 16.18 b. Phil 1.29 (NT var.)

142. To Marcellus,[1] Archimandrite of the Acoimetoi[2]

Your Reverence enjoys the distinction of your exemplary way of life, an image on earth of the life of the angels, yet your life gains more splendor still from your zeal in the cause of the apostolic faith. What the keel is to a ship, the foundation to a house, such is truth based on gospel doctrine for those who choose to adhere to orthodoxy. You stepped forward in courageous defense of the truth when an assault was mounted against it—not that you thought it without force of its own and in need of a champion, but to show forth for all to see the love of God that you have within you. Indeed, the teaching of our Master Christ has its own unshakable foundation as we know from the promise our Savior made when he said, "The gates of Hell will not prevail against it."[a]

Thanks to the goodness and generosity of our Lord, we too have been deemed worthy to suffer disgrace and to be sent to our slaughter. You see, as we understand things, the disgrace was an honor, and violent death life, for we paid good attention to the words of the Apostle, who says, "To us has been given by God the grace not only to believe, but also to suffer on his behalf."[b] But, "like one who was sleeping, the

1. The addressee was the second successor of St. Alexander. Canivet (pp. 33f.) points out that Theodoret never mentions Alexander in the *H. rel.* though he lived until about 430 and founded monasteries in the Syrian countryside to the west of the Euphrates, the home of Theodoret's ascetic heroes. Perhaps Theodoret had reservations about Alexander's insistence that monks be supported by alms rather than by their own manual labor. The date of this letter must be subsequent to the death of Theodosius but prior to Marcian's lifting of the ban, which kept Theodoret in exile from his see. Azéma places this letter around the same time as *epp.* 134f.

2. The community of the "non-sleepers" was founded in Constantinople by St. Alexander in the early fifth century. By the mid-fifth century, the monastery had been moved to a location "on the eastern shore of the Bosporus." "Pledged to perpetual praise of God," the monks were divided into three choirs, each of which performed a daily shift of eight hours; *v.* Talbot and Taft. The proper English transcription is "Acoemetoi," the nominative of a second declension form (-ος). Jackson, who printed "Acoemetae," mistakenly understood the genitive Ἀκοιμήτων to be derived from a masculine noun (-της) of the first declension. On the title, "archimandrite," *v. ep.* 27 n. 1.

ἀνέστη δὲ τάχιστα, *ὡς ὁ ὑπνῶν, Κύριος*[c] καὶ ἐνέφραξε μὲν τὰ στόματα τὰ λαλοῦντα[d] κατὰ τοῦ Θεοῦ βλασφημίαν καὶ καθ᾽ ἡμῶν ἀδικίαν, τὰς δὲ τῶν εὐσεβούντων γλώττας εἰς τὴν συνήθη ἀποστολὴν τὰ νάματα προχεῖν παρεσκεύασεν. ἡμεῖς δὲ τῆς ἡσυχίας τοὺς ἀξιεράστους τρυγῶμεν καρπούς, καί, τὴν μὲν τῶν ἐκκλησιῶν ζάλην ὁρῶντες, ἀλγοῦμεν, γαννύμεθα δὲ καὶ εὐφραινόμεθα, φροντίδων ἀπηλλαγμένοι.

Τῇ δὲ Θεοσεβείᾳ Σου ἀεὶ μὲν συνήσθημεν διὰ πάντα θαυμαζομένῃ, μέχρι δὲ τοῦ παρόντος οὐκ ἐγράψαμεν, οὐ τῶν τῆς ἀγάπης νόμων ὀλιγωροῦντες, ἀλλ᾽ ἀφορμήν τινα λαβεῖν γραμμάτων προσμένοντες. αὐτίκα νῦν τοῖς εὐσεβεστάτοις καὶ συνετωτάτοις συντετυχηκότες μονάζουσιν, οἳ παρὰ Τῆς Σῆς Ὁσιότητος ἑτέρων ἕνεκα χρειῶν ἀπεστάλησαν, εὐθὺς δεδράκαμεν τὸ ποθούμενον, καί, τὴν θεοφιλῆ σου περιπτυσσόμενοι κεφαλήν, παρακαλοῦμεν πρῶτον μὲν ἡμᾶς ἀνέχειν ταῖς προσευχαῖς, ἔπειτα δὲ καὶ γράμμασιν εὐφραίνειν· διὰ γὰρ τὴν θείαν χάριν ὑπὲρ τῶν ἀποστολικῶν πεπολεμήμεθα δογμάτων.

c. Ps 78.65 (LXX var.) d. Ps 63.11

Lord has risen up"[c] all at once and shut up the mouths spouting[d] blasphemy against God and injustice against us while making the tongues of the orthodox pour forth their streams of eloquence in support of the apostleship they have always served. As for us, we are enjoying a harvest of that most excellent fruit of peace and quiet, and, though grieved at the storm that has overtaken the churches, we are more than glad to be freed from our cares.

We have always taken pleasure in Your Reverence, for whom we have nothing but admiration. Yet up to this moment we have never written you, not out of disregard for the laws of love, but with the intention of grasping the first good reason for a letter. And just now that we have made the acquaintance of the monks—men of exceptional piety and prudence—that Your Holiness had sent here on other business, we have lost no time in achieving the accomplishment of our desire. Wrapping our arms around your head dear to God, we entreat you to sustain us with your prayers and then to cheer us with a letter, for, through the grace of God, we are under siege for our adherence to apostolic doctrine.

143. ΤΩΙ ΑΥΤΩΙ

Καὶ ἤδη δι᾽ ἑτέρων γραμμάτων Τὴν Σὴν προσείπομεν Θεοσέβειαν, τοῖς τιμιωτάτοις ἀδελφοῖς τοῖς ὑμετέροις τὴν ἐπιστολὴν δεδωκότες, καὶ νῦν δὲ πάλιν προσφθεγγόμεθά Σου Τὴν Ἁγιότητα· προτρέπει γὰρ ἡμᾶς τοῦτο ποιεῖν καὶ ὁ ἀξιάγαστος ὑμῶν βίος καὶ ὁ ἀξιέπαινος ζῆλος ὃν ὑπὲρ τῆς ἀποστολικῆς ἐπεδείξασθε πίστεως, οὐ βασιλικὴν δείσαντες δυναστείαν, οὐκ ἐπισκοπικὴν συμφωνίαν· εἰ γὰρ καὶ τῶν συνεληλυθότων οἱ πλεῖστοι βιασθέντες συνέθεντο, ἀλλ᾽ οὖν ταῖς ὑπογραφαῖς τὴν καινὴν ἐκράτυναν αἵρεσιν. Τὴν δὲ Ὑμετέραν Φιλοθεΐαν οὐδὲν τούτων διέσεισεν, ἀλλ᾽ ἐπὶ τῶν παλαιῶν διεμείνατε δογμάτων, ἃ καὶ διὰ τῶν προφητῶν καὶ τῶν ἀποστόλων φρονεῖν τὰς ἐκκλησίας ὁ Δεσπότης ἐδίδαξεν.

Τούτους καὶ ἡμεῖς τοὺς ὅρους φυλάττειν εὐχόμεθα καὶ τὴν εἰς τὸν ἕνα Πατέρα, καὶ τὸν ἕνα Υἱόν, καὶ τὸ ἓν Ἅγιον Πνεῦμα πίστιν τε καὶ ὁμολογίαν μέχρι τέλους διατηρῆσαι· ἡ γὰρ ἐνανθρώπησις τοῦ Μονογενοῦς οὐκ ηὔξησεν τῆς Τριάδος τὸν ἀριθμόν, ἀλλὰ μεμένηκεν, καὶ μετὰ τὴν σάρκωσιν, Τριὰς ἡ Τριάς· οὕτως γὰρ ἐξ ἀρχῆς ἐμαθητεύθημεν, οὕτως ἐπιστεύσαμεν, οὕτως ἐβαπτίσθημεν, οὕτως ἐκηρύξαμεν, οὕτως ἐβαπτίσαμεν, οὕτω διατελοῦμεν δοξάζοντες.

Περὶ δὲ τοῦ πατρὸς τῶν λαλούντων τὸ ψεῦδος,[a] ὁ Κύριος ἔφη, *Ὅταν λαλῇ τὸ ψεῦδος, ἐκ τῶν ἰδίων λαλεῖ,*[b] ἁρμόττει δὲ τοῖς μαθηταῖς τὰ περὶ τοῦ διδασκάλου ῥηθέντα·[c] καὶ γὰρ οὗτοι, ταῖς καθ᾽ ἡμῶν ψευδολογίαις χρησάμενοι, ἐκ τῶν ἰδίων λαλοῦσιν, οὐ τὰ ἡμέτερα λέγουσιν. ἡμᾶς δὲ ὁ Δεσπότης ψυχαγωγεῖ λέγων, *Μακάριοί ἐστε ὅταν ὀνειδίσωσιν ὑμᾶς, καὶ διώξωσιν, καὶ εἴπωσιν πᾶν πονηρὸν* ῥῆμα *καθ᾽ ὑμῶν ἕνεκεν ἐμοῦ, ψευδόμενοι· χαίρετε*

l. 9 καινὴν *ZA, N*$^{s.l.m1}$, *Az.* : κεν- *N*$^{i.l.}$ *Cf. ep.* 141, *c. n.* (καινὴν).

a. *Cf.* Ps 5.6; Jn 8.44. b. Jn 8.44 c. *Cf.* Mt 10.24f.; Jn 15.20.

143. To the Same[1]

Having already addressed ourselves to Your Reverence through the letter we entrusted to your honorable brethren,[2] we now send greetings to Your Sanctity a second time. We feel encouraged to this by your admirable way of life and the praiseworthy zeal for the apostolic faith of which you gave proof when you refused to allow yourself to be cowed by imperial might or the concurrence of bishops.[3] The fact is that, even if the majority of those who attended the council signed the acts only under duress, they still lent strength with their signatures to that heresy of recent origin. But Your Piety remained unshaken; you stood firm on the ancient doctrine that our Master, through the prophets and the apostles, has taught the churches to hold as their belief.

It is our prayer that we as well may defend these established doctrines and adhere to the end to the faith that confesses one Father, one Son, and one Holy Spirit. When the Only-begotten became man, there was, of course, no addition to the number of the Trinity; even after he became flesh, the Trinity remained the Trinity.[4] This is the faith in which we began our discipleship, the faith of our belief, the faith of our baptism; this we have preached, in this we have baptized, this is the faith we continue to uphold.

Regarding the father of all liars,[a] the Lord declared, "When he speaks a lie, he speaks from what is his own."[b] Now, this statement regarding the teacher applies also to the disciples; when these men spread lies about us, they speak from what is their own, not what belongs to us.[c] But we draw comfort from the words of our Master, "Blessed are you whenever, for my sake, they revile you, persecute you, and spread lies attributing every sort of evil to you. Rejoice and

1. For the addressee and the date, *v. ep.* 142 n. 1.

2. *V. ep.* 142.

3. Theodoret refers to the violent tactics used by Dioscorus and his party at the Second Council of Ephesus in 449; *v.* Intro. secc. 4.7f.

4. *V. ep.* 144 n. 3.

καὶ ἀγαλλιᾶσθε, ὅτι ὁ μισθὸς ὑμῶν πολὺς ἐν τοῖς οὐρανοῖς.[d] καὶ Τὴν Σὴν δὲ παρακαλοῦμεν προσεύξασθαι Θεοσέβειαν μὴ τῆς τῶν ἀδικούντων ἡμᾶς γενέσθαι μερίδος, ἀλλὰ τῆς τῶν ἠδικημένων διὰ τὴν τῶν εὐαγγελίων ἀλήθειαν.

d. Mt 5.11f. (NT var.)

be glad, for you have a great reward in heaven."[d] And we request as well Your Reverence's prayers that we may be reckoned not among those who commit injustice, but among those who suffer injustice for the true teaching of the gospels.

144. ΑΝΔΡΕΑΙ ΜΟΝΑΖΟΝΤΙ ΚΩΝΣΤΑΝΤΙΝΟΥΠΟΛΕΩΣ

Οὔτε θεασάμενος πώποτε Τὴν Σὴν Θεοσέβειαν οὔτε διὰ γραμμάτων ὡμιληκώς, ἐραστὴς αὐτῆς ἐγενόμην θερμότατος, εἰργάσατο δὲ τὸ φίλτρον καὶ τοῦτο πυρσεύει διηνεκῶς τὰ παρὰ τῶν τοῦ σοῦ μέλιτος γεγευμένων συμφώνως λεγόμενα· θαυμάζουσι γὰρ ἅπαντες τῆς πίστεως τὴν ὀρθότητα, τὴν τοῦ βίου λαμπρότητα, τὴν εὐστάθειαν τῆς ψυχῆς, τὴν τῶν ἠθῶν ἁρμονίαν, τὸ τῆς συνουσίας ἐπαγωγὸν καὶ γλυκύ, καὶ τἄλλα ὅσα τὸν τέλειον ὑπογράφει τῆς φιλοσοφίας τρόφιμον. διὰ ταῦτα Τῆς Σῆς Φιλοθεΐας ἐξήρτημαι, ὁ δὲ πόθος καὶ γραμμάτων ἄρξαι πεποίηκεν, ἀλλ᾽, ὦ φίλη μοι κεφαλή, μετάδος ὡς τάχιστα τοῦ ποθουμένου καὶ τὴν διὰ γραμμάτων ἡμῖν πάρασχε διάλεξιν· ἱκανὴν γὰρ τοῖς διεστηκόσιν παρέχει ψυχαγωγίαν ἡ δι᾽ ἐπιστολῶν ὁμιλία.

Γράψεις δὲ οὐχ ἑτεροδόξῳ, ἀλλὰ τῇ τῶν ἀποστόλων ἐντεθραμμένῳ διδασκαλίᾳ καὶ Τριάδος, οὐ τετράδος, κήρυκι· τῷ ὄντι γὰρ παραπλησίως ὑπείληφα δυσσεβεῖς τούς τε τὰς δύο τοῦ Μονογενοῦς φύσεις εἰς μίαν συνάγειν τολμῶντας καὶ τοὺς τὸν Κύριον ἡμῶν Ἰησοῦν Χριστόν, τὸν Υἱὸν *τοῦ Θεοῦ τοῦ ζῶντος*,[a] τὸν ἐνανθρωπήσαντα Θεὸν Λόγον,[b] εἰς δύο μερίζειν ἐπιχειροῦντας υἱούς—εἴπερ ἄρα τινές εἰσιν· ἐγὼ γὰρ οὐκ οἴομαι· ἀλλὰ ταύτην ἀεὶ τὴν συκοφαντίαν κατὰ τῆς Ἐκκλησίας οἱ τῆς Ἀρείου, καὶ Εὐνομίου, καὶ μέντοι καὶ Ἀπολιναρίου συμμορίας ἀναίδην ἐξύφηναν. καὶ ῥᾴδιον γνῶναι τοῖς φιλοπόνοις ὡς οἱ

l. 1 θεοσέβειαν *codd.* : εὐσ- *edd.* **l. 23** ἀναίδην *ZA*, $N^{s.l.m1}$, *Az.* : ἀνέδην $N^{i.l.}$ = *"the false charge that the sectaries of Arius … have recklessly fabricated." The LSJ and the PGL both (ad uoc.) regard* ἀναίδην *as an incorrect spelling of* ἀνέδην *(derived from the verb* ἀνίημι*); in fact, the two forms would have been homophonous for the medieval scribes. Yet, the TLG cites more than 220 attestations of* ἀναίδην, *the great majority in later Byz. authors. I have preferred this spelling, since the form in -αι- seems to have a wider field of reference; like*

a. Mt 16.16 b. *Cf.* Sym. Nic-CP.

144. To Andrew, a Monk of Constantinople[1]

Though I've never seen Your Reverence or communicated with you by letter, I've become warmly enamored of you. This love burns within me, a constant flame, fed by what I hear from everyone who has had some experience of your honied eloquence. Your orthodox faith, splendid life, steady self-control, well-tempered character,[2] attractive and sweet address, and the other sure marks of the perfect devotee of wisdom have all become the object of universal admiration. The result is I'm now devoted to Your Piety, and my yearning for you has moved me to be the first to write, and you, my dear friend, please satisfy this yearning as soon as you can, granting us by letter the gift of your conversation. As we all know, the companionship afforded by correspondence is in itself capable of making up for the separation of a long distance.

You will be writing to no heretic, but to a man brought up on the teaching of the apostles, a herald of the Trinity, not some quaternity![3] For really, I regard as just about equally heretical those who have the temerity to unite into one the two natures of the Only-begotten and those who set about dividing our Lord Jesus Christ, "the Son of the living God,"[a] God the Word who took on humanity,[b] into two sons—if, indeed, there are any such people, because I don't really believe there are, though this is the false charge the sectaries of Arius, Eunomius, and Apollinaris as well have had the effrontery to fabricate against the Church. Anyone who wishes to take the trouble

1. This Andrew may possibly be identified with the archimandrite Andrew named among the signatories to the condemnation of Eutyches at the Synod of Constantinople summoned by Flavian in November 448; *v. Conc. chalc., Act. 1*, sec. 552, #31; Intro., sec. 4.2.

2. My "well-tempered character" represents Theodoret's τῶν ἠθῶν τὴν ἁρμονίαν. For the implications of the term "harmony," *cf. ep.* 22 n. 2.

3. Theodoret is referring to the notion that the humanity of Christ could be considered to extend the Trinity to a quaternity. Athanasius had attacked this notion in *ep. Epict.* 9, which Theodoret had quoted in *Eran. flor.* 2, sec. 23.

πανεύφημοι πατέρες ἡμῶν, τῶν ἐκκλησιῶν οἱ φωστῆρες,[c] παρὰ τῶν τῆς ἀληθείας ἐχθρῶν ταύτην τὴν κατηγορίαν ὑπέμειναν ἣν νῦν ἡμεῖς παρὰ τῶν βελτίστων ὑφιστάμεθα τῆς καινῆς προμάχων αἱρέσεως, ὧν ὁ πάνσοφος Δεσπότης ἐγύμνωσεν τὴν ἀσέβειαν, οὐκ ἀνασχόμενος τὴν ἀνοσίαν αἵρεσιν τῇ μακροθυμίᾳ κρατῦναι.

Πεισθεὶς τοίνυν ὡς ὁμοδόξοις, Δέσποτα, γράφεις· ῥᾴδιον δέ σοι τοῦτο καὶ ἐκ πολλῶν ἡμῶν συγγραμμάτων μαθεῖν· ἀντίδος τὰ γράμματα· ἔστιν γὰρ ταῦτα πάλιν, σὺν Θεῷ φάναι, τῆς ἀγάπης ἐκκαύματα. πρὸ δὲ τῶν γραμμάτων, δὸς τῶν προσευχῶν τὴν βοήθειαν καὶ τὸν ἀγαθὸν ἡμῶν ἀντιβόλησον Κύριον πρὸς τὴν ἀπλανῆ κατευθῦναι πορείαν τοὺς ἡμετέρους πόδας ἵνα μετὰ τῶν αὐτοῦ νόμων ἐξανύσωμεν τὸν λειπόμενον δρόμον·[d] ἔχων γὰρ τὴν ἐκ τῆς καθαρᾶς βιοτῆς παρρησίαν, ῥᾷστα πείσεις[e] τὸν εὐεργετεῖν ἐπειγόμενον.[f]

ἀνέδην, ἀναίδην *may denote rash, headstrong behavior, but it may also suggest shamelessness. Here Thdt. seems to tax the sectaries of Arius, Eunomius, and Apollinaris with shamelessness, rather than recklessness, in the bringing of a false accusation*; *cf. Suda, #2198, where the form with -αι- is associated with terms expressing both ideas: Ἀναίδην, ἀθρόως, σφοδρῶς, ἀπηρυθριασμένως. καὶ Ἀναιδῶς: ἀναισχύντως. καὶ Ἀναιδής, καὶ Ἀναίδεια, ἡ ἀναισχυντία.*
l. 26 καινῆς $N^{s.l.}$, *Az.* : κεν- $N^{i.l.}$, *Z*, A^{ac}. *Cf. ep.* 141, *c. n.* (καινὴν).

c. Phil 2.15 d. *Cf.* Acts 20.24; Heb 12.1. e. *Cf.* 1Jn 3.21f.
f. *Cf.* Ps 70.1.

will have no difficulty verifying that our celebrated fathers, the luminaries of the churches,[c] had to endure this same calumny from the enemies of the truth that we today have to put up with from the valiant champions of this recent heresy.[4] But their impiety has been laid bare by our Master, who, in his wisdom, refuses to stand by patiently and allow this profane heresy to grow in strength.

So then, my Master, quite confident that you are writing to a man of the same mind—you can easily determine this from the many works I have written—please answer this letter of mine. For, if God so wills, letters are the fuel of love. But before you write, grant us the support of your prayers, and entreat our Lord to guide our steps straight along the unerring course, so that, always keeping hold of his laws, we may complete the race that still lies before us.[d] As the purity of your life ensures a hearing for your prayers,[e] you will have no trouble persuading him who makes haste to do us good.[5f]

4. On the adaptation of the Pauline metaphor, "luminary" (φωστήρ), *v. ep.* 125 n. 7. As Garnier had first argued (p. 235), Theodoret must be referring to attacks made against the eminent eastern exegetes and theologians, Diodore of Tarsus and Theodore of Mopsuestia, the teachers of Nestorius; *v.* Intro., sec. 3.13 and *ep.* 16 n. 5. In a discussion of this passage in relationship with others from *epp.* 21, 104, 146, Koch (pp. 72–75) points out that, for Theodoret, the truly dangerous christological heresies were those that in some way limited the humanity of Christ and thus called into question the salvation of the human person; in contrast, he saw little or no real danger in the positions espoused by Nestorius; *cf. ep.* 104 n. 6.

5. In Theodoret's psalter, Ps 70.1 (69.2 LXX) reads, Ὁ Θεὸς, εἰς τὴν βοήθειάν μου πρόσχες· Κύριε, εἰς τὸ βοηθῆσαί μοι σπεῦσον ("Oh God, turn to help me; Lord make haste to aid me); *v. in Ps. ad loc.* and *cf.* Rahlfs' ed.

145. ΤΟΙΣ ΣΤΡΑΤΙΩΤΑΙΣ

(1) Μία μὲν πάντων ἀνθρώπων φύσις, αἱ δὲ τῶν βίων προαιρέσεις πολλαὶ καὶ διάφοροι· οἱ μὲν γὰρ ναυτικόν, οἱ δὲ πολεμικὸν αἱροῦνται βίον, καὶ οἱ μὲν ἀθλητικόν, οἱ δὲ γεωργικόν, καὶ οἱ μὲν τήνδε, οἱ δὲ τήνδε τὴν τέχνην μεταχειρίζουσιν, καί, ἵνα τὰς ἄλλας παραλίπω διαφοράς, οἱ μέν εἰσι τῶν ἀνθρώπων σπουδαῖοι καὶ ἐμμελεῖς περὶ τὰ θεῖα καὶ τῶν ἀποστολικῶν δογμάτων ἐκπαιδεύονται τὴν ἀκρίβειαν, οἱ δὲ γαστρὶ δουλεύουσιν καὶ τῶν αἰσχρῶν ἡδονῶν τὴν ἀπόλαυσιν εὐημερίαν ὑπολαμβάνουσιν,[a] ἄλλοι δέ γε μέσοι τούτων κἀκείνων εἰσίν, καὶ οὔτε τὴν ἐπαινουμένην ζηλοῦσι σπουδὴν οὔτε τὸν ἀκόλαστον ἀσπάζονται βίον, τὴν δὲ ἁπλότητα τιμῶσι τῆς πίστεως. ἡγοῦμαι τοίνυν τοὺς ἐπισκήψαντας ἐκείνῳ τῷ λόγῳ ὅς φησιν εἶναί τινα παντελῶς ἀδύνατα τῷ Θεῷ οὐ τῶν σπουδαίων εἶναι καὶ τὰ θεῖα πεπαιδευμένων, ἀλλ᾽ ἢ τούτων οἳ τὴν ἀκρίβειαν τῶν ἀποστολικῶν δογμάτων οὐκ ἴσασιν, ἢ ἐκείνων οἵ, ταῖς ἡδυπαθείαις δεδουλωμένοι, πρὸς τοὺς καιροὺς μεταβάλλονται καὶ νῦν μὲν ταῦτα, νῦν δὲ ἐκεῖνα πρεσβεύουσιν. ἐπειδὴ δὲ γράψαι περὶ τούτων ἡμᾶς ᾐτήσατε, σιγᾶν ἐπὶ τοῦ παρόντος βεβουλευμένος, βραχέα εἰπεῖν ἀναγκάζομαι, τῇ δεσποτικῇ πειθόμενος ἐντολῇ· *Παντί,* γάρ φησιν, τῷ *αἰτοῦντί σε δίδου.*[b]

(2) Ἡμεῖς τοίνυν πάντα μὲν δύνασθαί φαμεν τὸν τῶν ὅλων Θεόν, τῇ δὲ *πάντα* φωνῇ μόνα τὰ καλὰ καὶ τὰ ἀγαθὰ συμπεριλαμβάνεται· ὁ γὰρ φύσει σοφός τε καὶ ἀγαθὸς οὐδὲν τῶν ἐναντίων προσίεται, ἀλλὰ μόνα τὰ τῇ φύσει πρέποντα. εἰ δέ τινες ἀντιλέγουσιν τῷδε τῷ λόγῳ, ἔρεσθε αὐτοὺς εἰ δύναται ψεύσασθαι ὁ τῶν ὅλων Θεός, τῆς ἀληθείας ὁ Νομοθέτης, κἂν μὲν εἴποιεν δυνατὸν τῷ Θεῷ τὸ ψεῦδος, ὡς δυσσεβεῖς

l. 23 συμπεριλαμβάνεται *codd.* : -εσθαι *edd.*

a. *Cf.* Phil 3.19; Ti 1.12; 3.3. b. Lk 6.30 (NT var.)

145. To the Soldiers[1]

(1) There is just one human nature, but men choose many different ways of life: some devote themselves to a life at sea, others to a life on campaign, some to athletics, others to farming—the choice of profession differs from man to man—and, to put aside other sorts of differences, there are those who are serious-minded and diligent in their religion, people who get themselves a thorough instruction in true doctrine, and those who are slaves to their bellies, people who imagine that felicity consists in the satisfaction of degrading desires;[a] then there are others who take a position between the former and the latter—people, who have none of this praiseworthy zeal, but do not take up a life of license and prefer a simple unexamined faith. I suppose the people who have attacked the position that there are some things quite impossible for God are not to be counted among the serious-minded who know their religion well, but either among those who remain ignorant of the true import of the apostolic doctrine or those who are slaves to pleasure and change their beliefs to meet the needs of the moment—today advocates for one set of beliefs, tomorrow for another. Though, in the present circumstances, it had been my plan to remain silent, as you have requested a letter on this topic, I cannot but make a brief reply if I am to comply with the command of our Master, who said, "Give to all that ask of you."[b]

(2) We hold that the God of the universe has the power to do all things, but the scope of the term "all things" is limited to the virtuous and the good. Obviously, he who is wise and good by nature does not take to himself anything the opposite of those qualities, but only what comports with his nature. If people object to this argument, ask them if the God of the universe, the lawgiver who enjoins truthfulness, is capable of speaking a lie, and, if they affirm

1. The addressees are not identified. Perhaps they were members of the corps stationed in Theodoret's diocese (*v. ep.* 70.1). From Theodoret's remark (sec. 1) that his choice to answer the soldiers' query went against a previous decision to hold his peace we can conclude that *ep.* 145 was written during his exile; *v.* Intro., sec. 4.8.

καὶ βλασφήμους τῆς ὑμετέρας συμμορίας ἐξελάσατε. εἰ δὲ σύνθοιντο καὶ αὐτοὶ μὴ δυνατὸν εἶναι τοῦτο τῷ τῶν ὅλων Θεῷ, πάλιν προσερωτήσατε εἰ δυνατὸν ἄδικον γενέσθαι τὸν τὴν δικαιοσύνην πηγάζοντα, εἰ δὲ συνομολογήσαιεν καὶ τοῦτο ἀδύνατον εἶναι τῷ τῶν ὅλων Θεῷ, πυθέσθαι χρὴ πάλιν εἰ δυνατὸν ἄσοφον γενέσθαι τῆς σοφίας τὴν ἄβυσσον,[c] καὶ τὸν Θεὸν μὴ εἶναι Θεόν, καὶ τὸν Κύριον ὡσαύτως μὴ εἶναι Κύριον, καὶ τὸν Δημιουργὸν οὐ Δημιουργόν, καὶ τὸν ἀγαθὸν οὐκ ἀγαθόν, ἀλλὰ κακόν, καὶ τὸ ἀληθινὸν φῶς μὴ εἶναι φῶς,[d] ἀλλὰ τοὐναντίον. εἰ δὲ συμφήσαιεν ταῦτα πάντα καὶ τὰ τούτοις προσόμοια ἀδύνατα εἶναι τῷ τῶν ὅλων Θεῷ, εἰπεῖν χρὴ πρὸς αὐτούς, *Οὐκοῦν πολλὰ ἀδύνατα τῷ Θεῷ*, καί, ὅτι *Ταῦτα τὰ ἀδύνατα οὐκ ἀδυναμίας δηλωτικά, ἀλλὰ δυνάμεως μεγίστης σημαντικά*. οὐδὲ γάρ, περὶ τῆς ψυχῆς τῆς ἡμετέρας λέγοντες ὡς ἀδύνατον αὐτὴν ἀποθανεῖν, ἀσθένειαν αὐτῆς κατηγοροῦμεν, ἀλλὰ τῆς ἀθανασίας αὐτῆς τὸ δυνατὸν κηρύττομεν, οὕτω τοίνυν, ὁμολογοῦντες τοῦ Θεοῦ τὸ ἄτρεπτον, τὸ ἀπαθές, τὸ ἀθάνατον, οὔτε τροπήν, οὔτε πάθος, οὔτε θάνατον ἐκείνῃ προσάψαι τῇ φύσει δυνάμεθα. εἰ δὲ εἴποιεν, *Ἅπερ ἂν ἐθελήσῃ δύναται ὁ Θεός*, χρὴ πρὸς αὐτοὺς εἰπεῖν, ὅτι *Οὐδὲν βούλεται ποιεῖν ὧν μὴ πέφυκεν, πέφυκεν δὲ ἀγαθός, οὐκοῦν οὐ βούλεταί τι κακόν· πέφυκεν δίκαιος, οὐκοῦν οὐ βούλεταί τι ἄδικον· πέφυκεν ἀληθής, οὐκοῦν τὸ ψεῦδος βδελύττεται· πέφυκεν ἄτρεπτος, οὐκοῦν τροπὴν οὐ προσίεται, εἰ δὲ τροπὴν οὐ προσίεται, ἀεὶ κατὰ ταὐτὰ καὶ ὡσαύτως ἔχει·* τοῦτο γὰρ καὶ αὐτὸς διὰ τοῦ προφήτου φησίν· *Ἐγώ* εἰμι, *καὶ οὐκ ἠλλοίωμαι·*[e] καὶ ὁ μακάριος Δαυίδ, *Σὺ δὲ ὁ αὐτὸς εἶ, καὶ τὰ ἔτη σου οὐκ ἐκλείψουσιν.*[f] εἰ δὲ ὁ αὐτός ἐστιν, μεταβολὴν

ll. 52f. Ἐγώ εἰμι *scripsi* : Ἐγ. εἰ. ἐγ. εἰ. *codd., edd.* = *"I am, I am." Thdt. quotes Mal 3.6 four other times in the form I have printed (Eran. dial. 1, p. 67, l. 12; Eran. flor. 2, p. 162, l. 21; flor. 3.28; Inc. 19, p. 90, ll. 56f.), never with the repetition displayed in N. Though he printed the reading of N, Az. (vol. 3, p. 166, n. 1) rightly suggested that the repetition is to be ascribed to scribal inadvertence.*

c. *Cf.* Sir 1.3. d. *Cf.* Jn 1.9; 1Jn 2.8. e. Mal 3.6 (LXX var.)
f. Ps 102.27

that God is capable of lying, regard them as enemies of religion and blasphemers, and banish them from your company. But if even they should agree to the proposition that this is not possible for the God of the universe, then go on and ask if the very fountainhead of justice could possibly become unjust, and, if they also grant that this is an impossibility for the God of the universe, ask the further question whether the very abyss of wisdom could become foolish,[c] and God not be God, and, similarly, the Lord not be the Lord, and the Creator not be the Creator, and the good not good, but evil, and the true light not true light,[d] but its opposite. Now, if they should agree that all these and other things like them are impossible for the God of the universe, you should reply, "Well then, there are many things that are impossible for God, and these things he cannot do are not indicative of powerlessness, but signs of his unsurpassed power." After all, even when, speaking of our own human soul, we declare it cannot die, our point is not to attribute weakness to the soul, but rather to highlight the fact that it is imbued with the capacity to live forever. Similarly, when we confess that God is unchangeable, impassible, deathless, we cannot attribute change, passion, and death to his nature. Should they object that God can do whatever he desires, the answer is that it is not his will to do anything counter to his nature: his nature is good, so he wills no evil; his nature is just, so he wills no injustice; his nature is truth, so he abhors falsehood; his nature is unchangeable, so he admits no change within himself, and, if he admits no change, he remains just as he is. Indeed, this is precisely what he says through the prophet, "I am, and I remain unchanged,"[e] and the blessed David says, "You are the same, and your years will have no end."[f] Now, if he is the same, he has not been sub-

οὐκ ἐδέξατο, εἰ δὲ κρείττων ὑπάρχει μεταβολῆς καὶ τροπῆς, οὐ γέγονεν ἐξ ἀθανάτου θνητός, οὐδὲ ἐξ ἀπαθοῦς παθητός.

(3) Εἰ γὰρ τοῦτο γενέσθαι οἷόν τε ἦν, οὐκ ἂν τὴν ἡμετέραν προσέλαβε φύσιν, ἐπειδὴ δὲ ἀθάνατον ἔχει φύσιν, ἔλαβεν τὸ παθεῖν δυνάμενον σῶμα καὶ σὺν τῷ σώματι τὴν ἀνθρωπείαν ψυχήν, καί, τούτων ἑκάτερον τῶν τῆς ἁμαρτίας κηλίδων φυλάξας ἀμύητον, ὑπὲρ μὲν τῶν ἡμαρτηκυιῶν ψυχῶν δέδωκε τὴν ψυχήν, ὑπὲρ δὲ τῶν τεθνηκότων σωμάτων τὸ σῶμα, καί, ἐπειδήπερ *αὐτοῦ τοῦ μονογενοῦς Υἱοῦ τοῦ Θεοῦ σῶμα* τὸ ληφθὲν προσηγορεύθη σῶμα, εἰς ἑαυτὸν ἀναφέρει τὸ τοῦ σώματος πάθος. ὅτι δὲ οὐχ ἡ θεία φύσις, ἀλλὰ τὸ σῶμα, τῷ σταυρῷ προσηλώθη, μάρτυρες οἱ τέσσαρες εὐαγγελισταί· ἅπαντες γὰρ συμφώνως τοῦτο διδάσκουσιν· ὡς Ἰωσὴφ ὁ ἀπὸ Ἀριμαθείας, προσελθὼν τῷ Πιλάτῳ, ᾔτησεν τὸ σῶμα τοῦ Ἰησοῦ, καὶ ὅτι οὗτος ἀπὸ τοῦ ξύλου καθεῖλεν τὸ σῶμα τοῦ Ἰησοῦ, καὶ ὅτι, σινδόνι καλύψας, ἔθηκεν ἐν τῷ καινῷ αὐτοῦ μνημείῳ τὸ σῶμα τοῦ Ἰησοῦ,[g] καὶ ὡς αἱ περὶ Μαρίαν τὴν Μαγδαληνὴν ἦλθον εἰς τὸ μνημεῖον, ζητοῦσαι τὸ σῶμα τοῦ Ἰησοῦ, καί, μὴ εὑροῦσαι τὸ σῶμα τοῦ Ἰησοῦ, ἔδραμον πρὸς τοὺς μαθητὰς αὐτοῦ καὶ ἀπήγγειλαν ταῦτα.[h] ταῦτα οἱ τέσσαρες εὐαγγελισταὶ συμφώνως κηρύττουσιν.

Εἰ δέ φασιν οἱ ἀντιλέγοντες εἰρηκέναι τὸν ἄγγελον, *Δεῦτε,* βλέπετε *τὸν τόπον ὅπου ἔκειτο* ὁ Κύριος,[i] μαθέτωσαν οἱ ἀσύνετοι ὡς καὶ περὶ τοῦ καλλινίκου Στεφάνου φησὶν ἡ θεία Γραφή, *Συνεκόμισαν δὲ τὸν Στέφανον ἄνδρες εὐλαβεῖς,*[j] καίτοι τὸ σῶμα μόνον ἠξιώθη ταφῆς, ἡ δὲ ψυχὴ οὐ συνετάφη τῷ σώματι, ἀλλ' ὅμως τοῦ κοινοῦ ὀνόματος καὶ μόνον τὸ σῶμα μετέλαχεν. οὕτως ὁ μακάριος Ἰακὼβ τοῖς υἱέσιν ἔλεγεν, *Θάψατέ με μετὰ τῶν*

l. 67 Ἀριμαθείας *scr. Sir. Nös. Az.* : -θέας *codd. For the form first printed by Sirmond, v. Eran., flor. 3.27, where Ettlinger reports no variant. The form carried by the mss. is attested in only one other source, and that of very late date.*

g. Mt 27.57–60; Mk 15.42–46; Lk 23.50–53; Jn 19.38–42
h. Mt 28.1–10; Mk 16.1–8; Lk 24.1–11; Jn 20.1–10
i. Mt 28.6 (NT var.) j. Acts 8.2

ject to change; if he is above any and all change, he did not pass from immortal to mortal or from impassible to passible.

(3) Of course, if this were possible, he would never have added our nature to his own. It is because he is by nature deathless that he took up a body that was capable of suffering and along with the body a human soul, and, preserving both of these innocent of any stain of sin, made the offering of his soul on behalf of souls that had sinned and of his body on behalf of bodies that had died, and precisely because the body that was taken up may be termed the "body of the only-begotten Son of God," he takes to himself the passion of the body. As to the fact that it was not the divine nature but the body that was nailed to the cross, we have the witness of the four evangelists. They are in unanimous agreement in teaching that Joseph of Arimathea approached Pilate and requested the body of Jesus, that he took the body of Jesus down from the wood of the cross, that he wrapped the body of Jesus in a sheet and placed it in his own new tomb,[g] that Mary Magdalene and the women came to the tomb in search of the body of Jesus, and when they didn't find the body of Jesus, ran off to his disciples and reported this. This is what the four evangelists proclaim with a single voice.[h]

Now, if they object that the angel declared, "Come here, and look upon the place where the Lord lay,"[i] they are missing the meaning and should take note that the holy Scripture states in regard to the glorious Stephen as well, "Pious men carried Stephen out for burial,"[j] yet it was only the body that was given over to burial, and his soul was not buried with the body, but the name belonging to both body and soul is here applied to the body alone. Just so, the blessed Jacob commanded his sons, "Bury me with my fathers,"[k] and not

πατέρων μου,[k] καὶ οὐκ εἶπεν, *Θάψατέ μου τὸ σῶμα,* καὶ ἐπήγαγεν, *Ἐκεῖ ἔθαψαν Ἀβραὰμ καὶ Σάρραν, τὴν γυναῖκα αὐτοῦ, καὶ ἐκεῖ ἔθαψαν Ἰσαὰκ καὶ Ῥεβέκκαν, τὴν γυναῖκα αὐτοῦ, καὶ ἐκεῖ ἔθαψαν* τὴν *Λείαν,*[l] καὶ οὐκ εἶπεν, *Τὰ ἐκείνων σώματα,* καὶ μὴν τὰ ὀνόματα κοινὰ σωμάτων ἐστὶ καὶ ψυχῶν, ἀλλ᾿ ὅμως καὶ μόνα τὰ σώματα ἐκ τῶν κοινῶν ὀνομάτων ἐκάλεσεν. οὕτω καὶ ἡμεῖς πολλάκις τοὺς τῶν ἁγίων *ἀποστόλων καὶ προφητῶν* καὶ μαρτύρων σηκοὺς ὀνομάζομεν,[m] καὶ τὸν μὲν *Διονυσίου* τυχόν, τὸν δὲ *Ἰουλιανοῦ* ἢ *Κοσμᾶ,* καίτοι εἰδότες ὡς μικρὰ πολλάκις λείψανα σωμάτων ἐν τούτοις κατάκειται, αἱ δὲ ψυχαὶ ἐν θειοτέροις χωρίοις διαναπαύονται. κἂν τῇ κοινῇ δὲ χρήσει τοῦτο τὸ ἔθος ἔστιν εὑρεῖν· *Ὁ δεῖνα,* γάρ φαμεν, *ἀπέθανεν,* καὶ *ὁ δεῖνα ἐν τῷδε κατάκειται τῷ τόπῳ,* καὶ ταῦτα, εἰδότες ὡς ἀθάνατος ἡ ψυχὴ καὶ ὡς οὐ κοινωνεῖ τοῦ τάφου τῷ σώματι. οὕτω καὶ ὁ ἄγγελος ἔφη, *Δεῦτε,* βλέπετε *τὸν τόπον ὅπου ἔκειτο ὁ Κύριος,*[n] οὐ τὴν θεότητα περικλείσας τῷ τάφῳ, ἀλλὰ τοῦ Κυρίου τὸ σῶμα τῷ *τοῦ Κυρίου* προσαγορεύσας ὀνόματι.

l. 92 κατάκειται *scripsi* : -ειντ- *codd., edd. The third per. forms of the pres. impf. indic. of* κατακεῖσθαι *are notably less common than those of* ἀποκεῖσθαι; *cf. ep. 112, c. n.* (ἀπόκειται). *Yet the TLG offers exx. of the sg. with a pl. neut. subj.: e.g. Pall., H. laus., Vita 44.4, ll. 5f.: εἰσῆλθεν εἰς τὸ μαρτύριον …, ἐν ᾧ λείψανα κατακεῖται Ἰωάννου τοῦ βαπτιστοῦ. The pl. form* (κατάκεινται) *here, and elsewhere in the ms. tradition of Thdt. (v. Haer. com. 5.19 (PG, vol. 83, col. 513, l. 32) may be due to the influence of later liturgical usage. Cf. the 11th-c. Menaea Junii (Cod. Lesbiacus Leimonos 11), #28, ll. 63f.: Ἰατρεῖον ἀνεδείχθη τὸ σεπτὸν ἡμῶν τέμενος, ἀθληταὶ Κυρίου, ἔνθα τὰ ὑμῶν νῦν κατάκεινται λείψανα.*
l. 95 κατάκειται *scr. Cir., edd.* : -τετέθη *N* (κατέτε *Z*). *Ciriaco's correction is supported by the following prep. phrase (ἐν τῷδε … τῷ τόπῳ) indicative of rest, rather than motion. Cf. Gr. nyss., De sancto Theodoro (PG, vol. 46, col. 737, ll. 27–31, regarding the disposition of the martyr's body): σῶμα δὲ τὸ σεμνὸν … σεμνῶς ἐν ἱερῷ τόπῳ κατάκειται. The combination κατετέθη + ἐν + dat. is frequent in later, especially liturgical texts; cf. Io. Dam., Or. secunda in dormitionem Sanctae dei genetricis Mariae, sec. 18, ll. 16f. (the body of the Virgin Mary was brought into a church in Jerusalem): ἔνθα τὸ ζωηφόρον αὐτῆς σῶμα κατετέθη ἐν σορῷ.*

k. Gn 49.29 l. Gn 49.31 (LXX var.) m. Eph 2.20 (*Cf.* Eph 3.5; 4.11.) n. Mt 28.6 (NT var.)

"Bury my body." He went on, "That is where they buried Abraham and Sarah his wife, where they buried Isaac and Rebecca his wife, and where they buried Leah,"[l] and he did not say, "buried their bodies." Of course, the names belong to both their bodies and their souls, but he used the names belonging to both to refer to just the bodies. We ourselves frequently refer to the shrines of the holy apostles, prophets, and martyrs in exactly the same way,[m] when we say, for example, "the shrine of Dionysius," or "of Julian," or of "Cosmas," though quite aware that nothing more than tiny fragments of their bodies actually lie in these shrines, and that their souls are receiving refreshment in regions far from earth.[2] Even common parlance affords examples of this usage; for example, we say, "So and so has died," and "so and so lies in that place," though we know full well that the soul is deathless and does not share the tomb with the body. The angel was using this way of speaking when he said, "Come and see the place where the Lord lay."[n] It was not his intention to constrict the godhead within the limits of the tomb; he was just calling the body of the Lord by the name belonging to the Lord himself.

2. For the development of the argument, *cf. ep.* 131.4 and n. 8. Dionysius, a Syrian martyr, had a church in Cyrus; *v.* Thdt., *H. rel.* 2.21 and Delehaye (*Origines*), pp. 189f. For the martyr Julian, *v. ep.* 131 n. 7. The celebrated physician martyrs, Cosmas and his companion Damian, were buried at Cyrus, where they had a church; *v.* Thdt., *ep.* 25 (vol. 4, p. 266, ll. 40f. = *Coll. cas.* 221.2f.). Their cult spread throughout the East and was carried also to Rome, where Felix IV (526–30) dedicated to them a church in the forum; *v.* Delehaye (*Origines*), pp. 190f.

(4) Ὅτι δὲ καὶ τοῖς ἁγίοις πατράσιν ταῦθ᾽ οὕτως δοκεῖ, ἀκουσάτωσαν Ἀθανασίου, τοῦ πανευφήμου τῆς Ἀλεξανδρείας ἀρχιεπισκόπου, ὃς δι᾽ ὁμολογίας τὴν ἀρχιερωσύνην ἐκόσμησεν, βοῶντος, *Ζωὴ ἀποθανεῖν οὐ δύναται, μᾶλλον δὲ* καὶ *τοὺς νεκροὺς ζωοποιεῖ.*[o] ἀκουσάτωσαν καὶ τοῦ πολυθρυλήτου Δαμάσου, τοῦ τῆς ῥωμαίων ἐπισκόπου βοῶντος, *Εἴ τις εἴποι ὅτι ἐν τῷ* … σταυρῷ *πόνον ὑπέμεινεν* ἡ θεότης, *καὶ οὐχὶ* τὸ σῶμα *μετὰ τῆς ψυχῆς, … ἡ τοῦ δούλου μορφή,*[p] ἣν τελείαν ἀνέλαβεν …, *ἀνάθεμα ἔστω.*[q] ἀκουσάτωσαν καὶ τοῦ ἁγιωτάτου καὶ ὁσιωτάτου τῶν ῥωμαίων ἐπισκόπου, τοῦ Κυρίου Λέοντος, νῦν γεγραφότος, ὅτι *Ἔπαθεν ὁ Υἱὸς τοῦ Θεοῦ, ὡς παθεῖν ἠδύνατο, οὐ κατὰ τὴν λαβοῦσαν φύσιν, ἀλλὰ κατὰ τὴν ληφθεῖσαν· ἡ γὰρ ἀπαθὴς φύσις τὸ παθητὸν ἔλαβε σῶμα, καὶ αὐτὸ παρέδωκεν ὑπὲρ ἡμῶν ἵνα τὴν ἡμετέραν ἐργάσηται σωτηρίαν καὶ τὴν οἰκείαν φύσιν ἐφύλαξεν ἀπαθῆ·* καὶ πάλιν, *Οὐ γὰρ ἦλθεν ἵνα τὴν οἰκείαν ἀπολέσῃ φύσιν, ἀλλ᾽ ἵνα τὴν ἡμετέραν σώσῃ.*[r] εἰ τοίνυν κατηγοροῦσιν ἡμῶν εἰρηκότων ὅτι ὅσα βούλεται δύναται ὁ Θεός, βούλεται δὲ τὰ τῇ αὐτοῦ φύσει πρέποντα, τὰ δὲ μὴ πρέποντα οὔτε βούλεται οὔτε

ll. 104f. Δαμάσου τοῦ τῆς Ῥωμαίων ἐπισκόπου *NZ* : Δ. τοῦ τῆς Ῥώμης ἐ. *Cir.* : Δ. τοῦ τῶν Ῥ. ἐ. *scr. Az. The reading of N is both idiomatic and the lect. diff., Azéma's conjecture not only unnecessary, but, like Ciriaco's* Ῥώμης, *a banalization of the Greek; cf. ep. 83, l. 130, c. n.* (ἀντιοχέων).

o. Ps.-Ath., *Serm. fid.*, fr. 2
p. Phil 2.7
q. Dam., *Fid.* ll. 65–70 (*Cf.* Thdt., *H. e.* 5.11.)
r. Leo, *ep. deperdita* (?)

(4) Now, for proof that the holy fathers understood this language in the same way, they should listen to the blessed Athanasius, archbishop of Alexandria, who adorned his holy office with his confession of the faith and cries out, "Life cannot die; rather it gives life even to the dead."[3o] And they should listen to Damasus, the celebrated bishop of Rome, who cries out, "Should anyone assert that the godhead suffered on the cross, and not the body along with the soul, the form of the slave,[p] which the godhead assumed in its entirety, let him be anathema."[4q] And have them listen to my Lord Leo, his holiness, bishop of Rome, who has just now written, "The Son of God suffered as it was possible for him to suffer—not according to the nature which assumed, but according to that which was assumed. The impassible nature assumed the body capable of suffering and, in giving this over for our sake to accomplish the work of salvation, yet preserved the impassibility of its own nature"; and further, "He came not to destroy his own nature, but in order to save ours."[5r] If they should continue to criticize our position—that God is capable of doing whatever he wills, but that he wills only what

3. As a result of his staunch opposition to Arianism, Athanasius, archbishop of Alexandria (328–73), was exiled from his see in 335, 339, 356, and 365. He was exiled also in 362 during the reign of the hellene Julian; *v.* Baldwin, Kazhdan, and Ševčenko, "Athanasius," and *cf. ep.* 146.7. Theodoret here reuses a quotation that he had already cited in *Eran. flor.* 3, sec. 28. Though both there and in this letter, he refers the passage to Ath., *ep. Epict.*, it actually comes from the *Serm. fid.* (*CPG* #2803), a work long attributed to Athanasius, but more likely belonging to Marcellus of Ancyra; *v.* Quasten, vol. 3, pp. 30, 200.

4. On Damasus, bishop of Rome from 366–84, *v.* Livingstone, "Damasus, St." and Intro., secc. 1.3f. The passage here attributed to Damasus is an excerpt from the tome produced at a council of western bishops that he assembled in Rome in 382 to deal with trinitarian and christological disputes, including the Macedonian and Apollinarian heresies. For a discussion of the historical and theological context of the council, the constitution and significance of the tome, and for a necessary correction to Turner's text of the final article of condemnation (ll. 133–53), *v.* Galtier, esp. pp. 563–78. Theodoret had quoted this excerpt previously in a somewhat different and fuller form in *Eran. flor.* 3, sec. 36. He provides a Greek translation of almost the entirety of the conciliar tome in *H. e.* 5.11.

5. As the two *testimonia* attributed to Leo do not appear in any of his extant works, it may be, as Azéma (vol. 3, pp. 171f., n. 5) suggests, that both derive from a lost letter.

δύναται, κατηγορείτωσαν καὶ τῶνδε τῶν ἁγίων καὶ τῶν ἄλλων ἁπάντων ὅσοι ταῦτα πρεσβεύουσιν, κατηγορείτωσαν καὶ τοῦ Ἀποστόλου βοῶντος, *Ἵνα διὰ δύο πραγμάτων ἀμεταθέτων, ἐν οἷς ἀδύνατον ψεύσασθαι Θεόν·*[s] καὶ πάλιν, *Εἰ ἀπιστοῦμεν, ἐκεῖνος πιστὸς μένει, ἀρνήσασθαι … ἑαυτὸν οὐ δύναται.*[t]

(5) Ταῦτα τοῖς ἀντιλέγουσιν ὑπανάγνωτε, καί εἰ μὲν πεισθεῖεν, ὑμνήσατε τὸν ἀγαθὸν Κύριον, ὅτι, διὰ τῆς ὑμετέρας σπουδῆς, κἀκείνοις τὴν ὠφέλειαν προὐξένησεν, εἰ δὲ ἐπιμένοιεν ἀπειθοῦντες, μηδεμίαν πρὸς αὐτοὺς περὶ δογμάτων ποιεῖσθε διάλεξιν· ἀπαγορεύει γὰρ ὁ θεῖος Ἀπόστολος *λογομαχεῖν* εἰς *οὐδὲν χρήσιμον ἐπὶ καταστροφῇ τῶν ἀκουόντων.*[u] ὑμεῖς δὲ τὴν εὐαγγελικὴν διδασκαλίαν ἄσυλον διατηρήσατε ἵν', ἐν τῇ τῆς ἐπιφανείας ἡμέρᾳ, μετὰ τῆς προσηκούσης ἐργασίας τὴν παρακαταθήκην τῷ δικαίῳ προσενεγκότες Κριτῇ, τῆς τριποθήτου φωνῆς ἐπακούσητε· *Εὖ, δοῦλε ἀγαθὲ καὶ πιστέ· ἐπὶ ὀλίγα ἦς πιστός, ἐπὶ πολλῶν σε καταστήσω· εἴσελθε εἰς τὴν χαρὰν τοῦ Κυρίου σου.*[v]

s. Heb 6.18 t. 2Tm 2.13 u. 2Tm 2.14 (NT var.) v. Mt 25.21

comports with his nature and neither wills nor can do what is opposed to it—let them extend their criticisms to these saints and to all the others who defend this teaching. Why, they should criticize the Apostle himself for calling out, "So that through two irrevocable acts, in which it is impossible that God should tell a lie";[s] and again, "Even if we are faithless, he remains faithful; he cannot contradict himself."[t]

(5) Read out these passages to your opponents, and, if they change their mind, sing a hymn of praise to the good Lord, because, thanks to your effort, he came even to their aid. If, however, they persist in gainsaying you, have no further discussion with them on points of doctrine. The holy Apostle forbids us "to wrangle over words in pointless arguments that will achieve nothing but the ruination of those who listen to them."[u] Your responsibility is rather to keep the gospel doctrine inviolate, so that, in the day of his coming, you may present to the Judge the deposit he left with you along with the interest it has earned and hear that answer all long to hear, "Well done, my good and trustworthy slave! You were trustworthy over little; I shall put you in charge of much. Enter into the joy of your Lord."[v]

146. ΤΟΙΣ ΕΝ ΚΩΝΣΤΑΝΤΙΝΟΥΠΟΛΕΙ ΜΟΝΑΖΟΥΣΙΝ

(1) Οἱ κατὰ *τοῦ … Θεοῦ καὶ Σωτῆρος ἡμῶν*[a] τὰς γλώττας ὁπλίσαντες οὐδὲν καινὸν οὐδὲ παράδοξον δρῶσιν, καὶ τοὺς εὔνους αὐτοῦ θεράποντας τῷ ψεύδει τοξεύοντες· τῆς γὰρ δεσποτικῆς παροινίας μετέχειν ἀνάγκη τοὺς δι᾽ αὐτὴν λίαν ἀλγοῦντας οἰκέτας. τοῦτο δὲ καὶ αὐτὸς ὁ Κύριος προτεθέσπικεν, τοὺς ἱεροὺς αὐτοῦ ψυχαγωγῶν μαθητάς· ἔφη δὲ οὕτως· *Εἰ ἐμὲ ἐδίωξαν, καὶ ὑμᾶς διώξουσιν·*[b] *εἰ τὸν οἰκοδεσπότην* Βεελζεβοὺλ ἐκάλεσαν, *πόσῳ μᾶλλον τοὺς οἰκειακοὺς αὐτοῦ;*[c] εἶτα παρεθάρρυνεν αὐτούς, δείξας τὸ τῆς συκοφαντίας εὐφώρατον· ἐπήγαγεν γάρ, *Μὴ οὖν φοβηθῆτε αὐτούς· οὐδὲν γάρ ἐστι κεκαλυμμένον, ὃ οὐκ ἀποκαλυφθήσεται, καὶ κρυπτόν, ὃ οὐ γνωσθήσεται.*[d] τῆς δὲ θείας προρρήσεως τὴν ἀλήθειαν πολλάκις μὲν καὶ ἄλλοτε, μάλιστα δὲ νῦν, σαφῶς ἑωράκαμεν· οἱ γὰρ τὴν καθ᾽ ἡμῶν συκοφαντίαν ὑφήναντες καὶ παμπόλλων πριάμενοι χρημάτων τὰς ἡμετέρας σφαγὰς ὤφθησαν ἐναργῶς τὴν Βαλεντίνου καὶ Βαρδησάνου περικείμενοι λώβην. ἤλπισαν δὲ ὅμως τὴν σφετέραν καλύψειν ἀσέβειαν εἰ τῇ τοῦ ψεύδους θηγάνῃ τὰς γλώττας καθ᾽ ἡμῶν παραθήξαιεν· ἐπειδὴ γὰρ ἡμεῖς, τὴν πάλαι κατασβεσθεῖσαν αἵρεσιν ἀνανεουμένην ὑπὸ τούτων ὁρῶντες, διετελοῦμεν βοῶντες, διαμαρτυρόμενοι καὶ ἰδίᾳ καὶ δημοσίᾳ κἀν τοῖς ἀσπαστηρίοις οἴκοις κἀν τοῖς θείοις σηκοῖς,

l. 6 αὐτοῦ *codd., Sir.* : αὑ- *scr. Nös. Az.*

a. Ti 2.13 b. Jn 15.20 c. Mt 10.25 (NT var.) d. Mt 10.26

146. To the Monks of Constantinople[1]

It is hardly strange or surprising that those who armed their tongues against "our ... God and Savior"[a] should also aim their arrows of falsehood at his devoted servants. It cannot be otherwise than that the slaves of his household feel deep pain at, and so themselves share in, the violence offered their Master. The Lord himself gave his holy disciples forewarning of this violence as he spoke these words of encouragement: "If they have persecuted me, they will persecute you as well;[b] if they have called the master of the house 'Beelzebub,' they will do that all the more to the members of his household!"[c] Then, as you can see in what follows, he bade them keep up their courage by pointing out how easy it is to detect slander: "So then, don't fear them, for there is nothing that is hidden that will not be revealed, nor any secret that will not be made known."[d] We have frequently seen this divine prophecy proven true, but with remarkable clarity at the present moment, as those very people who have woven this web of false accusations against us, who spent fortunes to have us sent off to slaughter, are now set before us in plain sight for what they are: bearers of the leprosy of Valentinus and Bardaisan! Of course, they had hopes of covering up their own irreligion if they could just sharpen their tongues against us on the whetstone of deceit. Precisely because we could see they were rekindling this long-extinguished heresy and refused to hold our peace and denounced them privately and publicly—in friendly gatherings and in the precincts of God[2]—and revealed

1. It is not known to which monks this letter was addressed; *cf.* Frend (p. 130) who notes that the stiffest opposition to Antiochene christology was to be found among monks. Azéma dates this letter to the first half of 451, after the new emperor Marcian had permitted Theodoret to return to his diocese; *v.* Intro. sec. 5.

2. "In friendly gatherings" represents the phrase κἀν τοῖς ἀσπαστηρίοις οἴκοις, unattested elsewhere in Greek literature, but *cf.* Acts 20.20 (κατ' οἴκους). Perhaps, Theodoret is referring to private discussions of doctrinal questions among bishops; *cf. ep.* 102, where we find a similar contrast between what is said in private and

καὶ τὰς κατὰ τῆς πίστεως ἐγχειρουμένας ἐπιβουλὰς ἐξηλέγχομεν, λοιδορίας ἡμῶν κατέχεαν, ὡς δύο κηρυττόντων υἱούς.

Ἔδει δὲ παρόντας ἐλέγχειν καὶ μὴ διαβάλλειν ἀπόντας, οὗτοι δὲ τοὐναντίον δεδράκασιν· βασιλικοῖς γὰρ ἡμᾶς τῇ Κύρρῳ προσδήσαντες γράμμασιν, ἐρήμην δικάσαι τοὺς δικαιοτάτους ἠνάγκασαν δικαστὰς καὶ κατὰ τοῦ πέντε καὶ τριάκοντα σταθμοῖς ἀφεστηκότος τὴν ὀρθοτάτην ψῆφον ἐξήνεγκαν. τοῦτο δε οὔτε γοητείαν τις οὔτε νεκροσυλίαν κατηγορούμενος, οὐκ ἀνδροφόνος, οὐ γάμων ἐπίβουλος ὑπέμεινεν πώποτε.

(2) Ἀλλὰ τοὺς μὲν δικαστὰς ἐπὶ τοῦ παρόντος ἐάσω· ἐγγὺς γὰρ ὁ Κύριος, ὁ κρίνων *τὴν οἰκουμένην ἐν δικαιοσύνῃ* καὶ *λαοὺς ἐν εὐθύτητι*[e] καὶ πραττόμενος εὐθύνας οὐ μόνον ῥημάτων καὶ πραγμάτων, ἀλλὰ καὶ πονηρῶν ἐνθυμημάτων· τὴν δὲ γεγενημένην δίκαιον οἶμαι διελέγξαι συκοφαντίαν. ποίαν ἀπόδειξιν ἔχουσι τοῦ δύο λέγειν ἡμᾶς υἱούς; εἰ μὲν γὰρ τῶν σιγώντων ἦμεν, ἔσχεν ἂν χώραν ἴσως ἡ ὑποψία, ἐπειδὴ δὲ ἔργον εἴχομεν τοὺς ὑπὲρ τῶν ἀποστολικῶν δογμάτων ἀγῶνας, καὶ τοῖς τοῦ Κυρίου ποιμνίοις τὴν διδασκαλικὴν προσφέρομεν πόαν, καί, πρὸς τούτοις, πέντε καὶ τριάκοντα συνεγράψαμεν βίβλους, τήν τε θείαν Γραφὴν ἑρμηνεύοντες καὶ τὸ τῶν αἱρέσεων διελέγχοντες ψεῦδος, εὐέλεγκτος ἄρα ἡ παρὰ τούτων συντεθεῖσα ψευδολογία· πολλαὶ μὲν γὰρ ἀκροατῶν μυριάδες μαρτυροῦσιν ἡμῖν τὴν τῶν εὐαγγελικῶν δογμάτων πεπρεσβευκόσιν ἀλήθειαν, πρόκειται δὲ καὶ τὰ συγγράμματα τοῖς βουλομένοις εἰς βάσανον. οὐ

l. 32 κρίνων *codd., Az.* : κρινῶν *coni. Gilb. = "he who will judge all the world in justice." Edd. should consider whether here and in numerous other places in Greek patristic literature, the rarer act. pt. fut. masc. sg. nom. has been ousted by the far more common pres. form. The TLG cites only thirteen exx. of the former, none of them in the works of Thdt. Yet, Thdt. is quoting Ps 9.8, which begins: κρινεῖ τὴν οἰκουμένην ἐν δικαιοσύνῃ, a clause that appears also in Ps. 96.13 and 98.9. In his exposition of each place, Thdt. quotes the indic. fut. form. Cf. p. 432, l. 3, Catena in Marcum: ἥξει πάλιν κρινῶν τὴν οἰκουμένην; and document 1, Second Council of Nicaea, (787): ἔρχεται κρινῶν τὴν οἰκουμένην. Still, given the coördinated pres. pt. πραττόμενος, I have left* κρίνων.

e. Ps 9.8 (LXX var.); 98.9

the conspiracy they had mounted against the faith, they have poured out their abuse, claiming we preach a doctrine of two sons.

They ought to have examined me in person, not slandered me when I wasn't there, but they did the exact opposite. First, by means of the emperor's letter, they had me tied up in Cyrus, then they insisted that my most just judges reach their verdict in the absence of a defense, and then they passed their sentence, their most righteous sentence, against a man who was thirty-five days' journey away—something no man tried for black magic or grave-robbing, something no murderer or adulterer has ever had to endure!

(2) But, for the moment, I'll say no more regarding my judges, for the Lord is near at hand, he who "will judge all the world in justice and all its peoples in righteousness"[e] and exacts an accounting not only of our words and deeds, but even of our evil thoughts; rather, I shall refute the false charge that has been brought against me. Just what proof can they offer that I say there are two sons? Now, if I were such as to hold my peace, there might perhaps be some room for this suspicion, but, as I've made it my task to contend on behalf of the apostolic teachings, and I provide the sheep of the Lord's flocks with the food of my instruction, and, on top of this, have written thirty-five works commenting on Scripture and confuting heretical error, there can be no difficulty at all in rebutting their trumped-up charge; thousands upon thousands have heard me preach and can bear witness that I have commended the gospel teachings, and my writings are available for anyone who wishes to

what is proclaimed in church (καὶ γὰρ ἐπ᾽ ἐκκλησίας λεγόντων ἡμῶν πολλάκις ἀκήκοεν Ἡ Σὴ Θεοσέβεια καί, ἐν συλλόγοις ἑτέροις δογματικῶν ἡμῖν κινηθέντων λόγων, τοὺς παρ᾽ ἡμῶν εἰρημένους ἐπήκουσε = "Your Reverence has often listened to us preaching in church and has heard what we have said in other gatherings where issues of doctrine have been discussed among us").

γὰρ ὑπὲρ δυάδος υἱῶν, ἀλλ᾽ ὑπὲρ τοῦ μονογενοῦς Υἱοῦ τοῦ Θεοῦ καὶ πρὸς ἕλληνας καὶ πρὸς ἰουδαίους, καὶ πρὸς τοὺς τὴν Ἀρείου καὶ Εὐνομίου νόσον εἰσδεξαμένους, καὶ πρὸς τοὺς τὴν Ἀπολιναρίου φρενοβλάβειαν ἀσπαζομένους, καὶ μέντοι καὶ πρὸς τοὺς τῇ Μαρκίωνος σηπεδόνι κατεχομένους ἀγωνιζόμενοι διατετελέκαμεν· ἕλληνας μὲν πείθοντες ὅτι αὐτός ἐστιν ὁ τῶν ἁπάντων Δημιουργός, ὁ τοῦ ἀεὶ ὄντος Θεοῦ συναΐδιος Υἱός, ἰουδαίους δὲ ὅτι περὶ αὐτοῦ τὰς προρρήσεις οἱ προφῆται πεποίηνται, τοὺς δὲ Ἀρείου καὶ Εὐνομίου κληρονόμους ὅτι τοῦ Πατρὸς ὁμοούσιος ὁμότιμός τε καὶ ἰσοδύναμος, τοὺς δὲ τῆς Μαρκίωνος λύττης μετεσχηκότας ὅτι οὐκ ἀγαθός ἐστι μόνον, ἀλλὰ καὶ δίκαιος, οὐκ ἀλλοτρίων, κατὰ τὸν ἐκείνων μῦθον, ἀλλ᾽ οἰκείων ποιημάτων Σωτήρ. καὶ ἁπαξαπλῶς πρὸς αἵρεσιν ἑκάστην διαμαχόμενοι, τὸν ἕνα προσκυνεῖν παρρεγγυῶμεν Υἱόν.

(3) Καὶ τί δεῖ μακρηγορεῖν, ἐξὸν συντόμως διελέγξαι τὸ ψεῦδος; τοὺς γὰρ καθ᾽ ἕκαστον ἔτος τῷ παναγίῳ προσιόντας βαπτίσματι τὴν ἐκτεθεῖσαν ἐν Νικαίᾳ παρὰ τῶν ἁγίων καὶ μακαρίων πατέρων πίστιν ἐκμανθάνειν παρασκευάζομεν καί, μυσταγωγοῦντες αὐτοὺς ὡς προσετάχθημεν, βαπτίζομεν *εἰς τὸ ὄνομα τοῦ Πατρός, καὶ τοῦ Υἱοῦ, καὶ τοῦ Ἁγίου Πνεύματος,*[f] ἑνικῶς ἑκάστην προσηγορίαν προσφέροντες. καὶ μέντοι καὶ τὰς θείας λειτουργίας ἐν ταῖς ἐκκλησίαις ἐπιτελοῦντες, καὶ ἀρχομένης καὶ ληγούσης ἡμέρας καὶ αὐτὴν δὲ τὴν ἡμέραν κατὰ τριτημόριον διαιροῦντες, δοξάζομεν τὸν Πατέρα, καὶ τὸν Υἱόν, καὶ τὸ Ἅγιον Πνεῦμα. εἰ δὲ δύο υἱοὺς κατὰ τὴν τούτων συκοφαντίαν πρεσβεύομεν, τίνα δοξάζομεν, τίνα δὲ ἀπροσκύνητον καταλείπομεν; μανίας γὰρ ἐσχάτης δύο μὲν εἶναι πιστεύειν υἱούς, ἑνὶ δὲ μόνῳ τὴν δοξολογίαν προσφέρειν. τίς δὲ οὕτως ἐμβρόντητος ὡς, τοῦ θείου Παύλου βοῶντος ἀκούων, *Εἷς Κύριος, μία πίστις, ἓν βάπτισμα,*[g] καὶ πάλιν, *Εἷς Κύριος Ἰησοῦς Χριστός, δι᾽ οὗ τὰ πάντα,*[h] ἀντινομοθετῆσαι τῇ διδασκαλίᾳ τοῦ Πνεύματος καὶ διχῇ τὸν ἕνα τεμεῖν;

f. Mt 28.19 g. Eph 4.5 h. 1Cor 8.6

scrutinize their doctrine. Against Hellenes and Jews, against those infected with the heresies of Arius and Eunomius, against those who have made themselves crazy with the insanity of Apollinaris, and above all, against those contaminated with Marcion's leprosy, I have always contended on behalf of the only-begotten Son of God, never for a pair of sons; I have tried to convince the Hellenes that he is the Creator of the universe, the Son co-eternal with the ever-existing God; Jews that he is the one described in the prophecies of the prophets; Arians and Eunomians that he is of the same essence, worthy of the same honor, possessed of the same power as the Father; the frenzied Marcionites that he is not just good, but also just, not the savior of someone else's creation—as their story goes—but of his own. In a word, in my struggles with each and every heresy, I enjoin the worship of the one Son.

(3) What need is there to go on at length, when the briefest of arguments will be quite enough to show up this lie? Every year, we have the candidates for holy baptism learn by heart the creed composed by the holy and blessed fathers of Nicaea, and, as we confer the sacrament of initiation, we baptize them, according to the command that was given us, "in the name of the Father, the Son, and the Holy Spirit,"[f] and pronounce each of these appellations in the singular. Moreover, in the performance of the divine liturgy in the churches, both in the morning and the evening, and in our threefold division of the day itself, we glorify the Father, the Son, and the Holy Spirit. Now, if, as this lying calumny would have it, we espouse two sons, which one do we glorify, and which do we leave without worship? As anyone can see, it would be pure madness to profess faith in two sons and then make offering of praise to just one! When St. Paul calls out, "One Lord, one faith, one baptism";[g] and "One Lord Jesus Christ, through whom are all things,"[h] who could be such a gaping fool as to set himself in deliberate opposition to the teaching of the Spirit and divide the one into two?

Ἀλλὰ γὰρ μάτην ἀδολεσχῶ· οὐδὲ γὰρ οὗτοι φάναι τολμῶσιν, καὶ ταῦτα τῷ ψεύδει συντεθραμμένοι,[i] ὡς ταῦτα λεγόντων ἡμῶν ἀκηκόασιν πώποτε, ἀλλά, τὸ τὰς δύο φύσεις ὁμολογεῖν τοῦ Δεσπότου Χριστοῦ, δύο λέγουσι κηρύττειν υἱούς. καὶ συνιδεῖν οὐκ ἐθέλουσιν ὡς τῶν ἀνθρώπων ἕκαστος καὶ ψυχὴν ἀθάνατον ἔχει καὶ σῶμα θνητόν, καὶ οὐδεὶς μέχρι καὶ τήμερον δύο Παύλους τὸν Παῦλον ὠνόμασεν, ἐπειδὴ καὶ ψυχὴν ἔχει καὶ σῶμα, οὔτε τὸν Πέτρον δύο Πέτρους, οὔτε τὸν Ἀβραάμ, οὔτε τὸν Ἀδάμ, ἀλλ᾽ οἶδε μὲν ἕκαστος τῶν φύσεων τὸ διάφορον, δύο δὲ Παύλους οὐκ ὀνομάζει τὸν ἕνα· οὕτω τοίνυν καὶ τὸν Κύριον ἡμῶν Ἰησοῦν Χριστόν, τὸν μονογενῆ τοῦ Θεοῦ Υἱόν, τὸν ἐνανθρωπήσαντα Θεὸν Λόγον, καὶ *Υἱὸν Θεοῦ* καὶ *Υἱὸν ἀνθρώπου* προσαγορεύοντες, ὡς παρὰ τῆς θείας Γραφῆς ἐδιδάχθημεν, οὐ δύο φαμὲν υἱούς, ἀλλὰ τῆς θεότητος καὶ τῆς ἀνθρωπότητος ὁμολογοῦμεν τὰς ἰδιότητας. οὗτοι δέ, τὴν ἐξ ἡμῶν ληφθεῖσαν ἀρνούμενοι φύσιν, δυσχεραίνουσι τῶνδε τῶν λόγων ἀκούοντες.

(4) Ἡμᾶς δὲ δεῖξαι προσήκει πόθεν ταύτην ἠσπάσαντο τὴν ἀσέβειαν· Σίμων μὲν γὰρ καὶ Μένανδρος, Κέρδων καὶ Μαρκίων παντάπασιν ἀρνοῦνται τὴν ἐνανθρώπησιν καὶ τὴν ἐκ Παρθένου γέννησιν *μυθολογίαν* ἀποκαλοῦσιν, Βαλεντῖνος δέ, καὶ Βασιλείδης, καὶ Βαρδησάνης, καὶ Ἁρμόνιος, καὶ οἱ τῆς τούτων συμμορίας δέχονται μὲν τῆς Παρθένου τὴν κύησιν

ll. 80f. τὸ τὰς δύο φύσεις ὁμολογεῖν δύο λέγουσι κηρύττειν υἱούς *N[pcm1]?* : τῷ, *etc.* *N[ac]?, Onor. A, edd.* = *"They are really just saying that, because we confess the two natures of our Master Christ, this is the same as preaching two sons" (?). Most likely, the first hand, while writing the dative article, realized his mistake and attempted to change this to the accusative; he never added an iota subscript, and it looks as if he erased the second circlet of the omega. The clause must be factitive; the acc. art. marks τὰς … ὁμολογεῖν as the d.o. of λέγουσι; δύο κηρύττειν υἱούς is the d.o. complement. Cf. Eran., dial. 2, p. 121, ll. 20f.: (εἰπέ, τί λωβᾶται τὸ θεὸν καὶ ἄνθρωπον ὁμολογεῖν τὸν Χριστόν;), where the def. art. markes θεὸν … Χριστόν as the subject of λωβᾶται. The text as printed by previous editors could possibly be construed to make it meaningful, but the omission of any personal pron. to identify the subj. of the infinn.* ὁμολογεῖν *and* κηρύττειν *makes for very eliptical and inelegant syntax.* **l. 94** ἠσπάσαντο *edd.* : ἐσ- *codd.*

i. *Cf.* Jn 8.44.

But I'm just wasting words. Not even my opponents, though reared in falsehood,[i] will dare assert that they've ever actually heard me say anything of the sort. They're really just saying that to confess the two natures of our Master Christ is the same as preaching two sons. What they refuse to see is that, as each individual man has an immortal soul and a mortal body, and the fact that he has both soul and body has never been cause for anyone calling the one Paul two Pauls, the one Peter, two Peters, or Abraham or Adam—of course, everyone is aware of the difference between the natures, but no one calls the one Paul two Pauls—just so, as we have been taught by holy Scripture, we apply to our Lord Jesus Christ, the only-begotten Son of God, God the Word who became man, the appellations "Son of God" and "Son of Man," not to declare that there are two sons, but to confess the properties of the godhead and the humanity. But, these people deny the nature assumed from humanity and raise objections when they hear such statements.

(4) It is well to set out the sources from which they picked up this piece of irreligion. So then, Simon and Menander, Cerdo and Marcion flatly denied the incarnation and dismissed the virgin birth as a fairy tale. Valentinus, Basilides, Bardaisan, Harmonius, and all the members of their sect accepted both the virginal conception and

καὶ τὸν τόκον, οὐδὲν δὲ τὸν Θεὸν Λόγον ἐκ τῆς Παρθένου προσειληφέναι φασίν, ἀλλὰ πάροδόν τινα δι᾽ αὐτῆς, ὥσπερ διὰ σωλῆνος, ποιήσασθαι, ἐπιφανῆναι δὲ τοῖς ἀνθρώποις φαντασίᾳ χρησάμενον καὶ δόξας εἶναι ἄνθρωπος ὃν τρόπον ὤφθη τῷ Ἀβραὰμ καί τισιν ἄλλοις τῶν παλαιῶν. Ἄρειος δὲ καὶ Εὐνόμιος σῶμα μὲν αὐτὸν ἔφασαν εἰληφέναι, τὴν θεότητα δὲ τὰ τῆς ψυχῆς ἐνηργηκέναι ἵνα ταύτῃ τὰ ταπεινὰ καὶ τῶν ῥημάτων καὶ τῶν πραγμάτων προσάψωσιν. ὁ δέ γε Ἀπολινάριος καὶ ψυχὴν αὐτὸν μετὰ τοῦ σώματος ἔφησεν εἰληφέναι, ἀλλ᾽ οὐ τὴν λογικήν, ἀλλὰ τὴν *ζωτικὴν* ἤγουν *φυτικὴν* ὀνομαζομένην· *Τοῦ νοῦ*, γάρ φησιν, *τὴν χρείαν ἡ θεότης ἐπλήρου.*[j] ψυχῆς δὲ καὶ νοῦ τὴν διαίρεσιν παρὰ τῶν ἔξω μεμάθηκεν φιλοσόφων· ἡ γὰρ θεία Γραφὴ ἐκ ψυχῆς λέγει καὶ σώματος συνεστάναι τὸν ἄνθρωπον· Ἐποίησεν, γάρ φησιν, *ὁ Θεὸς τὸν ἄνθρωπον χοῦν ἀπὸ τῆς γῆς καὶ ἐνεφύσησεν εἰς τὸ πρόσωπον αὐτοῦ πνοὴν ζωῆς, καὶ ἐγένετο ὁ ἄνθρωπος εἰς ψυχὴν ζῶσαν,*[k] καὶ ὁ Κύριος ἐν τοῖς ἱεροῖς εὐαγγελίοις τοῖς ἀποστόλοις ἔφη, *Μὴ φοβεῖσθε ἀπὸ τῶν ἀποκτεννόντων τὸ σῶμα, τὴν δὲ ψυχὴν μὴ δυναμένων ἀποκτεῖναι.*[l] τὰ μὲν οὖν τῶν αἱρετικῶν δόγματα τοσαύτην ἔχει πρὸς ἄλληλα διαμάχην.

(5) Οὗτοι δέ, τὸν Ἀπολινάριον, καὶ μέντοι καὶ Ἄρειον, καὶ Εὐνόμιον ὑπερβῆναι τῇ ἀσεβείᾳ φιλονεικήσαντες, τὴν ὑπὸ Βαλεντίνου καὶ Βαρδησάνου πάλαι σπαρεῖσαν αἵρεσιν, εἶτα πρόρριζον ὑπὸ τῶν ἀρίστων ἀνασπασθεῖσαν γεωργῶν, φυτεῦσαι νῦν ἐπειράθησαν·[m] παραπλησίως γὰρ ἐκείνοις ἠρνήθησαν τὸ ἐκ τῆς ἡμετέρας φύσεως προσειλῆφθαι τοῦ Δεσπότου τὸ σῶμα. ἡ δὲ Ἐκκλησία, τοῖς ἀποστολικοῖς ἴχνεσιν ἑπομένη, καὶ θεότητα τελείαν καὶ ἀνθρωπότητα τελείαν ἐν τῷ Δεσπότῃ Χριστῷ θεωρεῖ· ὥσπερ γὰρ ἔλαβεν σῶμα, οὐ δεόμενος σώματος, ἀλλὰ πᾶσι τοῖς σώμασι δι᾽ ἐκείνου τὴν ἀθανασίαν πραγματευόμενος, οὕτω δὴ καὶ ψυχὴν ἔλαβεν τὴν κυβερνῶσαν τὸ σῶμα ἵνα πᾶσα

j. *V.*, *e.g.*, Gr. nyss., *Antir.* vol. 3.1, p. 227, l. 10 - p. 228, l. 17.
k. Gn 2.7 (LXX var.) l. Mt 10.28 m. Mt 13.24–30

birth, but said that God the Word took nothing from the Virgin, but passed through her as if through a water pipe and then, when he appeared to men, made use of a mere image—only seeming to be a human being—in the way he had appeared to Abraham and some other Old Testament figures. Arius and Eunomius, however, while affirming the assumption of a body, made the godhead supply the faculties of the soul, their intention being to attribute to the godhead all the words and deeds suggestive of subordination. Finally, Apollinaris asserted that God the Word assumed a soul as well as a body, but not the rational soul, just what he called the "vital" or "vegetative" soul, since, so he declared, "the godhead fulfilled the function of the rational mind."[3j] Now he learned this distinction between the soul and the rational mind from non-Christian philosophers, since, according to the holy Scripture, the human being consists of soul and body: "God," so it reads "created the human being, dust from the earth, and breathed into his mouth the breath of life, and the human being became a living soul."[k] Furthermore, in the holy gospels, the Lord declared to his disciples, "Don't be afraid of those who kill the body, but have no power to kill the soul."[l] As we see, the teachings of the heretics are in such disaccord they fairly fight against each other.

(5) But my opponents, in their eagerness to outdo the irreligion of Apollinaris and even Arius and Eunomius, have now tried to replant the heresy sown long ago by Valentinus and Bardaisan, one that had been entirely eradicated by the best of farmers;[m] indeed, it is apparent that they are just like them in denying that our Master's body was a body assumed from our nature. Yet, the Church, following in the footsteps of the apostles, contemplates in our Master Christ both perfect divinity and perfect humanity; though having no need of a body, he assumed a body, and made use of it to gain eternal life for all bodies, and, in the same way, he assumed the

3. On Apollinaris' anthropology, *v.* Intro., sec. 1.5; *cf. Eran. dial.* 1, p. 69, ll. 14–24.

ψυχὴ διὰ ταύτης μετάσχῃ τῆς ἀτρεπτότητος. εἰ γὰρ καὶ ἀθάνατοί εἰσιν αἱ ψυχαί, ἀλλ᾽ οὐκ ἄτρεπτοι· πολλὰς γὰρ καὶ ἀγχιστρόφους. μεταβολὰς ὑπομένουσιν, νῦν μὲν τούτοις ἀρεσκόμεναι, νῦν δὲ ἐκείνοις, οὗ δὴ χάριν καὶ πλημμελοῦμεν, ἐκτρεπόμενοι καὶ τὴν ἐπὶ τὰ χείρω ῥοπὴν εἰσδεχόμενοι. μετὰ δὲ τὴν ἀνάστασιν, ἀπολαύει μὲν ἀθανασίας καὶ ἀφθαρσίας τὰ σώματα, ἀπολαύουσι δὲ ἀπαθείας καὶ ἀτρεπτότητος αἱ ψυχαί. διά τοι τοῦτο καὶ σῶμα λαβὼν καὶ ψυχὴν ὁ μονογενὴς Υἱὸς τοῦ Θεοῦ, μώμου ταῦτα παντὸς ἐλεύθερα διεφύλαξεν καὶ τὴν ὑπὲρ τοῦ γένους θυσίαν προσήνεγκεν· διὰ γὰρ δὴ τοῦτο καὶ *ἀρχιερεὺς ἡμῶν* ἐχρημάτισεν, *ἀρχιερεὺς* δέ, οὐχ ὡς Θεός, ἀλλ᾽ ὡς ἄνθρωπος κέκληται, καὶ αὐτὸς προσφέρει μὲν ὡς ἄνθρωπος, δέχεται δὲ τὴν θυσίαν μετὰ τοῦ Πατρὸς καὶ τοῦ Ἁγίου Πνεύματος ὡς Θεός. εἰ μὲν γὰρ τοῦ Ἀδὰμ τὸ σῶμα μόνον ἐξήμαρτεν, ἔδει τοῦτο μόνον ἀπολαῦσαι τῆς θεραπείας, ἐπεὶ δὲ οὐ μόνον συνήμαρτεν, ἀλλὰ καὶ προήμαρτεν ἡ ψυχή· πρότερος γὰρ ὁ λογισμὸς διαγράφει τὴν ἁμαρτίαν, εἶθ᾽ οὕτως ταύτην διὰ τοῦ σώματος ἐνεργεῖ· δίκαιον ἦν δήπου καὶ ταύτην τῆς ἰατρείας τυχεῖν. ἀλλὰ γὰρ παρέλκον ἴσως ἐκ λογισμῶν ποιεῖσθαι τούτου τὰς ἀποδείξεις, τῆς θείας σαφῶς τοῦτο κηρυττούσης Γραφῆς· καὶ γὰρ Δαυὶδ ὁ θεσπέσιος καὶ ὁ θειότατος Πέτρος διαρρήδην τοῦτο διδάσκουσιν· ὁ μὲν πόρρωθεν προθεσπίζων, ὁ δὲ τὴν πρόρρησιν ἑρμηνεύων. φησὶν δὲ οὕτως τῶν ἀποστόλων ὁ πρῶτος· *Προφήτης … ὑπάρχων* ὁ Δαυὶδ *καὶ εἰδὼς ὅτι ὅρκῳ ὤμοσεν αὐτῷ ὁ Θεὸς ἐκ καρποῦ τῆς ὀσφύος αὐτοῦ* ἀναστήσειν κατὰ σάρκα τὸν Χριστὸν *καθίσαι ἐπὶ* τοῦ θρόνου *αὐτοῦ*, προειδὼς *ἐλάλησεν περὶ τῆς ἀναστάσεως* αὐτοῦ, *ὅτι οὐκ ἐγκατελείφθη εἰς* ᾅδου ἡ ψυχὴ αὐτοῦ, οὐδὲ *ἡ σάρξ αὐτοῦ εἶδεν διαφθοράν.*[n]

(6) Πολλὰ δὲ κατὰ ταὐτὸν ἡμᾶς διὰ τῶν ὀλίγων τούτων ἐξεπαίδευσε λόγων· πρῶτον μὲν ὡς ἡ ληφθεῖσα φύσις ἐκ τῆς ὀσφύος τοῦ Δαυὶδ κατάγει τὸ γένος, ἔπειτα δὲ ὅτι οὐ σῶμα μόνον, ἀλλὰ καὶ ψυχὴν ἀθάνατον ἔλαβεν, καί, πρὸς τούτοις,

n. Acts 2.30f. (NT var.)

soul, the helmsman of the body, so that, through his soul, every soul might acquire immutability. We all know that souls, though immortal, are not immutable but subject to any number of sudden changes as they draw pleasure from one source or another; this is how we are turned astray and sin and allow ourselves to be pulled toward the worse. After the resurrection, however, our bodies are immortal and incorruptible, and our souls impassible and immutable. This, then, is the reason the only-begotten Son of God assumed both body and soul, kept both free of blemish, and made his sacrifice on behalf of the human race—it is precisely because of this that he is called our "high priest," a name he has received not as God, but as man: on the one hand, he makes his offering as man; on the other, he receives the sacrifice along with the Father and the Holy Spirit as God. You see, if it had been just Adam's body that had sinned, just the body would have needed to be cured, but, as the soul not only shared in the sin, but sinned before the body—our rational faculty must first plan the sin before it makes use of the body to carry it out—it was only proper that the soul should also receive treatment. But perhaps all this proof from reason is quite unnecessary, since holy Scripture itself proclaims this for all to hear. This is the explicit teaching of David, inspired prophet, and Peter, holiest of saints, the former announcing what he saw from afar, the latter interpreting his prophecy. This is how the prince of the apostles put it: "David, being a prophet and knowing that God had sworn him an oath to raise up the messiah, according to the flesh, from the fruit of his loins to set him on his throne, spoke, with foreknowledge of what was to be, of his resurrection and said that his soul did not remain 'in death,' nor did his flesh 'see dissolution.'"[n]

(6) With just these few words Scripture has given us instruction on a great many points: first, that the assumed nature is descended from the loins of David; second, that he assumed not just a body, but also an immortal soul; third, that he gave these over to death, took

ὅτι ταῦτα τῷ θανάτῳ παραδέδωκεν ἅ, λαβὼν πάλιν, ἀνέστησεν ὡς ἠθέλησεν· αὐτοῦ γάρ ἐστιν φωνή, *Λύσατε τὸν ναὸν τοῦτον, καὶ ἐν τρισὶν ἡμέραις ἐγερῶ αὐτόν,*[o] μεμαθήκαμεν δὲ καὶ ὡς ἡ θεία φύσις ἀθάνατος· πέπονθεν γὰρ τὸ παθητόν, καὶ τὸ ἀπαθὲς μεμένηκεν ἀπαθές· ἐνηνθρώπησεν γὰρ ὁ Θεὸς Λόγος, οὐχ ἵνα παθητὴν ἀποφήνῃ τὴν ἀπαθῆ φύσιν, ἀλλ᾽ ἵνα τῇ παθητῇ φύσει διὰ τοῦ πάθους τὴν ἀπάθειαν δωρήσηται. καὶ αὐτὸς δὲ ὁ Κύριος ἐν τοῖς ἱεροῖς εὐαγγελίοις νῦν μέν φησιν, *Ἐξουσίαν ἔχω θεῖναι* τὴν ψυχήν μου *καὶ ἐξουσίαν ἔχω πάλιν λαβεῖν αὐτήν· οὐδεὶς αἴρει αὐτὴν ἀπ᾽ ἐμοῦ· … ἐγὼ τίθημι* αὐτὴν ἀπ᾽ ἐμαυτοῦ *ἵνα πάλιν λάβω αὐτήν·* νῦν δέ, *διὰ τοῦτο ὁ Πατήρ με ἀγαπᾷ, ὅτι ἐγὼ τίθημι τὴν ψυχήν μου* ὑπὲρ τῶν προβάτων·[p] καὶ πάλιν, *Νῦν ἡ ψυχή μου τετάρακται·*[q] καὶ αὖθις, *Περίλυπός ἐστιν ἡ ψυχή μου ἕως θανάτου.*[r] καὶ περὶ τοῦ σώματος δέ φησιν, *Ὁ δὲ ἄρτος ὃν ἐγὼ δώσω ἡ σάρξ μου ἐστίν,* ἣν ἐγὼ δώσω *ὑπὲρ τῆς τοῦ κόσμου ζωῆς·*[s] καί, τὰ θεῖα δὲ παραδοὺς μυστήρια καὶ τὸ σύμβολον κλάσας καὶ διανείμας, ἐπήγαγεν, *Τοῦτό μού ἐστιν τὸ σῶμα, τὸ ὑπὲρ ὑμῶν* θρυπτόμενον εἰς ἄφεσιν ἁμαρτιῶν·[t] καὶ πάλιν, *Τοῦτό μού ἐστιν τὸ αἷμα …, τὸ* ὑπὲρ *πολλῶν ἐκχυνόμενον εἰς ἄφεσιν ἁμαρτιῶν·*[u] καὶ αὖθις, Ἂν *μὴ φάγητε τὴν σάρκα τοῦ Υἱοῦ τοῦ ἀνθρώπου καὶ πίητε*

l. 163 ἃ *corr. Cir., scr. edd.* : ὃ *NZ, A^ac? Ciriaco's correction provides the expected pl. rel. pron. to stand in correlation to the preceding demonstr.* ταῦτα. *It is also necessary to Thdt.'s argument regarding the redemption of the whole man (v. ep. 144, n. 5).* **l. 164** φωνὴ *NZ* : ἡ φ. *Cir., edd. The TLG cites four other places in the works of Thdt. for the formula Αὐτοῦ γάρ (or δέ) ἐστιν ἡ φωνή. Thdt. may, however, have used the formula without the article; v. the comment on 1Cor 9.13 attributed to him in the Catena in epistulam I ad Corinthios e cod. Paris. gr. 227 (Cramer, J.A., Catenae graecorum patrum in Novum Testamentum, vol. 5, p. 173): αὐτοῦ [τοῦ Κυρίου] γάρ ἐστιν φωνὴ, ἄξιος γὰρ ὁ ἐργάτης τῆς τροφῆς αὐτοῦ ἐστιν. Certainly, the anarthrous noun is the lect. diff.*

o. Jn 2.19
p. Jn 10.17f. (NT var.)
q. Jn 12.27
r. Mt 26.38
s. Jn 6.51 (NT var.)
t. 1Cor 11.24 (NT var.)
u. Mt 26.28 (NT var.)

them back again, and raised them up according to his will; he is, after all, the one who spoke the words, "Destroy this temple, and in three days I shall raise it up."[o] Now, as we are aware, the divine nature is immortal—what suffered was the passible, while the impassible remained impassible—God the Word becoming man, not to make the impassible nature passible, but through his suffering to grant the gift of impassibility to the naturally passible. In the holy gospels, the Lord himself declares, "I have the power to lay down my soul and power to take it up again. No one can take it away from me. I put it off from myself in order to take it up again," and then "it is because I lay down my soul"[p] for my sheep "that the Father loves me"; and elsewhere, "Now is my soul troubled";[q] and again, "My soul is deeply troubled, unto death."[r] And with regard to the body he declares, "The bread I shall give is my flesh, which I shall give for the life of the world."[s] Moreover, in the transmission of the sacred mysteries, breaking and distributing the token,[4] he added, "This is my body, which is broken for you, for the remission of sin";[t] and elsewhere, "This is my blood, which is poured out for many, for the remission of sin";[5u] and again, "Unless you eat the flesh of the Son of man and drink his blood, you

4. On Theodoret's use of the term "token" to refer to the bread of the Eucharist, *v. ep.* 131 n. 9.

5. Neither of these is a true quotation; both appear to be liturgical developments of the words of institution. It is noteworthy that, in reference to the body of Christ, Theodoret employs τὸ ὑπὲρ ὑμῶν θρυπτόμενον, the reading of the sixth-century *codex Claromontanus*; this form of the words of institution is reflected also in *Const. apost.* 8.12.35 (τὸ περὶ πολλῶν θρυπτόμενον). In contrast, in *ep.* 131.4, his commentary on 1Cor 11.23–25, and in a *testimonium* of Athanasius included in *Eran. flor.* 2, 25c, he had quoted in place of the sparsely attested θρυπτόμενον the better attested participle κλώμενον; *cf. ep.* 131 n. 10. The words regarding the cup seem to draw on both of the parallel passages in Mk and Mt.

αὐτοῦ τὸ αἷμα, οὐκ ἔχετε ζωὴν ἐν ἑαυτοῖς·[v] καί, Ὁ ἐσθίων *μου τὴν σάρκα καὶ πίνων μου τὸ αἷμα ἔχει ζωὴν* ἐν ἑαυτῷ *αἰώνιον.*[w] καὶ ἕτερα δὲ τοιαῦτα μυρία ἔστιν εὑρεῖν κἀν τῇ παλαιᾷ κἀν τῇ καινῇ, καὶ τοῦ σώματος καὶ τῆς ψυχῆς δεικνύντα τὴν πρόσληψιν καὶ ὡς ἐξ Ἀβραὰμ καὶ Δαυὶδ ἕλκει ταῦτα τὸ γένος. καὶ Ἰωσὴφ δὲ ὁ Ἀριμαθαῖος, τῷ Πιλάτῳ προσελθών, ᾔτησεν τὸ σῶμα τοῦ Ἰησοῦ,[x] καὶ διδάσκει ἡμᾶς διαρρήδην τῶν ἱερῶν εὐαγγελίων ἡ τετρακτὺς ὅπως τε ἔλαβεν τὸ σῶμα, καὶ ὅπως *ἐνείλησεν τῇ σινδόνι,*[y] καὶ ὅπως τῷ τάφῳ παρέδωκεν.[z]

(7) Ἐγὼ δὲ θρηνῶ καὶ ὀδύρομαι ὅτι ἃς πρώην τοῖς τὴν Μαρκίωνος λύμην εἰσδεξαμένοις προσέφερον ἀποδείξεις· καὶ πλείους ἢ μυρίους διὰ τῆς θείας χάριτος πείσας, προσήγαγον τῷ παναγίῳ βαπτίσματι· ταύτας νῦν τοῖς νομισθεῖσιν ὁμοπίστοις ἡ ἐπισκήψασα νόσος προσφέρειν καταναγκάζει· τίς γὰρ πώποτε περὶ τούτων τοῖς τῆς Ἐκκλησίας τροφίμοις ἀμφισβήτησις γέγονεν; τίς δὲ τῶν ἁγίων πατέρων οὐ τήνδε τὴν διδασκαλίαν προσήνεγκε; πλήρη γὰρ ταύτης καὶ τὰ τοῦ μεγάλου Βασιλείου συγγράμματα, καὶ τὰ τῶν ἐκείνου συναγωνιστῶν Γρηγορίου καὶ Ἀμφιλοχίου, καὶ τῶν ἐν τῇ δύσει διαπρεψάντων ἐν τῇ διδασκαλίᾳ τῆς χάριτος· Δαμάσου τοῦ τῆς μεγάλης Ῥώμης, καὶ Ἀμβροσίου τοῦ Μεδιολάνων, καὶ Κυπριανοῦ τοῦ Καρχηδόνος, ὃς καὶ τοῦ μαρτυρίου τὸν στέφανον ἀνεδέξατο. ὑπὲρ τουτωνὶ τῶν δογμάτων Ἀθανάσιος, ἐκεῖνος ὁ πολυθρύλητος, πεντάκις

l. 200 Γρηγορίου *scr. Cir., edd.* : Γ. Γ. *NZ = "and in the writings of Gregory, and Gregory, and Amphilochius." It looks likely that N has erred by dittography. In other lists of authorities, Thdt. mentions only one Gr., most probably Gr. nys.; v. epp. 83, n. 3 and 89, n. 2. The pairing of the two brothers is very common in patristic sources; cf. ACO, vol. 2.1.2, p. 79, l. 6: παρὰ … Βασιλείου Γρηγορίου καὶ νῦν πάλιν διὰ τοῦ ἁγιωτάτου Λέοντος; cf. 2.2.2, p. 50, l. 34. Yet, analogous lists of authorities sometimes cite more than one Gregory; v., e.g. ACO, vol. 2.1.1, p. 101, l. 16: οὕτως ἐφεξῆς καὶ Ἀθανασίου καὶ τοῦ μεγάλου Γρηγορίου καὶ Γρηγορίου καὶ Γρηγορίου καὶ Ἀττικοῦ καὶ Πρόκλου τῶν ἁγίων ἐπισκόπων.*

v. Jn 6.53 (NT var.) w. Jn 6.54 (NT var.)
x. Mt 27.58 y. Mk 15.46
z. Mt 27.57–60; Mk 15.42–46; Lk 23.50–53; Jn 19.38–42

have no life within you";[v] and, "He who eats my flesh and drinks my blood has life eternal in him."[w] One could find in both the Old and the New Testament thousands upon thousands of such texts indicating the assumption of the body and the soul and proving that his body and soul are descended from Abraham and David. Furthermore, there is Joseph of Arimathea, who approached Pilate to ask for the body of Jesus.[x] And from the fourfold gospel-book we learn in no uncertain terms how Joseph took the body, "wrapped it in a sheet,"[y] and deposited it in the tomb.[z]

(7) I can only deplore the fact that I find myself constrained by the onset of this virus to put before men supposedly of the same faith the same proofs I long ago put before people—and there were more than ten thousand of them whom, through the grace of God, I was able to win over and present for holy baptism—who had been infected with Marcionism. When was there ever any argument about these issues among those brought up in the Church? Was there any holy father who did not teach this? The teaching of the Church is set out in full in the writings of the great Basil and in those of Gregory and Amphilochius, who contended at his side, and in the writings of westerners preëminent for their teaching of God's grace: Damasus of the great Rome, Ambrose of Milan, and Cyprian of Carthage, who received the crown of martyrdom. In defense of these very doctrines, Athanasius, the far-famed, was driven from his flock five times and

ἐξηλάθη τῆς ποίμνης καὶ τὴν ὑπερορίαν οἰκεῖν ἠναγκάσθη, καὶ Ἀλέξανδρος δέ, ὁ ἐκείνου διδάσκαλος, ὑπὲρ τούτων ἠγωνίσατο τῶν δογμάτων, καὶ Εὐστάθιος, καὶ Μελέτιος, καὶ Φλαβιανός, τῆς Ἀνατολῆς οἱ φωστῆρες,[ba] καὶ Ἐφραίμ, ἡ τοῦ Πνεύματος λύρα, ὁ τὸ σύρων ἔθνος ἄρδων ὁσημέραι τοῖς τῆς χάριτος νάμασιν, καὶ Ἰωάννης καὶ Ἀττικός, οἱ τῆς ἀληθείας μεγαλόφωνοι κήρυκες, καὶ οἱ τούτων ἔτι πρεσβύτεροι· Ἰγνάτιος, καὶ Πολύκαρπος, καὶ Εἰρηναῖος, καὶ Ἰουστῖνος, καὶ Ἱππόλυτος, ὧν οἱ πλείους οὐκ ἀρχιερέων προλάμπουσι μόνον, ἀλλὰ καὶ τὸν τῶν μαρτύρων διακοσμοῦσι χορόν. καὶ μὲν δὴ καὶ ὁ νῦν τὴν μεγάλην Ῥώμην ἰθύνων καὶ τῶν ὀρθῶν δογμάτων τὰς ἀκτῖνας ἐκ τῆς Ἑσπέρας πάντοσε ἐκτείνων, ὁ ἁγιώτατος Λέων, τοῦτον ἡμῖν τῆς πίστεως τὸν χαρακτῆρα διὰ τῶν οἰκείων δογμάτων προσήνεγκεν.

ba. Phil 2.15

compelled to live in exile. Alexander, his teacher, also fought for these doctrines. And what about Eustathius, and Meletius, as well as Flavian, the luminaries of the East?[ba] Ephrem, the lyre of the Holy Spirit, who, day after day, poured out streams of grace for the people of Syria? John and Atticus, the great-voiced heralds of the truth? And men of an earlier time: Ignatius, Polycarp, Irenaeus, Justin, Hippolytus, most of these not only shining bright among the ranks of the bishops, but adorning the chorus of martyrs as well?[6] And now, his Holiness Leo, guide of the great city of Rome, sends forth from the West in every direction the beaming light of orthodoxy, in his own doctrinal teaching commending to us a faith of this very same stamp.

6. On the adaptation of Paul's metaphor (Phil 2.15), *v. ep.* 125 n. 7. This catalogue is considerably longer than that in *ep.* 89 (to the patrician, Florentius). There Theodoret listed Basil of Caesarea, Gregory of Nyssa, Athanasius of Alexandria (for his five exiles, *v. ep.* 145 n. 3), Eustathius of Antioch, John Chrysostom, Ignatius of Antioch, all of whom are cited in the *florilegia* of the *Eran*. Here he has added seven more bishops also quoted in these *florilegia*: Amphilochius of Iconium (*ca.* 340–94; *v.* Baldwin, "Amphilochios of Ikonion"), Damasus of Rome (*ca.* 304–84; *v.* "Damasus, St.," Livingstone), Ambrose of Milan (*ca.* 339–97; *v.* Gregory, "Ambrose"), Flavian of Antioch (301–404; *v.* Gorce, "7. Flavien I[er]"), Atticus of Constantinople (bishop 406–25; *v.* Kazhdan, "Attikos"), Irenaeus of Lyon (*ca.* 130–*ca.* 200; *v.* Livingstone, "Irenaeus, St."), and Hippolytus (*ca.* 170–*ca.* 236; *v.* Livingstone, "Hippolytus, St."). Though Hippolytus was regarded at Rome as a schismatic, in the *Eran.*, he is regularly introduced only as "bishop and martyr"; *v.* pp. 99, l. 1; 155, l. 3; 230, l. 19; most likely Theodoret could not attach his name to a given see. In addition, this list, unlike that in *ep.* 89, includes the names of figures not quoted in the *Eran.* Four, Alexander of Alexandria (*ca.* 250–328; *v.* Papadakis, "Alexander"), Cyprian of Carthage (d. 258; *v.* Livingstone, "Cyprian, St."), Meletius of Antioch (elected bishop in 360; *v.* Gregory and Kazhdan, "Meletian Schism"), Polycarp of Smyrna (*ca.* 69–*ca.* 155; *v.* Livingstone, "Polycarp, St."), were bishops; two, Ephraem Syrus (*ca.* 306–73; *v.* Baldwin and Ševčenko, "Ephrem the Syrian") and Justin Martyr (*ca.* 100–*ca.* 165; *v.* Livingstone, "Justin Martyr, St."), were major theological authors, the first a deacon, the second a layman. Most likely, Theodoret had no access to any work by any of these six, or at least, to any work relevant to his present purpose. Alexander was remembered primarily for his excommunication of Arius; the others were martyrs (Cyprian, Polycarp, and Justin) or confessors (Meletius and Ephraem); *v.* Intro., n. 33. Thus, in *ep.* 89, Theodoret named authors whose works he had consulted; here he extended that bibliography but inserted as well the names of men he probably knew only as heroes of orthodoxy. The structure of the list, however, makes no distinctions, and the monks to whom he was writing might well have imagined that Theodoret could cite proof texts from, *e.g.*, Cyprian, as well as from Basil.

(8) Οὗτοι πάντες σαφῶς ἐξεπαίδευσαν ὡς εἷς Υἱὸς ὁ μονογενὴς τοῦ Θεοῦ Υἱὸς καὶ Θεὸς προαιώνιος ἐκ τοῦ Πατρὸς ἀρρήτως γεγεννημένος καὶ ὡς, μετὰ τὴν ἐνανθρώπησιν, καὶ *Υἱὸς ἀνθρώπου* καὶ *ἄνθρωπος* ἐχρημάτισεν, οὐκ εἰς τοῦτο τραπείς· ἄτρεπτον γὰρ ἔχει τὴν φύσιν· ἀλλὰ προσλαβὼν τὸ ἡμέτερον, καὶ ὅτι αὐτὸς καὶ ἀπαθὴς ἦν καὶ ἀθάνατος ὡς θεός, καὶ θνητὸς καὶ παθητὸς ὡς ἄνθρωπος, μετὰ δὲ τὴν ἀνάστασιν, καὶ κατὰ τὸ ἀνθρώπειον καὶ τὴν ἀπάθειαν καὶ τὴν ἀθανασίαν ἐδέξατο· εἰ γὰρ καὶ μεμένηκεν σῶμα τὸ σῶμα, ἀλλ᾽ ἀπαθές ἐστιν καὶ ἀθάνατον, καὶ θεῖον ὄντως σῶμα, καὶ θείᾳ δόξῃ δεδοξασμένον. καὶ τοῦτο σαφῶς ἡμᾶς ὁ μακάριος ἐδίδαξε Παῦλος, *Ἡμῶν γάρ*, φησί, *τὸ πολίτευμα ἐν οὐρανοῖς ὑπάρχει, ἐξ οὗ καὶ σωτῆρα ἀπεκδεχόμεθα Κύριον Ἰησοῦν Χριστόν, ὃς μετασχηματίσει τὸ σῶμα τῆς ταπεινώσεως ἡμῶν* εἰς τὸ γενέσθαι αὐτὸ *σύμμορφον τῷ σώματι τῆς δόξης αὐτοῦ*,[bb] καὶ οὐκ εἶπεν, *Τῇ δόξῃ αὐτοῦ*, ἀλλὰ *Τῷ σώματι τῆς δόξης αὐτοῦ*. καὶ αὐτὸς δὲ ὁ Κύριος, εἰπὼν τοῖς ἀποστόλοις, *Εἰσίν τινες τῶν ὧδε ἑστώτων οἵτινες οὐ μὴ γεύσωνται θανάτου ἕως ἂν ἴδωσιν τὸν Υἱὸν τοῦ ἀνθρώπου ἐρχόμενον ἐν τῇ* δόξῃ τοῦ Πατρός,[bc] παρέλαβεν αὐτοὺς *μετὰ ἓξ ἡμέρας εἰς ὄρος ὑψηλὸν* λίαν *καὶ μετεμορφώθη ἔμπροσθεν αὐτῶν, καὶ* ἐγένετο *τὸ πρόσωπον αὐτοῦ ὡς ὁ ἥλιος, καὶ τὰ ἱμάτια αὐτοῦ* … λαμπρὰ *ὡς τὸ φῶς*.[bd] ἐδίδαξεν δὲ διὰ τούτων τῆς δευτέρας ἐπιφανείας τὸν τρόπον καὶ ὡς ἀπερίγραφος μὲν ἡ ληφθεῖσα φύσις οὐκ ἔστιν· τοῦτο γὰρ μόνης τῆς θεότητος ἴδιον· τὰς δὲ τῆς θείας δόξης

l. 235 γεύσωνται *scripsi* (*cf. NTG*) : -σον- *codd., edd. Although Thdt. is quoting Mt 16.28, the clause* οὐ μὴ γεύσωνται θάνατον *appears also at Mk 9.1 and Lk 9.27. In all three passages, the NTG prints the subjunc. aor., without citing attestations of the indic. fut.; for tenth-c. scribes the two forms would be homophones* (*cf. ep. 147.6, c. n. ad* προσκυνήσωμεν). *This is the only passage where Thdt. quotes the clause, and both the aor. subjunc. and the fut. indic. appear in quotations of and references to this word of Christ in the printed texts of patristic authors. Both may express a strong denial regarding the fut.* (*v. Smyth, sec. 2755*), *but the subjunc. is the clear lect. diff.*

bb. Phil 3.20f. (NT var.) bc. Mt 16.28 (NT var.) bd. Mt 17.1f. (NT var.)

(8) It was the clear and explicit teaching of all of these that there is one Son, the only-begotten of God, God eternal, begotten in some ineffable manner from the Father; that after the incarnation, the Son received the appellations "Son of Man" and "man," not that he was changed into a human being—of course, his nature is immutable—but that he assumed what belongs to us; furthermore, that he was at once impassible and immortal as God and, as man, subject both to death and suffering; that after the resurrection, he received, even in his humanity, freedom from suffering and death, because, though his body is still a body, it is now impassible and immortal, a body truly belonging to God, glorified with the glory of divinity. This is the clear meaning of the teaching we have received from the blessed Paul, who says, "We are citizens of heaven, and it is from there that we await, with eager anticipation, our Savior, the Lord Jesus Christ, who will transform our lowly body to make it like his own glorious body."[bb] Now Paul did not say, "like his glory," but "like his own glorious body." Moreover, the Lord himself said to his apostles, "Some of you who are standing here today, will not taste death until they see the Son of Man coming in the glory of the Father,"[bc] and then "six days later," took them "to a lofty mountain where he was transfigured before their eyes, and his face became like the sun, and his garments shone bright as light."[bd] This was his way of teaching them the manner of his second coming. Now, while the nature that was assumed is not uncircumscribed—a property belonging to the godhead alone—his body will emit the radiance of the glory of

ἀφήσει μαρμαρυγὰς καὶ φωτὸς ἀκτῖνας ἐκπέμψει, τῆς ὀπτικῆς αἰσθήσεως ὑπερβαίνουσα τὰ μέτρα. μετὰ ταύτης ἀνελήφθη τῆς δόξης, οὕτως αὐτὸν ἔφασαν ἥξειν οἱ ἄγγελοι· αὐτῶν γάρ ἐστι φωνή, *Οὗτος ... ὁ ἀναληφθεὶς ἀφ᾽ ὑμῶν εἰς τὸν οὐρανὸν οὕτως ἐλεύσεται, ὅν τρόπον ἐθεάσασθε αὐτὸν πορευόμενον εἰς τὸν οὐρανόν.*[be] καὶ τοῖς θείοις δὲ ἀποστόλοις ὀφθεὶς μετὰ τὴν ἀνάστασιν, καὶ χεῖρας αὐτοῖς καὶ πόδας ὑπέδειξεν,[bf] τῷ δὲ Θωμᾷ καὶ τὴν πλευρὰν καὶ τῶν ἥλων καὶ τῆς λόγχης τὰς ὠτειλάς·[bg] διὰ γὰρ δὴ τούτους τοὺς ἄντικρυς ἀρνουμένους τῆς σαρκὸς τὴν ἀνάληψιν καὶ μέντοι καὶ τοὺς ἄλλους οἵ, μετὰ τὴν ἀνάστασιν, εἰς θεότητός φασιν μεταβεβλῆσθαι φύσιν τὴν τοῦ σώματος φύσιν, ἐφύλαξεν ἀκεραίους τῶν ἥλων καὶ τῆς λόγχης τοὺς τύπους. καὶ τἄλλα σώματα μώμου παντὸς ἐγείρων ἐλεύθερα, τῷ οἰκείῳ σώματι τὰ τῶν παθημάτων σημεῖα κατέλιπεν ἵνα καὶ τοὺς ἀρνουμένους τοῦ σώματος τὴν ἀνάληψιν διὰ τῶν παθημάτων πλανωμένους ἐλέγξῃ καὶ τοὺς εἰς ἑτέραν φύσιν μεταβεβλῆσθαι τὸ σῶμα νομίζοντας διδάξῃ διὰ τοῦ τύπου τῶν ἥλων ὡς ἐπὶ τῶν οἰκείων χαρακτήρων μεμένηκεν.

(9) Εἰ δέ τις ἀπόδειξιν ἔχειν οἴεται τοῦ μὴ μεμενηκέναι σῶμα μετὰ τὴν ἀνάστασιν τοῦ Κυρίου τὸ σῶμα ὡς, κεκλεισμένων τῶν θυρῶν, πρὸς τοὺς μαθητὰς εἰσελθεῖν,[bh] ἀναμνησθήτω πῶς ἐπὶ θαλάττης ἐβάδισεν, θνητὸν ἔχων ἔτι τὸ σῶμα,[bi] καὶ μέντοι πῶς ἐγεννήθη, τῆς παρθενίας ἀκήρατα φυλάξας τὰ σήμαντρα, καὶ αὖ πάλιν πῶς τῶν ἐπιβουλευόντων πολλάκις τὰς χεῖρας διέφυγεν, ὑπ᾽ ἐκείνων κεκυκλωμένος.[bj] καὶ τί λέγω τὸν Δεσπότην, ὅς οὐ μόνον ἄνθρωπος ἦν, ἀλλὰ καὶ Θεὸς προαιώνιος, καὶ ῥᾴδιον ἦν αὐτῷ πάντα ποιεῖν ὅσα βούλεται; εἰπάτωσαν πῶς ὁ Ἀμβακοὺμ ἐκ τῆς Ἰουδαίας εἰς Βαβυλῶνα ἐν ἀκαρεῖ τοῦ χρόνου μετέβη, καὶ διέβη τοῦ λάκκου τὸ κάλυμμα,

be. Acts 1.11 (NT var.) bf. Jn 20.19f. bg. Jn 20.25–27 bh. Jn 20.19
bi. Mt 14.22–33; Mk 6.45–52; Jn 6.16–21
bj. *Cf.*, *e.g.*, Lk 4.29f.; Jn 7.30; 10.39.

God and send forth rays of light that will be brighter than anything our eyes can see. This was the glory of his assumption into heaven, and, according to the angels, this is how he will come again. For this we have their word: "He who was taken up from you into heaven will come in the same manner as you have seen him go into heaven."[be] Furthermore, when he appeared to the holy apostles after the resurrection he showed them his hands and feet[bf] but, to Thomas, also his side and the wounds left by the lance and the nails.[bg] You see, he preserved the marks left by the nails and the lance, just as they were, on account of those who flatly deny the assumption of the flesh and also those who assert that, after the resurrection, the nature of the body was transformed into that of God. Though he raises all other bodies free of blemish, he left the signs of his passion in his own so that his sufferings might show the error of those denying the assumption of the body, and so that the imprint of the nails might teach those who believe that his body was changed into the other nature that it continues to exist within the limits of its own characteristics.

(9) Now, if anyone imagines he can prove that the Lord's body did not remain a body after the resurrection on the ground that he passed through closed doors to join his disciples,[bh] he should recall how the Lord walked on the sea while he still had a mortal body,[bi] and how he was born without violating the seal of virginity, and how he often evaded the clutches of his enemies even when they had him surrounded.[bj] And why should I speak of the Lord, who was not only man, but also God eternal, and thus could easily accomplish whatever he willed? I would have them explain how Habakkuk managed to travel, in no more than a moment of time, from Judea to Babylon, pass through the planking over the lions' pit, de-

καὶ τῷ Δανιὴλ προσενήνοχε τὴν τροφήν, καὶ αὖθις ἐπανῆλθεν, μὴ διαφθείρας τοῦ λάκκου τὰ σήμαντρα.[bk] ἀλλὰ μανία σαφὴς καὶ τῶν δεσποτικῶν θαυμάτων τοὺς τρόπους ἀνερευνᾶν. προσήκει δὲ καὶ τοῦτο πρὸς τοῖς εἰρημένοις εἰδέναι, ὡς, μετὰ τὴν ἀνάστασιν, καὶ τὰ ἡμέτερα σώματα ἄφθαρτα ἔσται καὶ ἀθάνατα, καί, τοῦ γεώδους ἀπαλλαττόμενα, κοῦφα γίγνεται καὶ μετάρσια. καὶ τοῦτο διαρρήδην σαφῶς ἡμᾶς ἐδίδαξεν ὁ θεῖος Παῦλος· *Σπείρεται*, γάρ φησιν, *ἐν φθορᾷ, ἐγείρεται ἐν ἀφθαρσίᾳ· σπείρεται ἐν ἀσθενείᾳ, ἐγείρεται ἐν δυνάμει· σπείρεται ἐν ἀτιμίᾳ, ἐγείρεται ἐν δόξῃ· σπείρεται σῶμα ψυχικόν, ἐγείρεται σῶμα πνευματικόν·*[bl] καὶ ἀλλαχοῦ, *Ἁρπαγησόμεθα*, φησίν, *ἐν νεφέλαις εἰς ἀέρα, εἰς ἀπάντησιν τοῦ Κυρίου.*[bm] εἰ δὲ τὰ τῶν ἁγίων σώματα κοῦφα γίγνεται καὶ μετάρσια καὶ ῥᾳδίως τὸν ἀέρα διαπερᾷ, οὐ δεῖ θαυμάζειν εἰ τὸ δεσποτικὸν σῶμα, τὸ τῇ θεότητι τοῦ Μονογενοῦς ἡνωμένον, μετὰ τὴν ἀνάστασιν γεγενημένον ἀθάνατον, κεκλεισμένων τῶν θυρῶν, εἰσελήλυθεν.

(10) Καὶ μυρίας δὲ ἑτέρας καὶ προφητικὰς καὶ ἀποστολικὰς μαρτυρίας παραγαγεῖν εὐπετές, ἀλλ᾽ ἀρκεῖ καὶ τὰ εἰρημένα δεῖξαι τὸν τῆς ἡμετέρας διδασκαλίας σκοπόν· πιστεύομεν γὰρ εἰς ἕνα Πατέρα, εἰς ἕνα Υἱόν, εἰς ἓν Ἅγιον Πνεῦμα καὶ ὁμολογοῦμεν μίαν θεότητα, μίαν κυριότητα, μίαν οὐσίαν, τρεῖς ὑποστάσεις· ἡ γὰρ ἐνανθρώπησις τοῦ Μονογενοῦς τὸν τῆς Τριάδος οὐκ ηὔξησεν ἀριθμὸν καὶ τετράδα τὴν Τριάδα πεποίηκεν, ἀλλὰ μεμένηκεν καὶ μετὰ τὴν ἐνανθρώπησιν Τριὰς ἡ Τριάς. ἐνανθρωπῆσαι δὲ πιστεύοντες τὸν μονογενῆ Υἱὸν τοῦ Θεοῦ, οὐκ ἀρνούμεθα ἣν ἔλαβε φύσιν, ἀλλ᾽ ὁμολογοῦμεν, ὡς ἔφην, καὶ τὴν λαβοῦσαν καὶ τὴν ληφθεῖσαν· ἡ γὰρ ἕνωσις οὐ συνέχεεν τὰ τῶν φύσεων ἴδια. εἰ γὰρ ὁ ἀήρ, ὅλος δι᾽ ὅλου τὸ φῶς εἰσδεχόμενος, οὐκ ἀπόλλυσιν τὸ εἶναι ἀὴρ οὔτε μὴν τοῦ φωτὸς διαφθείρει τὴν φύσιν, ἀλλὰ τοῖς μὲν ὀφθαλμοῖς ὁρῶμεν τὸ φῶς, τῇ δὲ ἁφῇ τὸν ἀέρα γινώσκομεν· ἢ γὰρ ψυχρὸς ἡμῖν ἢ θερμός, ἢ ὑγρὸς ἢ ξηρὸς προσπελάζει·

bk. Bel 31–39 bl. 1Cor 15.42–44 bm. 1Thes 4.17

liver the food to Daniel, and then get out of the pit without breaking the seals.[bk] But, after all, it's just foolishness to try to figure out how our Master works his miracles. In addition to what I've already said, there is the fact that, after the resurrection, even our own bodies will be incorruptible and immortal and, removed from the earthly, become light and capable of rising on high. For this we have the explicit teaching of St. Paul, who says, "Sown in corruption, raised up in incorruptibility; sown in weakness, raised up in power; sown in dishonor, raised up in glory; the body sown is carnal, the body raised is spiritual";[bl] and elsewhere he says, "We shall be snatched up in the midst of the clouds into the air to meet the Lord."[bm] If it is the case that the bodies of the saints become light and capable of rising on high and thus pass effortlessly through the air, there is no cause for wonder if the body of our Master, united to the godhead of the Only-begotten, having become immortal after its resurrection, passed through the closed doors.

(10) It would be an easy matter to adduce thousands upon thousands more testimonies from the prophets and the apostles, yet what has already been said is quite sufficient to indicate the thrust of our teaching. So then, we believe in one Father, in one Son, in one Holy Spirit, and we confess one godhead, one lordship, one essence, three persons,[7] because the incarnation of the Only-begotten did not increase the number of the Trinity to a quaternity, but, even after the incarnation, the Trinity remained a Trinity.[8] Yet, our faith in the incarnation of the Only-begotten does not entail denial of the nature that he assumed, but we confess, as I've said, both the nature that assumed and that which was assumed, since the union involved no confusion of the properties peculiar to these natures. If, for example, air, everywhere throughout its entire extent, is permeable to light without losing its existence as air or in any way corrupting the nature of light, and we can see light with our eyes while we sense

7. For "person," Theodoret here uses the term *hypostasis,* in earlier trinitarian discussion often a synonym for *prosopon*, which he will use in the last sentence of this same section; *cf.* Intro., sec. 1.2.

8. On the notion of quaternity, *v. ep.* 144 n. 3.

ἀνοίας ἐσχάτης *σύγχυσιν* ἀποκαλεῖν τὴν τῆς θεότητος καὶ τῆς ἀνθρωπότητος ἕνωσιν. εἰ γὰρ αἱ ὁμόδουλοι, καὶ ὁμόχρονοι, καὶ κτισταὶ φύσεις, ἑνούμεναι καὶ οἱονεὶ κεραννύμεναι, ἀκέραιοι διαμένουσιν καί, τοῦ φωτὸς ὑποχωροῦντος, μένει καθ' αὑτὴν τοῦ ἀέρος ἡ φύσις, πολλῷ δήπουθεν δικαιότερον τὴν τὰ πάντα τεκτηναμένην φύσιν, τῇ ἐξ ἡμῶν ληφθείσῃ συναφθεῖσάν τε καὶ ἑνωθεῖσαν φύσει, καὶ αὐτὴν ἀκραιφνῆ μεμενηκέναι ὁμολογεῖν καὶ ἣν ἔλαβεν ὡσαύτως ἀκεραίαν διαφυλάξαι. καὶ γὰρ καὶ ὁ χρυσός, τῷ πυρὶ προσομιλῶν, μεταλαμβάνει μὲν τῆς τοῦ πυρὸς καὶ χρόας καὶ ἐνεργείας, τὴν δὲ οἰκείαν οὐκ ἀπόλλυσι φύσιν, ἀλλὰ καὶ μένει χρυσὸς καὶ ἐνεργεῖ τὰ πυρός, οὕτω καὶ τὸ δεσποτικὸν σῶμα σῶμα μέν ἐστιν, ἀλλ' ἀπαθές, ἄφθαρτον, καὶ ἀθάνατον, καὶ δεσποτικόν, καὶ θεῖον, καὶ τῇ θείᾳ δόξῃ δεδοξασμένον· οὐ γὰρ κεχώρισται τῆς θεότητος οὐδὲ ἄλλου τινός ἐστιν, ἀλλ' αὐτοῦ τοῦ Μονογενοῦς Υἱοῦ τοῦ Θεοῦ, οὐδὲ γὰρ ἕτερον ἡμῖν ἐπιδείκνυσι πρόσωπον, ἀλλ' αὐτὸν τὸν Μονογενῆ, τὴν ἡμετέραν περικείμενον φύσιν.

(11) Ταύτην ἡμεῖς τὴν διδασκαλίαν διατελοῦμεν κηρύττοντες, οἱ δὲ τὴν ὑπὲρ ἡμῶν γεγενημένην οἰκονομίαν ἀρνούμενοι *αἱρετικοὺς* ἡμᾶς προσηγόρευσαν, προσόμοιόν τι ταῖς γυναιξὶ ταῖς ἀκολάστοις ποιοῦντες· καὶ γὰρ ἐκεῖναι, δημοσίᾳ πωλοῦσαι τὴν ὥραν, τοῖς ἑταιρικοῖς ὀνείδεσι τὰς σώφρονας περιβάλλουσιν καὶ τὰ τῆς οἰκείας ἀσελγείας ὀνόματα ταῖς τὴν ἀσέλγειαν βδελυττομέναις περιτιθέασιν. τοῦτο καὶ ἡ αἰγυπτία πεποίηκεν· τὴν γὰρ τῆς αἰσχρᾶς ἐπιθυμίας δουλείαν ἀσπασαμένη καὶ τὴν ἀνδραποδώδη κολακείαν προσενεγκοῦσα τῷ σώφρονι, εἶτα, μὴ δελεάσασα μηδὲ ταῖς τῆς ἡδυπαθείας περιπείρασα πάγαις, *ἀλλοτρίας εὐνῆς* ἀπεκάλει *λῃστὴν* τῆς σωφροσύνης τὸν ἐραστήν.[bn] ἀλλ' οὗτοι μὲν δώσουσι τῷ Θεῷ

l. 329 ἡδυπαθείας *scr. Cir.* (*uerbo scripto, cancellato, rescripto*), *edd.* : -αις *NZ*

bn. Gn 39.6–18

air by touch—since air is cold or hot, wet or dry as it reaches us—it is sheer unreason to refer to the union of the godhead and the humanity as "a confusion." After all, if these two created substances, both made to serve us within the temporal world, can unite and, so to speak, mix themselves together and yet remain unimpaired—the nature of air remaining in itself when light withdraws from it—it is with all the more reason that we should confess that the nature that constructed the universe, when joined to and united with the nature taken from humanity, remained itself unimpaired and likewise kept unimpaired the nature it had assumed. One might also mention that gold, when brought into contact with fire, takes on the color and the power of the fire with no loss of its own nature, but remains gold and, at the same time, performs the same functions as fire. Just so, the Master's body is a body, but impassible, incorruptible, and immortal, the body of the Master, the body of God, possessed of the divine glory, because it is not separated from the godhead, and it belongs to the only-begotten Son of God alone. This body presents to us only the Only-begotten, and no other person, clad in our nature.

(11) This is the doctrine I have always preached. But those who deny the redemption that took place on our behalf call me a heretic, in this behaving rather like immoral women. These, as you know, sell their beauty to all comers and then invest chaste women with volleys of insults appropriate for prostitutes—showering women who abhor such behavior with all the epithets that should really be applied to their own misbehavior. This is how that Egyptian woman behaved: it was she who was so eager to enslave herself to a foul lust, she the one who offered her servile flatteries to that chaste man, then—when she couldn't entice him, when she couldn't trap him in the snares of pleasure—began defaming him, the devoted lover of chastity, as "the thief of another man's bed."[bn] But they will have to

τὰς εὐθύνας καὶ τῶν κατὰ τῆς πίστεως μηχανημάτων καὶ τῶν καθ' ἡμῶν σκευωρημάτων. ἐγὼ δὲ τοὺς ὑπηγμένους ταῖς γεγενημέναις ψευδολογίαις παρακαλῶ θατέραν ταῖν ἀκοαῖν τῷ κατηγορουμένῳ φυλάττειν, καὶ μὴ τὰς δύο τοῖς κατηγοροῦσιν ὑπέχειν· οὕτω γὰρ τὸν θεῖον πληρώσουσι νόμον ὃς διαρρήδην βοᾷ, *Ἀκοὴν ματαίαν οὐ παραδέξῃ*,[bo] καὶ *Κρίσιν δικαίαν κρίνετε ἀναμέσον ἀνδρὸς καὶ ἀναμέσον* τοῦ πλησίον αὐτοῦ·[bp] διὰ γὰρ δὴ τούτων ὁ θεῖος νόμος παρεγγυᾷ μὴ πιστεύειν ταῖς κατὰ τῶν ἀπόντων διαβολαῖς, ἀλλὰ παροῦσι τοῖς κατηγορουμένοις δικάζειν.

l. 334 θατέραν ταῖν ἀκοαῖν *corr. Cir., scr. edd.* : θ. τὴν ἀκοὴν *NZ*, A^{ac}. *As the phrase carried by NZ and* A^{ac} *is attested nowhere else in Greek literature, the previous editors were doubtless right to accept Ciriaco's correction*; *cf. ep.* 83.2, *c. n.* (θατέραν ταῖν ἀκοαῖν).

bo. Ex 23.1 bp. Dt 1.16 (LXX var.) (*Cf.* Jn 7.24.)

render before God an accounting for their machinations against the faith and their dishonest attacks against me. I now call upon any who have been misled by their false statements not to give both ears to the prosecution, but to keep one for the defendant. In this, they will fulfill the law of God which explicitly proclaims, "You shall not give heed to an empty rumor";[bo] and "Render righteous judgment between a man and his neighbor."[bp] With these commandments, the law of God forbids us to give credence to calumny against the absent and requires that judgment be rendered in the presence of the accused.

147. ΙΩΑΝΝΗΙ ΟΙΚΟΝΟΜΩΙ

|N (1) |Ἐμοὶ μὲν ἡσυχία θυμήρης καὶ βίος φροντίδων ἐλεύθερος· διά τοι τοῦτο καὶ τοῦ μοναστηρίου τὴν αὔλειον ἀνῳκοδόμησα θύραν καὶ τῶν γνωρίμων τὰς συντυχίας ἐκκλίνω· ἐπειδὴ δὲ καινοτομίαν κατὰ τῆς εὐαγγελικῆς πίστεως κινεῖσθαι μεμάθηκα, οὐκ ἀκίνδυνον ὑπολαμβάνω τὴν σιωπήν. εἰ γάρ, ἀνθρώπου βασιλεύειν λαχόντος παρά τινων ὑβρισθέντος, οὐ κατὰ τῶν ὑβρικότων μόνον, ἀλλὰ καὶ κατὰ τῶν παρατετυχηκότων μέν, ἥκιστα δὲ τοὺς πεπαρῳνηκότας ἀμυναμένων κίνδυνος ἐπῃώρηται, ποίαν οὐκ ἂν δικαίως κόλασιν ὑποσταῖεν οἱ τὰς κατὰ *τοῦ … Θεοῦ καὶ Σωτῆρος ἡμῶν*[a] τολμωμένας βλασφημίας παρορᾶν ἀνεχόμενοι; τοῦτό με τὸ δέος ἐπὶ τοῦ παρόντος ἠνάγκασεν γράψαι νῦν καὶ δηλῶσαι ἃ παρά τινων καινοτομεῖσθαι μεμάθηκα.

Πολλοὶ γάρ, ὥς τινές φασιν, ἐν τῇ πόλει θρυλοῦσιν ὡς, πρεσβυτέρων τινῶν προσευξαμένων, καὶ τὸ σύνηθες τέλος ἐπιτεθεικότων τῇ προσευχῇ, καί, τῶν μὲν εἰρηκότων, ὅτι *Σοὶ πρέπει δόξα, καὶ τῷ Χριστῷ σου, καὶ τῷ Ἁγίῳ σου Πνεύματι,* τῶν δέ, *Χάριτι καὶ φιλανθρωπίᾳ τοῦ Χριστοῦ σου, μεθ᾽ οὗ σοὶ πρέπει δόξα σὺν τῷ Ἁγίῳ σου Πνεύματι,* ἐπέσκηψεν ὁ σοφώτατος ἀρχιδιάκονος μὴ χρῆναι λέγειν *τὸν Χριστόν,* ἀλλὰ *τὸν Μονογενῆ* δοξάζειν. εἰ δὲ τοῦτο ἀληθές, οὐδεμίαν ἀσεβείας ὑπερβολὴν καταλείπει· ἢ γὰρ εἰς δύο υἱοὺς μερίζει τὸν ἕνα Κύριον ἡμῶν Ἰησοῦν Χριστὸν καὶ τὸν μονογενῆ μὲν Υἱὸν ὑπολαμβάνει γνήσιόν τε καὶ φύσει γεγενημένον, τὸν δὲ Χριστὸν εἰσποιητόν τε καὶ νόθον καὶ διὰ τοῦτο δοξολογίας ἀνάξιον, ἢ πειρᾶται κρατύνειν τὴν νῦν εἰσκωμάσασαν αἵρεσιν. καὶ εἰ μὲν ὁ παγχάλεπος ἐπέκειτο κλύδων, ἐτόπασεν ἄν τις αὐτόν,

l. 27 ὁ παγχάλεπος *codd.* : π. *scr. Sir.* (*fort. recte*) *Nös. Az.* = *"if there were a severe tempest hovering above us." Since there has been no previous mention in this letter of the metaphorical storm, Sirmond's emendation, while not necessary, is appropriate enough. Elsewhere in the letters, the combination of*

a. Ti 2.13

147. To John,[1] the Steward[2]

I'm enjoying peace and quiet, a life free of care. Just for this reason, I've blocked up the front door of the monastery, and I avoid interaction with acquaintances. Yet, as I've learned there's a heretical effort afoot to make changes in the gospel faith, I think it quite unsafe to remain quiet. If someone subjects a mere man, but that man who happens to be emperor, to some act of violence; the threat of punishment hangs not just over the offenders, but also over any bystander who made no effort to protect the ruler from assault. So, is any punishment too severe for those who can stand by and permit "our … God and Savior"[a] to be attacked with insolent blasphemy? It is this fear that has compelled me to pick up my pen and expose these innovations, which, as I've been informed, some people are trying to introduce.

According to this report, there is much talk about how, when certain priests had offered a prayer and had just capped the prayer in the usual manner—some saying, "To you belongs glory, and to your Christ, and to your Holy Spirit," and others, "by the grace and loving kindness of your Christ, with whom you and your Holy Spirit are rightly glorified"—the archdeacon, in his great wisdom, objected that they should not make use of the title "Christ" but give glory to the "Only-begotten." If this is really true, I can imagine no greater piece of irreligion! He is either dividing our one Lord Jesus Christ into two sons and imagining that the only-begotten Son is the true son, born of God's nature, and Christ, just an adopted and illegitimate son and thus undeserving of glorification, or he is speaking in support of that heresy that has just recently burst through our doors.[3] Now, if there were some severe tempest hovering above

1. The recipient of this letter is otherwise unknown. The date must be subsequent to the death of Theodosius and the ascension of Marcian; *v.* sec. 1, where Theodoret refers to the change in ecclesiastical policy, and *cf. ep.* 136.2. Azéma suggests Lent 451.

2. On this title and the duties attached to it, *v. ep.* 105 n. 1.

3. Theodoret is probably referring to those, who, like Eutyches and the more

δεδοικότα τὴν δυναστείαν τῶν γεγεννηκότων τὴν αἵρεσιν, τῷ καιρῷ τὴν βλασφημίαν χαρίζεσθαι, ἐπειδὴ δὲ ὁ βλασφημούμενος ἐπετίμησεν τοῖς ἀνέμοις καὶ τῇ θαλάττῃ καὶ ταῖς χειμαζομέναις ἐκκλησίαις παρέσχεν γαλήνην,[b] καὶ πανταχοῦ γῆς καὶ θαλάττης τὸ τῶν ἀποστόλων καταγγέλλεται κήρυγμα, ποίαν ἔχει χώραν ἡ βλασφημία; ἀλλὰ γὰρ οὐδὲ οἱ τὴν *μίαν φύσιν* σαρκὸς καὶ θεότητος τοῖς ἐκκλησιαστικοῖς νῦν κακῶς κατασπείραντες δόγμασιν ἀπηγόρευσαν τὸν Δεσπότην ὑμνεῖσθαι Χριστόν,[c] καὶ ῥᾴδιον αὐτὸ τοῦτο μαθεῖν παρὰ τῶν ἐκεῖθεν ἐπανεληλυθότων.

(2) Ἐχρῆν δὲ αὐτὸν τῆς ἐκκλησιαστικῆς προστατεύοντα τάξεως τὴν θείαν εἰδέναι Γραφὴν[d] καὶ μαθεῖν ἐκ ταύτης ὅτι, καθάπερ τὸν μονογενῆ Υἱὸν τῷ Πατρὶ συντάττουσιν οἱ τῆς ἀληθείας κήρυκες, οὕτω δὴ πάλιν, τὴν τοῦ *Χριστοῦ* προσηγορίαν ἀντὶ τῆς τοῦ *Υἱοῦ* τιθέντες, ποτὲ μὲν τῷ Πατρί, ποτὲ δὲ τῷ Πνεύματι τῷ Παναγίῳ συναριθμοῦσιν, ἐπειδὴ οὐκ ἄλλος ἐστὶν ὁ Χριστὸς παρὰ τὸν μονογενῆ Υἱὸν τοῦ Θεοῦ. καὶ ἔστιν ἀκοῦσαι τοῦ θειοτάτου Παύλου κορινθίοις μὲν ἐπιστέλλοντος, τὴν δὲ οἰκουμένην διδάσκοντος, ὅτι *Εἷς Θεός, ὁ Πατήρ, ἐξ οὗ τὰ*

---

the noun κλύδων + the adj. παγχάλεπος is anarthrous; v. ep. 129 (μόνης δὲ τῆς Ἐκκλησίας χειμαζομένης, καὶ παγχαλέπῳ κλύδωνι περιπεσούσης) and cf. ep. 118 (Παγχάλεπος χειμὼν, etc.). Yet there is the counter example of H. e. 5.4.2 (τῷ παγχαλέπῳ κλύδωνι), and the use of the article here may perhaps reflect the pressure of the ongoing dogmatic controversy. **l. 28** γεγεννηκότων A^{pc} (*Car.?*), *Az.* : -ενη- *NZ*, A^{ac} **l. 41** τῆς τοῦ Υἱοῦ *scripsi* : Υἱὸς *codd., edd. Elsewhere, Thdt. always joins the genitive of Υἱὸς to forms of the noun προσηγορία. In this letter, v. sec. 3: καὶ τῷ Θεῷ καὶ Πατρὶ τὴν τοῦ Υἱοῦ προσηγορίαν συζεύγνυσι; sec. 6: τὴν τοῦ Υἱοῦ προσηγορίαν πολλοῖς ὁ μεγαλόδωρος Δεσπότης δεδώρηται. Here,* Υἱὸς *could be regarded as an appositive to an understood* προσηγορίας, *but that seems overly harsh. Cf. sec. 7: αὐτὴν γὰρ τὴν Θεὸς προσηγορίαν πολλοὶ μὲν ἔλαβον, where the nominative Θεὸς stands in apposition to an accusative, but προσηγορίαν is expressed, and the noun and its art. surround the appositive.*

b. Mt 8.26 c. *Cf.* Mt 13.24–30. d. *Cf.* Mk 12.24.

us, one might surmise that, fearing the influence of those who had produced this heresy, he blasphemes only in concession to the circumstances, but, now that the one against whom this blasphemy is spoken has rebuked the winds and the sea and granted peace to the churches that were battered by the storm,[b] and the message of the apostles is heard everywhere in the world, how can blasphemy receive any hearing? Why, not even those who have just recently cast the tares of the doctrine of the one nature of the flesh and the godhead amidst the teachings of the Church raised any objection to singing the praise of the Master Christ[c]—a fact you can easily ascertain from anyone who was there.[4]

(2) A man who holds a position of leadership in the hierarchy should know the holy Scripture;[d] he should have learned that, just as the heralds of the truth conjoin the only-begotten Son to the Father, they also use the name "Christ" instead of "Son" and sometimes place Christ on the same level with the Father, at others with Holy Spirit, precisely because Christ and the only-begotten Son of God are not two different persons. We need only listen to what St. Paul says, writing to the Corinthians and instructing the entire world: "There is one God, the Father, from whom are all things, ... and one Lord Jesus

---

extreme followers of Cyril, habitually overemphasized the divine nature of Christ. Cyril himself had usually referred to Jesus as "the Only-begotten" or "the Son," rather than "Christ." *V., e.g.*, his comment on the temptation (*serm.* 12, *in Luc.* 4.1f.): "There was no one of those upon earth who could rise up against his power (*i.e.* the power of Satan); but the Son rose up against him, and contended with him, having been made like unto us." Nestorius, in contrast, had always argued that, since Christ was both God and man, Mary could be correctly spoken of as "Christ-bearer" (Christotokos). The overzealous archdeacon has used a name preferred by both Cyril and the Eutychians and in so doing, opened himself up to the charge of dividing the one Christ into two sons, the divine Word and Jesus. Theodoret, thus, turns on his opponents the very accusation they had levelled against him.

4. Theodoret is referring to the Second Council of Ephesus and the Apollinarian-Cyrilian formula μίαν φύσιν τοῦ Λόγου σεσαρκωμένην that was commended there; *v.* Intro. sec. 4.7.

πάντα,… καὶ εἷς Κύριος, Ἰησοῦς Χριστός, δι᾽ οὗ τὰ πάντα,[e] καὶ τὸν αὐτὸν καὶ *Χριστόν,* καὶ *Ἰησοῦν,* καὶ *Κύριον,* καὶ *τῶν ὅλων Δημιουργὸν* ὀνομάζοντος. καὶ θεσσαλονικεῦσι δὲ γράφων, οὕτως ἔφη· *Αὐτὸς δὲ ὁ Θεὸς καὶ Πατὴρ ἡμῶν καὶ ὁ Κύριος ἡμῶν Ἰησοῦς* Χριστὸς *κατευθύναι τὴν ὁδὸν ἡμῶν πρὸς ὑμᾶς.*[f]

(3) Ἐν δὲ τῇ δευτέρᾳ τῇ πρὸς τούτους ἐπιστολῇ καὶ προτέταχεν τὸν Χριστὸν τοῦ Πατρός, οὐ τὴν τάξιν ἀνατρέπων, ἀλλὰ διδάσκων ὡς ἡ τάξις τῶν ὀνομάτων οὐκ ἀξιωμάτων καὶ φύσεων διδάσκει διαφοράν. λέγει δὲ οὕτως· *Αὐτὸς δὲ ὁ Κύριος ἡμῶν Ἰησοῦς Χριστὸς καὶ ὁ Θεὸς καὶ Πατὴρ ἡμῶν, ὁ ἀγαπήσας ἡμᾶς καὶ δοὺς παράκλησιν* αἰώνιον *καὶ ἐλπίδα ἀγαθὴν ἐν χάριτι, παρακαλέσαι ὑμῶν τὰς καρδίας καὶ στηρίξαι ἐν παντὶ ἔργῳ καὶ λόγῳ ἀγαθῷ.*[g] ἐν δέ γε τῷ τέλει τῆς πρὸς ῥωμαίους ἐπιστολῆς τινὰ παραινέσας, ἐπεισήγαγεν, *Παρακαλῶ οὖν ὑμᾶς, ἀδελφοί, διὰ τοῦ Κυρίου ἡμῶν Ἰησοῦ Χριστοῦ καὶ διὰ τῆς ἀγάπης τοῦ Πνεύματος,*[h] εἰ δὲ ἄλλον τινὰ παρὰ τὸν Υἱὸν ἠπίστατο τὸν Χριστόν, οὐκ ἂν αὐτὸν προέταξεν τοῦ Παναγίου Πνεύματος. κορινθίοις δὲ γράφων, ἐν αὐτῷ γε τῷ προοιμίῳ, μόνου τοῦ Χριστοῦ τὸ ὄνομα τέθεικεν, ὡς ἀρκοῦν καὶ μόνον τοὺς πιστεύοντας καταιδέσαι· *Παρακαλῶ οὖν ὑμᾶς, ἀδελφοί, διὰ τοῦ ὀνόματος τοῦ Κυρίου ἡμῶν Ἰησοῦ Χριστοῦ ἵνα τὸ αὐτὸ λέγητε πάντες.*[i] καὶ δὶς δὲ αὐτοῖς ἐπιστείλας, τοῦτο τοῖς γράμμασιν ||N ἐντέθεικεν τέλος· *Ἡ χάρις τοῦ Κυρίου ἡμῶν Ἰησοῦ Χριστοῦ,*|| *καὶ ἡ ἀγάπη τοῦ Θεοῦ* καὶ Πατρός, *καὶ ἡ κοινωνία τοῦ Ἁγίου Πνεύματος* εἴη *μετὰ πάντων ὑμῶν,*[j] καὶ προτέθεικεν ἐνταῦθα οὐ μόνον *τοῦ Πνεύματος,* ἀλλὰ καὶ αὐτοῦ *τοῦ Πατρός,* τὴν *τοῦ Χριστοῦ* προσηγορίαν· τοῦτο δὲ ἐν πάσαις ταῖς ἐκκλησίαις τῆς μυστικῆς ἐστι λειτουργίας προοίμιον.

Προσήκει τοίνυν κατὰ τὸν θαυμάσιον τοῦτον νόμον καὶ ἐκ τῶν μυστικῶν ἀπολειφθῆναι γραμμάτων τὸ σεπτότατον

e. 1Cor 8.6
f. 1Thes 3.11 (NT var.)
g. 2Thes 2.16f. (NT var.)
h. Rom 15.30 (NT var.)
i. 1Cor 1.10 (NT var.)
j. 2Cor 13.13 (NT var.)

Christ, through whom are all things";[e] here he calls the same person "Christ," "Jesus," "Lord," and "Creator of the universe." And this is what he says when writing to the Thessalonians: "May our God and Father himself and our Lord Jesus Christ make straight our way to you."[f]

(3) In the second Epistle to the Thessalonians, he even sets Christ before the Father, not to overturn the usual order, but to teach us that the order of the names is not to be interpreted as an indication of difference in rank or nature. These are his words: "May our Lord Jesus Christ and our God and Father, who has shown his love for us and graciously granted us a lasting consolation and a good hope, strengthen your hearts and confirm you in every good work and word."[g] Furthermore, toward the end of his Epistle to the Romans, after some words of encouragement, he adds, "I exhort you, brethren, by our Lord Jesus Christ and the love of the Spirit."[h] Now, had he understood that Christ was distinct from the Son, he would never have placed him prior to the Holy Spirit. Indeed, writing to the Corinthians, at the beginning of the letter, he set down no more than the name "Christ" as being in itself sufficient to call forth a sense of reverence among the faithful: "Therefore, brethren, I urge you, through our Lord Jesus Christ, to agree among yourselves."[i] And, in his second letter to them, his final words were: "May the grace of our Lord Jesus Christ, the love of our God and Father, and the fellowship of the Holy Spirit be with you all."[j] Here, he set the name of "Christ" before "Spirit," and even before "Father," and this verse serves throughout the Church as the beginning of our mystical service of God.

Yet, according to this excellent rule, we should also remove from the words of our sacraments the most holy name "of our ... God and

ὄνομα *τοῦ … Θεοῦ καὶ Σωτῆρος ἡμῶν*[k] Ἰησοῦ Χριστοῦ· ἀλλὰ γὰρ περιττὸν περὶ τούτου μηκύνειν· ἕκαστον γὰρ ἐπιστολῆς προοίμιον ὁ θεῖος Ἀπόστολος τῇδε τῇ προσηγορίᾳ λαμπρύνει, νῦν μὲν λέγων, *Παῦλος δοῦλος Ἰησοῦ Χριστοῦ, κλητὸς ἀπόστολος·*[l] νῦν δέ, *Παῦλος κλητὸς ἀπόστολος Ἰησοῦ Χριστοῦ·*[m] καί, *Παῦλος δοῦλος Θεοῦ, ἀπόστολος δὲ Ἰησοῦ Χριστοῦ.*[n] καί, τῷ προοιμίῳ τὴν εὐλογίαν συνάπτων, ἐκ ταύτης ταύτην ἀρύεται τῆς πηγῆς καὶ τῷ Θεῷ καὶ Πατρὶ τὴν *τοῦ Υἱοῦ* προσηγορίαν συζεύγνυσι λέγων, *Χάρις ὑμῖν καὶ εἰρήνη ἀπὸ Θεοῦ Πατρὸς ἡμῶν καὶ Κυρίου* ἡμῶν *Ἰησοῦ Χριστοῦ.*[o] καὶ τῶν ἐπιστολῶν δὲ τὰ τέλη τῇδε τῇ εὐλογίᾳ διακοσμεῖ· *Ἡ χάρις τοῦ Κυρίου Ἰησοῦ Χριστοῦ μετὰ πάντων ὑμῶν. ἀμήν.*[p]

(4) Καὶ ἑτέρας δὲ παμπόλλας ἔστιν εὑρεῖν μαρτυρίας δι᾿ ὧν καταμαθεῖν εὐπετὲς ὡς ὁ Κύριος ἡμῶν Ἰησοῦς Χριστὸς οὐκ ἄλλο πρόσωπόν ἐστι παρὰ τὸν Υἱόν, ἀλλὰ τὸ τῆς Τριάδος πληρωτικόν· ὁ γὰρ αὐτὸς πρὸ μὲν τῶν αἰώνων Υἱὸς ἦν μονογενὴς καὶ Θεὸς Λόγος, μετὰ δὲ τὴν ἐνανθρώπησιν ὠνομάσθη καὶ *Ἰησοῦς* καὶ *Χριστός*, ἀπὸ τῶν πραγμάτων τὰς προσηγορίας δεξάμενος. *Ἰησοῦς* μὲν γὰρ *Σωτὴρ* ἑρμηνεύεται· *Καλέσεις γὰρ τὸ ὄνομα*

l. 85 Κυρίου ἡμῶν Z^{ac}, A^{mg}. (*ms.* ἡμῶν), *Sir.* : K. *A*, Z^{pc} (*pron. gen. expunxit punctis s. l. scriptis*) *Nös. Az. Ciriaco followed the corrector of Z, almost certainly Onorio, and omitted the pronoun* ἡμῶν. *The marginal indication "ms.* ἡμῶν*" is almost certainly due to Sirmond, who found* ἡμῶν *in N, of which he was able to consult folios now lost; v. "Intro. to the Gk. Text," n. 51.* **l. 90** ἀλλὰ τὸ τῆς A^{mg}. : ἀ. τῆς *Z, Sir.* : τῆς *Nös. Az. Nösselt's reading, adopted by Azéma, is probably due, not to conjecture, but to the accidental omission of* ἀλλὰ *in the typesetting. The status of the neut. art. is unclear. It seems to be in the hand of Sirmond, and could, thus, be a word he found in the more complete copy of N that he consulted (v. "Intro. to the Gk. Text," n. 51) or his own conjecture; in any case, he did not adopt it in his text. It is to be taken as referring to the preceding πρόσωπόν; its omission following the masc. art. + Υἱὸν and preceding the fem. τῆς would be quite easy.*

k. Ti 2.13 l. Rom 1.1 m. 1Cor 1.1 n. Ti 1.1 o. Rom 1.7
p. Phil 4.23 (Byz./Majority text). *Cf.* Rom 16.20; Eph 6.24.

Savior"[k] Jesus Christ.[5] But it would be a waste of time to discuss this any further. It is with this name that the holy Apostle adorns the beginning of every one of his epistles. In one he says, "Paul, a slave of Jesus Christ, called to be an apostle";[l] in another, "Paul, chosen to be the apostle of Jesus Christ";[m] and then, "Paul, slave of God and apostle of Jesus Christ."[n] When he adds a blessing to the opening words, he draws his water from the same well: linking the name of the Son to that of God and Father, he says, "Grace to you and peace from God our Father and the Lord Jesus Christ."[o] And he uses the following blessing to adorn the conclusion of his letters: "May the grace of the Lord Jesus Christ be with you all. Amen."[p]

(4) One could find a great many more texts allowing the easy conclusion that our Lord Jesus Christ is not some person distinct from the Son, but the one constitutive of the Trinity. There is just one and the same person: the only-begotten Son and God the Word before all ages, who received the names Jesus and Christ after the incarnation, appellations drawn from historical fact. "Jesus," of course, means "Savior": "You will call his name 'Jesus,' because he will save

5. On Theodoret's use of the term "mystical," *v. ep.* 82 n. 6. In this discussion of the appropriate liturgical use of the name "Christ," Koch (pp. 104–08) sees evidence of a development in Theodoret's presentation of the unity of the Lord, which he understands to be due to a closer association of christology with the trinitarian teaching of the three persons. Rather than speaking of the union of the divine with the human (*i.e.* of two natures), Theodoret identifies the divinity with the person of the Logos, who has become man: "Gott sich im Menschen Jesus von Nazaret absolut und eschatologisch offenbart hat."

αὐτοῦ Ἰησοῦν, ὅτι αὐτὸς σώσει τὸν λαὸν αὐτοῦ ἀπὸ τῶν ἁμαρτιῶν αὐτοῦ·[q] *Χριστὸς* δὲ κέκληται, ὡς, κατὰ τὸ ἀνθρώπειον, τῷ Πνεύματι τῷ Παναγίῳ χρισθεὶς καὶ χρηματίσας *ἀρχιερεὺς ἡμῶν*, καὶ *ἀπόστολος*, καὶ *προφήτης*, καὶ *βασιλεύς*. Μωϋσῆς μὲν γὰρ ὁ θεσπέσιος βοᾷ πόρρωθεν, *Προφήτην* ὑμῖν *ἀναστήσει Κύριος ὁ Θεὸς … ἐκ τῶν ἀδελφῶν* ὑμῶν *ὡς ἐμέ*,[r] ὁ δὲ θεῖος Δαυὶδ κέκραγεν λέγων, *Ὤμοσεν Κύριος καὶ οὐ μεταμεληθήσεται· Σὺ … ἱερεὺς εἰς τὸν αἰῶνα κατὰ τὴν τάξιν Μελχισεδέκ*·[s] βεβαιοῖ δὲ τὴν προφητείαν ὁ θεῖος Ἀπόστολος καὶ πάλιν· *Ἔχοντες οὖν ἀρχιερέα μέγαν διεληλυθότα τοὺς οὐρανούς, Ἰησοῦν τὸν Υἱὸν τοῦ Θεοῦ, κρατῶμεν τῆς ὁμολογίας*.[t] ὅτι δὲ καὶ βασιλεύς ἐστι προαιώνιος ὡς Θεός, ἡ προφητικὴ πάλιν ἡμᾶς μελῳδία διδάσκει· *Ὁ θρόνος σου*, γάρ φησιν, *ὁ Θεός, εἰς τὸν αἰῶνα τοῦ αἰῶνος· ῥάβδος εὐθύτητος ἡ ῥάβδος τῆς βασιλείας σου*.[u] ὑποδείκνυσι δὲ ἡμῖν καὶ τὸ ἀνθρώπειον αὐτοῦ κράτος· ἔχων γὰρ τῶν ὅλων τὴν δεσποτείαν ὡς Θεὸς καὶ Δημιουργός, λαμβάνει ταύτην ὡς ἄνθρωπος, οὗ δὴ χάριν ἐπήγαγεν, *Ἠγάπησας δικαιοσύνην καὶ ἐμίσησας ἀνομίαν, διὰ τοῦτο ἔχρισέν σε ὁ Θεός, ὁ Θεός σου, ἔλαιον ἀγαλλιάσεως παρὰ τοὺς μετόχους σου*,[v] καὶ ἐν τῷ δευτέρῳ γέ φησιν ψαλμῷ αὐτὸς ὁ χρισθείς, *Ἐγὼ δὲ κατεστάθην βασιλεὺς ὑπ᾽ αὐτοῦ ἐπὶ Σιὼν ὄρος τὸ ἅγιον αὐτοῦ, διαγγέλλων τὸ πρόσταγμα Κυρίου· Κύριος εἶπε πρός με, Υἱός μου εἶ σύ, ἐγὼ σήμερον γεγέννηκά σε. αἴτησαι παρ᾽ ἐμοῦ, καί δώσω σοι ἔθνη τὴν κληρονομίαν σου καὶ τὴν κατάσχεσίν σου τὰ πέρατα τῆς γῆς*.[w] ταῦτα δὲ ὡς ἄνθρωπος εἴρηκεν· ὡς γὰρ ἄνθρωπος λαμβάνει ἅπερ ἔχει ὡς Θεός· καί, ἐν αὐτῷ γε τῷ τοῦ ψαλμοῦ προοιμίῳ, τῷ Θεῷ καὶ Πατρὶ συνέταξεν αὐτὸν ἡ προφητικὴ χάρις· *Ἵνα τί*, γάρ φησι, *ἐφρύαξαν ἔθνη, καὶ λαοὶ ἐμελέτησαν κενά; παρέστησαν οἱ*

q. Mt 1.21 (NT var.)
r. Dt 18.15 (LXX var.)
s. Ps 110.4 (*Cf.* Heb 7.21.)
t. Heb 4.14
u. Ps 45.6
v. Ps 45.7
w. Ps 2.6–8

his people from their sins."[q] He bears the appellation "Christ," as one, in his humanity, anointed with the chrism of the Holy Spirit, and who thus became our "high priest," "apostle," "prophet," and "king." Long ago, Moses cried out in inspired words, "The Lord God will raise up for you a prophet like me from among your brethren."[r] As the holy man David proclaimed, "The Lord has sworn an oath he will not take back: 'You are a priest forever according to the order of Melchisedek.'"[s] The holy Apostle demonstrates the fulfillment of this prophecy: "As we have a great high priest who has passed through the heavens, Jesus, the son of God, let us hold fast to our confession of faith."[t] As to the fact that, as God, he is king before all time—this once again, we learn from the prophetic psalmody: "Your throne, O God, is unto eternity, a scepter of righteousness is the scepter of your kingship."[u] This psalm indicates as well the power that belongs to him as a human being, for as man he receives the universal sway belonging to him as God and Creator; thus the psalmist adds, "You have loved justice and abhorred lawlessness, and for this reason God, your God, has anointed you with the oil of gladness to set you apart from your fellows."[v] Furthermore, in the second psalm, the messiah himself declares, "I have been appointed king by him on Sion, his holy mount, where I proclaim the decree of the Lord: The Lord said to me, 'You are my son; today have I begotten you. Ask of me, and I shall give you the peoples for your inheritance and the ends of the earth for your possession.'"[w] Such words are spoken as a human being, since, as man, he receives what he possesses as God. And, in the introduction to this psalm, the inspired prophecy sets him side-by-side with God the Father, saying, "Why have the nations become so arrogant, and the peoples plotted

βασιλεῖς τῆς γῆς, καὶ οἱ ἄρχοντες συνήχθησαν ἐπὶ τὸ αὐτὸ κατὰ τοῦ Κυρίου καὶ κατὰ τοῦ Χριστοῦ αὐτοῦ.[x]

(5) Μηδεὶς τοίνυν ἀνοήτως ἄλλον τινὰ τὸν Χριστὸν νομιζέτω παρὰ τὸν Υἱὸν τὸν μονογενῆ, μηδὲ σοφωτέρους ἑαυτοὺς ὑπολάβωμεν τῆς τοῦ Πνεύματος χάριτος, ἀλλ᾽ ἀκούσωμεν τοῦ μεγάλου Πέτρου βοῶντος, *Σὺ εἶ ὁ Χριστός, ὁ Υἱὸς τοῦ Θεοῦ τοῦ ζῶντος,*[y] καὶ ἀκούσωμεν τοῦ Δεσπότου Χριστοῦ, τήνδε τὴν ὁμολογίαν κρατύνοντος· *ἐπὶ ταύτῃ,* γὰρ ἔφη, *τῇ πέτρᾳ οἰκοδομήσω μου τὴν Ἐκκλησίαν, καὶ πύλαι ᾅδου οὐ κατισχύσουσιν αὐτῆς.*[z] διά τοι τοῦτο καὶ Παῦλος ὁ πάνσοφος, ὁ τῶν ἐκκλησιῶν ἄριστος ἀρχιτέκτων, οὐχ ἕτερον, ἀλλὰ τοῦτον αὐτὸν κατέπηξεν τὸν θεμέλιον· ἐγώ, γάρ φησιν, *ὡς σοφὸς ἀρχιτέκτων θεμέλιον* τέθεικα, *ἄλλος δὲ ἐποικοδομεῖ. ἕκαστος δὲ βλεπέτω πῶς ἐποικοδομεῖ· θεμέλιον γὰρ ἄλλον οὐδεὶς δύναται θεῖναι παρὰ τὸν κείμενον, ὅς ἐστι Ἰησοῦς Χριστός.*[ba] πῶς τοίνυν ἕτερον ἐπινοοῦσι θεμέλιον, οὐ πηγνύναι θεμέλιον, ἀλλ᾽ ἐποικοδομεῖν τῷ κειμένῳ προστεταγμένοι; ὁ δὲ θεῖος ἐκεῖνος ἀνὴρ τὸν Χριστὸν οἶδε θεμέλιον καὶ ταύτῃ τῇ προσηγορίᾳ λαμπρύνεται· καὶ νῦν μέν φησι, *Χριστῷ συνεσταύρωμαι· ζῶ δὲ οὐκέτι ἐγώ, ζῇ δὲ ἐν ἐμοὶ Χριστός·*[bb] νῦν δέ, *Ἐμοὶ … τὸ ζῆν Χριστός, καὶ τὸ ἀποθανεῖν κέρδος·*[bc] καὶ πάλιν, *Οὐ γὰρ ἔκρινα* τοῦ *εἰδέναι τι ἐν ὑμῖν εἰ μὴ Ἰησοῦν Χριστόν, καὶ τοῦτον ἐσταυρωμένον·*[bd] καὶ μικρὸν πρὸ τούτων, *Ἡμεῖς δὲ* κηρύττομεν *Χριστὸν ἐσταυρωμένον· ἰουδαίοις μὲν σκάνδαλον, ἔθνεσι δὲ μωρίαν, αὐτοῖς τε κλητοῖς, ἰουδαίοις τε καὶ ἕλλησιν, Χριστὸν Θεοῦ δύναμιν καὶ Θεοῦ σοφίαν.*[be] Καί, γαλάταις μὲν ἐπιστέλλων, ἔφη, *Ὅτε δὲ* ηὐδόκησεν … *ὁ ἀφορίσας με ἐκ κοιλίας μητρός μου καὶ καλέσας διὰ τῆς χάριτος αὐτοῦ ἀποκαλύψαι τὸν Υἱὸν αὐτοῦ ἐν ἐμοὶ ἵνα εὐαγγελίζωμαι αὐτὸν*

x. Ps 2.1f.
y. Mt 16.16
z. Mt 16.18
ba. 1Cor 3.10f. (NT var.)
bb. Gal 2.19f.
bc. Phil 1.21
bd. 1Cor 2.2 (NT var.)
be. 1Cor 1.23f. (NT var.)

in vain? The kings of the earth have gathered round, the rulers have come together against the Lord and against his anointed."[x]

(5) Therefore, no one should foolishly imagine that there is a Christ distinct from the only-begotten Son; no one should think he knows better than the revelation of the Spirit. Rather, listen to the great Peter who declared, "You are the Christ, the Son of the living God."[y] And pay attention to the Master Christ's confirmation of Peter's confession: "On this rock," he declared, "I shall build my Church, and the gates of Hell will not prevail against it."[z] For this reason, Paul in his wisdom, Paul that master builder of the churches, laid down Christ himself and no other as their foundation. As he says, "Like a master builder, I have laid the foundation on which another will build. It is up to each just how he will build, but nobody can lay any foundation other than that which is already in place, that is to say, Jesus Christ."[ba] How, then, do they imagine a different foundation when they have received the command not to lay a foundation, but to build on the one that has already been laid? That holy man recognizes Christ as the foundation and glories in the name of Christ. Now he declares, "I have been crucified with Christ; it is no longer I who live, but Christ who lives within me";[bb] now, "For me, life is Christ, death a gain";[bc] and then, "I had decided that, while I was with you, I should know nothing but Jesus Christ, and him crucified";[bd] and a bit before this, "Our preaching is of Christ crucified, a stumbling block for Jews, an absurdity for gentiles, but for the chosen, whether Jews or Hellenes, Christ the power and wisdom of God."[be] And in the Epistle to the Galatians, he said, "When it pleased him who had set me apart when I was still in my mother's womb and, in his grace, called me to make his Son known through

ἐν τοῖς ἔθνεσι,[bf] κορινθίοις δὲ γράφων, οὐκ εἶπεν, ὅτι *Ἡμεῖς μὲν κηρύττομεν τὸν Υἱόν, ἀλλὰ Χριστὸν ἐσταυρωμένον,* οὐκ ἐναντία ποιῶν οἷς προσετάχθη, ἀλλὰ τὸν αὐτὸν εἰδὼς καὶ Ἰησοῦν, καὶ Χριστόν, καὶ Κύριον, καὶ Μονογενῆ, καὶ Θεὸν Λόγον. τούτου δὴ χάριν, καὶ ῥωμαίοις γράφειν ἀρξάμενος, *δοῦλον* μὲν ἑαυτὸν ὠνόμασεν *Ἰησοῦ Χριστοῦ,* εἶπε δὲ ἀφωρίσθαι *εἰς εὐαγγέλιον Θεοῦ, ὅ προεπηγγείλατο διὰ τῶν προφητῶν αὐτοῦ ἐν Γραφαῖς ἁγίαις περὶ τοῦ Υἱοῦ αὐτοῦ, τοῦ γενομένου ἐκ σπέρματος Δαυὶδ κατὰ σάρκα, τοῦ ὁρισθέντος Υἱοῦ Θεοῦ ἐν δυνάμει,* καὶ τὰ ἑξῆς.[bg] καὶ τὸν αὐτὸν ἐκάλεσεν καὶ *Ἰησοῦν Χριστόν,* καὶ *υἱὸν τοῦ Δαυὶδ* κατὰ σάρκα, καὶ *Υἱὸν τοῦ Θεοῦ,* ὡς Θεὸν καὶ τῶν ὅλων Δεσπότην. καὶ μέντοι κἀν τῷ μέσῳ τῆς ἐπιστολῆς, ἰουδαίων μνημονεύσας, ἐπήγαγεν, *Ὧν οἱ πατέρες, καὶ ἐξ ὧν ὁ Χριστὸς τὸ κατὰ σάρκα, ὁ ὢν ἐπὶ πάντων Θεὸς εὐλογητὸς εἰς τοὺς αἰῶνας* τῶν αἰώνων. *ἀμήν.*[bh] καὶ τὸν αὐτὸν κατὰ σάρκα μὲν ἐξ ἰουδαίων ἔφη κατάγειν τὸ γένος, αἰώνιον δὲ εἶναι Θεὸν καὶ πάντων ὁμοῦ τῶν γενητῶν Δεσπότην παρὰ τῶν εὐγνωμόνων ὑμνούμενον. τὴν αὐτὴν δὲ ἡμῖν δικασκαλίαν προσήνεγκεν καὶ δι᾽ ὧν τῷ θαυμασίῳ γέγραφεν Τίτῳ· *Προσδεχόμενοι,* γάρ φησι, *τὴν μακαρίαν ἐλπίδα καὶ ἐπιφανείαν τῆς δόξης τοῦ μεγάλου Θεοῦ καὶ Σωτῆρος ἡμῶν Ἰησοῦ Χριστοῦ,*[bi] καὶ τὸν αὐτὸν καὶ *Σωτῆρα,* καὶ *μέγαν Θεόν,* καὶ *Ἰησοῦν Χριστὸν* προσηγόρευσεν· καὶ ἀλλαχοῦ, *Ἐν τῇ βασιλείᾳ τοῦ*

l. 155 δοῦλον μὲν *Z* : δ. *Cir., edd. The phraseology of Z well suits the argument by pointing a contrast between the the name "Jesus Christ" and the title "Son"; i.e. first Paul uses the name suggestive of humanity, then the title of divinity, but both refer to one and the same subject. Throughout the* corpus, *one observes Ciriaco's tendency to omit individual words and short phrases, a tendency even more marked in this last letter.* **l. 171** τὸν αὐτὸν *coni. et scr. Car.?, edd.* : τ. *Z. The pronoun, first conjectured in the margin, then introduced into the text by the same hand, is necessary to the sense of this passage.*

bf. Gal 1.15f. (NT var.) bg. Rom 1.1–4 (NT var.) bh. Rom 9.5 (NT var.) bi. Ti 2.13

me, to preach him among the gentiles."[bf] Writing to the Corinthians, he did not say, "We preach the 'Son,'" but rather "We preach 'Christ crucified,'" in no way acting in opposition to his commission, but fully aware that Jesus, Christ, the Lord, the Only-begotten, and God the Word are all the same person. This is why, at the beginning of the Epistle to the Romans, he first referred to himself as "the slave of Jesus Christ," and then said, "to set me apart for the gospel of God, the gospel previously announced by his prophets in the holy Scriptures, regarding his Son who was born of the seed of David according to the flesh, designated Son of God in power, *etc.*"[bg] In this passage, he referred to the same person as "Jesus Christ," "son of David" according to the flesh, and "Son of God" as God and Master of the Universe. What is more, in the middle of this epistle, when speaking of the Jews, he adds, "to whom belong the fathers, and from whom, according to the flesh, is also descended the Christ, God above all, to whom be praise for ever and ever, Amen."[bh] Here he declared that the same person is both descended from the Jews according to the flesh and God eternal, praised as the Master of all creation by those who give him his due. The Apostle has passed this same teaching on to us in his letter to St. Titus: "In the expectation of that blessed hope and the revelation of the glory of our great God and Savior Jesus Christ."[bi] Here he refers to the same person with the names "Savior," "great God," and "Jesus Christ"; then, in another passage,

Χριστοῦ καὶ Θεοῦ·[bj] καὶ μέντοι καὶ τοῖς ποιμέσιν ὁ τῶν ἀγγέλων ἔφη χορός, Ἰδοὺ τίκτεται *ὑμῖν σήμερον … Χριστὸς Κύριος ἐν πόλει Δαυίδ*.[bk] Ἀλλὰ γὰρ παρέλκον πάσας τὰς τοιαύτας συλλέγειν μαρτυρίας ἀνδράσι γράφοντι τοῖς μελετῶσιν *ἐν … νόμῳ Κυρίου … ἡμέρας καὶ νυκτός*,[bl] ἀποχρῶσί τε αὗται πεῖσαι καὶ τοὺς ἄγαν δυσπειθεστάτους τὰς θείας μὴ μερίζειν προσηγορίας.

(6) Ἐκεῖνο μέντοι παραλιπεῖν οὐκ ἀνέξομαι· φασὶ γὰρ αὐτὸν εἰρηκέναι χριστοὺς μὲν εἶναι πολλούς, Υἱὸν δὲ ἕνα. τοῦτο δὲ ἐξ ἀγνοίας αὐτὸν ὑπείληφα πλημμελεῖν· εἰ γὰρ τὴν θείαν ἀνέγνω Γραφήν, ἐγνώκει ἂν ὡς καὶ τὴν *τοῦ Υἱοῦ* προσηγορίαν πολλοῖς ὁ μεγαλόδωρος Δεσπότης δεδώρηται. Μωϋσῆς μὲν γὰρ ὁ νομοθέτης, ὁ τὴν παλαιὰν ἱστορίαν συγγράψας, φησίν, *Ἰδόντες … οἱ υἱοὶ τοῦ Θεοῦ τὰς θυγατέρας τῶν ἀνθρώπων ὅτι καλαί εἰσιν, ἔλαβον ἑαυτοῖς* ἐξ αὐτῶν *γυναῖκας*,[bm] αὐτὸς δὲ ὁ τῶν ὅλων Θεὸς πρὸς τοῦτον ἔφη τὸν προφήτην, Εἰπὲ πρὸς *Φαραώ, … Υἱὸς πρωτότοκός μου Ἰσραήλ*,[bn] κἂν τῇ Ὠιδῇ δὲ τῇ μεγάλῃ, *Εὐφράνθητε*, φησίν, *ἔθνη μετὰ τοῦ λαοῦ αὐτοῦ, καὶ ἐνισχυσάτωσαν αὐτῷ πάντες* υἱοὶ *Θεοῦ*,[bo] διὰ δὲ Ἡσαΐου τοῦ προφήτου φησίν, *Υἱοὺς ἐγέννησα καὶ ὕψωσα, αὐτοὶ δέ με*

l. 176 γράφοντι *Z*, A^{ac} : -τα $A^{mg.}$, *Az. The correction of* -τι to -τα *in A does not seem due to Ciriaco. The use of παρέλκον + dat. or acc. + infin. does not appear elsewhere in the works of Thdt. The expression here used seems a brachylogy in which the verb δοκεῖ is to be understood: cf. Chrys., Hom. 1.1 in Io.: περιττὸν εἶναί μοι δοκεῖ καὶ παρέλκον ταῦτα ἀναζητεῖν. Cf. also ep. 83.2:* ῥᾴδιόν *Σου Τῇ … Τελειότητι παρὰ τῶν ἐκεῖθεν αὐτόσε παραγιγνομένων … μαθεῖν; there BV offer the acc. Τὴν … Τελειότητα.* **l. 186** ἑαυτοῖς *scripsi* (*cf. LXX*) : αὐ- *ZA, Sir.* : αὑ- *Nös. Az.* : *The reflexive pronoun ἑαυτοῖς is the reading of the LXX, and this is followed in numerous patristic and late antique quotations; v. Thdt. himself* (*H. e.* 1.4.34, *p.* 17, *l.* 19); *Iul., Gal.* 290*C*; *Cyr., C. Iul.* (*bk.* 9, *sec.* 11, *ll.* 21–23). *There is no example of the non-reflexive form carried by ZA among the quotations of Gn* 6.2 *recorded in the TLG.*

bj. Eph 5.5 bk. Lk 2.11 (NT var.) bl. Ps 1.2
bm. Gn 6.2 (LXX var.) bn. Ex 4.22 (LXX var.) bo. Dt 32.43 (LXX var.)

"In the kingdom of Christ and God."[bj] Indeed, the chorus of angels proclaimed to the shepherds, "Behold, today in the city of David is born to you Christ the Lord."[bk] Yet, it's quite unnecessary to draw up an exhaustive list of such proof texts when writing to men whose study "day and night" is "in the law of the Lord";[bl] this much is quite enough to dissuade even the most obstinate from making division among the divine names.

(6) But, I really can't allow the following point to pass without remark. As I'm informed, he asserts that there are many Christs, but just one Son. I suppose this mistake is to be attributed to ignorance; if he had read the Scriptures, he would know very well that, in his generosity, our Master has conferred the gift of this appellation "Son" on more than a few. First of all, Moses, the lawgiver and the author of the ancient history, tells us that "The sons of God, beholding the beauty of the daughters of man, took some of them to wife."[bm] And then, the God of the universe himself said to the prophet, "Declare unto Pharaoh, 'Israel is my first-begotten Son.'"[bn] And in his great song, Moses declared, "Rejoice, ye nations along with his people, and may all the sons of God take strength in him."[bo] Through the prophet Isaiah, God says, "I begat sons and raised

ἠθέτησαν,[bp] καὶ διὰ τοῦ τρισμακαρίου Δαυίδ, *Ἐγώ,* φησίν, *εἶπα, Θεοί ἐστε καὶ υἱοὶ Ὑψίστου πάντες.*[bq] ὁ δὲ πάνσοφος Παῦλος ῥωμαίοις μὲν γέγραφεν οὕτως· *Ὅσοι γὰρ Πνεύματι Θεοῦ ἄγονται, οὗτοί εἰσιν υἱοὶ Θεοῦ· οὐ γὰρ ἐλάβετε πνεῦμα δουλείας πάλιν εἰς φόβον, ἀλλ᾽ ἐλάβετε πνεῦμα υἱοθεσίας, ἐν ᾧ κράζομεν, Ἀββᾶ, ὁ Πατήρ. αὐτὸ τὸ Πνεῦμα συμμαρτυρεῖ τῷ πνεύματι ἡμῶν ὅτι ἐσμὲν τέκνα Θεοῦ· εἰ δὲ τέκνα, καὶ κληρονόμοι, κληρονόμοι μὲν Θεοῦ, συγκληρονόμοι δὲ Χριστοῦ εἴπερ συμπάσχομεν ἵνα καὶ συνδοξασθῶμεν.*[br] γαλάταις δὲ ἐπιστέλλων, οὕτως ἔφη· *Ὅτι δέ ἐστε υἱοί, ἐξαπέστειλεν ὁ Θεὸς τὸ Πνεῦμα τοῦ Υἱοῦ αὐτοῦ εἰς τὰς καρδίας* ὑμῶν, *κράζον, Ἀββᾶ, ὁ Πατήρ, ὥστε οὐκέτι εἶ δοῦλος, ἀλλὰ υἱός· εἰ δὲ υἱός, καὶ κληρονόμος Θεοῦ διὰ* Ἰησοῦ Χριστοῦ.[bs] ταὐτὰ δὲ καὶ ἐφεσίους ἐδίδαξεν· *Ἐν ἀγάπῃ,* γάρ φησι, *προορίσας ἡμᾶς εἰς υἱοθεσίαν διὰ Ἰησοῦ Χριστοῦ εἰς αὐτόν.*[bt] Εἰ τοίνυν, ἐπεὶ κοινόν ἐστι τὸ ὄνομα *τοῦ Χριστοῦ,* δοξάζειν οὐ δεῖ τὸν Χριστὸν ὡς Θεόν, μηδὲ ὡς Υἱὸν αὐτὸν προσκυνήσωμεν· πολλοὶ γὰρ καὶ τοῦδε μετέλαχον τοῦ ὀνόματος.

(7) Καὶ τί λέγω *τοῦ Υἱοῦ;* αὐτὴν γὰρ τὴν *Θεὸς* προσηγορίαν πολλοὶ μὲν ἔλαβον, τοῦ Θεοῦ δεδωκότος· *Θεὸς θεῶν Κύριος ἐλάλησεν καὶ ἐκάλεσεν τὴν γῆν·*[bu] καί, *Ἐγὼ εἶπα, Θεοί ἐστε·*[bv] καί, *Θεοὺς οὐ κακολογήσεις.*[bw] πολλοὶ δὲ καὶ ἁρπάσαντες τήνδε

l. 204 ταὐτὰ *scripsi* : ταῦτα *ZA, edd.* = *"He imparts this teaching to the Ephesians."* **l. 207** μηδὲ … προσκυνήσωμεν *scripsi* : μ. … -σομ- *ZA, edd. The subjunc. aor., not the indic. fut., is expected in the formulation of the first per. pl. prohibition; cf. secc.* 5 (*μηδὲ σοφωτέρους ἑαυτοὺς ὑπολάβωμεν τῆς τοῦ Πνεύματος χάριτος, ἀλλ᾽ ἀκούσωμεν*) *and* 8 (*Μὴ … ἀποστερήσωμεν*) *above. Cf. c. n. ep. 146.8* (γεύσωνται). **l. 211** εἶπα *scr. Cir., edd.* (*cf. LXX; NTG, Jn 10.34*) : -πον *Z. Ciraco restored the less common first per. form printed by Rahlfs*

bp. Is 1.2
bq. Ps 82.6
br. Rom 8.14–17
bs. Gal 4.6f. (NT var.)
bt. Eph 1.4f.
bu. Ps 50.1
bv. Ps 82.6
bw. Ex 22.28

them up high, but they have rejected me";[bp] and through the blessed David, "I said, you are gods and sons of the Most High, all of you."[bq] Furthermore, Paul, a man endowed with all wisdom, wrote to the Romans, "Those who follow the lead of the Spirit of God are the true sons of God. You have received no slave's spirit so that you should relapse into fear; rather, you have received the spirit of adoption, in which we cry out, 'Abba, Father!' The Spirit himself joins our spirit in testifying that we are children of God. If children, we are also heirs, heirs of God and co-heirs with Christ, if, that is, we suffer with Christ so that we may also be glorified with him."[br] Then, in the Epistle to the Galatians, he said, "As you are sons, God has sent into your hearts the Spirit of his Son, which cries out, 'Abba, Father!' Thus, you are no longer a slave, but a son; if a son, also an heir of God through Jesus Christ."[bs] He imparted the same teaching to the Ephesians, saying, "In his love, having already chosen us for adoption as his children through Jesus Christ."[bt] Now if we are wrong to give glory to Christ, because the name "Christ" is not particular to him, then we shouldn't worship him as "Son" either, since this is also a name he shares with many others.

(7) And why should I confine myself to the name "Son" when many have received even the name of "God" by God's own gift: "The Lord, God of gods, has spoken and summoned the earth";[bu] and, "I said, 'You are gods'";[bv] and, "You shall not revile gods."[bw] Many others have unlawfully possessed themselves of this title; as you

τὴν κλῆσιν ἐσχήκασιν· οἱ γὰρ τοὺς ἀνθρώπους ἐξαπατήσαντες δαίμονες τοῖς εἰδώλοις τήνδε τὴν προσηγορίαν ἐπέθεσαν. οὗ δὴ χάριν Ἰερεμίας βοᾷ, *Θεοὶ οἳ τὸν οὐρανὸν καὶ τὴν γῆν οὐκ ἐποίησαν ἀπολέσθωσαν ἀπὸ* προσώπου *τῆς γῆς καὶ* ἀπὸ προσώπου *τοῦ οὐρανοῦ·*[bx] καὶ πάλιν, Ἐποίησαν ἑαυτοῖς *θεοὺς ἀργυροῦς καὶ* θεοὺς *χρυσοῦς.*[by] καὶ ὁ Ἡσαΐας, κωμῳδήσας τὴν τῶν εἰδώλων κατασκευήν, εἰρηκώς, ὅτι *Τὸ ἥμισυ αὐτοῦ κατέκαυσεν ἐν πυρὶ καί … ὀπτήσας κρέας, ἔφαγεν καὶ … εἶπεν, Ἡδύ μοι ὅτι ἐθερμάνθην καὶ εἶδον* φῶς, καὶ ἐπήγαγεν, *Τὸ δὲ λοιπὸν ἔγλυψεν ὡς Θεὸν … καὶ προσκυνεῖ αὐτῷ … λέγων, Ἐξελοῦ με, ὅτι θεός μου εἶ σύ,*[bz] οὗ δὴ χάριν, αὐτοὺς ὀδυρόμενος, λέγει, Γνῶθι *ὅτι σποδὸς ἡ καρδία αὐτῶν.*[ca] καὶ ὁ μελοποιὸς δὲ Δαυὶδ ψάλλειν ἡμᾶς ἐδίδαξεν, *Ὅτι πάντες οἱ θεοὶ τῶν ἐθνῶν δαιμόνια, ὁ δὲ Κύριος τοὺς οὐρανοὺς ἐποίησεν.*[cb]

Ἀλλὰ τὸ τῶν ὀνομάτων ὁμώνυμον οὐδὲν τοῖς εὐσεβεῖν ἐπισταμένοις λυμαίνεται· ἴσμεν γὰρ ὡς οἱ δαίμονες ψευδῶς σφίσιν τε αὐτοῖς καὶ τοῖς εἰδώλοις τὴν θείαν προσηγορίαν ἐπέθεσαν, οἱ δὲ ἅγιοι χάριτι ταύτην ἐδέξαντο τὴν τιμήν, ἀληθῶς δὲ καὶ φύσει Θεὸς ὁ τῶν ὅλων Θεός, καὶ ὁ μονογενὴς αὐτοῦ Υἱός, καὶ τὸ Πανάγιον Πνεῦμα. καὶ τοῦτο σαφῶς ὁ πανεύφημος ἐδίδαξεν ἡμᾶς Παῦλος· φησὶν δὲ οὕτως· *Καὶ γὰρ εἴπερ εἰσὶ λεγόμενοι θεοί* πολλοί, *εἴτε ἐν οὐρανῷ εἴτε ἐπὶ γῆς, ὥσπερ εἰσὶ* θεοὶ

in Ps 82.6 and the editors of the NTG; εἶπα *had already appeared in sec. 6 of this letter. Printed texts of Thdt. present both versions of this psalmic verse; cf. Eran., dial. 2, p. 129, l. 32.* **l. 234** θεοὶ πολλοί *ZA, Sir. Nös. :* θ. *Az. (cf. NTG). Z carries a form of 1Cor 8.5 that, though probably corrupted by dittography, is attested in the work of other late-antique authors; v. Epiph., Haer. vol 2, p. 323, l. 11; Chrys., Hom. 5 C. Anom., l. 209; and Cyr., Trin. dial. 3, sec. 488c. This version of the verse appears again in the ms. tradition of Thdt. at in Ps. 135.13 (PG, vol. 80, col. 1921, l. 13).*

bx. Jer 10.11 (LXX var.)
by. Ep Jer 4 (LXX var.)
bz. Is 44.16f. (LXX var.)
ca. Is 44.20 (LXX; LXX var.)
cb. Ps 96.5

know, the demons who misled the human race conferred this name on idols. So, Jeremiah cries out, "May those gods who did not create heaven and earth perish from the face of the earth and from the face of heaven!";[bx] and again, "They made for themselves gods of silver and gold."[by] Isaiah too in a passage mocking the fabrication of idols, first said, "Half of it he burned in the fire, broiled his meat, ate his fill, and declared, 'Such a comfort to get warm and to have some light!,'" and then he went on, "From the rest, he fashioned a god, and prostrating himself before it, said 'Save me, because you are my god.'"[bz] Weeping for such men, he declares, "See how their heart is just dust."[ca] And David, the psalmist, has taught us to chant, "The gods of the gentiles are all evil spirits; the Lord is the maker of the heavens."[cb]

Of course, this identity in names doesn't in the least bother those who understand true religion. We're well aware that demons falsely apply the divine name to themselves and their idols, and that the appellation "God" has been granted by grace to the holy as a special honor, yet it belongs properly and by nature to God, the God of the universe, his only-begotten Son, and the Holy Spirit. This is the clear meaning of the teaching given us by Paul whose word is everywhere revered. As he says, "Even if there is a multiplicity of so-called gods in heaven and on earth, as there is also a multiplicity of gods and

πολλοὶ καὶ κύριοι πολλοί, ἀλλ᾽ ἡμῖν εἷς Θεός, ὁ Πατήρ, ἐξ οὗ τὰ πάντα, καὶ ἡμεῖς εἰς αὐτόν, καὶ εἷς Κύριος, Ἰησοῦς Χριστός, δι᾽ οὗ τὰ πάντα, καὶ ἡμεῖς δι᾽ αὐτοῦ.[cc]

Καὶ *πνεῦμα* δὲ Θεοῦ τὸ Πανάγιον καλεῖται Πνεῦμα, ἀλλὰ καὶ ἡ τοῦ ἀνθρώπου ψυχή· *Ἐξελεύσεται*, γάρ φησιν, *τὸ πνεῦμα αὐτοῦ·*[cd] καί, *Εὐλογεῖτε, πνεύματα καὶ ψυχαὶ δικαίων, τὸν Κύριον.*[ce] καὶ τοὺς ἀγγέλους δὲ *πνεύματα* προσηγόρευσεν ὁ ὑμνοποιὸς Δαυίδ· *Ὁ ποιῶν*, γάρ φησι, *τοὺς ἀγγέλους αὐτοῦ πνεύματα καὶ τοὺς λειτουργοὺς αὐτοῦ* πυρὸς φλόγα.[cf] καὶ τί λέγω τοὺς ἀγγέλους καὶ τὰς τῶν ἀνθρώπων ψυχάς; καὶ γὰρ τοὺς δαίμονας οὕτως ὁ Δεσπότης ὠνόμασεν· Παραλήψεται, γάρ φησιν, *ἕτερα ἑπτὰ πνεύματα πονηρότερα ἑαυτοῦ καὶ* εἰσελεύσεται *εἰς αὐτόν, … καὶ* ἔσται *τὰ ἔσχατα τοῦ ἀνθρώπου ἐκείνου χείρονα τῶν πρώτων.*[cg]

(8) Ἀλλ᾽ οὐδὲ ἡ ὁμωνυμία τὸν εὐσεβῆ λωβᾶται· εἷς γὰρ φύσει Θεὸς ὁ Πατήρ, καὶ ὁ μονογενὴς αὐτοῦ Υἱός, καὶ τὸ Πανάγιον αὐτοῦ Πνεῦμα, καὶ εἷς φύσει Υἱὸς τοῦ Θεοῦ Μονογενής, ὁ

ll. 236f. εἰς αὐτόν … καὶ ἡμεῖς *add.* A[mg.]*(Car.?), scr. edd. : om. ZA. The corrector, most likely Sirmond, has prefixed* "ms" *to this supplement. As this passage is missing also in Z, the exemplar of A, only N, which is now here lacunose, seems a possible source; v. "Intro. to the Gk. Text," n. 51.* **l. 244** τὰς τῶν ἀνθρώπων ψυχάς *corr. Sir.?, scr. Az.* : τῶν ἀ. τὰς ψ. *corr. Car.?, scr. Sir. Nös.* : τῶν ἀ. ψ. *ZA The acc. art. is expected and needed; the phrase with anarthrous* ψυχάς *carried by the mss. has no parallels in the* corpus *of Thdt. The supplement has been written twice, and its insertion indicated both before τῶν and before ψυχάς; in the first place, the handwriting is probably that of Sirmond, in the second, that of Cariofilo. For the works of Thdt., the TLG lists four other exx. of τὰς τῶν ἀνθρώπων ψυχάς, none for τῶν ἀ. τὰς ψ.; cf. Eran. dial. 3, p. 219, ll. 1f.: Τί οὖν φαμεν καὶ τὰς ἀοράτους δυνάμεις καὶ τὰς τῶν ἀνθρώπων ψυχὰς … ἀθανάτους; Still Thdt. does use the latter word order with other fem. pl. acc. nouns: e.g.* ἁμαρτίας *(80, 1860, 48) and* πλημμελείας *(80, 1389, 20). It looks likely that Sirmond, the author of the correction Azéma and I have accepted, himself deferred to the expertise of Cariofilo.*

cc. 1Cor 8.5f. (NT var.) cd. Ps 146.4 ce. Dn 3.86 (LXX)
cf. Ps 104.4 (LXX var.) cg. Lk 11.26 (NT var.)

lords, we have but one God, the Father, from whom are all things and toward whom we look, and one Lord, Jesus Christ, through whom all things come, and thanks to whom we have our being."[6][cc]

Now the Holy Spirit is called God's "Spirit," and the soul of man is also spoken of as "spirit." As Scripture says, "His spirit will leave him"[cd]; and, "Praise the Lord, ye spirits and souls of the just!"[ce] The psalmist David has applied the name "spirits" to angels as well: "He who makes his angels spirits and his ministers a flaming fire."[cf] And why talk just about the angels and human souls? Our Master has applied this name even to demons: "He will take along with him seven more spirits, worse than himself, and enter into him, and, in the end, that man will be worse off than before."[cg]

(8) But this use of the same terminology will cause no trouble for the orthodox. As we know, there is but one who is God by nature, the Father, his only-begotten Son, and his Holy Spirit; and just one

6. This translation of Paul's difficult prepositional phrases εἰς αὐτὸν and δι' αὐτοῦ follows Theodoret's exposition of 1Cor 8.5f.: Τὸ δὲ, ἡμεῖς εἰς αὐτὸν, ἀντὶ τοῦ, Πρὸς αὐτὸν ἀπεστράφθαι ὀφείλομεν, εἰς αὐτὸν ἀφορᾶν, αὐτὸν διηνεκῶς ἀνυμνεῖν. Τὸ δὲ, καὶ ἡμεῖς δι' αὐτοῦ, οὐ τὴν δημιουργίαν, ἀλλὰ τὴν σωτηρίαν αἰνίττεται. Δι' αὐτοῦ μὲν γὰρ τὰ πάντα, ἡμεῖς δὲ οἱ πεπιστευκότες δι' αὐτοῦ τῆς σωτηρίας τετυχήκαμεν ("The phrase 'we to him' is equivalent to saying, 'We should be turned toward him, contemplate him, and ceaselessly sing his praises.' The phrase 'and we through him' refers not to creation, but to salvation. Of course, everything was made through him, but we who have believed have obtained our salvation through him").

ἐνανθρωπήσας Θεὸς Λόγος, ὁ Κύριος ἡμῶν Ἰησοῦς Χριστός, καὶ ἓν Πνεῦμα Ἅγιον, ὁ Παράκλητος, ὅς πληροῖ τῆς Τριάδος τὸν ἀριθμόν. οὕτω, πολλῶν ὀνομαζομένων πατέρων, ἕνα προσκυνοῦμεν Πατέρα, τὸν πρὸ τῶν αἰώνων Πατέρα, τὸν καὶ ταύτην τοῖς ἀνθρώποις τὴν ἐπίκλησιν δεδωκότα, κατὰ τὴν τοῦ Ἀποστόλου φωνήν· *Κάμπτω,* γάρ φησι, *τὰ γόνατά μου πρὸς τὸν Πατέρα* τοῦ Κυρίου ἡμῶν Ἰησοῦ Χριστοῦ, *ἐξ οὗ πᾶσα πατριὰ ἐν οὐρανῷ καὶ ἐπὶ γῆς ὀνομάζεται.*[ch]

Μὴ τοίνυν τῷ ἄλλους ὀνομάζεσθαι *χριστοὺς* ἀποστερήσωμεν ἑαυτοὺς τῆς τοῦ Κυρίου ἡμῶν Ἰησοῦ Χριστοῦ προσκυνήσεως· ὡς γάρ, πολλῶν ὠνομασμένων *θεῶν* τε καὶ *πατέρων,* εἷς ἐστιν ὁ ἐπὶ πάντων Θεὸς καὶ πρὸ αἰώνων Πατήρ, καί, πολλῶν κεκλημένων *υἱῶν,* εἷς ὁ ἀληθινὸς καὶ φύσει Υἱός, καί, πολλῶν προσηγορευμένων *πνευμάτων,* ἕν ἐστι τὸ Πανάγιον Πνεῦμα, οὕτω πολλῶν κληθέντων *χριστῶν, εἷς Κύριος, Ἰησοῦς Χριστός, δι᾽ οὗ τὰ πάντα.*[ci] μάλα δὲ εἰκότως ἡ Ἐκκλησία τοῦδε ἐξήρτηται τοῦ ὀνόματος· ἤκουσεν γὰρ τοῦ νυμφοστόλου Παύλου βοῶντος, *Ἡρμοσάμην … ὑμᾶς ἑνὶ ἀνδρί, παρθένον ἁγνὴν παραστῆσαι τῷ Χριστῷ·*[cj] καὶ πάλιν, *οἱ ἄνδρες, ἀγαπᾶτε τὰς γυναῖκας* ὑμῶν *ὡς καὶ ὁ Χριστὸς ἠγάπησεν τὴν Ἐκκλησίαν·*[ck] καὶ αὖθις εἰπών, *Ἀντὶ τούτου καταλείψει ἄνθρωπος τὸν πατέρα* αὐτοῦ *καὶ τὴν μητέρα* αὐτοῦ *καὶ προσκολληθήσεται πρὸς τὴν γυναῖκα αὐτοῦ, καὶ ἔσονται οἱ δύο εἰς σάρκα μίαν,* ἐπήγαγεν, *Τὸ μυστήριον τοῦτο μέγα ἐστίν· ἐγὼ δὲ λέγω εἰς Χριστὸν καὶ εἰς τὴν Ἐκκλησίαν.*[cl] ἄκουσον αὐτοῦ λέγοντος, *Χριστὸς ἡμᾶς ἐξηγόρασεν ἐκ τῆς κατάρας τοῦ νόμου, γενόμενος ὑπὲρ ἡμῶν κατάρα·*[cm] καὶ ἑτέρωθι, *Ἢ ἀγνοεῖτε ὅτι ὅσοι εἰς Χριστὸν …* ἐβαπτίσθητε *εἰς τὸν θάνατον αὐτοῦ*

ch. Eph 3.14f. (NT var.) ci. 1Cor 8.6 cj. 2Cor 11.2
ck. Eph 5.25 (NT var.) cl. Eph 5.31f. (NT var.) cm. Gal 3.13

who is by nature the Son, the Only-begotten of God, God the Word who became man, our Lord, Jesus Christ; and one Holy Spirit, the Paraclete, who completes the number of the Trinity. Thus, though many are called by the name of "father," we adore just one Father, the Father before all time, the one who, as the Apostle says, bestowed this name on mortal men: "I bend my knee before the Father of our Lord, Jesus Christ, the source from which all fatherhood in heaven and earth takes its name."[7ch]

Therefore, we must not deny ourselves the adoration of our Lord Jesus Christ, just because there are others who are called "christs." In the same way that many are called "god" and "father," but there is just one who is God over all things and Father before all time, and many are called "sons," but there is just one truly Son by nature, and many known as "spirits," but there is just one Holy Spirit, so, though many are called "christs," there is just one Lord Jesus Christ, through whom are all things.[ci] It is with good reason that the Church clings to this name. In this, she has shown her obedience to St. Paul, who gave her away at her wedding: "I betrothed you," he exclaims, "to one husband to present you as a holy virgin to Christ";[cj] and again, "Men, love your wives, just as Christ has loved his Church."[ck] Then, after declaring, "Because of this, a man will leave his father and his mother and be joined to his wife, and the two will become one flesh," he went on, "This is a great mystery; I say this in reference to Christ and the Church."[cl] Listen to his words: "Christ has ransomed us from the curse of the law, himself becoming a curse for us";[cm] and, in another passage, "Or could you be unaware that all of you who have been baptized into Christ have been baptized into his

7. While the Greek word πατριά normally means "family," in this passage and in sec. 12 below, Theodoret is clearly pointing to its etymological connection with πατήρ = "father"; *cf.* his remarks on this verse in *in Eph. ad loc.*: Κυρίως Πατὴρ, καὶ ἀληθῶς Πατὴρ ὁ Θεός. Οὐ γὰρ ἐγένετο πρῶτον υἱὸς, εἶτα Πατήρ· ἀλλ' ἀεὶ Πατήρ ἐστι καὶ φύσει Πατήρ· οἱ δὲ ἄλλοι πατέρες, εἴτε σωματικοί, εἴτε πνευματικοί, ἄνωθεν τὴν προσηγορίαν εἵλκυσαν ("God is properly and truly 'Father.' He did not become Father as the result of the birth of a son; rather he is always Father, Father by nature. All other fathers, whether physical or spiritual, have their title from that heavenly source"); *cf.* Jackson, p. 320, n. 6.

ἐβαπτίσθητε;[cn] καὶ ἀλλαχοῦ, *Ὅσοι … εἰς Χριστὸν ἐβαπτίσθητε Χριστὸν ἐνεδύσασθε·*[co] καὶ πάλιν, *Ἐνδύσασθε τὸν Κύριον Ἰησοῦν Χριστὸν καὶ τῆς σαρκὸς πρόνοιαν μὴ ποιεῖσθε εἰς ἐπιθυμίας.*[cp]

(9) Ταῦτα καὶ τὰ τούτοις προσόμοια μεμαθηκότες, οἱ τῶν θείων δωρεῶν τετυχηκότες ἔρωτι τοῦ φιλοδώρου Δεσπότου καὶ τὴν τριπόθητον αὐτοῦ προσηγορίαν ἐν τῷ στόματι περιφέρουσι καὶ τὰ τοῦ Ἄισματος Τῶν Ἀισμάτων βοῶσιν· *Ἀδελφιδός μου ἐμοί, κἀγὼ αὐτῷ·*[cq] *ἐν τῇ σκιᾷ αὐτοῦ ἐπεθύμησα καὶ ἐκάθισα, καὶ ὁ καρπὸς αὐτοῦ γλυκὺς ἐν λάρυγγί μου.*[cr] πρὸς δὲ τούτοις, καὶ τὴν ἐπέραστον προσηγορίαν ἣν ἔχομεν ἐκ τῆς τοῦ *Χριστοῦ* προσηγορίας ἐλάβομεν· *Χριστιανοὶ* γὰρ ὀνομαζόμεθα.[cs] περὶ τούτου τοῦ ὀνόματος προαγορεύων, ὁ τῶν ὅλων ἔφη Θεός, *Τοῖς δὲ δουλεύουσί* μοι *κληθήσεται ὄνομα καινόν, ὃ εὐλογηθήσεται* N| *ἐπὶ τῆς γῆς.*[ct] τούτου δὴ χάριν διαφερόντως ἡ Ἐκκλησία |τῆσδε τῆς προσηγορίας ἐξήρτηται· ὅτε γὰρ ἐνανθρώπησεν ὁ μονογενὴς τοῦ Θεοῦ Υἱός, τότε *Χριστὸς* ὠνομάσθη, τότε τῶν ἀνθρώπων ἡ φύσις τοῦ νοεροῦ φωτὸς τὰς ἀκτῖνας ἐδέξατο, τότε τῆς ἀληθείας οἱ κήρυκες τὴν οἰκουμένην κατηύγασαν. οἱ μέντοι τῆς Ἐκκλησίας διδάσκαλοι ἀδιαφόρως ἀεὶ ταῖς τοῦ Μονογενοῦς προσηγορίαις ἐχρήσαντο· ποτὲ μὲν γὰρ δοξάζουσιν τὸν Πατέρα, καὶ τὸν Υἱόν, καὶ τὸ Ἅγιον Πνεῦμα, ποτὲ δὲ τὸν Πατέρα σὺν τῷ Χριστῷ καὶ τῷ Ἁγίῳ Πνεύματι· ἀλλ᾽ ὅμως οὐδεμίαν ἔχει, κατὰ τὴν διάνοιαν, τοῦτο πρὸς ἐκεῖνο διαφοράν. διά τοι τοῦτο, τοῦ Κυρίου προστεταχότος βαπτίζειν *εἰς τὸ ὄνομα τοῦ Πατρός, καὶ τοῦ Υἱοῦ, καὶ τοῦ Ἁγίου Πνεύματος,*[cu] ὁ τρισμακάριος Πέτρος τοῖς τὸ κήρυγμα δεδεγμένοις, ἐρομένοις τί χρὴ ποιῆσαι, Πιστεύσατε,

l. 288 ἐπέραστον *coni. mg. et scr. Cir. (uocem tamquam coniecturam in mg. scriptam cancel. et in textum transtulit), edd.* : -ρατ- *Z*

cn. Rom 6.3 (NT var.) (*Cf.* Gal 3.27.)
co. Gal 3.27
cp. Rom 13.14
cq. Song 2.16
cr. Song 2.3 (LXX var.)
cs. *Cf.* Acts 11.26.
ct. Is 65.15f. (LXX var.)
cu. Mt 28.19

death?"[cn] and elsewhere, "All of you who have been baptized into Christ have clothed yourselves with Christ";[co] and again, "Clothe yourselves with the Lord Jesus Christ, and make no provision for the flesh to arouse its lusts."[8][cp]

(9) With an understanding of these and passages of similar import, those who have partaken of the bounty of God, in their passionate love for their kindly Master, bear about on their lips his name that they love, and, in the words of the Song of Songs, cry out, "My beloved is mine, and I am his;[cq] for his shadow I longed, and in it I took my rest. Sweet is the taste of his fruit."[cr] What is more, we derive the name that we ourselves bear and cherish from the name "Christ," since we call ourselves "Christians."[cs] In a prophecy regarding this name, the God of the universe declared, "My servants will receive a new name, a name that will be blessed over all the earth."[ct] The Church clings to this name with deep devotion, since the only-begotten Son of God received the name "Christ" after he became man, when human nature was illuminated by rays of spiritual light, when the heralds of the truth cast their light on all the world. Of course, the teachers of the Church make an undifferentiated use of the names given to the Only-begotten; sometimes they glorify Father, Son, and Holy Spirit, sometimes the Father with Christ and the Holy Spirit, but there is no difference of meaning between one formula and the other. So it is that the Lord gave the command to baptize in the name of the Father, the Son, and Holy Spirit,[cu] and yet, when asked by those who had received the gospel, what they should

8. *V.* Theodoret's comment on Rom 13.14: Paul did not mean to prohibit appropriate care for the body, but the luxury that would awaken vigorous desire (Μὴ σκιρτᾷν αὐτὴν παρασκευάζετε διὰ τῆς τρυφῆς; "Don't make the flesh go wild by pampering it").

ἔφη, *καὶ βαπτισθήτω ἕκαστος ὑμῶν εἰς τὸ ὄνομα* τοῦ Κυρίου ἡμῶν *Ἰησοῦ Χριστοῦ,*[cv] ὡς ταυτησὶ τῆς προσηγορίας πᾶσαν ἐχούσης τοῦ θείου κηρύγματος τὴν δύναμιν. καὶ τοῦτο σαφῶς ἡμᾶς ἐδίδαξεν ὁ μέγας Βασίλειος, ὁ τῆς καππαδοκῶν, μᾶλλον δὲ τῆς οἰκουμένης, φωστήρ·[cw] ἔφη δὲ οὕτως· *Ἡ γὰρ τοῦ Χριστοῦ προσηγορία τοῦ παντός ἐστιν ὁμολογία· δηλοῖ γὰρ τὸν Πατέρα τὸν … χρίσαντα, … τὸν Υἱὸν τὸν χρισθέντα, τὸ Πνεῦμα τὸ Ἅγιον ᾧ ἐχρίσθη.*[cx] καὶ οἱ ἐν Νικαίᾳ δὲ συνεληλυθότες τρισμακάριοι πατέρες, εἰπόντες χρῆναι πιστεύειν *εἰς ἕνα Θεόν, Πατέρα,* ἐπήγαγον, *Καὶ εἰς ἕνα Κύριον, Ἰησοῦν Χριστόν, τὸν Υἱὸν τοῦ Θεοῦ τὸν μονογενῆ,*[cy] διδάσκοντες ὡς ὁ Κύριος Ἰησοῦς Χριστὸς αὐτός ἐστιν ὁ μονογενὴς Υἱὸς τοῦ Θεοῦ.

(10) Χρὴ δὲ κἀκεῖνο προσθεῖναι τοῖς εἰρημένοις· ὡς οὐ χρὴ λέγειν, *Μετὰ τὴν ἀνάληψιν οὐκ ἔστι Χριστὸς ὁ Δεσπότης Χριστός, ἀλλὰ Υἱὸς μονογενής·* μετὰ γὰρ δὴ τὴν ἀνάληψιν, καὶ τὰ θεῖα εὐαγγέλια συνεγράφη, καὶ ἡ τῶν πράξεων ἱστορία, καὶ αἱ τοῦ Ἀποστόλου ἐπιστολαί. μετὰ τὴν ἀνάληψιν ὁ θεῖος βοᾷ Παῦλος, *Ἔχοντες … ἀρχιερέα μέγαν διεληλυθότα τοὺς οὐρανούς, Ἰησοῦν* Χριστόν, τὸν Κύριον ἡμῶν, *κρατῶμεν τῆς ὁμολογίας·*[cz] καὶ πάλιν, *Οὐ γὰρ εἰς χειροποίητα ἅγια εἰσῆλθε Χριστός, ἀντίτυπα τῶν ἀληθινῶν, ἀλλ᾽ εἰς αὐτὸν τὸν οὐρανὸν νῦν ἐμφανισθῆναι τῷ προσώπῳ τοῦ Θεοῦ ὑπὲρ ἡμῶν*[da] καὶ αὖθις, περὶ τῆς εἰς τὸν Θεὸν ἐλπίδος εἰπών τινα, ἐπήγαγεν· *Ἣν ὡς ἄγκυραν ἔχομεν … ἀσφαλῆ τε καὶ βεβαίαν καὶ εἰσερχομένην εἰς τὸ ἐσώτερον τοῦ καταπετάσματος, ὅπου πρόδρομος εἰσῆλθεν ὑπὲρ ἡμῶν Ἰησοῦς,*

l. 317 χρὴ *corr. Cir.?, scr. edd.* : χρῆναι *NZ*, A^{ac}? *A corrector of A, probably Ciriaco, has restored grammatical sense. The scribe of N may still have been thinking of the* χρῆναι *of the previous period, when he repeated it here.*

cv. Acts 2.38 (NT var.) cw. Phil 2.15 cx. Bas., *Spir.* 12.28
cy. *Sym. Nic-CP* cz. Heb 4.14 (NT var.) da. Heb 9.24

do next, the blessed Peter replied, "You must believe, and each of you must be baptized in the name of our Lord, Jesus Christ,"[cv] thus demonstrating his conviction that this name possessed all the potency of the divine commission. And this is exactly what is taught by Basil the Great, the luminary of Cappadocia, or rather, the entire world.[9cw] As he said, "The name 'Christ' contains within itself the entirety of our confession, since it signifies the Father who anointed, the Son who received the anointing, and the Holy Spirit in whom the Son was anointed."[cx] Furthermore, when the blessed fathers assembled in Nicaea declared the necessity of belief in one God the Father, they went on to add, "and in the one Lord Jesus Christ, the only-begotten Son of God,"[cy] thus teaching that the Lord Jesus Christ is one and the same as the only-begotten Son of God.

(10) I must add a further point, namely that we must not say, "After the ascension, the Master Christ is no longer Christ, but the only-begotten Son." As you know, the holy gospels, the history of Acts, and the epistles of the Apostle were all composed after the ascension. After the ascension, St. Paul calls out, "As we have a great high priest who has passed through the heavens, Jesus Christ, our Lord, let us hold fast to our confession of faith"[10cz]; and again, "It was no holy place made by human hands, an image of the real, that Christ entered, but heaven itself in order to appear before the face of God on our behalf."[da] Then there is the passage, where, after speaking of hope in God, he adds, "And we grasp this hope like an anchor safe and secure that passes through to the other side of the veil, where Jesus, as our forerunner, our eternal high priest after the order of Melchisedek, has

9. On Theodoret's adaptation of Paul's metaphor (Phil 2.15), *v. ep.* 125 n. 7.

10. Perhaps carried away on the force of his argument, which would be much strengthened by a reference to "Christ," Theodoret here quotes Heb 4.14 in a form quite different from that in which he had quoted the same verse earlier in this letter (*v.* sec. 4). The *NTG* cites no support in the NT manuscripts for this peculiar reading.

κατὰ τὴν τάξιν Μελχισεδὲκ ἀρχιερεὺς γενόμενος εἰς τὸν αἰῶνα·[db] καὶ τῷ μακαρίῳ δὲ Τίτῳ περὶ τῆς δευτέρας γράφων ἐπιφανείας, οὕτως εἶπεν· *Προσδεχόμενοι τὴν μακαρίαν ἐλπίδα καὶ ἐπιφάνειαν τῆς δόξης τοῦ μεγάλου Θεοῦ καὶ Σωτῆρος ἡμῶν Ἰησοῦ Χριστοῦ·*[dc] καὶ θεσσαλονικεῦσι δὲ τὰ παραπλήσια γέγραφεν· *Αὐτοὶ γὰρ περὶ ἡμῶν ἀπαγγελοῦσιν ὁποίαν εἴσοδον ἔχομεν πρὸς ὑμᾶς καὶ πῶς ἐπεστρέψατε πρὸς τὸν Θεὸν ἀπὸ τῶν εἰδώλων δουλεύειν Θεῷ ζῶντι καὶ ἀληθινῷ καὶ ἀναμένειν τὸν Υἱὸν αὐτοῦ ἐκ τῶν οὐρανῶν, ὃν ἤγειρεν ἐκ τῶν νεκρῶν, Ἰησοῦν, τὸν ῥυόμενον ἡμᾶς ἀπὸ τῆς ὀργῆς τῆς ἐρχομένης·*[dd] καὶ πάλιν, *Ὑμᾶς δὲ ὁ Κύριος πλεονάσαι καὶ περισσεύσαι τῇ ἀγάπῃ εἰς ἀλλήλους καὶ εἰς πάντας, καθάπερ καὶ ἡμεῖς εἰς ὑμᾶς εἰς τὸ στηρίξαι ὑμῶν τὰς καρδίας ἀμέμπτους ἐν ἁγιωσύνῃ ἔμπροσθεν τοῦ Θεοῦ καὶ Πατρὸς ἡμῶν ἐν τῇ παρουσίᾳ τοῦ Κυρίου ἡμῶν Ἰησοῦ* Χριστοῦ *μετὰ πάντων τῶν ἁγίων αὐτοῦ·*[de] καὶ αὖθις δὲ τοῖς αὐτοῖς ἐπιστείλας, καὶ ταῦτα N|| τέθεικεν· *Ἐρωτῶμεν δὲ ὑμᾶς,|| ἀδελφοί, ὑπὲρ τῆς παρουσίας τοῦ Κυρίου ἡμῶν Ἰησοῦ Χριστοῦ καὶ ἡμῶν ἐπισυναγωγῆς ἐπ᾽ αὐτόν·*[df] καὶ μετ᾽ ὀλίγα δέ, τοῦ Ἀντιχρίστου τὸν ὄλεθρον προθεσπίζων, ἐπήγαγεν, *Ὃν ὁ Κύριος …* ἀναλώσει *τῷ πνεύματι τοῦ στόματος αὐτοῦ καὶ καταργήσει τῇ ἐπιφανείᾳ τῆς παρουσίας αὐτοῦ·*[dg] καὶ ῥωμαίους δὲ εἰς ὁμόνοιαν προτρέψας, καὶ ταῦτα προστέθεικεν· *Σὺ δέ, τί κρίνεις τὸν ἀδελφόν σου, ἤ, καὶ σύ, τί ἐξουθενεῖς τὸν ἀδελφόν σου; πάντες γὰρ παραστησόμεθα τῷ βήματι τοῦ* Χριστοῦ· *γέγραπται γάρ, Ζῶ ἐγώ, λέγει Κύριος, ὅτι ἐμοὶ κάμψει πᾶν γόνυ, καὶ πᾶσα γλῶσσα ἐξομολογήσεται τῷ Θεῷ·*[dh] καὶ αὐτὸς

l. 335 ἡμῶν *scr. Nös. Az. (Cf. NTG)* : αὐτῶν *codd., Sir. = "They will themselves spread the word about their reception among you." Nösselt's correction restores the obvious sense of this clause of 1Thes 1.9. The first per. pl. pron. is the reading printed by the NTG, and appears in Thdt.'s quotation of this verse in his commentary ad loc. The false reading of N must be due to the preceding Αὐτοὶ.*

db. Heb 6.19f.
dc. Ti 2.13
dd. 1Thes 1.9f. (NT var.)
de. 1Thes 3.12f. (NT var.)
df. 2Thes 2.1
dg. 2Thes 2.8 (NT var.)
dh. Rom 14.10f. (NT var.)

entered before us."[db] In the Epistle to the blessed Titus, in a passage regarding the second coming, he says, "In the expectation of that blessed hope and the revelation of the glory of our great God and Savior Jesus Christ."[dc] And he writes much the same thing to the Thessalonians: "They will themselves spread the word about our reception among you, how you turned toward God and away from your idols, to serve the living, the true God and await his Son from heaven, Jesus, whom he raised from the dead, our Savior from the wrath that is to come";[dd] and again, "As he has done for our love for you, may the Lord increase more and more abundantly your love for each other and for all the world, so that your hearts will be fixed firm in innocence and holiness before our God and Father when our Lord, Jesus Christ comes with all his saints."[de] Then, in the second letter to the same community, he writes, "With regard to the coming of our Lord Jesus Christ when he will gather us to himself, we entreat you, brethren";[df] and then, a bit further on, in a prophecy of the downfall of the Antichrist, he adds, "whom the Lord will destroy with the breath of his mouth and annihilate with the brilliance of his second coming."[dg] Then, after enjoining concord on the Romans, he adds: "You there, why do you judge your brother? And you, why do you look down on your brother? We shall all take our place before the court of Christ, for it is written, 'As I live, says the Lord, every knee will bow before me, and every tongue will sing praise to God.'"[dh] And, in a prophecy

δὲ ὁ Κύριος, τὴν δευτέραν αὐτοῦ παρουσίαν προαγορεύων, πρὸς πολλοῖς ἄλλοις καὶ ταῦτα εἴρηκεν· *Τότε ἐάν τις ὑμῖν εἴπῃ, Ἰδοὺ ὧδε ὁ Χριστός*, ἰδοὺ ἐκεῖ, *μὴ πιστεύσητε*·[di] *ὥσπερ γὰρ … ἀστραπὴ ἐξέρχεται ἀπὸ ἀνατολῶν καὶ φαίνεται* εἰς δυσμάς, *οὕτως ἔσται ἡ παρουσία τοῦ Υἱοῦ τοῦ ἀνθρώπου.*[dj]

(11) Καὶ μετὰ τὴν τοῦ σώματος ἀθανασίαν καὶ ἀφθαρσίαν, *Υἱὸν ἀνθρώπου* ἑαυτὸν προσηγόρευσεν, ἀπὸ τῆς ὁρωμένης φύσεως ὀνομάσας· αὕτη γὰρ καὶ τότε φανήσεται. ἡ γὰρ θεία φύσις καὶ ἀγγέλοις ἀόρατος· *Θεὸν* γὰρ *οὐδεὶς ἑώρακεν πώποτε,*[dk] κατὰ τὴν αὐτοῦ τοῦ Κυρίου φωνήν, καὶ τῷ μεγάλῳ Μωϋσεῖ ἔφη, Οὐδεὶς ὄψεται *τὸ πρόσωπόν μου καὶ ζήσεται.*[dl] τὸ γὰρ *Οὐδένα οἴδαμεν κατὰ σάρκα· εἰ* δὲ *καὶ ἐγνώκαμεν κατὰ σάρκα Χριστόν, ἀλλὰ νῦν οὐκέτι γινώσκομεν*[dm] οὐκ εἰς ἀναίρεσιν τῆς ληφθείσης φύσεως ὁ θεῖος εἶπεν Ἀπόστολος, ἀλλ᾽ εἰς βεβαίωσιν τῆς ἐσομένης ἡμῖν ἀφθαρσίας τε καὶ ἀθανασίας καὶ πνευματικῆς ζωῆς· οὗ δὴ χάριν ἐπήγαγεν, *Ὥστε, εἴ τις ἐν Χριστῷ, καινὴ κτίσις, τὰ ἀρχαῖα παρῆλθεν· ἰδού· γέγονε* τὰ πάντα *καινά.*[dn] τὰ δὲ ἐσόμενα ὡς γεγενημένα εἴρηκεν· οὐδέπω γὰρ τῆς ἀθανασίας ἐτύχομεν, τευξόμεθα δέ, καὶ τυχόντες, οὐκ ἀσώματοι γενησόμεθα, ἀλλ᾽ ἀθανασίαν ἐνδυσόμεθα. *Οὐ θέλομεν,* γάρ φησιν ὁ θεῖος Ἀπόστολος, *ἐκδύσασθαι, ἀλλ᾽ ἐπενδύσασθαι ἵνα καταποθῇ τὸ θνητὸν ὑπὸ τῆς ζωῆς*·[do] καὶ πάλιν, *Δεῖ γὰρ τὸ φθαρτὸν*

l. 355 αὐτοῦ *ZA, Sir.* : αὐ- *Nös. Az.* **l. 366** ἐγνώκαμεν κατὰ σάρκα *scripsi (cf. NTG)* : ἐ. *ZA, edd. = "even if we did know Christ, we no longer know him." While the obvious sense of this truncated form of 2Cor 5.16 carried by ZA is unacceptable, a reader who mentally supplies the omitted prepositional phrase will elicit the sense intended. Yet, in his commentary ad loc., Thdt. cites the verse with the repeated* κατὰ σάρκα. *In this passage, the loss of the second identical prep. phrase is far more likely due to scribal haplography than to a choice by Thdt. to write something rough and difficult of comprehension; cf. Azéma, vol. 3, p. 228, n. 3.*

di. Mt 24.23 (NT var.)
dj. Mt 24.27 (NT var.)
dk. Jn 1.18 (*Cf., e.g.,* Jn 6.46.)
dl. Ex 33.20 (LXX var.)
dm. 2Cor 5.16 (NT var.)
dn. 2Cor 5.17 (NT var.)
do. 2Cor 5.4

of his second coming, among many other things, the Lord himself has declared, "Then, if someone say to you, 'Look, here is the Christ, or there he is, do not believe him,'"[di] "for as a bolt of lightning comes out of the east and is seen even in the west, so will be the coming of the Son of Man."[dj]

(11) He called himself "Son of Man," a title taken from his visible nature, even in reference to a time after his body had become deathless and incorruptible. This, of course, is the nature that will be visible at his coming, since the divine nature is invisible even to the angels. As we know from the Lord's own word, "No one has ever seen God,"[dk] and, as the Lord declared to Moses, "No one will look upon my face and live."[dl] The holy apostle's statement, "We know no one according to the flesh; even if we did know Christ according to the flesh, we no longer know him so,"[dm] is not meant to deny the nature he assumed, but to confirm the incorruption, immortality, and spiritual life that will one day be ours. Precisely for this reason, he adds, "Therefore, whoever is in Christ is a new creation; the old has passed away. Behold! All things have become new."[dn] Here he speaks of what will be as though it had already happened; of course, we haven't already received immortality, though we shall, and when we do, we won't become bodiless but rather put on immortality. As the holy Apostle declares, "It is not our desire to take off a garment, but to put on another over it, so that what is mortal may be swallowed up by life";[do] and again, "Because our corruptible body must put on

τοῦτο ἐνδύσασθαι ἀφθαρσίαν, καὶ τὸ θνητὸν τοῦτο ἐνδύσασθαι ἀθανασίαν.[dp] οὕτω τοίνυν τὸν Κύριον οὐκ ἀσώματον εἴρηκεν, ἀλλ᾽ ἄφθαρτον εἶναι καὶ τὴν ὁρωμένην φύσιν, καὶ ἀθάνατον, καὶ τῇ θείᾳ δόξῃ δεδοξασμένην πιστεύειν ἐδίδαξεν. τοῦτο γὰρ ἐν τῇ πρὸς φιλιππησίους σαφέστερον ἡμᾶς ἐξεπαίδευσεν· *Ἡμῶν γάρ,* ἔφη, *τὸ πολίτευμα ἐν οὐρανοῖς ὑπάρχει, ἐξ οὗ καὶ σωτῆρα ἀπεκδεχόμεθα Κύριον Ἰησοῦν, … ὃς μετασχηματίσει τὸ σῶμα τῆς ταπεινώσεως ἡμῶν* εἰς τὸ γενέσθαι αὐτὸ *σύμμορφον τῷ σώματι τῆς δόξης αὐτοῦ.*[dq] ἐναργῶς δὲ διὰ τούτων ἐδίδαξεν ὅτι σῶμα μέν ἐστι τὸ δεσποτικὸν σῶμα, θεῖον δὲ σῶμα καὶ τῇ θείᾳ δόξῃ δεδοξασμένον.

(12) Μὴ τοίνυν φύγωμεν προσηγορίαν δι᾽ ἧς ἀπελαύσαμεν σωτηρίας, δι᾽ ἧς ἀνεκαινίσθη τὰ πάντα ὡς αὐτὸς ἔφη ὁ διδάσκαλος, ἐφεσίοις γράφων· *Κατὰ τὴν εὐδοκίαν αὐτοῦ, ἣν προέθετο ἐν αὐτῷ εἰς οἰκονομίαν τοῦ πληρώματος τῶν καιρῶν, ἀνακεφαλαιώσασθαι τὰ πάντα ἐν τῷ Χριστῷ, τὰ ἐν τοῖς οὐρανοῖς καὶ … ἐπὶ τῆς γῆς ἐν αὐτῷ.*[dr] μάθωμεν δὲ παρὰ τῆς μακαρίας ταυτησὶ γλώττης καὶ ὅπως δεῖ δοξάζειν τὸν εὐεργέτην, τῷ Θεῷ καὶ Πατρὶ τὴν τοῦ Χριστοῦ προσηγορίαν προσάπτοντας· ῥωμαίοις μὲν γὰρ ἐπιστέλλων, ὧδέ φησι· *Τὸ εὐαγγέλιόν μου καὶ τὸ κήρυγμα Ἰησοῦ Χριστοῦ, κατὰ ἀποκάλυψιν μυστηρίου χρόνοις αἰωνίοις σεσιγημένου, φανερωθέντος τε νῦν διά τε γραφῶν προφητικῶν κατ᾽ ἐπιταγὴν τοῦ αἰωνίου Θεοῦ,* καὶ *εἰς ὑπακοὴν πίστεως εἰς πάντα τὰ ἔθνη γνωρισθέντος—μόνῳ σοφῷ Θεῷ διὰ Ἰησοῦ Χριστοῦ, ᾧ ἡ δόξα εἰς τοὺς αἰῶνας. ἀμήν·*[ds] ἐφεσίοις δὲ γράφων, οὕτως ὕμνησεν· *Τῷ δὲ δυναμένῳ ὑπὲρ πάντα ποιῆσαι*

dp. 1Cor 15.53
dq. Phil 3.20f. (NT var.)
dr. Eph 1.9f. (NT var.)
ds. Rom 16.25–27 (NT var.)

incorruptibility, and our mortal body immortality."[dp] Therefore, he clearly does not mean to say the Lord is now without body; rather he has taught us to believe that even Christ's visible nature has become incorruptible, immortal, and full of God's glory. This instruction he sets out more clearly in Philippians, "We are citizens of heaven, and it is from there that we await, with eager anticipation, our Savior, the Lord Jesus, who will transform our lowly body to have a glory like his own."[dq] His teaching in these passages is entirely clear: that the Master's body is a body, but a body belonging to God, full of God's glory.

(12) We must not, then, avoid that title through which we have our salvation, the title through which, as our teacher declared in the Epistle to the Ephesians, the entire universe has been reborn: "According to his good pleasure, which he had foredetermined in Christ for the working of his providential plan for the fulness of time: that all things, both in heaven and on earth, should be transformed in Christ."[11dr] So, we should learn from the speech of this saintly man how we are to honor our benefactor by placing the name of Christ alongside that of God the Father. In the Epistle to the Romans, he spoke as follows: "My gospel and the preaching of Jesus Christ, in accordance with the revelation of the mystery that was for untold ages kept in silence, but, in accordance with the decree of immortal God, has been revealed now and through the prophetic Scriptures and made known to all peoples so that they may receive it in obedient faith—let there be glory forever through Jesus Christ to God who alone is wise. Amen."[12ds]

11. This translation follows Theodoret's interpretation of Eph 1.9. For this translation of ἀνακεφαλαιώσασθαι, *v.* Thdt. *in Eph. ad loc.*: *Ἀνακεφαλαίωσιν* τοίνυν καλεῖ τὴν σύντομον τῶν πραγμάτων μεταβολήν. Διὰ γὰρ τῆς κατὰ τὸν Δεσπότην Χριστὸν οἰκονομίας, καὶ τῶν ἀνθρώπων ἡ φύσις ἀνίσταται καὶ τὴν ἀφθαρσίαν ἐνδύεται, καὶ ἡ ὁρωμένη κτίσις τῆς φθορᾶς ἐλευθερουμένη τεύξεται τῆς ἀφθαρσίας ("He uses the term *ἀνακεφαλαίωσις* to signify the sudden transformation of creation. Through the work accomplished in the Lord Christ, human nature is also raised up and clothed with incorruptibility; likewise, the visible creation, freed from decay, will acquire incorruptibility").

12. The translation follows Theodoret's articulation of this doxology, which, in his text of Romans, stood after 14.23; on the complex issues of the authenticity and the placement of these verses, *v.* Metzger, *A Textual Commentary, ad* Rm 14.23.

ὑπερεκπερισσοῦ ὧν αἰτούμεθα ἢ νοοῦμεν, κατὰ τὴν δύναμιν τὴν ἐνεργουμένην ἐν ἡμῖν, αὐτῷ ἡ δόξα ἐν τῇ Ἐκκλησίᾳ … ἐν Χριστῷ Ἰησοῦ εἰς πάσας τὰς γενεὰς τοῦ αἰῶνος τῶν αἰώνων. ἀμήν·[dt] καὶ μικρὸν δὲ τούτων ἔμπροσθεν, οὕτως ἔφη· *Τούτου χάριν κάμπτω τὰ γόνατά μου πρὸς τὸν Πατέρα* τοῦ Κυρίου ἡμῶν Ἰησοῦ Χριστοῦ, *ἐξ οὗ πᾶσα πατριὰ ἐν οὐρανῷ καὶ ἐπὶ γῆς ὀνομάζεται·*[du] καί, μετὰ πλεῖστα, Εὐχαριστοῦμεν, φησίν, *πάντοτε ὑπὲρ πάντων* ὑμῶν *ἐν ὀνόματι τοῦ Κυρίου ἡμῶν Ἰησοῦ Χριστοῦ τῷ Θεῷ καὶ Πατρί·*[dv] καὶ μέντοι καὶ τὴν φιλιππησίων φιλοτιμίαν ταῖς εὐλογίαις ἠμείψατο· *Ὁ δὲ Θεός μου* πληρώσαι *πᾶσαν χρείαν ὑμῶν κατὰ* τὸν πλοῦτον *αὐτοῦ ἐν δόξῃ ἐν Χριστῷ Ἰησοῦ·*[dw] ἑβραίοις δὲ οὕτως ἐπηύξατο· *Ὁ δὲ Θεὸς τῆς εἰρήνης, ὁ ἀναγαγὼν ἐκ* τῶν *νεκρῶν τὸν ποιμένα τῶν προβάτων, τὸν μέγαν ἐν αἵματι διαθήκης αἰωνίου, τὸν Κύριον ἡμῶν Ἰησοῦν, καταρτίσαι ὑμᾶς ἐν παντὶ ἔργῳ ἀγαθῷ εἰς τὸ ποιῆσαι τὸ θέλημα αὐτοῦ, ποιῶν ἐν ὑμῖν τὸ εὐάρεστον ἐνώπιον αὐτοῦ διὰ Ἰησοῦ Χριστοῦ, ᾧ ἡ δόξα εἰς τοὺς αἰῶνας. ἀμήν.*[dx]

(13) Οὐ μόνον δὲ δοξολογῶν, ἀλλὰ καὶ παραγγέλλων καὶ διαμαρτυρόμενος, συνάπτει τὸν Χριστὸν τῷ Θεῷ καὶ Πατρί. καὶ τῷ μακαρίῳ Τιμοθέῳ γράφων, βοᾷ, *Διαμαρτύρομαι ἐνώπιον τοῦ Θεοῦ καὶ Ἰησοῦ Χριστοῦ·*[dy] καὶ πάλιν, *Παραγγέλλω σοι ἐνώπιον τοῦ Θεοῦ, τοῦ ζωογονοῦντος τὰ πάντα, καὶ Χριστοῦ Ἰησοῦ, τοῦ μαρτυρήσαντος ἐπὶ Ποντίου Πιλάτου τὴν καλὴν ὁμολογίαν, τηρῆσαί σε τὴν ἐντολὴν ἄσπιλον,* ἀνεπίληπτον *μέχρι τῆς ἐπιφανείας τοῦ Κυρίου ἡμῶν Ἰησοῦ Χριστοῦ, ἣν* καιροῖς *ἰδίοις δείξει ὁ μακάριος καὶ μόνος δυνάστης, ὁ βασιλεὺς τῶν βασιλευόντων καὶ Κύριος τῶν κυριευόντων, ὁ μόνος ἔχων ἀθανασίαν, φῶς οἰκῶν ἀπρόσιτον, ὃν εἶδεν οὐδεὶς ἀνθρώπων* οὔτε *ἰδεῖν δύναται, ᾧ τιμὴ καὶ κράτος αἰώνιον. ἀμήν.*[dz]

Ταῦτα παρὰ τῶν θείων ἐδιδάχθημεν ἀποστόλων, ταύτην καὶ Ἰωάννης καὶ Ματθαῖος, τῶν εὐαγγελικῶν κηρυγμάτων οἱ μέγιστοι ποταμοί, τὴν διδασκαλίαν ἡμῖν προσήνεγκαν, ὁ

dt Eph 3.20f. du. Eph 3.14f. (NT var.) dv. Eph 5.20 (NT var.)
dw. Phil 4.19 (NT var.) dx. Heb 13.20f. (NT var.) dy. 2Tm 4.1
dz. 1Tm 6.13–16 (NT var.)

In the Epistle to the Ephesians, he offers praise "to him who can accomplish, through the power that is at work among us, far more for us than we could ever pray for or even think of—Glory be to him in the Church, glory … in Christ Jesus from generation to generation, evermore. Amen."[dt] And just a bit before that, he had declared, "This is why I bend my knee before the Father of our Lord, Jesus Christ, the source from which all fatherhood in heaven and earth takes its name."[13][du] Rather further on, he said, "We give thanks continually for all of you to our God and Father in the name of our Lord Jesus Christ."[dv] Furthermore, he blessed the Philippians for their generosity as follows, "May my God meet your every need, in accordance with his abundant wealth, with glory in Christ Jesus."[dw] In the case of the Hebrews, he prayed, "May the God of peace, who, by the blood of the everlasting covenant, raised up from the dead the great shepherd of the sheep, our Lord Jesus, make you capable of every good work so that you may do his will as he accomplishes in you what is pleasing in his sight through Jesus Christ to whom be glory forever. Amen."[dx]

(13) He places Christ alongside God the Father not only in doxologies, but also in passages of exhortation and adjuration. In a letter to the blessed Timothy, he calls out, "I adjure you before God and Jesus Christ";[dy] and again, "In the presence of God, who gives life to all things, and Christ Jesus, who made his courageous confession before Pontius Pilate, I charge you to keep your commission free of spot or reproach until the coming of our Lord, Jesus Christ, which God will make manifest at a time of his own choosing: God, the blessed, sole Ruler, King of kings and Lord of Lords, alone immortal, who dwells in unapproachable light, he whom no mortal has ever seen or can see, to whom be honor and might forever. Amen."[dz]

These are the lessons we have learned from the holy apostles, this the teaching poured out for us by John and Matthew, those mighty rivers of gospel preaching.[14] Of these, the latter declared, "This is the

13. *V.* n. 7 above.

14. These two passages are juxtaposed, though in reverse order, also in *Eran.*, *dial.* 2, p. 135, ll. 3–7.

μὲν εἰπών· *Βίβλος γενέσεως Ἰησοῦ Χριστοῦ, υἱοῦ Δαυίδ, υἱοῦ Ἀβραάμ,*[ea] ὁ δέ, τὰ πρὸ τῶν αἰώνων ἐπιδείξας, *Ἐν ἀρχῇ ἦν ὁ Λόγος, καὶ ὁ Λόγος ἦν πρὸς τὸν Θεόν, καὶ Θεὸς ἦν ὁ Λόγος. οὗτος ἦν ἐν ἀρχῇ πρὸς τὸν Θεόν,* καί, ὅτι *Πάντα δι᾽ αὐτοῦ ἐγένετο.*[eb]

ea. Mt 1.1 eb. Jn 1.1–3

genealogy of Jesus Christ, son of David, son of Abraham,"[ea] while the former revealed what was before all time: "In the beginning was the Word, and the Word was with God, and the Word was God. He was in the beginning with God," and then, "all things were made through him."[eb]

INDEX SCRIPTURISTICUS

I. Identifying Scriptural Quotations

In general, we define a quotation of Scripture as a phrase that matches in every respect of vocabulary and morphology the corresponding phrase printed in our sources for the biblical text.[1] For the OT, these are the Göttingen Septuagint and Rahlfs' edition of 1935 for those books (*e.g.*, Joshua) still unpublished by the Göttingen Academy. For the NT, we rely on the twenty-eighth edition of *The Greek New Testament* (*NTG*), edited by B. Aland *et al.*

In the Greek text, we use italics to set off every word that corresponds to our sources and points of ellipsis to note the absence of material contained in them. The abbreviations "(LXX var.)" for quotations of the OT and "(NT var.)" for quotations of the NT indicate that Theodoret has added one or more words that do not appear in our sources or has used at least one word that differs somehow (*e.g.*, in case or number) from their reading.[2] Thus, in the Greek text, the use of words that are not in our authorities and even a difference in the inflection of the same word will be signaled by the use of upright, rather than italic, font, and by the notation "(LXX var.)" or "(NT var.)." Simple examples include the insertion of an extra particle or the substitution of *Χριστόν* for *Κύριον*. Note that, in the *apparatus fontium*, the term *var.* does not refer to the *apparatus criticus* of the Göttingen Septuagint, or the *NTG* or, indeed, to the *apparatus* of any printed edition.

In the notes to the text, the parenthetical abbreviation "(LXX)" indicates that a verse or a portion of a verse is found in the Greek, but not in the Hebrew, or that the LXX carries material of such different meaning that it would be difficult for a reader to see the correspondence between the LXX

1. It sometimes happens that a single very rare word may be regarded as a quotation.

2. We do not use the term *var.* to point out a difference between text and source that is strictly orthographical, *i.e.* one that changes neither the number of syllables nor the pronunciation. Thus, in Theodoret's quotations of Mt 10.25 (*epp.* 109.1 and 146.1), οἰκειακοὺς is italicised though the *NTG* prints the homophone in οἰκι-.

and the MT.[3] Thus, the notation "Ps 70.1 (LXX)" referring to the first verse of the seventieth psalm of the MT, alerts the reader to the fact that the LXX version (Ps 69.2) quoted by Theodoret contains a clause that does not appear in the Hebrew original. In contrast, the notation (LXX var.) would have indicated that Theodoret's quotation contained more words than, or a word or words different from, those printed by Rahlfs.

In the English translation, we indicate quotations by the use of quotation marks. We enclose within quotation marks everything Theodoret seems to have regarded as part of the quotation, even words or phrases that do not completely match the corresponding material in our printed sources. Thus, a phrase in which Theodoret adapts a quotation of Scripture to the syntax of his prose (*e.g.*, when he changes the case of a noun or the mood or tense of a verb), or in which he employs a synonym for a word in our authorities, will be regarded as part of the quotation in the English. It would, after all, be of little use and frequently impossible to indicate by the English punctuation precisely where and how Theodoret's text differs from that of our authorities.

To the extent possible, in the notes to the text, we cite Theodoret's biblical references according to the chapter and verse of the *NRSV*, which follows the numeration of the MT. In this index, we include the chapter and verse divisions of the LXX in parentheses in cases where they differ from the MT (*e.g.* Ps 9–147). Yet in cases where his translation of the OT seems to have diverged markedly from the MT, in both the text and in this index, we follow the chapter and verse divisions of the LXX.

Thus, the reader will always find the fullest information about any one citation in the *ap. fontium* of the Greek text. In the English translation, we place between quotation marks words that do not stand in the Göttingen LXX or the *NTG*. And in this index, we do not supply the notations "(LXX var.)" and "(NT var.)" that would alert the reader to even small differences of wording between Theodoret's Greek and that of our authorities.

3. We do not use this abbreviation in places where the LXX contains nothing that is not in the MT, or where the difference of meaning between the MT and the LXX is slight; *v.* Petruccione and Hill, *Theodoret of Cyrus, Questions on the Octateuch*, LEC, vol. 1, pp. liiif., n. 80.

II. Typographical Conventions

A. Bold-faced numbers indicate direct quotation (*i.e.* verbal equivalences with our sources); those in normal typeface all other citations, whether paraphrases, allusions, or *comparanda.*

B. Citations within the *Epp.*

These are listed by letter or letter and subsection, those appearing in the introductions by the number of the page or footnote. A passage quoted or referred to more than once within a brief compass (*i.e.* within a letter lacking subdivision, a single subsection of a letter, or a single note to the translation) is listed only once. If any of these citations is a direct quotation, the number appears in bold face. Thus, in the context indicated by a bold-faced number, in addition to the direct quotation, the reader may find references to or paraphrases of the same verse(s).

C. Citations in the Notes to the Text and the Translation

These are listed separately even if they are also cited in the text of the work. Thus, the entry "Rom. 9.5: *epp.* **83.3**, 83.3 (εἰς τοὺς αἰῶνας τῶν αἰώνων)" indicates that Rom. 9.5 is quoted in the third subsection of the Greek text of *ep.* 83 and referred to in the critical note on the phrase εἰς τοὺς αἰῶνας τῶν αἰώνων. All critical notes that contain a reference to, or a quotation of, a biblical passage are identified by a lemma enclosed within parentheses. These lemmas are printed in bold-face when the note they introduce contains a direct quotation of Scripture.

D. Citations in the Introductions

As there are two introductions, one by I. Pástori-Kupán (to volumes 4 and 5) and the second by J.F. Petruccione (to the Greek text), and each has its own series of footnotes, an asterisk marks references to the pages and notes of the introduction to the Greek text.

Old Testament

New Testament

GENERAL INDEX

This index contains references to the Introduction to volumes 4f., the English translation, the historical notes to the English translation, and to some terms used in the Greek text. The more complex articles are subdivided; most often a collection of general references precedes more specific subheadings. The subheadings are arranged by a variety of criteria: alphabetical, chronological, thematic; to facilitate reference we have sacrificed complete consistency of arrangement. The order of references is (1) to the introduction, cited by section and, where relevant, page number; (2) to the notes in the introduction; and (3) to the letters and historical notes, cited by letter number (including subdivisions if relevant) and footnote number. To avoid confusion between subdivisions of a letter and notes on the letter, nonconsecutive references are joined by "and." For example, "*ep.* 42.1f. and 4, 42 nn. 1–3, 7, and 10" refers to *ep.* 42 sections 1, 2, and 4, and *ep.* 42 footnotes 1–3, 7, and 10. In cross-references, commas divide consecutive references within an article, semi-cola divisions between different articles. Thus, the cross-references at the end of the entry for "Jerusalem"—"*Cf.* Church, 2.3.3.7; Cyril (Bishop of Jerusalem)"—refer the reader to a subdivision of the entry for "Church"and to the entry regarding the fourth-century bishop Cyril.

General Index

General Index

General Index

General Index

General Index

General Index

General Index

General Index

General Index

General Index

General Index

INDEX OF MODERN AUTHORS

This index contains references to and citations of the authors mentioned in the Introduction to Theodoret's Life and Works, the Introduction to the Greek text, and the historical notes to the English translation of *epp.* 1–147. We define as "modern" those authors active since the invention of the printing press. Figures of the earlier period are identified first by the Latin, and then by the vernacular, version of their names. Our term "author" is used broadly to include as well editors and scholars who may not have written anything. We have tried to catch all the places where an author's name appears but have not traced all those where he or his work is referred to without name. When an author is mentioned in both the body of the text and in a footnote to that portion of text, we have reported only the reference in the footnote. In this index, "Intro." refers to the Introduction to Theodoret's Life and Works. For other details of organization and abbreviation, *v.* the introduction to the General Index.